The Front-Runner of the
Catholic Reformation

Dedicated to Rudolf K. Markwald

The Front-Runner of the Catholic Reformation

The Life and Works of Johann von Staupitz

FRANZ POSSET

ASHGATE

Published by
Ashgate Publishing Limited
Gower House
Croft Road
Aldershot
Hants GU11 3HR
England

Ashgate Publishing Company
Suite 420
101 Cherry Street
Burlington, VT 05401-4405
USA

Ashgate website: http://www.ashgate.com

British Library Cataloguing in Publication Data

Posset, Franz
    The front-runner of the Catholic Reformation: the life and works of Johann von Staupitz. – (St Andrews studies in Reformation history)
    1. Staupitz, Johann von 2. Catholic Church – Germany – History – 16th century 3. Theologians – Germany – Biography 4. Abbots – Germany – Biography 5. Reformation – Germany 6. Church history – 16th century
    I. Title
    230.2'092

Library of Congress Cataloging-in-Publication Data

Posset, Franz.
    The front-runner of the Catholic Reformation : the life and works of Johann von Staupitz / Franz Posset.
        p. cm. – (St. Andrews studies in Reformation history)
        Includes bibliographical references and index.
    1. Staupitz, Johann von, d. 1524. I. Title. II. Series.

BX4705.S813 P67 2002
230'.2'092–dc21

2002074534

ISBN 0 7546 0866 2

This book is printed on acid-free paper

Typeset in Sabon by Laserscript, Mitcham, Surrey, Great Britain
Printed and bound in Great Britain by MPG Books Ltd, Bodmin, Cornwall

Contents

St Andrews Studies in Reformation History

List of Plates

Foreword

In a letter of March 27, 1545, Martin Luther wrote to Elector John Frederick: 'Doctor Staupitz is first of all my father in this doctrine and he has given birth to me in Christ.' The conviction that Johann von Staupitz had been Luther's spiritual father and that everything had started with him can often be found in Luther's works, and less than a year before his death he remembers him with much gratitude. However, Luther's own view of Staupitz's significance for him was seldom fully appreciated. Moreover, in contrast to Luther, Staupitz was generally underexposed. The Roman Catholic Church put his writings on the index of forbidden books. The Protestants underlined the theological originality of Luther and in that view Staupitz could only be seen as a forerunner of the Reformation, who at his best has had some sort of pastoral influence on Luther.

This theological biography, presented by Dr. Franz Posset, wants to put the life and work of Staupitz into a new perspective. Anyone who closely considers Catholic theology before the Council of Trent will discover much more than just variations of scholastic theology. By means of the renewal of the religious Orders, of theology and especially of preaching, some strong reform efforts became evident which made up the cradle of both the Catholic and the Protestant Reformations. In this regard, Staupitz made an important contribution as vicar general of the observant Augustinian friars. He aimed at a reform of the Christian life within the contemporary context of biblical humanism, monastic humanism, and devotional theology, all of which wanted to return to the ancient sources of the faith that is to the Bible and the Church Fathers, especially Augustine.

The title of Franz Posset's study already reveals his view of Staupitz. He does not want to see him only as a forerunner, but rather as a *front-runner* of the Reformation. There is no reason to play down Staupitz's great significance for Luther for the sake of safeguarding the latter's originality. Staupitz has to be seen as a reform theologian in his own right. He wanted to bring the Gospel closer to the ordinary people of his time and considered this task to be the mission for the Augustinian friars. Luther, in his own peculiar way, fulfilled Staupitz's vision of reforming the Church through the reform of preaching.

Definitely, Franz Posset also wants to pursue an ecumenical interest with his historical–theological study. He sees Staupitz's theology and spirituality not only as 'a genuine Catholic possibility in proximity to Augustine' in the Reformation period but also for us today. This gives his book a special dimension. He has earned our gratitude for this rich and fascinating biography.

Theo M.M.A.C. Bell
Utrecht

Preface

My principal reason for writing this book is to make available to the English-speaking reader insights into the extraordinary life and work of a largely underestimated German theologian of the Reformation, an actor in the drama of the early sixteenth century, Johann von Staupitz. Most recent studies and the critical edition of Staupitz's works are written in German. In this volume I have tried to process the research results of the past 130 years or so, starting with J.K.F. Knaake's unfinished edition of Staupitz's works of 1867. At the beginning of the new millenium, my intention is to provide a preliminary synthesis of the life and work of Staupitz, as it may not be possible to produce a definitive biography until all of the sources are available in critical editions. Nonetheless, one can investigate the essential traits of his life as it unfolds over the years within the context of the Catholic reform movement around 1500 and in the first decades of the sixteenth century.

Staupitz is primarily remembered as the superior and admired mentor of Friar Martin Luther within the reformed branch of the Order of St Augustine in German-speaking lands, however, to date no full biography of him has been written. Staupitz displayed a remarkable openness to the various intellectual and religious challenges of his time, and for this he earned his place of honour in the history of pastoral care. It seems to me that the Reformation in Germany cannot be understood fully and properly without a thorough knowledge of Staupitz's spirituality and pastoral/practical theology. In a sense, this biography may be read as a theological introduction to the early Reformation in Germany. Staupitz is to be appreciated here for his own decisive contribution to the Catholic Reformation, of which Luther, in his earlier phase, was a part, until he was excommunicated. This is a theological biography written by a lay theologian for other theologians and for historians. My main concern is to bring forth Staupitz's 'Catholic spirituality', that is, his understanding of the relationship of man to God, of which he so often speaks in his sermons.

I am grateful to Dr Bruce Gordon of the St Andrews Reformation Studies Institute in Scotland for his helpful, critical review of this study and for including it in his series of *St Andrews Studies in Reformation History*. For further collegial, scholarly advice and helpful hints I am indebted to my Lutheran friends in Wisconsin, Rudolf K. and Lynn Markwald, and Kenneth and Aldemar Hagen, who critiqued earlier drafts of this book. I dedicate it to Rudolf K. Markwald, translator of Staupitz's 1520 sermons, who in 1999 celebrated his 80th birthday.

Franz Posset
Beaver Dam, Wisconsin, USA

Abbreviations

AAug	*Analecta Augustiniana.*
ABR	*The American Benedictine Review.*
AELK	*Allgemeine Evangelisch-Lutherische Kirchenzeitung.*
ARG	*Archiv für Reformationsgeschichte.*
BBKL	Friedrich Wilhelm Bautz (ed.), *Biographisch-Bibliographisches Kirchenlexikon*, vols 1–2 (Hamm, 1990), vols 3–18 (Herzberg, 1992–2000), vols 19–21 (Nordhausen, 2001–2003)
CR	Carolus Gottlieb Bretschneider (ed.), *Corpus Reformatorum*, 28 vols (Halis Saxonum, 1834–60)
CSQ	*Cistercian Studies Quarterly.*
Dictionnaire	Marcel Viller SK et al. (eds), *Dictionnaire de Spiritualité Ascétique et mystique, doctrine et histoire*, 17 vols (Paris, 1937–95).
Jeremias, *AELK*	Alfred Jeremias, 'Johannes Staupitz, Luthers Vater un Schüler', *Allgemeine Evangelisch Lutherische Kirchenzeitung*, **61** (1928), pp. 345–50.
Kleine Schriften	Otto Clemen, *Kleine Schriften zur Reformationgeschichte (1897–1944)*, ed. Ernst Koch, 9 vols (Leipzig, 1907; reprinted 1983).
Kunzelmann	Adalbero Kunzelmann, *Geschicte der deutschen Augustiner-Eremiten*, 7 vols (Würzburg, 1979–83).
LQ	*Lutheran Quarterly.*
LW	Jaroslav Pelikan and Helmut T. Lehmann (eds), *Luther's Works*, 55 vols (St Louis, MO, 1955–86).
NCE	*New Catholic Encyclopedia*, prepared by editorial staff of the Catholic University of America (New York, 1967–).
PL	*Patrologia Series Latina.*
RGG	*Religion in Geschichte und Gegenwart, Handwörterbuch für Theologie and Religionswissenschaft*, 7 vols (Tübingen, 1957–65).
SBOp	Jean Leclereq et al. (eds), *Sancti Bernardi Opera*, 8 vols (Rome, 1957–77).
SCJ	*Sixteenth Century Journal.*

Staupitz, I.	Lothar Graf Zu Dohna and Richard Wetzel (eds), *Johann von Staupitz: Sämtliche Schriften, Abhandlungen, Predigten, Zeugnisse*, Volume I, Tübinger Predigten (Berlin and New York, 1987).
Staupitz, II.	Lothar Graf zu Dohna and Richard Wetzel (eds), *Johann von Staupitz: Sämtliche Schriften, Abhandlungen, Predigten, Zeugnisse*, Volume II, [Advent Sermons at Nuremberg] (= Libellus de exsecutione aeternae praedestinationis) (Berlin and New York, 1979).
Stupperich	Robert Stupperich, *Reformatorenlexikon*, (Gütersloh, 1984).
WA	*D Martin Luthers Werke: kritische Gesamtausgabe*, Weimarer Ausgabe (Weimar, 1883–). References to this edition are abbreviated in line with the following example: *WA* 39,2. 100,3 = *WA* vol. 39, part 2, page 100, line 3.)
WABR	Weimarer Ausgabe *Briefe* (Letters).
WATR	Weimarer Ausgabe *Tischreden* (Table Talks).
ZKG	*Zeitschrift für Kirchengeschichte*.

1   Portrait of Johann von Staupitz as Abbot of St Peter's at Salzburg. Bibliothek
St Peter, Salzburg, Austria. Photo: Oskar Anrather.

Ein seligs newes Jar

von der lieb gottes: Gegeben von dē
hochgelarten wirdigen hern Doctori Johanni von
Staupitz Augustiner ordens ꝛc. Im ꝗviij.
Jhesus.

Lieb got ober alle dingk.

2 Title-page of Staupitz's *Ein seligs newes Jar von der lieb gottes* ('On the Love of God') with Martin Luther's signature. Staatsbibliothek zu Berlin, Germany, Preußischer Kulturbesitz; Sig. 1: Libr. impr. rar. Quart 196. Photo: Oskar Anrather.

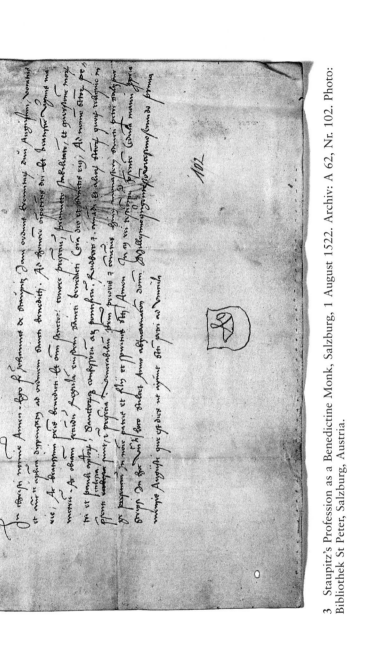

3   Staupitz's Profession as a Benedictine Monk, Salzburg, 1 August 1522. Archiv: A 62, Nr. 102. Photo: Bibliothek St Peter, Salzburg, Austria.

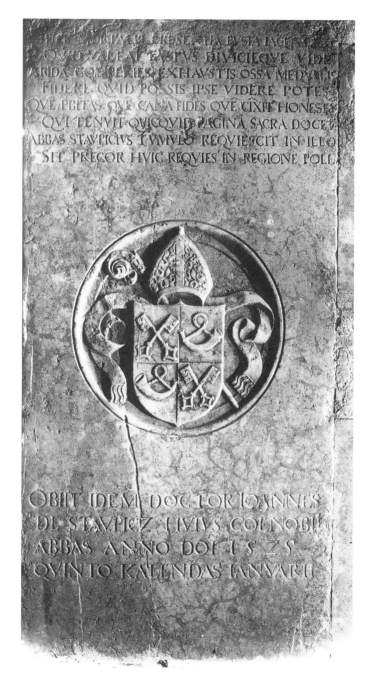

4   Epitaph on Staupitz's Grave, St Mary's Chapel at St Peter's Archabbey, Salzburg. Bibliothek St Peter, Salzburg, Austria. Photo: Oskar Anrather.

Introduction

'I am yours, save me' is the motto of Staupitz's life and work. He recommended this verse, taken from Ps. 118 (119): 94, to the dying person as a final prayer – as we find in the conclusion of his booklet on this subject, his first publication from the year 1515 – and also placed it on the title-page of both the Latin and German editions of his Advent sermons of 1516 (printed in 1517), in the Vulgate version, *Tuus sum ego, salvum me fac*. Further, he used it in a letter to a confrère in 1516.

His life and work are permeated by the Word of God; as the epitaph on his grave at Salzburg testifies, 'he's held to whatever the sacred page teaches'. This biblical scholar is the key figure in the transition from the reforms of the religious Orders in the fifteenth century to the Reformation of the early sixteenth century. As the leader of the reformed (observant) Augustinian Order, he exercised enormous influence on the reform of piety through preaching and writing, a task to which this Order was committed at that time. Plate 1 shows Staupitz in his Abbot's robes; he was Abbot of St Peter's, Salzburg from 1522 to 1524.

The significance of Staupitz is difficult to overestimate; one could even ask: is Staupitz the Reformation? Yes and no. Yes in terms of much of Reformation theology. Yes, because he is an exponent of what is usually associated with the Reformation theological principles of 'grace alone', 'faith alone', and 'Scripture alone'. No, because he was not a proponent of nationalistic German anti-Roman politics so virulent at this time. No, also in terms of ecclesiastical reform politics; he was a 'critical' thinker, but he nevertheless remained loyal to the Church.

Staupitz's Reformation theology is worth investigating in the framework of a biography. This volume will show that he provided the decisive spiritual and theological impulses for his more famous confrère, Martin Luther. In terms of theology, therefore, Staupitz may be called not simply a forerunner of the Reformation, but the front-runner. Luther himself indicated that through Staupitz the light of the gospel had entered his heart. This is precisely so because Staupitz's pastoral theology was convincing as theology, rather than psychology, and not because of any pastoral counselling methods. One would do Staupitz an injustice if one belittled his thoroughly theological way of approaching pastoral care.[1] Luther himself confirmed that in his own case it was Staupitz's pastoral theology, that is, his great preaching of the gospel and of the cross, which was of decisive help.

Staupitz's life and work, his theological and spiritual insights will be presented in as chronological a sequence as is possible, and as they were made explicit in his sermons and tracts year after year, as far as these are accessible to us today. Staupitz himself did not present a systematic theology. He mainly preached to fellow friars and nuns, although also to the common people, including intellectuals, of major cities of that time. His principal medium was the 'sermon', augmented by booklets based on his preaching.

In Chapter 1 the scene is set with a background sketch of the reform efforts of the religious Orders in the fifteenth and early sixteenth centuries. Chapter 2 will study Staupitz's early Latin 'sermons', also called a 'book', which he wrote in 1497/98 at Tübingen. These sermons, which are permeated by the concept of the priority of grace in human life, were probably not delivered orally to an audience, but carefully composed and written, very likely for a fraternal readership. This chapter also describes the other tasks Staupitz had to master during the first decade of the new century as the vicar general of the reformed Augustinians, including his opening up to the contemporary humanist movement: conducting business for his Order, mediating in political matters, and even becoming a matchmaker. We will meet him as professor of the 'sacred page'. Chapter 3 is dedicated to his position as prominent preacher and author at Salzburg, Nuremberg, and Munich, between 1512 and 1517. In Chapter 4 we will focus on the years after his resignation from his professorship at the University of Wittenberg in 1512, when around 1515 he was considered for the bishopric at Salzburg-Chiemsee, and when he had to cope with Friar Martin Luther and his determination to reform pastoral care and challenge publicly the abuses in the indulgence business. In Chapter 5, we will again find Staupitz as a preacher and curate of souls (*Seelsorger*) at Salzburg, at the 'anus of the world', as he 'stands up for the evangelical truth' in 1520. By now he has ended his career as vicar general of the Augustinian

---

[1] Unfortunately, Gerhard Ebeling appears to do just that, saying that Staupitz as 'pastor' to Luther lacked theological thoroughness (*theologische Durchbildung*) and therefore pastoral effectiveness (*seelsorgerliche Durchschlagskraft*), in *Luthers Seelsorge: Theologie in der Vielfalt der Lebenssituationen an seinen Briefen dargestellt* (Tübingen, 1997), p. 477. The theological biography of Staupitz which is presented here, will demonstrate Staupitz's pastoral effectiveness precisely because of his biblical, theological expertise, that is his *seelsorgerliche Theologie*. See M. Wriedt, 'Staupitz und Luther. Zur Bedeutung der seelsorgerlichen Theologie Johannes von Staupitz für den jungen Luther', in J. Heubach (ed.), *Luther als Seelsorger* (Erlangen, 1991), pp. 67–108.

Reformed Congregation. Chapter 6 will deal with Staupitz as the Benedictine abbot of St Peter's Abbey in Salzburg (1522–24), delivering his last major series of sermons. From that same time, a text is extant on the Christian faith which was published after his death by his friend, the ex-friar Wenceslaus Linck (printed at Augsburg, 1525). Also from the latter part of his life (1523), we have his expert opinion (*Consultatio*) about the confessions of his former confrère Stephan Agricola who was accused of heresy and whom Abbot Staupitz was able to save. Chapter 7 will then treat Staupitz's theological testament and the remembrance by friends and foes of later times and, finally, all the above threads will be brought together in the concluding chapter.

This theological approach to Staupitz's life and work will show that there was no sharp division between the pre-Reformation and Reformation periods. This insight concurs with what scholars of popular piety have begun to realize, namely that the 'newer perspectives increasingly transcend the divide between the pre-Reformation and Reformation periods'.[2] The fifteenth century was a time of great reform efforts which were inspired by the biblical directive 'reform yourselves' as found in Rom. 12: 2 (Vulgate: *reformamini*).[3]

Studying Staupitz's life and work will reveal these reform efforts and will prove wrong the perception of the general 'unresponsiveness' of the Church of that time.[4] Staupitz's reform work within the Church demonstrates the complexities of the Catholic Reformation. It would be too deceptively simplistic to try to paint a picture of the Church in accelerating decay during the fifteenth century and then to let the Protestant Reformation shine all the brighter against such a backdrop. Reformation theology and historiography no longer need the construct of a 'deformation' in the fifteenth-century church and society in order to explain (in a mono-causal way) the reactions of *the* (Protestant) 'Reformation' of the sixteenth century. This is so because one may actually find a continuum between the various reform efforts of the religious Orders of previous centuries and the sixteenth-century 'Reformation'. Therefore, it is time to focus on the 'catholicity of the

---

[2] Bob Scribner, 'Introduction', in B. Scribner and T. Johnson (eds), *Popular Religion in Germany and Central Europe, 1400–1800* (New York, 1996), p. 1.

[3] See J. Helmrath, 'Theorie und Praxis der Kirchenreform im Spätmittelalter', *Rottenburger Jahrbuch für Kirchengeschichte* 11 (1992), pp. 41–70 (p. 48). On the history of the notion of 'reform', see K. Repken, 'Reform', in H.J. Hillerbrand (ed.), *The Oxford Encyclopaedia of the Reformation* (4 vols, New York, 1996), III, pp. 392–5.

[4] See L.G. Duggan, 'The Unresponsiveness of the Late Medieval Church: A Reconsideration', *SCJ*, 9 (1978), pp. 3–26; F. Rapp, *L'Eglise et la vie religieuse en Occident à la fin du Moyen Age* (Paris, 1971), pp. 296–331; A. Angenendt, *Geschichte der Religiosität im Mittelalter* (Darmstadt, 1997), p. 29.

Reformation'.[5] A case in point are the recent studies of Bernard of Clairvaux and his impact on theology and devotion around 1500,[6] and specifically on Luther[7] and Calvin.[8] Another case would be the very basic concept of 'visitations' of cloisters with the purpose of inspecting their status of reform. Such undertakings may very well have been the matrix for the later reformers' 'visitations' of the parishes in the various territories. What Staupitz accomplished by his visitations of the friaries, the later reformers tried to emulate with their pastoral visits of parishes.

When in the course of this investigation we refer to 'German lands' (*Deutsche Lande*) we are aware of the historical fact that there was no 'Germany' at that time. There was the 'Empire' (*Reich*) which during Staupitz's lifetime (that is, after 1492) began to be called the 'Holy Roman Empire of the German Nation'. Even then there was no unified 'nation'. In the Middle Ages, the province of a religious Order might include, for example, the 'nations' of Austria, Bavaria, Swabia, Alsace and Brabant.[9] Staupitz moved within these regions ('nations') on his visitation journeys and was thus an 'internationalist' by contemporary standards.

By working closely with the sources we will arrive at a new image of Staupitz as an eminent theologian, preacher and curate, more specifically as an 'academic city preacher' in the major urban centres in the south of the German-speaking territory. He belonged to the 'elite of preachers' of his time,[10] not to the class of 'pastors' (*Pfarrer*, *Pfarr-Herr*) who at that time, were primarily 'rectors' of a local church building, their main concern being the co-ordination of the liturgical activities of the numerous priests, especially their celebrations of Masses at the various altars in a given church.[11] In contrast, Staupitz was an outstanding

---

[5] See C.E. Braaten and R.W. Jenson (eds), *The Catholicity of the Reformation* (Grand Rapids, MI, 1996).

[6] See F. Posset, 'Saint Bernard of Clairvaux in the Devotion, Theology, and Art of the Sixteenth Century', *LQ*, 21 (1997), pp. 308–52.

[7] See T. Bell, *Divus Bernhardus: Bernhard von Clairvaux in Martin Luthers Schriften* (Mainz, 1993). My own studies on Bernard and Luther, published since 1987, are gathered in my book *Pater Bernhardus: Martin Luther and Bernard of Clairvaux* (Kalamazoo, MI, 1999).

[8] See A.N.S. Lane, *Calvin and Bernard of Clairvaux* (Princeton, NJ, 1996); D.E. Tamburello, *Union with Christ: John Calvin and the Mysticism of St. Bernard* (Louisville, KY, 1994).

[9] E. Schubert, *Einführung in die Grundprobleme der deutschen Geschichte im Spätmittelalter* (Darmstadt, 1992), pp. 26–32.

[10] *Predigerelite* and *akademischer Stadtprediger* are designations that are applied to mendicant preachers in general by Angenendt, *Geschichte der Religiosität*, pp. 444 and 479.

[11] See Schubert, *Einführung*, p. 260.

curate,[12] who correctly takes his place of honour in the history of pastoral care[13] and preaching, and its reforms, which constitute an essential part of any definition of the Catholic Reformation.

---

[12] See Wriedt, 'Staupitz und Luther' (above n. 1), and *idem*, 'Seelsorgerliche Theologie am Vorabend der Reformation: Johann Staupitz als Fastenprediger in Nürnberg', *Zeitschrift für Bayerische Kirchengeschichte*, **63** (1994), pp. 1–12.

[13] See M. Wriedt, 'Johann von Staupitz', in C. Möller (ed.), *Geschichte der Seelsorge in Einzelporträts*, 3 vols (Göttingen, 1994–96), II, pp. 45–64. It is curious that the chapter on Luther (II, pp. 25–44) precedes that on Staupitz, who was the older of the two and Luther's teacher.

CHAPTER ONE

The Augustinian Order and the Struggle for Reform in the Late Medieval Period

There is an inner unity which manifests itself in the Catholic Reformation of the late Middle Ages; it is well described by John C. Olin (who however did not have Staupitz in mind at all when he elaborated on the Catholic Reformation):

> Two characteristics run like a double rhythm through the Catholic Reformation: (a) the preoccupation of the Catholic reformers with the reform of the individual, and (b) their concern for the restoration and renewal of the Church's pastoral mission. Catholic reform, in short, had a marked personal and pastoral orientation.[1]

The life and work of Johann von Staupitz must be seen not only in the wider context of the 'observant movements' of the late Middle Ages comprising monasteries and friaries, but also and specifically in connection with Order of 'Friars Hermits of St Augustine' that Staupitz joined as a young man. The Order's name is something of a misnomer, because its members were not 'hermits' in the strict sense. In fact, by the beginning of the sixteenth century it was a powerful, mobile, international religious organization that numbered about 20 000 friars, living in around 1000 friaries, grouped into 26 provinces. The early reform movement was concerned with the proper community life in those friaries. All private property, as well as the numerous dispensations from all kinds of tasks, were to be given up, although, from the beginnings of the Order, individual members had been able to possess private property and indeed friars responsible for alms collection were allowed to keep some of the income for themselves. In addition, common meals and worship were stressed as important for any reformed friary, as this had not always been the case in the past. Especially during times of pestilence in the fourteenth century, it had been recommended that not more than three friars live under one roof in order to reduce the

---

[1] J.C. Olin, *Catholic Reform From Cardinal Ximenes to the Council of Trent 1495–1563* (New York, 1990), p. 35. For a historical review of the Augustinians' involvement in pastoral care, see D. Gutierrez, *The Augustinians in the Middle Ages 1357–1517 (History of the Order of St. Augustine)* trans. T. Martin, 2 vols, (Villanova, 1979–83), I, pp. 177–94.

possibility of infection – with the effect that friars had to live outside the friary and return only for prayer or Mass. The reform movement sought the abolition of this rule which had come into existence during times of necessity and the observant friars wanted to return to the strict rules of the Order. Their efforts found official recognition in 1493.[2]

While much of the reform effort went into the renewal of life in the local friaries, the mendicants per se were (and still are) not bound by the monastic oath of loyalty to one locality (*stabilitas loci*) whereby a monk or nun entered a particular monastery and remained there until death. In contrast, mendicant friars were moved around to wherever they were needed. Their loyalty was not to the place where they made their profession (as is the case with monks), but to the rule of their mendicant Order as such, within which they could be assigned and reassigned according to need. This specific characteristic of the mendicants may help explain Staupitz's (and others') mobility from friary to friary, both as a student and as a leading officer in his Order. It also may account for his personnel politics in that it allowed him to transfer subordinates from place to place – a prerogative of which he made ample use, as we shall see.

The mendicant Orders had adapted the monastic life to the urbanized civilization that had developed in Europe during the course of the twelfth and thirteenth centuries. They lived in friaries located within the cities, in contrast to the traditional monasteries of the Benedictines and Cistercians which were generally located in remote regions. To this day, the members of the mendicant Orders are mobile, 'begging friars'; not 'monks' in the proper sense, such as the Benedictines or the Cistercians who live in solidly established and usually well-funded monasteries and adhere to the rule of permanent residence in one location.

It was in the mid-thirteenth century that the papacy had recognized the religious needs of the urban centres of Europe and entrusted the care of souls to the mendicant friars. The Augustinian hermits became Augustinian friars who kept the official name 'Friars Hermits of St Augustine' when they began to teach and preach the Word of God in the cities. They deserve more than honourable mention in any history of pastoral care.

The 'observant movement' of the Middle Ages affected not only the Augustinians, but also the Franciscans and the Dominicans. Within the

---

[2] See A. Kunzelmann, *Geschichte der deutschen Augustiner-Eremiten* (7 vols, Würzburg, 1969–76), V, pp. 383–6; A. Zumkeller, 'Johannes von Staupitz und die klösterliche Reformbewegung', *AAug*, **52** (1989), pp. 31–49, esp. p. 36; A. Borromeo (trans. Robert E. Shillen), 'Augustinians', in Hillerbrand, *The Oxford Encyclopedia of the Reformation*, I, p. 100; K. Walsh, 'The Observance: Sources for a History of the Observant Reform Movement in the Order of Augustinian Friars in the Fourteenth and Fifteenth Centuries', *Rivista di Storia della chiesa in Italia*, **31** (1977), pp. 40–67.

Franciscan Order, there had been a long-term struggle, that still continued, between those who wanted to maintain complete adherence to the ideals of St Francis (the observants) and those who wanted to live a more relaxed religious life (the conventuals). In 1517, the Franciscan observants received their independence by papal decree and declared themselves the true Order of St Francis.[3] Great religious figures between 1490 and 1520 were members of the 'observant movement' – for example, such as Francisco Ximenes de Cisneros of the Franciscan Order in Spain, and Girolamo Savonarola of the Dominican Order in Florence. They were not only concerned with reforms within their Orders, but also made their influence felt in the wider Church and in society. Cardinal Ximenes de Cisneros wanted every student of the Bible to quench his thirst 'at the fountainhead of the water that flows unto life everlasting and not to have to content himself with rivulets alone'.[4] He was the chief editor of the *Polyglot Bible* which included both Testaments in the original languages, in six folio volumes, compiled between 1513 and 1517, and published in 1522.[5] Friar Savonarola's preaching and writings exercised great influence outside monastic walls, and were 'virtual best-sellers'.[6] He incurred, however, the wrath of Pope Alexander VI (d. 1503) and, after a short time in prison, died at the stake in 1498.[7]

The observant movements were of considerable importance for the religious history of the late Middle Ages in central Europe. This is not the place for a detailed review of the different non-Augustinian reform movements;[8] however, it should be noted that Franciscans and Augustinians in German-speaking lands contributed decisively to the Roman Catholic and the Lutheran Catholic (later called 'Protestant') 'Reformation'. Numerous Augustinians and several Franciscans became Lutheran preachers in the cities.[9]

---

[3] See K.S. Latourette, *A History of Christianity*, 2 vols (New York, 1975), I, p. 655.

[4] 'Prologue to the Books of the Old and New Testaments Printed in Their Various Languages', in Olin, *Catholic Reform*, pp. 62–64 (p. 63).

[5] See ibid., p. 6.

[6] See B. Gordon, '"This Worthy Witness of Christ": Protestant Uses of Savonarola in the Sixteenth Century', in B. Gordon (ed.), *Protestant History and Identity in Sixteenth-Century Europe*, 2 vols (Aldershot, 1996), I, pp. 93–107 (p. 93).

[7] See Introduction in J.P. Donnelly (ed. and trans.), *Prison Meditations on Psalms 51 and 31 by Girolamo Savonarola, O.P.* (Milwaukee, WI, 1994); D. Weinstein, *Savonarola and Florence: Prophecy and Patriotism in the Renaissance* (Princeton, NJ, 1970).

[8] See L. Lemmens, *Die Provinzialvikare der Sächsischen Observanten* (Düsseldorf, 1910); F. Doelle, *Die Observanzbewegung in der Sächsischen Franziskanerprovinz bis zum Generalkapitel von Parma (1529)* (Münster, 1918).

[9] See K. Blaschke, 'Reformation und Modernisierung', *ARG Sonderband* (1993), pp. 511–20 (p. 518).

The Augustinian observant movement which Staupitz joined is summed up in seven characteristics by Francis X. Martin, a historian of the Augustinian Order during the Renaissance:

> 1) It [the Augustinian observant movement] owed a great deal to the example of the Franciscan observants; 2) it was Italian in origin and of continuing influence; 3) it upheld the eremitical ideal as a main principle, and looked back in particular to the Hermits of St Augustine in Tuscany in the early middle ages as the link with St Augustine; 4) it was formally initiated in 1385 by the Augustinian prior general, the central authority of the Order in Rome, and was consistently supported by a succession of priors general up to the time of the Protestant Reformation and later; 5) the observants remained under the jurisdiction of the priors general, who became their protectors. Several of the priors general were observants; 6) the observant movement was not co-terminous with the Augustinian Order. It was encouraged, but not imposed, by the priors general. It depended on local support for its beginnings in different countries, but inevitably this was a matter of chance and opportunity; 7) the observants encouraged learning. This was a policy of the Augustinian Order since the late thirteenth century, and owed much to the example of the Dominicans.
>
> To be an observant friar meant that one belonged to a reformed house or branch of the Order .... The reformers did not expound revolutionary policy. Their purpose was to observe strictly, yet as far as humanly possible, the vows of poverty, chastity, and obedience, the *Rule* of St Augustine, and the constitutions of the Order.[10]

The hermitage of Lecceto in Tuscany became the first centre of the reform among the Augustinians. According to legend, St Augustine himself had lived at Lecceto for some time. It was known as a place of spiritual renewal and mystical piety, and was associated also with St Catherine of Siena. The seal of the Lecceto friary showed three mountains, symbols of the mystical ascent to God, beneath which ran the motto '[Christ] by his cross and blood redeemed us'.[11] When the Augustinians decided in 1385 to promote officially the observant movement within their Order, they selected Lecceto as the first house of the observance. From there, the 'observant movement' spread throughout Italy. Usually, the reform-minded friars formed certain communities where they could pursue the 'perfect community life' (*vita communis perfecta*) or the 'observance' (*observantia*), which meant that they gave up any private property and participated, on a regular basis, in community activities such as communal prayers and meals in the dining hall. By 1404 the reforms reached Saxony, when the first observant friary

---

[10] F.X. Martin, *Friar, Reformer, and Renaissance Scholar: Life and Work of Giles of Viterbo* (Villanova, 1992), pp. 77f., 85.

[11] See ibid., p. 81; and pp. 21f. See Gutierrez, *The Augustinians*, I, pp. 82–6 and 93–4.

was founded at Waldheim near Dresden. In 1419 reforms were begun at Ramsau, Bavaria, and Erfurt joined the reform movement in 1466. In the course of time such reformed friaries separated from the others and gathered in so-called 'reform congregations'. As early as 1397 a general chapter meeting for observant friaries had taken place at Munich. It was in this Bavarian city where 100 years later, in the 1490s, Staupitz most likely entered the Augustinian Order, probably because the friary belonged to the observant movement. He definitely professed his religious vows at Munich. In the late fifteenth century a growing number of friaries in the province of Bavaria (including Ramsau, Kulmbach, Nuremberg, Mindelheim, Memmingen, Regensburg and Munich) belonged to the reformed Augustinians and fell under the direct supervision of their general in Rome. This growth and the direct connection to Rome may have been factors in Staupitz's decision to join the friary at Munich, which was one of the most important at that time. Perhaps he imagined that in this group of reformed friaries he could make a career, possibly similar to that of the former prior of Munich, Johann Perger (= Berger, d. 1481), who had become auxiliary bishop of Freising and Brixen.[12]

Especially since the reform Council of Basel in 1434/35, efforts had been under way to reform the Augustinian Order from the top down to the local level. The general of the Order, Gerard de Rimini, was a participant in the Council of Basel and pushed for the reform of his Order. He found a collaborator at the Nuremberg Friary in Heinrich Zolter. The Order's province of Saxony was reformed according to the wishes of the Council of Basel. Since 1459 there has been a separate Saxon/German congregation of observant friaries. ('Congregation' by that time definitely meant a unit of reformed friaries distinct from the Order's provinces.) Staupitz belonged to the Saxon/German unit and eventually became its leader. The appearance of Augustinian observants in any region was almost always due to some young friar who had studied in Italy where he came into contact with the 'observant movement',[13] and also with the humanist movement there. So it

---

[12] See J. Hemmerle, *Die Klöster der Augustiner-Eremiten in Bayern* (Munich-Pasing, 1958), pp. 12–14, 51 (on Friar and Bishop Johann Perger); Kunzelmann, III, p. 251; V, p. 388. On Erfurt, see A. Zumkeller, 'Martin Luther und sein Orden', *AAug*, 25 (1962), pp. 254–90 (p. 258); English translation in J.E. Rotelle (ed.), *Theology and History of the Augustinian School in the Middle Ages* (n.p., Augustinian Press, 1996), pp. 207–37.

[13] See Kunzelmann, V, p. 390; Martin, *Friar, Reformer*, pp. 82–4; Walsh, 'The Observance', pp. 40–67; Zumkeller, 'Staupitz und die klösterliche Reformbewegung', p. 36. On Gerard de Rimini and Heinrich Zolter, see J. Helmrath, 'Theorie und Praxis: der Kirchenreform in Spätmittelalter', *Rottenburger Jahrbuch für Kirchengeschichte*, 11 (1992), pp. 41–70 (p. 64).

happened at that time that a friar such as Caspar Amman (*c.* 1450–1524) studied in Italy and became *Doctor sacrae paginae et pontificiorum canonum* (Doctor of Sacred Scripture and Canon Law). He was later the provincial of the Rhenish-Swabian province and was concerned about the observance. He also was one of the most learned Hebraists of his time and a sympathizer of the Lutheran Reformation, although he did not, however, break with the old Church. Provincial Caspar Amman, General Egidio da Viterbo (d. 1532) and Friar Felix Prato Israelita (d. 1539) were the three outstanding Hebrew scholars within the Augustinian Order in the first half of the sixteenth century.[14]

The great leader of the observants in Germany, Andreas Proles from Dresden (d. 1503), had also been sent to Italy where he had been a teacher of theology at Perugia in 1455. He was 'a zealot of implacable resolve' and the leader of the Saxon reform congregation of 27 friaries.[15] Staupitz became his immediate successor, both in terms of general spiritual outlook and in the office of vicar general of the observants in Germany. Staupitz was recommended for this job by Friar Johann von Paltz (*c.* 1444–1511) who had been a theology professor at Erfurt from 1485 to 1495, and also a preacher against the Turks and the Bohemians. Although he was concerned about reform within the friaries, Paltz's pastoral orientation was directed primarily toward the believers outside the friaries and their spiritual well-being. In all this he preached Augustinian theology. Friar Paltz was so well known that he was invited to preach before the Elector Frederick the Wise of Saxony. His sermons, delivered in the vernacular, were first published in 1490 under the title *Himlische Funtgrube* ('Heavenly Mine'), and were subsequently reprinted more than 20 times up to 1521; in 1502 they appeared in a Latin translation as *Coelifodina*. Paltz's pastoral efforts were aimed at the practice of piety under the general theological insight that God is merciful to all sinners. He urged the people to trust in God's mercy and

---

[14] On Amman, see A. Wagner, 'Der Augustiner Kaspar Amman', *Jahresbericht des Historischen Vereins Dillingen*, 7 (1894), pp. 42–64; H. Vonschott, *Geistiges Leben im Augustinerorden am Ende des Mittelalters und zu Beginn der Neuzeit* (Berlin, 1915; reprinted Vaduz, 1965), pp. 103–6. On the three Hebraists, see Gutierrez, *The Augustinians*, II, p. 143. See also my entry 'Amman' in *BBKL*, 16 (1999), pp. 49–52.

[15] See A. Zumkeller, 'Proles, André', *Dictionnaire*, XII, pp. 2406–9. The most recent monograph on Proles is R. Weinbrenner: *Klosterreform im 15. Jahrhundert zwischen Ideal und Praxis: Der Augustinereremit Andreas Proles (1429–1503) und die privilegierte Observanz* (Tübingen, 1996). Proles's sermons were edited by the Dominican Petrus Sylvius and the first set of five sermons was printed by Valten Schumann in 1530: *Sermones dominicales des gnadenreichen Predigers Andree Prolis ... vom neuen Jare erstlich angefangen. Durch Sylvium vleißig zusamm gelesen. Editio Prima* (Leipzig, 1530); see N. Paulus, *Die deutschen Dominikaner im Kampf gegen Luther (1518–1563)* (Freiburg, 1903), pp. 65f.

goodness. To what degree Staupitz became familiar with Paltz's theology, spirituality and reform efforts is difficult to assess. It is not surprising that with Paltz's predilection for Augustine some occasional similarities emerge between his writings and those of Staupitz's, as both relied heavily on Augustine.[16]

The purpose of the Order of St Augustine from 1256 was to produce biblical preachers equal to the Dominicans and the Franciscans. Indeed, it brought forth magnificent preachers as spiritual sons of the monk-bishop-preacher St Augustine. The Order's constitutions of 1290 made compulsory the study of theology, which was seen as the basis of the Order. The Augustinians spent much of their energies on preaching in the developing urban centres, so much so that preaching became a feature of their role in all of their provinces. Some of these preachers of the fourteenth and fifteenth centuries are still known by name: Christian Prezner of the Munich friary (d. after 1389); Stephen Wirtenberger of the Hagenau friary (d. c. 1400); Angelus Dobelinus originally of the Grimma friary (d. c. 1420) and the Saxon provincial Johann Zachariae of the Erfurt friary (d. 1428), both esteemed preachers at the Council of Constance. Johann Bocholt of the Wesel friary in Westphalia, Johann Screyen of the Königsberg friary and Johann of Wiedenbrück of the Osnabrück friary were the best known preachers of the first half of the fifteenth century. From the second half of that century we know of Konrad von Zenn (d. 1460), who was an influential member of the observant friary at Nuremberg, and the author of a book on the religious life. Also at Nuremberg, Friar Johann Vogt had become a popular preacher in around 1488. He preached in the Augustinians' new and much larger church, St Vitus, which had to be built (between 1479 and 1488) because of the huge crowds which their preachers regularly

---

[16] See T. Kolde, *Die deutsche Augustiner-Congregation und Johann von Staupitz: Ein Beitrag zur Ordens und Reformationsgeschichte nach meistens ungedruckten Quellen* (Gotha, 1879), pp. 96–165; W. Hümpfner, 'Äussere Geschichte der Augustiner-Eremiten in Deutschland (Von den Anfängen bis zur Säkularisation)', in *St. Augustin 430–1930* (Würzburg, 1930), pp. 147–96. Sermon 3 of Paltz's *Coelifodina* may have influenced Staupitz's booklet of 1515 on the art of dying; see M. Wriedt, 'Staupitz und Augustin: zur Kirchenväterrezeption am Vorabend der Reformation', in L. Grane et al. (eds), *Auctoritas Patrum: Contributions on the Reception of the Church Fathers in the 15th and 16th Century* (Mainz, 1993), pp. 227–57 (p. 236); on Paltz's *Werke 3, Opuscula*, and its use of Bernard see my 'Saint Bernard of Clairvaux in the Devotion, Theology, and Art of the Sixteenth Century', *LQ*, **11** (1997), pp. 306–52 (pp. 325–8). For a detailed investigation of Paltz's work, see B. Hamm, *Frömmigkeitstheologie am Anfang des 16. Jahrhunderts: Studien zu Johannes von Paltz und seinem Umkreis* (Tübingen, 1982). See also A. Morisi, 'Traditionalism, Humanism, and Mystical Experience in Northern Europe and in the Germanic Areas in the Fifteenth and Sixteenth Centuries', in G. D'Onofrio (ed.), *History of Theology*, trans. M.J. O'Connell, 3 vols (Collegeville, MN, 1996), III, pp. 338f.

attracted. Johann von Dorsten at Erfurt (d. 1481) was another great preacher of the Augustinians. There was, also, the preacher Reinhard of Laudenburg (d. 1503), author of a book on the passion of Christ, who worked at the friaries of Heidelberg and Nuremberg.[17]

Good preaching requires preparation and study. Thus, the Augustinians stressed learning, including secular vernacular learning, while, for instance, the Franciscan spirituals favoured devotion and stressed poverty. The Augustinians dutifully studied the Scriptures and theology, and they cultivated the ideal of the 'devotion to the common good'.[18] The Roman humanist Paul Cortese (d. 1510) asserted that among the best preachers in Italy were Bernardino of Siena, Savonarola and the two Augustinian generals, Mariano de Genazzano (d. 1498) and Egidio da Viterbo = Giles Canisio, d. 1532. Mariano was placed at the head of the Augustinians in 1495, Egidio in 1506. In Germany, Johann von Staupitz is counted among the most widely known, learned preachers after the older Johann von Paltz.[19]

Staupitz, like friars of other Orders, held preacher positions which had begun to be established from the late fourteenth century and which now, by the early sixteenth century, could be found in most if not all cities in Germany. Such urban *Prädikanten-Stellen* were not identical with the position of pastors. In fact, pastors may have said Mass on Sunday mornings without a sermon. On Sunday afternoons, the urban 'preachers' (usually from the ranks of mendicant Orders) took over and offered liturgies of the Word or some sort of religious adult education in complete separation from the celebration of the Eucharist. This phenomenon of the mendicants' preaching activities may have been the forerunner of the later worship practice of Protestants which consisted primarily of liturgies of the Word that were then returned to Sunday morning worship settings. This late medieval practice of sermonizing separate from the Mass in the churches of the mendicant Orders contributed to the decline of the significance of the Mass liturgy.[20]

---

[17] See A. Zumkeller, 'The Augustinian School of the Middle Ages', in Rotelle, *Theology and History*, pp. 11–79. On Nuremberg's Church of Saint Vitus, see J. Rosenthal-Metzger, 'Das Augustinerkloster in Nürnberg', *Mitteilungen des Vereins für Geschichte der Stadt Nürnberg*, 30 (1931), pp. 1–103 (pp. 14f.); Friar Vogt is listed as preacher on p. 101. On Dobelinus and Zachariae, see A. Zumkeller, 'The Augustinians at the Councils of Constance and Basle' in Rotelle, *Theology and History*, pp. 166f. On Bocholt, Screyen and Wiedenbruck, see A. Zumkeller, 'Teachers of the Spiritual Life Among the German Augustinians from the Thirteenth Century to the Council of Trent', in Rotelle, *Theology and History*, p. 135; Gutierrez, *The Augustinians*, I, p. 187; Martin, *Friar, Reformer*, pp. 19 and 86.

[18] See Martin, *Friar, Reformer*, p. 85.

[19] See Gutierrez, *The Augustinians*, I, 38–42; 186f.

[20] On the mendicants' custom of afternoon preaching, see M. Menzel, 'Predigt und Predigtorganisation im Mittelalter', *Historisches Jahrbuch*, **111** (1991), pp. 337–84;

Staupitz, himself, practised his preaching mainly during the seasons of Lent and Advent, and he tried to fill such preacher positions with talented friars drawn from his own reformed Augustinian Order. Historians have begun to investigate what was preached during the 'early years' of the Reformation, but so far they have paid little attention to the years immediately prior to what became known as the 'Reformation Year of 1517'. We shall see that focusing on the cross of Christ in preaching was not a uniquely post-1517, Protestant preaching prerogative, and that Luther, with his famous 'theology of the cross', is probably viewed best within the cross-centred spirituality of his observant Augustinian Order that had chosen the already mentioned motto: '[Christ] by his cross and blood redeemed us'. That such cross-centred preaching took place on the eve of the 'Reformation' can be observed in particular in Staupitz's Lenten sermons of 1512, in the last of which he quoted 1 Cor. 1: 23: 'We preach Christ, and him crucified.'[21]

The Augustinians were very much in touch with the currents of their times. In Italy they were friends of the humanists Petrarch (d. 1374) and Boccaccio (d. 1375), the two luminaries of the early Renaissance. By a happy coincidence of circumstances, the scholarship of the Renaissance and the Augustinian observant movement became associated at an early stage.[22] Petrarch provided the preface to the *Milleloquium sancti Augustini* written by the Augustinian Bartolomeo da Urbino (d. *c.* 1335), who completed a collection by another friar of about 15 000 excerpts from Augustine's works, under the maxim 'back to the sources'.[23] Friar Luigi Marsigli (d. 1394) was probably the first humanist member of the Augustinian Order who caught the attention of artists, scholars, and literati as the 'apostle and soul of the literary

---

A. Angenendt, *Geschichte der Religiosität im Mittelalter* (Darmstadt, 1997), p. 479. On preacher positions at cathedral churches in German-speaking lands, see A. Schmid, 'Die Anfänge der Domprädikaturen in den deutsch-sprachigen Diözesen', *Römische Quartalschrift*, **89** (1994), 78–110. On the impact of the preachers in the late Middle Ages and their significance for the introduction of the Reformation, see R. Herrmann, 'Die Prediger im ausgehenden Mittelalter und ihre Bedeutung für die Einführung der Reformation im Ernestinischen Thüringen', *Beiträge zur Thüringer Kirchengeschichte*, **1** (1929–31), pp. 20–68.

21 See Sermon 12; F. Posset, 'Preaching the Passion of Christ on the Eve of the Reformation', *Concordia Theological Quarterly*, **59** (1995), pp. 279–300 (pp. 279–82).

22 See Vonschott, *Geistiges Leben*; R. Arbesmann, *Der Augustiner-Eremitenorden und der Beginn der humanistischen Bewegung* (Würzburg, 1965); *idem*, 'Forerunners and Representatives of Humanism', in Gutierrez, *The Augustinians*, I, pp. 159–73; Martin, *Friar, Reformer*, pp. 87–9. On Petrarch and other humanists and theologians of the Renaissance, see C. Vasoli, 'The Theology of Italian Humanism in the Early Fifteenth Century', in D'Onofrio, *History of Theology*, III, pp. 22–60.

23 See Gutierrez, *The Augustinians*, I, pp. 161f.; Zumkeller, 'The Augustinian School of the Middle Ages', p. 14.

renaissance in Florence'. He became known at the same time as a reformer of the Church. He gathered a sodality of humanists at his friary Santo Spirito in Florence.[24] Perhaps modelled after this circle around Marsigli in Florence, the Nuremberg humanists formed their Staupitz Sodality, most likely inspired by Friar Nicholas Besler (Pesler/Peßler) who had been stationed in Florence for some time,[25] and who was one of Staupitz's confidants. Egidio da Viterbo, as the international leader of the Order of the Augustinians from 1506 to 1518, was a humanistic linguist, observant friar and reformer.[26] It was an Augustinian friar by the name of Augustinus Dodo Phrysius who worked on the humanist edition of Augustine's works published in 1506 by Johann Amerbach in Basel.[27]

The Augustinian Order had a scholastic master in Egidio da Roma (= Aegidius Romanus/Giles of Rome, d. 1316) whom they were expected to study according to their own regulations of 1290,[28] just as the Dominicans had their Thomas Aquinas (d. 1274), and the Franciscans had their Duns Scotus (d. 1308). To what degree Staupitz adhered to his Order's regulation is difficult to assess because there is no surviving systematic theological tract from him to parallel the commentary on the Sentences of Egidio da Roma. Staupitz was less interested in Scholastic theology and more concerned with good preaching and with a 'theology-for-piety' (*seelsorgerliche Theologie* or *Frömmigkeitstheologie*), a spiritual theology for practical use in the care of souls. Thus Staupitz was a *Seelsorger* (curate of souls), an observant monastic reformer, an Augustinian friar familiar with Scholastic theology but open to the humanist trends of his time, a professor of the 'sacred page', and a spiritual writer; but most of all, he was a great preacher.

These developments within the Augustinian Order and its pressure group, the observants, occurred within the wider context of the general reform movement in the Church. One of its high points was the Council of Constance (1414–18) while one of its chief actors, Jean Gerson

---

[24] See Vonschott, *Geistiges Leben*, pp. 20–23; Arbesmann, *Der Augustiner-Eremite-norden*, pp. 74–6; idem, 'Forerunners and Representatives', in Gutierrez, *The Augustinians*, I, pp. 63f.; P. Gallagher, 'Luigi Marsigli, the Florentine Humanist, 1342–1394' (Doctoral disseration, University College, Dublin, 1972); Vasoli, 'The Theology of Italian Humanism' in D'Onofrio, *History of Theology*, III, pp. 26–32.

[25] See F. Machilek, 'Klosterhumanismus in Nürnberg um 1500', *Mitteilungen des Vereins für Geschichte der Stadt Nürnberg*, **64** (1977), pp. 10–45 (p. 42).

[26] See J.W. O'Malley, *Giles of Viterbo on Church and Reform: A Study in Renaissance Thought* (Leiden, 1968).

[27] See H. Junghans, *Der junge Luther und die Humanisten* (Weimar, 1984), p. 44.

[28] See A. Zumkeller, *Johannes von Staupitz und seine christliche Heilslehre* (Würzburg, 1994), p. 211; idem, 'The Augustinian School of the Middle Ages', in Rotelle, *Theology and History*, pp. 17–29.

(1363–1429), became one of Staupitz's favourite writers. Gerson had transcended the traditional divisions of the Scholasticism and opted for the reform of theology in terms of a 'theology-for-piety'; he may be considered its initiator.[29]

Augustinian friars became famous for their preaching at the Council of Constance; among them were the already mentioned Friars Dobelinus and Zachariae. This Council had the *causa reformationis* on its agenda, but failed to decide much on it. This council was followed by recurring calls to reform. From the 1430s we know of a pamphlet which, in the name of Emperor Sigismund (d. 1437), called for radical reforms in state and church. It was spread under the title *Reformatio Sigismundi*; it originated probably at Basel and is attributed to a priest in the service of Duke William of Bavaria. Such calls, and included in them were the various complaints (*gravamina*), were taken up at the Council of Basel (1431–49) which was held under the protection of the said Duke William. These demands for reform were heard throughout the years to come, especially at the imperial diets of the Empire up to the Diet of Augsburg in 1518 and the Diet of Worms in 1521; it was to the latter that Martin Luther was summoned.[30]

The reform ideas were kept alive by the observant friars (among others). At the Fifth Lateran Council, at the beginning of the sixteenth century, the Augustinian prior general, Egidio da Viterbo, an eminent humanist, gave an impressive speech in favour of reform. Staupitz had Egidio's speech printed at Grunenberg's press which was located at the Augustinian friary in Wittenberg. Its title reads: *Oratio Prima Synodi sive concilii Lateranensis ... habita in aede Lateranensi Quinto Nonas Maias 1512. Impressa Wittenburgii per Ioannem Gronenbergk Apud Augustinianos.*[31]

---

[29] On 'theology-for-piety', see J. Wicks, *Luther's Reform: Studies on Conversion and the Church* (Mainz, 1992), p. 121. Wicks uses this expression as his own genial and felicitous translation of the less fortunate German expression *Frömmigkeitstheologie* which was introduced by Hamm in his *Frömmigkeitstheologie am Anfang des 16. Jahrhunderts* in 1982 (on Gerson, see p. 479). On Staupitz's concern for pastoral care, see M. Wriedt, 'Johann von Staupitz (ca. 1465–1524)', in C. Möller (ed.), *Geschichte der Seelsorge in Einzelportraits*, 3 vols (Göttingen, 1994–96), II, pp. 45–64.

[30] On Bavaria, see K. Bihlmeyer and H. Tüchle, *Kirchengeschichte*, 3 vols (Paderborn, 1960), II, p. 508. On the national interests and complaints of the Germans, see the 'Complaints of the German Nation Against the Roman See' at Augsburg in 1518, see G. Schmidt, 'Luther und die frühe Reformation – ein nationales Ereignis?', in S.E. Buckwalter and B. Moeller (eds), *Die frühe Reformation in Deutschland als Umbruch. Wissenschaftliches Symposion des Vereins für Reformationsgeschichte 1996* (Gütersloh, 1998), pp. 54–75 (p. 63).

[31] Egidio's speech is found in translation in Olin, *Catholic Reform*, pp. 47–60. On the printing of this speech in Germany, see M. Großmann, *Wittenberger Drucke 1502 bis 1517* (1971), no. 76; also R. Wetzel, 'Staupitz antibarbarus: Beobachtungen zur Rezeption heidnischer Antike in seinen Tübinger Predigten', in A. Mehl and W.C. Schneider (eds),

It could be inferred that, at the beginning of the sixteenth century, and during the early days of the Lutheran Reformation, reforms were demanded and carried out mostly by members of the Augustinian Order. In the past, the fact that a significant number of Augustinian friars sided with their confrère at Wittenberg, Martin Luther, was occasionally interpreted as proof of the decadence of the Augustinian Order itself.[32] This is not necessarily so, as this fact may alternatively be interpreted as indicating that those friars were in the forefront of the Catholic reform movement under the leadership of Staupitz, up to about 1520. Only in the 1520s did the Augustinian reform movement split into oppositional camps, for and against Luther. Early in 1521, the former general of the Augustinian Order, Cardinal Egidio da Viterbo, turned against Luther in some sort of an expert opinion or instruction written for the pope with the purpose of outlining the course of action that the emperor should take against Luther, whom Egidio called 'the father of lies' and the 'minister of Satan'.[33] It would need a detailed investigation of local church histories to demonstrate that the presence of Augustinian friars in a city brought about the spread of reform ideas in its region, and that their reform ideas flowed into what became most of the time, but not always, the Lutheran Reformation. In other words, the introduction of the Lutheran Reformation in imperial cities and elsewhere in German-speaking lands was channelled chiefly, although not exclusively, through the Augustinian friars in their midst, who had opened up to humanist ideas and spiritual reform. It is apparent that the first imperial cities which accepted the Reformation early in the 1520s had not only been exposed to the humanist movement[34] but also housed reformed

---

Reformatio et Reformationes: Festschrift für Lothar Graf zu Dohna zum 65. Geburtstag (Darmstadt, 1989), pp. 107–30 (p. 110).

[32] See F.X. Martin, 'The Augustinian Order on the Eve of the Reformation', *Miscellanea Historiae Ecclesiasticae. Bibliothèque de la Revue d'histoire ecclésiastique*, **44** (1967), pp. 71–104. On the role of the mendicants in France, see Robert Sauzet, *Mendiants et Réformes. Les réguliers mendiants acteurs du changement religieux dans le royaume de France (1480–1560)* (Tours, 1994).

[33] *Contra patrem mendacii, ministrum sathanae, Martinum*, in Egidio's *Informatio pro concilio contra Lutheranos*, partly edited in H. Tüchle, 'Des Papstes und seiner Jünger Bücher: Eine römische Verteidigung und Antwort auf Luthers Schrift "Warum des Papstes und seiner Jünger Bücher von D. M. Luther verbrannt sind" aus dem Jahre 1521', in R. Bäumer (ed.), *Lutherprozess und Lutherbann: Vorgeschichte, Ergebnis, Nachwirkung* (Münster, 1972), p. 67.

[34] See S.E. Ozment, *The Reformation in the Cities: The Appeal of Protestantism to Sixteenth-Century Germany and Switzerland* (New Haven, CT, 1975); B. Moeller, *Imperial Cities and the Reformation: Three Essays* (Durham, NC, 1982). However, the reform spirit of the Augustinians is not always taken into account. Often the connection between humanism and the Reformation is made, while the significance of the Augustinian friars and friaries remains underexposed.

Augustinian cloisters like, for example, Wittenberg and Nuremberg. Augustinian friars were often instrumental in the introduction of reform ideas, if not of the Reformation as such. The following list offers brief details of more than twenty friars whose contributions to the Reformation movement in the cities where they worked, were deemed so impressive as to merit individual entries in the Protestant dictionary of the (Protestant) Reformers (*Reformatorenlexikon*, Gütersloh, 1984) compiled – incompletely – by Robert Stupperich:

1 *Friar Stephan Agricola* (= Kastenpaur, d. 1547), who was saved by Staupitz from further persecution by the Salzburg authorities, became a reformer at Augsburg, and was a participant at the Marburg Colloquy.
2 *Friar Ludwig Agricola* (= Bauer, d. after 1540) became a reformer at Kulmbach, in the friary of which he had been the preacher.
3 *Friar Leonhard Beier* (= Beyer, year of death unknown), with a master's degree from Wittenberg, was persecuted at Munich in 1522, and became the reformer at Guben and Zwickau.
4 *Friar Adrian Buxschott* (d. 1561) originally belonged to the friary of Antwerp, which Staupitz had promoted and visited. He held a master's degree from Wittenberg, granted in 1518. After being persecuted in Holland, he became a reformer at Bremen and elsewhere in northern Germany.
5 *Friar Johann Dreyer* (d. 1544), from the friary of Osnabrück, was a reformer at Herford and Minden.
6 *Friar Augustin Gschmus* (d. 1543), entered the Augustinian Order at Basel, called himself an Erasmian and then a Lutheran. He is known as the reformer of Mühlhausen (Mulhouse), Alsace.
7 *Friar Caspar Güttel*, well known to Staupitz, originally belonged to the friary at Neustadt (Orla) from 1514; he was preacher and prior at the new friary at Eisleben until its dissolution in 1523, when he became the preacher and reformer of that city.
8 *Friar Gerhard Hecker* (d. 1538) had been provincial of the Saxon province in 1500 and later. In 1518 he was ordered by the prior general in Rome to take Luther, and possibly Staupitz, prisoners when they were at Augsburg; apparently he let both of them escape.
9 *Friar Heinrich Himmel*, whose dates are unknown, studied at Wittenberg from 1516; he gave lectures in the Cologne friary from 1521. The theology faculty of Cologne sought to prevent this, but without success. He was a reform-minded preacher not only in Cologne, but also at Wittenberg's castle church.
10 *Friar Johann Lang* (d. 1548), Staupitz's protégé, was the known humanist and reformer of Erfurt.

11 *Friar Wenceslaus Linck* (d. 1547), one of the first students at Wittenberg, succeeded Staupitz as dean of the theology faculty, as prior and preacher in Munich, and as vicar general of the observants; he became a key figure in the German Reformation. Simultaneously, for a short period of time, he was the vicar general of the Augustinians and the local preacher at Altenburg in 1522/23. He transferred to Nuremberg in 1525.

12 *Friar Johann Lonicer* (d. 1567) received his master's degree from Wittenberg, was preacher at the friars' church at Esslingen in southern Germany, and a professor of Greek at Strasbourg, and then at Marburg.

13 *Friar Johann Mantel* (d. 1530), had entered the Augustinians at Nuremberg, was with Staupitz at Tübingen, became prior of the Nuremberg friars from 1500 to 1502 and later was a reform-minded preacher at Stuttgart and elsewhere. He had to flee to Strasbourg and died in Switzerland as a more or less Zwinglian preacher.

14 *Friar Jacob Propst* (d. 1562), was the prior at the Antwerp friary from 1519; after being persecuted he ended up as the reformer of Bremen.

15 *Friar Nicholas Prugener* (d. 1553) became a reformer in the Alsace region.

16 *Friar Tilemann Schnabel* (d. 1557) was a friar at Erfurt and Wittenberg together with Luther and became a doctor of theology in 1514. He was provincial of Thuringia, and eventually became the reformer of Alsfeld.

17 *Friar Michael Stiefel* from Esslingen (d. 1567), was a preacher at Mansfeld and in Austria for some time. He then became pastor at Lochau.

18 *Peter Martyr Vermigli* (d. 1562), Augustinian prior at Naples, became pastor to the evangelicals from Italy who, like himself, ended up in Cambridge.

19 *Friar Johann Westermann* (year of death unknown) studied at Wittenberg in 1510, became prior at Lippstadt, and is known as the reformer of Geismar.

20 *Friar Heinrich Winkel* (d. 1551), from the friary at Halberstadt, was instrumental in the Reformation of Braunschweig.

21 *Friar Henry van Zutphen* (d. 1524) was a student at Wittenberg when Staupitz was Bible professor there. He became subprior of the Cologne friary in 1514, then prior at Dordrecht. He was close to the two Augustinian friars, Johann van den Essen and Johann Voss, who were executed in Brussels. He himself was executed in Heide, in Northern Germany.

22 *Friar Gabriel Zwilling* (d. 1558), was close to Staupitz at Wittenberg in 1512, came under the influence of Karlstadt and began reforms of his own at Wittenberg in 1521.

To these individual biographies of Augustinians who took a stand for Luther in the 1520s, should be added others, such as that of Friar Wolfgang Volprecht, a reform-minded friar who was appointed to the position of preacher at the friary at Nuremberg in the early 1520s. By 1525 the Augustinians were the only mendicants who were allowed to preach and hear confessions in that city; the Dominicans, Franciscans and Carmelites lost this privilege. Only at Volprecht's friary was holy communion distributed under both kinds at Easter in 1523.[35]

One must recall that the entire reform congregation of the Augustinians was in turmoil and transition. Much more historical research is needed in order to trace the role of Augustinian friars – who either contributed to Luther's Reformation, or who stayed within the Catholic reform movement of the sixteenth century, such as Johann Nathin and Bartholomäus Arnoldi von Usingen. There were a number of friars who had studied at Wittenberg and remained within the Catholic Church; for example, Konrad Helt (who was to become prior at Heidelberg), Johann Bethel von Spangenberg, Johann Ferber, Ludwig von Kochritz, Andreas Hofrichter (who was to become provincial of Franconia), Johann von Mecheln (who was to become vicar of the reform congregation in the Low Countries), Johann Herrgott (who was dean of the theology faculty at Wittenberg in 1516/17), Johann Pictor (also called Meler, who from 1518 to 1530 was a bishop in Münster and Osnabrück), and Wolfgang Kappelmaier (also called Ostermayer, who had received his doctorate in theology at Wittenberg in 1509).[36] Kappelmaier taught alongside Luther at Wittenberg, but turned against him and later on helped to preserve the Munich friary for the traditional Catholic faith.[37] Another Augustinian friar who remained with the 'old church' was the Swiss Konrad Treger (d. 1542) whose teaching came so

---

[35] See G. Vogler, 'Erwartung – Enttäuschung – Befriedigung: Reformatorischer Umbruch in der Reichsstadt Nürnberg', in Buckwalter and Moeller, Die frühe Reformation, pp. 381–406 (pp. 393 and 400). On the turmoil in the order, see Zumkeller, 'Martin Luther and his Order' in Rotelle, Theology and History, pp. 224–33. Stupperich's Reformatorenlexikon also omits two other Augustinian friars who became Lutheran pastors: Martin Glaser OSA was the prior of the friary in Ramsau and later the evangelical preacher in Franconia (see LW 48: 124); and Wolfgang von Zeschau OSA, prior of the friary in Grimma and later the evangelical preacher in a neighbouring town (see WABR 1. 227, n. 1).

[36] See N. Paulus, Die deutschen Augustiner in der Reformationszeit (Freiburg, 1891); idem, Der Augustinermönch Johannes Hoffmeister (Freiburg, 1891); idem, Bartholomäus Arnoldi von Usingen (Freiburg, 1893); Zumkeller, 'Martin Luther and his Order' in Rotelle, Theology and History, pp. 219–20.

[37] For the history of the Munich friary, see J. Hemmerle, Geschichte des Augustinerklosters in München (Munich-Pasing, 1956).

close to Luther's that some people even thought that he was a 'Lutheran'.[38]

From among the friars whom Staupitz knew personally or whom he promoted to positions in the reform movement, several adhered to the reform concepts within their Order. Nicholas Besler, who had been the prior at Nuremberg – first in 1491 and then again during 1495–99, 1513–14 and once more in 1515 – became Staupitz's successor as prior in Munich from 1503 to perhaps 1508. Besler was co-inspector of the friaries in the Low Countries together with Vicar Linck in 1521; however, the latter soon got married, while Besler fled from Nuremberg in 1524 and became prior at Cologne from 1525 to 1529.

Another one of Staupitz's friends, Friar Gregor Mayr, also remained with the religious community of the Augustinians. He had studied at Wittenberg in 1502/03 and earned his master of arts degree there; he had been in charge of the building project of the Wittenberg friary in 1504. Mayr was prior at Munich from 1508 to 1510, and again from 1517 to 1520. Both friars, Mayr and Besler, lived with Staupitz for a while at the branch office of their Order at Salzburg, during the winter months of 1520/21. However, a few years later, during the Peasants' War, Friar Mayr attempted to follow in the footsteps of Staupitz by applying for admission to the Benedictines of Salzburg. His request was denied by the Roman authorities. From 1523 to 1529 Friar Mayr was the main preacher (*concionator*, *Stiftsprediger*) at Salzburg.[39] Thus the reform-minded Augustinian Order around Staupitz produced not only 'Lutherans', as they were later called, but also prominent Catholic reformers[40] – the 'Staupitzians'.

As the present investigation of the life and work of Johann von Staupitz – as a friar, prior, and vicar general of the observant Augustinians in German lands – will make plain, Staupitz was a master of balanced Catholic spirituality, all of whose writings were thoroughly permeated by the teachings of Augustine, and who significantly contributed to the Reformation (both Catholic and Protestant). He

---

[38] See A. Zumkeller, 'Konrad Treger OESA (ca. 1480–1542)', in E. Iserloh (ed.), *Katholische Theologen der Reformationszeit* (Münster, 1988), pp. 74–80.

[39] On Besler, see Kunzelmann, VI, p. 363; VII, p. 384; on Mayr, see ibid, VI, pp. 339, 341 and 363. For the complete list of priors, subpriors, and friars of the friary at Nuremberg up to 1525, see Rosenthal-Metzger, 'Das Augustinerkloster in Nürnberg', pp. 94–103. On Besler and Mayr with Staupitz at Salzburg, and on Mayr's attempt to join the Benedictines, see J. Sallaberger, 'Johann von Staupitz, Abt von St. Peter (1522–1524) und die Salzburger Mendikantentermineien', *Studien und Mitteilungen zur Geschichte des Benediktinerordens und seiner Zweige*, **103** (1992), pp. 87–188 (pp. 146–9 and 158–65).

[40] See F.X. Martin, 'The Augustinian Observant Movement', in K. Elm (ed.), *Reformbemühungen und Observanzbestrebungen im spätmittelalterlichen Ordenswesen* (Berlin, 1989), pp. 325–45.

was recognized by his contemporaries as a true reformer and Luther himself always maintained that Staupitz was his 'reverend father in Christ'. Staupitz was to him the 'herald of grace and the cross' (1521); 'I have everything from Doctor Staupitz who got me started' (1532); 'Staupitz told me: One must look at the man who is Christ. Staupitz started the teaching' (1533); and finally (1535):

> I recall that when my movement [*initio cause meae*] first began, Dr. Staupitz, a very worthy man and the vicar of the Augustinian Order, said to me: 'It pleases me very much that this doctrine of ours gives glory and everything else solely to God and nothing at all to men; for it is as clear as day that it is impossible to ascribe too much glory, goodness, etc., to God'. So it was that he consoled me.

Interestingly, this was the wording Luther used in the publication of his *Commentary on Galatians* in 1535, where he gave proper credit to Staupitz in speaking of 'this doctrine of ours'. In later editions (after 1538) the editors censored Luther's own statement and made him remember Staupitz as saying 'the doctrine that you [Luther] preach', rather than 'our doctrine'.

Even during his final years Luther properly credited Staupitz for having been of decisive help with his pastoral care and theology. Luther confessed that otherwise he would have 'drowned' in his spiritual anxieties 'and ended up in hell' (1542). 'He [Staupitz] is first of all my father in this doctrine and he has given birth to me in Christ' (1545). In Luther's last letter to Staupitz, we read of the compliment that it was Staupitz through whom 'out of the darkness the light of the Gospel first began to shine in our hearts'.[41] Thus, with Steinmetz, one may state that 'if Luther is to be believed, then Staupitz is not merely a forerunner but the father of the Protestant Reformation'.[42] This observation is to be corroborated here, even though Steinmetz himself is not inclined to believe Luther's self-assessment; nor were other scholars before Steinmetz, such as the Protestant Ernst Wolf and the Catholic Reinhoud Weijenborg. One must no longer minimize Staupitz's significance when

---

[41] See *WA* 5. 21,25 (*Operationes in Psalmos*, Preface, 1521). *WATR* 1. 80,6f. (no. 173, 1532); 1. 245,9–12 (no. 526, Spring 1533); *WABR* 2. 264,48 (no. 376); *WABR* 3. 155,7–156,1 (no. 659); *WABR* 11. 67,7f. (Luther to Elector John Frederick, 1545); *WA* 40, 1. 131, 21–5 (on Galatians, 1535); see L.G. zu Dohna, 'Staupitz und Luther: Kontinuität und Umbruch in den Anfängen der Reformation', *Pastoraltheologie*, 74 (1985), pp. 452–65 (p. 457).

[42] D.C. Steinmetz, *Luther and Staupitz: An Essay in the Intellectual Origins of the Protestant Reformation* (Durham, NC, 1980), pp. 4 and 144. Steinmetz's book demonstrates the strange fact that Luther's own clear testimony regarding Staupitz's influence on him is not always accorded proper consideration by those researching Luther's life and work. Many such studies are preoccupied with preserving the originality of Luther and his work. On this, see Dohna, 'Staupitz und Luther', pp. 455f.

one wants to introduce *Reformation Thought*, as Alister E. McGrath still did in 1988.[43]

Not only did Luther himself give due credit to Staupitz, but so did the less friendly papal nuncio, Jerome Aleander (= Girolamo Aleandro, 1480–1542). Having analysed the situation, he declared that it was Staupitz 'who was the first to begin to speak up against the common school of theologians, although not with as much courage as Luther'.[44] These hints at a close connection between Staupitz and Luther are not meant to confirm the thesis that Staupitz was the mediator of a specific Augustinian school of thought to Luther; indeed, it is rather doubtful that such a specific school existed.[45] Nevertheless, Staupitz's and Luther's early theology are very similar, if not identical.

Despite the emphasis placed here on the significance of Staupitz and the Augustinian Order with its reform-minded friars for the development of both the Catholic and Protestant Reformations, the 'professional rivalry' between the Augustinians and the Dominicans which pervaded these developments should not be downplayed. The main purpose of both groups of friars was to preach. The Dominicans officially call themselves *Ordo Praedicatorum* (O.P.), that is 'Order of Preachers'. The rivalry and discrepancies between Augustinians and Dominicans can be observed, for example, in Florence where the Augustinians sided with their general Mariano de Genazzano, and the Dominicans with their confrère Savonarola.[46] The same rivalry became apparent at Tübingen at the time of Duke Eberhardus Barbatus (1445–96) who at first wanted Dominicans to teach at his new university, although it was the Augustinians who had already established a friary there. The Augustinian Johann Nathin was instrumental in averting the eviction of the Augustinians from Tübingen by reforming their friary there in 1483 according to the wishes of the Duke, their

---

[43] See E. Wolf in *RGG*, 6 (1962), col. 343; R. Weijenborg, in *Lexikon für Theologie und Kirche*, 2nd edn (Freiburg, 1962), IX, col. 1026; A.E. McGrath, *Reformation Thought: An Introduction* (Oxford and New York, 1988), pp. 62f. One may agree, however, with McGrath that Staupitz was not a typical representative of some so-called *schola Augustiniana moderna*.

[44] P. Kalkoff, *Aleander gegen Luther. Studien zu ungedruckten Aktenstücken aus Aleanders Nachlass* (Leipzig and New York, 1908) pp. 137–40 (p. 138).

[45] See D.C. Steinmetz, 'Luther and the Late Medieval Augustinians: Another Look', *Concordia Theological Monthly*, 44 (1973), pp. 245–9. M. Wriedt, 'Via Guilemi – Via Gregorii: Zur Frage einer Augustinerschule im Gefolge Gregors von Rimini unter besonderer Berücksichtigung Johannes von Staupitz', in R. Melville et al. (eds), *Deutschland und Europa in der Neuzeit. Festschrift für Otmar Freiherr von Aretin zum 65. Geburtstag* (Stuttgart, 1988), 1. Halbband, pp. 111–31.

[46] See Martin, *Friar, Reformer*, p. 15. At Florence, rivalry existed also between Dominicans and Franciscans; see Donnelly, *Prison Meditations*, p. 13.

territorial lord.[47] Staupitz for a brief period of time would be a member of the Tübingen friary.

Differences between the Orders were most obvious in the controversy over the humanist Reuchlin when the Dominican Hochstraten stood up against him, while the Augustinian general in Rome, Egidio da Viterbo, 'unhesitatingly' supported Reuchlin in 1513.[48] The rivalry continued during the indulgence controversy when the Dominican Johann Tetzel was attacked by Luther, who himself was instigated by Staupitz. Furthermore, it was the Dominican Order that set in motion the heresy charges against Luther; and Luther's papal interrogator in 1518, Cardinal Cajetan (1468–1534), was a Dominican. The Dominicans in Rome even made a Martin-in-effigy out of paper and burned, cursed and execrated it in a public square, the Campo di Fiore.[49]

Rivalry among the friars of different Orders was apparently commonplace both at Rome and at home. Both Orders, Augustinians and Dominicans, were also present at Wittenberg. The Dominicans of Magdeburg possessed a *terminus* station at Wittenberg as did the Augustinians of Herzberg. (A *terminus* was a branch office with living quarters for the friars and a warehouse for the storage of goods which the friars gathered ('begged').) Thus an economic factor also contributed to the rivalry between the two mendicant Orders. However, the main duty of the officers of such a *terminus* was not the collection of donations, but preaching and the hearing of private confession. The goods that the friars received were given in exchange for the pastoral care, especially their good preaching, which they provided for the people of the region or town which belonged to a given *terminus*.[50]

The Dominicans, like the Augustinians, sent young friars as students to the University of Wittenberg. Twelve Dominicans studied there between 1503 and 1520. One of them, Johann Mensing (d. 1547), was a student there in 1515/16, but never became a 'Lutheran', although he esteemed Luther's commentary on Galatians of 1519.[51] However, one must also note that not all Dominicans were automatically counter-reformers. We know of at least two exceptions: Martin Bucer who died

---

[47] See Kunzelmann, V, p. 444.

[48] See Martin, *Friar, Reformer*, p. 122.

[49] Luther was well aware of this incident: '*Dicitur mihi papyraceus Martinus in Campo fiore publice combustus ...*' (Luther's letter to Martin Glaser of 30 May 1519, *WABR* 1. 408,13f. with n. 6; *LW* 48. 125). There were about 30 Dominicans in the Saxon Order Province that, between 1518 and 1563, entered the battle against Luther, according to Paulus, *Die deutschen Dominikaner*.

[50] The main job of a *terminarius* was preaching in a certain territory (*terminus praedicationis*), not begging (*terminus mendiationis*); see Sallaberger, 'Johann von Staupitz, Abt von St. Peter', p. 91.

[51] See V. Pfnür, 'Johannes Mensing (+1547)' in Iserloh, *Katholische Theologen*, pp. 48f.

at Cambridge in 1551; and another Dominican who joined the Lutheran Reformation, Gallus Korn, who became a preacher at the Dominican friary at Nuremberg.[52]

Professional rivalry between the mendicant Augustinians and the mendicant Franciscans was less forceful, but it did still exist. When Staupitz published his first booklet in 1500 on the issue of Mass attendance in one's parish church, he met immediate opposition from the Franciscan Caspar Schatzgeyer (1463–1527) who published a defence of the mendicants' interests, which mentioned Staupitz's name in its title.[53] Later on, Schatzgeyer became a vocal opponent of the Lutheran Reformation. The Franciscans and Augustinians were also divided on the issue of interpreting Matt. 16: 18 ('You are Peter...'). When in 1520 the Franciscan Thomas Murner (1475–1537) wrote on the papacy as the highest authority of the Christian faith and in this context used Matt. 16: 18 in a way that irritated others, the Christian Hebraist and Augustinian Friar, Caspar Amman (c. 1450–1524) retaliated with a pamphlet, published in 1522, 'on the true exposition of the words of Christ, "You are Peter and on this rock I will build my church"'.[54] However, there were some other Franciscans who early on sided with the Wittenberg reformers. In the 1520s the Franciscan Johann Brießmann (1488–1549) got into trouble with his superior Jacob Schwederich for his 'Lutheran' tendencies. When the Franciscans held their provincial chapter meeting at Wittenberg in the autumn of 1519, Schwederich delivered his disputation on the stigmata of St Francis 'against Luther', *Quaestio disputata de S. Francisci stigmatibus contra Lutherum*, apparently

---

[52] 'On Bucer, see Stupperich, p. 47. On Korn, see J. Schilling, *Klöster und Mönche in der hessischen Reformation* (Gütersloh, 1997), pp. 143f.

[53] *Tractatulus de audienda missa diebus festivis editus per v. p. f. Casp. Schatzgeyer contra p. fr. Johannem Staubitz*; see Zumkeller, *Heilslehre*, pp. 13 and XIX. Schatzgeyer's tract is extant in manuscript form in the university library at Munich (Cod. ms. Oct. 34, bl. 200–210).

[54] T. Murner, *Uon dem babstentum, das ist von der hochsten oberkeyt* (Strasbourg: Johann Grieninger, 1520); C. Amman, *M Gasparis Amman vera expositio verborum christi Tu es Petrus et super hanc petram edificabo ecclesiam meam ... Contra falsam expositionem doctoris Thome Murner Ex fonte Hebreo hausta* n.p., 1521); edited by O. Clemen, "Eine Abhandlung Kaspar Ammans", *ARG*, 4 (1906), pp. 162–83, reprinted in E. Koch (ed.) *Kleine Schriften zur Reformationsgeschichte (1897–1944)*, 9 vols (Leipzig 1907; reprinted 1983), II, pp. 510–31. On the controversial interpretations of the 'rock' in Matt. 16: 18, and on the catholicity of Staupitz's and Luther's interpretation, see F. Posset, '"Rock" and "Recognition": Martin Luther's Catholic Interpretation of "You are Peter and on this rock I will build my Church" (Matthew 16: 18) and the Friendly Criticism from the Point of View of the "Hebrew Truth" by his Confrère, Caspar Amman, Doctor of the "Sacred Page"', in T. Maschke et al. (eds), *Ad fontes Lutheri: Toward the Recovery of the Real Luther. Essays in Honor of Kenneth Hagen's Sixty-Fifth Birthday* (Milwaukee, WI, 2001), pp. 214–52.

implying that Luther had preached *contra stigmata* (as the upset Luther wrote to Staupitz).[55] The Swabian Johann Eberlin, a member of the observant Franciscans, after having read Luther's works, eventually became the reformed pastor at Wertheim.[56] Bernardino Ochino, born in Siena, Italy, was first an observant Franciscan, then joined the newly founded Capuchin Order, becoming their general in 1539, until he had to flee to Protestant lands in 1542.[57]

These examples may suffice to illustrate two points. First, the personal biographies of numerous observant friars from different Orders demonstrate that – at least during Staupitz's lifetime – both developments were possible; that is, either to join the Protestant Reformation, or to retain one's place within the Catholic Reformation, as Staupitz did. Secondly, there was a long-standing element of professional rivalry among these Orders which had dedicated themselves to preaching and to pastoral care in the cities, a rivalry that was carried over into the religious conflicts of the early sixteenth century. Thus, the history of the early Reformation, especially in its early phase, may appear at times to be reducible to the quarrelling among friars (*Mönchsgezänk*) of differing affiliations: Augustinians against Dominicans, and Augustinians against Franciscans.

Details of such rivalries make it all the more anachronistic to employ a simplistic concept of *reformatio*. This term was used by many reform-minded friars of various shades; the call to reform was heard everywhere at the turn of the fifteenth to the sixteenth century. 'Everyone wanted reform, or professed to want reform. How to reform and what to reform was not so clear.'[58] Egidio da Viterbo, the worldwide leader of the Augustinians, wrote in 1517 to an unidentified province about the 'holy reformation'[59] within their religious Order. Generally, the term meant most of all the improvement of the ecclesiastical life, the reform of the church's head and members. The papacy, however, for a long time showed itself immune to any reforms of the 'head'. Yet, in the summons

---

[55] See Luther's letter to Staupitz of 3 October 1519 (*WABR* 1. 513–15 (no. 202), here 514,60f). On Schwederich, see J. Madey, 'Schwederich' in *BBKL*, 9 (1995), pp. 1183f. On Brießmann, see Stupperich, pp. 44–6.

[56] See Stupperich, p. 73.

[57] See ibid., pp. 155f.; also E. Campi, 'Bernardino Ochino's Christology and "Mariology" in his Writings of the Italian Period (1538–42)', in Gordon, *Protestant History and Identity* (see n. 6 above), pp. 108–22.

[58] O. Chadwick, *The Reformation* (Baltimore, MD, 1964), p. 12.

[59] Martin, *Friar, Reformer*, p. 376. On the various modern concepts of 'Reformation', see B. Hamm, 'Von der spätmittelalterlichen reformatio zur Reformation: der Prozess normativer Zentrierung von Religion und Gesellschaft in Deutschland', *ARG*, 84 (1993), pp. 27–33. B. Hamm, B. Moeller et al., *Reformationstheorien. Ein kirchenhistorischer Disput über Einheit und Vielfalt der Reformation* (Göttingen, 1995).

to the Fifth Lateran Council in 1512, Pope Julius could no longer avoid the issue.[60] In contrast, the 'members' of numerous religious/monastic communities were ready for it. What Staupitz meant by this will be developed in the following chapters.

The time was ready for reform, not only of academic theology, but also of pastoral care – which always included the reform of preaching. It may be symptomatic that at that time manuals for pastoral care and preaching appeared on the book market; for example, the *Manuale sacerdotum (curatorum)* of 1503 (1508?) by the pastor and professor, Ulrich Surgant, at Basel, or the *De arte predicandi* which the layman Johann Reuchlin published in 1504. Both books were preceded by the *Parochiale curatorum* of Michael Lochmaier (or Lochmayer), printed first in 1497 at Nuremberg, then reprinted in 1514 by Michael Furter in Basel.[61] This great concern for the reform of pastoral care/preaching, shared by Staupitz, is best understood against the backdrop of a widespread lack of care of souls among the higher clergy. The notion of pastoral care had so declined amongst the bishops that many of the prelates lived according to the ideals of secular lords, possessing tyrannical power and pursuing the enjoyment of life. 'These prince-bishops were not simply priest-bishops who were also princes, dukes and counts. They were predominantly only the latter.'[62]

While most prince-bishops were not in a mood for *reformation*, many monks and friars were. Here it is appropriate to recall the numerous monks of the Benedictine tradition who had worked toward reform for a long time and were encouraged by the reform councils of Constance and Basel. Best known are the efforts of several Benedictine congregations. For example, in Germany after 1380 the Benedictine reform group from the monastery of Kastl disseminated its ideas into many Bavarian monasteries. Other monasteries in Bavaria, and yet others in Swabia and Austria, were reached by the 'Union of Melk' which was established around 1418. In northern and western Germany, the Bursfelde Congregation (near Göttingen) made its reform felt from 1434 on.[63]

---

[60] See Stupperich, *Reformatorenlexikon*, p. 8.

[61] See Bihlmeyer and Tüchle, *Kirchengeschichte*, II, p. 459; E. Schubert, *Einführung*, *in die Grundprobleme der deutschen Geschichte im Spätmittelalter* (Darmstadt, 1992), p. 278. A copy of Lochmaier's 1514 edition is extant at the Cambridge University Library.

[62] J. Lortz, *The Reformation in Germany*, trans. R. Walls, 2 vols (London and New York, 1968), I, p. 94.

[63] In 1517 the Bursfelde congregation alone comprised almost 100 monasteries; see W. Ziegler, *Die Bursfelder Kongregation in der Reformationszeit: Dargestellt an Hand der Generalkapitelsrezesse der Bursfelder Kongregation* (Münster, 1968); Schilling, *Klöster und Mönche*, pp. 99–101; K. Schreiner, 'Benediktinische Klosterreform als zeitgebundene Auslegung der Regel. Geistige, religiöse und soziale Erneuerung in spätmittelalterlichen Klöstern Südwestdeutschlands im Zeichen der Kastler, Melker und Bursfelder Reform',

Under its influence, the Benedictine Abbot, Johann Trithemius (1462–1516), a great representative of monastic and biblical humanism, worked toward reform. He not only demanded the return to the biblical sources but, as a disciple of Reuchlin, himself copied the Greek text of St John's Gospel for his library at Sponheim. In 1486 he also wrote a biblical hermeneutic, *De investigatione sacrae scripturae*.[64] There still survives on an arch above a door at his monastery the trilingual inscription in Latin, Greek, and Hebrew: 'This gate is the Lord's; the just shall enter it' (Psalm 117: 20).[65] Some of his works (and, for instance, those of the French humanist Jacobus Faber Stapulensis) were available at the library of the Benedictine Abbey of St Peter at Salzburg,[66] where Staupitz became abbot in 1522.

The reforms issuing from the Benedictine centres of Kastl, Melk and Bursfelde led to the blossoming of the spiritual and scholarly life in most of the monasteries connected to them. In view of this long-standing climate of reform in the Benedictine monasteries north of the Alps, it is not all that surprising that the reform-minded Staupitz would also eventually become attracted to this monastic humanism, and that, late in his life, he himself would become the abbot of the Benedictine Arch-Abbey of St Peter at Salzburg.

Inner-monastic reforms alone may not have been the decisive factor which drew Staupitz to Salzburg. Other contributing factors that made the city appealing to him may have included the concerns of the Benedictines for pastoral care in the surrounding towns, the stability of this monastery, a friendly archbishop nearby, and perhaps the humanist side of the monastic reforms. We do know of the Benedictine Abbey of St Peter at Salzburg that it was a stimulating intellectual and spiritual centre from the middle of the fifteenth century on. No other monastery

---

Blätter für württembergische Kirchengeschichte 86 (1986), pp. 105–95; Helmrath, 'Theorie und Praxis', pp. 50–70.

[64] See K. Arnold, *Johannes Trithemius (1462–1516)* (Würzburg, 1971), pp. 46–51; N.L. Brann, *Abbot Trithemius 1462–1516: The Renaissance of Monastic Humanism* (Leiden, 1981); D.I. Howie, 'Benedictine Monks, Manuscript Copying and the Renaissance: Johannes Trithemius' "De Laude Scriptorum"', *Revue bénédicte de critique, d'histoire et de littérature religieuses*, **86** (1976), pp. 129–54. Perhaps, Staupitz read Trithemius's laments on the sad state of monasticism and on monastic reform, *Liber penthicus seu lugubris de statu et ruina ordinis monastici* (Mainz, 1493). This would not be too far-fetched, as we know that the young Luther had access to it and entered marginalia into chapter 4 of his copy of the *Liber penthicus*, see WA 9. (104) 114.

[65] See P. Becker, 'Benediktinische Reformbewegungen und klösterliches Bildungsstreben', *Rottenburger Jahrbuch für Kirchengeschichte*, 11 (1992), pp. 161–74 (p. 170).

[66] On (monastic and non-monastic) humanism in the Salzburg region including St Peter's Abbey, see C. Bonorand, *Joachim Vadian und der Humanismus im Bereich des Erzbistums Salzburg* (St Gallen, 1980) with valuable information on numerous humanists; here p. 80 (on St Peter's library holding works by Stapulensis and Trithemius).

possessed more texts in the vernacular than St Peter's library, a fact that mirrors great concern for pastoral care for the laity. Its scriptorium reflects the determination of an unknown director who wanted to make Latin religious literature available to wider circles by offering vernacular translations of works by Augustine, Bernard, Gerson, Johann Nider, Thomas à Kempis, Heinrich von Langenstein, Nicolaus von Dinkelsbühl and others.[67] Thus, the oldest Benedictine cloister in the German-language area (it was founded in 696 at the foot of the towering Castle Hohensalzburg, the residence of Salzburg's prince-bishops), must have appealed to Staupitz as a good place for pursuing fruitful pastoral work, somewhat protected by a huge fortress that could withstand the storms of the times that he may have anticipated in the early 1520s.

The general religious climate before and during Staupitz's lifetime favoured the tendency toward individualized and simplified piety. This *Tendenz* emerged due to the impact of Renaissance humanism and of the *Devotio Moderna* which was especially strong in the Low Countries, the birthplace of the prince of the humanists, Erasmus of Rotterdam.[68] The religious literature that came into existence at that time was often addressed to the individual; its concern was personal devotion and a virtuous, grace-filled life. This appealed to Staupitz. Late medieval treatises intended for personal reading, like Henry Suso's works, had a large readership.[69] Suso had written of the religious practices of the past (*antiquae consuetudines*) in contrast to those of the 'modern devout' (*moderni devoti*)[70] of his time. His wording may have been the matrix for our historiographic concept of 'modern devotion' which, along with religious humanism, had been on the rise and contributed to the colourful backdrop for Staupitz's life and work. There is at times a striking similarity between Suso's and Staupitz's expressions; however, Staupitz never mentioned Suso by name.

Late medieval reform efforts did not only focus on the individual devotion, but also on the reform of pastoral care. We may assume that Staupitz was familiar with, or at least shared, the concerns that found expression in contemporary manuals for priests such as the *Manuale curatorum predicandi* ... by the humanist pastor and professor, Ulrich Surgant. In his widely used and reprinted work (first published in 1502 at

---

[67] See R. Newald, 'Beiträge zur Geschichte des Humanismus in Oberösterreich', *Probleme und Gestalten des deutschen Humanismus* (Berlin, 1963), pp. 67–112 (p. 99); on monastic humanism in the fifteenth and sixteenth centuries, see pp. 82–102.

[68] See Vonschott, *Geistiges Leben*, pp. 68–96.

[69] See I.W. Frank, *A Concise History of the Mediaeval Church*, trans. J. Bowden (New York, 1995), pp. 148–51.

[70] P. Künzle (ed.), *Heinrich Seuses Horologium Sapientiae* (Fribourg, Switzerland, 1977), p. 408, lines 14–19.

Basel) Surgant wrote that 'the Sacred Scripture is the fitting material for preaching' (*congrua materia praedicationis est Sacra Scriptura*).[71] We may imagine that this is exactly what Staupitz wanted to hear and recommend.

In the following chapters we will pay close attention to the traces of late medieval spiritualities on the one hand and to any elements of biblical and monastic humanism on the other hand, as they appear in the life and work of Staupitz. All in all, we shall see Staupitz and many of his observant Augustinians as 'pioneers' of religious and pastoral reforms.[72]

---

[71] *Manuale Curatorum predicandi prebens modum tam latino quam vulgari passim quoque gallico sermone practice illuminatum. Cum certis aliis ad curam animarum pertinentibus. Omnibus curatis tam conducibilis quam salubris* (Basel, 1502). See 'Homiletics', in *Catholic Encyclopedia* (internet). See E. Wenneker, after Johann Ulrich, in *BBKL*, **11** (1996), pp. 273–5.

[72] Joseph Hemmerle spoke of 'the Augustinians, of the strict observance' as the spiritual pioneers for the Reformation: 'die geistigen Bahnbrecher für die Reformation', in *Die Klöster der Augustiner-Eremiten in Bayern*, p. 14.

CHAPTER TWO

The Early Years: Sermonizer, *Reformator*, Friend of Humanists, and Concern for Pastoral Care (1460s–1512)

The early years

Johann von Staupitz, one of the six children of Günther and Katharine von Staupitz, was born at Motterwitz (or Mutterwitz), near Grimma and Meissen, in Saxony,[1] and although the year of his birth is unknown, most scholars agree that he was born between 1463 and 1468. Thus he was about the same age or a little bit older than Desiderius Erasmus of Rotterdam, whose birthdate is also not known, but is assumed to be between 1466 and 1469. Staupitz was the descendant of an old noble Saxon-Meissen family which still exists today. The family's coat of arms shows a red post-horn on a silver background, the emblem being crowned with a helmet and a jumping hart.[2] When his father died in 1494, Johann was already an Augustinian friar, so the inheritance went to his three brothers. Günther was apparently the oldest, followed by Rahfolt, then Heinrich. His older sister, whose name is not known, married Albrecht Gernod. Her dowry consisted of half of the village of Leippen. The youngest sister, Magdalene, was six years of age when their father died. As a 13-year-old girl she was sent to the Cistercian nunnery at nearby Nimbschen for an annual fee of two *gulden* which the oldest brother Günther paid every year. The family owned land in Dabrun near Wittenberg.[3]

---

[1] According to the local researcher, Dieter Moebius, Motterwitz is located 15 km southeast of Grimma, Germany; Moebius's letter of 10 April 1992 to Rudolf K. Markwald, co-editor of *125 Years of Staupitz Research: 1867–1992. An Annotated Bibliography of Studies on Johannes von Staupitz (c. 1468–1524)* (St Louis, MO, 1994), p. 11. The most recent biographical sketches on Staupitz (in English) are to be found in the introduction to *125 Years of Staupitz Research*, and in D.C. Steinmetz, 'Staupitz', in H.J. Hillerbrand (ed.), *The Oxford Encyclopedia of the Reformation*, 4 vols (New York and Oxford, 1996), IV, pp. 109–11.

[2] See J. Sallaberger, 'Johann von Staupitz, Luthers Vorgesetzter und Freund, und seine Beziehungen zu Salzburg', *Augustiniana*, **28** (1978), pp. 108–54 (p. 152, n. 197).

[3] See A. Jeremias, 'Johannes Staupitz, Luthers Vater und Schüler', *AELK*, **61** (1928), pp. 345–50 (pp. 346–47); hereafter, 'Jeremias, *AELK*'.

Staupitz grew up as a childhood friend of the future Duke and Elector of Saxony, Frederick the Wise, who was born in 1463 at Torgau, south east of Wittenberg, and north east of Leipzig, and died in 1525. Staupitz may also have been a friend of Johann von Schleinitz (c. 1470–1537), who was born at Mügeln, east of Leipzig, and was the prince-bishop of Meissen from 1518 to 1534. All three boys may have gone to the same school for the local nobility at Grimma. According to George Spalatin, the Elector Frederick himself had once remarked to him, when they were both at Grimma: 'Here it was where I went to school', pointing toward the 'black tower' which housed the school.[4] Staupitz stayed in close contact with Frederick for most of his life. Frederick's epithet 'the Wise' had originally been conferred on him for his expertise in courtly etiquette, but he soon merited it also for his wisdom in governing the land. He was a man of great piety, as he collected relics in the traditional way, occasionally with the help of Staupitz, as will be seen below. He was a modest man and 'wise' enough not to seek to become emperor of the Holy Roman Empire of the German Nation after Maximilian's death in 1519. Staupitz, in growing up in such illustrious company, obviously was not destined to remain an obscure and simple friar, when he joined the Order of the Augustinians. If there is doubt about him being educated at Grimma, one may assume that he was educated in the company of young Frederick at the electoral castle at Torgau.

In the city of Grimma an Augustinian friary, at first unaffiliated, had existed since the thirteenth century; its church still exists. Here Frederick the Wise liked to spend Easter every year and did so as late as 1520. It was probably here that Staupitz first got to know the Order of the Hermits of St Augustine in which he was to play an important leadership role. He may have joined the Order there, but it is more likely that he did so in Munich. In Staupitz's time the Grimma friary already belonged to the observant – that is, the strict reform – congregation of the Augustinians whose primary task was known as the 'work of preaching

---

[4] The information that Frederick went to school at Grimma is based on Spalatin's biography of the elector; see Jeremias, *AELK*, p. 347. I. Ludolphy, *Friedrich der Weise. Kurfürst von Sachsen 1463–1525* (Göttingen, 1984), p. 45, questions the likelihood of Frederick having been taught in a school rather than by private tutors. M. Wriedt, 'Johannes von Staupitz als Gründungsmitglied der Wittenberger Universität', in S. Oehmig (ed.), *700 Jahre Wittenberg: Stadt, Universität, Reformation* (Weimar, 1995), p. 175, n. 7, also points out that there is no solid proof for Staupitz and Frederick having been schooled together. Not much is known of Johann von Schleinitz; see, however, W. Rittenbach and S. Seifert, *Geschichte der Bischöfe von Meißen 968–1581* (Leipzig, 1965), pp. 360–67; P. Dittrich, *Die Meißener Diözese unter der Kirchenpolitik der Landesherren des 16. und 17. Jahrhunderts*, 2nd edn (Leipzig, 1982), p. 92; R. Schwarz, *Luther* (Göttingen, 1986), pp. 73–4 (on Schleinitz's later action against Luther's sermon on the Lord's Supper), W. Kohl, 'Schleinitz, Johann von', in *BBKL*, 9 (1995), pp. 272f.

and of religious information' (*opus praedicationis et religiosae informationis*).[5]

Staupitz's education seems to have been somewhat peripatetic. He began his studies with the liberal arts at the distant University of Cologne where he may have matriculated in May 1483, receiving his bachelor of arts degree in November 1484. Cologne was the greatest city of Germany in the late Middle Ages, an economic, ecclesiastical and cultural centre. The following year, Staupitz spent one semester (from summer 1485 to the end of October 1485) at the University of Leipzig, which was close to his home territory. He then returned to Cologne where, in summer 1489, he received his master of arts degree. On 30 October 1489 he was listed as a member of the faculty of arts at Leipzig, but it is not known whether he gave any lectures there.[6]

One may wonder why Staupitz studied at these two cities. The fact that the universities of Cologne and Leipzig were known as centres of humanism may have influenced his choice. Classicists like Conrad Celtis (d. 1508) and Petrus Mosellanus (d. 1524) worked at Leipzig; while the humanist Hermann von Neuenahr (d. 1530) was the chancellor of the University of Cologne, which was devoted to theology, medicine and the natural sciences. It was at Cologne that the works of the French spiritual writer, Jean Gerson, *Opera Omnia*, were published in 1483/84, at the time when Staupitz was finishing his undergraduate studies there. Staupitz's Tübingen sermons of 1497/98 are permeated with references and allusions to Gerson's works on the spiritual life of the soul, on the consolation of theology, on the *Magnificat*, on the simplicity of the heart, on the passions of the heart, and similar topics (see pp. 47–9, 54–9, 65).

These two universities – Leipzig and Cologne – represent, however, not only the climate of humanism, but also that of scholasticism. Nevertheless, the humanists inspired the study especially of Augustine, and they thus created some sort of an 'Augustine renaissance' in the late Middle Ages. The reformed Augustinian Order contributed much to this development and the prior of the Augustinian friary at Cologne, Theodoricus Wichwael, was sympathetic to the humanist movement. In 1509, under prior Johann von Huysden, a friend of Staupitz, the friary switched to the Saxon province. Their friendship led to the establishment

---

[5] Tübingen Sermon 20 (Staupitz, I. 319). See Jeremias, *AELK*, p. 347; Sallaberger, 'Johann von Staupitz, Luthers Vorgesetzter und Freund', pp. 114–15; A. Zumkeller, 'Johannes von Staupitz und die klösterliche Reformbewegung', *AAug*, 52 (1989), pp. 31–49; Zumkeller, *Heilstehre*, p. 33 (Würzburg, 1994) p. 15. On the buildings at Grimma, see Institut für Denkmalpflege der DDR (ed.), *Martin Luther: Stätten seines Lebens und Wirkens* (Berlin, 1983), p. 36.

[6] See A. Kunzelmann, V, pp. 434–5; A. Zumkeller, 'Staupitz', in *Dictionnaire*, XIV, p. 1184.

of a *studium generale* in Cologne. During the Reuchlin controversy, the Cologne friary of the Augustinians unequivocally supported with Reuchlin against the Dominicans.

At Leipzig, too, one could find humanists who eventually began to challenge the scholastic teachers. For example, Martin Pollich von Mellerstad and Hermann von dem Busche sided with the humanists against the scholastic Conrad Wimpina.[7] Nothing, however, is known as to which side, if either, Staupitz favoured when he was in Leipzig and Cologne. His later actions in finding professors inclined to humanism for the new university at Wittenberg, and the fact that he and Martin Pollich were instrumental in building up the University of Wittenberg, indicate his preference for the movement of the humanists, as well as his distaste for the *rixosa theologia*, the 'quarrelling theology', of the scholastics.

'Who will liberate me from this quarrelling theology?' (1497–1500)

The exact date of Staupitz's entry into the Augustinian Order is not known. Quite possibly it could have been shortly after he had finished his studies at Cologne where he came to know the humanistic Augustinians. He may have made the decision to become a friar in 1490, or perhaps as late as 1495. The Augustinians possessed more than 100 friaries in Germany. He could have picked any one of them once he determined that this Order was the right one for him. If the intellectual climate of humanism in general and monastic humanism in particular was a factor for the young Staupitz's selection, then becoming a member of the Augustinian Order was the logical choice because this Order had been most closely involved in the humanist movement since its beginnings in Italy. Not only the Italian, but also the German friaries had opened up to

---

[7] See Introduction in Staupitz, I. 18–19; Zumkeller, 'Johannes von Staupitz und die klösterliche Reformbewegung'; M. Wriedt, *Gnade und Erwählung. Eine Untersuchung zu Johann von Staupitz und Martin Luther* (Mainz, 1991), p. 205. The Universities of Leipzig and Cologne are mistakenly understood as exclusively being schools of scholasticism in D.C. Steinmetz, *Reformers in the Wings* (Philadelphia, 1971), pp. 18–29; M. Brecht, *Martin Luther. His Road to Reformation 1483–1521*, trans. J.L. Schaaf (Philadelphia, PA, 1985), p. 54. See also J.V. Mehl, 'Humanism in the Hometown of the "Obscure Men"', *Studien zur Geschichte der Universität zu Köln* (Cologne, Weimar and Vienna, 1991), p. 32; Mehl, 'Hermann von dem Busche's *Vallium humanitatis*: A German Defense of the Renaissance *studia humanitatis*', *Renaissance Quarterly*, 42 (1989), pp. 480–506. For the situation at Leipzig, see J.H. Overfield, *Humanism and Scholasticism in Late Medieval Germany* (Princeton, NJ, 1984), pp. 173–85; E. Rummel, *The Humanist–Scholastic Debate in the Renaissance and Reformation* (Cambridge, MA, and London, 1995), pp. 69–70.

this movement which at first co-existed peacefully with the scholastic traditions.[8]

It is very likely that Staupitz joined the Order at Munich, because he made the profession of his final vows there. Having become a friar, Staupitz wore the black habit of the Order and a leather belt. Why this Saxon went to Bavaria remains unclear. Perhaps he got to know the southern region through the Saxon court councillor Degenhart Pfäffinger who came from the region east of Munich (his name is associated with the locations Pfäffing and Wasserburg).

The friary at Munich is located on Neuhauser Street, and since the fifteenth century had belonged to the branch of the strict observers of the Rule of St Augustine. Perhaps Andreas Proles, the vicar general, assigned Staupitz to the Munich friary in order to strengthen the reforms there, which had been introduced only a few years earlier. Furthermore, we know from the library catalogue of the Munich friary, that its library housed books of ancient authors and writers of the Italian Renaissance, which may have been attractive to the young Staupitz. The number of humanist books in friaries in the south (Bavaria, Austria) was greater than in those of the north, where he came from.[9]

The date of Staupitz's ordination to the priesthood is unknown. Equally uncertain is where he received further training. It has been suggested that from Munich he may have been sent for further studies to the friaries at Prague or Vienna, both of which belonged to the Bavarian province.[10] However, this is not very likely because the Munich friary

---

[8] See R. Arbesmann, *Der Augustiner-Eremitenorden und der Beginn der humanistischen Bewegung* (Würzburg, 1965). On humanists and Augustinian friars in Italy, see K. Elm, 'Mendikanten und Humanisten im Florenz des Tre- und Quadrocento. Zum Problem der Legitimierung humanistischer Studien in den Bettelorden', in O. Herding (ed.), *Die Humanisten in ihrer politischen und sozialen Umwelt* (Boppard, 1976), pp. 51–86. We know that monastic humanism was present, for example, in Nuremberg with the Benedictines, Carthusians, Carmelites and Dominicans as well as with the Augustinians; their libraries at Nuremberg contained a considerable amount of humanist literature; see F. Machilek, 'Klosterhumanismus in Nürnberg um 1500', *Mitteilungen des Vereins für Geschichte der Stadt Nürnberg*, **64**, pp. 10–45.

[9] On the Munich library catalogue, see H. Vonschott, *Geistiges Leben, im Augustinerorden am Ende des Mittelalters und zu Beginn der Neuzeit* (Berlin, 1915; reprinted Vaduz, 1965), p. 121; H. Junghans, *Der junge Luther und die Humanisten*, (Weimar, 1984; Göttingen, 1985), p. 26.

[10] See W. Günter, 'Johann von Staupitz (ca. 1468 bis 1524)', in E. Iserloh (ed.), *Katholische Theologen der Reformationszeit* (Münster, 1988), pp. 11–31 (on the possiblity of Staupitz studying at Prague and Vienna); with Zumkeller, *Heilslehre*, p. 3, one may question Günter's assumption. On the Munich friary, see C.-J. Roepke, *Die Protestanten in Bayern* (Munich, 1972), p. 17. For the history of the Augustinian friary at Vienna, see F. Rennhofer, *Die Augustiner-Eremiten in Wien: Ein Beitrag zur Kulturgeschichte Wiens* (Würzburg, 1956).

was observant/reformed at that time and thus no longer belonged to the conventual Bavarian province of the Augustinians. The Munich friary had, since 1481, been a member of the reformed branch in the Saxon-Thuringian province.

It is not impossible that the young friar received some of his training in one of the reformed friaries such as that at Erfurt. The religious and theological climate at Erfurt around 1500 is well documented. The Augustinian friary was probably dominated by its own teaching friars who appear to have made a strong differentiation between philosophy and theology, and were open-minded as regards humanist ideas.[11] The constitutions of the Augustinian Order from 1290 decreed that all theological studies were to follow the lines of thinking of Egidio da Roma (d. 1316). The general chapter of the Order renewed this decision in 1491 in order to counteract certain attempts made to introduce the teachings of Gregory of Rimini (d. 1358).[12] This regulation may have been in effect also at Tübingen where we find Staupitz at the end of May 1497.

Tübingen at that time was a little town of about 3000 inhabitants. Since 1490 the theology faculty of the University of Tübingen had its lecture hall in the Augustinian friary – an indicator of the close integration of faculty and Order. The choir area of the church also served the university as the location for academic celebrations; the university paid rent to the cloister. Thus, Staupitz experienced here a model of cooperation between friary and university that served him well later on, when he was invited to help build up the new University of Wittenberg.

Friar Johann von Staupitz, Friar Nicholas Besler (originally from Nuremberg), and Friar Gregor Mayr (also Mayer; originally from Munich) matriculated at the same time at Tübingen in the spring of 1497. Both Besler and Mayr were to become Staupitz's lifelong co-workers. Apparently it was the vicar general of the reformed Augustinians, Proles, who recommended them for the advanced study of theology at the general chapter meeting in Rome in 1497. Staupitz soon became a *Baccalaureus Biblicus*, and the prior of the reformed

---

[11] See Zumkeller, *Heilslehre*, p. 3, n. 2. J. Sallaberger, 'Johann von Staupitz, die Stiftsprediger und die Mendikanten-Termineien in Salzburg', *Studien und Mitteilungen zur Geschichte des Benediktinerordens und seiner Zweige*, **93** (1982), pp. 218–69 (p. 241). On the religious climate at Erfurt, see A. Zumkeller, *Erbsünde, Gnade, Rechtfertigung und Verdienst nach der Lehre der Erfurter Augustinertheologen des Spätmittelalters* (Würzburg, 1984); H. Junghans, *Der junge Luther*, pp. 31–56; for a recent summary of the religious situation at Erfurt (and Wittenberg), see B. Lohse, *Luthers Theologie in ihrer historischen Entwicklung und in ihrem systematischen Zusammenhang* (Göttingen, 1995), pp. 29–35.

[12] See Zumkeller, *Heilslehre*, p. 211.

friary, that is from the autumn of 1498 until 1500. Professor Wendelin Steinbach (1454–1519) entered into the records of the theological faculty that 'Magister Johannes Staupitz ... prior of the Tübingen convent' began his Bible lectures on 29 October 1498.[13]

Staupitz lived at an old Augustinian friary at Tübingen. Founded in the second half of the thirteenth century, this friary was built on the banks of the Neckar River, below the castle, in the centre of the city. In 1464 a new building had been erected, and the cloister church had been rebuilt at the same time. Only a few years before Staupitz's arrival the stone pulpit had been carved: it shows the Virgin and Child and the four Church Fathers, Gregory, Jerome, Ambrose and Augustine. At the time of the founding of the university in 1477 the friars had been pressured into reforms, namely to return to the strict observance of their Rule. The local government of Count Eberhard wanted only reformed friars in its city, as he had learned from his relatives at the Heidelberg court that the reform of the Augustinians at Heidelberg in 1476 had been successful. If the cloister at Tübingen had not reformed itself, the friars would have had to relocate elsewhere and the rival, and at that time perhaps more learned, Dominicans would have taken their place. In 1478 Andreas Proles (leader of the observants since 1460) succeeded in reforming the friary and thus guaranteed the Augustinians' stay at Tübingen. The reform, however, did not take effect officially until October 1483.

In order to secure this reform process, Proles assigned the north-German Friar Johann Nathin to this southern friary. Nathin appears to have been the first of the learned Augustinian friars at Tübingen. He left Tübingen in 1488 to continue his studies at Heidelberg, and afterwards taught at Erfurt. Johann Brüheym from Gotha appears to have taken Nathin's place at the Tübingen friary and was its prior while he pursued

---

[13] 'Magister Johannes Stupitz [sic] ord. herem. s. August. conventus tüwingensis prior, principiavit in cursum biblie Die antepenultimam octobris Anni 1498 [29 October 1498]; in sentencias vero 10. Jan. 1499 ...; recepit licentiam 6. Juli 1500 et insignia magistralia die sequente', as quoted in Kunzelmann, V, p. 434; and in Staupitz, I. 6, n. 13. On Besler's simultaneous presence at Tübingen, see W. Schneider-Lastin (ed.), *Johann von Staupitz, Salzburger Predigten 1512. Eine textkritische Edition* (Tübingen, 1990), p. 4. On some of the better known friars that were at Tübingen during 1483–1500 (such as Nathin, Bickel, Brüheym, Themmen, Epp, Mantel, Luft, Mayer), see Kunzelmann, II, pp. 142–7. On the history of the Tübingen friary, see M. Brecht, 'Das Augustiner-Eremiten-Kloster zu Tübingen', in *Mittelalterliches Erbe* (Tübingen, 1962), pp. 45–91 (p. 64), as quoted by B. Neidiger, 'Die Observanzbewegungen der Bettelorden in Südwestdeutschland', *Rottenburger Jahrbuch für Kirchengeschichte*, 11 (1992), pp. 175–96 (p. 194); R. Huber, *Die Universitätsstadt Tübingen* (Tübingen, 1968), pp. 40–62. On Proles and the general chapter meeting, see T. Kolde, *Die Deutsche Augustiner-Congregation und Johann von Staupitz*, (Gotha, 1879) p. 213.

graduate studies in theology. He and Friar Hertwig Themmen from Goslar graduated together in 1494 as doctors of theology. Two other learned friars are known who became professors at Wittenberg; one was Dionysius Bickel, the other Sigismund Epp. The latter, upon his return from Wittenberg, became rector of the University of Tübingen in 1504/05, while another friar, Johann Kreuss (or Kruss), held this position in 1516. Altogether the names of almost 50 Augustinians appear in the university records up to 1530. Among them was Staupitz who, in 1497, was sent to Tübingen both for the purpose of study and in order to take on the office of prior of the friary in 1498. Staupitz played a key role there, especially in its study programme, as in him the friary gained a reform-minded leader. His approach towards the internal affairs of the Order meshed with the general tendencies at Tübingen university where the overall inclination was towards humanism and toward a general 'reformation of the church in head and members'. This institution, with its four classical faculties of philosophy, theology, jurisprudence and medicine, was only 20 years old when Staupitz moved to Tübingen.

Reform of the friaries and of university studies went hand in hand, much to Staupitz's liking. Shortly before his arrival, the teaching of the Latin language at the friary had been revised through the introduction, in 1496, of new, more humanist textbooks. For this the friars employed their own Latin language instructor. While Johann Reuchlin and others at Tübingen began to study Hebrew and Greek at that time, nothing is known of such studies at the Augustinian friary.[14]

During these years the significance of the city of Tübingen was on the rise, as it had become not only a university town, but also, after Stuttgart, the second largest city of the state of Württemberg. In 1495, Tübingen had become the second place of residence for its territorial lord. Besides the count's determination to accept only reformed Augustinians, he favoured the Brethren of the Common Life who lived according to the principles of the *Devotio Moderna*. This group had been invited by the same Count Eberhard and settled a few miles north east of Tübingen, shortly before Staupitz's arrival there. Professor Gabriel Biel (1410–95) was a member of the Brethren.

---

[14] See Brecht, 'Das Augustiner-Eremiten-Kloster zu Tübingen', pp. 73–85; M. Schulze, 'Tübinger Gegenätze. Gabriel Biel und Johannes von Staupitz: von spätmittelalterlicher Reform zu Luthers Reformation', *Tübinger Blätter*, **72** (1985), pp. 54–9. As early as 22 April 1476, Friar Heinrich Stirer wrote to the secretary of Duke Ludwig of Bavaria-Landshut that 'years ago' Stirer had been asked to help with the 'reformation' of the friary at Tübingen, but was unable to do so because it was outside his own province, and he lacked the necessary extra personnel at his disposal. This letter is preserved in the *Chronik des Lauinger Augustinerklosters* (Archive of the city of Lauingen) and was published in *Jahresbericht des Historischen Vereins Dillingen*, **8** (1895), pp. 168f.

The reform-minded climate at Tübingen suited Staupitz well. Having completed the obligatory lectures on the Bible, which, as mentioned, he had begun in October 1498, he became *Sententiarius* on 10 January 1499. With this advanced degree in systematic ('dogmatic') theology he now lectured on the *Sentences*. If he followed the Order's constitutions, he would have studied the books of Egidio da Roma on the *Sentences*. That he actually did this is evident from the numerous traces and long quotations from the first two books of Egidio's work which are to be found in Staupitz's Tübingen sermons. Since the twelfth century, theological studies had concentrated on both Holy Scripture and the *Sentences* of Peter Lombard. The commentaries on the Scriptures and on the *Sentences* were the most important literary genres of scholastic theology. For about three centuries Lombard's systematizations were the official texts for teaching in the 'schools' (hence the label 'scholasticism'). We do not have any of Staupitz's lectures of that time, neither his biblical nor his systematic-dogmatic ones. However, we do have his 'sermons' on Job, which indicate Staupitz's decision to concentrate on commenting on the Scriptures rather than on any *Sentences*, and to do so in the form of 'sermons'.

It is probable that at Tübingen at that time Staupitz would have been exposed to the thought-world of the four most widely known theologians and preachers: the Bible scholar Wendelin Steinbach (1454–1519) who became known for his commentaries on Pauline letters; the Franciscan Friar Paul Scriptoris (*c.* 1462–1505); the humanist Konrad Summenhart (1458–1502); and the *Stiftsprediger*, that is, a preacher who is paid from an endowment fund, at St George's church, Martin Plantsch (1460–1533), whose sermon manuscripts are extant.[15]

Scriptoris had learned Greek from Reuchlin in order to enhance his Bible studies. He was somehow forced to leave Tübingen because he was suspected of holding heretical views, and had to join the Franciscans at Basel. From there he fled to Vienna in fear of being imprisoned, and from Vienna to Italy where he died in 1505. Scriptoris was a very popular lecturer on Scotus, and indeed was called the most keen and sharp expert (*acutissimus Scotista*). Scriptoris's lectures on Ockham with their Scotist colouring were available in print (Tübingen: Othmar, 1498). Scotism was

---

[15] H. Feld, 'Konrad Summenhart. Theologe der kirchlichen Reform vor der Reformation', *Rottenburger Jahrbuch für Kirchengeschichte*, **11** (1992), pp. 85–116. Johann Eck largely agreed with the assessment that these theologians were of significance, as he mentioned three of them as his own teachers at Tübingen (in his spelling – D. *Chunrat Sumerhart*, D. *Wendel Stainbach* and F. *Paulus Scriptoris*; Eck also listed D. Jacob Lemp, but not Martin Plantsch; see Eck, *Schutz red kindtlicher unschuld wider den Catechisten Andre Hosander* [Andreas Osiander] *und sein schmach büchlein* (Eichstätt, 1540); Feld, 'Konrad Summenhart', p. 86, n. 6.

always well represented at the University of Tübingen, from its beginnings, with Heynlin von Stein (1477/78) and Walter von Wervee (1480). Scriptoris was an advocate of change in theology and in the Church, and he is often considered a reformer before the Reformation. Staupitz had made sure that his subordinate friars at Tübingen took Scriptoris's courses. Indeed, it is said that Staupitz daily led all the students of his friary to Scriptoris's lectures on Scotus. Moreover, it appears that later on Staupitz continued this practice at Wittenberg where the young friars also had to study Scotus (more so than Augustine).[16] However, one need not overstate any dichotomy between Scotus and Augustine because the Franciscan-Scotist school of thought incorporated much of Augustine.

The University of Tübingen at Staupitz's time had primarily come under the influence of the humanist Konrad Summenhart who had been teaching on Scotus since 1492. He was rector of the university in 1500 when Staupitz earned his graduate degree in theology. As a professor of sacred theology, he too learned the biblical languages from Reuchlin. Like other humanists he did not identify with any theological movement of his time. Summenhart was concerned that Aristotle had gained too much influence in theology. In 1492 he had deplored the fact that in the schools of theology Averroes as a commentator on Aristotle was heard louder than Christ and the apostles. Summenhart and Scriptoris wanted to push back scholastic studies, and, along with them, Aristotle and Averroes. The distancing from such an influence on theology was nothing new as there were a number of late medieval theologians in the Order of St Augustine who expressed their strong reservations in this regard. Besides being apprehensive about Aristotle's influence in theology, both theologians also shared interests in a practical theology directed toward piety, and in conciliarism. Summenhart, in particular,

---

[16] On Scotism at Tübingen, see Neidiger, 'Die Observanzbewegungen', p. 190. The title of Scriptoris' lectures is *Scriptoris, Paulus, o. Min., Lectura declarando doctoris subtilis* [Ockham] *sententias circa Magistrum in primo libro*. On Scriptoris, see L. Keller, *Johann von Staupitz und die Anfänge der Reformation. Nach den Quellen dargestellt* (Leipzig, 1888; reprinted Nieuwkoop, 1967), pp. 7–13; H. Tüchle, 'Scriptoris, Paulus' in *Lexikon für Theologie und Kirche*, 11 vols, 2nd edn, (Freiburg, 1957–65) IX, pp. 553f. Zumkeller, *Erbsünde*, p. 459; *idem*, *Heilslehre*, p. 213. On Staupitz at Tübingen, see B. Riggenbach (ed.), *Das Chronikon des Konrad Pellikan* (Basel, 1877), p. 12, as quoted by Junghans, *Der junge Luther*, p. 50. For Luther's reminiscence on Scotus, see his table talk: '[Augustinus] est summus theologus, qui post apostolos scripserunt. Sed nos monachi non legimus eum [Augustinum], sed Scotum' (*WATR* 4. 611, 6–8 (no. 5009; May/June 1540)). A recent introduction to Scotus is provided by A. Broadie, *The Shadow of Scotus: Philosophy and Faith in Pre-Reformation Scotland* (Edinburgh, 1995). On medieval scholarship, Lombard, the *Sentences* and scholasticism, see the succinct description in I.W. Frank, *A Concise History of the Mediaeval Church*, trans. J. Bowden (New York, 1995) pp. 101–7.

opposed the excessive use of art in monasteries and for devotion, and may be considered a follower of St Bernard of Clairvaux on this issue. Summenhart was a preacher of the incarnation; two of his Christmas Eve sermons on the humanity and divinity of Christ were published in 1498.[17]

Summenhart fought tooth and nail against the pigeon-holing of theologians into specific schools of thought. He also pleaded for an openness to the diversity of theological currents and emphasized the need for biblical studies at the university. Staupitz remembered Summenhart's slogan: 'Who will free me from this quarrelling theology?' This exclamation was so striking that Martin Luther, who heard it from Staupitz, mentioned it in one of his table talks as late as in summer 1540:

> Staupitz was vicar of over 30 monasteries. He was the first who restored the Bible to his monasteries .... A fine impetus must have been at work in this man. He laboured hard on establishing the university [of Wittenberg]. In his lectures he often cited Doctor Summenhart of Tübingen as saying: 'Who will free me from this quarreling theology?'.... [Staupitz] was the first who restored [the study of] the Bible in his monasteries.[18]

This general trend towards intensified Bible studies is aptly characterized as 'Biblical Humanism'. This movement was also represented by Wendelin Steinbach, who may have been Staupitz's other professor at Tübingen. Steinbach was known as an industrious researcher of the Bible and, according to the humanist Philipp Melanchthon (d. 1560), of Augustine's works. At Tübingen, Staupitz may also have known Melanchthon's great-uncle, Johann Reuchlin, the famous German humanist and Hebrew expert who had lectured there since 1481. It is not known, however, whether Staupitz actually was Reuchlin's student. Furthermore, Staupitz came to Tübingen in the same year that the humanist Heinrich Bebel (1472–1518) became professor of

---

[17] On Summenhart, see F.X. Linsenmann, *Konrad Summenhart: Ein Culturbild aus den Anfängen der Universtät Tübingen* (Tübingen, 1877); on his criticism of Aristotelianism, see H.-G. Hofacker, 'Vom alten und nuen Gott, Glauben und Ler', in J. Nolte et al. (eds), *Kontinuität und Umbruch: Theologie und Frömmigkeit in Flugschriften und Kleinliteratur an der Wende vom 15. zum 16. Jahrhundert* (Stuttgart, 1978), p. 148. On his understanding of indulgences, see Feld, 'Konrad Summenhart', pp. 113–14; on his conciliarism, p. 96; on his iconoclastic tendencies, pp. 102–7; on his published Christmas Eve sermons, pp. 100–102; on his anti-Aristotelianism, p 104. On the Augustinians and their criticism of Aristotle, see A. Zumkeller, 'Die Augustinertheologen Simon Fidati von Cascia und Hugolin von Orvieto und Martin Luthers Kritik an Aristoteles', *ARG*, **54** (1963), pp. 13–57; *idem, Heilslehre*, p. 19.

[18] 'De Staupitio ... . Saepe citavit in lectionibus Doctorem Summerhand [sic] Tubingensem dicentem: Quis liberabit me ab ista rixosa theologia? ... Is primus restituit biblia suis monasteriis' (*WATR* 5. 99, 12–18 (no. 5374)).

poetry and rhetoric. Bebel openly fought against the scholastic teaching method as his *Disputation with a Theologian* reveals. In it, he objected to allowing theologians to speak 'ungrammatically'; to him it was 'a novel and unusual privilege to let theologians speak like barbarians'. Bebel – sounding just like Summenhart with his lament on the 'quarrelling' theologians – expected theologians to imitate the church fathers and refrain from 'obscuring the theological truth with their minute, morose, and inextricably knotty questions'.[19] Thus, all in all, Staupitz lived at Tübingen in a milieu of Augustinian reforms and of an emerging critical attitude toward scholastic theology. It is therefore perhaps noteworthy that Staupitz never referred to any work of the best known Tübingen professor, Gabriel Biel, except once, and then on a rather insignificant issue.[20]

Sermonizer on the priority of God's mercy (1497–98)

Staupitz's spiritual writings at Tübingen are extant, and are known as his 'Tübingen Sermons'. In them he covered the first two chapters of the Book of Job. The sermons, which may or may not have been delivered orally to his friars, may have come into existence between 1 June 1497 and the end of 1498.[21] They are his earliest works and are preserved in

---

[19] As regards Bebel at Tübingen, see Rummel, *The Humanist–Scholastic Debate*, pp. 41–8. See also O. Clemen, 'Staupitz', in A. Hauck (ed.), *Realencyclopädie für protestantische Theologie und Kirche*, 3rd edn, (Leipzig, 1896–1913), XVIII, pp. 781–6 (p. 781). On Reuchlin, see L. Geiger, *Johannes Reuchlin* (Leipzig, 1871); L.W. Spitz, 'Reuchlin's Philosophy: Pythagoras and Cabala for Christ', in his *The Religious Renaissance of German Humanism* (Cambridge, MA, 1963). M. Goshen-Gottstein, 'Reuchlin and his Generation', in A. Herzig and J.H. Schoeps (eds), *Reuchlin und die Juden* (Sigmaringen, 1993), pp. 151–60.

[20] Concerning the relationship between Biel and Staupitz, one should probably abandon the view (uncritically repeated by Wriedt, *Gnade und Erwählung*, p. 205), that Staupitz knew Biel's works quite well, but rather say, with Zumkeller, that 'one is not certain that he [Staupitz] studied the works of Gabriel Biel' ('Staupitz', *Dictionnaire*, XIV, p. 1189).

[21] On the dating of these 'sermons', see G. Buchwald and E. Wolf, *Staupitz. Tübinger Predigten* (Leipzig, 1927) p. XIV. Staupitz's dedication preface: 'post multam deliberationem coniectis oculis in Iob affectum firmius stabilivi' (Staupitz, I. 45). In his Sermon 1 of 1512 Staupitz gave a similar instruction for practising meditation: 'tue die augen zue' ('close your eyes') (Schneider-Lastin, *Johann von Staupitz, Salzburger Predigten 1512*, p. 28). Similar advice for meditating 'with closed eyes' would later reappear in Luther; see F. Posset, 'Bible Reading "With Closed Eyes" in the Monastic Tradition: An Overlooked Aspect of Martin Luther's Hermeneutics', *ABR*, 38 (1987), pp. 293–306. Staupitz's Prologue: 'Erit in omni processu huius libri textus punctatim sermonibus distinctus; neque enim scholastice disputando, sed de ambone ad vulgum praedicando praesentem statui discutere materiam'. (Staupitz, I, 46). 'Omnes huius libri sermones sub unico themate propono; erit tale: "Dominus dedit ..." Iob 1, etc.' (Staupitz, I. 47).

his own handwriting, collected into a book-length manuscript, but never published by him. These sermons actually form a *tractate* which he dedicated to the man who perhaps inspired him to write them, Johann Brüheym, a doctor of theology and former prior at Tübingen. Brüheym was the commissioner of the reformed friaries within three of the four Augustinian provinces in the south and west of what is today Germany, namely the provinces of Bavaria, Rhineland-Swabia and Cologne (thus excluding Saxony-Thuringia). He became prior of the new friary Mühlheim-Ehrenbreitstein in 1495, before Staupitz had come to Tübingen. This may mean that Staupitz knew Brüheym through other, earlier connections which now prompted him to dedicate his sermons to him. Alternatively, he may have wanted to be on good terms with this commissioner who supervised all the reformed friaries in German-speaking lands except Saxony-Thuringia.

Staupitz's 34 sermons were written in Latin. In the preface he indicated that he had been commissioned to write these sermons; yet, he was apparently free to choose his topic. After much meditation 'with closed eyes' he settled on Job, but not in the way of a 'scholastic disputation', as he wrote in the Prologue. Evidently he wanted to provide a devotional theology and therefore he decided to discuss the matter in sermon form. He took as his biblical *leitmotif* the verse 'The Lord has given it, the Lord has taken away; as it pleased the Lord so it was done; blessed be the name of the Lord' (Job 1: 21). At the beginning of each single 'sermon' he repeated the main theme, 'The Lord has given ...', and then he entered into the subject matter which he divided into three parts. In all this he understood the figure of Job as a 'figure of Christ' (*figura Christi*) in the traditional typological interpretation of Christ's suffering, an interpretation which left its traces, for instance, also in a contemporary illustration of the booklet *Die himlische funtgrub* ('The heavenly mine') of his confrère Johann von Paltz. In a manuscript edition from 1508 of Paltz's text, the picture of Christ's flagellation is framed by the words of Job 1: 21 in German, to be read from bottom to the top: *GOT GAB / GOT NAM / GOT SY / GEBENEDIT*.[22] Evidently, Job provided much food for meditative thought to the Augustinians of that time. Reproduced below is the table of contents of Staupitz's Tübingen sermons:

Part I:
  1 On the mercy of God.
  2 On the simple heart.
  3 On the upright heart.

---

[22] C. Burger et al. (eds), *Johannes von Paltz, Werke 3, Opuscula* (Berlin and New York, 1989), p. 189 (with illustration 8); hereafter 'Paltz, *Werke*'.

4 On the fear of God.
5 On evil.
6 On marriage.
7 On riches.
8 On honour, fame, and power.
9 On banquets.
10 On parental care.

Part II:
11 On temptations and tribulations.
12 On the call to penance.
13 On the diabolic way.
14 On the Lord's help.

Part III:
15 On virtue and grace.
16 On the power and licence for tempting.
17 On the devil and his temptations.
18 On the balance of the soul.
19 On the abuse of spiritual power.
20 On the manner of correcting.
21 On the abuse of secular power.
22 On parental neglect in educating the children.
23 On neglecting the intellect.
24 On neglecting the will or emotion, or on devotion.
25 On detraction and silence.
26 On angels.
27 On the devil working on Job.
28 On the truth about Job's equanimity and patience.
29 On the ultimate power or licence conceded to the devil, concerning temptations.
30 On the life of nature, grace, virtue.
31 On sin coming from the heart.
32 On punishment and suffering.
33 On detrimental compassion.
34 On fraternal correction.
35 [*only extant as a draft*].
[*Part IV was planned, but not executed*].

Staupitz's first sermon featured the mercy of God, his main theme for all of his sermons. He developed it from Rom. 15: 9, 'the Gentiles glorify God because of his mercy'. The sermonizer correlated this to the gentile Job and his relation to God. God's glory stems from his mercy, and God's great mercy is shown to us in Job. God is to be honoured and praised for his mercy. However, God cannot be praised unless his mercy 'precedes'. Concerning this concept of prevenient grace, Staupitz was dependent upon Augustine's interpretation of Psalm 62 as he readily admitted: 'I give praise to You, through your mercy I praise You, says St Augustine.' Then Staupitz quoted Ps. 62: 4 and addressed his 'most dear brothers' (that is, the listeners or readers) by saying that Job and everyone else is conceived and born in sin (alluding to Ps. 50: 7); 'and the divine mercy precedes us' through the institution of the sacraments so that we may receive grace. 'The mercy of God alone' does all this, since we did nothing good to deserve it. The gentile Job received his perfect life 'from God's mercy alone'.[23] Already here, the principle of 'grace alone' is stated explicitly, including the concept of God's 'prevenient grace' (mercy). Staupitz carried this theme throughout his *tractate* – always mindful of 'The Lord has given it ...'. He repeatedly spoke of the prevenient God (alluding to Ps. 20: 4) and God's free will and man's consent to God's grace, but not as a human achievement. As is typical of him, he always started with his central theological theme, namely the goodness of God. In this he primarily followed Augustine and Egidio da Roma.[24] Staupitz explicitly took up the theme of 'prevenient grace', in a later sermon, based on Romans 7, saying that the grace of God came to us through Jesus Christ.[25] From his first sermon on, Staupitz dealt with the theme of grace and the mercy of God, making no distinction between 'grace' (*gratia*) and 'mercy'

---

[23] 'Vere honorandus est deus super misericordia sua, qui nec laudari posset, nisi praecederet misericordia sua: 'Dono tuo te laudo, per misericordiam tuam te laudo, inquit sanctus Augustinus; et sanctus David: Quoniam melior est misericordia tua super vitas, labia mea laudabunt [Ps. 62: 4]. Recogitemus, o fratres carissimi, quoniam gentilis hic erat, et nos, aliquando inter gentes computati, in peccatis concepti [see Ps. 50: 7] sumus et nati, et praevenit nos divina misericordia institutione sacramentorum, ut gratiam reciperemus. Sola misericordia hoc fecit .... Iob ergo gentilem cum cogitaverimus perfectionem habuisse virtutum, ex sola dei misericordia recipisse confiteamur' (Sermon 1, Staupitz, I. 49). David Steinmetz correctly placed Staupitz's entire theology under the theme *Misericordia Dei: The Theology of Johannes von Staupitz in Its Late Medieval Setting* (1968). However, Steinmetz's opinion of the Tübingen Sermons is wanting according to Oberman, '*Duplex Misericordia*: The Devil and the Church in the Early Theology of Johann von Staupitz', in *The Impact of the Reformation* (Grand Rapids, MI, 1994), p. 43.

[24] '... totum dei, quia sine ipso praeveniente quantum ad divinam motionem nullum bonum, totum hominis, quia non infunditur nobis gratia, nisi motui divino consentiamus. Iustificat enim deus nos, nobis consentientibus. Haec Aegidius de Roma in 2 Scripto distinctione 28 quaestione 1 quaestiuncula 3' (Sermon 15, Staupitz, I. 271); see Steinmetz, *Misericordia Dei*, p. 114), who points out that Staupitz is in agreement with Thomas Aquinas in affirming the impossibility of meriting either election or justifying grace. Zumkeller (*Heilslehre*, p. 59), emphasizes Staupitz's use of Augustine and Egidio at this point.

[25] 'Gratia dei per Iesum Christum dominum nostrum' (see Rom. 7: 24f.). Hac utique gratia praeventus est sanctus Iob' (Sermon 27, Staupitz, I. 399).

(*misericordia*). He would take up this great theme of his life repeatedly in his later sermons. Here, in his Tübingen sermons, he insisted, along with Thomas Aquinas, that no one is denied grace who does what is in him, *facere quod in se est*.[26] He saw no contradiction between the radical principle of 'grace alone' including the 'prevenient grace' and the concept of 'doing what is in oneself'. For Staupitz, everything is done under God's grace, as 'the Lord has given it' (Job 1: 21).

There is no reason to postulate that in developing his theology Staupitz would have had to be familiar with Gregory of Rimini as the leader of a school of strict Augustinian anti-Pelagianism. He did not mention the name of Gregory of Rimini anywhere in these sermons. It is unlikely that Staupitz belonged to a definite Augustinian school, that is the so-called *via Gregorii*;[27] rather, he returned directly to the Bible and to the church fathers, especially St Augustine. Grace cannot be merited, and everything good that is done is done by nothing else but by grace. Staupitz grounded his teaching in the Scriptures, drawing from Isa. 64: 5, that our good works are like dirty rags, and that thus we are in need of grace. It is striking how closely he adhered to Pauline theology in all his sermons, saying at one point: 'This is what St Paul preached in almost all his Epistles, that we do not believe that we are justified by works, but by grace.'[28] Staupitz continued that our sins are not 'imputed' because of the 'most rich mercy of the Redeemer', speaking with Ps. 31: 1–2 ('Happy the person whose fault is taken away, whose sin is covered. Happy the person to whom the Lord imputes not guilt, in whose spirit there is no guile'). He expanded his considerations with explicit quotations from Jean Gerson;[29] on whom he also depended when

---

[26] 'Sanctus Thomas non credit 'facienti quod in se est' posse negari "gratiam"' (Sermon 5, Staupitz, I. 95).

[27] On the controversy over the *via Gregorii*, see M. Wriedt, 'Via Guilelmi – via Gregorii. Zur Frage einer Augustinerschule im Gefolge Gregors von Rimini unter besonderer Berücksichtigung Johannes von Staupitz', in R. Melville et al. (eds), *Deutschland und Europa*, pp. 111–31. U. Köpf, 'Monastische Traditionen bei Martin Luther', in C. Markschies and M. Trowitzsch (eds), *Luther – zwischen den Zeiten. Eine Jenaer Ringvorlesung* (Tübingen, 1999), pp. 17–35 (pp. 22–6.) On 'Augustinianism', see D.C. Steinmetz, 'Luther and the Late Medieval Augustinians: Another Look', *Concordia Theological Monthly*, 44 (1973), pp. 245–60; D.R. Janz, 'Towards a Definition of Late Medieval Augustinianism', *Thomist*, 44 (1980), pp. 117–27; Zumkeller, *Heilslehre*, p. 211 (on Staupitz and Egidio).

[28] 'Hoc est quod sanctus Paulus in omnibus epistulis suis fere praedicavit, ne in operibus sed gratia iustificari credamus' (Sermon 23, Staupitz, I. 354–55 p. 355).

[29] 'Quod autem non imputatur, hoc agit misericordia copiosissima redemptoris' (Sermon 23, Staupitz, I. 355); for his reference to Gerson's *De vita spirituali animae*, see Staupitz, I. 357f. Staupitz again declared in this context with reference to the non-imputation of sins according to Ps. 31 (Vulgate) that no sin can be forgiven except by God's free non-imputation of it; see Staupitz, I. 356.

discussing the opinions of other 'doctors' who dealt with this crucial Psalm 31. Staupitz's doctrine of the non-imputation of sins is the consequence of his reflections on the wording of the Vulgate Psalm 31 (*Beatus vir*). The sermonizer concluded that we are not good and righteous because of our good works. Grace cannot be merited. As we came forth from our mother's womb without our doing, so 'we came forth from the womb of Mother Church without our merits'.

Staupitz owed much of his theology of grace to Egidio da Roma, whom he mentioned by name more than a dozen times – almost in every other of his Tübingen sermons (3, 5, 6, 10, 11, 12, 15, 23, 24, 25, 30 and 31) – usually referring to him as *dominus Aegidius de Roma*. 'Lord Egidio' was the teaching authority of the Augustinian Order according to its own constitutions which had been reinforced recently, in 1491. Egidio had been a student of Thomas Aquinas, although he was an Augustinian friar; he later become a bishop. In following Egidio da Roma and also Augustine, whose Letter 194 (*ad Sixtum presbyterum*) he quoted, Egidio thus appeared as one of Staupitz's most important theological mentors who led him back to St Augustine and to St Paul.[30] The Tübingen sermons reveal Staupitz most of all as one who preached the priority of God's grace and mercy. It is not surprising then that the expression *misericordia Dei* (mercy of God) occurs in them about one hundred times.[31]

These sermons reveal him also as a reformer of the religious life, something the local government of Count Eberhard expected from him. Staupitz pursued the ideals of the observants. He was critical of the non-reformed mendicant friars. In his mind there was a connection between the devotion and work of the friars and that of the common people. After all, the friars were entrusted with preaching to them. If the friars are not reformed themselves and live in sin and vice – and people complain about their 'perversion' (*perversitas*) – they are unable to eradicate the vices among the people. Such friars would be more decadent than the laity and the secular clergy.

Staupitz's call to reform was accompanied by his moral teaching for he presented Job as the model of Christian living, who, as a spiritual

---

[30] 'Quod gratia ex condigno mereri non potest. Quod certe pulchre satis dominus Aegidius 2 Sententiarum distinctione 27 triplici via declarat .... Unde sanctus Augustinus ad Sixtum presbyterum... : 'Quid.' inquit, 'est meritum hominis ante gratiam, cum omne bonum meritum nostrum non in nobis faciat nisi gratia?' .... Unde aperte concludimus, quod sine nostris meritis, ex utero matris ecclesiae progressi sumus' (Sermon 23, Staupitz, I. 354–60 (pp. 359–60). Habes istorum declarationem ampliorem domini Aegidii 39 distinctione 2 Sententiarum' (Sermon 25, Staupitz, I. 377); see Zumkeller, *Heilslehre*, pp. 211–13.

[31] See Zumkeller, *Heilslehre*, p. 30, n. 134.

athlete, fought evil. Job was the model not only for the vowed religious, but also for every Christian. 'False brethren' were the real temptation of the time. Young Staupitz put the reform of the cloisters at the service of the reform of Christianity. He contrasted the conventual friars (*non reformati*) with the reformed ones (*reformati*). The Holy Spirit is poured into the hearts of the 'reformed' (Rom. 5: 5). For God's sake they gave up all worldly possessions; the less they are concerned with possessions, the more they are eager to work for the cause of God. In thinking this he was influenced by Gerson's spiritual writings which in turn appear to be based on Augustine's zeal for reform in the Church. Staupitz followed the Augustinian-Gersonian principle that the proper zeal is to correct ecclesiastical abuses, if that is possible; but if it is not, such zeal would have to tolerate them, while still deploring them. Augustine mentioned this in his tract on the Gospel of John. Gerson talked about it in his *Consolatio theologiae*, from which Staupitz copied almost literally, as he added further Gersonian thoughts to his Sermon 20.[32]

Staupitz's pastoral concerns at Tübingen went beyond traditional preaching on *exemplum* and virtues. He felt compelled to deal with the problem of temptations. In possessing a God-centred spirituality he declared temptations to be signs of God's care. This was meant as a consolation to anyone who is tempted. 'Those who contemplate the infallibility of the divine knowledge, will become confident that every temptation comes forth from God's ordinance.'[33] Furthermore, Staupitz as a religious leader developed a theology of lowliness within a typical monastic theology. Job was the model for such a *humilitas*-theology. As mentioned, Staupitz presumed the insufficiency of human works for salvation. He connected his concern for humility and self-accusation with the typical monastic theological acknowledgement of God's sole righteousness. The sinner who practices self-accusation demonstrates that he or she is in need of divine redemption. Thus the truly humble person is safe with God. Staupitz may have taken this important spiritual

---

[32] 'Sunt enim in veritate laicis et clericis saecularibus magis dissoluti. Sed e contrario reformati zelose agere consueverunt, … . Ideo sunt tanto amplius zelosi, quanto minus fuerint proprietarii (Sermon 20, Staupitz, I. 319); see M. Schulze, *Fürsten und Reformation. Geistliche Reformpolitik weltlicher Fürsten vor der Reformation* (Tübingen, 1991), p. 10. Re Augustine and Gerson, see Staupitz, I. 320–22; see Zumkeller, *Heilslehre*, pp. 18 and 105.

[33] 'Hi vero qui divinae scientiae infallibilitatem contemplantur, ex dei ordinatione procedere omnem temptationem confitentur …'. (Sermon 11, Staupitz, I. 190). On several occasions in the 1530s Luther recorded being consoled by Staupitz's advice (*WATR* 1. 240, 12–20 (no. 518); *WATR* 2. 26, 4–6 (no. 1288) and 112, 9–11 (no. 1490)); on 23 February 1542 he wrote to Albrecht of Mansfeld: 'oder viel mehr Gott durch Doctor Staupitz' (*WABR* 9. 627, 23–25, no. 3716); in his lectures on Genesis: 'Nisi Staupitius eadem me laborantem liberasset' (*WA* 43. 461, 1–13 (on Gen. 26: 9)); see Brecht, *Martin Luther, 1483–1521*, pp. 68f.

concept of self-accusation from Augustine's commentary on John or from the sermons of Bernard of Clairvaux, or directly from the Bible – Prov. 18: 17, in the Vulgate version. He used it several times in his later works, such as in an Advent sermon of 1516, in his booklet *On God's Gracious Love*, and in one of his Passion sermons of 1520.[34]

As to Staupitz's theological sources, a few observations should be made. All signals which Staupitz himself had sent through his sermonizing point directly to Augustine as his main theological source. His Tübingen sermons demonstrate that, early on, he must have considered himself a direct disciple of that church father. Staupitz depended on Augustine not only as regards the concepts of grace and sin and self-accusation, but also as regards the use of the distinction between 'use-enjoy' (*uti-frui*) and the goodness of God (*bonitas dei*). If he did not lift these ideas from Augustine's works directly, he may have received them from his reading of Thomas Waley's commentary on Augustine's *City of God* of 1489.[35] While Staupitz also used other authorities, such as Gregory the Great's *Moralia,* one observes that Augustine remained nearly omnipresent in all of his thinking. Staupitz quoted, for instance, more than 30 passages from Augustine's *Enarrationes in psalmos.* Indeed, his Tübingen sermons were shaped by the 'Augustinian homiletic literature'.[36] Equally important to him was Augustine's *City of God*, which would again show its influence nearly

---

[34] Augustine: 'Quia qui confitetur peccata sua, et accusat, peccata sua, iam cum Deo facit' (*In Joannis Evangelium* XII, 13 PL 35. 1491). Bernard: '...'Omnis homo mendax.' ... In illo ... seipsum diiudicat ... omnis homo miser et impotens, qui nec se, nec alium possit salvare', (*SBOp*, III. 28, 21–6). 'Superbus excusat peccatum suum, humilis accusat ... si nosmetipsos iudicaverimus, non utique iudicabimur' (1 Cor. 11: 31, *SBOp*, III. 227, 13–15). 'Diligit enim animam, quae in conspectu eius et sine intermissione considerat, et sine dissimulatione diiudicat semetipsam. Idque iudicium non nisi propter nos a nobis exigit, quia si nosmetipsos iudicaverimus, non utique iudicabimur' (1 Cor. 11: 31, *SBOp*, IV. 181, 4–7); see J.R. Sommerfeldt, *The Spiritual Teachings of Bernard of Clairvaux* (Kalamazoo, MI, 1991), p. 58. Staupitz: 'Iustus in principio est accusator sui' (speaking with Prov. 18: 17 [Vulgate] in his Tübingen Sermon 20) (Staupitz, I. 319); see also Sermon 22 (Staupitz, I. 348). Staupitz's Advent Sermon 23 (1516), (Staupitz, II. 286–7 and 290–91); and again in *John Staupitz On God's Gracious Love*, trans. J.J. Stoudt, *LQ*, 8 (1956), Chapter XXI, p. 243. Staupitz in his Lenten Sermon 5 of 1520 again used the concept of self-accusation, see R.K. Markwald, *A Mystic's Passion: The Spirituality of Johannes von Staupitz in his 1520 Lenten Sermons. Translation and Commentary* (New York, 1990), pp. 135–7. For Staupitz on humility, see M. Schulze, 'Der Hiob-Prediger Johannes von Staupitz auf der Kanzel der Tübinger Augustinerkirche', in K. Hagen (ed.), *Augustine, the Harvest, and Theology (1300–1650). Essays Dedicated to Heiko Augustinus Oberman in Honor of his Sixtieth Birthday* (Leiden, 1990), pp. 60–88. The concept of self-accusation is prominent also in Luther, see F. Posset, *Pater Bernhardus: Martin Luther and Bernard of Clairvaux* (Kalamazoo, MI, 1999), pp. 227–31.

[35] See Staupitz, I. 14–20 (Introduction); see Steinmetz, *Misericordia Dei*, pp. 35–8.

[36] See Steinmetz, 'Luther and the Late Medieval Augustinians', p. 257.

20 years later in Staupitz's book on discipleship and the art of dying, *Von der nachfolgung des willigen sterbens Christi*.[37] Due to the impact of the *City of God*, a fully fledged doctrine of original sin was present in these early sermons.[38] With Augustine's *City of God* and with Egidio da Roma, Staupitz believed that Adam and Eve in Paradise possessed the original righteousness (*iustitia originalis*). He maintained that the first parents suffered, as a consequence of their disobedience, a new movement in their flesh which they could no longer control. Through their sin, all humanity is now 'infected'; here he used the term *infectum* (Sermon 10), which includes the meaning of 'stained', and even 'poisoned'. The Fall brought with it the rotting (*putredo*) of the sin of the flesh, a sin which, so to speak, is now our second nature (*connaturale*), as he pointed out in his Sermon 32.[39]

Staupitz, however, was not a theological pessimist. He made good use of another strand from the broad patristic and medieval tradition – the traditional, often mystical, talk of the 'sweetness of God'. Staupitz spoke of this several times in these early sermons (especially nos 13, 18 and 24). He preached Christ as the 'most sweet donor' (*dulcissimus dator*). In regard to this topic, Staupitz again turned out to be a follower of Augustine, and his passages on the 'sweetness of God' are usually found within an Augustinian context, that is to say in a context where he referred explictly to Augustine's writings. Staupitz spoke of the Christian faith and of eternal life as belief in Christ who was sent from the Father (speaking with John 17: 3) so that people recognize him as good (*bonus*) and thus would recognize his unique sweetness.[40] Next Staupitz quoted Pseudo-Augustine's *soliloquia* (chapter 21), on the great mercy of God, our good creator, who created all things good and very delectable, and so sweet (*quam dulcia*). If all this is found here on earth, how much more will one find in the heavenly kingdom. 'For according to the multitude of your greatness there is also the great multitude of your sweetness which you have in store for those who fear you [Ps. 30: 20]. For you are great, my God, and immense, and there is no limit to your greatness.'[41] The believer in Christ must be elevated from the sweet things of this world

---

[37] Ernst Wolf counted 163 quotations from 24 of Augustine's books, see his *Staupitz und Luther: Ein Beitrag zur Theologie des Johannes Staupitz und deren Bedeutung für Luthers theologischen Werdegang* (Leipzig, 1927; reprinted: New York, London, 1971).

[38] See R. Wetzel, 'Staupitz Augustinianus: An Account of the Reception of Augustine in his Tübingen Sermons' in H.A. Oberman and F.A. James III (eds), *Via Augustini. Augustine in the Later Middle Ages, Renaissance and Reformation. Essays in Honor of Damasus Trapp, O.S.A.* (Leiden, 1991), pp. 72–115.

[39] See Zumkeller, *Heilslehre*, pp. 30–46, for an excellent summary of the doctrine of sin.

[40] See Staupitz, I. 250 (Sermon 13); see F. Posset, 'The Sweetness of God', *ABR*, 44 (1993), 143–78; here 155–57.

[41] *PL* 40: 881.

'toward the higher sweetness where God is being tasted in His sweetness'. He then referred directly to Augustine's *On the Trinity* 13, 3.[42] Accompanied by these two explicit references to Augustine, he proclaimed the 'sweetness of God'.[43] The Latin wording which Staupitz used here was close to Augustine's *On the Spirit and the Letter*, which is the only passage in that text which uses the expression 'sweetness of God'.[44] It can happen that one gets tired of elevating oneself toward this higher sweetness. This tiredness stems from the fact that God is not recognized as the donor of all good things. Only the 'sweetness' (*suavitas*) of the fruit received will generate a pleasant feeling (*dulcem affectum*) toward the giver in the recipient. People should recognize that with 'the most sweet donor' everything is good and sweet.[45] Staupitz continued with a quotation from Augustine's *Confessions* (Book 3,1) deploring any false 'sweetness':

> Thus the holy father Augustine in Book III of his *Confessions* exclaims: 'My God, my Mercy, with how much gall did You, who are so good, besprinkle for me that [fleshly] sweetness? For I was loved myself, and I reached the point where we met together to enjoy our love, and there I was fettered happily in bonds of misery so that I might be beaten with rods of red-hot iron – the rods of jealousy and suspicions, and fears and angers and quarrels'.[46]

Staupitz's image of Christ was essentially that of the generous giver, as he called him in these sermons and as he would call him again with a similar expression in an Advent sermon of 1516, speaking of Christ as the 'most generous giver' (*liberalissimus dator*).[47]

In his sermon on Job 1: 21, Staupitz returned to the contrast between the worldly pleasures and the 'sweetness of God'. First, he pointed out, again along Augustinian lines, that if we taste sweet to ourselves, we are caught up in self-love, and consequently God cannot taste sweet to us. God becomes bitter all the more we remain in self-love, and so unfortunately we turn away from God to ourselves. This is where sin starts.[48] Then, after explicitly referring to Augustine, he quoted Aristotle's ethics saying that God provides enjoyment. Because of that, man cannot be sad; he is elevated affectionately and sweetly to the

---

[42] *PL* 42: 1017.

[43] See Sermon 13 (Staupitz, I. 251).

[44] See *De spiritu et litera*, Chapter 30 (*PL* 44: 233).

[45] 'Ut in omni bono dulcissimum datorem recognoscant' (Sermon 13, Staupitz, I. 253).

[46] *PL* 32: 683, as quoted in Sermon 13 (Staupitz, I. 254f).

[47] Advent Sermon 18 of 1516 (Staupitz, II. 226/27).

[48] 'Amaricatur deus' (Sermon 24, Staupitz, I. 368); see Steinmetz, *Misericrdia Dei*, pp. 66f. with n. 4. In the same Sermon 24, Staupitz deliberated on faith, hope and love; see B. Hamm, 'Warum wurde für Luther der Glaube zum Zentralbegriff des christlichen Lebens?', in Buckwalter and Moeller (eds), *Die frühe Reformation*, pp. 106f.

fountain of sweetness where there is nothing sad, but everything is most sweet.[49] Our moral actions must conform to the first truth, beauty, power, and sweetness.[50] In this context he referred to *Confessions* 2,6, that we must seek to imitate God in our works. Reliance on God's truth solidifies our faith. We rest upon him who is the best and the sweetest, as this reliance strengthens our charity, too.[51] Those who do not realize this are those of whom Apoc. 3: 17f. speaks, who are neither cold nor warm, and who therefore will be vomited from God's mouth. They do not arrive at the 'sweet taste'.[52]

As is evident by now, Staupitz was a great teacher of the priority of the grace and the sweetness of God. He found this concept connected to Ps. 33: 9 ('Taste and see that the Lord is sweet', Vulgate), which he paraphrased and combined with other Bible verses. Direct quotations or allusions to this verse were featured several times in his Tübingen sermons:

1 In his Sermon 9 on the notion of 'feast' (*convivium*), taken from Job 1: 4, which he interpreted in a spiritual way, he said that at this feast 'wisdom' comes and brings the 'sweetness of the divine goodness' because the Spirit of the Lord is good and sweet to those who taste, see, hear, and embrace him. All this happens by grace and not by natural recognition.[53]

2 In Sermon 13 he spoke of the Christian faithful who needed to be lifted from earthly sweetness to the higher sweetness where God is being tasted in his sweetness.[54]

3 In Sermon 24 he spoke of those who may not taste it after all.[55]

4 Finally he alluded to this psalm (33: 9) in Sermon 29, and here twice, stressing again that one tastes the sweetness of the Lord in one's faith and that God's decisions are sweet.[56]

The topic of 'sweetness' will become even more evident in the later sermons. Staupitz, of course, used other psalms besides those that contain verses on the 'sweetness of God'. One of them he presented at great length, in the middle of Sermon 10, where he quoted from Psalm 36

---

[49] See Sermon 24 (Staupitz, I. 370).

[50] See ibid. (Staupitz, I. 371).

[51] See ibid. (Staupitz, I. 372).

[52] See ibid. (Staupitz, I. 374).

[53] See Sermon 9 (Staupitz, I. 161–2); see Steinmetz, *Misericordia Dei*, pp. 71f., where, however, other aspects of Staupitz's sermons are featured.

[54] See Sermon 13 (Staupitz, I. 252).

[55] See Sermon 24 (Staupitz, I. 374).

[56] See Sermon 29 (Staupitz, I. 422–3).

(Vulgate) a total of 27 verses (9–36).[57] In Sermon 30 he quoted Ps. 87: 11–13,[58] and in conjunction with other scriptural texts he developed his teaching on grace once again, namely that by grace human beings are reborn to become children of God.

As Staupitz preached on the 'sweetness of God', the related notion of the spiritual senses, including the spiritual 'palate', necessarily had to come into play. He said that we see 'with the eyes of the mind' (*mentis oculis*), speaking here with Gregory the Great (*Moralia* 2, chapter 1), whom he had quoted at length. Interestingly, most of these Tübingen sermons on Job began with a quotation from Gregory's meditations on Job (*Moralia*).[59] As to the 'spiritual senses', Staupitz also worked with the concept of the 'mouth of the heart', perhaps under the direct influence of the late medieval spiritual author, Henry Suso. Staupitz used this notion in his fourth sermon,[60] in which he also said that fear of God eventually changes into sweetness, as God becomes sweet to us.[61] In his last extant sermon of Tübingen, on the sweetness of God's judgment, he worked with the spiritual notion of the 'not yet healed palate of the soul', most likely following in this regard the tradition that was shaped by Augustine, Gregory, Bernard and Suso: 'As someone with a fever wrongly takes a sweet drink to be bitter, so the sweetness and pleasantness of the divine judgment is to the not yet healed palate of the soul nothing but punishment.'[62]

As the influence of patristic and medieval spiritual authors has become apparent in these sermons of 1497/98, it needs to be said that Staupitz highly esteemed as well the French spiritual writer Jean Gerson, whose thoughts also played a significant role in these sermons. As mentioned above, Staupitz may have come to know Gerson's works at Cologne where they were printed for the first time in 1483/84.[63] Staupitz

---

[57] See Sermon 10 (Staupitz, I. 169–70); here he quoted two pages of psalm verses.

[58] See Sermon 30 (Staupitz, I. 427).

[59] 'Inquit sanctus Gregorius 2 Moralium capitulo 1, mentis oculis quasi quoddam speculum opponitur, ut interna nostra facies in ipso videatur' (Sermon 11, Staupitz, I. 186). In Sermon 6, Aristotle takes the place of Gregory, in Sermon 8 it is Thomas Aquinas, in Sermon 22 it is Gerson, and in Sermon 24 it is Hugo of Saint Victor. It should be noted that Staupitz did not use the term *gustus internus*.

[60] 'Ad os cordis haec interrogatio mittenda est et interrogati responsio audienda' (Sermon 4, Staupitz, I. 80).

[61] 'Et dulcescit deus' (Sermon 4, Staupitz, I. 77).

[62] 'Sane quem ad modum febricitans iniuste accusat de amaritudine potum dulcem, sic palato animae non sano poena est suavitas et iucunditas divini iudicii' (Sermon 34, Staupitz, I. 480).

[63] Gerson's works were printed in Cologne in 1483/84 and reprinted by Grüninger at Strasbourg in 1488; Staupitz may have used either edition. On Gerson, see B.P. McGuire, *Jean Gerson: Early Works* (New York, 1998).

quoted him next to Augustine and Gregory the Great, with precise source references. In this same Sermon 29 he again operated with the notion 'palate' (of the heart), as he dealt with temptation and consolation. He utilized 1 Cor. 2: 9, James 1: 12, and Ps. 33: 9, saying that God has prepared what none of the senses can feel, but what is felt by the faith which 'has the foretaste' of this 'sweetness'.[64] Staupitz also quoted 'St David's Psalm' (118: 39), and 1 Pet. 2: 3, and perhaps Ps. 118: 103. At this point he reminded his brethren, speaking with Augustine (*Confessions* 7,6), as far as the 'sick eyes are concerned, that 'we have a palate not yet healed, and sick eyes, so that it happens that we hate the light and that we think that the most sweet judgment of the divine paternity would be bitter'. Staupitz continued with words of Ps. 115: 11–13 and spoke then of the 'interior sense':

> I said in my excess: 'Every man is a liar', from which he soon subsumes: 'How shall I make a return to the Lord for all the good he has done to me? The cup of salvation', he says, 'I will accept'. I do not say, that the bitter [cup] should be replaced by the natural [drink], but that we ourselves be changed toward being better able to taste the interior sense.[65]

At issue here is the vision of the divine face, a vision which shows so much sweetness that nothing bitter can be found any more. Staupitz pointed out that we know of this by faith. As we believe those people who saw some things invisible, so we believe those who learned of what is in the immaterial light and even removed from our interior sense.[66] Like Augustine, he said that those who believe in Christ are elevated from the sweet things of this world to the sweetness above, where God is tasted in his sweetness.[67] Like Augustine and Suso, he warned that the

---

[64] 'Nec oculus vidit nec auris audivit nec in cor hominis ascendit, quanta praeparavit deus diligentibus se, verumtamen fides quandam praegustat illius suavitatem [Ps. 33: 9]' (Sermon 29, Staupitz, I. 422). Gerson is quoted selectively also in Sermon 23. Steinmetz noted that Staupitz cited only those passages from Gerson 'which he wishes to use' (*Misericordia Dei*, p. 54).

[65] 'Satis enim dulcis est deus [1 Peter 2: 3] suntque iudicia eius dulcia [taking up again Ps. 118: 39], quibus profecto cognitis, dulcescunt et ea quae prius amara videbantur. Habemus, fratres, palatum non sanum et aegros oculos, quo fit, ut odio lucem habeamus et amarum dulcissimum divinae paternitatis iudicium iudicamus ... [Ps. 115: 11–13]. Non dico, amarum amisisse naturam, sed nos mutasse utique in melius gustandi interiorem sensum' (Sermon 29, Staupitz, I. 422–3). 'Est divinae faciei intuitio quae tantam complectitur suavitatem, ut non iam dulcia sint amara, sed nec amarum ibi quidquam reperire est' (Sermon 29, Staupitz, I. 423). On the history of the concept 'palate of the heart', see F. Posset, 'Sensing God with the Palate of the Heart', *ABR*, 49 (1998), pp. 356–86; on Staupitz, see p. 381.

[66] 'Ita et de his quae a nostro sensu interiore remota sunt his nos oportet credere qui haec in illo incorporeo lumine disposita didicerunt' [see Augustine, *De Civitate* 11, 2] (Sermon 13, Staupitz, I. 245).

[67] 'Hoc modo debent elevari Christifideles etiam ex dulcibus huius mundi et praesentis

inner sense can be lost easily, as can be observed with young people (*adulescentulis*) who turn to bad thoughts, being deprived of their interior sense. This is so because man is easily instigated to evil, as Gen. 8: 21 says. Concerning the *sensus interiores* Staupitz relied also on a certain 'Book 2' with the title *De anima*, without specifying the author of that work.[68]

In addition to the theological and spiritual authorities who have so far been mentioned, there was Henry of Friemar (d. 1340), a member of the same Augustinian Order, who with his concept of the sweetness of God and his understanding of the union with God was another author whom Staupitz had read. This is evident from his third Tübingen sermon,[69] where he used the almost identical sentence on the soul's union with God which is found in Henry of Friemar's work on the coming of the Word into the human heart: it is a spiritual union in terms of the conformity of the will rather than an identity of substance.[70] It is all the more likely that Henry was Staupitz's source as his home town was Friemar near Erfurt, and he, like Staupitz, was a member of the Augustinian Order.[71]

With Staupitz, the biblical (Vulgate) concept of the 'sweetness of God' (and not the image of the angry Judge) had gained priority. The concept of the goodness of God deemed him most suitable and nourishing for hungry and troubled souls. Pastoral concerns appeared as his guiding principles. Consequently, it is no surprise that Bernard of Clairvaux's book on pastoral care, *On Consideration*, was also on his mind (especially in Sermon 19). Staupitz quoted Christ's phrase for Peter on 'feeding the sheep' of the Church (John 21: 15–17) and gave the full source reference as follows: 'As St Bernard says to Eugene in the Book *On Consideration.*' Staupitz could have lifted the quotation directly from Bernard's book, or from Gerson, whose wording in *Super victu et*

---

temporis quorum etiam ipse deus dator est, qui nec peccati actum sua privat dulcedine ad illam supernam dulcedinem ubi deus in sua degustatur suavitate ...' (Sermon 13, Staupitz, I. 252).

[68] 'Depravati sensu interiori' (Sermon 20, Staupitz, I. 324). The editors of Staupitz's sermons refer us to Aristotle, *De anima* 2, 8, and to Thomas Aquinas's terminology; and also to Gerson, *De passionibus animae consid.* Ch. 20.

[69] 'Unde unus spiritus fit per voluntatis conformationem, non substantiae identitate' (Sermon 3, Staupitz, I. 71).

[70] See A. Zumkeller (ed.), *Henrici de Frimaria O.S.A. Tractatus ascetico-mystici tomus I complectens Tractatum de adventu Verbi in mentem, Tractatum de adventu Domini, Tractatum de incarnatione Verbi* (Würzburg, 1975), p. 42; see also *idem*, 'Staupitz', *Dictionnaire*, XIV, p. 1193. This parallel is not indicated in the new critical edition of Staupitz's works. However, Zumkeller's reference does not prove beyond doubt that Staupitz read Henry of Friemar; he could equally have found this concept in Bernard of Clairvaux who is listed in the apparatus of the critical edition.

[71] See Zumkeller's Introduction in *Henrici de Frimaria*.

pompa praelatorum he may have used.[72] Regardless of whether Staupitz quoted Bernard directly or indirectly, he was as concerned as Bernard about the lack of pastoral care which many popes and prelates displayed. Also in Sermon 19, Staupitz lamented the worldly, scandalous behaviour of the clergy, their *Jasonica perversitas* (see Jason, the high priest in 2 Macc. 4: 13–16), their concubinage and other misconduct, and the fact that they did not care about the people. Staupitz apparently also included in his criticism the contemporary Pope Alexander VI, although he did not mention his name, when he spoke of the vicar of Christ as someone who acted like a robbing and unjust wolf. Our sermonizer declared him an enemy of the people as he was a 'satellite of Satan'. God may punish such a monstrous crime, especially when it is a crime that is committed by someone who does not recognize another superior on earth (as is the case with the popes).[73]

In Tübingen, Staupitz had begun his career as an Augustinian preacher of the priority of divine grace and sweetness, and as a reformer of the monastic life and of pastoral care. He had made a typical contemporary (if you will, 'humanist') turn, away from late medieval scholasticism as represented by Biel, towards the earlier sources, that is the church fathers and the Bible. Although he had a certain preference for the spiritual authors just mentioned, his greatest concern was to conform with Augustine whom he called his 'father and teacher, yes, and also of the holy church, [Augustine] who is of the most profound intellect'.[74] Thus, in by-passing or neglecting, for instance, Biel's influential scholastic teachings, Staupitz returned to the mainstream Catholic tradition as shaped by Augustine, Gregory the Great, and Bernard of Clairvaux. His return to these esteemed teachers was accompanied by typically humanist concerns which he indicated in the preface to his Tübingen

---

[72] 'Unde sanctus Bernardus ad Eugenium libro De consideratione' (Sermon 19, Staupitz, I. 311). The critical edition suggests at this point a dependence upon Gerson's *Super victu et pompa prelatorum* (Staupitz, I. 309 and 311, n. 81 and 100). Perhaps under Staupitz's influence, this same Bernardine passage would be quoted by Luther, 18 years later, in his 1516 lectures on Romans 15: 'For thus Blessed Bernard explains in *Ad Eugenium* that threefold "Feed"' (*WA* 56. 137, 26f.); see F. Posset, 'Recommendations by Martin Luther of St Bernard's *On Consideration*', *CSQ*, 25 (1990), pp. 25–36; Posset, *Pater Bernhardus*, pp. 353–77.

[73] See Staupitz, I. 308–9; Zumkeller, *Heilslehre*, pp. 50–51.

[74] '[Augustinus] pater et doctor meus est, immo et sanctae ecclesiae, intellectu profundissimus' (Sermon 7, Staupitz, I. 124); see F. Posset, 'Pater et Doctor Meus Est, Immo Sanctae Ecclesiae Intellectu Profundissimus', in F. Van Fleteren et al. (eds), *Collectanea Augustiniana: Augustine. Mystic and Mystagogue* (New York 1994), pp. 513–43. Another example of Augustine's great and continuous significance for Staupitz are the closing words of his Lenten Sermons, delivered at Salzburg in 1520; see Markwald, *A Mystic's Passion*, p. 167. See also Zumkeller, 'Staupitz', *Dictionnaire*, XIV, p. 1188; Wetzel, 'Staupitz Augustinianus', pp. 72–115; Wriedt, 'Staupitz und Augustin', p. 230.

sermons – concerns of fostering *scientia* and *eloquentia*. With a humanist frame of mind he mentioned in these sermons many Latin classical authors including Cicero, Horace, Juvenal, Lactantius, Livy, Ovid, Persius, Plato, Sallust, Seneca, Terentius, Valerius Maximus, Virgil and Xenophon. Not even the Roman deities were absent from these early sermons. One may suspect that Staupitz borrowed all this from the works of his beloved Augustine. Indeed, Staupitz, in reading the church father in this way, thus participated in the contemporary humanist reception of Augustine at the turn of the century. His use of classical antiquity via Augustine was to demonstrate his humanist, 'anti-barbarian' programme,[75] which placed him within the wider context of Renaissance humanism that sought to return to the sources. In religious terms, this meant the return to the church fathers and ultimately to the sacred texts of the Bible. In using Greek phrases Staupitz also indicated that he wanted to join the humanist movement which began to return to the original text version of the New Testament.

While Staupitz was still at Tübingen, and also at Munich, he must have liberated himself from the quarrels of scholastic theology by moving in the tracks of biblical humanism to which he was exposed especially in Tübingen's humanist milieu. Although his Tübingen sermons displayed at times a great similarity with the analytical, scholastic method of dissecting and taking apart an issue, he indicated that he would not want to pursue a certain topic any further, leaving all this to 'the schools'.[76] He felt that he had discussed Job 1: 7 extensively enough, having included also a reference to Thomas Aquinas. In a way this was Staupitz's way of by-passing scholasticism by benign neglect, as he had announced already in his *Prologus*. Furthermore, he may have realized that too sophisticated a treatment of biblical texts may not have been very helpful for the care of souls and for spiritual edification; which perhaps explains why he never completed the treatment of the Book of Job as he had planned.

Already one of his primary concerns in these Tübingen sermons was the proper image of God as derived from Job 1: 21: 'The Lord has given

---

[75] 'Iupiter, Romulus' (Staupitz, I. (index)). See Wetzel, 'Staupitz antibarbarus: Beobachtungen zur Rezeption heidnischer Antike in seinen Tübinger Predigten', in A. Mehl and W.C. Schneider (eds), *Reformatio et reformationes: Festschrift für Lothar Graf zu Dohna zum 65. Geburtstag* (Darmstadt, 1989), pp. 107–30. Incidentally, Wetzel, as editor, acknowledged the mistakes in his 1979 edition of Staupitz which Reinoud Weijenborg had made known in his review of *Johann von Staupitz, Sämtliche Schriften*, vol. 2 (*Revue d'Histoire Ecclesiastique*, 76 (1981), 394–400). Wetzel's main goal in his article was to present the reception of pagan antiquity in Staupitz's Tübingen sermons (1497/98); he rightly criticizes Wolf and Steinmetz for interpreting these sermons as if they were written as scholastic disputations.

[76] 'Scholis hoc remittendum melius fore existimo' (Sermon 12, Staupitz, I. 218).

it ... Blessed be the name of the Lord.' They are filled with talk of God's abundant mercy and grace, and give us a taste of God's sweetness. In fact, there was hardly any mention in these sermons of God being angry with us, a concept which is sometimes taken as the predominant medieval image of God, allegedly found in all and every late medieval piety. Staupitz's sermons demonstrate that this was not the case. He would return to preaching on the figure of Job more than two decades later, in his Lenten Sermons at Salzburg in 1520 on the passion of Christ. This continuity in his later sermons was not accidental, however, because Job was considered a typological figure of the suffering Christ.

One passage in Staupitz's Tübingen Sermon 11 seems to sum up much of his unique spirituality, as in it he (like Augustine) called upon his 'most sweet God' and upon divine wisdom in times of trouble (quoting Wis. 9: 1–2 and 4–6, and 1 Cor. 15: 10):

> I, a man about to be tempted, call upon You before I feel temptation, that You may confer upon me the strength and unchangeable perseverance with which I can conquer the enemy, increase grace, and merit eternal life. This, most merciful Lord and most pious Saviour, I now pray with a tranquil heart. For I know myself, know, I say, my infinite imperfections; and I have often experienced in myself that with suffering being present I judge less correctly your benevolence. Therefore, I come before Your face in confession, seeking mercy and grace. I do not ask, most sweet God, I do not ask that You take temptation away from me, which in Your wisdom You have determined, but that You comfort me, that You help me that I do not succumb. God of my fathers and Lord of mercy, You have made everything by Your word and in Your wisdom You established man. Give me wisdom, the attendant at Your throne, and reject me not from among Your children, for I am Your servant, the son of Your handmaid, a man weak and short-lived and lacking in comprehension of judgment and of laws. Indeed, though one be perfect among the sons of men, if wisdom, who comes from You, be not with him, he shall be held in no esteem. By the grace of God we are what we are.[77]

In his quest for spiritual renewal Staupitz appears always to have grounded himself in the Scriptures. In following Augustine, he saw in the Bible the unique authority in which we trust, and in which everything is found that is necessary for salvation, and what cannot be found within ourselves. In following Gerson, Staupitz refuted those who belittled the Bible because of its simplicity.[78] Occasionally he began to criticize the representatives of the Church for their lack of interest in pastoral care

---

[77] 'Te invoco homo temtandus .... Haec, misericordissime domine et piissime salvator .... Non rogo, dulcissime deus, non rogo, ut auferas a me temptationem ...' (Sermon 11, Staupitz, I. 189–90); see Steinmetz, *Misericordia Dei*, p. 167.

[78] See Zumkeller, *Heilslehre*, 21.

and for their scandalous behaviour. He was a reformer in the making. Yet, the secular government came under his criticism as well, especially when the neglect of the defense of Christianity against the Turkish threat became apparent, as when he spoke of the 'Mohammedan sect' (*Mahametica secta*) in his Tübingen Sermon 7. We will see him return to the criticism of the heads of church and state for their poor governing and shepherding in his Salzburg sermons of 1512.

One of the advantages of Staupitz's progression from university to university especially during his early years was that he was exposed to a variety of movements of the time and so also to the local book markets connected to the universities. We may assume that Staupitz was aware of the contemporary publication trends, and that he knew of the new editions of the classical authorities of Christianity and of the spiritual literature that came off the printing presses. Thus we may assume further that he became aware, for instance, of the books, and anthologies of works, of Augustine and Bernard of Clairvaux which became available at that time. In 1489 Augustine's *Opuscula plurima* was printed in Strasbourg, and his *De trinitate* and *De civitate dei* at Basel. This humanist Augustine edition was completed in 1506 and comprised 11 volumes. Thomas Waley's Commentary on Augustine's *City of God* was also published in 1489; we know Staupitz used this edition for his sermonizing as he even copied some of the mistakes that were made in it.[79]

The result of earlier humanist investigations into Augustine's works had become most visible with one of the best known works of this 'Augustine renaissance', the *Milleloquium S. Augustini* compiled by the Augustinian friar, and later bishop, Bartolomeo da Urbino (d. 1350). Bartolomeo collected excerpts from Augustine's works for approximately 1000 catchwords, for which he included the precise source references. At the end of his work he put the *Distinctio librorum* in which he listed and reviewed in detail Augustine's letters, books, and sermons, thus providing a very helpful introduction to Augustine's writings. One may assume that Augustinians who, like Staupitz, held this church father in such high esteem, also used this *Milleloquium S. Augustini*.[80] As to the spiritual works of St Bernard, Staupitz may have used one of the 300 or so printed editions which appeared on the book market between 1464 and 1500.[81]

---

[79] See Staupitz, I. 407f. with n. 19.

[80] On the *Milleloquium*, see Arbesmann, *Der Augustiner-Eremitenorden*, pp. 38–44; Junghans, *Der junge Luther*, pp. 127–8. Unfortunately, the new critical edition of Staupitz's works does not take into consideration the *Milleloquium* as a possible (indeed likely) source for Staupitz.

[81] On the Bernard *Florilegium* of 1472, see F. Cavallera, 'Bernard (Apocryphes attribué à saint)', *Dictionnaire*, I, pp. 1499–1500. On the Bernard editions of *c.* 1500, see Posset,

What other contributions to the intellectual, spiritual, and pastoral setting in which Staupitz moved came into existence at that time? A look at some contemporary publications helps to shed light on this. In 1490 the booklet of the Augustinian friar of Erfurt, Johann von Paltz, in which he published the sermons he had delivered before Frederick the Wise, *Die himlische funtgrub* or 'The heavenly mine' (mentioned above) became available. With this title Paltz alluded to the local industry of mining, as he declared that in this book one may find the heavenly ore, 'that is the grace of God'. Only someone concerned with the care of souls could have come up with such a metaphor that spoke to a wider audience.[82]

In the following year, 1491, Amerbach published Cassiodorus' commentary on the Psalms, *Cassiodori Clarissimi Senatoris in Psalterium expositio*. In 1492, Nicholas of Lyra's Bible commentary, *Nicolai de Lyra Super toto corpore bibliae cum suis additionibus*, was printed at Strasbourg. Staupitz the scriptural scholar must have been quite interested in publications such as these. Also in 1492, the first complete edition of the works of the church father Ambrose became available, printed in three volumes by Amerbach at Basel. Publications of spiritual writings in 1494 included Johannes Mauburnus' *Rosetum exercitiorum spiritualium* (spiritual exercises), Johann Reuchlin's *De verbo mirifico* (on the miracle-working word), and Sebastian Brandt's *The Ship of Fools*. By the end of the fifteenth century, prophetic books such as Johann Lichtenberger's *Prenostication* of 1497 predicted the wreck of the Church which was perceived as a ship in perilous waters, as an illustration in Lichtenberger's book demonstrates.[83] Although we do not know whether Staupitz knew this particular book, it is neverthess symptomatic of the feeling of the time in which he lived, at the turn of the century.

From 1498 the *Aeglogae* of the Italian humanist and Carmelite Friar, Baptista Mantuanus (d. 1516), were published all over Europe, as this booklet had become very popular. It, too, was filled with pastoral concerns and it contained remarks critical of the church. Among the numerous places where the *Aeglogae* were published were Leipzig and

---

'Saint Bernard of Clairvaux in the Devotion, Theology, and Art of the Sixteenth Century', *LQ*, **11** (1997), pp. 309–15.

[82] On Paltz's work, see C. Burger and F. Stasch (eds), *Johannes von Paltz, Werke: Coelifodina* (Berlin and New York, 1983); H. Lauber and W. Urban (eds), *Opuscula* (Berlin and New York, 1989), with the vernacular version of *Die himlische funtgrub*, pp. 155–3. On Paltz's theology, see B. Hamm, *Frömmigkeitstheologie am Anfang des 16. Jahrhunderts: Studien zu Johannes von Paltz und seinem Umkreis* (Tübingen, 1982).

[83] See A.G. Dickens, *Reformation and Society in Sixteenth-Century Europe* (London, 1968), with an illustration from the *Prenostication* of 1497 on p. 11.

Tübingen, in both of which Staupitz had lived.[84] As already mentioned, the humanist Franciscan Paul Scriptoris published his lectures on Scotus; these were printed at Tübingen in 1498. In the same year Savonarola wrote his prison meditations on the psalms, which soon became so famous that they were translated and published in Germany. One edition is known to have been printed in Reutlingen near Tübingen; another, with a preface by Martin Luther, was edited in 1523.[85] Gabriel Biel's 225 sermons were edited by Wendelin Steinbach in 1499/1500, and printed by Johann Othmar in Tübingen.[86] One may assume that Staupitz the preacher was aware of this edition as well, but he never quoted from it. Knowledge of the existence of such books does not necessarily mean that he read them, or that he agreed with their content.

Some, if not all of these spiritual and humanist authors may have helped Staupitz liberate himself from the quarrelling theology of the schoolmen and may have helped him to turn to issues of pastoral care. In this he, like a humanist, returned to the sources. Only the Tübingen sermons of the 'humble lector of sacred theology' – as he called himself in the preface – provide us with insights into the sources that he exploited at that time. Only in these early sermons did he readily reveal his sources by name and book, something which he never did to the same extent in later years.

As already mentioned, Staupitz's favourite authors were Augustine, Gregory the Great, Egidio da Roma (see Sermons 3 and 5), Jean Gerson (see Sermons 3 and, especially, 28), and also Thomas Aquinas (see Sermons 3, 5, 15 and so on), whose works he quoted directly and several times. He also made direct use of Boethius (for instance, in Sermon 23), Gratiani's *Corpus Iuris Canonici*, Peter Lombard (in Sermons 3, 4 and 5), Nicholas of Lyra (as for instance in Sermons 25 and 32) and Florus (*Epitomatae*, in Sermon 28).

In Sermon 7 on wealth and possessions, Staupitz quoted by name the medieval teacher of rhetoric Geoffrey de Vinsauf, an Englishman (Gaufredus de Vinosalvo, d. *c.* 1210) who wrote the *Poetria Nova*, a polished poem about writing poetry, dedicated to Pope Innocent III.

---

[84] On Baptista Mantuanus, see F. Posset, '"Heaven is on Sale". The Influence of the Italian Humanist and Carmelite Baptist Mantuanus on Martin Luther', *Carmelus*, 36 (1989), pp. 134–44.

[85] See J. Nolte, 'Evangelicae doctrinae purum exemplum. Savonarolas Gefängnismeditationen im Hinblick auf Luthers theologische Anfänge', in Nolte et al., *Kontinuität und Umbruch* (see n. 17 above), pp. 59–92; J.P. Donnelly (ed. and trans.), *Prison Meditations on Psalms 51 and 31 by Girolamo Savonarola O.P.* (Milwaukee, WI, 1994), p. 18.

[86] W.M. Landeen, 'Gabriel Biel and the Devotio Moderna in Germany', *Research Studies. A Quarterly Publication of Washington State University*, 27 (1959), pp. 135–76; and 28 (1960), pp. 21–45; 61–95 (p. 39).

He wrote in verse about verse, in contrast to authors like Virgil who wrote in verse, but not about verse; or others who wrote about verse, but in prose. Evidently, Geoffrey was still considered a significant authority in Staupitz's days; Erasmus, too, mentioned Geoffrey in a letter of 1489. The typical rhetorical style of grouping in 'threes' any material that is to be talked about is found in Geoffrey's book, a method which appears in Staupitz's sermons on a regular basis. Staupitz actually quoted a few words of Geoffrey with the following introduction:

> This is the teaching: A person uses wealth the best the more he or she shies away from adverse causes when prospering; and so Gaufredus says:
>   'Always fear that the good conceals the worse! Trust not in things: after the honey comes poison. And black night puts an end to day, as clouds the clear sky.'[87]

At this point he was apparently less interested in rhetorical theory than in the content of Geoffrey's saying which helped him to illustrate his point on wealth. Staupitz may have come across this passage when he studied the *Poetria Nova* for the purpose of becoming a good orator and preacher. The *Poetria Nova* and the other works mentioned above must either have been represented in Staupitz's library before the turn of the century, or else he must have had access to them somehow through the friary or university.

Staupitz may also have read Henry von Friemar's *De incarnatione Verbi*, Henry Suso's *Horologium Sapientiae*, Denis the Carthusian's *Ennarationes* and Hugo Cardinalis' *Postilla* (as used perhaps in his Sermons 5, 7, 11, 16, 19, 20 and 22). These names and works are not explicitly mentioned in his sermons, however, Staupitz may have been thinking of them when at times he referred to certain 'authorities' (such as in Sermon 21). In contrast, Staupitz did quote by name the following authorities: Thomas de Argentina (that is, of Strasbourg; in Sermon 19), Ambrose (in Sermons 7 and 25), Jerome and Eusebius (both in Sermon 3), Isidore (in Sermons 7 and 13), Leo the Great (in Sermon 19), and Bonaventure (in sermon 4). When in Sermon 12 Staupitz quoted several lines from 'a certain sermon of St Ambrose',[88] he actually used Pseudo-Ambrose, that is Maximus of Turin (d. *c.* 465) whose

---

[87] E. Gallo (ed.), *The 'Poetria nova' and its Sources in Early Rhetorical Doctrine* (Latin text and English translation; The Hague and Paris, 1971), lines 287–9. Staupitz's quotation (Staupitz, I. 134): 'Unde Gaufredus: Sub meliori statu semper peiora caveto! Nulla fides rerum: Sequitur post mella venenum. Et claudit nox atra diem nebulaeque serenum' deviates slightly from the original: 'Sub meliore statu semper cavere. Nulla fides rerum: sequitur post mella venenum. Et claudit nox atra diem, nebulaeque serenum'. On Geoffrey, see M.C. Woods (ed.), *An Early Commentary on the 'Poetria nova' of Geoffrey of Vinsauf* (New York and London, 1985), Introduction.

[88] Sermon 12 (Staupitz, I. 227).

sermons must have been available to him; perhaps they were part of the three volumes which were published in 1492.

A peculiar case among Staupitz's sources is Origen. Sermon 13 contains a reference to Origen whose book Staupitz quoted by its Greek title, *Peri archon*, which he translated immediately into Latin with *De principiis*.[89] On another occasion, in Sermon 23, Staupitz used another Greek expression, the famous phrase, 'Know Thyself', which he quoted in Greek as part of his Latin quotation from Juvenal's *Satires* (*Saturae* 11, 27f.).[90] Those are the only two loci in these early sermons where Staupitz employed Greek words (in Latin transcription). It is doubtful that Staupitz actually knew Greek; rather it appears that he wanted to look like a learned humanist who was familiar with this sacred language. Later on, in one of his Advent sermons of 1516 which he delivered in the presence of Nuremberg's humanists, he again used Greek. This time it was the term *tetragrammaton*. He also mentioned the Hebrew word 'Messiah',[91] probably being influenced in this regard by Johann Reuchlin's *De verbo mirifico* which had been published at Basel by Amerbach in 1494. In it, Reuchlin explained that the Hebrew name of God, YHVH (a *tetragrammaton*), which must not be pronounced, became expressible by inserting the Hebrew letter *shin* into it, YHSVH ('Y'hoshua') which then reads 'Jesus' in Hebrew.[92]

All in all, however, in these Tübingen sermons Staupitz did not approach the Book of Job in the original Hebrew. Hardly anybody among non-Jewish scholars at that time was learned enough to do so. Reuchlin noted in the *Preface* to his *Rudimenta* of 1506 that although Hebrew Bibles may be bought in Italy at a low cost, there was hardly anybody who was able to teach the Christians the language of the Jews.[93] Apparently this was the case with Staupitz. As his Tübingen sermons do not contain any references to the Hebrew text of Job, therefore, one must assume that he did not master Hebrew, nor did he employ any of the philological skills of the humanists. Nevertheless he shared with them the concern for

---

[89] 'Hic Origenes iure culpatur. In libris enim quos appellat Peri archon, id est: De principiis, hoc sensit, hoc scripsit' (Sermon 22, Staupitz, I. 247).

[90] 'Iuvenalis dicit: "E coelo descendit gnothi seauton, figendum et memori tradendum pectore"' (Sermon 23, Staupitz, I. 352).

[91] 'The wise men among the Jews perceived this when they established the truth that no one except the *messias* was allowed intelligibly to pronounce the *tetragrammaton* of God's name, so that the four letters in that name may not make any completely [good] sense in any word, and would not lead, without the *messias*, to any understanding of what is designated by them' (Staupitz II. 88); Scheurl's vernacular version of these Advent sermons leaves both alien words untranslated (Staupitz II, 89).

[92] See J. Friedman, *The Most Ancient Testimony. Sixteenth-Century Christian-Hebraica in the Age of Renaissance Nostalgia* (Athens, OH, 1983), p. 77.

[93] See Goshen-Gottstein, 'Reuchlin and his Generation', p. 153.

returning to the sources, that is to the church fathers and the Bible. Staupitz was surely an admirer of humanists such as Reuchlin.[94]

Other (non-biblical) authorities whom Staupitz mentioned by name, may have been familiar to him through secondary literature: Virgil (in Sermon 28) may have been mediated to him via Augustine's *City of God*; from Waley's commentary on Augustine he may have lifted a saying of Orosius (in Sermon 28). He may have borrowed from Egidio da Roma's scholastic commentary certain ideas of Plato, Aristotle, Averroes (whom he referred to as 'the commentator' [on Aristotle], but not by name, as in Sermon 11), also from Proclus (in Sermon 2), Hilary (in Sermon 24), Johannes Damascenus (in Sermons 5, 11 and 25), and Anselm. Ideas from Bernard of Clairvaux (in Sermon 19), Hugo of St Victor (in Sermon 24) and William of Auvergne (in Sermon 24) were most likely mediated to Staupitz via Gerson; and Pseudo-Dionysius (in sermon 20) via Thomas Aquinas, Egidio or Gerson.

There were other sources which Staupitz must have used, without giving their names, such as in Sermon 29, where he most likely relied on *The Golden Legend* for the examples from the lives of saints. *The Golden Legend* was reprinted by Michael Greyff at nearby Reutlingen in 1483. When Staupitz did not explicitly mention any names, or *florilegia*, or handbooks, it is very difficult to determine with certainty his exact sources (the critical edition mentions numerous other possibilities and indicates parallels of thought, such as with Cassiodorus at the end of Sermon 4, or with the *Florilegium Morale Oxoniense* as a possible source for an idea in Sermon 25). Staupitz's deeper knowledge of the tradition remains difficult to analyse, as it is not always easy to determine what he learned from secondary literature and what he studied in the original.

Like the humanists, Staupitz was interested in proverbs, as these Tübingen sermons show. Erasmus's collection of proverbs was published in 1500 under the title *Adages*. Also, over time contemporary books on Christ's life and passion by fellow Augustinians may have become known to Staupitz; for example, the *Passio Domini nostri Jesu Christi* (Nuremberg, 1501) written by the Nuremberg lector Reinhard von Laudenburg (d. 1502), or the new edition of *De Gestis Domini Salvatoris* of Blessed Simon Fidati de Cascia, edited by the Regensburg Friar Stephan Sutor (Basel, 1517).[95]

---

[94] See Kolde, *Die Deutsche Augustiner-Congregation*, p. 272. See also D.C. Steinmetz, 'Hermeneutic and Old Testament Interpretation in Staupitz and the Young Martin Luther', *ARG*, 70 (1979), pp. 24–58, esp. pp. 28–40.

[95] On proverbs, see Index 'proverbia' in Staupitz, I. 521. On the contemporary Augustinian editor Friar Sutor, see M.G. McNeil, *Simone Fidati and his De Gestis Domini Salvatoris* (Washington, DC, 1950), pp. 15, 61 and 71; *De gestis Domini Salvatoris/Simon Fidati de Cassia; quod edendum curavit Willigis Eckermann; cooperantibus, Franz-Bernhard*

From the mass of theological and other kind of sources which Staupitz processed in these sermons, one may conclude that his sermonizing was not meant at all for the general public at Tübingen. Although Staupitz himself called these texts *sermones*, they were probably not preached orally in the conventional sense. Latin *sermo* is not necessarily the English 'sermon', because the meaning of *sermo* in Latin may also comprise 'discourse', 'conversation', and simply 'talk'. It is most likely that Staupitz conceived of these *sermones* as a 'book' since he himself referred to them in Latin as a *liber* of several parts which he described at the beginning of his *sermo* 15.

Concern for pastoral care

The care of souls was Staupitz's first priority. In one of his Tübingen sermons (Sermon 19) he had spoken out against the pastoral negligence which was evident at the highest levels; but he was also concerned about it at the local level. At issue was the location where people should receive their pastoral care: whether parishioners should go to Mass on Sundays and Holy Days in their own parish church or whether they could attend services at a (mendicant) cloister church. He dealt with this question in his *Decisio questionis de audientia misse in parrochiali ecclesia dominicis et festiuis diebus. Cum ceteris annexis*, his first publication (we must remember that his Tübingen sermons of 1497/98 were not printed during his lifetime). Staupitz argued for Mass attendance at the parish church against the interests of the mendicant Orders (evidently including his own). Normally a layperson was not to hear Mass anywhere else except in his or her home parish, as the precept of the Church required. If, however, a just cause prompted someone to go to another church, no serious sin would be committed. Staupitz's position was criticized by the Franciscan Friar, Caspar Schatzgeyer.[96] The controversy between them rumbled on, on a different level, as Schatzgeyer became an early opponent of the Reformation. Staupitz's *Decisio* was in part a canonistic text, utilizing works by Gratiani and Panormitanus, but perhaps even more so it was a pastoral and theological one, as in it he also quoted from Scotus, Bonaventure and others.

Staupitz's booklet was an expression of the pastoral concern which he shared with contemporary pastoral leaders at Tübingen such as

---

Stammkötter, Virginie Riant et Catrin Finsterhölzl (Würzburg, 1998). On Laudenburg, see Zumkeller, *Heilslehre*, p. 105.

[96] Schatzgeyer responded with his *Tractatus de audienda missa diebus festivis … contra p. fr. Johannem Staubitz*, which is extant at the University of Munich; see Zumkeller, 'Staupitz', *Dictionnaire*, XIV, p. 1187; Schulze, 'Tübinger Gegensätze' (see n. 14 above), pp. 54–9.

Summenhart whose two sermons, mentioned above, were also printed by Othmar in 1498 as the *Tractatus bipartitus*. Summenhart's speech to monks at Hirsau on monastic shortcomings, *Tractatulus exhortatorius*, was published by Othmar in the same year. Staupitz's text was one of the first known (or extant) printed products from a printer's press at Tübingen. The press belonged to Othmar who was invited from neighbouring Reutlingen to Tübingen in 1498 by Andreas Proles, the same Augustinian superior, who had most likely ordered Staupitz to go to Tübingen. There must have been a close connection between this printer and the Augustinians, and especially Staupitz. The first letter we possess from Staupitz's pen is the one he wrote to Othmar, on 30 March 1500, which forms his preface to the *Decisio*. Staupitz deplored the state of morals, and declared that one cannot wait patiently any longer as did the father in the gospel (Luke 15), because one deals here with the truth, and therefore the enemy has to be destroyed on the threshold. This first publication of Staupitz demonstrates his concern for pastoral care as he included in it his catechetical reflections on 'what a Christian needs to know' – for example, such as the various commandments, precepts and ordinances, including the 'Golden Rule' and the Ten Commandments. He also provided a list of holy days, and concluded the booklet with the text of the Nicene Creed. It thus offered a kind of catechism for the home.[97]

Othmar's other most famous printings were the works of outstanding German preachers and spiritual writers (not academic scholastics). He published works by Henry Suso, John Tauler, Johann Geiler von Kaisersberg, as well as the anonymous *Theologia Germanica*, and (pre-Lutheran) German Bibles. He also brought out the commentary on the Mass by the Tübingen Professor Gabriel Biel (published first in 1488 when his printing shop was still located in nearby Reutlingen) and Biel's sermons on *The Passion of Our Lord* (printed in 1489, also at Reutlingen). This edition of Biel's sermons is no longer extant; another edition came out in 1509 in Mainz.[98]

---

[97] Staupitz's letter to Othmar/preface is edited by Kolde, *Die Deutsche Augustiner-Congregation*, pp. 436f. Kolde called the booklet some sort of a *Hauskatechismus*, ibid., p. 219. On the wider context, see M. Grossmann, *Humanism in Wittenberg 1485–1517* (Nieuwkoop, 1975), p. 45; Jeremias, *AELK*, p. 348; L. Keller, *Johann von Staupitz und die Anfänge der Reformation*. On Summenhart's pastoral texts, see Feld, 'Konrad Summenhart', pp. 100–102: 'Tractatus bipartitus in quo quod deus homo fieri voluerit: quodque messias in lege et prophetis promissus ... per Magistrum Conradum Summenhart de Calw sacre theologie professorem in generali studio Tüwingensi editus (1498); Tractatulus exhortatorius ad attendum super decem defectibus virorum monasticorum: per Magistrum Conradum Summenhart de Calw: sacre theologie professorem (1498)'; Calw is a town in the Black Forest.

[98] See A. Jeremias, *Johann von Staupitz: Luthers Vater und Schüler* (Sannerz and Leipzig, 1926), p. 22. The information on Biel's *Canonis Missae Expositio* is found in

It can be presumed that during his years at Tübingen Staupitz became familiar with these spiritual and pastoral texts and sermons, and with those early German Bibles which Othmar printed. Tübingen was a place of biblical and monastic humanism, and the Augustinian friary under Staupitz's leadership certainly was open to that milieu. With his pastoral theological concern for people's piety (his devotional theology), as we find it expressed in his *Decisio*, Staupitz showed himself to be a proponent of the same theology which the other professors at Tübingen pursued: in *c.* 1483 Scriptoris questioned the pastoral usefulness of forcing certain penitents to do penance in public; in 1507 Plantsch preached and wrote against 'witch hunts'; and Summenhart tried to correct misconceptions about the indulgences, as a manuscript of his demonstrates.[99]

While Staupitz was at Tübingen, a friar by the name of Johann Mantel (1470–1530) was also there. He became prior of the Nuremberg friary from 1500 to 1503 and remained in close contact with Staupitz. Being appointed as the organizer of the new University of Wittenberg, Staupitz summoned Mantel to Wittenberg for graduate studies. Here Mantel became a theology professor after having received his doctorate from that university in 1507, at the age of 37. He later accepted a position as preacher in Stuttgart in southern Germany. Afterwards he worked at Strasbourg in the Order's general studies programme. Two other friars from Tübingen, Sigismund Epp and Dionysius Bickel (originally from the friary at Weil der Stadt near Tübingen), were among the first professors of the faculty at Wittenberg. Friar Augustin Luft from Tübingen would be the prior at Heidelberg at the time of the Augustinians' famous Heidelberg Disputation in 1518. Friar Konrad Treger was also at Tübingen at that time; he later became an opponent of the Reformation, when he was the leader of the Rhenish-Swabian province of the Augustinians. Gregor Mayr was another friar, and later preacher, who was with Staupitz at Tübingen at the same time, and who later was of service to him at Salzburg. Besides Mayr and Mantel, there also was Besler who had matriculated at the university with him. All these connections proved to be rather useful to Staupitz in his endeavours. One may further assume that Staupitz himself kept up with his Order's tradition of providing good preachers for various assignments in the major cities and that he sought to be a good preacher himself. We may surmise that he gave great sermons when he became a 'professor of the sacred page', even though none of Staupitz's sermons or recordings

---

Schulze, 'Tübinger Gegensätze', p. 55. On Biel, see Landeen, 'Gabriel Biel and the Devotio Moderna in Germany', p. 36.

[99] See Feld, 'Konrad Summenhart', p. 85 with n. 4 (on Plantsch); p. 113 with n. 133 (on Summenhart); and pp. 115–16 (on Scriptoris).

thereof have survived, nor any references to them, dating from the years 1498 to 1510. We may further assume that his proclamation of God's mercy would have continued through these years. His grace-filled message would become tangible again in 1512 and in the following years. Thus we find in the early work of the young Staupitz, in his observations on the mercy of God, the foundations of the principles that will allow him, in the 1520s, to see the state of the Church clearly and call it as he sees it – a Babylonian captivity – and yet to remain in captivity and bear it patiently.[100]

Reformator of the Order of St Augustine and of the University of Wittenberg

As a reform-minded prior at the friary at Tübingen Staupitz became involved in the case of a fellow friar, Dr Conrad Holzinger. This friar, who did not want to live in voluntary poverty, had left his friary (possibly Weil der Stadt) after 1480, when under the Order's leadership of Andreas Proles, it became an observant cloister. A few years later, Holzinger had become prior of the conventual friary at Lauingen, but must have departed from there by 1485, when Caspar Amman held this position. It is possible that Holzinger may have left the Order altogether, without permission, and became the councillor, chancellor and chaplain of the count of Württemberg. However, as a result of political quarrels he had to leave this position, whereupon his political opponents, who received legal advice from the humanist lawyer Johann Reuchlin, arranged his capture and imprisonment with papal permission. He was brought to Tübingen and was jailed at the castle for some time. (Reuchlin's comedy, *Sergius*, is said to include satirical attacks on Holzinger and his political machinations.) After being in and out of prison, Holzinger was once again in captivity in 1498, and this time was handed over to the Augustinian authorities at Tübingen where Staupitz was now the prior. As the leader of that friary he had to keep Holzinger in monastic imprisonment. On the Monday after the feast of the Epiphany in 1499, Staupitz (together with another friar) received Holzinger's possessions and an inventory of his books, as a document written in German shows.[101]

---

[100] See Brecht, 'Das Augustiner-Eremiten-Kloster zu Tübingen', p. 77; on J. Mantel, see Stupperich, pp. 137–8. On Mayr, see Schneider-Lastin, *Johann von Staupitz, Salzburger Predigten 1512*, p. 4, n. 8. Oberman, '*Duplex Misericordia*', p. 47.

[101] 'Fr. Johannes de Stubitz zu den Augustinern zu Tuwingen und mit im Fr. Bernharden Lindaw auch desselben Ordens hend uff Montag nach trium regum anno CCCCIC Doctor Cunrat Holzungs Dinglach genomen, wie das von item zu item hernach

It was during these turbulent times that Staupitz studied toward his doctorate in theology. After three years at Tübingen he received his licentiate in theology on 6 July 1500, and his doctor's degree on the following day. He then returned to Munich, where, it is thought, he had previously made his final vows, and took on a leadership position within the already reformed friary. He was head of this friary from 1500 until at least April 1503 and, in this function, was able to participate at the meeting of the Bavarian congregation of Augustinians at Regensburg on 14 August 1502. The Munich friary, had possessed since 1407 a *terminus* – that is, a branch office or outpost with the privilege of alms collections in a designated area – at Salzburg. The facility included storage rooms for the donations, and housing for the administrator of the outpost, who usually had to be a good preacher as well, and was usually a friar with a graduate degree in theology. If such a *terminus* needed a full-time administrator, that person was called a *stationarius*, or holder of the station. Some of the friars from Munich were assigned to the *terminus* at Salzburg both to preach and to collect alms. (Although the latter is sometimes referred to as 'begging', it is more likely to have been meant as an honorarium or stipend for preaching.) As the prior of Munich, Staupitz probably had to supervise the *terminarius* and ask the Salzburg authorities for permission for alms collections and for the other duties connected with it. Another *terminus* of the Munich Augustinians was located in nearby Bad Reichenhall (south-west of the city of Salzburg), still within the Archdiocese of Salzburg. The Munich friary also had two branch offices in the diocese of Freising: one in Erding (north-east of Munich) and one in Bad Aibling (south-east of Munich). In April 1503, Staupitz asked the administrator of the diocese of Freising to order the diocesan clergy to support the friars in their collections of alms in a document that named Staupitz as prior of Munich under the date of 15 April 1503. With these four extension offices the Munich friary covered much of the region along the northern edge of the Alps. In addition, the friary of Seemannshausen in lower Bavaria had three *termini*: one in Mühldorf, which was an enclave belonging to the Archbishopric of Salzburg, and one in Braunau (both located east of Munich in the Inn Valley), and the third in Burghausen on the Salzach River, north of Salzburg. These were important cities at the time. Burghausen still houses Germany's largest fortress, which was built in the fifteenth century as a bulwark against the Turkish armies then

geschriben stet'. For biographical data on Holzinger and for this document with Staupitz's name, see D. Stievermann, 'Der Augustinermönch Dr. Conrad Holzinger – Kaplan, Rat und Kanzler des Grafen bzw. Herzogs Eberhard d. J. von Württemberg am Ende des 15. Jahrhunderts', in J. Engel (ed.), *Mittel und Wege früher Verfassungspolitik* (Stuttgart, 1979), pp. 356–405 (n. 171).

advancing from the Balkans toward central Europe. Being stationed at Munich, Staupitz became very familiar with the regions of Bavaria and Salzburg and their political and ecclesiastical conditions. It is not unlikely that Staupitz himself, as prior of the Munich friary, visited the Salzburg *terminus* sometime between 1500 and 1503.[102]

Staupitz's stay at his home friary at Munich was interrupted because Frederick the Wise, Elector of Saxony, called him to develop the University of Wittenberg which was established in 1502. The elector provided Staupitz with the *probstey*, that is the office of provost. The friars were given the property at the Holy Spirit Hospital where they started to construct the friary in 1504, using the old church as their chapel. At a leadership conference at Nuremberg on 16 May 1504 (when the revised constitutions were approved) the deal with the elector of Saxony was approved with the stipulation that, in exchange for receiving the necessary funds for building the new friary at Wittenberg, the friars were to pray for the eternal salvation of the elector's ancestors. This meant the holding of vigils and celebration of masses for the deceased, especially on the anniversaries of their deaths.[103]

It would appear that Staupitz and his Order were determined to make Wittenberg the most prestigious place of study for their members. Every Augustinian friary ran a study programme for its members, called the *studium locale*, the purpose of which was to provide education in grammar and logic. In addition, every province within the Order ran one if not more *studia generalia* intended to provide an introduction to philosophy and theology for those destined to be ordained as priests. Usually these *studia generalia* were placed in cities with universities.

In the Middle Ages, Paris was the dominant centre of study for the Augustinians. The university there was pre-eminent in theological studies, the other French centre being Toulouse. In Italy, Bologna, Florence,

---

[102] On Staupitz and the Bavarian congregation, see H. Tüchle, 'Zur Geschichte der bayrischen Provinz der Augustinereremiten im Jahrhundert vor der Reformation. Mitteilungen aus dem Kollektaneenbuch des P. Hieronymus Streitel', in C.P. Mayer and W. Eckermann (eds), *Scientia Augustiniana. Studien über Augustinus, den Augustinismus und den Augustinerorden. Festschrift für P. DDr. Adolar Zumkeller OSA zum 60. Geburtstag* (Würzburg, 1975), pp. 638–40. On Staupitz in the Salzburg region, see Kunzelmann, V, p. 434 (with n. 2172); Sallaberger, 'Johann von Staupitz, Luthers Vorgesetzter und Freund', pp. 122–3. However, there is no record in the Salzburg archives for these activities (alms collection etc.). The first contact of Staupitz with Salzburg is to be assumed for 1510. Sallaberger, 'Johann von Staupitz, Luthers Vorgesetzter und Freund', p. 121. On the required qualities of a preacher at a *terminus*, see K. Elm, 'Mendikantenstudium, Laienbildung und Klerikerschulung im spätmittelalterlichen Westfalen', in B. Moeller et al. (eds), *Studien zum städtischen Bildungswesen des späten Mittelalters und der frühen Neuzeit* (Göttingen, 1983), pp. 586–617 (p. 609f.).

[103] See Kunzelmann, V, pp. 447f.

Padua, Pavia, Siena, Naples and Rome were the principal cities, while, north of the Alps, Louvain and Krakow were the centres for their respective regions. Members of friaries in the Cologne area used to go to Louvain; however, from the fourteenth century onwards the Augustinians at Cologne had a study programme of their own. The Bavarian province had two study centres, Vienna and Prague; the Rhenish-Swabian province had theirs at Strasbourg and Constance, and later at Heidelberg. The Saxon-Thuringian province usually sent their friars to Magdeburg and Erfurt. By the close of the Middle Ages, the other friaries with *studia generalia*, incorporated into universities, in the German-speaking lands, were those in Basel, Freiburg in the Black Forest, and Tübingen. To these, Staupitz would add the one at Wittenberg for the elector of Saxony. Remarkably, three important cultural and political centres which Staupitz frequented – Nuremberg, Munich, and Salzburg – did not have any *studia generalia* for the Augustinians. Salzburg did not even have an Augustinian friary in its midst.

Usually a *regens* was the director of studies, assisted by *professores sacrae paginae*. A *regens* had the power to confer degrees, in the name of the Order's general, on the members of his *studium generale*; the most gifted members were then sent to major universities for further study. Frederick and Staupitz may have envisioned that Wittenberg would develop into such a centre of higher learning for Frederick's people, mainly to prepare administrators for his government offices, and to provide physicians, lawyers, teachers and priests for his territory. The new school should rival the prestigious university in neighbouring Leipzig where Staupitz had studied. The university lectures actually took place under the Wittenberg friars' roof once the construction was finished, just as happened at Tübingen and Heidelberg. As the territorial lord, Frederick used Wittenberg as the city of his residence, and he now wanted to increase its significance by establishing a university there. His castle had been under construction since 1490, but was not finished until 1525, the year of his death.[104]

From the beginning of the thirteenth century, it was customary, when a new university was established, for numerous teaching positions to be given to clergymen with benefices (*Pfründen*). Frederick maintained this custom

---

[104] On the organization of studies within the Augustinian Order, see Vonschott, *Geistiges Leben*, p. 100; A. Zumkeller, 'The Augustinian School of the Middle Ages' in J.E. Rotelle (ed.), *Theology and History*, p. 40. On Wittenberg, see H. Junghans, 'Wittenberg and Luther: Luther and Wittenberg', trans. K. Gustavs, in T. Divino and R. Kolb (eds), *Martin Luther in Two Centuries. The Sixteenth and The Twentieth* (St Paul, MN, 1992), p. 16; Ludolphy, *Friedrich der Weise*, p. 350. G. Wentz, 'Das Augustinerer-emitenkloster in Wittenberg', in F. Bünger and G. Wentz (eds), *Germania Sacra* (Berlin, 1941), pp. 443ff. See also Institut für Denkmalpflege der DDR, *Martin Luther* (see n. 5 above), p. 30.

and determined that of the 22 professorships to be established, 12 should go to the clergymen with the respective benefices for funding and three to the friaries of Wittenberg. The elector himself therefore had only to finance the remaining seven positions. On 11 November 1504, Staupitz and two other officials of the Augustinian Order agreed definitely to provide personnel from their ranks for (at least) two professorships at this university. The two other officials were Johann Vogt, the district vicar for Saxony and Thuringia, and Johann Brüheym (or Brüheim), the district vicar for Bavaria and the Rhineland (including Cologne). Staupitz himself remained professor of the theological faculty,[105] while the other position was filled by Friar Wolfgang Ostermair from Munich (also known as Ansermaier or Cäppelmair) who was to teach philosophy within the faculty of arts. Staupitz may have known Ostermair from Tübingen where the latter matriculated at the beginning of 1501. In 1507 Ostermair was professor of the Bible, and in 1509 became the first Augustinian to graduate with a doctor's degree in theology from the new University of Wittenberg. In the autumn of 1510 he was dean of the theology faculty, apparently replacing Staupitz who held this office in 1508/09, then, in summer 1510, he returned to his friary in Munich. Staupitz made sure that a few other friars with whom he had been acquainted in Tübingen came to Wittenberg in order to complete their studies there. Among them was Gregor Mayr (or Mayer) who was transferred from Tübingen for the winter semester 1502/03 and who, after graduating with a master of arts degree in 1503, became prior of the friary of Wittenberg. He later returned to Munich. Staupitz also transferred Friar Christoph Fladensteyn from Tübingen to Wittenberg. He later became the prior of the friary at Kulmbach. Staupitz sent a total of 13 friars to Wittenberg at the opening of the new university,[106] even though there was very little living space for them.

---

[105] 'Doctor Staupitz probst. als churfurst Friedrich Doctori Staupitz die probstey zu Wittenberg hat eingereumet' (*WATR* 5. 290, 1f. (no. 5641, undated)). 'Ordinaria in biblia und ein lection in morali philosophia', document no. 14, in W. Friedensburg, *Urkundenbuch der Universität Wittenberg* (Magdeburg, 1926); see H. Boehmer, *Martin Luther: Road to Reformation*, trans. J.W. Doberstein and T.G. Tappert (New York, 1960, 3rd printing), p. 46; W. Landgraf, *Martin Luther. Reformator und Rebell. Biografie*, 2nd edn (Berlin, 1982), p. 61; C. Burger, 'Der Augustinereremit Martin Luther in Kloster und Universität bis zum Jahre 1512' in G. Ruhbach and K. Schmidt-Clausen (eds), *Kloster Amelungsborn 1135–1985* (Hannover, 1985), pp. 174–6 and 185, n. 71. Burger points out, that Staupitz's professorship was not necessarily always intended to be the Bible professorship, as in one document it is simply referred to as *lectur zu wittenberg* (ibid., pp. 176–7).

[106] On Friar Ostermair, see Kunzelmann, V, p. 495 with n. 2410; Wriedt, 'Johannes von Staupitz als Gründungsmitglied' (see n. 4 above), p. 179; on Ostermair and his Good Friday sermon of 1514, see A. Zumkeller, 'Der Münchener Theologieprofessor Wolfgang Ostermair und seine Karfreitagspredigt vom Jahre 1514', *AAug*, 29 (1966), pp. 214–54. On Fladensteyn, see Kunzelmann, V, pp. 495f. with n. 2411.

Up to that time, Wittenberg did not have a friary of its own, but was home of a *terminus* that belonged to the Augustinian friars of Herzberg, located south-east of Wittenberg. The Wittenberg *terminus* had one house available where the friars stayed during their collection campaigns. However, Staupitz somehow managed to also house there those friars who were designated to teach or to study at Wittenberg, as he was determined to establish a study programme for the Order. This meant that the Augustinians' *terminus* of Wittenberg had been converted into a full friary under Staupitz's leadership; an expansion programme by which Staupitz intended to secure the success of the new university. He thus may be rightly called one of the 'fathers' of the university at Wittenberg.

Undoubtedly because of Staupitz's impact as an Augustinian friar and Bible scholar and because of the humanists' preference for St Paul, this apostle was made the patron saint of the theology faculty, and St Augustine the patron saint of the entire university, while St Catherine of Siena, a favourite saint among local miners, became the patroness of the faculty of arts. St Ivo was named the patron of the law school. The selection of St Augustine as patron of the university and St Paul as patron of the faculty of theology perhaps indicates Staupitz's theological agenda; both patrons stand in marked contrast to Jerome, who was patron of the theology faculty of Erfurt. However, having St Augustine as patron saint was not unique since the University of Basel was also placed under his patronage.[107] Staupitz being newly appointed to this leadership role at Wittenberg brought additional benefits and prestige for the elector when he persuaded several scholars and students from within the Order to come to Wittenberg from Tübingen.

Besides Dr Staupitz, Dr Martin Pollich von Mellerstad had been invited to join in establishing the University of Wittenberg. Pollich and Staupitz knew each other from Leipzig, where Pollich had been involved in a literary controversy with Conrad Wimpina (1465–1531), which continued even after Pollich's move to Wittenberg. Wimpina was a Thomist and became an early opponent of the reformers. Nevertheless, at the beginning of the year 1503, Staupitz accompanied his elderly superior Proles to the University of Leipzig in order to attend to

---

[107] The new university was not the only one north of the Alps dedicated to St Augustine, and was thus not a complete 'novelty' in Germany, as Giancarlo Pani thinks in 'Novita' A Wittenberg Prima Dell' Arrivo Di Lutero', *Studi storico-religiosi*, 4 (1980), pp. 135–53. On Basel, see Kolde, *Die Deutsche Augustiner-Congregation*, p. 220. St Catherine was a patron saint of miners along with St Margaretha and St Barbara; on this, see Ludolphy, *Friedrich der Weise*, p. 359, n. 141. On the patron at Erfurt, see the critical edition of Johann von Paltz, *Werke*, p. 368, n. 79.

the doctoral promotion of Wimpina there. This may have been Proles's way of testing Staupitz's leadership qualities and of grooming him as his successor in the office of the vicar general of the reformed Augustinians. Staupitz became one of the mediators in the controversy between Pollich and Wimpina, along with Archbishop Ernest of Magdeburg and Goswin of Orsoy, Chancellor of the University of Wittenberg. The feud ended in 1504. Pollich represented the forward-looking forces at Leipzig, and later also at Wittenberg. As the first rector of Wittenberg he was concerned that Aristotle had too great an influence in matters of theology. In this regard he apparently joined the chorus of contemporary humanists that we found also at Tübingen.[108] Evidently Wimpina was not to play any role at the University of Wittenberg.

On 6 July 1502 Emperor Maximilian I signed the university's foundation document during his stay at the imperial city of Ulm in southern Germany. On 24 August 1502 Frederick published the invitation to students to register at his new university, where they were able to begin their studies on 18 October 1502, the feast day of St Luke. It was a novelty that this official invitation was sent out in German, and not in Latin. The curriculum consisted of the liberal arts, church law and civil (Roman) law, medicine, *poeterei* (humanist studies), and Sacred Scriptures.[109] Interestingly, the original text speaks of the study of the 'sacred scripture', and not of 'theology', an emphasis that is most likely due to Frederick's love of the Bible and to the influence of Staupitz who, as a Bible scholar, wanted to foster biblical theology at this new university. Staupitz managed to attract his nephew, Nicholas von Amsdorf (1488–1565) to a teaching position at Wittenberg. (They were related through Amsdorf's mother.) At Wittenberg Amsdorf received his master's degree in 1504 and in 1508 he became a canon at All Saints' church there. He earned his licentiate in 1511 and became a professor of philosophy at the university, where he was assigned to lecture on Scotus, whose thought was highly esteemed by Staupitz. Previous instructors on Scotism, Jerome Schurf (also Schurpf or Schurff, 1481–1554) and Sigismund Epp, did not last very long in these positions. Although Amsdorf's appointment may smack of nepotism, it seems more probable that Staupitz wanted to make sure that at 'his'

---

[108] See Vonschott, *Geistiges Leben*; Grossmann, *Humanism*, p. 44; Zumkeller, *Erbsünde*, p. 501. On Staupitz and Proles at Leipzig, see Kolde, *Die Deutsche Augustiner-Congregation*, pp. 164f.

[109] See Ludolphy, *Friedrich der Weise*, p. 318; M. Treu, 'Die Leucorea zwischen Tradition und Erneuerung. Erwägungen zur frühen Geschichte der Universität Wittenberg' in H. Lück (ed.), *Martin Luther und seine Universität. Vorträge anlässlich des 450. Todestages des Reformators* (Cologne, Weimar and Vienna, 1998), pp. 31–51.

university a philosophy more to his liking was taught. An intellectual move from Scotist to Augustinian thinking was in fact not a great step as one may trace a continuum from Augustine to Scotus. Amsdorf was encouraged to study directly Augustine's thought world; he received from Luther a complete set of this church father's works.[110] Staupitz (and Luther) also persuaded Professor Karlstadt to turn to Augustine although Karlstadt had begun his teaching assignment with lectures on Thomas Aquinas. Evidently, Staupitz played a key role in the formation of the Wittenberg theology by directing his younger colleagues to the study of Augustine.[111]

At first, the new university struggled for its existence; that is why it opened its doors to as many schools of thought as possible, including the humanists – whose movement was on the rise, even if that movement cannot be defined clearly and sharply. Staupitz and Pollich set up the University of Wittenberg along humanist lines. This meant a return to the sources of the Bible and the church fathers, and the study of these sources in their original languages. The university was also known by its grecized name *Leucorea* ('Wittenberg' = 'white hill' in Old German). Such grecizing and latinizing of names of places and persons was a typical contemporary humanist phenomenon.

Staupitz took the constitution of the University of Tübingen, where humanists had already gained professorships, as his model for the University of Wittenberg. The statutes of Wittenberg repeated almost word for word those of Tübingen. Staupitz began to hire professors who were trained in the humanist studies, among them Jerome Schurf. Schurf, a Swiss who had studied law at Tübingen since 1501, had brought his humanism from Basel. At Tübingen he was a student of Konrad Summenhart, who perhaps had told Staupitz about Schurf's capabilities. Alternatively, Staupitz and Schurf may have met in Summenhart's classroom. In any case, he came to Wittenberg as a professor of Scotism (*via Scoti*), but immediately in Spring 1505 he switched to the law school where he remained for 45 years. Staupitz also brought from Tübingen the canon lawyer, Wolfgang Staehelin, the first dean of the law school, and the humanist jurist Ambros Volland who had received his law degree from Padua, and who became professor of civil law at Wittenberg, but

---

[110] See R. Kolb, *Nikolaus von Amsdorf (1483–1565): Popular polemics in preservation of Luther's legacy* (Nieuwkoop, 1978); Stupperich, pp. 25f.; E.G. Schwiebert, *Luther and his times: The Reformation from a new perspective* (St Louis, 1950), p. 271; H. Bornkamm, *Luther in Mid-Career 1521–1530*, ed. K. Bornkamm, trans. E.T. Bachmann (Philadelphia, PA, 1983), p. 277.

[111] See B. Lohse, 'Zum Wittenberger Augustinismus. Augustins Schrift De Spiritu et Littera in der Auslegung bei Staupitz, Luther und Karlstadt', in Hagen, *Augustine, the Harvest*, pp. 89–109.

not even for a full year. Dr Volland eventually settled at Salzburg in 1523 in the service of Cardinal Lang, probably upon the recommendation of Staupitz.[112]

Furthermore, Staupitz introduced two Augustinian friars from Tübingen as new professors at Wittenberg. One was the Scotist Sigismund Epp who became the first dean of the faculty of arts (between 1502 and 1504); while in this office he became professor of theology in the spring of 1503, but left the following year and returned to Tübingen. The other friar was Hertwig Temmen (= Themmen, or Heydewicus Themen, or Herdewich Demen, or Diemann), a professor of biblical theology. Temmen had been a friar at Himmelpforten from where he was sent to Leipzig in 1482 to study. In November 1483 he received his Bachelor of Arts degree from the University of Heidelberg, and in October 1485 he received his Master of Arts degree. At Easter 1487 he matriculated at the Univerity of Erfurt, from where he went to Tübingen in December 1491. Here he lectured on the Bible between March and October 1492, and afterwards on the Sentences. At Tübingen he became master of theology in April 1494; he then must have returned to Himmelpforten where records show him as 'doctor of the Sacred Scripture' in 1499. In the winter of 1503/04 he was professor of theology at the University of Wittenberg. It appears that at times there were three theology professors among the Augustinians at Wittenberg.

Known humanists were hired, too, such as the professor of rhetoric Hermann von dem Busche (c. 1468–1534), who came with Pollich from Leipzig. Busche gave the opening lecture at the new university and thus gave a signal to the world that this establishment was sympathetic to humanism. Also hired, as the professor of Greek, was Nicholas Marschalk (c. 1470–1525), one of the best Greek scholars in northern Germany. He was at Wittenberg from the opening of the university, but stayed there only until 1505. After his departure, Greek was taught by Hermann Trebelius (c. 1475 – c. 1514), Johannes Draco (1494–1566), Tilmann Conradi (c. 1485 – c. 1522), the Augustinian friar John Lang (1487–1548), John Rhagius Aesticampianus (1457–1520), until Philipp Melanchthon (1497–1560) was hired in 1518. In Friar Johann Lang, who joined the Augustinians in 1506, Staupitz's Order gained a young humanist and scholar of the Greek language, who had been trained by Marschalk. The fact that Lang joined the Augustinians demonstrates the fact that there was a certain openness to humanism in

---

[112] On Volland, see J. Sallaberger, *Kardinal Matthäus Lang von Wellenburg (1468–1540): Staatsmann und Kirchenfürst im Zeitalter von Renaissance, Reformation und Bauernkriegen* (Salzburg, 1997), pp. 192f (hereafter 'Sallaberger, *Kardinal*'). On the other aspects, see Grossmann, *Humanism*, p. 44–8; M.J. Harran, *Martin Luther: Learning for Life* (St Louis, 1997), pp. 107–13.

Staupitz's Order, since for a long time numerous Italian humanists had belonged to the Augustinian Order.[113]

Although moving in a humanist milieu, Staupitz's own writings were neither typically humanist, nor anti-humanist. He was esteemed in humanist circles, especially by Erasmus who told John Lang in October 1518: 'I like this great man Staupitz.'[114] At Wittenberg, sometime between 1504 and 1507, the humanist John Crispus published the second edition of the grammar book by the Italian humanist Johannes Sulpitius Verulanus (b. 1475), an edition which he dedicated to Staupitz and Pollich. From Crispus's preface we know that Staupitz and Pollich had ordered the adoption of this textbook as the replacement of the *Doctrinale* which had been written by Alexander Gallus around 1200. With this change, the humanist programme was confirmed; it stressed the linguistic training. Here follows Crispus's preface to the textbook which was called *Posterior editio Sulpitiana in partes tres divisa quae complectuntur: Prima Examen puerorum*, addressing Staupitz and Pollich:

> Day after day, your great diligence comes more and more to light, a diligence with which you labour toward leading the tender young people – as fast as possible – away from the slime to the genuine gems. You do this by having established for our Academy of Wittenberg, which is highly celebrated and firmly planted, the Grammar of Sulpitius which is to be read along with the poems and the refinements of [J. Badius] Ascensius. [You decreed this] in order that from now on it is no longer possible that out of stupidity a weak foundation is laid for our studious alumni, as was the case for almost 300 years with the chapters in the textbook of Alexander Gallus, first because of the completely barbaric edition of his verses, and secondly because of the arrogant ignorance of its interpreters, as [from this old textbook] all of us had been taught, with grave distress and loss, O what a pain.[115]

[113] See Schwiebert, *Luther and his times*, pp. 268–72; Wriedt, 'Johannes von Staupitz als Gründungsmitglied', pp. 179–81; Zumkeller, 'Martin Luther und sein Orden', p. 260; Sallaberger, 'Johann von Staupitz, die Stiftsprediger', p. 116; Junghans, *Der junge Luther*, p. 57. On Schurf, see Kolde, *Die Deutsche Augustiner-Congregation*, p. 221, and W. Schaich-Klose, *D. Hieronymus Schürpf. Leben und Werk des Wittenberger Reformationsjuristen 1481–1554* (Trogen, Switzerland, 1967); on Themmen, see Kunzelmann, V, pp. 223, 446–7 and 494–5.

[114] See *Letter* 872 (and 1166) in the Allen edition (Oxford, 1906), III. 408; I. Guenter, 'Staupitz', in P.G. Bietenholz and T.B. Deutscher (eds), *Contemporaries of Erasmus* (Toronto, 1987), III, pp. 282–3; H. Scheible (ed.), *Melanchthons Briefwechsel*, 10 vols (Stuttgart-Bad Cannstatt, 1977–), I, p. 64; Wetzel, 'Staupitz antibarbarus', p. 111.

[115] See Grossmann, *Humanism*, p. 53; Junghans, *Der junge Luther*, p. 58; Wetzel, 'Staupitz antibarbarus', p. 107 with the addendum on pp. 129–30 re the recent discovery of the *Editio Sulpitiana*, and announcing that this preface is to be edited for the first time in vol. 6 (not yet appeared) of the new critical edition of Staupitz's works.

Staupitz thus was recognized as having been instrumental, together with Pollich, in laying the humanist foundations for the linguistic training at Wittenberg. Evidently, Staupitz must have appeared like a humanist to these humanists. 'Sacred philology' began to take a central place for theology.[116] The leading men of the University of Wittenberg were called 'reformers' (reformatores). Their task was to advise the territorial lord, Frederick the Wise, on matters of university reform. One of these university reformers had to be the rector of the institution. In having four reformatores at the top, Wittenberg's university followed the model of Bologna, and as such was the only university in Germany with official 'reformers' in charge. The traditional division into 'nations' was no longer tolerated at Wittenberg.[117]

Vicar general of the Saxon reform congregation

Helping the elector establish the new university at Wittenberg did not mean, however, that Staupitz settled there as the permanent dean of the theology faculty; he was far too busy organizing the observant movement within the Order. On 7 May 1503, as candidate for the leadership position in the Order, he presided over the general chapter meeting of the reformed friaries at the observant friary of Eschwege, west of Erfurt. Among those present at this decisive gathering was Andreas Proles, the long-time vicar of the reformed branch who had resigned, after 30 years in the position of vicar general, having been in charge of almost 30 friaries. Also present were Johann Vogt, the district vicar of the 12 friaries in Saxony-Thuringia and Johann Brüheym (a Bible professor), the district vicar of the friaries in Bavaria, the Cologne region, and of the five friaries in the Rhine-Swabian region (Tübingen, Esslingen, Weil der Stadt, Mindelheim and Heidelberg). Also belonging to the reformed branch were the three friaries in Franconia (Nuremberg, Königsberg and Kulmbach), the two in Hesse (Alzey and Eschwege), one under construction in Sternberg in the distant Mecklenburg region, one recent foundation at Mühlheim/Ehrenbreitstein near Koblenz in the lower Rhine region, two Dutch friaries (one at Haarlem and one at Enkhuizen), and the large Bavarian friary at Munich. Besides Proles,

---

[116] On 'sacred philology', see P.O. Kristeller, Renaissance Thought: The Classic, Scholastic, and Humanistic Strains (New York, 1961), p. 79.

[117] 'Joannem de Staupicz Augustinianum, Martinum Polichium Mellerstatinum, devotos nostros magistros et doctores, in quatuor studii generalis reformatores' (Frederick's statutes of the University of Wittenberg of 1 October 1508; as quoted by M. Schulze, Fürsten und Reformation (Tübingen, 1991), p. 79, n. 137); Ludolphy, Friedrich der Weise, p. 322.

Vogt and Brüheym, we know of a few other leading friars in attendance, namely the theology professors Johann von Paltz, Johann Nathin and Hertwig Themmen.

Here, at Eschwege, Staupitz was elected vicar general of the reformed (observant) Augustinians, succeeding Andreas Proles, who, about one month after Staupitz's election died on 5 June 1503, at the age of 74 at the friary at Kulmbach. Very probably, Proles had suggested Staupitz as his successor. Staupitz was about 35 years of age at that time and now held the highest office within the reformed congregation of the Hermits of St Augustine in Saxony. The position of vicar general was comparable not so much to that of a provincial in the conventual branch, as to the general of the entire Order. His main task was to make an annual visitation to each friary.[118]

Nathin had directed the general studies programme of the friars at Erfurt since 1493. A decade earlier, in 1483, he had introduced the strict observance of the Rule at the friary of Tübingen and had thereby saved the Augustinians from eviction from that university city. Remarkably, however, Staupitz dedicated his Tübingen sermons on the Book of Job neither to Nathin nor to Themmen, but to Brüheym who apparently was the most powerful leader. He was, as has been said, in charge of the observant friaries in three major provinces – Cologne, Bavaria and Rhine-Swabia – and he was a Bible scholar like Staupitz. Great differences of opinion must have arisen between Nathin and Staupitz, as Nathin turned out to be vehemently opposed to Staupitz's plan to unite the Saxon reform congregation with the Saxon province of the Order. He signed the protest document against Staupitz in 1510. It was Nathin who sent Luther to Rome on behalf of the strict observant friary of Erfurt in order to counteract Staupitz's plans. Incidentally, it was Nathin, not Staupitz, who recommended that Luther, in his preparation for ordination to the priesthood, should read the *Canonis Missae expositio* by Gabriel Biel. Although none of Nathin's works are extant, it may be assumed that under his leadership no Occamist theology was taught, which is significant for the type of theology to which the young friars were exposed.[119]

---

[118] See Kolde, *Die Deutsche Augustiner-Congregation*, p. 225; Kunzelmann, V, pp. 181, 435–47; on Proles, see Zumkeller, entry 'Proles, André', *Dictionnaire*, XII, pp. 2406–9; on the friaries, see J. Sallaberger, 'Abt Johann von Staupitz (1522–1524), Luthers einstiger Vorgesetzter und Freund', in Salzburger Landesregierung, *Das älteste Kloster im deutschen Sprachraum: St. Peter in Salzburg* (Salzburg, 1982), p. 92.

[119] See Zumkeller, *Erbsünde*, pp. 503–4. Zumkeller's conclusion is very significant because it means that the young friars, including Luther, were not really exposed to Occamist theology at Erfurt. However, it must be said that at Erfurt there was no explicit Augustinianism either; see Burger, 'Der Augustinereremit', pp. 163–6. On Nathin, see Kunzelmann, V, pp. 443–6.

The reform movement among the Augustinian friars came, like the humanist movement, from Italy. These reformed or observant friaries gathered themselves in 'congregations'. One of the earliest, founded in 1387, had its centre at Lecceto to which the humanist Egidio da Viterbo was later temporarily connected. There were other Italian congregations, such as the one at Perugia founded in 1436, and, most important for the Germans, there was from 1419 the Lombard congregation in northern Italy, with which Staupitz tried to connect his Saxon reformed congregation. The Spanish reformed congregation had appeared in 1431; the one in Dalmatia emerged as late as 1511. These congregations were governed by their own vicars who were subject directly to the general in Rome. On the local level, Staupitz either found the divisions of the territory of his jurisdiction already established into smaller districts with 'district vicars' as immediate supervisors, or else he himself invented this system. He, together with those assembled at Eschwege (where he was elected), were determined to realize the reform programme. While Proles had carried out the *reformatio* of the friaries with the help of the 'secular' authorities and had great success with this approach, Staupitz, although not neglecting the input from the local governments, pursued more far-reaching plans – which ended in disaster. Staupitz planned to create a supranational movement of reformed (observant) friaries by seeking union with the northern Italian friaries.

After his return from his first visitiation tour in Saxony and Thuringia in the summer of 1504, he did not settle in Wittenberg in order to teach, but went back to Munich where we find him in December 1504.[120] In January 1505 Staupitz sent his confrère and confidant Besler to Italy. Besler, then prior at Munich, having succeeded Staupitz in that position, was to take on the task of procurator of the Saxon reformed congregation in Rome. He received the directive of primarily maintaining a strong position for their congregation vis-à-vis the Order's general at Rome. Staupitz had known him since their days at Tübingen. Besler had also been inclined toward humanism as a prior at the Nuremberg friary in 1491/92, and again from 1495 to 1499. Besler's other assignment in Italy was to achieve the union of the Saxon/German reform congregation with the Lombard congregation. He attended the chapter meeting of the Lombard congregation at Vercelli on 19 April 1505. The arrangement was approved on 21 June 1505 by a bull of Pope Julius II (d. 1513). Staupitz's hopes that his congregation would now

---

[120] See Kolde, *Die Deutsche Augustiner-Congregation*, p. 226; Kunzelmann, V, pp. 435–48; Zumkeller, 'Johannes von Staupitz und die klösterliche Reformbewegung', p. 32. For the history of the Augustinian reformed congregations, see 'Augustinians', *NCE*, I. 1073.

share the rich privileges of the Lombard congregation – mainly a considerable degree of autonomy from the central government of their Order in Rome – seemed to come true. (The Lombard congregation had been granted relative autonomy by Pope Alexander VI as early as in 1498.) Staupitz apparently began to act as if he were independent like the vicar of the Lombards, directly subordinated only to the pope, and not any longer to the general of the Order. He had some right to feel this way because on 15 March the pope ordered the archbishops of Mainz, Magdeburg and Salzburg solemnly to publish the papal bull of June 1505 that was addressed to the reform congregation. However, Besler, who had obtained the approval of the union of 1505 without the consent of the Order's general, Agostino Faccioni de Terni (also known as 'Interamna'), was in deep trouble. This general, who was elected on 1 September 1505, 'hated the German observants'. He interrogated and threatened Besler with imprisonment and would have excommunicated him and fined him a large sum of money, had he left the city of Rome. Besler lived in constant fear of secretly being killed. The new general of the Order did not even want to see any friars of the reform congregation attend the general chapter meeting.[121]

In the meantime, the provincial of the Rhenish-Swabian province travelled to Rome as well, in order to regain control of the five friaries over which he had lost jurisdiction to Staupitz. He received a warm welcome at the Order's central administration and, although he did not regain control completely, in March 1506 he achieved the annulment of the privileges, which Staupitz and Besler had sought – from the same pope who had approved them. After Staupitz's plan to make his reformed congregation relatively independent from the Order's general in Rome by joining the German congregation with the Lombardian in the union of 1505, was aborted, Staupitz wanted to try something else. Since an international union was not possible, he now attempted to unite the conventuals (non-reformed) and the observants (reformed) in the German-speaking lands.[122]

Staupitz soon became involved in the Order's affairs at the local level, too. In April 1505 he wanted the construction of the new friary of Sternberg to be resumed. In 1492 this little town in Mecklenburg had

---

[121] '... ne recipiant fratres Congregationis Alemaniae' (Kunzelmann, V, p. 450 with n. 2550). On the publication of the papal bull of 1505, see ibid., V, p. 449. See also Kolde, *Die Deutsche Augustiner-Congregation*, p. 228–9.

[122] See M. Wernicke, 'Die deutschen Augustiner von 1500 bis 1520', in *Egidio da Viterbo, O.S.A. e il suo tempo: Atti del V Convegno dell'Instituto Storico Agostiniano, Roma-Viterbo, 20–23 ottobre 1982* (Rome, 1983), p. 22; Martin, *Friar, Reformer*, p. 122. See R. Weijenborg, 'Staupitz', in *Lexikon für Theologie und Kirche*, 2nd edn (Freiburg, 1964), IX, p. 1026. On Besler, see Machilek, 'Klosterhumanismus', pp. 32f.

become famous because of the rumour that a Jew had buried consecrated hosts there. In order to atone for this act, the political leaders had undertaken to build a chapel at the spot in question. Adjacent to the chapel they had started to build a cloister for the Augustinians, which in 1505 remained unfinished. Staupitz, who at the time was at the elector's court in Weimar, therefore wrote a letter, dated 24 April 1505, to the two territorial lords, asking for their continued support and apologizing for the shortcomings of the local friars of his Order. As he was unable personally to take care of this matter, he sent two friars who were both doctors of theology, Johann Vogt and Johann Paltz.[123]

Having to deal with local issues like that did not prevent Staupitz from remaining involved in more far-reaching matters. In the autumn of 1506, having now been the leader of the reformed friaries for some years, he went to Italy himself – for the first time. He had several tasks to fulfil. One part of his mission was to obtain papal privileges for the University of Wittenberg. This was granted on 21 December 1506 by Pope Julius II in Bologna (which at that time belonged to the Papal States). Under the date of 12 June 1507, Julius II confirmed the accreditation of the university with all the rights necessary and with its connection to the All Saints Foundation at Wittenberg. The other part of his mission was to bring relief to Friar Nicholas Besler, and to secure his release from the restrictions placed on him. Staupitz also had to rebuild relations with the central office under the new superior of the Order in Rome, Egidio da Viterbo, whom the pope had appointed as general on 17 August 1506. Egidio's predecessor, the inimical Agostino Faccioni de Interamna, who had been in office only for a short time (1505/06), had died on 26 June 1506. One may assume that Staupitz would not have dared to come to Rome if the old general of the Order had still been alive or in office. Now, however, such reconnecting was a relatively easy task.

Egidio was about Staupitz's age. Born in 1469 as Egidio Antonio Canisio in Canepina (near Viterbo), Italy, he had entered the Augustinian Order at the age of 18. He was a master of Latin, Greek, Hebrew and Arabic. (To be at least trilingual was the ambitious goal of any Renaissance biblical humanist.) The new general favoured the uniform observance of the new constitution of their Order, and he and Staupitz made plans to carry out the reform in Germany by expanding it to the conventual houses. This plan was hardly Staupitz's very own because Staupitz could not have pursued such far-reaching plans without the superior's consent. Moreover, the intended union between the two

---

[123] See Kunzelmann, V, pp. 490–91. V. Honemann, 'Die Sternberger Hostienschändung und ihre Quellen', in H. Boockmann (ed.), *Kirche und Gesellschaft im Heiligen Römischen Reich des 15. und 16. Jahrhunderts* (Göttingen, 1994), pp. 75–102 (p. 79).

branches had a model to follow. It was to follow the procedure adopted in the province of Castile where the province of the Order had become observant in character and control, while canonically it was a conventual province under the leadership of the prior general in Rome.

Under the new leader, Friar Besler was freed from all the restrictions which he had endured. Besler reported his liberation to Staupitz in a letter from Bologna on January 1507.[124] Staupitz was in Rome at the end of January/beginning of February 1507. While there, he must have stayed either at the Augustinian friary next door to Santa Maria del Popolo, or at the friary of S. Agostino. It was probably the latter, because Egidio also lived there when he was in the city; moreover the friars of the cloister by Santa Maria del Popolo were known as opponents of Staupitz's plans to form a union. They had held Besler in confinement.[125]

The third task of Staupitz's mission in Italy had been to attend the graduation of the Nuremberg citizen Christoph Scheurl (1481–1542) before Christmas 1506 at Bologna's law school where he earned the degree *Dr utriusque iuris*, 'doctor of both laws', secular and ecclesiastical. Scheurl had spent some time at the University of Heidelberg in 1496/97, before going to Bologna in November 1498. Bologna had developed as the most important centre for the study of canon and civil law; it was internationally recognized. The commencement exercises were a magnificent spectacle due to the fact that the Pope himself, Julius II, was present. By agreement with the territorial lord Frederick, Staupitz hired Scheurl for the new University of Wittenberg. Soon Staupitz and Scheurl travelled home, but by separate routes. According to Scheurl's travel log, he arrived at the Elector Frederick's residence at Weimar on 1 April, where he met Staupitz again. Evidently, Staupitz had not attended the Order's general chapter meeting in Naples on 21 May 1507; the reasons for his absence are unknown. From Weimar, Scheurl travelled to Wittenberg, accompanied by two friars whom Staupitz assigned to him.[126] Scheurl started teaching on 13 April 1507 and soon after, on 1 May, was elected as the rector of the university – at the age of 25. About 200 students were enrolled at that time. They

---

[124] See Jeremias, *AELK*, p. 348; Martin, 'The Augustinian Order on the Eve of the Reformation', pp. 96–100; Wernicke, 'Die deutschen Augustiner', p. 22.

[125] On Besler in Rome, see Kunzelmann, V, p. 452. See also H. Jedin, 'Die römischen Augustiner-Quellen zu Luthers Frühzeit', *ARG*, 25 (1928), pp. 256–70 (pp. 265–70).

[126] 'Weymar ... do er den Churfürsten sambt Doctor Staupitzen fand' (Wilhelm Graf, *Doktor Christoph Scheurl von Nürnberg*, Berlin and Leipzig, 1930), p. 35; also pp. 36–40); Grossmann, *Humanism*, p. 63; M. Wriedt, 'Scheurl', *BBKL* IX, pp. 178–85 (1995); Sallaberger, 'Johann von Staupitz, Abt von St. Peter (1522–1524) und die Salzburger Mendikantentermineien', pp. 172–5. Kolde assumed that Staupitz attended the meeting at Naples (*Die deutsche Augustiner-Congregation*, p. 232).

were taught by 12 professors with doctoral degrees. Two other jurists, who were trained at Bologna, the Italian Peter of Ravenna (*c*. 1448–?) and the Saxon Johann von Kitzscher (d. *c*. 1520), also came to teach at Wittenberg. Kitzscher had been a member of the humanist circle around Cardinal Ascanio Sforza in Rome.[127] Scheurl brought with him from Bologna the *rotulus* (schedule of courses) and – being the rector – he published a similar prospectus of courses for Wittenberg on 1 May 1507, the day he took office.

Since the fourteenth century it had been possible to study at Bologna for a master's degree in *sacra pagina*, or *theologia* as it was also known. In general, the scholastics often simply spoke of *sacra scriptura* and meant 'theology'.[128] Modelled after Bologna's terminology, the Wittenberg *rotulus* listed five men as teachers in theology – including Staupitz who was described as inactive because of other duties. In this remarkable document, drawn up by the humanist Scheurl, two other professors, Martin Pollich and John Mantel, were listed as 'masters of the sacred page'; while Jodocus Trutfetter (who was hired by Staupitz in 1506), Ludwig Henning (or Henign) and Staupitz himself were called professors of *sacrae theologiae*. There is probably no difference between the two designations (*sacra theologia and sacra pagina*).[129] Friar Mantel had belonged to the Order since 1495 and was prior of the friary at Nuremberg between 1500 and 1503. He received his graduate degree in theology in 1507 and may have substituted for Staupitz. In 1511 he did not become Staupitz's successor, but instead was appointed to a preacher position in Stuttgart in south-western Germany where in 1520 he was persecuted as an advocate of the Reformation. Mantel died in 1530 as a preacher in Switzerland, by which time he had embraced Zwinglian ideas.[130]

Staupitz had brought another one of his friars to Wittenberg, the prior of the friary of Nordhausen, Johann Herrgott, who at the time of his

---

[127] See Grossmann, *Humanism*, pp. 50f.

[128] See J. de Ghellinck, '"Pagina" et "Sacra Pagina". Histoire d'un mot et transformation de l'object primitivement désigné', in *Mélanges Auguste Pelzer* (Louvain, 1947), pp. 23–59 (p. 52). For the church fathers, 'sacred page' is synonymous with 'Scripture'. For the twelfth and thirteenth centuries the meaning extended to include 'theology'. Unfortunately, Ghellinck does not extend his research into the Renaissance and Reformation period, except for his reference to Vincent Ferri (d. 1702) who is called Doctor in *sacra pagina* (p. 52).

[129] 'Magistri sacrae paginae', in *Rotulus doctorum Vittemberge profitentium*, (Friedensburg, document no. 17); Grossmann, *Humanism*, p. 55; Wriedt, 'Johannes von Staupitz als Gründungsmitglied', pp. 179f. In a document of 5 May 1512 concerning the Nuremberg friary, Staupitz called himself 'sacre theologie professor et vicarius generalis' (Kolde, *Die deutsche Augustiner-Congregation*, p. 438).

[130] See Wriedt, 'Johannes von Staupitz als Gründungsmitglied', pp. 179f.

matriculation was already a *lector theologiae*. In 1516/17 he was the dean of the theology faculty. Johann Vogt, another friar professor of theology at Magdeburg came to Wittenberg in 1505/06. In 1516 he was back at Magdeburg as prior of the friary. Still another friar, Wenceslaus Linck, was at Wittenberg, first as a student from 1503, then as prior of the friary after succeeding Herrgott in 1512. Staupitz had promoted Linck to the doctorate in theology in September 1511. After Staupitz's and Ostermair's departures from Wittenberg, Linck became dean of the theology faculty in 1512/13 and 1514/15. It may seem surprising that the office of dean of the faculty changed hands so often. Evidently it was not meant at all as an appointment for life. Anyone with a doctoral degree, after a waiting period of about one year upon such a promotion, was eligible. The dean's tasks included, among other things, the keeping of the keys and the seal, taking care of the correspondence, making sure that the statutes were read to the assembly of docents and students within ten days of taking office, providing the schedule of the lectures, and collecting the registration fees. As regards the theology faculty at Wittenberg, any records (*Dekanatsbuch*) were kept only after 1508 for sure (that is, demonstrably), following recognition of the university by the pope in 1507. It is therefore open to doubt whether Staupitz had already been officially the 'dean' of the theology faculty in 1502. He may have been designated for this position in 1502. The new establishment was just beginning to take shape at that time, and the number of students was small.[131]

Staupitz's friend Scheurl was listed (as mentioned above) among the canon lawyers. As his salary was rather small, he asked Staupitz to help him get appointed to the elector's court as a lawyer and judge. He gained this position and Staupitz presided over the ceremony when he took his oath of office. Scheurl also wrote new constitutions for the Wittenberg University which took effect from October 1508. In typically humanist fashion these read that the university was established to the glory of the 'best and greatest God' (*dei optimi maximi*) and with the approval of the pope, the 'greatest bridgebuilder Julius' (*Julius pontifex maximus*). The theology faculty was placed under the protection of 'St Paul', who in similarly typical humanist style was called *divus Paulus*. The patron of the university as a whole was St Augustine, who was called the 'protective god of our school' (*gymnasii nostri tutelaris deus*).[132] Busy as he was with the further development of the university and the friary,

---

[131] Kolde, *Die deutsche Augustiner-Congregation*, p. 244, n. 1, has Staupitz as dean in 1502/03 and 1508/09. On Linck, see Graf, *Doktor Christoph Scheurl*, p. 44. On the duties of a dean at that time, see Wriedt, 'Johannes von Staupitz als Gründungsmitglied', pp. 182–3.

[132] See Wriedt, 'Johannes von Staupitz als Gründungsmitglied', pp. 178–9.

Staupitz nevertheless made plans to preach at Wittenberg at least for 'half of the Advent season' of 1507. His honorarium was to be used to help finance the construction of the Wittenberg friary.[133] No records of these sermons are extant.

This promotion of the University of Wittenberg as a place of study for Staupitz's friars meant correspondingly increased competition for, and weakening of, the older places of study for the Augustinians, namely Magdeburg and Erfurt. Staupitz was determined to carry out the reforms at a new location. The revision of everyday life in the friaries was then known as 'reformation' (*reformacie*);[134] so were, as we have seen, the curricular revisions at the university. During that time Staupitz embarked on his first visitations of his friaries in order to inspect them on the progress of the *reformacie*. He was accompanied by Friar Besler from Munich. In the summer and autumn of 1504 they went to Saxony and Thuringia. Their visitations included the friary of Neustadt on the Orla River in the Archdiocese of Mainz. This friary had been reformed since 1474 when Andreas Proles had made sure that Johann von Paltz became prior there. In September 1504, while Staupitz was present at Neustadt he also summoned some leaders of the reformed friaries to the friary. He wanted to prepare them for the realization of his long-held plan of uniting the Saxon province of Augustinians with the reform congregation. This gathering was not a formal chapter meeting, but a 'convocation'.[135]

Staupitz always had religious reforms on his mind. He planned to unite his own reformed segment of the Order, which practised a strict observance of the religious rules, with the more easy-going 'conventuals'. However, fearful for their independence and for a watering-down of their values, the *reformati* in Saxony resisted this effort. Perhaps to appease them, Staupitz in his new leadership position quickly began to revise the constitutions of the Order, which dated from 1287/90. A gathering of leaders had been planned for 23 April 1504 at Mindelheim in order to approve the revisions, but war had broken out over the issue of the inheritance of the Landshut territory (*Landshuter Erbfolgekrieg*), so the meeting had to take place at Nuremberg on 16 May 1504. There, the revised constitutions were accepted; they exhorted all friars eagerly to read the Bible and meditate on it. Staupitz insisted upon the study of the Bible as the greatest task for the friars – religious reform thus meant a return to Bible studies! Staupitz wrote the preface to the new

---

[133] See Kolde, *Die deutsche Augustiner-Congregation*, p. 244.

[134] See Jeremias, *AELK*, p. 348.

[135] See Kunzelmann, V, pp 166 and 447f.; Zumkeller, 'Johannes von Staupitz und die klösterliche Reformbewegung', p. 38, n. 11.

constitutions and, soon after Pentecost 1504, had them printed on the friars' own printing press at Nuremberg under the title 'Constitutions of the Hermit Brothers of St Augustine, with apostolic privileges, for the reformation of Germany'. Again, religious reform of the Order was called 'reformation'. The booklet comprised 54 pages and dealt with the external regulations of the Order. It appears that it represented the first constitutions to be produced by that new medium, the printing press.

In his preface, Staupitz traced the history of the monastic reformation which began with the Order's generals, Augustine of Rome and Gerard (incorrectly printed as 'Gregory') de Rimini. The Popes Eugene IV, Pius II and Sixtus IV had freed the reformed friaries from the jurisdiction of their provincial superiors and granted many other privileges. The generals were concerned with the 'stability' of the reforms (*stabilitas reformationis*) and therefore gave the Order new constitutions. Staupitz also mentioned his two predecessors in the office, Simon Lindner (1467–73) and Andreas Proles (1461–67 and 1473–1503), who had worked for the 'reformation'. What they had started, he himself wanted to complete. However, Staupitz's revised constitution for the Order was in breach of the decision, reached in 1497 by the general chapter in Rome under General Mariano de Genazzano (d. 1498), whereby the individual congregations (such as Staupitz's in Saxony) were prohibited from breaking away from the *corpus Augustinianum*. It seemed to many people that exactly this took place under Staupitz's leadership, even though he did not want to break away completely from the Order as such. After his preface to the constitutions Staupitz inserted a brief dedication under the date of Pentecost Eve 1504, in which he called himself 'vicar by apostolic authority of the friaries of the privileged reformation throughout Alemania' (*conventuum privilegiate reformationis per alemaniam auctoritate apostolica vicarius*). He felt himself to be in charge of the reform of the friaries not only in Saxony but in *Alemania* (Germany). In the text of the constitutions the job title 'provincial' was always replaced by 'vicar' in order to indicate the exemption from the jurisdiction of any provincials of the Order.[136]

Meanwhile, the need for printing presses in the friaries became urgent. The Augustinian friary at Tübingen already had its affiliated press (that of Othmar, see p. 67); so did Nuremberg. Now it was Wittenberg's turn. In 1508, probably upon Staupitz's initiative (or at least with his approval), Johann Grunenberg, a printer by profession, set up shop at

---

[136] See *Gutachten und Satzungen*, ed. L. Graf zu Dohna and R. Wetzel (Berlin, 2001), vol. 5 of the critical edition. The only extant copy of the *Constitutiones* is currently held in the university library at Jena; see Kolde, *Die deutsche Augustiner-Congregation*, p. 223 with n. 1; Zumkeller, 'Johannes von Staupitz und die klösterliche Reformbewegung', pp. 37–8; Schulze, *Fürsten und Reformation*, pp. 167–8.

the Augustinian friary at Wittenberg. As the university itself did not have a printing press, the friars were thus in the forefront of modern technology, most likely as a result of Staupitz's influence. The first book printed on this press was Professor Karlstadt's *Distinctiones Thomistarum*, edited in 1508, in which – as a novelty – even Hebrew type was included, following humanist practice. Since this printing press was sited at an Augustinian friary under humanist influence, works of humanist editors were part of its publishing programme; for example, the edition of Nilus's *Morales Sententiae* which was translated from the Greek into Latin by the eminent humanist W. Pirckheimer (1470–1530), and republished early in 1516 by Grunenberg 'at the press of the friars of Aurelius Augustinus', *Apud Aurelianos* as the title-page says. In 1513 Grunenberg's press printed the first Greek text, Homer, edited by Thiloninus Philymnus Syasticanus. It also produced teaching aids for Luther's lectures and, in 1517, Luther's famous *95 Theses* on indulgences.[137] Evidently, scholastic, humanist, and reformation works were printed by the Augustinians' press at that time.

Accepting a troubled young man (1505–06)

The friary at Erfurt, where the Order's general studies programme was located, had been a renowned and major centre of the reformed Augustinians since 1473. Here, in July 1505, Martin Luther 'moved in', but perhaps not yet as a postulant. Why Luther 'moved' into this friary and eventually became a friar himself is hotly debated.[138] There are probably two major reasons for Luther joining the Augustinian Order: one had to do with the attractiveness of this reformed Order; the other, perhaps, with Luther's personal situation.

First, there was the fact that this Order had a very 'progressive' image at that time in the sense of being open to the contemporary humanist

---

[137] Grossmann, *Humanism*, pp. 94–5 (n. 32) lists the variations of imprints which Grunenberg used: 'Apud Augustinianos', 'bei den Augustinern', 'Apud Aurelianos', 'apud collegium novum', 'in aedibus Iohannis Grunenbergii apud Augustinianos'. Grunenberg's edition of Nilus is mentioned in K. Hagen, 'An Addition to the Letters of John Lang. Introduction and Translation', *ARG*, **60** (1969), p. 27, n. 5: 'Wittenberg in aedibus Ioannis Grunenbergi. Anno MDCXVI. Apud Aurelianos.' Schwiebert, *Luther and his Times*, p. 225, mentions that Grunenberg's press printed Luther's lecture notes on Romans. On Thiloninus Philymnus Syasticanus (Thilemann Conradi), the instructor of Greek at Wittenberg, and also of Hebrew from 1516, see Ludolphy, *Friedrich der Weise*, p. 327.

[138] Luther himself said that around 16 July he 'had moved' (*gezogen*) into the friary at Erfurt: '16. Iulii, in die Alexii, dicebat: Heute ist die jerige zeit, do ich in das kloster zu Erffurt gezogen' (*WATR* 4. 440, 5f. (no. 4707)). See D. Emme, *Martin Luthers Weg ins Kloster. Eine wissenschaftliche Untersuchung in Aufsätzen* (Regensburg, 1991), p. 21.

movement and to the promotion of biblical studies. Whether there is a
connection between Staupitz's revised version of the Augustinian
constitutions and Luther's knowledge of and attraction to that reformed
Order together with Staupitz's insistence on Bible studies is hard to
prove, but it is not unlikely. In any case, what motivation caused Luther
to enter specifically the Augustinian Order at Erfurt? According to
Luther's own testimony, Bible reading served him as medicine against
melancholy when he was still 'a young *magister* at Erfurt'. He decided to
turn to the Bible after he, as a *magister*, had tried in vain to derive
comfort from Boethius's *De Consolatione Philosophiae*.[139] If, as a
layman, he was so very interested in studying the Bible, this Order gave
him the best opportunity for continuing with it. Luther may have
observed the Augustinians' expertise in the Sacred Scriptures when they
preached to the public at Erfurt. Known as an Order of preachers, the
Augustinians had been under instruction to preach since the fourteenth
century. A text of 1357 stipulates: 'Those to whom the grace of
preaching has been given by God are obliged to carry out the ministry.
On a monthly basis at least, they must preach to the faithful in the
vernacular.'[140] Luther may have been exposed to the Augustinians'
preaching in the main church of Erfurt, but, it is also known that they
held preaching positions at St Peter's church of the Benedictine monks
and at the church of the Cistercian nuns, both at Erfurt.[141] This much is
certain, the Augustinian Order in the German-speaking lands produced
attractive preachers and authors.[142]

Not only was the renewal of the religious life in the friaries and the
curriculum revisions at the university referred to as 'reformation', as we
have seen already, but the emphasis on biblical studies was also
associated with the Augustinians' 'reformation'. The Order's revised
constitutions emphasized the study of the Scriptures and they even
referred to such studies as the centre of the 'reformation' (*reformacie*) of
the spiritual life in the friaries. Staupitz's statutes enjoin upon all the duty
of 'reading the Bible with fervour, to hear it read with devotion, and to
learn it with assiduity'.[143] This monastic practice is an essential
component of what we associate today with the notion of 'the
Reformation'. The dutiful 'divine reading' (*lectio divina*) may have
been very attractive to the young Luther. As a friar, he began to do
exactly what Staupitz wanted the friars to do, that is to read and
meditate on the Bible. Luther in retrospect recalled that up to about the

---

[139] See *WATR* 4. 647, 11 (no. 5082b).
[140] As quoted by Gutierrez, *The Augustinians*, p. 186.
[141] See Burger, 'Der Augustinereremit', p. 170.
[142] See Gutierrez, *The Augustinians*, p. 187.
[143] See Jeremias, *AELK*, p. 348.

year 1504, when he was twenty years old, he had not yet seen a complete Bible:

> I thought that there were no gospels and epistles except those which were written in the Sunday postils. Finally I found a Bible in the library and forthwith I took it with me into the monastery. I began to read, to reread, and to read it over again, to the great astonishment of Dr Staupitz.

According to Luther, there was not a day 'on which the Word of the Scriptures was not perceived abundantly by ear and intellect. It came to be a permanent companion, a monitor and comforter, a judge and a benefactor.'[144] He remembered in 1540 that Staupitz had 'restored the Bible for his monasteries'.[145] It is not too difficult to imagine that the Augustinians at Erfurt and elsewhere were known as biblical humanists, especially to those who, like the young Luther, were in close contact with the humanist circle at Erfurt. Furthermore, the alternative Orders which were represented at Erfurt did not appeal to him at all; he perceived the Dominicans as 'learned, but haughty', the *Schottenmönche* (Scottish Benedictines) as 'exclusively haughty', and the Franciscans as being inimical to any scholarly work.[146] Reviewing his options, Staupitz's reformed Order must have looked the best to Luther as a young intellectual.

Besides the probability of Luther's familiarity with and consequent attraction to the Augustinian Order because of their fondness for Bible studies and biblical preaching, there is perhaps another, very personal and tragic reason why Luther entered Staupitz's Augustinian Order. It may actually have been his only choice: the Erfurt friary was willing to accept Luther even though he was being sought by the Erfurt authorities for having participated in a duel. The local authorities wanted to arrest him for allegedly having killed another student, Jerome Buntz, during a duel in January 1505, at an unknown location.[147] Luther mentioned this fact in a table talk, preserved in a macaronic version by Veit Dietrich, based upon the very reliable manuscript of Georg Rörer: 'Because of God's extraordinary decision I was made a friar, so that they could not

---

[144] 'Incepi legere, relegere et iterum legere bibliam cum summa admiratione Doctoris Staupitii' (WATR 3. 598, 14f. (no. 3767)). 'Endlich fand ich in der Liberei zu Erfurt eine bibel, die las ich oftmals mit großer Verwunderung D. Staupitzen' (*WATR* 3. 599, 13f. (no. 376, 21 February 1538)); Schwiebert, *Luther and his Times*, p. 121.

[145] '*Is* [= Staupitz] primus restituit biblia suis monasteriis' (*WATR* 5. 99, 14–16 (no. 5374)).

[146] See Burger, 'Der Augustinereremit', p. 170.

[147] See Emme, *Martin Luthers Weg*, pp. 11, 18 and 24; Brecht, *Martin Luther. 1483–1521*, pp. 46–7. Brecht does not discuss the issue of the duel; he propounds the theory that Luther got hurt by accident while travelling and that Buntz died of the plague.

capture me. Otherwise, I very easily would have been captured. But now they could not, because the entire Order took care of me.'[148]

As one is here completely dependent on Luther's table talks (which occasionally turn out to be unreliable), there is, of course, no certainty regarding such incidents in the life of the young Luther. In the table talk mentioned above, Luther admitted that he 'was made a friar'. The passive form is peculiar. The reason, he said, was 'so that they could not capture me', which can be interpreted to mean that he could thus avoid imprisonment – a hint which, taken literally, could mean that he was ordered to move into a cloister instead of going to jail. What is remarkable for our purposes here is Luther's suggestion that 'the entire Order' took care of him. 'The entire Order' included, of course, Staupitz as the head of the reformed congregation. Why would 'the entire Order' have to 'take care' of a young man who wanted to join them? If Luther's application to join the Order had been completely normal, 'the entire Order' would not have had to 'take care' of him. However, by virtue of the political and juridical situation at Erfurt, only the reformed Augustinian Order in Germany had the privilege of exemption from the jurisdiction of local governments including episcopal governments, such as there was at Erfurt. In addition, the

---

[148] 'Singulari Dei consilio factus sum monachus, ne me caperent. Alioqui essem facillime captus. Sic autem non poterant, quia es nahm sich der gantz orden mein an' (WATR 1. 134, 32–5 (no. 326)); see Emme, Martin Luthers Weg, p. 39. The renowned Catholic Luther expert, Otto Hermann Pesch, strongly refuted Emme's interpretation; see Pesch, 'Warum ging Luther ins Kloster? Eine Polemik gegen eine neue alte Luther-Legende und ihre Anhänger', Catholica, 39 (1985), pp. 255–78, esp. pp. 268–9 for Table Talk no. 326; and idem, 'Warum wurde Martin Luther Mönch? Warnung vor einer neuen alten Luther-Legende und ihrem theologischen Mißbrauch', Stimmen der Zeit, 110 (1985), pp. 592–604. Disregarding the polemics (by Emme and by Pesch), Pesch's interpretation of Table Talk no. 326 remains unconvincing, and however preferable the ecumenical consensus reached by Lutheran and Catholic Luther researchers may appear, it is difficult not to accept Emme's interpretation. Even if Emme's other comments regarding the circumstances of Luther's entry into the cloister were misinterpretations, his reference to, and understanding of, Table Talk no. 326 cannot be dismissed so easily. In a critical review of Emme's thesis, Martin Treu (Theologische Literaturzeitung, 117 (1992), pp. 678–9), also finds all kinds of flaws with Emme's interpretation, but does not discuss or disprove Emme's understanding of that table talk. E.H. Erikson, Young Man Luther. A Study in Psychoanalysis and History (New York, 1962), p. 92, also pointed out that Luther felt compelled to become a friar; but Erikson did not take into consideration Table Talk no. 326. Luther's statement, made later in his life, that he felt compelled to join a religious order (drungen und gezwungen; coactum et necessarium, WATR 4. 440, 5–19 (no. 4707)) does not have to be understood exclusively in terms of the 'vow' to which he was provoked by the thunderstorm near Stotternheim. It could also be his way of saying that, of the duel and its unfortunate outcome, he had no other choice. On other aspects of Luther's entry into the friary, see H. Puchta, 'Luthers Stotternheimer Gelübde: Versuch einer Deutung', ARG, 84 (1993), pp. 311–18.

local university wanted to keep the incident quiet because of the fear of riots – other students were killed in duels around that time, including a protégé of a French cardinal.[149] It was undoubtedly in the interest of saving the good image of the University of Erfurt to let the unfortunate young man disappear quietly from their midst. Up to July 1503, the University of Erfurt took care of its own affairs through its own court and prison system. After 1503 the university could no longer do so, as it renounced this legal set-up and became subordinated to the general courts of the city of Erfurt, that is, the local archbishop's court. The episcopal authorities, however, would never have dared to lay hands on any friar because of their privilege of exemption from local control, as Luther indicated in another table talk.[150] Neither the university authorities nor the episcopal authorities could 'capture' him if he joined the Augustinians, as Luther himself said (even though he was not yet a member of the Order at the time of the duel). On the basis of the canon law of that time, the penalty of imprisonment (either temporary or permanent) in a cloister was a real possibility. This may have been the primary reason for Luther 'moving' into the cloister where this recent Master of Arts may have found refuge or 'asylum' on 16/17 July 1505.

At first, however, according to Luther's own words, the friars harrassed him, the refugee or asylum-seeker. They let him perform the most menial tasks for them and, although he was a master of arts, he was not allowed to do any scholarly work. It appears that Luther was in effect a domestic servant of the cloister, required to 'beg, make cheese, and clean the latrines'. During the period from 16/17 July 1505 to the end of that year he was apparently not even a postulant or a lay brother. Only after this initial period of asylum or monastic imprisonment was he accepted into the formal novitiate (at the end of 1505) which itself ended after one year (at the end of 1506), when he made his final vows. Interestingly, the first tract that is attributed to Luther (falsely?), of 1517, dealt with the ecclesiastical right to asylum;[151] he may have published it in order personally to justify himself.

---

[149] See Emme, *Martin Luthers Weg*, pp. 84f.

[150] See *WATR* 1. 182, 27 (no. 416); see Emme, *Martin Luthers Weg*, p. 60.

[151] *Tractatulus Doctoris Martini Luttherii, Ordinarii Universitatis Wittenbergensis, De his qui ad Ecclesias confugiunt, tam iudicibus secularibus quam Ecclesie Rectoribus et Monasteriorum Prelatis perutilis* (*WA* 1. 3–7; tract on asylum); see B. Emme and D. Emme (eds and trans.), *Martin Luther. Traktat über das kirchliche Asylrecht* (Regensburg, 1985); D. Emme, 'Über die Bedeutung der biographischen Lutherforschung', in R. Bäumer and A. von Stockhausen (eds), *Luther und die Folgen für die Geistesgeschichte. Festschrift für Theobald Beer* (Weilheim-Bierbronnen, 1992), pp. 31–40. On this issue, see *WA* 60. 311f. The new perspective on Luther's entry into Staupitz's reform congregation is supported once again by Luther himself, in 1521, when he wrote that he did not become a friar

As a member of Staupitz's religious Order, Luther was now immune from arrest and imprisonment, whether he was guilty or not. The advice to join the Augustinians may have come originally from Luther's priest-friend John Braun of Eisenach. Entry into the Order may have been facilitated also through the help of Professor Trutvetter[152] who had known Luther as a student when he had enrolled him at the University of Erfurt in 1501.[153] A hint in Luther's letter to Trutvetter of 9 May 1518, may be interpreted as expressing his gratitude for assistance in 1505.[154] Trutvetter was also Staupitz's acquaintance and had been called by him, in 1506, to a teaching position at Wittenberg. Perhaps it was upon the recommendation of Trutvetter that Staupitz accepted the young man Luther into the privileged Order. The local friars at Erfurt, known as they were for being concerned about their observance, apparently could not, or would not, readily take in a hunted fugitive. Thus it may have happened that the 'entire Order' (according to Luther's words) needed to become involved, which meant, presumably, the approval of Staupitz as the superior. According to the statutes of the Augustinian Order, the vicar general (in this case, Staupitz) was empowered to decide on any extraordinary applications. Luther's entry was certainly extraordinary!

Given his problems, it is little wonder that Luther had occasionally been depressed prior to his entry into the Order. The Order's generous acceptance of him and their 'medicine' against depression (that is, Bible studies), meant decisive spiritual support for Luther in his situation. No wonder that later on, in the spring of 1509, Luther told his priest-friend, John Braun, that he (Luther) lived now in 'sweetness' (*suavitas*) according to God's will – that is, having experienced several years of life in the Augustinian Order – and that he would rather study theology (that is, the Bible) than philosophy, to which he was currently assigned.[155]

While Staupitz was presumably involved in the decision to accept this young *magister*, Martin Luther, into his Order, it is not known

---

voluntarily, but was driven by the terror over a sudden death, see *WA* 8. 573, 32–574, 1 (*De votis monasticis*). 'Lutherus iam magister coactus est mendicare, caeeos et pulsare et verrere latrinam' (*WATR* 5. 99, 20f. (no. 5375, summer 1540)), and by the end of the year 1505 he became a friar (a formal novice): '1505 monachus in fine anni eiusdem' (*WATR* 5. 76, 27 (no. 5347)).

[152] See Emme, *Martin Luthers Weg*, pp. 88–90.

[153] See Schwiebert, *Luther and his times*, p. 128.

[154] See Emme, *Martin Luthers Weg*, p. 90.

[155] 'Sum itaque nunc iubente vel permittente Deo Wittembergae. Quod si statum meum nosse desideres, bene habeo Dei gratia, nisi quod violentem est studium, maxime philosophiae, quam ego ab initio libentissime mutarim theologia, ea inquam theologia, quae nucleum nucis et medullam tritici et medullam ossium scrutatur. Hic est Deus noster, ipse reget nos in suavitate et in saecula' (*WABR* 1. 17, 39–46 (no. 5, 1509)).

whether he had to meet with him beforehand, or whether he actually met him in person on his arrival. Staupitz as the vicar general had his hands full with manoeuvring in the Order's politics. During his extensive travels he participated in chapter meetings – at Mindelheim in 1504, and in Mühlheim near Ehrenbreitstein in 1505, where on 28 August he may have approved Luther's admission into the Erfurt friary.[156]

One can only speculate as to when Staupitz met the new Friar Martin in person. If it was not in April 1506, it may have been in July, about a year after Luther had 'moved' into the friary, on the occasion of Staupitz's visit to Erfurt on 3 July 1506; in other words, about six months into Luther's novitiate. Staupitz's presence was required for the signing of a contract with the city of Erfurt that related to a piece of property on which the Erfurt friars could erect a new building, and also included an agreement to the demand that no further buildings were to be purchased without the knowledge and permission of the city council. This contract was signed by representatives of the local friary and by 'Johann von Staupicz [sic], Doctor of the Sacred Scriptures and Vicar General of the Augustinian Order of the German Nation'.[157]

Staupitz recognized the great potential of this new Friar, Luther, who showed so much interest in the Bible as the book of spiritual consolation; being a Bible scholar himself, he consequently took Luther under his wing. Gradually Staupitz helped Luther change his perception of God, from a merciless Judge to a merciful Father.[158] Luther himself understood his entry into the cloister always as an act of divine intervention: he 'was made' a friar 'because of God's extraordinary decision'. On another occasion he interpreted his entry as follows: 'God has understood my vow in Hebrew: "Anna" means "under grace"'.[159] (He was convinced that God understood him 'in Hebrew' and placed him under his divine grace ('Anna').) Luther wrote to his humanist friend Melanchthon in 1521 that he came into the religious life 'more seized [raptus] than drawn'. Interestingly, Melanchthon, in his biographical sketch of Luther of 1546, did not say anything about St Anne and/or

---

[156] On Mindelheim in 1504, see Hemmerle, *Die Klöster der Augustiner-Eremiten in Bayern*, pp. 48f. On the chapter meeting at Mühlheim, see Brecht, *Martin Luther. 1483–1521*, p. 71 with n. 1.

[157] See A. Overmann, *Urkunden der Erfurter Stifte und Klöster, Teil 3: Urkunden des Augustiner-Eremitenklosters (1331–1565)* (Magdeburg, 1934), p. 255 (no. 373). Emme, *Martin Luthers Weg*, pp. 90–91.

[158] See F. Posset, 'The Sweetness of God', *ABR*, 44 (1993), pp. 143–78 (p. 172).

[159] *WATR* 4. 440, 10f. (no. 4707). See A. Dörfler-Dierken, 'Luther und die heilige Anna. Zum Gelübde von Stotternheim', *Lutherjahrbuch*, 64 (1997), pp. 19–46 (pp. 42–5).

Stotternheim; but he clearly pointed out that Luther had been scared to death when a fellow student had lost his life.[160]

Staupitz had become the driving force of the observant movement within his Augustinian Order.

Professor of the 'sacred page' – open to humanism (1508–11)

The call to assist in the foundation and development of the University of Wittenberg gave him the opportunity to shape an institution that would serve the purpose of training his friars in the theology that he saw fit for the main tasks of his Order – pastoral care and biblical preaching. How much lecturing Staupitz did in those years is hard to tell because no lecture notes of any sort are extant.

The study of Sacred Scripture within the Augustinian Order was the most noble task for the friars, a kind of divine service. The constitutions of the Augustinian Order of 1287/90 exhort the friars 'to read the Scriptures eagerly, to hear them devoutly, and to learn them zealously'.[161] Moving in this medieval tradition, Staupitz recognized the unique authority (*eminentissima auctoritas*) of the Bible as holy writ (*sancta scriptura*). He spoke of the biblical authority in one of his Tübingen sermons using Augustine's words from *The City of God* that the Bible has supreme authority to which we give credence concerning all those things which we ought to know and yet, by ourselves, are unable to learn. With Jean Gerson's words from his *De consolatione theologiae* he criticized those who held the *scriptura sacra* in low esteem because of its alleged simplicity.[162] Gabriel Biel's idea that Bible studies might not be appropriate for young theology students may not have been acceptable to Staupitz at all.[163] In a 1512 sermon Staupitz would stress that nobody is so great that he does not need the life-giving Word.[164] With this frame of mind he must have lectured on the Sacred Scriptures at Wittenberg, where in the autumn of 1508 he became dean of the theology faculty, after the new university had been accredited on 12 June 1507 by Pope Julius II (see pp. 81–82).

---

[160] See *WABR* 2. 384, 80 (no. 428) of 9 September 1521; *CR* 6. 158 (Luther biography).

[161] As quoted by R.D. Balge, 'Martin Luther, Augustinian' in E.C. Fredrich, S.W. Becker et al. (eds), *Luther Lives: Essays in Commemoration of the 500th Anniversary of Martin Luther's Birth* (Milwaukee, WI, 1983), p. 8. See Zumkeller, 'The Augustinian School of the Middle Ages', in Rotelle, *Theology and History*, p. 11.

[162] Augustine, Book XI, 3, as quoted in Staupitz's Tübingen Sermon 13 (Staupitz, I. 245); see also Staupitz, I. 74; Zumkeller, *Heilslehre*, p. 21.

[163] On Biel's attitude, see Junghans, *Der junge Luther*, p. 107.

[164] '… es ist das lebentigmachund wart' [*sic*; *wort* = 'word' in English] (Sermon 9, Schneider-Lastin, *Johann von Staupitz, Salzburger Predigten 1512*, p. 94).

During that time Staupitz arranged the transfer from Erfurt to Wittenburg of the young friar, Martin Luther (who was ordained to the priesthood probably on 4 April 1507) in order that Luther might take up the post of substitute instructor in moral philosophy. This was one of the two positions that the Augustinian Order had to fill besides the one that Staupitz held himself. Staupitz was certainly involved in this transfer; Luther himself told his dinner guests in summer 1540: 'Staupitz ... appointed me to lecture and to preach.'[165] Nonetheless, Staupitz is unlikely to have played any role in guiding Luther to a priestly career – that must likely be credited to the local superiors at Erfurt.

From about October 1508 until Pentecost 1509, Staupitz seems to have stayed at Wittenberg. One wonders how long Staupitz as the vicar actually managed to remain there, after his leadership position in the Order had been confirmed at the chapter meeting in Munich in 1508. Due to his obligation to make visits to all the friaries, his sojourns at Wittenberg appear to have been rather brief. Other professors of theology from the Augustinian Order who were assigned to Wittenberg did not last long there either. None seems to have stayed for an extended period of time. During the first decade of the new university's existence (1502–12), teaching there did not appear very attractive. Friar Epp, the Scotist, briefly taught in the theology faculty in 1503 and returned to Tübingen the following year. Friar Themmen arrived for the winter semester 1503/04, but we do not know how long he lasted. Friar Mantel was listed as a theology professor in Scheurl's *rotulus* of 1507, but he left in 1509, apparently because he wanted to join the Rhenish-Swabian province. Friar Herrgott came as a lector of theology in 1505, and became a doctor of theology in 1511; in 1516/17 he was dean of the faculty. Friar Vogt arrived as a professor for the winter semester 1505/06, but we do not know how long he stayed. Friar Ostermair lectured on the Scriptures from 1507, became a doctor of theology in 1509 (the first doctoral promotion at Wittenberg) and dean of the faculty in 1510; he returned to Munich in spring 1511. Friar Linck, who had been one of the first students at Wittenberg in 1503 but had interrupted his studies there and gone elsewhere for a while, became a faculty member in 1508, doctor of theology in 1511 and, after Staupitz's resignation from Wittenberg, served as dean in 1512/13, and again in 1514/15.[166] Friar Luther started his teaching career at Wittenberg in 1512/13 and was the only one who remained there for the rest of his life.

---

[165] '[De studiis Lutheri] ... Non ita longe post transferebar huc per Staupitium. Hic incidi in sophisticam ... . Ego vero metiu doctorum sententias damnare. Sed Stupitius revocavit me et praefecit me, ut legerem et praedicarem ...' (*WATR* 5. 75, 20 – 76, 6).

[166] See Kunzelmann V, pp. 494–9; Grossmann, *Humanism*, pp. 44f.

The university slowly began to take shape as a humanist institution. Staupitz in general influenced the intellectual 'atmosphere' at Wittenberg and within the Order. It was an atmosphere of openness, of the beginning of the decline of scholasticism, and of a deliberate turning towards other traditions. It was a milieu in which the deepened exposition of the Bible was esteemed and the revival of the Augustinian heritage fostered. Besides the theological 'openness' which Staupitz created,[167] his personality and personal integrity must have exercised considerable influence. This theological 'openness' makes it difficult to classify him, except to say that he was a biblical theologian unhappy with the brawling theologians of the scholastic sort. Staupitz may have passed on his aversion to the scholastics to his disciples.

As for Staupitz's Bible professorship, it is noteworthy that the sources speak of him as teacher of the 'sacred page', as in the document for the doctoral promotion of Peter Lupinus, dated 15 November 1508, where Staupitz was listed along with Pollich and Trutfetter as the *magistri sacrae paginae*.[168] The expression 'sacred page' is synonymous with 'sacred theology'. 'Bible professor' may thus mean 'theology professor', as this document and the *rotulus* demonstrate. The Augustinian friars from north and south of the Alps, who were heavily influenced by humanism, may have preferred the designation 'professors of the sacred page'. In 1350 the German provincial of the Augustinians, Henry of Friemar, was called *sacre pagine professor* [*sic*]; and, in 1477, Caspar Amman, Augustinian friar at Lauingen in southern Germany, came home from his studies in Italy with the degree of *doctor sacrae paginae et pontificiorum canonum*. Amman was a specialist in the Hebrew language – which once again demonstrates the happy symbiosis of humanism and theology within the Augustinian Order. In 1514 the German Provincial of the Augustinians, Gerhard Hecker, was called *sacre pagine professor* [*sic*].[169] In 1518, Pope Leo appointed the Italian Gabriel della Volta, who was *professor sacrae paginae*, as the new Augustinian general, succeeding Egidio da Viterbo.[170] Staupitz was master of the 'sacred page', or of 'theology', and he also called himself *Frater Joannes de Staupitz, divinarum litterarum humilis professor*

---

[167] See Wriedt (*Gnade und Erwählung*), who doubts that Luther's subjective judgment can ever be verified when he says: 'Staupitz has started this doctrine'. In contrast to Wriedt, one may take Luther's own evaluation to be rather apt.

[168] See Friedensburg, document no. 23; see Burger, 'Der Augustinereremit', p. 185, n. 74.

[169] See Kunzelmann, V, pp. 376 and 384, n. 1942. O. Clemen, 'Eine Abhandlung Kaspar Ammans', in *Kleine Schriften*, II, pp. 510–31 (p. 511). A. Wagner, 'Der Augustiner Kaspar Amman', *Jahresbericht des Historischen Vereins Dillingen*, 7 (1894), pp. 42–64.

[170] See Kunzelmann, V, p. 476.

(professor of 'divine letters') in a legal document, a contract between two monastic groups.[171]

While *sacra pagina* was the favourite term among Italian and German humanist friars of the Order of St Augustine, the notions 'sacred letters' or 'divine letters' were the expressions for the Bible favoured primarily among non-theological Renaissance humanists raised in non-monastic circles. They appear to have approached the Bible in terms of 'sacred literature', like the Wittenberg humanist and undergraduate teacher of Greek, Philipp Melanchthon;[172] he was not a 'monastic theologian', but a layman. The notions 'theology' and 'sacred doctrine' (*sacra doctrina*) appear to have been the preferred expressions of the scholastics since Peter Abelard who in his theological approach had moved from *sacra pagina* to *theologia*.[173] Still, Thomas Aquinas had a master's degree in *sacra pagina*.[174] When humanists early in the sixteenth century used the medieval synonymous expressions *theologia* and *sacra pagina*, they reveal in their usage that they were not yet sharply opposed to scholasticism (if scholasticism stands for the preferential use of the notion *theologia*). In this regard, then, Staupitz fits the category of an intellectual hybrid, a semi-scholastic and a semi-humanist Bible scholar. Staupitz appeared as a man who approached the 'Scriptures' in a less scholastic way, and more in a 'monastic theological' way by letting the 'sacred page' speak to him. Staupitz certainly did not want to be a professor of ancient 'literature', however sacred it may be.

---

[171] See Schneider-Lastin, *Johann von Staupitz, Salzburger Predigten 1512*, p. 5, n. 18.

[172] See K. Hagen, *Luther's Approach to Scripture as seen in his 'Commentaries' on Galatians 1519–1538* (Tübingen, 1993), pp. 10 and 38. Hagen points out that Melanchthon and Erasmus regarded Scripture as classical, sacred literature in much the same way as they treated ancient pagan literature. Luther's approach is different, as the Bible is the 'sacred page' or 'Word of God'.

[173] See Y. Congar, *A History of Theology*, trans. and ed. Hunter Guthrie (New York, 1968), pp. 51–77. Congar shows the development from 'sacred page' to 'sacred doctrine' with the early scholastics, but also notes that 'theology' was then essentially and exclusively biblical, and therefore properly called the study of the sacred page or of the sacred scripture. See Hagen, *Luther's Approach to Scripture*, pp. 38–46. The various approaches to the Bible may be assigned to certain locations or groups of scholars: the study of the Bible as 'sacred page' to the monastery, 'sacred doctrine' to the medieval schools (scholastics), and 'sacred letters' to the humanists' printing presses of the Renaissance (ibid., pp. 38–42, n. 93). Luther called himself 'professor of sacred theology' (*sacrae Theologiae Professor*) in his letter of 1 May 1516 to John Bercken (*WABR* 1. 39, 26 (no. 13)), and was thus addressed by the Benedictine monk and humanist Veit Bild (*WABR* 1. 206, 1f. (no. 95)). The monastic humanists themselves were apparently not bound to the designation of either 'sacred letters' or 'sacred page'.

[174] See J.A. Weisheipl, *Friar Thomas D'Aquino. His Life, Thought, and Work* (Garden City, NY, 1974), p. 110.

He was the dominant figure (along with Pollich), as the *Dialogus* of Magister Andreas Meinhardi of 1508 also shows. This was a pamphlet, written in humanist Latin, praising the University of Wittenberg as a centre of humanism, designed to attract students from all over the world. It introduced the teaching staff with Staupitz and Pollich listed first, Staupitz being called 'doctor of the liberal arts and professor of the Sacred Page', the 'greatest and most eloquent public crier of the divine word', and the 'pillar of the new gymnasium'. Its title-page is a woodcut showing the influence of Staupitz, the Augustinian, as it displays the Order's patron, St Augustine, in his bishop's robe with a book.[175] Apparently, this document's humanist terminology equates *gymnasium* with 'university'.

Staupitz's early life and work had been shaped by the milieu of various universities, but most of all by that at Tübingen where humanism was flourishing. This experience served him well in building up the new University of Wittenberg. Although he had in the past utilized Thomas Aquinas (d. 1274) and Egidio da Roma (d. 1316) numerous times, he appears to have been influenced most of all by Augustine, the church father whom the humanists preferred (together with Jerome). His study of Augustine meshed with his interest in Scotus (d. 1308) whose thinking was largely Augustinian, and whom he had studied under the Scotist Paul Scriptoris (d. 1505) at Tübingen. As the prior of the friary, he had personally led his entire monastic community into Scriptoris's lecture hall.[176] Yet, Staupitz quoted Scotus only once – in his *Decisio* of *c.* 1500.[177] Nevertheless Scotus's theology appears to have had some influence, perhaps only temporarily, on the young Staupitz's view of the merits of good works in terms of being acceptable to God (*acceptatio divina*), a wording which he used in his *Decisio*; however, Staupitz did not follow Scotus's doctrine on the human ability to love God by natural capacity. Yet, Scotus's Mariology remained acceptable to Staupitz,[178] as is evident in his sermons of 1512. All in all, Staupitz probably preferred the Franciscan Duns Scotus over the Dominican Thomas Aquinas in so far as Scotus's theology had a greater affinity with his, and many humanists', beloved

---

[175] 'Religiosus pater dominus Joannes Staupitz, artium liberalium doctor et sacrae paginae professor Tubingensis, ordinis heremitarum vicarius, divini verbi praeco maximus et facundissimus, uno novi gymnasii columna, Dialogus' (as quoted in Wriedt, 'Johannes von Staupitz als Gründungsmitglied', p. 173); Grossmann, *Humanism*, pp. 56–7; see *The Dialogus of Andreas Meinhardi: a utopian description of Wittenburg and its university*, 1508/edited and translated into English with introd. and notes by Edgar C. Reinke (Ann Arbor, MI, 1976).

[176] See Junghans, *Der junge Luther*, p. 50.

[177] See Zumkeller, *Heilslehre*, pp. 28–29, 179 and 210.

[178] See ibid., pp. 122 and 178–79; p. 96 (on Mary).

Augustine. It remains conspicuous that Staupitz was always concerned to ensure that he had a representative of the Scotist way of thinking on the faculty at Wittenberg. The first one was Sigismund Epp in 1503 who, however, returned to Tübingen; then in 1504 it was Jerome Schurf until his move to the law school in 1505, and finally it was Staupitz's own nephew Nicolaus von Amsdorf who started to teach Scotist philosophy in 1511.

If it is true that Staupitz was more of a Scotist than anything else, it would explain why he had little interest in the Occamist tradition to which Gabriel Biel belonged. Biel had died in 1495, that is prior to Staupitz's arrival in Tübingen. Only once do we find Staupitz refer to Biel – in a document where Scotus's name also is found – quoting him in connection with the sinfulness of missing Mass in one's own parish. Biel had expressed this view in his manual on the Mass, *Canonis missae expositio*.[179] Thus, one cannot clarify with certainty whether Staupitz had really studied Biel's works thoroughly, and whether he would perhaps have been influenced by them. It appears that Staupitz and Biel had little in common.

Staupitz must instead have loved the ideas of the Tübingen humanist Heinrich Bebel (d. 1518) who, in a poem of 1501, invited the students of theology to study carefully the Bible and the ancient Fathers.[180] It was the milieu of biblical humanism that appears to have made a lasting impression on Staupitz. He favoured a theology which was based on the Bible and on Augustine. Staupitz also incorporated the practical theology in the service of devotion as it was exemplified by Jean Gerson (d. 1429), a theology which proclaimed the mercy of God for the consolation of the sinner. In this context it remains noteworthy that Staupitz had already used the expression *misericordia Dei* (mercy of God) about one hundred times in his Tübingen sermons of 1497/98.[181] Furthermore, in following Gerson he recommended that Christians should learn 'Christian customs' rather than 'philosophical reasoning'.[182] He definitely disliked the scholastic sophistications as he repeated the outcry of the rector of the university of Tübingen, Konrad Summenhart (d. 1502): 'Who will liberate me from this quarreling theology?' Summenhart, who was also fond of Scotus, welcomed, along with his colleague Scriptoris, the revival of the study of the Bible and Augustine.[183] If one had to rank the

---

[179] See ibid., p. 215.

[180] See Junghans, *Der junge Luther*, p. 108. Curiously, this poem is attached to Biel's *Collectorium*, which is his commentary on the *Sentences*, edited by Wendelin Steinbach in 1501.

[181] See Zumkeller, *Heilslehre*, p. 30, n. 134.

[182] See Tübingen Sermon 3 (Staupitz, I. 75); Zumkeller, *Heilslehre*, p. 35.

[183] See Junghans, *Der junge Luther*, p. 50; Zumkeller, *Heilslehre*, p. 29, follows Junghans in this regard.

authorities which Staupitz listened to, one must place the Sacred Scriptures first and above all, then Augustine whom he had called 'his teacher' since his Tübingen sermons, and then perhaps Scotus, Gerson and others. With this theological and spiritual background he approached his various duties as a professor, preacher, spiritual counsellor, pastor and *reformator* both of the University of Wittenberg and of his Order.

More reform business, political mediation and potential matchmaking (1508–12)

From 1504 to 1508, Staupitz had taken care of the construction of the new friary at Wittenberg. Due to his close association with the territorial lord Frederick, in 1507/08 the government contributed 400 florins to the construction of the new Augustinian friary on the site of the former hospital for the poor at the Elster Gate. Soon afterwards Staupitz had to appeal to Frederick again: 'We desire that Your Grace would favour us with some bricks from your own building [at the castle] so that we shall not be at a standstill.'[184] Furthermore, in order to finance his project Staupitz was apparently compelled to sell certain income rights of the Wittenberg friary to the All Saints Foundation of the castle church at Wittenberg, according to a document dated 5 May 1509 which appears to have been written by Staupitz himself.[185] He secured further funding from other sources within his Order. The friary of Nordhausen, located north of Erfurt, contributed 100 florins, in exchange for room and board for one of their friars who would be a student at Wittenberg. A similar arrangement was made with the Munich friary whereby, in exchange for 200 florins, one friar from Munich could study there free of charge. A total of 77 Augustinian friars matriculated at the University of Wittenberg between 1502 and 1511.[186]

Staupitz himself must have spent a considerable time at the Munich friary, limiting his stay at the University of Wittenberg. He was listed as a great benefactor of the friary of Munich, since he had the sanctuary of the

---

[184] The letter (not dated) is edited by Kolde, *Die Deutsche Augustiner-Congregation*, pp. 435–6. Staupitz signed it with 'Undertanigster Caplan bruder Johannes von Staupitz augustiner'.

[185] 'Pergamenturkunde des Wittenberger Augustiner-Eremiten Klosters über den Verkauf eines Jahreszinses an das Allerheiligenstift [Schloßkirche], 5. Mai 1509', as shown in the exhibition catalogue *Martin Luther 1483 bis 1546*, 2nd revised edn (Berlin, 1993), p. 61.

[186] See Zumkeller, 'Martin Luther and his Order', p. 219; Burger, 'Der Augustinereremit', p. 174.

church expanded and the chapel of St Monica (the mother of St Augustine) erected. While he was at the Munich friary, he was asked to become a member of a committee which was to deal with grievances at the Benedictine monastery at Andechs, south-west of Munich. The committee invited him to join them on 1 September 1508. The Benedictine Abbot, Balthasar, of the Abbey Benediktbeuren (south of Munich) also served on that committee; which did indeed uncover certain abuses.[187]

Apparently, Staupitz, the Augustinian, moved with ease in the Benedictine circles of Bavaria. Operating either from Munich or from Salzburg, Staupitz worked out a deal with Rome for the abbess of the Benedictine Abbey at Frauenchiemsee in Bavaria, later in 1508. This abbess was Ursula Pfäffinger (1463–1528) whose sister Regina was the abbess of the Nonnberg Abbey at Salzburg. Staupitz obtained certain dispensations from fasts and clothes the Benedictine nuns had to wear, and he secured Mass stipends for them. Staupitz was on friendly terms with the Pfäffingers, an old Bavarian noble family, because he knew their brother, Degenhart Pfäffinger (1471–1519), who had been chamberlain and diplomat in the service of Frederick the Wise since 1493. It was Degenhart who handed over to Staupitz the sum of money from the Elector which was needed to pay for Luther's doctoral promotion in 1512.

Staupitz cultivated other contacts besides those with the nobility, such as the Pfäffingers. In 1508 he connected his Order with Albrecht II of Ellwangen (south-west of Nuremberg) in the form of a brotherhood of prayer. Staupitz also had a cordial relationship with Duke Albrecht IV of Bavaria who died in 1508. Staupitz dedicated to Albrecht's widow Kunigunde, the sister of Emperor Frederick III (d. 1493) his booklet on the love of God (published in 1518). Kunigunde arranged donations of five gulden annually to the friary at Munich, starting in 1509. Staupitz also persuaded Duke Wolfgang (the younger brother of Duke Albrecht IV) to become a benefactor to his Order.[188]

---

[187] See Hemmerle, *Geschichte des Augustinerklosters*, pp. 15–20; O. Clemen, 'Staupitz', in Hanck, *Realencyclopädie* (see n. 19 above) (1906), XVIII, pp. 781–6. On the visitation at Andechs, see J. Hemmerle, *Das Bistum Augsburg. 1. Die Benediktinerabtei Benediktbeuren* (Berlin and New York, 1991), p. 493.

[188] See Sallaberger, 'Johann von Staupitz, die Stiftsprediger', pp. 256–9; R. Angermeier, 'Salmanskirchen: Kirche, Herrschaft, Hofmark. 480 Jahre St. Johann Baptist' (manuscript; I am grateful to the Katholisches Pfarramt Ampfing for sending me this text). Degenhart was instrumental in finding experts in gold-mining who would be willing to move from Salzburg to Saxony. The elector of Saxony had asked the prince-bishop of Salzburg to send him experienced miners, since valuable findings were made in the Elector's territory, in the *Erzgebirge*. In the early 1500s, the Saxon town Annaberg became the centre of mining, and with 12 000 inhabitants it was at that time larger than cities like Leipzig or Dresden. The miners of Annaberg built the largest church in Saxony in honour of their patroness, St Anne, after whom their town was named. Correspondence from the years 1507 and 1508

While Staupitz resided at Munich, he arranged the chapter meeting of the reform congregation to be held there on 18 October 1508. Its purpose was to prepare the unification of the reformed and the conventual friaries; and perhaps also to cope with the anticipated objections of the friars of Nuremberg to this plan. From Munich he sent Friar Gregor Mayr as his confidant to Rome in order to represent his interests to the general of the Order concerning the union between the reform congregation and the Saxon province.[189]

In Munich Staupitz used the incoming funds for renovations of the monastic properties; for example, at Bad Reichenhall in Bavaria he rebuilt the *terminus* facilities, which had been in the possession of the Munich friary since 1370, and purchased a garden for it in 1509. In 1513 he had the Augustinian *terminus* at Salzburg, where one of the friars always was in residence, remodelled. It is quite possible that Staupitz renovated the place for his own convenience, as he may have planned, if not to stay at Salzburg permanently, at least to visit there on a regular basis.[190]

All in all, Staupitz was rather successful, not only in securing the material basis of his friaries through the support of the local nobility, but also in taking care of spiritual matters. At the end of his stay at Salzburg in the spring of 1512, on behalf of his Order Staupitz entered a prayer contract with the Salzburg Benedictine nuns who lived at the Nonnberg Abbey (all the members of which had to be of noble birth). This cloister had always been wealthy, as it was supported by the nobility, and Staupitz must have been well aware of these circumstances. Indeed, this abbey was so important that its abbess had a seat next to the prelates in the local *Landtag* (a sort of parliament). In Staupitz's time, the Nonnberg convent was under the leadership of Abbess Regina Pfäffinger (d. 1516), to whom Staupitz may have been introduced by her younger brother Degenhart (b. 1471) who was known to Staupitz from his dealings with the Elector's court at Wittenberg. (As mentioned above, their other sister, Ursula Pfäffinger, was abbess at Frauenchiemsee.) This prayer contract which covered more than 50 Augustinian friaries,[191] is documented and

---

between Archbishop Keutschach and the Bavarian Degenhart Pfäffinger at the Saxon court, concerning this transfer of technology, is in the archives at Salzburg. On Duke Wolfgang and the Munich friary, see Hemmerle, *Geschichte des Augustinerklosters*, p. 17.

   [189] See Kunzelmann, V, pp. 453–4.

   [190] See Sallaberger, 'Johann von Staupitz, Luthers Vorgesetzter und Freund', pp. 122–4.

   [191] 'Frater Joannes de Staupitz, divinar[um] litterar[um] humilis professor, Thuringiae et Saxoniae ordinis fratr[um] Eremitar[um] S[ancti] Augustini Prior provincialis as sacrae unionis reformatae per Allemaniam eiusdem ordinis Ap[osto]lica auctoritate generalis vicarius.' Schneider-Lastin, *Salzburger Predigten 1512*, p. 5, n. 18; Sallaberger, 'Johann von Staupitz, die Stiftsprediger', p. 257. On the Abbey of Nonnberg, see N. Backmund, 'Nonnberg, Abbey of', in *NCE*, X, 491–2.

dated 9 April 1512, and signed by Staupitz. It is of particular interest insofar as it lists Staupitz's three professional roles at that time: (1) professor of the Bible (at Wittenberg, a position he held until the autumn of 1512), (2) Prior Provincial of the Order's province of Thuringia and Saxony (held until May 1512), and (3) Vicar General of the German Reformed Branch of the Order (held until 1520).

As this prayer contract indicated, Staupitz was both the vicar of the Reform Congregation and provincial of Thuringia and Saxony. From 1507 to 1512 he had worked toward the unification of the two branches of the Augustinian Order, the conventuals and the reformed friaries. Now, as the leader of the reformed friars, he planned to expand the reform to all friaries within the province of Thuringia and Saxony. The revised constitution of the Order (Nuremberg, 1504) was observed by almost 30 reformed friaries, while another 25 friaries (the conventuals) remained un-reformed. Staupitz had probably visited these 25 houses in the previous three years and tried to win them over. One year after his first personal visit to Rome in 1506/07, the official document of unification was delivered and published at Memmingen in southern Germany on 15 December 1507. Memmingen is located at the crossroads of important medieval highways leading into Switzerland and Austria; this south-east of Tübingen, south-west of Augsburg and west of Munich. The Memmingen friary was reformed, and it had as one of its members a friar by the name of George Spenlein who studied at Wittenberg in 1512. The document, known as the 'Memmingen Bull', was presented by the papal legate Bernardin de Carvajal. It summarized the history of the reform congregation and expressed both the desire of the leaders of the Saxon province to be united to the reformed congregation, and the vicar's readiness to accept them as long as this unification was not detrimental to the observance. The committee for the unification should comprise two representatives of the reform congregation and two from the province. The new leader should be a friar who was trained in the reform movement. All this, however, must not lead to any separation from the Order with its headquarters in Rome. The new leader must recognize the general in Rome as his superior.[192]

Staupitz thus added these friaries to the 34 already reformed ones within the province of Thuringia and Saxony. Staupitz's plan had come true, but only on paper. It was announced that an election was to be held at Munich in 1508 when the vicar of the congregation would be chosen. Indeed, Staupitz was elected for a third term in the reformed branch.

---

[192] R. Weijenborg, 'Neuentdeckte Dokumente im Zusammenhang mit Luthers Romreise', *Antonianum*, **32** (1957), p. 152. On Friar Spenlein, see correspondence with Luther in *WABR* 1. 33–6 (no. 11).

It appears that by this time he had also been elected as the provincial of the entire province of Saxony and Thuringia – at the chapter meeting at Münnerstadt, near Bad Kissingen, in 1509, which the provincial Gerhard Hecker had arranged. When, at the beginning of 1510, Staupitz travelled to Italy he already had the titles of vicar of the reform congregation and provincial of the Saxon province.[193]

Staupitz would have received additional help had General Egidio been able to come to Germany. A journey Egidio had planned for the spring of 1508 did not take place and he then promised Staupitz that he would come in the autumn, apparently in order to preside over the meeting of the Reform Congregation at Munich. Meanwhile he advised Staupitz to proceed in a peaceful and pious way with their plans. However, Egidio did not come to the Munich meeting in October either, so Staupitz himself presided over the gathering. Egidio entered a memorandum in his office files, dated 23 April 1509, that he would come to Germany when the times were 'tranquil'.[194]

Staupitz apparently felt strong enough to override any opposition, such as that of the Cologne friary, a house which the local government wanted to see reformed. Asked by the city council of Cologne to carry out the monastic reform, on 31 May 1509 he simply incorporated the friary into his reformed congregation against the protests of Anton Rath, the provincial concerned, and even against the wish of the Order's general who threatened him with the punishment of excommunication. Only five weeks after this takeover, the general empowered the provincial of Cologne to expel Staupitz's observants – within ten days. On 15 October 1509 Edigio renewed this privilege.[195] Staupitz had clearly proceeded too rashly for even the reform-minded Egidio.

Furthermore, there arose opposition to Staupitz's plans in some friaries which had been reformed for quite some time. Surprisingly, this was not from the non-reformed friaries, but from the strictest and most

---

[193] 'Vicarius congregationis Alemanie et provincialis electus provincie Saxonie Romam se confert' (1 May 1510, no. 588), A. de Meijer (ed.), *Aegidii Viterbiensis (O.S.A. Resgestae Generalatus*, 2 vols (Rome, 1988), I, p. 202. See H. Jedin, 'Die römischen Augustiner-Quellen zu Luthers Frühzeit', p. 258; Kunzelmann, V, pp. 374 and 455.

[194] '[To Staupitz] Vicario reformate congregationis Alamanie, ut, quoniam nos illuc ire non potuimus, curaret omnia pacifice et sancte agi, pollicentes ut cum tranquilla erunt tempora, nos illuc ituros' (no. 210; Meijer, *Aegidii Viterbiensis I*, p. 95). See Wernicke, 'Die deutschen Augustiner', p. 23; as to Münnerstadt, see S. Back and A. Zumkeller, *Das Augustinerkloster in Münnerstadt: Ein Gang durch seine Geschichte* (Würzburg, 1975), p. 55.

[195] 'Mandatum est provinciali Coloniensi magistro Antonio ut fratres congregationis reformate nisi in spacio octo dierum conventum Coloniensem exirent eos excommunicatos publicaret' (no. 387; Meijer, *Aegidii Viterbiensis*, I, p. 148). See Kunzelmann, VII, 8; Zumkeller, 'Johannes von Staupitz und die klösterliche Reformbewegung', pp. 44f.

important friaries, including those at Nuremberg and Erfurt. At Nuremberg, not only were the friars unwaveringly opposed to Staupitz's plans, but so and perhaps even more vehemently, was the city government. The city even withheld drinking water from the Augustinians in 1508 until the Nuremberg friars approached 'their Doctor Staupitz' to petition for their independence from him and his Saxon Congregation and for their transfer to direct dependence upon Rome. The Nurembergers enjoyed the strict observance of their friary and the privileged, direct submission to Rome. A leading citizen and council member, Willibald Pirckheimer, accused Staupitz of 'poisoning' them and bringing shame to the Augustinian Order, by mixing the reformed with the non-reformed friaries in one union.[196]

The situation was so extreme that Egidio himself, aware of the opposition that Staupitz's progress had aroused, felt the need to travel from Rome to Germany. However, war between the emperor and Venice once more prevented him from coming. Therefore, in the spring and summer of 1510, Staupitz himself travelled to Italy again in order to obtain Egidio's full approval for his plans. They met in April 1510 at the friary at Monte Cimino near Viterbo, where Staupitz convinced the general that he wanted to do everything in his power to end the quarrels among the friars in the German lands. Later, Egidio entered a memorandum in his files in Rome on 25 May 1510 that he had exhorted the friars of the congregation in Germany to keep the peace and not to make any changes while Staupitz was in Rome.[197] By 10 May 1510 Staupitz had apparently given up jurisdiction over the reformed friary of Cologne. On 17 June that year Egidio also removed the five reformed friaries in Swabia from Staupitz's jurisdiction and placed them under his own direct control.[198] In compensation, a few days later, on 26 June

---

[196] 'Das sy Iren doctor Staupitz so nach ains Ratsschrifft auch schreiben und bitten zu bewilligen, das sie zu Rom arbaiten Ires closters freiheit zu derogiren' (Nuremberg, 1508); as quoted by Schulze, *Fürsten und Reformation*, pp. 173–4, n. 225; Schwiebert, *Luther and his times*, p. 181. On Pirckheimer and Staupitz, see F. Reicke (ed.), *Willibald Pirckheimers Briefwechsel* (Munich, 1956), II, pp. 55–60, as referred to by Schulze, *Fürsten und Reformation*, pp. 177–8.

[197] 'Hortamur patres congregationis Alamanie ad pacem et charitatem, mandamusque ut dum vicarius est Rome nihil innovent' (25 May 1510, no. 612), Meijer, *Aegidii Viterbiensis*, I, p. 209. 'Te Provincialem Saxoniae et Vicarium congregationis Alamaniae decernimus' ... (Letter of Egidio to Staupitz on 26 June, 1510) as quoted in Meijer, *Aegidii Viterbiensis*, I, p. 218, n. 1; see Kunzelmann, V, p. 457; Zumkeller, 'Johannes von Staupitz und die klösterliche Reformbewegung', p. 42; Martin, *Friar, Reformer*, pp. 112–13.

[198] 'Conventus Eslingen, Tubingen, Wila, Heidelberga et Alzeia nostre potestati subiicimus, mandamusque ut vocales istorum quinque conventuum vicarium eligant quem confirmamus, nullusque se intromittat de commixtione cum aliis' (no. 636; Meijer, *Aegidii Viterbiensis*, I, p. 215). See Kunzelmann, V, p. 457.

1510, Egidio confirmed in writing that Staupitz was now both the vicar of the German Reformed Congregation and the provincial of the non-reformed province of Thuringia and Saxony.[199] This decision meant that the reform-minded Staupitz was actually to be accepted by the conventual Augustinians. He held the double position until May 1512. The expectation was, of course, that the conventual friaries would eventually be reformed. The prior general praised Staupitz for all that he had done to foster unity among the German friars and, on 29 July 1510, he even commanded the members of the congregation to accept their vicar general under pain of incurring the penalties of rebellion, presumably because he had become aware of the resistance to Staupitz's authority.[200] Egidio then entered into his files the note of 30 July 1510 that he ordered Staupitz to 'compel' the itinerant friars who were outside his congregation to return to their cloisters.[201]

Staupitz stayed with the Order's general at Monte Cimino probably until the beginning of August 1510. Upon his return from Italy he stopped at Salzburg later in August, which is the earliest date that can be established for Staupitz's presence there.[202] He was in friendly contact with the local Archbishop Leonhard von Keutschach (d. 1519); but, in contrast, his own confrères at the important friaries of Nuremberg and Erfurt were not so friendly. He met with them on 8 September 1510 at Neustadt on the Orla River (south-east of Erfurt), where he reported to them about his trip to Rome and about the result of the unification which he had achieved. Staupitz reminded them of the meeting at Münnerstadt in 1509 at which he had been elected provincial of the entire province of Saxony and Thuringia. The meeting at Neustadt was attended by the representatives of the reformed branch who supported him in the double position (vicar and provincial), in which he had been confirmed (*decernimus*) by the prior general of the Order, Egidio. Staupitz was now the legitimate provincial of the Saxon province (formerly, the conventuals) on the one hand and the head of the German reformed congregation on the other hand.[203]

At this point in time, thinking that he had gained the support of the reformed friaries, Staupitz published the Memmingen Bull, together with other documents, from the headquarters of the Order. All of these were

---

[199] 'Confirmamus in vicarium congregationis Alamanie et in provincialem provincie Saxoniae magistrum Ioannem Staupitz' (26 June 1510, no. 644; Meijer, *Aegidii Viterbiensis*, p. 218).

[200] Letter to Staupitz (Weijenborg, 'Neuentdeckte Dokumente', pp. 156–7).

[201] 'Magistro Iohanni Staupiz vicario congregationis Alamanie mandatum, ut fratres qui extra congregationem sunt redire compellat' (no. 679; Meijer, *Aegidii Viterbiensis*, I, p. 228).

[202] See Sallaberger, 'Johann von Staupitz, die Stiftsprediger', p. 238.

[203] See Weijenborg, 'Neuentdeckte Dokumente', pp. 147–202.

printed by Johann Rhau-Grunenberg in Wittenberg's Augustinian friary (*apud Augustinianos*).[204] Staupitz also included a circular letter to the members of the reformed congregation, in which he defended himself against the charge that he had destroyed the congregation when he unified it with the province and he admonished his cavillers to be obedient.[205] As of 30 September 1510 the union became official, but was still opposed by some strictly reform-minded friers who were afraid that reforms would be slowed down or diluted.

The unhappy friars of Erfurt sent Professor Nathin and young Friar Luther (by now a *baccalarius sententiarius*) to Halle in order to register their protest at the court of Archbishop Ernest of Magdeburg, via the senior pastor of Magdeburg, Adolf von Anhalt. Nathin and Luther were to obtain from the archbishop, who happened to be a member of the governing Wettin family, a letter of recommendation that would facilitate an appeal to the pope against Staupitz's unification. Their attempt failed, because the archbishop was not willing to accept a mediation role in this case.[206] However, Staupitz's opponents sent two of their friars to Rome anyway, without any letters of recommendation. One of them was Luther from Erfurt; the other one was a friar from Nuremberg whose name is not known. Both these friaries were very strict in their reform efforts and opposed any weakening which they feared would arise from any collaboration with the conventuals. Perhaps journeying via Munich (a reformed friary), the two eager friars arrived in Rome in November 1510, hoping to appeal to the general of their Order against Staupitz's union plans. They had no success, however, as Egidio upheld those plans. Luther may actually have returned from Rome as a fresh supporter of Staupitz. It was likely Egidio himself who convinced Luther and his companion that their local superiors at home had not done the right thing in opposing Staupitz's leadership. In January 1511, General Egidio, as a friend of Staupitz's reforms, entered a memorandum in his files that read: 'The Germans are not allowed to appeal'. Friar Johannes Klein was sent to Staupitz with this message.[207] For a moment it looked as though Staupitz had won, and that all German reform friaries had to obey him.

---

[204] See Kunzelmann, V, p. 458; Staupitz, I. 7 (Introduction).

[205] See Kunzelmann, V, p. 458; Zumkeller, 'Johannes von Staupitz und die klösterliche Reformbewegung', pp. 42–3.

[206] See Schwiebert, *Luther and his times*, p. 181; Kunzelmann, V, p. 462; Burger, 'Der Augustinereremit', pp. 171–2.

[207] 'Appellare ex Legibus germani prohibentur. ut res germanae ad amorem et integram obedientiam redigerentur, Fr. Johannes Germanus' [Johannes Klein] ad Vicarium missus est' (no. 811; Meijer, *Aegidii Viterbiensis*; I, p. 258); see Kunzelmann, V, p. 463; Wernicke, 'Die deutschen Augustiner', p. 24.

In March 1511, Luther and the other friar returned empty-handed via Augsburg to Nuremberg, where representatives of the seven oppositional observant convents were gathered. The convents sent a new delegation to Rome that explained their position to Egidio. He was impressed by the standpoint which the powerful Nuremberg city council had communicated to him on 2 April 1511, signalling the city's opposition to Staupitz's plans and indicating that Egidio should settle the dispute.[208] The Nurembergers were proud of their reformed friary and did not want any lessening of its quality. The friars there possessed a large church, St Vitus (in use since 1486, construction having begun in 1479),[209] which had become known as an outstanding religious centre where good sermons could be enjoyed. The Nurembergers did not want to run the risk of losing this great reputation.

Staupitz ran into trouble also at the friary of Sangerhausen, near Eisleben. Here, however, he was apparently able to influence the territorial lord, Duke George, to side with him against the friars.[210] Evidently, as the cases of Nuremberg and Sangerhausen illustrate, at that time the local governments played a large role in the lives of their friaries. However, not even the political intervention at Sangerhausen on Staupitz's behalf helped him in his plans. Indeed, he appears to have given in, after all, to the strong opposition from Nuremberg. Both Staupitz and Egidio must have realized that their far-reaching reform plans in fact went too far, and that they had proceeded too fast.

In the summer of 1511 Staupitz made a long visitation journey to the Low Countries, via Ehrenbreitstein (near Koblenz). He returned to Westphalia and Saxony. On 16 September 1511 he presided over the doctoral promotions of four of his friars: Johann von Mecheln, Johann Hergott, Wenceslaus Linck and Johann Bethel von Spangenberg. From Wittenberg Staupitz then travelled to Nuremberg, where he stayed on 28 October, before going on, via Regensburg, to Salzburg, where he arrived probably in November 1511 in the company of Friar Nicolas Besler.[211] In between all these meetings he managed to be at Jena in July 1511.

---

[208] See H. Boehmer, *Luthers Romfahrt* (Leipzig, 1914), pp. 166–7; W. Eckermann, 'Neue Dokumente zur Auseinandersetzung zwischen Johann Staupitz und der sächsischen Reformkongregation', *AAug*, 40 (1977), pp. 279–96 (pp. 285–6 with n. 14); Sallaberger, 'Johann von Staupitz, Luthers Vorgesetzter und Freund', p. 125.

[209] See Machilek, 'Klosterhumanismus', p. 33.

[210] See Schulze, *Fürsten und Reformation*, p. 176.

[211] See A. Feutry (ed.), 'P. Nicolai Beslerii nurimbergensis eremitae autobiographia', *AAug*, 4 (1911–12), pp. 293–4; Eckermann, 'Neue Dokumente', pp. 284f.; Schneider-Lastin, *Johann von Staupitz, Salzburger Predigten 1512*, p. 3. On the four graduated friars, see Kunzelmann, V, p. 499. It is not clear whether Staupitz presided over the graduation in his role as vicar of the Order or as dean of the theology faculty. He needed permission from the general in Rome to graduate Friar Hergott (see Kunzelmann, V, p. 498, n. 2420).

He had summoned those friars inclined towards strict reform to meet him there. Staupitz explained to them that he could not renounce his double function of vicar and provincial; nonetheless he appeared conciliatory, and a preliminary agreement was achieved. Even so, there still remained seven oppositional cloisters who refused to give their approval. Their opposition was taken so seriously that the general of their Order, Egidio, had to threaten them with the punishment of excommunication if they did not comply. The opposition leader was Simon Kayser, who now called himself vicar of the German reformed congregation. He assembled the opposition at the Nordhausen friary (west of Eisleben, but in the diocese of Mainz) in September 1511. Their renewed appeal to Pope Julius II, directed against Staupitz, was denied. In this appeal of 10 September 1511, the protesters maintained that they were accountable exclusively to the central office in Rome, and thus not to Staupitz. This direct line of command was a privilege which had the purpose of letting them lead their monastic lives in strict observance of their Rule. Staupitz was accused of violating this privilege and of endangering the fundamental goal of reform by unifying them with the conventual friaries. The recently discovered copy of this appeal, found at Madrid, eliminates the uncertainty concerning the names of the seven oppositional friaries. These are Erfurt, Nuremberg, Himmelpforten (near Wernigerode), Kulmbach, Nordhausen, Sangerhausen and Sternberg (thus, not Königsberg in Franconia, nor Ehrenbreitstein, as had occasionally been assumed).[212]

The Nuremberg city council remained opposed and on 19 September rejected the compromise that had been reached at Jena because its friary would have become subordinated to the provincial of Saxony.[213] A minority of friars – including Luther at Erfurt – began to side with Staupitz, thus accepting the 'Jena decision' in the belief that the unification process would bring the desired reform to the non-reformed friaries, and that further opposition was out of order and not good for the Church. It appears that at this point the humanist John Lang left Erfurt to go to Wittenberg, where he is known to have matriculated on 17 August 1511. That same summer Luther, too, was moved from Erfurt to Wittenberg, probably on Staupitz's orders. Since both these friars were open to humanist philology, one may assume that with their transfer to Wittenberg

---

[212] The document was edited in 1977 by Eckermann, 'Neue Dokumente', pp. 292–5. On the excommunication of the oppositional friaries, ibid., p. 286, n. 16; on Simon Kayser's self-designation, ibid., pp. 293f.: 'Ego praelibatus Frater Symon cesaris [= Kayser] auctoritate apostolica Vicarius'. This title indicates that Kayser had been elected to this position (perhaps only by the seven oppositional convents) after Staupitz had become the provincial of Saxony. Staupitz thus was no longer their superior.

[213] See Kunzelmann, V, p. 465; Wernicke, 'Die deutschen Augustiner', p. 24.

Staupitz intended to strengthen the new direction of studies, that is humanism with its interest in the sacred languages. Lang, who tutored Luther in the Greek language as he prepared for his lectures on Romans in 1515/16, returned to Erfurt to become prior of the friary in 1516.[214]

Staupitz now began to groom two energetic and promising young friars for leadership roles: one was Luther, the other was Wenceslaus Linck. These two were about the same age. Linck, whose hometown was Colditz, only a few miles south of Grimma, Staupitz's former neighbourhood, had become a friar very early in his life. He may have joined the Order of St Augustine at Waldheim, a few more miles southeast of Grimma. He was one of the first students in 1503 at the new University of Wittenberg. Although he finished his master's degree elsewhere, Linck returned to Wittenberg in 1508 in order to earn his doctoral degree in theology, which he received in September 1511. He was the prior of the Wittenberg friary from 1511 to 1515, and also the dean of the theology faculty at Wittenberg when Luther received his own doctoral degree in 1512, and again in 1514/15. Luther and Linck were close friends, perhaps from childhood on when both went to school at Magdeburg. This early friendship between them and the fatherly Staupitz lasted their lifetimes. We might call them the Augustinian trio that would form a united front in the years to come. They became each other's confidants. Much of the early reformation efforts may be attributed to the fact that these three friars encouraged each other in pursuing the reform of spirituality, devotional theology, preaching and Christian living.[215] As we shall see, this trio would be supportive of each other, first in the controversy over the indulgences in 1517, and then at Augsburg in 1518 when Staupitz and Linck would take up their positions at Luther's side before the Dominican Cardinal Cajetan. Thus their friendship would make history.

Furthermore, Staupitz was selected by Luther to be his confessor when he happened to be in town in 1511 and 1512. The scrupulous young Luther must have brought to confession all kinds of things that on one occasion made Staupitz exclaim in exasperation: 'Look here, Brother Martin. If you are going to confess so much, why don't you go and do something worth confessing? ... Stop coming in here with such flummery and fake sins!'[216]

One day, probably still in September 1511, he and Luther were conversing under the pear tree in the cloister yard at Wittenberg.

---

[214] On Lang, see Stupperich, p. 127; R.W. Scribner, 'The Erasmians and the Beginning of the Reformation in Erfurt', *The Journal of Religious History*, 9 (1976–77), pp. 14–15.

[215] On Linck, see Stupperich, pp. 131–3.

[216] See *WA* 18. 719; *LW* 33. 191; Schwiebert, *Luther and his times*, pp. 193f.

Staupitz challenged Luther to study for the doctorate in theology and become a preacher, which Staupitz meant as an antidote to Luther's spiritual anxieties. Staupitz had noticed Luther's strong inclinations toward Bible studies. This does not mean, however, that Staupitz merely wanted to give Luther 'something to do' in terms of 'occupational therapy' as Staupitz reportedly had said to Luther: 'You must become a doctor; then you will have something to do.' Luther in retrospect added that Staupitz's prophecy was actually fulfilled as the debate began over 'penance, indulgences, and the other traditions of the pope'. Interestingly, the main mandate for Luther was to become a preacher; and for this, in order to become a good one, a doctorate in theology was required as the best preparation. Luther at first resisted vigorously – perhaps his reservations had something to do with the obligatory monastic humility that was expected when such an offer was made. He even objected that such studies would kill him, although in spring 1509 he had written to a priest friend that he would prefer the study of theology to that of philosophy. Perhaps Luther's initial reservation was resistance to the prospect of being assigned to preaching rather than an objection to being assigned to the study of theology and the Bible. Ultimately Luther obeyed Staupitz who talked to him again a few days later and jokingly insisted: 'Don't you know that our Lord God has many great matters to attend to? For these He needs clever people to advise Him. If you should die, you will be received into His counsel in heaven, for He, too, has need of some doctors.' Staupitz successfully applied this kind of disarming charm to Luther's scruples. About a year later, Luther did indeed receive his doctoral degree in theology from the University of Wittenberg. Staupitz had designated the young friar for succession to his own chair at the university. The fact that Staupitz recognized the young man's potential as a preacher and teacher of the Word of God, and overrode his vehement objections, marks him as a man of 'therapeutic courage as well as of administrative shrewdness'.[217] Staupitz knew that he could trust Luther.

---

[217] 'Stupitius semel dixit ad me: Magister Martine, suscipite gradum doctoratus, so krigt ir etwas zu schaffen. Sequenti anno impleta est haec prophetia; movit enim tunc quaestionem de poenitentia, indulgentiis, et de traditionibus aliis papae' (WATR 1. 442, 9–12; no. 885; early 1530s). 'Stopitz, prior meus, sub piro, quae etiam hodie stat in medio curiae meae, cogitabundus aliquando sedens tandem dixit ad me: Domine Magister, vos suscipietis gradum doctoratus, ßo krigt yhr etwas zu schaffen.... Stopicius: Wist yhr nicht, das unser Hergott viel grosser sachen hatt außrichten? Da bedarf es viel kluger vnd weyser leute zu, die yhm helffen raten. Wen yhr den ymer sterbet, ßo must yhr sein radgeber sein ...' (WATR 2. 379, 7–19; no. 2255a, autumn 1531); see also WATR 3. 188, 14–16 (no. 3143); WATR 4. 130, 1 (no. 4091, in 1538). 'Sub hac arbore convenit me Staupitius ...' (WATR 5. 98, 21–9; no. 5371, summer 1540); WATR 5. 655, 3–8 (no. 6422, undated). Erikson, Young Man Luther, p. 166.

Some time after September 1511, Staupitz left Wittenberg for visitations to the friaries at Nuremberg and Regensburg. At Nuremberg the opposition against his plans remained as adamant as in 1508 when the city had turned off the friary's water supply. The Nuremberg city council sent two letters on 19 September 1511 with basically the same message. In the one to Staupitz, the city council reiterated that the Nurembergers were afraid that their friary would lose its privileges if it were annexed by his province; under no circumstances was their cloister to be subordinated to any provincial of Saxony. The other letter was sent to the prior general in Rome, Egidio, communicating the same message. Since opposition to Staupitz had not faded, and apparently Erfurt and Nuremberg refused to abide by the decision reached at Jena, Staupitz himself may have concluded by about September 1511 that it was useless to continue the fight for the unification of the conventuals and observants. After all, what good would the seven reformed, but oppositional, friaries be to him and his plan after their excommunication by the prior general, which took effect on 1 October 1511.[218] How long this excommunication lasted and how much importance was attached to it is not known. Staupitz travelled to Nuremberg in order to meet with the opposition. He was now convinced that the planned unification would not work and, having decided to give it up, he sent Friar Dr Johann von Mecheln to Rome in order to inform the general about his decision. When the friar returned from Rome on 25 February 1512, he presented his report to Staupitz and Besler at Salzburg, telling them that Egidio approved of his decision. This meant that the dissident observants had won their battle to reject the plan for unifying the observants (reformed) and the conventuals (non-reformed), while simultaneously preserving the general's control over the observants.[219]

Having encountered so much opposition from the friaries in the north (Nuremberg, Erfurt and Nordhausen), Staupitz chose to stay in the south, at Salzburg, during the winter of 1511/12. After all, he once had successfully left the quarrelling (scholastic) theologians behind, and now he was confronted with the quarrelling friars who were overly zealous in preserving their reform – which Staupitz, of course, wanted too. Evidently

---

[218] 'Das unser Closter in kaynerlay weiss einem provincial von Sachsen underworffen …werd', as quoted by Eckermann, 'Neue Dokumente', pp. 284–5; Zumkeller, 'Johannes von Staupitz und die klösterliche Reformbewegung', p. 37. On the letter to Egidio, see T. Kolde, 'Innere Bewegungen unter den deutschen Augustinern und Luthers Romreise', *ZKG*, 2 (1878), pp. 470–72; Schulze, *Fürsten und Reformation*, p. 174. On the excommunication of the seven friaries, see Martin, *Friar, Reformer*, p. 115.

[219] See Kolde, *Die Deutsche Augustiner-Congregation*, p. 241; Jedin, 'Die römischen Augustiner-Quellen zu Luthers Frühzeit', pp. 256–69; Martin, 'The Augustinian Order on the Eve of the Reformation', pp. 101–2. See n. 11 in *WABR* 1. 52 (no. 20). Kunzelmann, V, p. 466.

Staupitz was more successful as a *reformator* ('reformer') in the academic than in the monastic realm. Apparently it was easier to reform universities than friaries. He was called *reformator,* a designation which, in the sixteenth century, hardly conveyed what one would understand by the term today, as it was applied more to the reform of university and monastic life. It is found in the preface written by the humanist Friar Altenstaig who called Staupitz a *reformator* of the friaries.[220] With this preponderant meaning in the language of the time it is then not surprising that the notorious Martin Luther rarely, if at all, called himself a *reformator.* He only occasionally spoke of his work as a *reformatio.*[221]

Staupitz remained a key figure in the monastic and spiritual *reformatio,* but with only limited success. He exercised his power wisely and for the benefit of the spiritual life in the friaries. On one occasion he removed a friar from a certain leadership position because that friar could not keep his spiritual priorities straight. We know of this incident from a reminscence of Luther during his lectures on Genesis 30. It is extraordinary that this story occurred to Luther so long after the event and in such a context:

> I remember that Staupitz told me a story about a prior in a certain friary who continually complained that the income of the friary was too slender for him to be able to procure the food and necessities for the friars from this source. Finally, Staupitz demanded from him a statement of the income and the expenditures. Here he saw that the property of the friary had been notably increased every year. Therefore after summoning him to his presence he removed him from office, saying: 'You are not a man of faith. Consequently, it is impossible for you to further the interests of the friary.'[222]

Staupitz took very seriously the guiding principle of his reforms, namely that the friars must be men of faith, and nothing may surpass this spiritual priority. He knew, of course, that he had to work with those who were under his command, and so he used to sigh that he had to play with the cards which he was dealt. 'Thus when our Staupitz wished and desired to promote the best men to all positions, he could not do so. "One must", he used to say, "plow with the horses one has".'[223]

---

[220] Altenstaig in his *Vocabularius Theologi[a]e* (1517; numerous reprints up to 1619): *Reuerendo in Christo patri Ioanni de Staupitz ... reformator.* On the humanist Friar Altenstaig, see Vonschott, *Geistiges Leben,* pp. 134–6 and; 149–52.

[221] See B. Lohse, 'Luthers Selbsteinschätzung', in *Evangelium in der Geschichte. Studien zu Luther und der Reformation* (Göttingen, 1988), pp. 162–6.

[222] ... *Tu non es homo fidei* (WA 43. 658, 18–24, here lines 23f. (on Gen. 30: 2); LW 5. 333).

[223] 'Sic Stupitius noster cum vellet ac cuperet omnibus officiis optimos praeficere, non tamen potuit. Man mus (aiebat) mit den pferden pflugen, die man hat' (WA 20. 97, 22–4 (on Eccl. 5: 7, 1526); LW 15. 83).

What seemed to irk Staupitz most was ingratitude within his monastic circles. When any of those young friars whom he had helped to promote by selecting them for graduate studies turned against him, he became really upset and did not hold back in saying so. 'When he had found a gifted young friar, he made him study for the degree of a doctor or master. But how [did such young men] return that favour? [Staupitz] said this: "After I have lifted them up, they shit into my hands".' And in a similarly boorish expression Staupitz was reported to have said: 'I made many brethren deacons, abbots, priors, and once I have lifted them up to the highest positions, they shit through my hands onto my head.'[224] Luther was never to become one of those ingrates, as he always remembered Staupitz with great admiration and gratitude. He recalled as late as in the summer of 1540 that Staupitz had even eased his burden of praying at the prescribed monastic prayer times. Staupitz had absolved him, the young Bible professor, from attending morning prayers at the time when he delivered his first lectures on the psalms. Staupitz also assigned a *famulus* (an assistant) to him.[225] As the scholar of the 'sacred page', Staupitz knew what the job of a Bible professor entailed, and he had no problem with releasing Luther from praying the psalms during morning prayers, as he dealt with them thoroughly during the daytime lectures.

It is open to question how much time Staupitz spent – from the autumn of 1508 on – as a professor of theology at Wittenberg. Little is known about this period of his career, but one gets the impression that he was more absent than present at Wittenberg. He also became very much involved in correcting abuses at the Augustinian friaries. Since the Order's general, Egidio, was unable to preside over the 1508 meeting of the Reformed Congregation at Munich (as mentioned earlier), he had to do so himself. At the same time as doing all these things, Staupitz was still officially employed by the University of Wittenberg, where he was listed along with Pollich and Trutfetter as 'master of the sacred page'. Whether this proves his actual presence at the university or his permanent residency elsewhere is not certain. He appears to have been preoccupied with reforming the Order, and may therefore have spent little, if any, time preparing lectures. No lectures, no student lecture notes and no sermons are known from Staupitz's pen at that time. It was

---

[224] 'Ich dencke an meinen Staupitz, wo der einen geschickten jungen Munch hette, macht er jn zu eim doctor, magister, Sed quam referebant gratiam? dicebat: wenn ich sie embor hab gehoben, haben sie mir ynn die hand geschissen' (*WA* 37. 148, 9–12 (sermon at home, on 14 September 1533)). Table Talk: '. . . *so schißen sie mir durch die hend auff den kopff*' (*WATR* 5. 417, 10–12 (no. 5989, undated)).

[225] 'Sed Staupitius, cum legeret Doctor Psalterium, absolvit eum a matutinis et addidit fratrem famulum' (*WATR* 5. 100, 1f. (no. 5375)).

probably during his scholarly work on the Bible that his hermeneutical conviction was formed, which he expressed in a table talk in 1517, namely that 'any issues and matters of Christian doctrine and teaching are contained in the Gospel, as one does not encounter anything that is Christian which is not contained in Sacred Scripture and in the Gospel'.[226]

In 1509–10 Staupitz entered politics when he became a mediator in the conflict between the city of Erfurt and the state of Saxony. The year is known as the 'mad year' when local tax increases caused riots and protests against the city council. The conflict widened: the city's lower classes supported the archbishop of Mainz who had certain rights in these affairs, while the upper class generally desired Saxony's protection. The riots also affected the University of Erfurt, resulting in the destruction of the Great College. In this situation, Staupitz was asked by the city of Erfurt to mediate, as apparently he was known to have good connections with the court of Saxony. The dispute was settled. When he was asked how God could deal with people so frightfully and 'Who can serve God as long as he strikes people down right and left?', he told the questioner to change his image of God: 'My dear fellow, you have to see God in a different way!'[227] This individual was Luther.

It was in the capacity of mediator in religious disputes that Staupitz, together with Christoph Scheurl, was sent by Frederick the Wise to a chapter meeting of another Order within Frederick's territory – a meeting of the Franciscans that took place in Berlin on 28 September 1511. Staupitz, as a known promoter of union plans, was sent to the Franciscans to further their unification. However, the address to them was delivered by Scheurl, the lawyer from the electoral court, in the name of the elector. The message was that the territorial lord wanted only reformed friars who led holy lives, and who were able to tame the common people in his lands; their disunity was detrimental to pastoral care and could have unwanted political consequences.[228] This message echoed the convictions which Staupitz had held since his Tübingen

---

[226] 'Das all fell und sachen cristlicher leren und underweisung im Evangelio sind begriffen; dann nichtzet cristlichs mag ainem menschen begegnen, das in der heiligen Schrift und dem Evangelio nit begriffen sei' ('Nuremberg Table Talk', in J.K.F. Knaake (ed.), *Johann von Staupitzens sämmtliche Werke. Erster Band: Deutsche Schriften* (Potsdam, 1867), p. 43).

[227] '. . . Tunc Doctor Staupizius respondit mihi: Lieber, lerned ihr yhn anderst [ansehen]' (*WATR* 1. 35, 14–20 (no. 94), *LW* 54. 11); for the historical context, see Brecht, *Martin Luther. 1483–1521*, pp. 23–6.

[228] See Ludolphy, *Friedrich der Weise*, pp. 370–71; Schulze, *Fürsten und Reformation*, pp. 184–7; L.G. zu Dohna, 'Von der Ordensreform zur Reformation: Johann von Staupitz', in K. Elm (ed.), *Reformbemühungen und Observanzbestrebungen im spätmittelalterlichen Ordenswesen* (Berlin, 1989), pp. 571–84.

sermons before the turn of the century; the Saxon elector sounded just like Duke Eberhard of Tübingen.

Staupitz was not only an adviser, but also a friend to Frederick the Wise. On one occasion, Frederick confessed to him the difficulty of being a good ruler of his land. We know about this conversation only because Staupitz apparently mentioned it to Luther who remembered it so well that he brought it up on several occasions in later years. The first time Luther was reminded of it was during his lectures on the Canticle in the 1520s, when on Cant. 1: 7 (about pasturing the flock) he said that 'Duke Frederick of Saxony told Staupitz that he knew less and less how to administer his duchy and yet there was no one to whom he could safely entrust any matter'. This reference to Staupitz came up again in the context of Luther's exposition of Psalm 101: 6, in 1534/35, a decade after Staupitz's death: 'I have heard Doctor Staupitz say that several times Duke Frederick lamented, that the longer he was a ruler the less he was able to rule.'[229] Two more times Luther remembered what Staupitz and the elector talked about, during his last lectures, on Gen. 30: 5–8 and on Gen. 41: 45.[230]

Furthermore, Staupitz was selected to find a suitable wife for Frederick. Once again, we know of this from Luther's recollections. Apparently in 1509 the elector's councillors thought it advantageous that Frederick should get married, although he had a concubine who had given him three sons and one daughter, whose names Luther also mentioned. The Duchess Mary of Jülich-Berg (in the region west of Cologne) was evidently ready to get married. Born in 1491, she was almost 30 years younger than Frederick. However, in 1496 as a five-year-old girl, she had been engaged to the duke of Kleve. Pressured by his advisers, the elector sent Staupitz out to take a look at the prospective bride from the Rhineland. Staupitz probably did so during his visitation trip to the Netherlands in 1509. He returned with the message that she would not be the right match for the elector. They would not 'rhyme', he said. Frederick's concubine's reaction was that she did not think that Frederick would marry the duchess as long as she herself was alive.[231]

---

[229] 'Sic Dux Saxoniae Fridericus ad Staupitium dixit ...' (WA 31, 2. 617, 38 – 619, 23 (printed version); LW 15. 204). 'Ich hab horen von Doctor Staupitz sagen, wie Hertzog Fridrich hette etliche mal geklagt, je lenger er regirte, je weniger er kundte regirn' (WA 51. 255, 15f. (on Psalm 101, 1534/35)); see also WA 20. 67, 10–12. Ludolphy, Friedrich der Weise, pp. 38f.

[230] WA 43. 664, 27–34; LW 5. 341f. (on Gen. 30: 5–8); and WA 44. 442; LW 7. 192f. (on Gen. 41: 45).

[231] 'Et cum elector a nobilibus suis persuasus, ut duceret ducem Gulicensem ... misit eo Staupitium ad considerandam sponsam, sed is dissuadens electori personam: Die reyme sich nicht zu ihme ... .' (WATR 4. 322, 1–11 (no. 4455), from the year 1539); see ibid., p. 376, 34–9 (no. 4555). On the life of Frederick, his concubine and children, see Ludolphy, Friedrich der Weise, pp. 47–58.

Luther's reminiscences provide insights which otherwise we would not have, not only about Staupitz as a councillor and friend of the elector, but also about Luther's own close friendship with Staupitz. He evidently discussed many matters with his younger confidant, including conversations which he had with the prince. Staupitz also shared with Luther his thoughts about his lack of success in reforming the Order. Luther remembered Staupitz saying that one must let go of things, and that somebody else would have to continue as vicar of the Reformed Order.[232]

With all the problems that some of the friars of the strict observance represented, it is understandable that Staupitz sought a more welcoming place: he spent the winter of 1511/12 at Salzburg. The following spring would turn out to be rather eventful for his career. He had just finished his Lenten sermons in Salzburg when, at the end of April 1512, the Nuremberg city council added to his difficulties over the reform of the friaries. The council sent a letter to the upcoming Augustinian chapter meeting at Cologne, in which opposition was expressed to Staupitz's plans for uniting reformed and non-reformed friaries into one Augustinian Order. This interference from the local government was particularly aggravating because Nuremberg was both the political centre of Europe and Europe's market place. In the face of mounting opposition from this important city, Staupitz renounced his plans at the chapter meeting in May 1512 in Cologne, abandoning the unification plan in order to keep the peace within his own reformed branch of the Order. Although he was able to add the new friary at Eisleben to his reformed congregation in that same year 1512, and later, in 1514, the friary of Rappoltsweiler (today Ribeauville, Alsace), he helplessly had to watch the secession of some of the reformed friaries. Those who returned to their former provinces included the friaries of Tübingen and Heidelberg, and three other cloisters at Esslingen, Weil der Stadt and Alzey. (Esslingen and Weil der Stadt were neighbours of the Tübingen friary, while Alzey is located north-west of Heidelberg and Worms.) However, these five friaries kept their reformed status as they returned to the jurisdiction of their original Rhenish-Swabian province. Staupitz was more successful in the great city of Antwerp where, in 1513, the reformed friars started a new friary. Staupitz appointed his confidant Johann von Mecheln as its prior and also as the district vicar for that area. Staupitz had known him from his studies at Wittenberg in 1507 and from his doctoral promotion there in 1511. In June 1516 Staupitz himself inspected the new friary.[233]

---

[232] 'Mitto vadere, sicut vadit, quia vult vadere, ut vadit (laß gehen, wie es gehet) ... es muß ein ander triennium vicariatus kommen!' (*WATR* 3. 188, 25–7 and 189, 16–18 (no. 3143)).

[233] See Kunzelmann, IV, p. 181 with n. 769; and pp. 505f. Friar Johannes von Mecheln became prior of Dortrecht in 1520–21, and in 1522 vicar general of the reformed

Let us return to the year 1512. At the meeting at Cologne in May 1512 Staupitz was re-elected vicar general of the Reformed Congregation, an office to which he would be re-elected periodically until 1520. At that same meeting Luther was appointed subprior for the Wittenberg friary, which made him master of novices. On 18 October 1512, at Wittenberg, Luther received the doctoral degree in theology, which he had pursued on the orders of Staupitz. That he had begun his graduate studies under compulsion is evident from Luther's letter of invitation to the graduation celebration which he extended on 22 September 1512 to the friars of Erfurt where he had entered the Order: 'On that day [of St Luke, 18 October 1512], in obedience to the fathers [friars] and the Reverend Father Vicar [Staupitz], I shall be solemnly graduated as a Doctor of Theology.'[234]

Staupitz wanted to bring to a close his original assignment to build up the University of Wittenberg and its faculty of theology. He went to the Leipzig Fair that took place in October 1512 in order to meet there the court official Degenhart Pfäffinger who gave him 50 *gulden*, the fee for Luther's doctoral promotion at Wittenberg. Upon his return to Wittenberg, Staupitz made Luther sign the receipt for this fee; this has subsequently become the oldest extant document from Luther's pen.[235] Luther publicly thanked Frederick the Wise for this payment in the preface to his *Commentary on Galatians*. Staupitz had to promise the elector that Luther would remain a Bible professor at the University of Wittenberg to the end of his life.[236] Shortly after Luther's doctoral promotion, probably also in October 1512, Staupitz must have resigned from his own teaching position at Wittenberg[237] and thus made Luther his successor.

Staupitz's occasional presence at, and permanent influence from afar on, the development of the University of Wittenberg attracted numerous friars who enrolled there between 1502 and 1511. They came not only from the neighbouring reformed friaries in Thuringia and Saxony, but also

congregation of the Low Countries, which was then independent from the Saxon reformed congregation. On the friary at Antwerp, see Clemen, 'Das Antwerper Augustiner-Kloster', in *Kleine Schriften*, I, pp. 434–41.

[234] 'Ex obedientia Patrum et Reverendi Patris Vicarii' (*WABR* 1. 18, 6f. (no. 6); *LW* 48. 6).

[235] See *WABR* 1. 20 (no. 7) with n. 3 on Pfäffinger; Sallaberger, Johann von Staupitz, die Stiftsprediger', p. 256; Brecht, *Martin Luther, 1483–1521*, p. 126. Brecht, however, has Luther and Staupitz arrive at Leipzig together.

[236] See Jeremias, *AELK*, p. 349.

[237] Scheurl mentioned Staupitz's abdication from Wittenberg in his letter of 5 November 1512 to Trutvetter: 'Sed fuit apud nos d. Staupitz qui et ipse Vittenberga se abdicavit' (F.F. von Soden and J.K.F. Knaake (eds), *Christoph Scheurl's Briefbuch, ein Beitrag zur Geschichte der Reformation und ihrer Zeit*, 2 vols, (Potsdam, 1867–72; reprinted Aalen, 1962), I, p. 104 (no. 66)).

from Cologne, Antwerp, Ghent, Nuremberg, Munich, Lippstadt and Tübingen.[238] Having nurtured its development up to this point, Staupitz may have felt that his mission was completed as far as the new university was concerned. The Bible professorship was now in good hands with his successor. The reform plans for the integration of conventual friaries were relinquished officially at the meeting in Cologne. What could possibly hold him in these northern territories? Nothing. There was, moreover, another factor that may have contributed to Staupitz's return to the southern region. In the spring of 1512, with effect from 12 April, his friend Scheurl had accepted a city government post in his home town of Nuremberg which paid 200 *gulden* a year.[239] Staupitz may also have wanted to move on. He had been instrumental in hiring Scheurl for the university as a canon law professor, and he was involved in facilitating Scheurl's appointment to a second job with a better salary as successor of a recently deceased judge at the electoral court. Staupitz had accepted Scheurl's oath of office on 26 July 1508. On the latter's invitation, he now came to the imperial city of Nuremberg, in the autumn of 1512, delivering sermons in October and November, which, however, are no longer extant. After this stopover at Nuremberg, Staupitz returned to Salzburg for the winter season of 1512/13. We do not know whether he preached the Advent sermons there at that time, nor whether he preached during the Lent of 1513. It is unlikely because during that spring Staupitz was preparing to depart from Salzburg for his third business trip to Rome, which he had previously visited in 1506 and in 1510. This trip of 1513 combined several objectives: to do business on behalf of his friend, Salzburg's Archbishop, Leonhard von Keutschach; to pay the required tax to the central office of the Augustinian Order; and to attend the general chapter meeting of the Order in Rome that confirmed Egidio in his office as general of the Order. In November 1511 it had been Friar Johannes Parvus (Klein) who had delivered the assessment for the years 1510 and 1511 on behalf of Staupitz nomine provincialis [prov. Saxoniae] magistri Ioanni de Stupiz', as the entry in Egidio's records shows.[240]

---

[238] See Zumkeller, 'Martin Luther and his Order', p. 219.

[239] See Graf, *Doktor Christoph Scheurl*, pp. 44–55.

[240] See Kolde, *Die deutsche Augustiner-Congregation*, p. 257. On the taxes for 1510 and 1511, see Meijer, *Aegidii Viterbiensis*, I, p. 274 (no. 874). See also Eckermann, 'Neue Dokumente', p. 284. Staupitz's presence at Nuremberg can only be assumed at that point. Kunzelmann also has Staupitz deliver sermons in October 1512; Sallaberger, 'Johann von Staupitz, die Stiftsprediger', p. 253; Machilek, 'Klosterhumanismus', p. 42; Christoph Scheurl's letter of 22 May 1513 to Staupitz, in Soden and Knaake, *Christoph Scheurl's Briefbuch*, I, p. 118 (no. 75). On Keutschach, see Newald, 'Beiträge zur Geschichte des Humanismus in Österreich', p. 100 and www.salzburginfo.or.at/kennenl/rundgang/ keutschach.

Staupitz must have liked the climate at Salzburg – not only in terms of temperature, but also in terms of its openness to spiritual reform. His friend, Leonhard, had been prince-bishop there since 1495 and was known as a promoter of monastic discipline much like Staupitz himself. He had also straightened out the economic problems which he had inherited, and reformed the pastoral care in his domain. Reform of the care of souls was, of course, ever Staupitz's burning interest. In 1511 the Archbishop Leonard's *Agenda* was printed at Basel by Jacob Pforzheim. This document contained the regulations of the administration of the sacraments and of the rituals that were to be observed for blessings and processions. Furthermore, in 1518 this Catholic Reform programme included the edition of a new Mass Book, again printed at Basel. His fellow reformer, Berthold Pürstinger, had earlier been made suffragan bishop of Salzburg-Chiemsee, in 1508.[241]

Staupitz now became involved in Salzburg's local ecclesiastical politics. The priests at Salzburg cathedral had been Augustinian canons (not friars) since 1120. They wanted to become secular priests and sought help from the diplomat Matthew Lang of Wellenburg near Augsburg (d. 1540). Lang had studied law at Tübingen and Vienna and was well-connected to humanist circles; he was also hungry for wealth and prestige. He collected ecclesiastical titles without being ordained (he was finally ordained in 1519 when he became archbishop of Salzburg). These included several Austrian parishes and the Cistercian monastery Viktring, besides being the 'Bishop of Gurk', as a suffragan of Salzburg. Lang also received from Pope Julius II (d. 1513) the title 'Cardinal Deacon of Sant'Angelo', which was proclaimed by Leo X in 1514. The canons of Salzburg knew that Cardinal Lang had been secretary of the Emperor Maximilian and that he was thus well-connected and influential. Lang himself was determined to become co-adjutor in the Salzburg archbishopric under Leonhard von Keutschach, as this would guarantee him the succession as archbishop of one of the largest and richest dioceses. Pope Julius II eventually appointed Lang to the desired post.[242] The reigning Archbishop Leonhard was an Augustinian canon himself and wanted to keep the status quo as far as the priests at his cathedral were concerned. Wishing to appeal to Rome in order to keep everything as it was and knowing Staupitz to be aquainted with the Roman administration, Leonhard requested him to travel to Rome on his behalf, during the spring/summer of 1513.

---

[241] See J. Sallaberger, 'Der Chiemseer Bischof Berthold Pürstinger (1464/65–1543). Biographische Daten zu seinem Leben und Werk', *Mitteilungen der Gesellschaft für Salzburger Landeskunde*, **130** (1990), pp. 427–84.

[242] See H. Wagner, 'Kardinal Matthäus Lang' in G.F. von Pölnitz (ed.), *Lebensbilder aus dem bayerischen Schwaben* (Munich, 1965), pp. 45–69; Sallaberger, *Kardinal*.

In Rome, the Fifth Lateran Council was currently in session; it had been convoked by Pope Julius II in 1511 and begun in April 1512. The Council was intended to improve discipline in the Church. Julius had promised to the cardinals who elected him in 1503 that he would conduct such an 'ecumenical' council. It took him, a rather reluctant reformer, almost a decade to get the council under way, and its results were rather meaningless as far as the thorough reform of the Church was concerned. Seemingly Julius II was more motivated by politics than by ecclesiastical reform. This 'ecumenical' Council was dominated by Italian prelates; Duke George and Elector Joachim of Brandenburg were represented at the Council, but Frederick the Wise was not.[243]

The prior general of the Augustinian Order, Egidio da Viterbo, had by now gained so much prestige in Rome that he had been asked to address the initial assembly of about 100 council fathers on 3 May 1512. He was one of the most renowned scholars and preachers in Italy at that time. This general of the Augustinians, who, together with Staupitz, had been so involved in reform of religious life, appealed to the Council before him to take action to reform the Church and help cure its ills. The Augustinian friars were in the forefront of the reform movement; they were the real fathers of reform early in the sixteenth century. In the opening paragraph of his address, Egidio had hinted at this role and specifically at his own previous reform activities; and it is not too far-fetched to think that he was thinking also of the reform efforts which were under way in German lands under Staupitz:

> There is no one here, I believe, who does not wonder, when there are so many men in the city who are famed indeed for their ability to speak with dignity and eloquence, why I, who can in no way be compared with these brilliant men, should be the one to appear before us and should dare to speak on so important a matter and in so great an assembly that the world has none more esteemed or more sacred. I might indeed say that something has intervened, and for this reason I have been preferred over the others, not because of any excellence but because of earlier times and activities. And so for this reason I seem to have been invited as the first to cast a spear in this conflict and to begin the holy Lateran Council.[244]

---

[243] See Ludolphy, *Friedrich der Weise*, pp. 373–4.

[244] This follows the English translation in Olin, *Catholic Reform*, pp. 47–60 (pp. 47–50). On Egidio da Viterbo, see F.X. Martin, 'The Problem of Giles of Viterbo: A Historiographical Problem,' *Augustiniana*, 9 (1959), pp. 357–79 and 10 (1960), pp. 43–60; Martin, 'Giles of Viterbo and the Monastery of Lecceto: The Making of a Reformer', *AAug*, 25 (1962), pp. 225–53; J.W. O'Malley, *Giles of Viterbo on Church and Reform* (Leiden, 1968). When Egidio was in Rome, he lived at the S. Agostino Friary; see Jedin, 'Die römischen Augustiner-Quellen (see n. 125), pp. 265–70.

In terms similar to Staupitz's Pauline theology, Egidio told the council fathers and the pope that 'without faith we cannot please God'. No wonder in view of their likemindedness that Staupitz was quick to arrange the printing of Egidio's opening address. It was published by the Augustinians' printing press in the Wittenberg friary, under the supervision of the printer Johann Grunenberg: *Oratio Prima Synodi sive concilii Lateranensis ... Impressa Wittenburgii per Ioannem Gronenbergk Apud Augustinianos.*[245]

The Lateran Council continued to meet for five more years, until March 1517, by which time Pope Julius II had died. His successor was the 37-year-old son of Lorenzo de' Medici, Leo X (1513–21), who had become a cardinal at the age of 13, and who narrowly escaped an assassination attempt in 1517. Under Leo X the Augustinians did not fare as well as under Julius II, at least in the perception of the Augustinian circles at Wittenberg, where a horror story emerged about two friars at the friary of St Augustine in Rome (where Egidio used to have his residence). Distressed about un-Christian and unjust papal behaviour, these two friars had spoken out in sermons against Leo X. 'And lo and behold, during the night two assassins visited them in the friary and murdered them by cutting off their heads; they cut out their tongues and stuck them into their anuses', as Luther told this story at table some time in 1531. In the next breath he pointed out that 'Pope Julius had treated Egidio, a very learned man, in a more civilized manner, even though he [Egidio] had criticized him in his speech' (in May 1512). Luther also thought it was Julius II who had made Egidio a cardinal, while in reality it was Leo X in 1519.[246]

As far as Staupitz was concerned, he had orders to congratulate the young Pope Leo X on his election, and, more importantly, to work for the repeal of the recent unwelcome appointment of Cardinal Matthew Lang as 'co-adjutor' with the right of succession to the prince-bishop of Salzburg (Keutschach). Cardinal Lang had landed this job because he was well connected to the mighty House of Hapsburg. The Salzburg archbishopric was clearly more important to him than any ecumenical council and pope, for it seems that when later in the same year, in November 1513, Lang himself went to Rome, he did not come as a participant in the ecumenical council which was in session, but as the emperor's proxy, in order that he might pledge allegiance to the pope. As Leo X wanted to be on good terms with the Hapsburgs, and Cardinal Lang was so closely connected to them, Staupitz's mission was destined to fail, possibly clouding any future relationships between him and the

---

[245] On the Wittenberg print of this speech, see Wetzel, 'Staupitz Antibarbarus', pp. 109f.
[246] See *WATR* 2. 347, 32–348, 8 (no. 2174).

cardinal (who did become archbishop of Salzburg after Keutschach's death in 1519). Staupitz had to bear another failure on 22 September 1515, when the pope decreed that the canons at Salzburg cathedral could indeed become secular priests.[247] This effectively terminated the Augustinian canons' presence at the cathedral, where they had been since the beginning of the twelfth century.

As a small positive by-product of his visit to Rome on behalf of Salzburg's archbishop, Staupitz did manage to achieve something for his reformed congregation. He was able to arrange the incorporation of the friary of Rappoltsweiler in Alsace under his authority as vicar of the Reformed Congregation in Germany. This move was decided during a meeting with his Order's General, Egidio, in 1513 and finally approved by Leo X on 23 April 1514.[248] With his personal experiences in dealing with the papacy in Rome, it is not too difficult to imagine that the reform-minded Staupitz was not hopeful concerning the reform of the Church, or that it would come about quickly. How disappointed he was is unknown.

Returning from Rome, Staupitz again lodged at Salzburg. Here he became involved in the expansion of the Augustinian branch office, the local *terminus*, which was supervised by the Munich friary. In 1513 he bought a new building large enough to store the collected goods. Of the 700 *gulden* needed for the purchase, Staupitz contributed 180 *gulden* from his own funds.[249] When the place was sold in 1519, Staupitz was paid back the same sum which he had contributed six years earlier. Busy with these tasks and with preparing his forthcoming visitation journey to the Low Countries, it is unlikely that he gave the 1514 Lenten sermons, at least not in Salzburg. We know that he was at Munich from February to April 1514, where he accepted the annual gift of 100 *gulden* for the Munich friary from Duke Wolfgang IV of Bavaria (1508–50).[250]

During his visitation journey to the Low Countries in the autumn of 1514, Staupitz was involved in resolving a number of conflicts. One concerned a challenge to the legitimacy of the new foundation of the friary at Antwerp. The secular clergy there had to come to an agreement

---

[247] See I. Friedhuber, 'Kaiser Maximilian I. und die Bemühungen Matthäus Langs um das Erzbistum Salzburg', in A. Novotny and O. Pickl (eds), *Festschrift Hermann Wiesflecker zum sechzigsten Geburtstag* (Graz, 1973); Sallaberger, 'Johann von Staupitz, Luthers Vorgesetzter', pp. 130–31; Sallaberger, *Kardinal*, pp. 87–95.

[248] See Kolde, *Die deutsche Augustiner-Congregation*, p. 257; Kunzelmann, V, pp. 469–70; Zumkeller, 'Johann von Staupitz und die klösterliche Reformbewegung', pp. 45–6.

[249] See Sallaberger, 'Johann von Staupitz, die Stiftsprediger', pp. 253–4; on Duke Wolfgang and Staupitz, see Sallaberger, 'Johann von Staupitz, Luthers Vorgesetzter', p. 144 with n. 165.

[250] 250. See Sallaberger, 'Johann von Staupitz, Luthers Vorgesetzter', pp. 122–4.

with the Augustinians on preaching. The friars were allowed to give sermons only at times when there was no scheduling conflict with the secular clergy. This contract was approved by Pope Leo X on 12 September 1514. Staupitz then assisted in establishing the friary at Antwerp under its first prior, Johann von Mecheln, with seven other members, at the beginning of October 1514. In the case of the friary of Dordrecht, Staupitz simply went ahead and annexed it. He displayed the same irregularity and disobedience as he had previously displayed in 1509 when he brought the Cologne friary under his control. This time, however, the Order's general, Egidio, in a letter of 15 May 1514 threatened him and his followers with excommunication if he proceeded with his plan. In the end, Staupitz prevailed because the Emperor Charles V and the city government of Dordrecht itself wanted to see their friary incorporated into his reformed congregation. In the autumn of 1516 he sent Friar Johannes Bethel von Spangenberg to Dordrecht to make the annexation official and appointed Henry van Zutphen, who had been subprior at Cologne, as prior of the friary. Henry pushed for reforms at Dordrecht against some resistance; he left for Wittenberg in 1520. He ended up being burnt at the stake in December 1524, shortly before Staupitz died at Salzburg. Johann von Mecheln succeeded Henry at Dordrecht in 1520 and became the vicar general of the newly reformed congregation of the Low Countries in the summer of 1522, which became independent from the one in Saxony. He declared himself an anti-Lutheran.[251]

In regards to the friary at Ghent in Belgium, Staupitz received permission by the *breve* of Pope Leo X of 28 September 1514 to bring it into his reformed flock, with the condition that Ghent remain part of the Cologne province. Nevertheless, Staupitz later incorporated it into his own Reformed Congregation by appointing in 1520 as prior of Ghent a friar of his choosing from Dresden. In 1521 Linck formally inspected the friary as the successor of Staupitz. Soon afterwards the connection with the Saxon Congregation was broken off and the friary was attached to the reformed congregation of the Low Countries under Johann von Mecheln.[252] The friary of Mecheln was also brought under Staupitz's control with the help of Emperor Charles V who sent a letter of support dated 25 February 1515 to the Mecheln city government. Nevertheless, Staupitz's control was incomplete as the friary remained with the province of Cologne.[253]

---

[251] See Kolde, *Die deutsche Augustiner-Congregation*, p. 261; Kunzelmann, VII, pp. 113–14; Stupperich, pp. 226–7.

[252] See Kunzelmann, VII, pp. 137–8; Zumkeller, 'Johann von Staupitz und die klösterliche Reformbewegung', pp. 44–5.

[253] See Kunzelmann, VII, p. 143.

To return to Staupitz in 1514. Before he returned from the Low Countries to his winter residence at Salzburg for the winter months of 1514/15 he had to deal with a local incident at Sternberg. Due to his support the friary there had begun to blossom which was resented by the local secular clergy and the clerical schoolmaster. One day the drunken schoolmaster violently interrupted the friars' evening prayers, so they arrested him. This laid them open to excommunication by the local bishop because they had laid their hands on a cleric. When, without any investigation, the bishop duly excommunicated them, Staupitz protested and appealed to the pope. Staupitz agreed to the mediators whom the pope assigned in this matter, and in September 1514 the ecclesiastical ban was lifted.[254]

After his return to Salzburg Staupitz was employed as a preacher for the Benedictine Abbey of St Peter. He probably preached the Advent sermons there in 1514, as we know from a payment which he received in January 1515 for this service, although the sermons themselves are not extant. Another invoice, dated April 1516, from the same abbey, indicates that Staupitz again received a stipend, this time probably for sermons delivered during the Lenten season of 1516.[255] From Lent 1512 on, Staupitz appears to have preached on a regular basis during the Advent and Lenten seasons in the south, either in Munich, Nuremberg or Salzburg. With the exception of Advent 1519, he appears to have continued this practice up to the Lenten season of 1520. All three cities were significant power centres in the political, economic and religious spheres.

Summary

Let us sum up the achievements of Staupitz as vicar general of the Reformed Congregation of the Augustinians in German lands following his election at Eschwege in 1503. In that same year, he accepted property to build a friary at Wittenberg. He arranged the printing of the constitutions and privileges of the Augustinians. He undertook his first visitations of friaries in Saxony and Thuringia in the summer and autumn of 1504. The chapter meeting of the Saxon Reformed Congregation of May 1505 at Mühlheim confirmed him in his leadership position for a second term. From 1505 he sought to unite his Congregation with the Lombardian Congregation, although this ultimately failed. In 1506/07 he journeyed to Rome for the first time to meet Egidio da Viterbo, the new general of all the Augustinians. He

---

[254] See Kunzelmann, V, p. 492.

[255] 'Item pro Stopiz 21d.' (Sallaberger, 'Johann von Staupitz, die Stiftsprediger', p. 254).

also obtained papal confirmation of the foundation of the University of Wittenberg at that time. On 15 December 1507 he received the papal bull at Memmingen which confirmed the controversial union of his Reformed Congregation in Germany with the Province of the Augustinians of Saxony and Thuringia. In September 1508 he was involved in the visitation to the Benedictine monastery at Andechs in Bavaria, while he was stationed in Munich.

As dean in Wittenberg Staupitz transferred Luther to Wittenberg. In October 1508, his Reformed Congregation held its chapter meeting at Munich, while he was in his third term as vicar general. Also in 1509 he was elected provincial of the Saxon province at Münnerstadt, and thus from 1509 to 1512 he simultaneously held the position of vicar general of the German reformed Augustinians and that of provincial of the conventual Augustinians of Saxony. In the spring of 1509 he annexed the friary of Cologne to his congregation. In September 1509 he was in Munich. In the spring of 1510 he travelled to Rome a second time to see Egidio regarding the unification issue. In the summer of 1510 he was again in Munich. In that year he and Besler conducted the first visitations in the Low Countries and Westphalia. In September 1511, he conferred the doctorate in theology onto several friars at Wittenberg. In the same month he was involved in reforming the Saxon Franciscans in Berlin.

At the end of January 1512, Staupitz wanted to initiate the construction of a new facility for the recently reformed friars of Ramsau, moving them from their remote location to the nearest trade centre, the city of Haag (north-west of Salzburg and east of Munich; then within the diocese of Freising). The Ramsau friary had belonged to Staupitz's Reformed Congregation since January 1509.[256] From his residence at Salzburg Staupitz petitioned the bishop of Freising on the grounds that the friars should not live like monks in remote monasteries, but in the cities where they could contribute to the pastoral care for the citizens.[257] However, for some unknown reason the new construction for the Ramsau friars was never begun. By the year 1517, Vicar Staupitz had reformed not only Ramsau, but also the friaries of Cologne, Nordhausen in Thuringia, Rappoltsweiler in Alsace, Dordrecht in the Netherlands and Ghent in Belgium, besides founding two new friaries, one in Eisleben in Saxony and the other in Antwerp in Belgium.

After 1511 Staupitz chose to live in Salzburg. During Lent 1512 he delivered sermons there; the Benedictine nuns took notes and thus

---

[256] See Sallaberger, *Kardinal*, p. 240 with n. 4.

[257] Staupitz's letter is extant in Bayerisches Hauptstaatsarchiv, Munich (*KL Ramsau, No. 2, fol. 23r*); see Sallaberger, *Kardinal*, p. 242, n. 6.

preserved them as the earliest vernacular sermons that we have from him. In May 1512 he gave up his grandiose unification plans, but remained vicar general of the reformed friars for a fourth term, and ultimately until 1520. He handed his professorship at Wittenberg over to Luther who had become a doctor of theology in October 1512. A year later, on 6 October 1513, Egidio da Viterbo as the head of the Augustinian Order appointed Luther to the lectorate at the friary of Wittenberg, that is, to the Order's study programme.[258] During late October and early November 1512 Staupitz delivered a few sermons at Nuremberg, and then returned to Salzburg, where he spent the winter at the *terminus* of the Munich friars.[259] There is no doubt that Salzburg had become and remained his preferred residence. His presence there can be documented from the extant sources for the following times: winter and spring 1511/12, winter and spring 1512/13; Lent 1514; winter 1514/15; spring 1516; spring, Lent, summer and autumn 1518; winter 1519/20; and Lent 1520. From the summer of 1520 onward he made his permanent residence in Salzburg.[260]

---

[258] '1513. Oktobr. 6 Fratrem Martinum Wittenberg. Lectorem facimus', in D.G. Kawerau, 'Aus den Actis generalatus Aegidii Viterbiensis', *ZKG*, **32** (1911), pp. 603–6 (p. 604).

[259] See Kolde, *Die deutsche Augustiner-Congregation*, pp. 254–7 with n. 2; Kunzelmann, V, pp. 453–69. On Staupitz in the Salzburg *terminus*, see Sallaberger, *Kardinal*, p. 242.

[260] See Sallaberger, *Kardinal*, pp. 242f., esp. n. 10–15, where the source material is listed.

CHAPTER THREE

Prominent Preacher and Author (1512–17)

Preaching on Christ's passion at Salzburg (1512)

It is a characteristic of the fifteenth and sixteenth centuries that preaching was taken very seriously, and this was indeed a period of great preachers, with Dominicans, Franciscans, Carmelites and Augustinians dominating and competing in the field. In the 1450s at Lyons in France the city government invited the local Carmelites and Dominicans to submit nominations for Lenten preachers; the latter won the assignment. Elsewhere the Orders took turns during Lent or Advent; the first Sunday was given to the Dominicans, the second to the Franciscans, the third to the Augustinians and the fourth to the Carmelites. In Florence, Italy, things were different again; the Franciscans directed their attention and preaching to the proletariat, while the Dominicans turned to the *popolo grasso*.[1]

The priest or religious who held a preaching position in German-speaking lands was called a *Prädikant* ('preacher'). These preaching positions were not identical to the pastors' offices, but were funded by city governments or by private donors. When the magistrates of a city wanted to introduce religious reforms, they had to use the institution of the preaching position and not the pastorate, since the hiring of preachers in the late Middle Ages had come under the control of the city governments, rather than that of the pastors or even local bishops. Thus the 'secular' authorities could exploit appointments to preaching positions to bring about reforms which they wished to make. Furthermore, the job of preaching was not particularly closely tied to the traditional and well-established ecclesiastical organization of the administration of the sacraments which was usually in the hands of the pastors. A city could thus attract a qualified preacher, who would remain relatively independent from the pastors. Such a preacher was required to

---

[1] On Florence, see D.R. Lesnick, *Preaching in Medieval Florence: The Social World of Franciscan and Dominican Spirituality* (Athens, GA, 1989). On France, see L. Taylor, *Soldiers of Christ: Preaching in Late Medieval and Reformation France* (New York and Oxford, 1992), pp. 20f. H. Martin, *Le metiér du prédicateur à la fin du Moyen Age, 1350–1520* (Paris, 1988). A. Zawart, *The History of Franciscan Preaching and of Franciscan Preachers (1209–1927)* (New York, 1928).

have, first, an advanced degree, usually a doctorate in theology, and, secondly, personal credibility as far as his lifestyle was concerned. Thus, for instance, the donor of an endowment fund at the imperial city of Isny in south-western Germany specified that the preacher to be hired must be a person 'whose words and deeds correspond to each other', evidently the result of the medieval spirituality of teaching by 'word and example' (*verbum et exemplum*).[2] Very often these preachers came from the ranks of the so-called mendicant Orders. Preaching positions which were held by the most reform-minded Augustinian friars were to become the gateways for the propagation of spiritual reform in the free imperial cities of the German-speaking lands.

Many medieval cities of central Europe instituted endowment funds for financing these positions, and it appears that there was much competition among them to obtain illustrious preachers for their main churches. In Strasbourg, Alsace, such a position to be maintained 'eternally', was funded in 1478 by a wealthy citizen. Johann Geiler von Kaisersberg (d. 1510), who accepted the post at Strasbourg's principal church, became arguably the most popular preacher of his time – at least as far as the German-speaking lands were concerned.[3]

In south-western Germany, in what is today Württemberg, 46 such foundations for preaching positions came into existence between 1400 and 1517.[4] This number is a clear indication of how important preaching was to the citizens of the imperial cities of the empire. Even at such a relatively small place as Isny, a preaching post had been established in 1462 which included the funding of a library for that particular preacher. One of Isny's preachers was Paul Fagius who shortly before his death in 1553 became professor of Hebrew at the University of Cambridge.

---

[2] 'Das sine wort und werk ainander glich syen', as quoted in Wolfgang Kehr (ed.), *Handbuch der historischen Buchbestände in Deutschland*, 8 vols (Hildesheim, Zurich and New York, 1994), VIII, p. 17. On preaching positions and the history of preaching in Germany, see J.B. Schneyer, *Geschichte der katholischen Predigt* (Freiburg, 1969), pp. 189–230; Schneyer 'Die Predigt im Mittelalter', in *Lexikon für Theologie und Kirche*, 2nd edn (Freiburg, 1962), VIII, col. 710. K. Bihlmeyer and H. Tüchle, *Kirchengeschichte*, 3 vols (Paderborn, 1960) II, pp. 458–60. K. Ruh, 'Geistliche Prosa', in W. Erzgräber (ed.), *Neues Handbuch der Literaturwissenschaft*, 8 vols (Wiesbaden, 1978), Vol. VIII *Europäisches Spätmittelalter*, p. 582. M. Menzel, 'Predigt und Predigtorganisation im Mittelalter', *Historisches Jahrbuch*, **111** (1991), pp. 337–84. On the medieval background of teaching by word and example, see C.W. Bynum, *Docere Verbo et Exemplo: An Aspect of Twelfth-Century Spirituality* (Missoula, MT, 1979).

[3] See O. Ritter, 'Geiler von Keisersberg und die Reformation in Strassburg', *Sechsundzwanzigster Jahresbericht des Königlichen Realgymnasiums und der Landwirtschaftschule zu Döbeln* (Döbeln, 1895), p. VI; see also Ruh, 'Geistliche Prosa', p. 583.

[4] See J. Rauscher, 'Die ältesten Prädikaturen Württembergs', *Blätter für Württembergische Kirchengeschichte*, (1921), pp. 107–11. Rauscher shows that such preaching posts were established in 1415 at Riedlingen and in 1420 at Giengen an der Brenz.

Another was John Marbach who left his position in order to study theology at Wittenberg, where in 1543 Professor Luther made him discuss a sentence from Staupitz as part of his doctoral disputation.[5]

Even the then small city of Wittenberg had established such a preaching post in the fifteenth century. It was Staupitz who assigned Luther to it in 1514 after the latter had been the preacher at their friary for some time.[6] The main churches of Nuremberg had full-time preachers who were required to have undergone theological training. At Nuremberg's St Lorenz church (with its famous Angelus sculpture, created by Veit Stoss, and financed by Anton Tucher) the position of preacher was funded in part by a wealthy widow. She, however, made the stipulation that the funding would end when Andreas Osiander, who was appointed to it in March 1522, departed from that position; thereafter the money would go to the poor. At Nuremberg's St Vitus church (which belonged to the Augustinians) the best Augustinian preachers were employed. The Nuremberg chronicles reveal that, in 1488 and 1489, when the new and very large church building of St Vitus had just been finished, the popular preacher Johann Vogt was reassigned to a prior's position elsewhere. The Nuremberg city council then intervened as the city wanted to keep this great preacher in their midst.[7] In 1516 Staupitz would enter into this tradition of good preaching at Nuremberg.

As every major and minor city in central Europe tried to hire good preachers, so too did the great city of Salzburg, which was the largest spiritual principality in the entire empire. Staupitz was well aware of the fact that Salzburg was the ecclesiastial centre for the surrounding episcopal sees including Vienna, Seckau, Gurk and Levant, all located to the east of Salzburg; Brixen (Tyrol) to the south; Chiemsee, Freising, Passau and even Regensburg to the west and north. To live and work in

---

[5] See I. Kammerer and G. Kopff, *Die Nikolaikirche in Isny und ihre Bibliotheken* (Munich, 1976). On Fagius, see Stupperich, pp. 77f.; on Marbach, see ibid., pp. 138f.; on Marbach's disputation, see *WA* 39, 2. 227, 31f. (with Staupitz's sentence).

[6] In a table talk Luther recalled having been first assigned to preaching to the brethren in the refectory (*WATR* 3. 188, 3 (no. 3143)). On the preaching situation at that time, see F. Posset, 'Preaching the Passion of Christ on the Eve of the Reformation', *Concordia Theological Quarterly*, 59 (1995), pp. 279–300.

[7] See I. Höss, 'Das religiös-geistige Leben in Nürnberg am Ende des 15. und am Ausgang des 16. Jahrhunderts', *Miscellanea Historiae Ecclesiasticae*, 2 (1967), p. 20. On Osiander, see G. Müller (ed.), *Andreas Osiander d. Ä. Gesamtausgabe, vol. 1: Schriften und Briefe 1522 bis März 1525*, 5 vols (Gütersloh, 1975), I, p. 18. On Vogt at Nuremberg, see H. Vonschott, *Geistiges Leben im Augustinerorden am Ende des Mittelalters und zu Beginn der Neuzeit* (Berlin, 1915; reprinted Vaduz, 1965), p. 155; Kunzelmann, III, p. 275 with n. 1050. For the situation in Switzerland, see E. Lengwiler, *Die vorreformatorischen Prädikaturen der deutschen Schweiz von ihrer Entstehung bis 1530* (Fribourg, 1955).

Salzburg must have been a most attractive proposition to any intellectual or learned preacher. There is evidence for a well-funded preaching position in the city, established since 1399. The post was financed by an endowment fund which was independent both from the cathedral and from the court of the local prince-bishop. This fund, which had been established by two Salzburg citizens, Virgil Säppel and Ott Hofpekch, was administered by three representatives of the local city government and the senior pastor of the city, who had to hire priests for this position. The three representatives on any search committee for new appointments to the post apparently had to be the leading officer of the city's social services, the hospital administrator (called *Spitalmeister*) and the mayor; the archdiocese had no say in this. The endowment fund stipulated that the priest who held this position must sing a Mass daily, in honour of the Virgin Mary, to be celebrated at the city church, and that he must include prayers for the donors and the poor souls in purgatory. In his singing of the Mass he was to be supported by two pupils. Secondly, such an office holder was to preach every Saturday night after vespers so as to prepare the audience for the first reading from the Bible scheduled for the following Sunday. Thirdly, during Advent and Lent he had to preach daily during the first Mass on the gospel of the day. The holder of the position was called a 'foundation preacher' (*Stiftsprediger*), or 'prebendary of the foundation' (*Stiftsherr*), or simply 'chaplain'. In around 1477 the city of Salzburg could afford to provide for his residence and to pay him a better salary than, for instance, a professor at the neighbouring University of Ingolstadt would have earned.[8]

In 1510, the longtime holder of the preaching position in Salzburg, Magister Nikolaus Vitzthum, retired; he had held it for 28 years, from 1482.[9] Staupitz most likely substituted for this preacher during the Lenten season of 1512, probably as a guest preacher, but it is unlikely that he would have assumed the rest of the duties connected to this endowed position. The name of Staupitz emerged in connection with Vitzthum's retirement, as on that occasion the book-keeping was reviewed. An invoice is preserved that shows Staupitz's name – the earliest hint of his connection with Salzburg. The entry is not dated, and it is not absolutely certain that one can prove Staupitz's presence at Salzburg by that document; but other hints make it likely.

---

[8] See Sallaberger, 'Johann von Staupitz, die Stiftsprediger' und die Mendikanten-Termineien in Salzburg', *Studien und Mitteilungen zur Geschichte des Benediktinerordens und seiner Zweige*, 93 (1982) pp. 218–69 (pp. 224–33); he emphasizes that the designation *Domprediger* ('preacher at the cathedral') was not used in Staupitz's time. Nor was Staupitz a 'court preacher', as Kolde assumed in 1879; he was substituting for the 'foundation preacher' (*Stiftsprediger*).

[9] See Sallaberger, 'Johann von Staupitz, die Stiftsprediger', p. 237.

In summer 1510 Staupitz visited the general of the Order, Egidio da Viterbo, at Monte Cimino near Viterbo (north-west of Rome). Being absent from Rome the general wrote to Staupitz from nearby Soriano on 26 June 1510 that the two leading offices of the Saxon Province and the German Reformed Congregation should be his. Staupitz must have returned to Germany soon after this, probably via Salzburg, as we find him on 8 September 1510 at Neustadt an der Orla in Thuringia.[10] In August 1510, Staupitz made sure that certain unknown goods were handed over from the property of the retiring Vitzthum to the Augustinian Order at Salzburg with its branch office (*terminus*). It is also very likely that contacts between Staupitz and the archbishop of Salzburg existed, because the Order's friars required the archbishop's permission for preaching and hearing confessions, and these two activities were always connected to collecting donations. The Salzburg branch office was subject to the main office at Munich where Staupitz had been superior from 1500 to 1503.[11]

We know that Staupitz spent the winter months of 1511/12 at Salzburg, but not whether he gave Advent sermons there in 1511. Staupitz is known to have been at the Munich friary on 27 January 1512, and a month later, by 25 February 1512, he was back in Salzburg in order to meet Friar Johann von Mecheln. This friar had returned from Rome, where he had been sent by Staupitz to inform Egidio about Staupitz's decision to drop the unification plans for the reformed and non-reformed branches of their Order. Staupitz then had sent both Johann von Mecheln and Besler from Salzburg to Cologne entrusting them with the preparations for the next chapter meeting of their Order in May 1512.[12]

Staupitz himself would now concentrate on good preaching and writing. Previously in the Prologue to his Tübingen sermons of 1497/98, Staupitz had hinted at the task he planned to fulfil, namely that of preaching to the people. He wanted to instruct and to console, and if necessary to correct what needed to be corrected; which might include the correction of pastors or other authorities. He felt he had to obey God more than human authority.[13] Staupitz, however, did not want to kill the

---

[10] See Kunzelmann, V, pp. 457–59; see Sallaberger, 'Johann von Staupitz, die Stiftsprediger', pp. 238–41.

[11] See Sallaberger, 'Johann von Staupitz, die Stiftsprediger', pp. 241f.

[12] See Zumkeller, 'Johannes von Staupitz und die klösterliche Reformbewegung', *AAug*, 52 (1989), pp. 31–49 (p. 267); W. Schneider-Lastin (ed.), *Johann von Staupitz Salzburger Predigten 1512*, Einer textkritische Edition (Tübingen, 1990) pp. 4f. Johann von Mecheln died some time after 1524, but never became a Lutheran, see Zumkeller, 'Johannes von Staupitz und die klösterliche Reformbewegung', p. 272.

[13] See Tübingen Sermon 21; see A. Zumkeller, *Johann von Staupitz und seine christliche Heilslehre* (Würzburg, 1994), p. 17.

'patient' while fighting the 'illness'. In this he closely followed the lead of St Augustine and Jean Gerson's *De consolatione theologiae*; he wanted to edify, that is, to build up the Christian life. He understood his preaching to be the proclamation of the 'life-giving Word'.[14] As a preacher he wanted to be a *weglaiter*, 'a leader on the way' or 'pathfinder', who is ordained by God to show the sinner the consoling and right way.[15] Apparently his homilies made such an impact in Salzburg that of the sermons delivered during Lent 1512 the last 12 (given between 23 March and 7 April 1512, the last two weeks before Easter) were recorded by local Benedictine nuns who at that time were known as *Petersfrauen* ('St Peter's [religious] ladies'). Salzburg's double monastery of St Peter housed both monks and nuns, who, of course, lived in separate quarters. The convent of the 'St Peter's ladies' was adjacent to the city church of St Mary (*Stadtpfarrkirche*; today the church of the Franciscans) where the nuns worshipped. From their pews they were able to listen to the sermons which were preached to the townspeople; thus they formed part of Staupitz's audience. The fact that Staupitz preached in the city church (and not in an exclusively monastic church) is an indication that he fulfilled the requirements set down by the endowment fund for the 'foundation preacher' for that particular church. He was probably substituting for the ordinary preacher whose identity for that year cannot be determined with certainty. It may have been Paul Speratus, the later famous Lutheran reformer and bishop of Pomerania, or perhaps Friar Gregor Mayr who had been Staupitz's friend since the time they spent together at Tübingen from 1497 to 1500.[16]

Staupitz may have begun his series of sermons shortly after Ash Wednesday, but none of the sermons were recorded until Tuesday after the fourth Sunday of Lent (*Laetare*) when the nuns began to write them down. On that day, 23 March 1512, Staupitz began to preach on the passion narrative. He continued his daily preaching for 12 days until the Wednesday before Holy Thursday, 8 April, except for Sundays and feast days.[17] Wishing to keep the audience's attention focused on Christ, he arranged his 12 sermons according to the perceived sequence of events in Christ's last days that led to the crucifixion:

---

[14] 'Das lebentigmachund wart' (Schneider-Lastin), *Salzburger Predigten 1512*, p. 94. See Zumkeller, *Heilslehre*, pp. 17f. and 21.

[15] Nuremberg sermon, as quoted by Zumkeller, *Heilslehre*, p. 15.

[16] See Sallaberger, 'Johann von Staupitz, die Stiftsprediger', pp. 252f.; Schneider-Lastin, *Salzburger Predigten 1512*, pp. 5–9 (with the information on the architecture of the church where Staupitz preached). On 'St Peter's ladies', see M. Schellhorn, 'Die Petersfrauen: Geschichte des ehemaligen Frauenkonventes bei St. Peter in Salzburg', *Mitteilungen der Gesellschaft für Salzburger Landeskunde*, 65 (1925), pp. 164–85.

[17] See Schneider-Lastin, *Salzburger Predigten 1512*, pp. 8f.

1   Departure from Mary at Bethany.
2   Departure from the disciples at the Last Supper.
3   Departure 'from himself' at Mount Olive.
4   Arrival of Judas at Mount Olive.
5   Imprisonment; interrogation before Annas; Peter's denial.
6   Accusations before Caiphas and the Sanhedrin; mistreatment.
7   Transfer from Caiphas to Pilate.
8   Standing before Pilate and Herod.
9   Flagellation by the Romans; condemnation.
10 Flagellation by the Jews, *Via Dolorosa*.
11 Crucifixion; Mary under the cross.
12 Death and deposition.

Staupitz followed the lines of the biblical accounts of the passion of the Lord, but he embellished the narrative with scenes not found in the biblical text. This tendency to fill in some details and to add legendary material to the biblical passion narratives was a typical trait of late medieval 'passion literature'. Staupitz created with these sermons a sort of *horologium* not unlike the famous devotional work with this title by Henry Suso, which was essentially a re-creation of the last days of Jesus Christ. It was also similar to Ludolph of Saxony's *Vita Jesu Christi*, or perhaps an emulation of the passion of Bonaventure's *The Tree of Life* (*Lignum Vitae*) and *The Mystical Vine* (*Vitis mystica*), the latter being long attributed to St Bernard of Clairvaux. These and other spiritual authors may have been Staupitz's favourites, as numerous parallels of thought with them are found in his sermons.[18] Staupitz let Mary follow Jesus all the way to the cross; he let Jesus be scourged twice (he thought he had evidence for this from the gospels of Matthew and John). Furthermore, Staupitz let Christ heal a legendary blind soldier by the name of Longinus beneath the cross. Yet at several points Staupitz as a former Bible professor conscientiously related his sermons back to 'the text' or to 'the story'. However, he did not follow one specific gospel text, but rather, seems to have had in mind a passion narrative according to some sort of gospel harmony. All in all, the chief source of his preaching remained the Bible, which is hardly surprising given that Staupitz had been professor of the Bible at the University of Wittenberg for the previous ten years. In his preaching he emphasized the immense

---

[18] See W. Haug and B. Wachinger (eds), *Die Passion Christi in Literatur und Kunst des Spätmittelalters* (Tübingen, 1993) with contributions by U. Köpf, 'Die Passion Christi in der lateinischen religiösen und theologischen Literatur des Spätmittelalters', pp. 21–41; and G. Steer, 'Die Passion Christi bei den deutschen Bettelorden im 13. Jahrhundert', pp. 52–75. For a brief discussion of Staupitz's spiritual sources for these sermons, see Schneider-Lastin, *Salzburger Predigten 1512*, pp. 15–17.

suffering which Christ endured in the course of his passion. The overall goal of his preaching according to his announcement in the opening passage of his first sermon was the meditation on the salvific suffering of Christ:

> ... I want to present to you your Captain, Jesus Christ, who will lead you to victory over your enemies. Therefore, be happy and rejoice, the triumph is won and death is overcome and gone. The trust in your righteous God shall never depart from your hearts.
>
> The first main point [is this]: All our suffering and all our illness is completely tied up and overcome in His suffering. We need to contemplate [His suffering] in great gratitude. Truly, if one does not contemplate His suffering, it does not taste, it does not taste sweet [at all]; then, what would serve for one's salvation is not pleasing.[19]

Staupitz communicated the salvific 'sweetness' of Christ's bitter suffering in traditional devotional language, speaking of the 'sweet Jesus' as his 'noble and tender God'.[20] In doing so his preaching was completely focused on Christ whose suffering alone brings about the believer's 'deification': 'Who would not want to be glad knowing that the mercy of God swallowed up one's sin completely? Christ's suffering deifies man. There is nothing more blessed on earth than Christ's suffering, because all salvation depends on it.'[21]

The preacher's second point was this: 'Nobody who contemplates will receive any sweetness from it unless that person enters into full contemplation of the body of Christ, then one arrives at [His] soul and passes through it and [finally] arrives at His divine nature.'[22] Staupitz operated here with the strange concept of Christ's 'three natures', which he used as a structual principle for most of his sermons of 1512, perhaps derived from his reading of Bernard, Henry of Friemar, and/or Ludolf of Saxony:

---

[19] Schneider-Lastin, *Salzburger Predigten 1512*, p. 25.

[20] 'Süesser Jesus' (ibid., pp. 30f). 'Wellet ir wol und recht betrachten das leiden Christi, so müest ir ansehen dreu stuck heut und auch in allem leiden, von dem ich sagen wirt. Erstlich: seinen heiligen leib, und in dem besichten di straich und peindlichait, und zu got schreien: "O du edler, zarter got und mein herr, wie pistu durch mich zerrissen, zerschniten, gegaiselt, gekrönt!"' (ibid., p. 26). On God's sweetness according to Augustine, Bernard and Staupitz, see F. Posset, 'The Sweetness of God', *ABR*, **44** (1993), 143–78; Posset, '*Christi Dulcedo*: The "Sweetness of Christ" in Western Christian Spirituality', *CSQ*, **30** (1995), 245–65. On Suso, see F. Tobin (ed.), *Henry Suso, The Exemplar, With Two German Sermons* (New York and Mahwah, NJ 1989) with numerous expressions of the sweetness of God.

[21] Schneider-Lastin, *Salzburger Predigten 1512*, pp. 25f. On the late medieval spiritual/theological concept of 'deification' (*Vergottung*), see F. Posset, '"Deification" in the German Spirituality of the Late Middle Ages and in Luther: An Ecumenical Historical Perspective', *ARG*, **84** (1993), pp. 103–26.

[22] Schneider-Lastin, *Salzburger Predigten 1512*, p. 26.

The divine person has three natures – body, life [soul], and divinity – in which body and soul are united and make a happy being, but remain one person. If you want to meditate well and rightly on the suffering of Christ, you must look at three aspects today and in every suffering of which I will speak.

Firstly, [let us look at] His holy body and, in looking at it, at the strokes and painful marks, and let us pray to God: 'O You, tender God and my Lord, how are You torn up because of me, cut up, scourged, and crowned!' Only a hardened person would not feel sorry and take [these things] to heart; if it were a little dog or animal that you see tortured in this way, you would have mercy with it.

Take note: eagerly meditate upon the suffering of Christ; do not stop until you find in your heart some compassion or motion of your heart. When you feel that, do not stand still, but proceed to the soul [of Christ] and think – this is the second point: 'O you most noble soul, how are you? The body is already maltreated. What do I notice in you? [I see] a complete, perfect obedience to the Heavenly Father; and you did not want to walk away from suffering, but to be obedient unto death. O, my God, grant that I may follow you obediently as is your will.'[23]

Staupitz in a meditative way guided his audience to speak to God in Christ directly. He then turned to his hearers with this exhortation:

And do not stand still here either; penetrate through the suffering of the soul and see what the divinity adds to it: the third [nature]. Thus you will find that the suffering of the body and the obedience of the soul flow out together from the fountain of God's mercy. 'O my God, now I see your love; I recognize your grace and your mercy; as I was your enemy, you did this [for me]. Was there ever anyone who suffered death for his enemy? Who deserved this from you since we all were your enemies?' But it flows out [from you]; there is nothing but mercy; and finally it was mercy which devoured sin; hope [which

---

[23] 'Die götlich perschon hat drei natur – ainen leib, ain leben und ain gothait …' (ibid., pp. 26f.). The concept of the three essences/natures of Christ may have been inspired by Bernard of Clairvaux's *Sermo 3 in vigilia nativitatis Domini*, 9: 'Verbum enim, et anima, et caro in unam convenere personam; et haec tria unum, et hoc unum tria, non in confusione substantiae, sed unitate personae' (*SBOp*, IV. 217, 29–218, 2). The concept is used also by the fourteenth-century author Marguerite Porete (d. 1310), *The Mirror of a Simple Soul*, Chapter 14, trans. E.L. Babinsky (New York and Mahwah, NJ, 1993), p. 96. It is found again in the work of the Augustinian Henry of Friemar (d. 1350) who explicitly relied on Bernard in this regard: 'Haec autem tres substantiae fuerunt substantia Verbi, animae rationalis et ipsius carnis. Quae quidem tria sunt ita distantia, quod secundum Bernardum nequam possent misceri, nisi ea coniungeret "glutinum Spiritus Sancti"' (A. Zumkeller, *Henrici de Frimaria O.S.A. Tractatus* (Würzburg, 1975), pp. 136f). Ludolf of Saxony (d. 1378) also has it: *Vita Jesu Christi*, I. 43a–44a, as identified by Schneider-Lastin, *Salzburger Predigten 1512*, p. 26, n. 12; Schneider-Lastin, however, does not take the Bernardine matrix of this concept into consideration. In his Salzburg Sermon 3 of 1523, Staupitz will use the concept again: 'alle drey natur' (all three natures [of Christ]); as quoted by D.C. Steinmetz, *Misericordia Dei: The Theology of Johannes Staupitz in its Late Medieval Setting* (Leiden, 1968), p. 147, n. 3.

devoured] fear, joy [which devoured] sadness, triumph [which devoured] suffering and grief, strength [which devoured] weakness, life [which devoured] death, and God [who devoured] man.

See, my child, and learn from it, what use and fruit come to you from [his] suffering. If someone meditates in one's heart upon the suffering of Christ and really sinks into it, then he must be filled with more joy than with sadness. O what sweet tears flow from the loving soul who in contemplation enters into God. If you taste the body's [suffering] alone, it is a bitter taste; but if you look at the soul's [suffering], it brings some joy. But when you enter into the Godhead, it is the most sweet thing. You should not remain with the meditation of the suffering of His body, but come forth and enter into discipleship: he suffered, and so we suffer, too; he struggled, and so we struggle, too. Keep in mind the three points: fellowship in suffering is in the body, discipleship is in the soul, joy is in the Godhead. You know what a consolation the sweetness of the Godhead was to Mary, the noble Queen ....[24]

At this point Staupitz made a critical reference to a contemporary devotional practice, and in so doing he was probably following the advice of spiritual directors of his time,[25] namely to be careful with the use of depictions and with rhetorical devices of leading the audience to fantastic flights of imagination. He pointed out that looking at holy cards or pictures is not enough. One must proceed in meditation 'with closed eyes' and finally reach the 'kernel of sweetness' or as Suso said, 'the inner sweetness of the kernel':

---

[24] 'O mein got, gib mir, das ich dir nachfolg mit gehorsam, wie du wildt. Und in dem stee nit still, tring hinein durch das leiden der sel und lueg was, die gothait darzu tue – das drit –; so findestu, das das leiden des leibs und di gehorsam der sel fliessen her aus dem prunn der parmherzikait gots .... Da fleust es heraus, da ist nichts dann parmherzikait, da ligts an dem end und hat di parmherzikait die sündt verschlickt, die hoffnung di forcht, dy frölichait das trauern, der triumpf das leiden und trübnüß, di sterk di krankhait, das leben den tod, und got den menschen.

Siech, mein kind, und daraus nim ain ler, was nutz und frucht dir aus dem leiden kümbt. Es ist nit müglich, so der mensch das leiden Christi herzenlich betracht und sich dareinsenkt, er mues mer freid dann trauern haben. O was süesser zächer flissen daher aus der liebhabunden sel, die sich einsenkt in got! Smeckst du es alain, als es aus dem leichnam hie ist, so ist es ain pitter ding; siechstu es aber an, als es aus der sel hie ist, so iss lustig; aber geestu ein in di gothait, so iss as allersüessist ding .... Merkt dreu ding: Mitleiden ist jm leib, nachfolgen ist in der sel, freid in der gothait. Was mainst, das ain trost sei gewesen Maria, der edeln künigin, dann di süssikait der gothait ...' (Sermon 1, Schneider-Lastin, Salzburger Predigten 1512, pp. 27f).

[25] See F.O. Schuppisser, 'Schauen mit den Augen des Herzens', in Haug and Wachinger, *Die Passion Christi*, pp. 169–210 (pp. 183f.). Artistic depictions as aids to meditation were not uncommon, as can be seen from P.E. Webber (ed.), *A Late Medieval Devotional Anthology From Salzburg ('Nonnberg Passion': Huntington Library HM 195). Commentary and Edition* (Göppingen, 1990), which includes pictures that may stem from the Nonnberg nunnery with which Staupitz had contact.

> Many people make holy cards for themselves. I do not condemn this practice, but I also do not praise it. Such things are useful for becoming mindful [of Christ's suffering]. But, as soon as you are enkindled in your contemplation, close your eyes, but do not remain there. The external picture of the [tortured] body only shows you Christ's suffering in the body, while contemplation of the soul [of Christ] makes this suffering fruitful to you, and it is in the divinity [of Christ] where one finds hidden the kernel of sweetness. It is to be sought deep down in the well of mercy.[26]

Staupitz's sermons were centred on Christ and on grace. He aimed at the heart of the listener who needs to taste the 'sweetness' which is to be found only in the suffering of the divine Christ. He wanted to lead his hearers beyond the external observation of depictions of Christ's suffering towards a spiritual understanding or to the religious meaning of the suffering of the Son of God for us and our salvation. In these otherwise Christo-centric sermons Staupitz also managed to feature Mary. She followed Christ in discipleship; she stood 'by the soul of Christ', and she went through Christ's soul to the 'sweetness of God'.[27] With this thought he concluded his first sermon.

In his second sermon, he continued to speak of the 'most sweet Jesus Christ' who had now departed from his mother. The preacher then invited his listeners to turn their eyes to God (he meant the divine Christ) in order to see his loneliness and his seven griefs. Christ shared his feelings only with John, the beloved disciple, who rested on his side at the Last Supper. The preacher then let some of the other apostles, engaged in farewell conversations with Christ, pass review in front of his audience's mental eyes: Judas, Peter, Thomas and Philip. At this point, when dealing with the apostles' failures, Staupitz added his own criticism of contemporary leaders of the Church. He had been critical of them earlier in his Tübingen Sermon 19, as we have seen. Here now, in 1512, he said that Christ takes upon himself the sorrow over the damage done by the 'heads of the Church who govern so badly and do not lead their sheep with eagerness'. Staupitz then concluded his second sermon with these consoling thoughts:

---

[26] 'Viel leit machen manigerlai priefel für sich. Ich schilts nit, so kan ichs auch nit loben. Es ist wol guet zu ermanen; aber alspald du anzünt wirst in der betrachtung, so tue die augen zue, stee nit darauf. Das ausser gesicht oder pild des leibs, das zaigt dir an das leiden Christi, die betrachtung der sel macht dirs fruchtper, in der gothait ligt der keren der süessikait verporgen. Es is teuf, wenn du es suechst im prunn der parmherzikait ...' (Sermon 1, Schneider-Lastin, *Salzburger Predigten 1512*, p. 28); on Suso and the 'sweetness of the kernel' (*inre suezikeit des kernen*), see K. Bihlmeyer (ed.), *Deutsche Schriften im Auftrag der Württembergischen Kommission für Landesgeschichte* (Stuttgart, 1907; reprinted Frankfurt, 1961); see Tobin, *Henry Suso*, p. 216.

[27] 'Und nun steet Maria pei der sel Christi im willen und geet dadurch ein zu der süessichait gots' (Schneider-Lastin, *Salzburger Predigten 1512*, pp. 32f.).

... People who meditate upon the suffering of Christ, find sadness and pain in Christ's body, in [His] soul the will and wish to suffer, and in [His] divine nature the mercy. When you now ponder what sufferings Christ had to endure when Judas departed, you see [only] the suffering of the body .... But enter into the suffering of Christ which redeems you from the cries of the damned; it is the suffering of the soul [of Christ]. Thirdly, through the Godhead [of Christ] your sins are forgiven you. Peter asked for forgiveness a thousand times, you [Lord] forgave him. In Peter the forgiveness of sins is shown; in Thomas we are shown that God [i.e. Christ] is the Way, the Truth, and the Life; and in Philip [who had asked to 'Show us the Father'] we are shown the sweetness of God. Abandoning the world has brought you God's presence which God may grant us all. Amen.[28]

Conspicuously, Staupitz's second sermon, in dealing with Christ's farewell from the disciples at the Last Supper, totally neglected any consideration of the institution of the sacrament of the Eucharist. At this point Staupitz's spirituality is completely Christ-centred, rather than sacrament-centred.

In his third sermon, he took up the topic of Christ's 'departure' (*schaiden*) with the focus on Christ's 'departure' from himself, meaning the separation of Christ's mind from his soul, which is the highest and greatest 'departure'. In this context Staupitz said that the 'heavenly Father stabbed his [Christ's] heart'.[29] He killed His own Son. Staupitz introduced at this point the typological interpretation of Abraham and Isaac climbing the mountain to symbolize God the Father sacrificing the Son.[30] Every sin of the world is placed on Christ who wanted to do penance and contrition for all. 'O what an inexplicable penance this is that the most loving God divorced Himself from Him and handed over His body to suffer and His soul to mourn, in order that the entire man [*mensch*] become deified!'[31] When Christ was completely ready to die, 'the divine mind separated from his most holy soul'.[32] At this point, towards the end of the third sermon, Staupitz made use of traditional bridal mysticism when 'Love' speaks to the Bride:

You are a wretched bride, what did he get from accepting you? Not a bride worth a hundred or a thousand *gulden*, not even a penny's worth. But what did he get with you? A common, miserable, poor,

---

[28] See ibid., pp. 36–48. Staupitz's criticism is on p. 38: '... schaden, der aus den häubtern der kirchen kümbt, so die übel regieren und iren schäflein nit mit fleis vor sein.'

[29] 'Der himlisch vater hat dir das herz abgestochen .... Der himlisch vater wirt dich dötten' (ibid., p. 41).

[30] See ibid., p. 42.

[31] Ibid., p. 44.

[32] 'Da schied sich der götlich geist von der allerheiligisten sel mit ganzer verwilligung zu sterben' (ibid., p. 46).

wretched bride; [this is so, in order that] he decorate you and make you rich with everything good....[33]

Staupitz ended with a direct reference to the Song of Songs 2: 6; 'You will place your hand under my head' and 'I sweetly rest on it.'[34]

With Sermon 4 Staupitz kept his audience at the scene on Mount Olive. He showed them Christ as the 'strong hero' (*stark held*) who did not flee from his enemies. Christ is the Saviour (*hailmacher*) in whom is disclosed 'divine wisdom', 'divine power', 'divine goodness', 'divine justice/righteousness' and 'divine patience'.[35] Since Christ did not run away, for our sake, we should not run away from suffering either. 'Do you see that Christ died for your sake? And he gives grace gratis to you .... May God grant that his imprisonment [at Gethsemane] may set us free. Amen.'[36]

In his fifth sermon, he wove several diverse topics into one sermon. As usual, he addressed his audience with the opening phrase, 'Friends of Christ', and then he made a brief connection with previous sermons before he entered into the explanation of his new topic, the imprisonment of Christ and the denial of Peter. Staupitz tied these points together with remarks on the role of 'the Jews' in the suffering of Christ. He also utilized mystical terminology as he had Christ speak to the mystical 'bride', who represents the individual believing soul. Here is a lengthy passage from his fifth sermon:

> Friends of Christ, you have heard how Christ, our Saviour and strong hero, stood up at the arrival of the Jews who wanted to capture Him; how Christ showed them in seven ways His true divinity: In the order and measure within which they were to capture Him and in no other way, in power, in wisdom, in goodness, in mercy, and in patience. Today, look at his imprisonment; there are three points to it.
>
> First, Christ, our Lord and God, gave courage to the approaching Jews, who at that time had been beaten down, so that now they would stand up and regain their evil will as before. For he wanted to offer Himself as a sacrifice, give up everything that would belong to a man of strength, have His eyes closed, let His hands be tied, and become silent like a lamb.
>
> Three things took place at His imprisonment: the devil was depressed and imprisoned; the devil regained his strength; and third, the disciples fled.
>
> First, He caught the devil in the net of the fear of God. Record in your heart that the devil has recognized God [in Christ], but the people did not. When the Lord convinced the people with one word

---

[33] Ibid., pp. 46f.
[34] Ibid., p. 47.
[35] Ibid., pp. 52–55.
[36] Ibid., pp. 55f.

– 'It is me' [John 18: 5] – the devil thought: 'Now the truth is out: He is the true God; no human being could have done what He did.' And the devil gave up his efforts to bring about His death. [The devil] gave it a rest and remained quiet in the hearts of the Jews.

Secondly, however, when the evil spirit saw that He [Christ] let Himself be captured and tied so miserably, he began again and thought to stir up again the devilish hatred. Therefore, the hearts of the Jews were awakened again to envy and hatred of the Lord. My God and my Lord, why is it that you let yourself be caught so infamously by the Jews? Why do you do that? Response: 'O my child, who gave you the strength to sin? Who gave you the mouth to speak evil words? I did it, because all strength is of God. Why should I not provide also that from which you would be cleansed? I gave my hands to be tied, so that your hands might be cleansed from evil works. I was spat in the face, so that your face might be cleansed. Let it be, my bride; I must pay the debt which you ran up.' Yes, my Lord, if this is so, that it was your will, then it is all right, because you really helped to bring it about. Therefore, my God and my Lord, much has been written of you by the prophets, how people beat you, torture you, and cause you pain. If it is so written, we must do it. Therefore, my Lord, be patient; we must do it, as the truth must be fulfilled completely in you, the truth that is prophesied of you.

Thirdly, as the Lord now prepared His head and His entire body to be delivered, the disciples realized that it is all over: O Peter, He is going to die! As soon as He let them, these hungry dogs [see Ps. 21: 17, Vulgate] grabbed Him as if they wanted to tear Him totally apart even in their first attack. As they attacked Him, the disciples fled from the garden.

This imprisonment was so pitiful because among all those scoundrels there was none not full of hatred. What are they up to with this perverted hatred? A person so hateful hates even a dead body and beats or pushes it although it no longer feels anything. However, the Jews do so without any reason. For no one punishes someone so hatefully whom one wants to seize legally for his debts and evil deeds; such a person is punished leniently and reluctantly. Therefore, his pain is that much less. But when it happens out of hate, it hurts beyond measure. Thus the hatred and envy of the Jews against the Lord was most painful, a pain inflicted on Him externally. If it had been for a debt or in mercy, it would have been easy to take. Secondly, the hate of the leaders is even greater yet. Thirdly, the hate of Judas was the greatest [of all] and his concern was that He [Christ] might escape.[37]

The embellishment of the story of Judas within the sermons on Christ's passion had become especially popular from the twelfth century when the 'Judas Legend' came into existence.[38] Staupitz apparently was not untouched by this popular tendency. He continued:

---

[37] Ibid, pp. 57–59.

[38] See B. Wachinger, 'Die Passion Christi und die Literatur', in Haug and Wachinger, *Die Passion Christi, p.* 8.

> O what misery have you seen when watching them all gang up on Him! It was impossible for Him to stay on His feet. He had to fall. O devout Child [Son], your Father deserted you! Here you lie below your enemies: one lies on your neck, the other on your heart. O you strong God, how you must suffer and let this happen to you. The most noble being in heaven and on earth lies here in so much pain. O stop that struggle! It is enough! All participated in this thing, no one wanted to miss it. They shouted: 'Seize the evildoer! Seize Him!' And their leaders, who came with a great crowd, grabbed Him; every one wanted to hurt Him. Look, here He lies, poor Lazarus, tied up and in fetters![39]

At this point in his sermon Staupitz reminded his hearers that 'the Christian Church meditates on His imprisonment at midnight and gives Him thanks and praise'. 'Midnight' refers to the monastic observance of the 'canonical hours'. Staupitz then dramatized Christ's suffering further:

> 'The second aspect [is this]: When the Lord Jesus was imprisoned thus, they took Him first to Annas, and here He suffered the greatest blow on His head. Note: Jesus was bound and a prisoner when they brought Him with a great noise. At times He walked, at times He was dragged. One could see the blood on the stones [in the street, or on the stairs] when they brought Him to Annas and without mercy they jostled Him up the stairs. 'Up, up, we bring you the scoundrel! Hurry, hurry!' And they accused Him of misleading the people with His teaching.[40]

Finally the learned preacher arrived at the scene of Peter's denial which gave him the opportunity to clarify what is meant by the 'rock' as he ventured into an interpretation of Matt 16: 18 ('On this Rock I will build my Church'). In this endeavour he relied on patristic and medieval interpretations.[41] He had the following basic options at his disposal from the theological, exegetical and canon law traditions: the Rock is Christ; the Rock is Faith; or the Rock is Peter. He opted for the first when he concluded his sermon by saying that we must rely 'on Christ alone, who is the Rock'. He led up to this conclusion with a dramatic sequence of rhetorical questions: 'Peter's denial hit the Lord much harder in His heart

---

[39] Schneider-Lastin, *Salzburger Predigten 1512*, p. 59.

[40] Ibid., p. 60.

[41] See J.E. Bigane, III, *Faith, Christ or Peter: Matthew 16:18 In Sixteenth Century Roman Catholic Exegesis* (Washington, DC, 1981). On Augustine's interpretation of Christ as the Rock, see Zumkeller, *Heilslehre*, p. 105, n. 669. An overview of the history of interpreting Matt. 16: 18 is given in F. Posset, '"Rock" and "Recognition": Martin Luther's Catholic Interpretation of "You are Peter and on this rock I will build my Church" (Matthew 16: 18) and the Friendly Criticism from the Point of View of the "Hebrew Truth" by his Confrère, Caspar Amman, "Doctor of the Sacred"', in T. Maschke et al. (eds), *Ad fontes Lutheri: Toward the Recovery of the Real Luther. Essays in Honor of Kenneth Hagen's Sixty-Fifth Birthday* (Milwaukee, WI, 2001), pp. 214–52.

than the Jew hitting Him on His cheek. O Peter, Peter, what are you doing? Are you the rock on whom to build? [No], You are a sick rock up to this day.'[42] He then exclaimed: 'O Peter, Peter, what are you doing to your good God? Why do you dare do this when you are so afraid? Why the devil do you get caught up in bad company!'[43] Staupitz emphasized the graveness of Peter's denial since Peter was not just any ordinary man: 'O how much this [behaviour] hurt the Lord! ... This was not done by an ordinary man, but by a rock of the Church'.[44] Staupitz offered the following explanation for Peter's weakness in the conclusion of his sermon, with words which could not be more Christo-centric: 'The whole world is misled. Peter fell [by denying Christ] in order that no one should think that the church is built on him; and that one might see and recognize that one must build on Christ alone, who is the Rock, and on no one else .... Amen.'[45] With this Christo-centric interpretation of the 'rock' Staupitz simply followed the teachings of outstanding members of his own Order including Egidio da Roma, Jacobus de Viterbo and Blessed Simon Fidati de Cascia, who drew their understanding from Augustine's *Retractationes*.[46]

In Sermon 6 of this *cyclus* of 12 sermons, Staupitz featured the accusations and the mistreatment of Christ and his salfivic 'sweetness' by becoming a prisoner and by his suffering. 'O you beautiful Son of God, how mistreated you are!' 'See your Lord stand there, see your God and Saviour!' 'The righteous God is silent like a lamb.' Perhaps Staupitz had been mindful of his younger friend Luther whom he had directed to the meditation of Christ's suffering,[47] when he now shared his personal conviction with his Salzburg audience, in concluding this sermon:

> I truly believe that the person who really seeks God will never have a saddened heart. Penetrate that suffering! Float in on the water of compassion [with Christ], and enter into the troubled mind [of Christ], and into the heart of God [Christ] .... Do not stop until you reach the most sweet Godhead! .... Truly, you must not blind-fold your eyes, but open them up and fix them on the suffering of Christ.
> He who only devours and does not chew the passion of Christ finds it bitter and hard. Bite into it, and it will become sweet to you.

---

[42] 'Ain kranker fels pistu auf den tag ...' (Schneider-Lastin, *Salzburger Predigten 1512*, p. 62).

[43] Ibid., p. 63.

[44] Ibid., p. 63.

[45] 'Die ganz welt ist verfüert; das man nit gedächt, auf Petre stuendt die kirchen, darumb ist er auch gefallen, das man säch und erkent, das alain auf Christum, den fels, zu pauen ist und sünst auf nimet' (ibid., p. 64).

[46] See ibid., pp. 68–70.

[47] 'Sed Staupicius meus dicebat: Man mus den man ansehen, der da heyst Christus. Staupicius hat die doctrinam angefangen' (*WATR* 1. 245 (no. 526); *LW* 54. 97).

It can happen that a person lives through the years and does not realize the sweetness of Christ's suffering; as he does not chew on it and does not really deal with it and recognize all its parts. One does not harvest much fruit, if one wants to contemplate twenty pieces or the entire passion within one hour. That is not worth much. You should bite into it, and take it piece by piece and chew it well, one after the other; then you will find the bitterness of suffering in the body; [you will find] the hard shell [to be cracked] in the soul as you fulfill the Father's will; you will find the kernel of sweetness and mercy in the divinity. [God's] Mercy is so great and so sweet that He cannot reject anybody who asks for grace .... Amen.[48]

This sixth sermon testifies to Staupitz's conviction that human understanding of God's mercy is completely dependent on the meditation of Christ's passion. Thus, Staupitz's spirituality is not so much the product of any scholastic school of thought, but rather it rests on the tradition which became prominent with Bernard of Clairvaux and which focused on the wounds of Christ. Staupitz shared such devotional theology with his confrère Johann von Paltz and his sermons on *The Heavenly Mine*, an edition of which featured coloured illustrations of the passion of Christ, especially the five wounds of Christ.[49]

With Sermon 7 Staupitz led his audience to the scene of Christ's transfer from Caiphas to Pilate. Here the preacher repeatedly spoke of the suffering of God and of the 'death of God' (meaning Christ as the second person of the Trinity): 'That God must suffer.' 'God must die' for our salvation, as He is our Saviour (*hailmacher*).[50] In this context Staupitz spoke of 'the Jews' who without remorse disregarded and

---

[48] '... Fürwar, du muest die augen nit zupinten, sundern auftain und stecken in das leiden Christi.'

Der das leiden Christi schlint und nit keut, dem ist es pitter und hert. Peis darein, so wirt es dir süeß. Da get es her, das der mensch lange jar hinget und nit entpfindt der suessikeit des leiden Christi, das ers nit keut und recht fürsich nimt und aller stücklein wol warnimt. Der pringt nit vil frucht, der in einer stund zwainzig stückel oder das ganz leiden wil betrachten. Das ist nichts wert. Ir sült wol dareinpeissen, und nembt klaine pisel und keuts wol, ains nach dem andern, so fint ir im leib pitrikait des leiden, in der sel ligt die hert schal: den väterlichen willen volpringen, in der gothait den kern der süessikait und erparmung. Die parmherzigkeit ist so gros und so süess, das si niemant verzeichen mag, der pitt umb genad. Wann die spaichel euch rain machen werden, so wirt euch eur leiden, eur unlust süess zu tragen. Darzue helf uns got. Amen' (ibid, pp. 71f.); part of this text is quoted in H.A. Oberman, '"Tuus sum, salvum me fac." Augustinreveil zwischen Renaissance und Reformation', in C.P. Mayer and W. Eckermann (eds), '*Scientia Augustiniana.' Studien über Augustinus, den Augustinismus und den Augustinerorden. Festschrift P. Dr. theol. Dr. phil. Adolar Zumkeller OSA zum 60. Geburtstag* (Würzburg, 1975), pp. 349–94 (p. 380, n. 119).

[49] See Paltz, *Werke 3, Opuscula*, ed. C. Burger et al. (Berlin and New York, 1989), col. pl. 2. On the Bernardine matrix of the devotion to the wounds of Christ, see S.F. Chen, 'Bernard's Prayer Before the Crucifix That Embraced Him: Cistercians and Devotions to the Wounds of Christ', *CSQ*, **29** (1994), pp. 23–54.

[50] See Schneider-Lastin, *Salzburger Predigten 1512*, pp. 74f.

'killed' the Saviour of the world. The Jews, Staupitz said, have sinned more severely than Pilate who was a righteous man at first, but who lacked insight. He was also afraid of them; they were downright wicked. If Pilate had had as much insight as the Jews, he would certainly not have condemned Jesus. He washed his hands. With this thought Staupitz ended Sermon 7 rather abruptly.

The tendency to excuse Pilate and to blame the Jews was carried over into Sermon 8. Staupitz even conceded that Pilate recognized Christ's kingdom as spiritual and not as temporal. To Staupitz the Jews were learned in the law, but did not keep it, and are therefore 'damned'. By contrast, Herod was a fool who only wanted to see new miracles and tricks. When Staupitz spoke of 'the Jews', he had the contemporaries of Jesus in mind, and not the Jews of his own times. One has the impression that Staupitz used the stereotypes of 'the Jews' as 'dogs' and 'swine', or the 'poisoned will of the Jews' and related denigrating labels as the dark foil from which Christ's tremendous suffering was to shine forth, as this was really the centre of his attention. Yet, these labels were not exclusively used for 'the Jews' since he also called the Romans 'dogs' who contributed to Christ's torture. The use of the term 'swine' for 'the Jews' occurred only once in the 1512 sermons and was not much elaborated on. His use of 'the Jews' was probably not unavoidable. Therefore, an evangelical, theological anti-Judaism does not appear to be essential to Staupitz's theological thinking. 'The Jews' did not occupy a central place in his sermonizing. He did not want to thematize 'the Jews' at all, as he had indicated in his opening sermon. It would be a mistake simply to declare Staupitz's thinking anti-Judaistic. The topic of 'the Jews' in Staupitz's sermons is more complex than that; for example, he spoke of Judas's hatred being greater than the Jews' hatred, and Peter's denial being more cruel than the Jew hitting Jesus.[51]

In Sermon 9, Staupitz repeated his favourable view of Pilate, but now also added his displeasure. He spoke of the 'Synagogue' as the 'whore' (*püebin*) who crowned Jesus with the crown of thorns.[52] The Jews remained the wicked ones,[53] because they demanded Christ's execution; however, Jesus himself was even more eager to be crucified than the Jews who wanted his crucifixion.[54] Staupitz's main concern was not to instigate hatred of 'the Jews' but to foster spiritual values which he

---

[51] See ibid., pp. 75–85; and on the opening sermon, see ibid., p. 29.

[52] Ibid., p. 90.

[53] 'O du pöser jud! Pilatus gibt dir zu erkennen, das dein natur ist herter dann ain swein; das hat erparmung mit seiner natur...' (ibid., p. 91). H.A. Oberman, *The Roots of Anti-Semitism in the Age of Renaissance and Reformation*, trans. J.I. Porter (Philadelphia, 1984), p. 137 is mistaken when he assumes that his source proof is found in 'Sermon X' (it is Sermon 9).

[54] See Schneider-Lastin, *Salzburger Predigten 1512*, p. 93.

summarized at the end of Sermon 8 as follows: (1) Do not pay too much attention to persecution, nor to praise. (2) Value any suffering and distress as much as any luck you may have. (3) 'The sweetness of my Godhead will teach you that death will taste better to you than life .... Lift up your heart toward the mercy of God. Then, the foolishness will become sweeter to you than any wisdom.'[55]

Finally at the end of Sermon 9 the preacher reiterated the spiritual goal which we are to reach (without any trace of anti-Judaism):

> Learn to enjoy in God all your suffering and sorrows. Bitterness is already taken out of [suffering] so that you may taste the divine sweetness. From all [of Christ's] veins and bones his divine blood, which has the taste of the divine mercy, flows out. Nowhere [on his body] is there any wound or opening that would be too small to enter. So enter in and advance to the soul [of Christ] and through his soul to his divinity. There you shall taste and try his most sweet mercy. God may grant this to me and to you. Amen.[56]

With Sermon 10 Staupitz took his listeners on to the *via dolorosa*, the way of the cross. In this context he stated that no human virtue can help the heathens to gain eternal life. Rather, both pagans and Jews will be drawn to Christ once he is lifted up (see John 12: 32).[57] It is the sinfulness of both pagans and Jews that called for Christ's atoning suffering and death. With this theological concern about the sinfulness of all humanity (gentiles and Jews) Staupitz displayed a genuine Augustinian theology here. He did not hold the death of Christ up against the Jews, but against every human being. He also retained the Augustinian view of the Jews which stands in contrast to the view developed by the Dominican friars in Spain from the late thirteenth century who began to look at them in a new way by treating them like heretics.[58] Staupitz may have acerbated

---

[55] Ibid., p. 87.

[56] 'Lernt euch freuen in got in allen peinen und leiden; es ist alle pitrikait herausgezogen, auf das ir die götlich süessichait mügt smecken. Da fleust aus allen adern und painen das götlich pluet heraus, das smeckt nach der götlichen parmherzikait. Es ist nindert ain so klains wündlein noch löchlein, du mügst wol dadurch eintringen zu der sel und durch die sel zu der gothait. Da soltu smecken und kosten die allersüessisten parmherzikait. Das verleich mir und euch got. Amen' (ibid., pp. 94f).

[57] See ibid., pp. 97f.

[58] On Augustine and medieval anti-Judaism, see B. Blumenkranz, *Die Judenpredigt Augustins. Ein Beitrag zur Geschichte der jüdisch-christlichen Beziehungen in den ersten Jahrhunderten* (Basel, 1946), pp. 190–95; A. Funkenstein, 'Basic Types of Christian Anti-Jewish Polemics in the Later Middle Ages', *Viator*, 2 (1971), pp. 373–82; J. Cohen, *The Friars and the Jews. The Evolution of Medieval Anti-Judaism* (Ithaca, NY, and London, 1982); Cohen, 'The Jews as the Killers of Christ in the Latin Tradition', *Traditio*, 40 (1983), pp. 1–32; T. Rasmussen, 'Jacob Perez of Valencia's "Tractatus Contra Judeos" (1484) in the Light of Medieval Anti-Judaic Traditions' in K. Hagen (ed.), *Augustine, the Harvest and Theology (1300–1650)* (Leiden, 1990), p. 41.

anti-Judaistic feelings, however, when he dealt with the strange concept of the two flagellations of Christ. In perhaps following Jean Gerson he assigned the first scourging to the Romans and the second to the 'damned Jews'.[59] The biblical texts (Matt. 27: 26; John 19: 1) mention only Pilate, a Roman, as having ordered a flagellation.

Staupitz invited his audience to follow Christ on the way to Calvary. Where Christ met the women, including his mother, he addressed them and took on their suffering, too, as an embellishment has it, in following Bernard of Clairvaux and Ludolf of Saxony.[60] Staupitz reiterated the typology of Abraham and Isaac who prefigured God the Father and the Son; however, while Isaac was saved, Christ was not because there was no one else to take his place in suffering. Staupitz added a further spiritual explanation as he interpreted the meaning of mixing wine and gall that was offered to Jesus on the cross. The mixture stands for the fact of life that rarely is anything done for the exclusive praise of God. Often things are done in a self-serving way. Then God becomes more bitter than gall. Only if one seeks God, and God alone, does God become 'sweet'. Once you leave yourself, you will find out what God is.[61] Staupitz concluded his sermon by saying that Christ wanted to die for all of us who constitute his spiritual Bride; 'so that my Bride will be saved soon'.[62]

In his penultimate sermon, speaking about the crucifixion, Staupitz made three points. First, Christ's sacrifice is the unique offer to the heavenly Father. This first point is subdivided into several aspects of the process of the crucifixion, noting the number of nails used, and that Christ's feet were nailed one over the other (according to the ecclesiastical tradition); only three nails were used supposedly in order to increase Christ's pain, because 'the Jews' wanted him to be attached the more painful way.[63] Christ's body was stretched until the bones cracked noisily and could not be stretched any further. He was stretched as one stretches sweet-sounding music strings: 'From this [cross] sounds the sweet voice of God.'[64] ('Sweet' means 'salvific' here as it usually does

---

[59] See Schneider-Lastin, *Salzburger Predigten 1512*, pp. 96–9; and on Staupitz borrowing the concept of two flagellations from Jean Gerson, see ibid., p. 96, n. 3. Staupitz also employed the concept of two chastisements again in his Salzburg Sermon 10 of 1520.

[60] See Schneider-Lastin, *Salzburger Predigten 1512*, pp. 102f. with n. 49 (on the possible backdrop as provided by Ludolf and Bernard).

[61] 'Geistlich:... Got ist nichts süess, du suechest in dann alain. Erst entpfindest du, was got ist, so du dich selbs verläst' (ibid., pp. 104f).

[62] Ibid., p. 106.

[63] See ibid., p. 107.

[64] 'Sie haben darnach strick angelegt an hendt und füess und also erpärmlich zogen, das alles das kracht hat und zertent ist, das kain saiten nimer also ausgespant wirt als di süess lautent saiten, daraus erklingt di süess stim gots' (ibid., pp. 107f).

in Staupitz's sermons.) 'Here the living book [the crucified Christ] is stretched out; in it is written the salvation for the soul.'[65] Staupitz probably borrowed the image of 'book' (then made of stretched material) for Christ from Suso's *Book of Eternal Wisdom,* or perhaps from Paltz.[66] Still as part of the first point, Staupitz invited the audience to fix their eyes on the cross and to be thankful to God.[67] In a colloary passage, he explained that 'paradise' is being moistened from the fountain which is the heart of Christ. Having shed his blood for all, Christ claims that all sinners are his property according to the Father's decision.[68]

Staupitz's second point was that the atmosphere was poisoned and filled with blasphemers like the one who was hanging next to Christ, while Jesus, as the patient lamb, was silent.[69] When this blaspheming was going on, Christ turned to the one at his right who felt 'in a blink of the eye the divine sweetness'.[70] Again Staupitz mentioned the Father's decree that Christ has the right, based on the merits of his passion, to claim the sinner as his property, who thus becomes safe with Christ. Here the Bernardine thought that Christ earned the right to heaven (*ius ad coelum*) for the sinners may have been influential.[71]

The third point which Staupitz made concerned the persons under the cross; the suffering 'Mother of God', Mary Magdalene, and John. Probably in leaning on the idea of the three stages of the spiritual life in Bernard's introductory sermons on the Canticle with the topic 'Let him kiss me with the kiss of his mouth', Staupitz declared that Mary, his mother, kissed Jesus on his 'mouth of sweetness', the disciple John yearned to rest on the breast of his love, while Mary Magdalene kissed the feet of his mercy.[72] Bernard had explained the 'spiritual kiss' as follows: sinners and converts in their early stage, like Magdalene, are granted the kiss on his feet. Those who are advanced in spiritual love may kiss Christ's hand (Staupitz substituted the kiss on the hand with

---

[65] 'Da ist das lebentig puech gots ausgespant, darinn das hail der sel geschriben stet' (ibid., p. 108).

[66] See Tobin, *Henry Suso,* p. 217 (ch. 3); Paltz, 'Die himlische funtgrub', *Werke,* III, p. 228.

[67] See Schneider-Lastin, *Salzburger Predigten 1512,* p. 108.

[68] 'Die sünder sind rechtlich all dein' (ibid., p. 109).

[69] See ibid., p. 110.

[70] 'In im ainen plick der götlichen süessichait' (ibid., p. 111).

[71] On the story about St Bernard with its characteristic phrase *ius ad caelum,* as found in *The Golden Legend* and taken up by both Staupitz and Luther, see Posset, 'St Bernard's Influence on Two Reformers: John von Staupitz and Martin Luther', *CSQ,* **25** (1990), pp. 175–87.

[72] 'mund der süessichait .... füess der parmherzikait ... Johannes lust nach meiner prust der lieb' (Schneider-Lastin, *Salzburger Predigten 1512,* p. 113).

John's resting on Christ's breast), while only the perfected ones may receive the kiss of the mouth.[73] This perfect person is Mary.

With the last sermon for that season (Sermon 12) Staupitz returned to his initial theme of 'departure'. In Christ's leaving (*abschid*) we find our salvation, consolation and joy. Again, as always, Staupitz followed the threefold pattern that he employed in these sermons by utilizing a medieval homiletic device. His Point 1 dealt with the aversion of all nature against the suffering which the Saviour had to endure. He developed this point in seven subsections, stating that 'nature by itself cannot achieve anything on its own', and does not want to tolerate that its creator has to suffer so much. The sun in the sky even objected to the hiddenness of the 'Light of the world' and to the 'darkening of the eternal sun'.[74]

In Point 2 he explained the death of Christ as His departure from his human 'nature' as He yearned for the salvation of all. When He cried out, 'My God, my God, why have you forsaken me', all creatures and the devils were terrified; even 'the lions and the elephants became scared'.[75] In seven subsections he explained himself: first, there was the 'departure' or 'separation' of Christ's soul from his mind. The upper part of His soul which is called 'the spirit' (*Geist*) still enjoyed the vision of the highest Godhead as this part did not suffer, but had the enjoyment of God'. Here the Augustinian *frui deum* (enjoy God) was at work. Only the lower part of the soul experienced pain and sorrow. However, there was communication between these contradictory experiences.[76] Staupitz articulated here in the vernacular the most speculative Christological dogma and the communication of the idioms of Christ's two natures in one person. Second, Christ left his soul in suffering. This explains His highest sadness, as perfect joy creates perfect sadness. Third, there was the departure of His rational consciousness (*vernunft*) caused by all His pain and suffering. One may observe that persons in great pain or on the point of dying often become unconscious. This was not the case with our Lord who, although in the greatest pain, remained with a complete consciousness.[77] The fourth separation refers to the departure of the soul from itself. Staupitz cited here St Paul (2 Cor. 12: 2–4) and St Augustine's mother as examples; Monica was totally beside herself because of (her mystical) *excessus* in 'sweetness'.[78] The fifth departure took place when

---

[73] See Bernard of Clairvaux, *On the Song of Songs*, Sermons 1 to 4, 4 vols (Kalamazoo, MI, 1981), I, p. 1–24.

[74] Schneider-Lastin, *Salzburger Predigten 1512*, pp. 115f.

[75] Ibid., p. 118.

[76] 'Und vor dem leiden haben sich die öbristen kreft in der niessung der gothait auch mittailt oder ausgossen den untristen kreften der sel' (ibid., p. 118).

[77] Ibid., p. 119.

[78] Ibid., pp. 119f.

the Godhead (*gothait*) deserted mankind (*menschait*).[79] The sixth separation concerned virtue and feeling. Staupitz simply asked here the rhetorical question: what good is virtue if one does not feel it in effective grace? On the final part of his second major point, Staupitz said that the Saviour was left without *rue* (contemporary German: *Ruhe*, here in the sense of 'composure') as He who is the 'fountain of living water' became very thirsty and cried for water. It was His thirst for the salvation of the 'bride's soul' (that is, all humanity).

The preacher then invited his listeners to open their 'inner ears', to lift up their hearts, and to realize the 'final departure and struggle' of the Lord.[80] With this thought Staupitz arrived at the third major point of his last sermon, the culmination of all his sermonizing: the great victorious 'encounter', or 'hit', or 'blow' (all of which meanings are comprised in Staupitz's vernacular expression *treffen*). It is the encounter between the Lord and death, the devil, and the world. The victory is already won, when the Lord said 'it is finished'. In this 'last, lordly' final encounter or blow, the death of heart, hands, feet, eyes, mouth, and the entire body occurs. The hands and feet which are nailed down are no longer usable for the battle. The heart alone is able to do battle. Now his death has swallowed up death (a paraphrase of 1 Cor. 15: 54f.), so that miserable man may enter eternal life.[81]

Staupitz then shifted his attention to Mary under the cross. He spoke to her directly, saying that normally a mother's heart would have been broken by now. However, Mary inwardly was filled with divine consolation, since 'God is in you'. Staupitz explained this as follows: 'Her spirit always enjoyed the sweetness' [of God's presence] as much as this is possible for a human being. 'And thus her highest and her lowest powers [of the soul and mind] were always filled with divine sweetness.'[82] Staupitz reiterated this thought and in doing so made it plain that 'sweetness' means spiritual consolation: 'In her sorrows under the cross, her soul was never deserted by the spirit, and therefore her soul and spirit were totally filled with divine consolation and sweetness.'[83]

From focusing on Mary, Staupitz then turned to his audience and addressed each individual with 'you' in the singular (*du*), in his typical form of address:

---

[79] Ibid., p. 120.

[80] 'Tuet di innern oren auf, erhebt eur herz und merkt den lesten abschid und streit meins herren' (ibid., p. 121).

[81] Ibid., pp. 121f.

[82] (On Mary): 'Und in dem sind ir öbrist kreft und nidrist kreft alweg erfült gewesen götlicher süessichait' (ibid., p. 122).

[83] Ibid., p. 123.

Be happy now, you devout soul, this is the day that the Hero has dealt the final blow, and the spear is broken. Remember today the seven aspects of this encounter which benefited you. Remember this sentence: first, you are allowed to be free from all judges except for the judge of mercy, because now the hellish judgment is broken. Miserable sinner, make your appeal before *your* Jesus on the cross. If you run to him, it is impossible that you would not be granted mercy. Second, the miserable human nature is placed above all the angels. Third, see what today God has achieved for you in His *treffen* [encounter]: His passion is better than His action. He does passion better, and it tastes better to Him than virtue. It has come to this today, and you should teach this to your children: it is more pleasing to God that you patiently suffer what He loads upon you than that you fulfill what He commands you. Today, suffering was lifted up and honoured. Fourth, the failures in virtue become fruitful. What would all our virtuous actions be, if they were not made fruitful by the power of Christ's passion! Fifth, with the *treffen* on the cross today, the Lord earned what the heavenly Father bestowed on him [thinking of Phil. 2: 9f.]: a name that is above every other name, so that at his name every knee must bend, that is in heaven, on earth, and in hell. Nothing is more honoured in heaven or on earth. Sixth, today He made it so that nothing will be more honoured than the cross. Today, death is better than life, as St Paul says [see Phil. 1: 21]: Life is good, but dying is better to me. Therefore, death is sweeter than life, and in death we enter life .... Seventh, what is given to us in this *treffen* is this: misery and poverty are now better than paradise. This we received through the death of Christ. Write this on your heart: before He departed, His heart had to be broken once more.[84]

Now, having covered Christ's salvific departure in all its aspects, Staupitz turned the spotlight to the soldier with the legendary name, Longinus, who was saved according to the legend which Staupitz told here. He connected this to the motif of the cross as the 'Book of Life' which he mentioned for the second time at this point:

Longinus, that blind man, had come and pierced the sacred heart. Water and blood ran down his shaft and hit him in the eyes, and he came to see and recognized that this was the true God. Longinus, poke into it and see: Christ is dead! Be a true witness that God who is the highest good is dead. From now on, the cross is no more a disgrace, but instead is an honour. 'We now preach nothing but Christ Crucified' [1 Cor. 1: 23]. He is the 'Book of Life'. Devout soul, you do well when you read in this book! If [the reading in this book] is not to your taste, turn the page, rip open the wounds, but not in the way of causing pain as the Jews did, but in love so that you may draw from it the sweetness of God. May God grant this to me and to you. Amen.[85]

---

[84] Ibid., pp. 123f.

[85] 'Was predigen wir nun mer dann Christum, den gekreuzigten? Er ist das puech des leben. Andechtige sel, erlis dich wol in disem puech! Wil es dir nit smecken, wirf die plätel

Staupitz here said the same as Henry Suso once did in contemplating the divine suffering, that Christ's life 'is a living book' in which 'is found everything that is necessary for salvation'.[86] Staupitz must have liked this image of the crucified Christ as 'The Book of Life' so much that he elaborated on it again in a sermon in 1523, when he compared the 'skin of Christ' to the stretched-out parchment of 'The Book of Life'.[87]

In reviewing these sermons in the vernacular of 1512, the earliest ones that we have from Staupitz, several points may be noted by way of summary. Good preaching enjoyed great esteem in late medieval cities; it demanded much more of a priest than simply the ability to mumble his way through the missal. Doctors of theology usually assumed the responsibility of preaching in the vernacular, as was the case here with Staupitz. His sermons provide an indication of the religious situation of that time. We see a lively preacher with a genuine religiosity. This is a picture at odds with the simplistic but popular myth of the total absence of pastoral care and preaching in all the German-speaking lands. In effect it is no longer possible to generalize and claim that there was nothing but eccesiastical decadence and deformation at that time. Lack of good preaching may have been true for many rural areas in Europe, but not for the imperial cities and cultural centres in the German-speaking lands where great pride was taken in creating endowment funds for preaching positions. There were abuses, it is true, and Staupitz and others pointed them out; however, it would be a mistake to brand everything at that time as corrupt and abuse-ridden, deformed and decayed.

Staupitz's sermons of 1512 demonstrate the high quality of preaching on the passion of Christ. They support what has been pointed out by scholars like A. Zumkeller concerning late-medieval sermon literature,

---

herumb, reis auf die wunden, nit in pein weis als die juden, sunder in lieb, das du heraus wellest ziechen die süessichait der gotthait. Das verleich mir und euch got. Amen' (ibid., p. 125); Steinmetz, *Misericordia Dei*, p. 126, n. 3.

[86] 'Es ist doch ein lebendig buch …' (Bihlmeyer, *Deutsche Schriften*, p. 256); Tobin, *Henry Suso*, p. 250. Suso also in his *Horologium*: 'Velut quidam liber vitae, in quo omnia saluti necessaria inveniuntur' (P. Künzle (ed.), *Horologium* (Fribourg, Switzerland, 1977), p. 494); see Posset, 'The Sweetness of God', pp. 157–9. Suso's eternal wisdom says: 'In the school of wisdom this is the beginning that one reads from the open, outstretched book of my crucified body' (Bihlmeyer, *Deutsche Schriften*, p. 209; Tobin, *Henry Suso*, p. 217).

[87] *Die Haut Christi* ('the skin of Christ'), as found in Jeremias, *Johannes Staupitz*, pp. 239f. In handwriting it is hard to distinguish between *Haut* and *Hand*. I suspect that Staupitz spoke of *Haut* ('skin') in following Suso. R.K. Markwald, *A Mystic's Passion: The Spirituality of Johannes von Staupitz in his 1520 Lenten Sermons. Translation and Commentary* (New York, 1990), pp. 102 and 120 (Sermon 4) and p. 147 (Sermon 5), points out that the *Codex Salzburgensis b* V8 has 'skin' instead of 'hand' in the 1520 Sermons 4 and 5.

namely that excellent sermons were being delivered which were Christ-centred and also fostered the spirituality of the imitation of Christ, without any emphasis on human merits or righteousness acquired through good works. These 1512 sermons also include some critical thoughts about ecclesiastical leadership. They were delivered not to a select or academic audience, but to the general population of one of the most important ecclesiastical centres north of the Alps, Salzburg. Evidently Staupitz's sermons in the vernacular were perceived as so significant that the local Benedictine nuns were prompted to make special efforts to record and preserve them. Staupitz's fifth sermon, in particular, demonstrates one of the various Catholic possibilities of interpreting Matt. 16: 18 at that time; that Christ alone remains the 'Rock' in whom we are to trust.

In these sermons Jesus was often spoken of as 'God'. The medieval concept of the 'three natures' of Christ (body, soul, divinity) was a characteristic of these sermons, as was Staupitz's proclamation of the 'sweetness of God' in Christ. Yet, his Christ-centredness also tolerated fine thoughts about the Virgin Mary. In his attempt to remain close to the 'text' or the biblical 'story', the preacher was still medieval inasmuch as he drew upon legendary material to embellish the biblical text. The preacher attempted an actualization of the story of the passion by speaking of 'bishops' when he was talking about the leaders of the Jews.[88] With this modernization some criticism of the contemporary scene may have entered Staupitz's sermons as he had a clear concept of a bishop's duties which, however, he did not find realized in his own days.

These sermons displayed an anti-Judaistic tendency which was especially strong when the preacher contended that 'the Jews' were responsible for not only one, but two flagellations of Christ. Having said this, one may state that Staupitz's sermons have to be scrutinized not only in regards to what he said, but also in regards to what he did not say. His later sermons (in 1520) on the same subject – with the reduced use of the cliché of the vicious Jews – indicate that he did not necessarily need this stereotype for the enforcement of the message of the Gospel. Staupitz's derogatory use of 'the Jews' was not essential for his theology and was thus not 'unavoidable'; it has more the character of a rhetorical tool. Staupitz's God-centred spirituality has God in absolute control, as the heavenly Father who is ready to have the Son sacrificed for all. Staupitz affirmed Christ's saying: 'When I am lifted up' on the cross, 'I will draw every one to myself', heathens and Jews (Sermon 10). As an Augustinian friar, Staupitz displayed here a certain faithfulness to

---

[88] See Posset, 'Preaching the Passion of Christ', pp. 290f. where the translation of the entire relevant passage from Sermon 5 is given.

Augustine's general theological view of all humans as sinners in need of salvation. The universality of sin calls for the universality of salvation through Christ's death on the cross – for all the world, both gentiles and Jews.

At the end of his stay at Salzburg in the spring of 1512, Staupitz, on behalf of his Order, entered a prayer contract with a second group of Salzburg Benedictine nuns, those of the nearby Nonnberg Abbey. Applicants had to be of noble birth in order to be accepted there. This cloister had always been wealthy, as it was supported by the nobility, and Staupitz must have been very aware of these circumstances. The prayer contract is documented and dated 9 April 1512, and is signed by him. The practice of signing prayer contracts between the Benedictines of Salzburg and the friars of the Augustinian Order had originated more than a century earlier when such agreements were made between the Bavarian province of the Augustinians and the Nonnberg Abbey in 1377 and with St Peter's Abbey in 1399. It appears that Staupitz revived these old connections. This contract of 1512 is of particular interest insofar as it lists Staupitz's three professional roles at that time: professor of the Bible (at Wittenberg, held until the autumn of 1512); provincial of the Augustinian Order's province of Thuringia and Saxony (held until May 1512); and vicar general of the German Reformed Congregation of the Augustinian Order (held until 1520). The prayer contract covered more than 50 Augustinian friaries.[89]

On preparing to die as a disciple of Christ: Staupitz's first publication in German (1515)

Staupitz probably preached exclusively in German from 1512 on, if not earlier. The subject of Christian discipleship had an important place in his theology and preaching. Many of his sermons ended with an exhortation to look to Christ as the model for the believer's action. Staupitz connected the topic of discipleship to the traditional subject of the art of dying, as is evident in his book *Ein büchlein von der nachfolgung des willigen sterbens Christi* ('A booklet on discipleship of

---

[89] 'Frater Joannes de Staupitz, divinar[um] litterar[um] humilis professor, Thuringiae et Saxoniae ordinis fratr[um] Eremitar[um] S[ancti] Augustini Prior provincialis ac sacrae unionis reformatae per Allemaniam eiusdem ordinis Ap[osto]lica auctoritate generalis vicarius' (F. Esterl, *Chronik des adeligen Benediktiner-Frauen-Stiftes Nonnberg in Salzburg* (Salzburg, 1841), p. 90, n. 1; as quoted in Schneider-Lastin, *Salzburger Predigten 1512*, p. 5 with n. 18); see J. Sallaberger, 'Johann von Staupitz, Abt von St. Peter (1522–1524) und die Salzburger Mendikantentermineien', *Studien und Mitteilungen zur Geschichte des Benediktinerordens und seiner Zweige*, 93 (1982), pp. 218–69 (p. 143).

Christ in accepting death'). Staupitz's text may be the result of reflections in two phases: the first during the years around 1512; the second during the summer of 1515.[90] Dedicated to the Countess Agnes of Mansfeld, it was published at Leipzig in 1515, with a second edition appearing in 1523. This first work published under his name was clearly intended to reach a wide audience as it was written in German. Staupitz was concerned about being understood in both upper and lower Germany, both regions having their own differing dialects. The reprint of 1523 displayed a greater linguistic uniformity than the first edition, and regional expressions were now avoided.[91] Staupitz's references to religious authorities of the past also diminished and he progressively inclined toward the principle of 'Scripture alone' as his biblical quotations demonstrate. In the 1523 edition, the names of authorities were omitted, while the biblical references (especially to St Paul) increased. This drift toward Pauline theology would be observed and reflected also by the Nurembergers in their reactions to his sermons of the following year. To them Staupitz was 'the disciple of Paul', even the 'voice of Paul'.[92] This booklet was published in eight editions altogether from the sixteenth to the twentieth century.

For Staupitz, the imitation of Christ was more than mere outward action. It was a disciple's way of life that draws upon God's fullness and shares it with others. One may ask whether his book was more concerned with discipleship in suffering (as Steinmetz viewed it in 1968) or with the individual's preparation for dying (*ars moriendi*). Part V of the book may corroborate its classification as *ars moriendi* literature; however, Staupitz did not concentrate exclusively on the hour of death.

Luther published a similar book, *On Preparing to* Die, printed by the same press, four years later. A comparison between Staupitz's book and Luther's shows that both differ from traditional works on this subject. However, quite unlike Luther, Staupitz did not refer to the sacraments (confession, communion, anointing) when it comes to dying.[93] Whatever

---

[90] *Ein büchlein von der nachfolgung des willigen sterbens Christi.* This text was supposed to appear in Vol. 3, *Deutsche Schriften 1,* of the new critical edition but this has not yet been published. The text was first published in Knaake (ed.), *Sämmtliche Werke,* pp. 51–88. See also A. Endriss, 'Nachfolgung des willigen Sterbens Christi. Interpretation des Staupitztraktates von 1515 und Versuch einer Einordnung in den frömmigkeits-geschichtlichen Kontext', in J. Nolte et al., *Kontinuität und Umbruch,* pp. 93–141. See also the Introduction in Staupitz, I. 6.

[91] See C. Fasola, *Die Sprache des Johann Staupitz. I. Lautlehre* (Philosophical dissertation, Marburg, 1892).

[92] 'Alii Pauli discipulum immo linguam, alii euangelii praeconem', Soden and Knaake, *Christoph Scheurl's Briefbuch,* no. 114.

[93] See Endriss, 'Nachfolgung', pp. 101f.

the main genre of Staupitz's book, the purpose of writing it was pastoral in nature; it was intended as spiritual consolation.

Father George Spalatin (1484–1545), a secular priest, who had become the tutor of the sons of Frederick the Wise in 1509, then the prince's librarian, court chaplain, private secretary and confidant, understood Staupitz's book as a contribution to the art of dying. It must have been in his role as confidant and spiritual adviser, that, in May 1517, he asked Luther, who apparently was known as Staupitz's literary agent, for a copy of it. Luther had distributed all of the copies which he himself had available, except his own, which he was ready to lend to Spalatin. In a letter of 8 May 1519 Luther recommended the booklet as a work 'on imitating Christ's death' (*Staupitii libellus de imitanda morte Christi*). He admitted that Staupitz did a better job than he had managed with his own sermon on this topic, which he published in November 1519.[94]

In terms of content Staupitz turned directly to Augustine and Gerson. The latter had written 'On the art of dying' (*De arte moriendi*); which may have given this genre its name.[95] Thus it is not surprising that Staupitz, already fond of Gerson, used his work in this regard, too. Staupitz included Gerson's and Augustine's considerations on original sin and on the three deaths of a human being. Original sin is innate sin which is almost man's nature, although God created human beings in his image. Staupitz, however, did not explain his view as to whether concupiscence is to be understood as an essential part of original sin or as its consequence. In any case, because of Adam's sinful disobedience, all humans live a miserable life which – speaking with Augustine – should rather be called a long process of dying. Death of the body occurs when the soul departs; death of the soul, when deserted by God; the death of both when the deserted soul departs from the body. Staupitz

---

[94] 'De Arte Moriendi [ut te vocas] hoc unum pro me habeo, omnia alia sunt distributa' (Luther's letter to Spalatin of May 1517; *WABR* 1. 96, 5f. (no. 39)). 'Vernaculus ille Staupitii libellus de imitanda morte Christi, In quo & melius [pro dote sua] rem tractavit quam sperem a me tractari posse, donec ociosior fiam' (*WABR* 1. 381 (no. 171)); W. Goez, 'Luthers "Ein Sermon von der Bereitung zum Sterben" und die mittelalterliche ars moriendi', *Lutherjahrbuch*, **48** (1981), pp. 97–114. See *LW* 42. 99–115.

[95] See Knaake (ed.), *Sämmtliche Werke*, pp. 53–5; for the marginalia referring to Augustine in the 1515 edition, see Zumkeller, *Heilslehre*, p. 25, n. 108, also pp. 33–6 and 46; M. Wriedt, 'Staupitz und Augustin: zur Kirchenväterrezeption am Vorabend der Reformation' in L. Grane et al. (eds) *Auctoritas Patrum. Contributions on the Reception of the Church Fathers in the 15th and 16th Century* (Mainz, 1993), pp. 227–57 (pp. 235f.). On Gerson's impact on Staupitz with regard to the understanding of original sin, see Staupitz's Tübingen Sermon 4 (Staupitz, I. 84), where Gerson's *A deo exivit* is quoted in describing human nature as *labilis et prone ad casum et defectum*. Staupitz also made a single reference to the *Summa* of William of Auxerre in the margin of his chapter 5.

found these distinctions in Augustine's *The City of God*. In the margins of the first printing of this text (Leipzig, 1515), a total of seven references to it may be found. One must die to oneself in order to live in Christ and hope in his 'grace alone'.[96] With this Augustinian perspective on sin and grace Staupitz evidently distanced himself from other opinions.

The principle of divisions for these chapters was taken from the words of Christ on the cross or from the events during the crucifixion such as the reactions of the Jews, of the women, and of the disciples under the cross. In Chapters 6 to 15 he dealt with physical dying, trials, and turning to God. When Staupitz spoke of 'merits' he used the opportunity to highlight the principle of 'grace alone'.[97] Using traditional mystical elements, he spoke of the birth of Christ in the soul, and of Christ as the spouse of the individual soul.

Staupitz's Chapter 7 comes very close in content to an anonymous contemporary work with the title *Libellus* on the same subject, with which Henry Suso's *Horologium* or *Little Book of Eternal Wisdom* was incorporated.[98] Staupitz's spiritual affinity to Suso may suggest the possibility that Staupitz himself was its author. Because of its popularity it was printed several times and translated into two German dialects.[99] The themes 'most sweet saviour', 'temptation and predestination', and the reference to 'preaching Christ and him crucified' (1 Cor. 2: 2) appear in both Staupitz's and the anonymous text.

---

[96] See M.A. Schmidt, 'Rechtfertigungslehre in Staupitz' "Nachfolgung" (Korrekturthesen zu Albrecht Endriss)', in Nolte et al., *Kontinuität und Umbruch*, pp. 142–4. Schmidt rightly criticizes Endriss's interpretation of Staupitz's doctrine of justification. and correctly points out that Staupitz used the notion of merit in order to highlight the principle of grace alone. Staupitz must also be seen as a proclaimer of *sola gratia* and *sola fide*.

[97] See M. Brecht, 'Der "Libellus auro praestantior de animae praeparatione in extremo laborantis, deque praedestinatione et tentatione fidei": Eine unbekannte frühe Predigt Luthers?' in G. Hammer and K.-H. zur Mühlen (eds), *Lutheriana. Zum 500. Geburtstag Martin Luthers von den Mitarbeitern der Weimarer Ausgabe* (Cologne and Vienna, 1984), pp. 333–50. On Suso within this anononymous text, see pp. 345–6 with n. 50 and 51.

[98] See ibid., pp. 340f. As Luther never quoted Suso, it is more likely that the author is Staupitz rather than Luther, or some unknown Staupitzian.

[99] See ibid., p. 347. Markus Wriedt questioned both Staupitz's and Luther's authorship of this anonymous booklet, in 'Ist der "Libellus auro praestantior de animae praeparatione in extremo laborantis, deque praedestinatione et tentatione fidei" eine Lutherschrift?', *Lutherjahrbuch*, 54 (1987), pp. 48–83. Brecht was not convinced by Wriedt's arguments and clarified his position further. He now finds a close connection between this *Libellus* and Staupitz's theology (see *Nachfolgung*, ch. 7); see Brecht, 'Zum Problem der Identifizierung namentlich nicht gekennzeichneter Lutherschriften', *Lutherjahrbuch*, 56 (1989), pp. 51–67. I would not exclude Staupitz as a possible author of the text under debate, as Luise Klein also established the connection between Staupitz and this anonymous booklet in her dissertation 'Die Bereitung zum Sterben. Studien zu den frühen reformatorischen Sterbebüchern' (Heidelberg, 1958).

Staupitz's *Ein büchlein von der nachfolgung des willigen sterbens Christi* is not only *ars moriendi* literature, but also a tract on justification![100] The Pauline-Augustinian doctrine of justification is present throughout, and is of central significance. Earlier, in his Tübingen sermons, Staupitz had vilified human merits, saying that all our righteousness is like a soiled cloth (following Isa. 64: 5, 'All our good deeds are like polluted rags'; Sermon 23). Now, in 1515, in his Chapter 11, he used a new and different metaphor for his explanation of the merits of good works: 'A *mensch* [human being] must become like a *weib* [woman] who wants to give birth to the fruits of eternal life.' By this he meant that the divinity is active and must make the passive human soul pregnant through the Holy Spirit in order to give birth to any meritorious works. The devout soul keeps completely non-active if she wants to become 'God's bride, God's child, God's woman'. According to this view, God always remains the author of any human works. Staupitz understood the role of the female as completely passive in the act of conception: 'A woman may receive the male seed, be pregnant with child, nurture [the embryo], and give birth.' The image of female passivity for the proper role of all humans in doing good deeds vis-à-vis God served him quite well also in 1519, when he declared that Christ actively fathers any good works within the human soul, just like in a passive mother whose only role is to receive the seed. She does not act herself.[101]

Moreover, for the proper teaching on the art of dying the concept of 'self-accusation' needed to be brought into focus. Staupitz developed it from thoughts of Augustine and Bernard. Traditionally, the concept of self-condemnation (self-accusation) was closely tied to the doctrine of salvation. Those who judge and condemn themselves do not need to be condemned further by God. Staupitz, who had utilized the concept of self-accusation as early as in his Tübingen sermons,[102] now did so again, in 1515. Here, too, he showed continuity.

As part of his conclusion (in Chapters 14 and 15), Staupitz made use of the then popular legend of St Bernard's dialogue with the devil. Bernard encountered the devil who claimed to have knowledge of several psalm verses which, if prayed daily, would save a person from sudden death. Bernard was eager to learn those verses; however, the devil, in order to tease him, would not reveal them. Bernard then cleverly responded by saying that from now on he would pray the entire psalter every night in order to make sure that the verses in question were

---

[100] See Schmidt, 'Rechtfertigungslehre in Staupitz', pp. 142–4.

[101] 'nuer tragen und nit wurchen' [*wirken*, in modern High German] (Knaake, *Sämmtliche Werke*, p. 78); for the quotation of Staupitz's Sermon 4 of 1519, see Zumkeller, *Heilslehre*, p. 184.

[102] See Staupitz's Tübingen Sermons 20 and 22 (Staupitz, I. 319 and 348).

included in his daily prayers. Astounded by this reaction, the devil revealed them to him, because he did not want Bernard to increase his prayers even more. The celebrated psalm verses read as follows:

> Give light to my eyes
> that I do not fall asleep when dying:
> so my enemy may never say:
> 'I prevailed against him' (12: 4b–5).

> Into your hands I commend my spirit:
> You have redeemed me, O Lord, God of truth (30: 6).

> I was told in my own language:
> Make known to me my end, O Lord.
> And what is the number of my days,
> that I may learn how frail I am (38: 5).

> Grant me a proof of your favour,
> that my enemies may see, to their confusion,
> that you, O Lord, have helped and comforted me (85: 17).

> You have loosed my bonds:
> To you will I offer sacrifice of thanksgiving:
> and I will call upon the name of the Lord (115: 16b–17).

> I have lost all means of escape;
> there is no one who cares for my life.
> I cry out to you, O Lord; I say,
> 'You are my refuge,
> my portion in the land of the living' (141: 5f).[103]

These 'Eight Verses of St Bernard', as this compilation of psalms was known, enjoyed immense popularity. Staupitz did not seem to object to praying them, nor did he ridicule the superstitious use of them, as had Erasmus of Rotterdam in *The Praise of Folly* of 1509.[104] If these verses

---

[103] Knaake, *Sämmtliche Werke*, p. 87. The Latin version of the prayer is found in *WA* 4. 442, n. 1 and in *WA* 55–I.887–79; see F. Posset, *Pater Bernhardus: Martin Luther and Bernard of Clairvaux* (Kalamazoo, MI, 1999), p. 71.

[104] A French prayerbook includes the *Septem versiculi sancti bernardi* (Lyons, 1480/90) with an illustration, shown in the exhibition catalogue edited by Peter Jezler: *Himmel, Hölle, Fegefeuer: Das Jenseits im Mittelalter* (Zürich, 1994), p. 208. The prayer is also found in a prayerbook from Salzburg (or Augsburg?) according to U. Köpf, 'Die Rezeptions- und Wirkungsgeschichte Bernhards von Clairvaux. Forschungsstand und Forschungsaufgaben', in K. Elm (ed.), *Bernhard von Clairvaux: Rezeption und Wirkung im Mittelalter und in der Neuzeit* (Wiesbaden, 1994), p. 62 and illustration 4. The German version speaks of eight verses, as in the laypeople's prayerbook of 1516, *Hortulus animae*, by Johann Koberger; see on this, V. Hasak, *Dr. Martin Luther und die religiöse Literatur seiner Zeit bis zum Jahre 1520* (Regensburg, 1881; reprinted Nieuwkoop, 1967), p. 214. On this and Erasmus' criticism, see Posset, 'Saint Bernard of Clairvaux in the Devotion, Theology, and Art of the Sixteenth Century', *LQ*, 11 (1997) pp. 306–52; pp. 321f. and illustration 6 showing Bernard and the devil discussing certain psalm verses.

helped to achieve inner peace, why not use them? This must have been Staupitz's line of thinking. He had a person's spiritual goal in mind, namely a peaceful heart and inner silence, where one may hear the secret words of God, rather like the mystics of the Middle Ages. Being lifted up one prays: 'O sweet inhabitant of the soul, you most secret friend, give me the silence where nothing is heard except you, and say one word . . . . Such a word nobody can speak but you alone.'[105]

Staupitz concluded his booklet with one of his favourite psalm verses: 'I am yours, save me' (Ps. 118/119: 94; Vulgate: *Tuus sum ego, salvum me fac*), which he recommended to the dying person as the final prayer:

> At the end, all people should do what Christ did, to hand themselves over into the heavenly Father's hands, and say what Christ said: 'Father, into your hands I commend my spirit' or better the spirit which belongs to you, which you commended to me, your own image, your likeness, for whom you shed your blood; into your hands from where nobody can take or rob anything, into your strong hands for protection; into your clement hands for reward, 'for I am yours, save me' [Ps. 118: 94]. Amen.[106]

Staupitz also used this last psalm verse in his letter of 14 November 1516 to Friar Lang,[107] and had it printed on the title-page of both the Latin and the German editions of his Advent sermons of 1516 (published in 1517) to which we will turn our attention in the following section.

Staupitz's book was so highly esteemed by the Franciscan Friar Jacob Vogt, who was the father confessor of Frederick the Wise, that he sent it to Princess Margaret von Anhalt on 29 February 1516. The Benedictine nuns at Salzburg loved it, too. A century later (1618) it was re-edited along with prayers by Eckhart and Tauler. In still later editions, prayers of St Thomas Aquinas and St Brigit were added.[108]

Preaching at Nuremberg on God being sweet for us (Advent 1516), and on free will, discipleship, and conscience (Lent 1517)

Staupitz was in Munich in September 1516, but by November he was in Nuremberg, from where he wrote on 14 November to the humanist Prior

---

[105] See Knaake (ed.), *Sämmtliche Werke*, p. 83; Steinmetz, *Misericordia Dei*, p. 83, n. 3.

[106] Knaake (ed.), *Sämmtliche Werke* (ch. 15), p. 88; Zumkeller, *Heilslehre*, p. 226, mistakenly referred to verse 54; it should read Ps. 118 (119): 94. Oberman, 'Tuus sum ego, salvum me fac', pp. 349–94.

[107] See Kolde, *Die deutsche Augustiner-Congregation und Johann von Staupitz* (Gotha, 1879), p. 307 with n. 2.

[108] See Endriss, 'Nachfolgung des willigen Sterbens Christi', pp. 93–141. On Vogt sending the booklet to the princess, see I. Ludolphy, *Friedrich der Weise. Kurfürst von Sachsen 1463–1525* (Göttingen, 1984), p. 361.

John Lang at Erfurt, asking him for a demonstration of their Order's humanist erudition by writing a letter in Greek and in Latin to the Nuremberg humanist Willibald Pirckheimer, 'so that he finally will acquit our Augustinian congregation of barbarism'.[109] Staupitz wanted his Order to shine in the eyes of the Nuremberg humanists. Monastic humanism had for some time permeated the cloisters of the Augustinians, Benedictines, Carthusians, Carmelites and Dominicans of that city, whose libraries contained numerous examples of contemporary humanist literature (according to the library catalogues that are extant).[110]

We have already noted in his Tübingen sermons some evidence of humanist interests, especially his quotation of the 'Know yourself' axiom in Greek (*gnothi seauton*) in Sermon 23. Staupitz used a Greek notion again (the *tetragrammaton*) and then also a Hebrew one (*messias*) here in the Latin translation of his Advent sermons of 1516. As for his reflections on the Hebrew name of God, he declared that the Hebrew letters YHVH make sense only when read with the Messiah 'Jesus' in mind, as Reuchlin had suggested that these letters need to be complemented by the letter 'S' to make the name YHSVH (that is, JESUS):

> The wise men among the Jews perceived this when they established the truth that no one except the *messias* was allowed to intelligibly pronounce the *tetragrammaton* of God's name, so that the four letters in the foresaid name may not make any completely [good] sense in any word, and would not lead, without the *messias*, to any understanding of what is designated by them.[111]

Thus, Staupitz's concerns in this regard (mixing Greek and Hebrew in his texts in some sort of humanist mannerism) show him as a 'hybrid', open to contemporary humanism without being a humanist philologist himself. He was a biblical humanist *in nuce*; yet he was not a skilled trilingual scholar. The humanist Conradus Mutianus (1470–1526)

---

[109] 'Illi scribas graece et latine qui tandem August[ini]anam nostram congregationem absoluat omni modo barbaria' (Staupitz's letter of 14 November 1516 to Lang, as edited in Kolde, *Die deutsche Augustiner-Congregation*, pp. 439–40); see R. Wetzel, 'Staupitz antibarbarus. Beobachtungen zur Rezeption heidnischer Antike in seinen Tübinger Predigten' in A. Mehl and W.C. Schneider (eds) *Reformatio et reformationes. Festschrift für Lothar Graf zu Dohna zum 65. Geburtstag* (Darmstadt, 1989), pp. 107–30 (p. 107).

[110] The library catalogues of the friaries are preserved at the Saxon State Library at Dresden; see R. Machilek, 'Klosterhumanismus in Nürnberg um 1500', *Mitteilungen des Vereins für Geschichte der Stadt Nürnberg*, 64 (1977), pp. 10–45 (p. 43).

[111] Staupitz, II, 88 (ch. 3); the vernacular version of these Advent sermons leaves both alien words untranslated (see Staupitz, II. 89). Reuchlin's *De verbo magnifico* is the most likely source for Staupitz's deliberations on the name of God. See Wetzel, 'Staupitz antibarbarus', p. 109. See above, p. 64.

acknowledged Staupitz's scholarship and counted him among the *docti*, or learned, and urged the humanist Spalatin to approach him. Christoph Scheurl in his humanist Latin called Staupitz a *nobilis et humanissimus praesul* ('noble and most learned performer', literally, 'dancer') which seems to indicate that Staupitz was claimed for the humanists' camp.[112]

At Nuremberg, Staupitz was among educated lay people who admired him. Among them was Scheurl, the city's lawyer, who was at that time working on reforming the city's constitution. Staupitz must have been interested in and inquired about the city's constitution (*Von policeischer ordnung*), as Scheurl dedicated it to Staupitz with an *Epistula ad Staupitium*. In this work, which he finished in December 1516, Scheurl summarized Nuremberg's aristocratic city constitution, including descriptions of the city council with its 42 members, the office of the 26 'mayors', half of whom were 'jurors', and the function of the city's treasurers/senators (*Losunger*), the most senior among them being the highest officer of the entire city council. The text was translated into German and Italian. Its German title reads in translation: 'On Polity Regulations and Good Government of the Glorious City of Nuremberg'.[113] Surely a somewhat secular and political work to be dedicated to Staupitz, who was primarily a religious leader!

Here at Nuremberg Staupitz brought the year 1516 to a meaningful close with a series of stunning sermons in the vernacular, delivered at the Augustinians' church of St Vitus.[114] His preaching appealed to the city's intellectuals and leaders and his sermons must have been considered very important as they were gathered into a booklet called *Libellus*, which was published early in 1517 at Nuremberg. Scheurl was asked to produce a German edition due to popular demand; he mentioned this fact in a letter to Luther of 2 January 1517:

> Our very good friend [Staupitz] has preached about the eternal predestination with such great attendance and applause of the people ... that your church [the Augustinian church at Nuremberg] often could not hold them. The most intelligent among us praise and

---

[112] See Scheurl's epilogue to the *Libellus* (Staupitz, II. 306). Staupitz is called a hybrid (*Zwischengestalt*) by Berndt Hamm in 'Reichsstädtischer Humanismus in Nürnberg' in Mehl and Schneider, *Reformatio et reformationes*, pp. 131–93 (p. 170).

[113] *Von policeischer ordnung und gutem regiment der loblichen stat Nurmberg*, as this title is quoted in the critical Staupitz edition of 1987 (Staupitz, I. 72, n. 2). The original text is found in *Gedruckte Chroniken der deutschen Städte* (Leipzig, 1874; reprinted Göttingen, 1961), pp. 785–804; the English translation of this Epistle to Staupitz is found in G. Strauss, *Nuremberg in the Sixteenth Century. City Politics and Life between Middle Ages and Modern Times* (Bloomington, IN, and London, 1976), pp. 58–67. Strauss (p. 58) enigmatically speaks of Staupitz as Scheurl's 'one-time classmate'. On Scheurl's text, see also W. Graf, *Doktor Christoph Scheurl von Nürnberg* (Berlin and Leipzig, 1930), p. 57.

[114] See C.-J. Roepke, *Die Protestanten in Bayern* (Munich, 1972), pp. 13f.

admire this man's eloquence, mature judgment and skill. With one word, they state publicly that they have not heard anybody like him before. I omit that some call him the disciple of Paul, yes even his tongue, others call him the herald of the gospel and a true theologian. His friendliness [*humanitas*] and affability make this yet more splendid. Even the most influential [patrician citizens] consider it as something desirable to solicit his friendship and consider it an honour... to dine with Dr Staupitz .... The entire city [*civitas*] looks forward to his return.[115]

On 14 January Scheurl wrote to Dr Johann Eck (1486–1543) that Staupitz, his best friend, had preached sermons this past Advent season to the people and that they listened 'with great devotion'. The notion *favor* which he employed here means 'devout stillness' in classical Latin, when used in the context of worship. Scheurl in the same letter also said that he translated the sermons, edited them in both languages, and then sent a copy to Eck.[116] In his preface, Scheurl wrote that during the five years which he spent at Nuremberg nobody was ever honoured by the Nurembergers in the way that Staupitz was.

These sermons (published in 24 chapters) came off the printing press of Friedrich Peypus (or Pypius) in their German version as early as 19 January 1517, followed by the Latin version on 6 February.[117] This sequence of publishing, with the German version preceding the Latin, makes one wonder which was the original and which Scheurl's translation. Scheurl, as the editor/translator, wrote to Staupitz in a letter of 22 January 1517, that he (Staupitz) should accept his 'translation' which had appeared two days before, while the Latin version was being printed at that moment.[118]

The fact that the German version came off the press first (on 19 January) might suggest that it was the original, or that it was most in demand, and therefore was given preference by the editor and printer. The popular demand (*tantopere efflagitatus*) does not necessarily mean

---

[115] 'Amicissimus meus Johannes de Staupitz hunc sacrum adventum apud nos praedicavit et magno quidem populi favore executionem aeternae praedestinationis; ego traduxi et utraque lingua edo' (Letter to Luther, in Soden and Knaake, *Christoph Scheurl's Briefbuch*, II. 1–2 (no. 114)).

[116] Letter to Eck, in ibid., II. 3 (no. 115).

[117] These dates are derived from original printings found in the Salzburg archives; see Sallaberger, 'Johann von Staupitz, die Stiftsprediger', p. 262, n. 255.

[118] 'Publicae devotionis argumentum fuit quod tractatus executionis tantopere efflagitatus ... implevit fama eius totam ferme urbem. Latinus [tractatus] imprimitur; interea accipe traductionem nostram' (Soden and Knaake, *Christoph Scheurl's Briefbuch*, II. 5 (no. 117)). Jeremias (*AELK*, p. 350), thinks that they were delivered in Latin and on popular demand translated into German. This thesis is, however, questioned in Weijenborg's review of vol. 2 (1979) of the critical edition in *Revue d' Histoire Ecclesiastique*, 76 (1981), pp. 394–400.

that the people wanted a translation of what was preached in Latin, but it could very well mean that they wanted now to read in print what they had heard in German. Staupitz is known to have preached in the vernacular as early as 1512. Why should it be different at Nuremberg during Advent in 1516, when, according to tradition, the Augustinians were expected to preach to the people? It is therefore very likely that the original sermons were delivered in German, and the people listened to them 'in great devout stillness' (*magno favore*), as Scheurl observed. Upon popular demand they were then published in German, along with the Latin version which Scheurl edited for a more learned readership, including Professor Eck to whom he wrote that he would soon receive a copy. One reconstruction of events is derived from the note written on the back of the title-page of a 1518 copy of these sermons: 'Written in Latin by Doctor Staupitz, Vicar and Doctor, which Christopher Scheurl translated into German, and which Friedrich Pypius printed at Nuremberg on the Eve of St Sebastian Day [20 January], 1517, Nuremberg, 1 January 1518'.[119] However, this entry does not invalidate the assumption that Staupitz preached in the vernacular, then gave Scheurl a Latin draft which was translated back into the vernacular for publication. Such an assumption is further supported by the following observations: the subtitle of the vernacular edition indicated that the booklet was based upon Staupitz's 'preaching during holy Advent of 1516 at Nuremberg, to the glory of God and for the common welfare',[120] while the subtitle of the Latin edition does not mention that this *Libellus* was based on sermons delivered at Nuremberg. The Latin postscript states that Scheurl 'revised' the *Libellus*, meaning that he edited the Latin text which he had received from Staupitz. The German postscript reads that 'the booklet ... was hastily written in Latin by the reverend theologian Father Johannes von Staupitz, Vicar, as he was urged by good friends, and point by point translated into German by Christoph Scheurl, and printed by Friderich Peypus, at Nuremberg on the eve of the feast of St Sebastian in the year 1517'.[121]

---

[119] 'In tergo tituli inscriptum est: in Latein beschrieben von dem Doctor Staupitz Vicari und Doctor, das Christoffel Schewerl geteutscht und Friedrich Pypius gedruckt hat zu Nurnberg am Abend Sebastiani 1517 Nurnberg 1. Jenner 1518.' This note is quoted by A.D. Geuder, *Vita Joannis Staupitii* (inaugural dissertation, Theological Faculty Göttingen, 1837), p. 44, n. 74.

[120] 'Ein nutzbarliches büchlein von der entlichen volziehung ewiger fürsehung, wie das der wirdig vatter Joannes von Staupitz, Doctor und der reformirten Augustiner Vicarius Das heilig Advent das 1516 Jars zu Nurmberg got zu lob und gemeiner wolphart gepredigt hat' (Staupitz, II. 69). *Libellus de Executione eterne predestinationis Fratris Ioannis de Staupitz. Christi & Augustinianae obseruantie serui, utinam non inutilis* (Staupitz, II. 68).

[121] 'Wie das zu götlichem lob und gemeiner wolfart der erwirdig gotßgelert vater Johannes von Staupitz, vicari, auf emsig anregen guter freund eilent in latein beschriben

Thus, the following sequence is most likely: Staupitz wrote a draft in Latin, a practice which was not uncommon,[122] preached from it in German, and finally gave Scheurl the Latin version for translation and editing purposes. The German version which we have today, therefore, is not Staupitz's own wording nor a direct recording by a listener, but Scheurl's translation of the Latin text which Staupitz hastily had written down for Scheurl as the editor of the Latin text and as the translator of it into German.

The picture on the title-page in the German and in the Latin editions is identical: it shows at the top three male figures, representing the Trinity, each holding up his right hand in a gesture of blessing. The banderole in Latin is given in both the Latin and German edition; it is a quotation from Rom. 9: 18: *[Ergo] cuius vult miseretur [et] Quem vult indurat* ('[Consequently, God] has mercy upon whom he wills, and he hardens whom he wills'). This Pauline verse was Staupitz's preaching theme for Advent of 1516. At the bottom of the title-page we see in the right-hand corner the mouth of hell wide open with a devil driving people into it. On the left side the sun shines over the gate of heaven – where a gatekeeper with the keys and the papal tiara controls the entrance. The incoming people are accompanied by two angels. The caption of the Latin title-page reads: *15 Jhesus 17. Tuus sum ego, saluum me fac*, which is given in the German edition as: *15 Jesus 17. Dein bin ich/mach mich selig*. The numbers 15 and 17 which flank the name of Jesus represent the year 1517; the words are those of Ps. 118: 94, 'I am yours; save me'. The last line on the title-page gives the author's name in abbreviated form: *B(ruder) J(oannes) V(on) S(taupitz)*. In addition, the German version indicates Staupitz's religious affiliation and function: 'Reverend Father Johannes von Staupitz, Doctor, and Vicar of the reformed Augustinians'. The Latin title-page presents him simply as 'Johannes von Staupitz, servant of Christ and of the Augustinian Observance'.

Staupitz dedicated these sermons in their published form to a senator of Nuremberg, Jerome Ebner (1477–1532), with the wish for a happy new year. Similarly, he would dedicate the publication of the Advent sermons *On the Love of God* of the following year to the widow of the duke of Bavaria, wishing her a happy new year. Possibly the dedication to Ebner was a tactical move on Staupitz's part as he wanted to appease the Nurembergers' leaders, some of whom he had angered by seeking to incorporate Nuremberg's reformed friary into the union with

---

und doctor Christoffel Scheurl von puncten zu puncten getreues fleis geteutscht und Friderich Peypus getruckt hat. Zu Nurmberg am abent Sebastiani anno 1517' (Staupitz, II. 305).

[122] See A. Linsenmayer, *Geschichte der Predigt in Deutschland* (Munich, 1886; reprinted Frankfurt, 1969), pp. 38–40, as cited in Paltz, *Werke 3, Opuscula*, p. 164, n. 34.

non-reformed friaries. In the process he had encountered the vehement opposition of the local government. Subsequently, the friars of Nuremberg had not sent any of their junior members to Staupitz's theological faculty at Wittenberg for five years (1507–12).[123]

Staupitz's German preface indicated that he and the senator had fraternized (*gebrudert*), whatever that may mean. It may indicate that they became good personal friends, as the Latin version suggests; or that the senator was accepted into the lay brotherhood of the Augustinian Order (confraternity); or, perhaps most likely, that Staupitz expressed with this hint that Senator Ebner was a member of the illustrious 'Staupitz Sodality' at Nuremberg. Here follow excerpts from the Latin version:

> To the noblest Jerome Ebner, Senator of Nuremberg, from Johann von Staupitz, servant of God and of the Reformed Congregation of the Augustinians .... I have often longed to be of service in some way to the people of Nuremberg. Now at last during this Holy Advent it has been accomplished by divine disposition that by preaching Christ I have applied myself to give an elucidation of the decree of eternal predestination. Compelled by the devotion of the hearers – and perhaps a little unwillingly – I have brought together into one booklet what I had preached, so that the pious reader might be able to correct my errors frankly and return me to the truth – which I would have him do immediately – if he should find any errors or rash words .... Accept this, therefore, as a little gift by which in these best of days a friend usually honours a friend, as is the ancient custom. Accept this present made of paper in the same spirit in which it is sent: as a lasting monument of my regard for you .... As for me, I, together with my people, will pray to God that he save you and your people .... Given at Nuremberg from the Augustinian friary, New Year's Day 1517.[124]

These Advent sermons may be considered Staupitz's commentary on Rom. 8: 30 (*vocatio, iustificatio, glorificatio*). Although he claims they were shaped into a tractate 'a little unwillingly', we do not really know the reason for this uneasiness. Was it a theological concern, or was he simply hesitant to go ahead with their publication? Why did he pick this difficult topic of predestination in the first place? We may speculate that this issue was a 'hot' topic at that time, especially when we further consider that Conrad Wimpina (d. 1531), a friar of the rival Dominican Order and a scholastic professor at Frankfurt on the Oder River (he, incidentally, would side with Tetzel in the indulgence controversy of the following autumn) dealt with it in three volumes: *De praedestinatione et*

---

[123] See Staupitz, II. 72, n. 5.

[124] Ibid., 72–4; translation in A.L. Henry, *Catholicity and Predestination in the Theologies of Johann Eck and Johannes von Staupitz, 1513–1517* (Th.D. dissertation, Graduate Theological Union, Berkeley, CA, 1971 [microfilm]), pp. 148–50.

praescientia divina, quid sentiendum quidve ad vulgus praedicandum, et concordantia praedicantium de his nonnumquam diversa adversaque contionantium libri tres. Whether or not Staupitz's sermons were meant as a direct commentary on or reaction to Wimpina's work on this subject is hard to tell, especially as long as the publication date of 1516/17 for Wimpina's work cannot be clarified.[125]

Staupitz's tractate dealt in the first 14 chapters with more or less doctrinal issues: the purpose of creation and its reparation, the need to praise God, the lack of praise, the predestination of the saints, the call to faith and salvation, the justification of the sinner, the works of the justified person, the spiritual marriage between Christ and the Christian, how the highest mercy of God corresponds to the greatest misery of man, the transfer of our sin on to Christ, the extinction of the sins of the elect, Christ's perpetual love for the Christian, and the peace of mind which is restored to the justified sinner.

In the second half of the book, Chapters 15 to 24, Staupitz's thoughts became rather mystical and ascetical, in dealing with the foretaste of salvation, the alleviation of the burden of the law, the sweetness of Christ's word spoken into the heart of the Christian, Christ's feasting with the Christian, the salvific vision that may be received already in this world, the perception of Christ's Spirit in hating sins, the tongue of a Christian, the preservation of the Christian from the diabolic venom, and what a Christian can do for spiritual mortification.

After Staupitz elaborated on the spiritual marriage between Christ and the believer, he continued with the proclamation of the sweetness of the Lord, that God was 'made sweet for us', and that we may have a foretaste of his 'future sweetness'. Where the German version has *sues*, the Latin uses *suavis*;[126] it is a wording which is almost identical with Augustine's expression that Christ 'was made sweet for us'. The critical edition of Staupitz's works lists this phrase as a reference to Psalm 144 or Ps. 99: 5, the latter of which has the wording *suavis Dominus*. However, a more precise parallel is found not so much in the Vulgate Psalm wording as in Augustine's sermons.[127] The mystery and marvel of Christ's life is to be seen, according to Staupitz, not so much in the union of the

---

[125] Wimpina's work was published at Frankfurt (on the Oder River) in either 1516 or 1517. See Zumkeller, *Heilslehre*, p. 79. See Staupitz, II. 234f., n. 42.

[126] Chapters 9 and 10, Staupitz, II. 150–55.

[127] Augustine: 'Factus est tibi suavis' (Sermon 145); and 'Ipse est mediator inde factus est suavis' (on Psalm 134). Cf. Staupitz: 'Unde deus suavis nobis factus est' (ch. 10, 1516); and 'Est factus nobis gratus placitusque' (ch. 16, 1516). On this, see Posset, 'The Sweetness of God', pp. 159–61; Posset 'Pater et Doctor Meus Est, Immo Sanctae Ecclesiae Intellecta Profundissimus, in F. van Fleteren et al. (eds) *Collecteanea Augustiniana* (New York, 1994), pp. 513–43.

two natures of Christ in one person, but in the sweet condescension of divine mercy for the redemption of the human misery. Thus, the incarnate and the suffering Christ is always the 'sweet Saviour', literally the 'sweet bliss maker'.[128] Earlier in his sermonizing he had quoted Augustine verbatim on the Incarnation mystery, saying that 'our Augustine' was not able by natural enlightenment to make sense of the mystery that is expressed in the biblical verse: 'the Word became *mensch*'. What is needed here, according to Staupitz, is true faith in Christ. This, by the way, is the only direct reference to an authentic text of Augustine in these Advent sermons. No other theological authority was mentioned by the preacher besides, of course, the Sacred Scriptures. Evidently Augustine's theology had a fundamental impact on Staupitz: Christ 'has been made sweet for us'. 'Christ is sweeter than everything'.[129] The sweetness of Christ's word is spoken to the Christian heart'.[130] Christ's word in Luke 23: 43, 'this day you will be with me in paradise' is the 'most sweet word'.[131] His task is to be our sweet redeemer: 'It is your office, O sweet Saviour, to seek and to save that which is lost'.[132]

In Chapter 15, on the foretaste of salvation, Staupitz elaborated with Ps. 33: 9 (Vulgate) on the tasting of the sweetness of God, that one cannot really communicate such an experience. The preacher's Latin version explicitly utilized the traditional expression *dulcedo dei*, 'sweetness of God', translated into German as *süse gots*. Here follows the essential part of the sermon in a rather literal translation:

> It is true, that no one can ever say enough about this experience in specific cases, in which God is more tasted than seen, except God who scrutinizes the hearts. This is so because whoever tasted the sweetness of God is unable to explain and inform satisfactorily others about such taste so that they would taste it, too. For whatever is learned from experience alone cannot be described properly in the form of a doctrine.
>
> Therefore, these things must be ladled from God's doctrine and kept warm by referring to similarities, figures of speech, and human persuasion.

---

[128] 'O sueser Seligmacher/dulcis salvator' (Staupitz, II. 152–3).

[129] 'Dulcior est Christus omnibus'/'Christus sueser ist dann alle andre dingk' (ibid., 194f., no. 119 (ch. 15)); see Oberman, *Forerunners of the Reformation*, trans. P.L. Nyhns (New York, 1966), p. 195.

[130] 'De dulcedine sermonis Christi ad cor christiani'/'Von der süse des zusprechens Christi in das herz des christen' (Staupitz, II. 206f).

[131] Ibid. 194f, no. 117 (ch. 15).

[132] 'Officii tui est, o dulcis salvator, quaerer et salvum facere quod perierat'/'Dein ampt ist, dir geburt, o sueser seligmacher, zu suchen und selig ze machen, das verdorben was' (ibid. 152f., no. 67 (ch. 10)); see Oberman, *Forerunners*, p. 189. The Augustinian wording is continued when Staupitz uses Augustine's title for Christ, 'physician' (*medicus*). Here the critical edition refers to Augustine (Staupitz, II. 150f., no. 66 (ch. 10)).

As you heard me saying before [in Chapter 9] that matrimony between a man and a woman most obviously is an image for the matrimony of Christ and the Church; and that marital love, that is a wife's love for her man and vice versa, can be compared most of all – but nevertheless only through imitation – to Christ's love for the faithful soul and to the faithful soul's love for Christ.

Christ's love cannot be imagined more pure, sweet, righteous, honest, fruitful and stable than through those signs by which the Groom shows the Bride his love and vice versa the Bride to the Groom. Thus, through such signs the innocent love gives testimony of the most innocent and most salutary love.

When you are perturbed that indecent love may produce more signs than holy love, take the signs of love, but exclude the vices of the lover. Guilt of indecency does not consist in the contact of the bodies but in the perversion of the [natural] order, that is when temporal enjoyment is given preference to eternal ones.

Certainly, the acts of a fornicator and that of a spouse are the same, although the latter is in accord with the law, while the former is a violation of the law. What is not against the law is allowed, provided that it does not cause scandal to the little ones. The [moral quality of the] acts as such depend[s] on the goodness or the maliciousness of love: If love is chaste, the signs of love are chaste; if love is impure, the signs are impure, too.

Therefore, in the Scriptures, the love-manifestations of the eternal Spouse – be they kisses, embraces, or copulation of the naked with the naked etc – are presented chastely to the chaste, but are interpreted according to the [pure or dirty] frame of mind of the reader.

On this the Scriptures say [see Cant. 6: 7–8] that there are four different souls which Christ embraces with the love of a spouse: there are the adolescents in faith; there are the concubines and their divided love ... ; there are the queens who despised the world with its temptations for the sake of the love for the heavenly Spouse; and there is the one love of Christ, the perfect one of Christ, unique to the Mother [of God], the choice of the one who gave birth, whom angels and humans admire, praise, and proclaim as the most blessed one.

In the first stage, they love and are being loved, but do not receive any special signs of love. God grabs them that they may not be seduced by malice or fraud. And they rejoice in this most sweet word that they will not die until Christ will speak to their heart: 'Today you will be with me in paradise'. This is to be understood of adults, while the little ones triumph on the basis of Christ's merit alone.

In the second stage, the Groom is loved above everything else, but he is loved not alone, but along with him also is creation. God calls them away from their work to refresh them, and often as a comfort he lets them know how vehemently he loves them, yet fleetingly, because their fleeting love cannot take continuous solace.

It seems to me from experience that those who sweat [while working hard] have a greater enjoyment of the sweetness in Christ than others who find themselves in better conditions – about them

we will talk later. One thing I must still add about the concubine
souls: they taste that Christ is sweeter than everything.

In the third stage there are the queens. They are naked and
copulate with the naked one. They taste that outside Christ there is
nothing sweet, and they enjoy [his] continuous sweetness. This is so
because the naked Christ cannot deny himself to these naked ones.
He allows at times strong vehemence in their love relations, but they
have no doubts at all that by comparison they receive hundredfold
corporeal riches and pleasures, here and now and in the eternal life
to come.

In the fourth stage the virgin Mary alone who is the Mother of
God, is found. She alone tasted how sweet he is: Jesus is subjected to
her, and he smiles when she wants him to, or he weeps, or he flatters
her with his talk, or throws kisses at her, sleeps naked with her naked
and he shows other signs of such love.[133]

One needs to remember that the 'naked Christ' is also the humiliated,
suffering Lord on the cross, on whom the contemplatives like Bernard in
his *Fasciculus Myrrhae* (Sermon 43 on the Canticle) meditate. Bernard's
thoughts may perhaps have come to Staupitz's attention through Jean
Gerson, whose sermon on the feast of St Bernard could be the immediate
source for Staupitz.[134] Here Staupitz followed in the Bernardine mystical
tradition which also influenced Henry Suso. Indeed, Staupitz sounded
here much like Suso on love (*minnespil*) and on the crucified Christ as the
'naked Godhead'.[135] From this contemplation of the naked Christ on the
cross, the meditating person draws spiritual sweetness as if one chewed
on the 'sweet wood', as Suso stated in alluding to the vernacular term
suzholze for 'liquorice', that is 'sweet wood'.[136]

The climax of mystical contemplation occurs when the naked souls
are 'coupled' to the naked Christ,[137] and thus enjoy the 'continuous
sweetness'[138] since the naked Christ (*nudus Christus*) cannot refuse the
naked souls. They are certain of their salvation. The fourth and last level
is the experience which Mary had who alone has tasted how sweet he is.
Jesus sleeps naked with her, that is he as the Christ child, or in general
the human Christ.[139]

---

[133] Staupitz, II. 188f–196f (ch. 15).

[134] See ibid., 188, notes 17, 18 and 20.

[135] See Suso in Bihlmeyer, *Deutsche Schriften: Minne spil*, p. 234; *blozen gotheit*,
pp. 254 and 272; Tobin, *Henry Suso*, pp. 236, 250 and 255.

[136] *Suezholze* (Bihlmeyer, *Deutsche Schriften*, p. 257); see Tobin, *Henry Suso*, p. 251,
where, however, the imprecise translation 'unchewed candy' is given for Suso's vernacular
suezholze which means 'liquorice' (lit., 'sweet wood'; *Süßholz* in modern German).

[137] 'Hae nudae copulantur nudo' (Staupitz, II. 196f., no. 120 (ch. 15)).

[138] 'Gaudent continua dulcedine/erwollustigen sich steter suese' (ibid.).

[139] See Staupitz, II. 196f., no. 121 (ch. 15); see Oberman, *Forerunners*, p. 193. On the
nudus motif, see M. Bernards, 'Nudus nudum Christum sequi', *Wissenschaft und Weisheit*,
14 (1951), pp. 148–51; G. Constable, 'Nudus Nudum Christum Sequi and Parallel

Staupitz had already pointed out in one of his Salzburg sermons that Christ's 'little bed of enjoyment' (*lustpetel*) is not a soft bed, but the cross.[140] With this interpretation, one realizes that there is nothing erotic in this contemplation by the poor ('naked') soul on the *nudus Christus*, as Christ is the salvific ('sweet') Lord on the cross. He is God made sweet for us.[141] Staupitz displayed here a theology and spirituality which meditates on the sweetness of God and his 'loveliness' (*lieblichkeit*); the latter appears to be another German synonym for the traditional Latin expressions *suavitas* and *dulcedo*.[142] In these sermons, the medieval spiritual tradition which is shaped by Augustine, Bernard and Suso clearly shines through.

While Bernardine spirituality seems to have had little direct impact on Staupitz's Tübingen sermons of 1497/98, this had changed by 1516, almost 20 years later, as his Nuremberg sermons reveal, especially Sermons 7 to 9.[143] A passage from *The Golden Legend* about St Bernard must have provided the inspiration for some elements in these Advent sermons of 1516. Unfortunately, the new critical edition of Staupitz's sermons does not consider Bernard as a source for Staupitz's expression 'right to heaven' (*ius ad caelum*) which is found in the Bernard story of *The Golden Legend*, but not in a genuine text of Bernard. The story very succinctly summarizes Bernard's Christo-centric spirituality:

> I admit I am unworthy, and unable by merits of my own, to gain entrance to the kingdom of heaven. On the other hand, my Lord Jesus Christ has won the kingdom by a twofold right, namely by inheritance from his Father, and by the merit of his passion. The first he has reserved for himself but the second he gives to me; and by that gift I assert my right, and shall not be confounded.[144]

Such Bernardine thinking formed a considerable part of the matrix of Staupitz's sermons. There is an undeniable theological congeniality

---

Formulas in the Twelfth Century', in F.F. Church and T. George (eds), *Continuity and Discontinuity in Church History. Essays Presented to George Hunston Williams on the Occasion of his 65th Birthday* (Leiden, 1979), pp. 83–91. Constable argues that the *nudus* is the poor person who follows the poor Christ to the cross. However, Staupitz's concept of the nude soul sleeping with the nude Jesus is different, because he refers to Mary the mother who has her child with her.

[140] *Das kreuz ist sein lustpetel*, Schneider-Lastin, *Salzburger Predigten 1512*, p. 108 (Sermon 11). Staupitz may have alluded to the *lectulus* ('little bed') of Cant. 1:15.

[141] 'Deus suavis nobis factus est'/'ist uns got sues' (Staupitz, II. 152f., no. 64 (ch. 10)).

[142] Note, however, the exception in Chapter 7 (Staupitz, II. 128f. (no. 44)), where the Latin term for the German *lieblich* is *decorus*, as Staupitz was referring probably to Cant. 2: 14: 'vox tua dulcis et facies tua decora.'

[143] See esp. Staupitz, II. 126f., 148f. and 300f. (nos. 44–62 and 252); see Posset, 'St Bernard's Influence on Two Reformers', pp. 179–82.

[144] *Jacobus de Voragine, The Golden Legend*, trans. W.G. Ryan (2 vols, Princeton, NJ, 1993), II, p. 102f.

between Bernard and Staupitz in their Christo-centrism and focus on Christ's cross and grace alone for the justification of the sinner; their common Pauline concern was always 'to preach Christ crucified' (1 Cor. 1: 23 and 2: 2). Staupitz had this to say:

> We ought not to doubt, however, the merits of Christ, knowing, as we do, that he is both God and man and that his claim to be equal with God was not presumptuous. Therefore the merits of Christ entitle us to enter the eternal kingdom .... Christ went on to say: '[Settle down] within the holes in the rock', that is, in the wounds of Christ and in the open cave, that is, in the opening to the heart of Christ, from where the forces of the sacraments flow.[145]

Staupitz also pointed to the sacraments here, as he connected the power (*virtutes*) of sacraments to the heart of Christ. The flow of water and blood from Christ's wound in his side was understood as the flow of the water of baptism and the flow of the blood of the Eucharist. Here, Staupitz wanted to instil a spiritualized concept of the sacraments; this was one of the rare occasions on which he mentioned them.

Later on, Staupitz dealt with the question of how Christ's merits really become ours. He used the concept of the mystical marriage between Christ and the Christian, and the 'marital right' derived from it,[146] a concept that is, of course, also very prominent with Bernard of Clairvaux.[147] In other words, Christ says: 'The Christian is my possession, the Christian is my concern, the Christian is I.' The spouse responds, 'Christ is my possession, Christ is my concern, Christ is I.' Finally, 'if Christ is I, I have a right to heaven [*ius ad caelum*], I have hope, and I glory in that hope which belongs to the children of God'.[148]

In the concluding Chapter 24, Staupitz connected to the concept of spiritual marriage and the 'right to heaven' another idea, namely the total resignation to, and acceptance of, the will of God for one's life. God

---

[145] '... Merita igitur Christi ius ad regnum aeternum conferunt'/'Demnach geberen die verdinst Christi gerechtikeit zu dem ewigen reich' (Staupitz, II. 126f., no. 44 (ch. 7)); see translation in Oberman, *Forerunners*, p. 184.

[146] *Ius matrimonii* (ch. 9), see Posset, 'St Bernard's Influence on Two Reformers', p. 181; for a translation, see Oberman, *Forerunners*, p. 186.

[147] See Posset, 'St Bernard's Influence on Two Reformers', pp. 175–6. Bernard is not quoted by name in this context, but his thought pattern is there.

[148] 'Si Christus est ego, ius ad caelum habeo/ Ist Christus ich, so hab ich gerechtikeit [i.e. recht auf] zum himel' (Staupitz, II. 148f., no. 62 (ch. 9)); see Oberman, *Forerunners*, pp. 187f. The same Bernardine expression, *ius ad caelum*, is employed in Staupitz's concluding sermon (i.e. ch. 24), Staupitz, II. 300f., no. 252). Oberman does not realize the Bernardine background of this concept, nor does Steinmetz in *Misericordia Dei*, pp. 54f., nor even Zumkeller in *Heilslehre*, p. 202. The concept of the 'right to heaven' belongs to soteriological Christology, as Christ earned for the sinner the right to enter heaven; it only secondarily belongs to the doctrine of God or the doctrine of election.

cannot be glorified better than by letting God's will take its course, even if this means giving up one's 'right to heaven'. With the concept of 'resignation', a concept that he had mentioned in his Tübingen sermons of 1497/98, and that he would bring up again in 1520, he may have been following John Tauler. This is what Staupitz said at Nuremberg:

> If God is served better through our non-existence than through our existence, we should prefer to return to nothing rather than to live. If his glory is served better by our resigning from all use of our merits, then not only are we to resign from all of our nature, but also from the fruits of gifts and grace. If the glory of God can increase by my renouncing Christ and his merits and his right to heaven, then I renounce.[149]

If one compares Staupitz's theology of predestination as presented in these sermons of 1516 with John Eck's *Chrysopassus* of 1514, one may observe that both Staupitz and Eck agree on the divine will as the matrix of predestination. Election and predestination are the same. Categories such as *potentia absoluta* and *potentia ordinata* were not used here. Staupitz may have followed Scotus in emphasizing the sovereignty of God's will apart from divine foreknowledge. Staupitz summarily denied the principle that *faciens quod in se est* meant that man may merit first grace and that man is capable of *meritum* before justification.[150] However, most of all, his teaching on God and grace, creation and the fall of man, is characterized by a strong Augustinian colouring. All in all, Staupitz's sermons definitely mirror a spirituality that is rather different from that of Gabriel Biel.[151]

On the works of the justified person, Staupitz had this to say: 'The man who is predestined, called, and justified surely does not live his life without good conduct and holy works. The justified man cannot but love ....'[152] Here the Scotist view of 'justification' as being closely connected to, if not identified with, 'love' shines through Staupitz's thinking. He continued: 'Therefore, human acts performed without faith in Christ cannot serve God but only mammon. Hence I shall not even consider such works but pass them by as useless, not to say, impediments to salvation.'[153] Those works which we do in Christ, renewed by grace, are

---

[149] Staupitz, II. 298–301; see his Tübingen Sermon 28 (Staupitz, I. 412); and his Salzburg sermons of 1520 in Markwald, *A Mystic's Passion*, pp. 36, 48f., where the connection is made to Tauler's and Suso's spirituality.

[150] Henry, *Catholicity*; see Zumkeller, *Heilslehre*, p. 202.

[151] See Schulze, 'Tübinger Gegensätze. Gabriel Biel und Johannes von Staupitz: von spätmittelalterlicher Reform zu Luthers Reformation', *Tübinger Blätter*, **72** (1985), pp. 54–9, for the comparison of Biel and Staupitz.

[152] For a translation of Sermon 8, see Oberman, *Forerunners*, p. 185.

[153] Ibid., pp. 185f.

works that issue from the love of God. These works are not self-centred but Christ-centred. Those works become good which they would not be without faith. These works display love which brings faith alive.[151] Good works as merits remain God's gifts in the Augustinian sense that *Deus non praemiat nisi sua opera*. 'Only Christ's own merits can one call merit full of worthiness [*meritum condigni*], and it was already determined by God before the creation of the world that no one would be able to do good works without the grace of Christ.'[155] Only Christ's merits are sufficient to save all of Christianity:

> Since justification is due to grace and not to nature, since acceptance of works performed in grace is grace, ... it is appropriate to attribute the whole Christian life to grace. And thus the claim for man, namely, that he is master over his works from beginning to the end, is destroyed. So, therefore, the origin of the works of Christian life is predestination, its means is justification, and its aim is glorification or thanksgiving – all these are the achievements not of nature but of grace.[156]

This text implied an anti-Aristotelian sentiment, which can probably be traced as far back as to Staupitz's studies at Tübingen, at the time when he had encountered Summenhart and his critical attitude toward Aristotle.[157] The Greek philosopher taught that we as 'human beings are from the beginning to the end the masters of our actions'.[158] In contrast, Staupitz in his eighth sermon declared that our 'rational nature' is out of order, defunct, 'deleted'.[159]

This Staupitzian sermon of 1516 may actually have been the source for one of Luther's theses against scholastic theology which he wrote in 1517. Staupitz's anti-Aristotelian position appears to be tacitly quoted by Luther's Thesis 39 in which Luther categorically stated: 'We are not masters of our actions, from beginning to end, but servants. This is in opposition to the philosophers.'[160] Even if Luther did not copy this

---

[154] See ibid., p. 186.

[155] '... Et sic ante mundi constitutionem conclusum fuit: neminem sine Christi gratia bene facere posse' (Staupitz, II. 94 (ch. 4)), see Oberman, *Forerunners*, p. 179 (and 186); see Steinmetz, *Misericordia Dei*, p. 70.

[156] Sermon 8; Oberman, *Forerunners*, p. 186.

[157] On Summenhart's criticism of Aristotelianism, see H.-G. Hofacker, 'Vom alten und nuen Gott, Glauben und Ler', in Josef Nolte et al., *Kontinuität und Umbruch*, p. 148.

[158] Aristotle: 'Operationum quidem enim a principio usque ad finem domini sumus' *Ethica* 3, 8.

[159] 'Et in ipso deletur quod naturae rationali concedunt, puta dominium operum a principio usque in finem' (Staupitz, II. 140, no. 52 (ch. 8); this edition does not disclose the parallel with Aristotle).

[160] See Luther's *Disputation Against Scholastic Theology*, LW 31: 9–16; on this, see R. Wetzel, 'Staupitz und Luther', in V. Press and D. Stievermann (eds), *Martin Luther:*

statement from Staupitz's sermon, it still demonstrates the congeniality of these two Augustinian friars. We do know, however, that Luther received Staupitz's printed sermons from Scheurl, as on 6 May 1517 Luther wrote him a letter thanking him for sending them.[161] A direct dependence upon Staupitz can therefore be inferred. The congeniality between mentor and protegé is confirmed by the fact that Staupitz held Luther in high regard when he talked about him to his friends at Nuremberg (as Scheurl reported to Luther in his letter of 1 April 1517[162]). Staupitz's sermons were in such demand at Wittenberg that in the autumn of 1517 Scheurl had to send 15 additional copies to Luther.[163] He sent them via Erfurt; however, they had not arrived in Wittenberg by 11 December, according to Luther in a letter to Scheurl of that date.[164]

On the basis of his sermons we may assume that Staupitz sided with the late medieval anti-Aristotelianism that had emerged in humanist theology in the fourteenth century,[165] and that he drew many of his insights directly from Bernard and Augustine. There are hardly any points of connection between him and Gregory of Rimini.[166] It is debatable whether Staupitz's sermons were influenced by him: any possible parallels may stem from Augustine directly. Indeed, Staupitz cannot be claimed for any definite late medieval school at all. Any similarities with specific representatives of a certain reception of Augustinian thought in the late Middle Ages are probably accidental, and not the result of a conscientious handing down of a particular scholastic tradition. It cannot be demonstrated that Staupitz made a deliberate turn to the

---

Probleme seiner Zeit (Stuttgart, 1986), p. 85, where Wetzel corrects his own editorial annotations in the critical edition of Staupitz's sermons.

[161] See *WABR* 1. 93, 4f. (no. 38).

[162] See *WABR* 1. 91, 7f. (no. 36).

[163] See *WABR* 1. 107, 20–22 (no. 47).

[164] See *WABR* 1. 126, 36–40 (no. 54).

[165] See Zumkeller, *Heilslehre*, p. 19. On the emerging anti-Aristotelianism, see C. Vasoli, 'The Theology of Italian Humanism in the Early Fifteenth Century', in G. D'Onofrio (ed.), *History of Theology*, trans. M.J. O'Connell, 3 vols (Collegeville, MN, 1996), III, pp. 49–52.

[166] Heiko A. Oberman and Manfred Schulze maintain that Staupitz may be considered a representative and intermediary of the so-called *via Gregorii* for Luther (that is, the school of Gregory of Rimini from the fourteenth century). To summarize their thesis: some of the candidates of the school of Gregory of Rimini (insofar as their names are encountered in secondary literature) are Alfonso Vargas of Toledo, Hugolin of Orvieto, Johannes Klenkok, Frater Guido, Konrad of Erbach (a Cistercian), Augustinus Favaroni, and Jacob Perez of Valencia. Staupitz was allegedly a particularly important channel of late medieval Augustinianism for Luther; see Oberman, 'Headwaters of the Reformation'; Schulze, '"Via Gregorii" in Forschung und Quellen', in H.A. Oberman (ed.), *Gregor von Rimini. Werk und Wirkung bis zur Reformation* (Berlin and New York, 1981), pp. 1–126.

theology of Gregory of Rimini.[167] Rather, it is on the sound basis of the spirituality that was shaped by the Augustinian and Bernardine concept of God (Christ) becoming sweet to us, and not the other way around, and thus as an effect of divine grace, that Staupitz developed his distinct interpretation of *gratia gratum faciens* in these Advent sermons of 1516. On the basis of his insights into the 'sweetness of God' as revealed in Christ the Saviour, Staupitz departed from the concept of man becoming pleasing to God, 'as it has often been interpreted'.[168] Apparently this was a deliberate move away from such a concept, which had so often been interpreted before him, and to which he had adhered in his Tübingen Sermon 30.[169] Now, however, in 1516, Staupitz declared that with the help of divine grace, God becomes sweet and pleasing to us. It is Staupitz alone who has this new interpretation of grace that makes God pleasing to man.[170] As a consequence of this thinking Staupitz had very little to say about Christ as the stern Judge; for him, the image of the angry Judge of the world turns into an image of God who is pleasing to man. His predominant image of Christ is that of the 'Saviour', not the 'Judge'.

---

[167] See Steinmetz, 'Luther and the Late Medieval Augustinians. Another Look', *Concordia Theological Monthly*, **44** (1973), pp. 245–60; in his *Luther and Staupitz* (Durham, NC, 1980) Steinmetz rightly questioned the hypothesis that Staupitz is the mediator of Augustinianism to Luther, and points out that he is not a Thomist either (against Wolf). Berndt Hamm (*Frömmigkeitstheologie am Anfang des 16. Jahrhunderts: Studien zu Johannes von Paltz und seinem Umkreis* (Tübingen, 1982), p. 330 states that the Augustine-School did not exist in the Middle Ages; see also Wriedt, 'Via Guilelmi – via Gregorii', in R. Melville et al. (eds), *Deutschland und Europa in der Neuzeit* (Stuttgart, 1988), pp. 111–31; S.H. Hendrix, 'Luther's Loyalties and the Augustinian Order', in Hagen, *Augustine, The Harvest*, pp. 236–58.

[168] 'Sicut multi exponunt'/'als es vil auslegen' (Staupitz, II. 116f., no. 36 (ch. 6)).

[169] In his Tübingen Sermon 30 Staupitz spoke of the person becoming pleasing to God by grace (Staupitz I. 432–3), see on this, Zumkeller, 'Staupitz', *Dictionnaire*, XV, p. 1190; Zumkeller, *Heilslehre*, pp. 126–8.

[170] 'Haec est gratia gratum faciens: non hominem deo, sicut multi exponunt ... sed solum deum facit placere et gratum esse homini per caritatem... qua deo, non nobis, et recte et iuste sumus et vivimus' (Staupitz, II. 116–17, no. 36 (ch. 6)); see nos. 40, 131 and 152. In my essay 'The Sweetness of God', I showed Augustine's concept of the 'sweetness of God' and Staupitz's dependence upon it in all his sermons from 1497/98 on. Following Steinmetz, *Misericordia Dei*, p. 84, n. 3: 'It is clear that Staupitz deviates from the main scholastic tradition by defining *gratia gratum faciens* in this new way.' See also D.C. Steinmetz, *Reformers in the Wings* (Philadelphia, 1971). It is doubtful whether Staupitz was inspired to this deviation by late medieval authors. He may have been inspired by Augustine directly or via Peter Lombard's reference to Augustine's *De Spiritu et Littera* 56; see Oberman who is mentioned in connection with this by Zumkeller, *Heilslehre*, p. 12, n. 828. However, a direct reference or quotation from Augustine's *De Spiritu et Littera* cannot be demonstrated; on this, see B. Lohse, 'Zum Wittenberger Augustinismus: Augustins Schrift De Spiritu et Littera in der Auslegung bei Staupitz, Luther und Karlstadt', in Hagen, *Augustine, The Harvest*, pp. 95f.

Staupitz made predestination simple to understand by redefining justifying grace (*gratia gratum faciens*) as the grace that makes God sweet and pleasing to the believer. This is Staupitz's great and revolutionary theological discovery; one in which Luther followed him. Staupitz was able to help the young friar to conquer the vulgar misconceptions of a bad theology that had led him to unnecessary spiritual anxieties about Christ as the stern Judge. It is not at all surprising then that Luther, too, spoke of the 'sweetness of God' and of God himself becoming lovely, pleasing, and sweet to our hearts.[171]

Someone may explain Staupitz's unconventional theme as a 'scholastic translation' of a maxim that was developed by Augustine who says that it is the mark of the justified person that he or she is pleased with God.[172] Perhaps it was a 'translation', but 'scholastic' it is not – one should not force Staupitz into a scholastic mould. Staupitz's new insight appears to have emerged directly from his readings of Augustine in combination with the Holy Scriptures. There is no question that these sermons of Advent 1516 echoed much of Augustine's anti-Pelagian and predestinarian thought, even though Staupitz hardly ever quoted Augustine directly. He only mentioned him twice by name; first in order to protect him from a misinterpretation and second in order to paraphrase his *Confessiones*.[173] Staupitz was perceived by his Nuremberg audience primarily as a scriptural scholar and as a spokesman of St Paul's theology.

Staupitz's theological position indeed turned Gabriel Biel's upside down, as in Staupitz's view it is not important to do what one can, but what God does in Christ.[174] Staupitz's theology and spirituality always developed from his God-centredness. He reached certainty of faith by calling upon salvation through Christ and his thinking is summed up in his biblical motto *Tuus sum ego, salvum me fac* (Ps. 118: 94), which, as has been mentioned above, graced the title-page of both the German and the Latin editions of his Advent sermons.

With his devotional theology, shaped by biblical, and especially Pauline, Augustinian and Bernardine insights, Staupitz in 1516 was at ease in straightening out his Nuremberg audience on the issue of indulgences. Toward the end of his sermon *cyclus* he declared that personal satisfaction

---

[171] '... *Szo kompt die sussickeyt gottis. Da wirt gott dem hertzen szo lieblich unnd gefellig unnd susz*' (WA 8. 379, 2–21).

[172] See Steinmetz, 'Luther and Late Medieval Augustinianism', p. 258. See also Zumkeller, *Heilslehre*, pp. 128–30 for a brief discussion of this issue.

[173] See Wriedt, 'Staupitz und Augustin', p. 242. The critical editors of these sermons point out more than 400 loci where Staupitz may have been mirroring Augustine's thought.

[174] See Zumkeller, 'Staupitz', *Dictionnaire*, XV, p. 1189. It is doubtful whether Staupitz read Biel; Biel had been a Brother of the Common Life at Tübingen, but died before Staupitz's arrival there; see Schulze, 'Tübinger Gegensätze', pp. 54–9.

for one's sins is more useful and praiseworthy than gaining an indulgence. Staupitz thus publicly corrected the indulgence ideology as early as Advent 1516. Here is what he proclaimed to the Nurembergers:

> Liberation from sins through satisfaction is more commendable and more useful than through an indulgence: it is certainly more commendable because it is done with a greater love of justice, more useful because it augments merit, makes one secure and anxious to avoid sin. And such a person [that is the one who is doing satisfaction] has no enemies because he or she firmly believes that everything that happened to such a person occurred for his or her best.[175]

Almost one year prior to Luther's famous public challenge with his 95 Theses[176] Staupitz practically did the same thing. He was in step with other criticisms of the indulgence practices at that time. The Augustinians of Antwerp, and a Benedictine abbot, for instance, voiced their objections. The latter published a booklet on this issue, in the vernacular, in Deventer in 1516.[177]

In considering Staupitz as an influence on Luther, one may, furthermore, review the concept of self-accusation which was alive and well in the late-medieval Augustinian tradition. Staupitz, in his Sermons 20 and 22 on Job at the end of the fifteenth century, had preached about this topic, and in his Advent sermons of 1516 he declared that, if God is on your side, nobody dares to be against you, as there is no accuser left, that is if God is the justifier. This is so because in Christ we have our advocate, not our judge. The person who practises self-accusation first, can count on being made just by God himself.[178] In the following year, in his Munich sermons *On God's Gracious Love*,[179] Staupitz would speak

---

[175] *Indulgentia / ablas* (Staupitz, II. 254f. (ch. 20, no. 195)); this is the only instance during his 1516 Advent sermons where Staupitz mentioned the indulgences as a problem. Höss, 'Das religiös-geistige Leben in Nürnberg', p. 19, speaks of Staupitz's *scharfe Kritik*, which is an exaggerated interpretation.

[176] See Luther's 95 Theses, esp. nos. 1–4, 39f., and 93–95; *WA* 1. 99ff. Luther had already raised the issue in a sermon delivered on 30 May 1517; see J. Wicks, '*Fides Sacramenti – Fides Specialis*: Luther's Development in 1518', in Wicks *Luther's Reform: Studies on Conversion and the Church* (Mainz, 1992), p. 120.

[177] On the criticism of the indulgences in Holland prior to Luther, see O. Clemen, 'Das Antwerper Augustiner-Kloster bei Beginn der Reformation (1513–1523)', in *Kleine Schriften*, I, pp. 434–41 (pp. 436f.).

[178] Sermon 20 (Staupitz I. 319); Sermon 22 (Staupitz I. 348). 'Non habet accusatorem, quia deus ipse iustificat; non potest habere iudicem damnantem, quia habet Christum interpellantem' (Staupitz, II. 286, no. 238 (ch. 23)); German version in Staupitz, II. 287, no. 238 (ch. 23); 'das der gerecht zuvorderst sein selbst ankleger ist; Latin: quod iustus in principio accusator sui est' (Staupitz, II. 290f., no. 242 (ch. 23)); see Staupitz I: 319 (ch. 20).

[179] Chapter 21. See translation by J.J. Stoudt, 'John Staupitz on God's Gracious Love', *LQ*, 8 (1956), pp. 225–44 (p. 243). (This is the first modern English version of Staupitz's *On the Love of God*. I use it as a check on my own translation of *Lieb gottes*.)

of the sinner's self-accusation again, and still later would mention it again in his fifth Lenten sermon of 1520.[180] As he used this concept on a regular basis, it is not hard to imagine that Luther came across it in Staupitz's proclamations (as well as or instead of reading about it directly in Bernard and/or in Augustine).[181]

Staupitz had become so well known by early 1517 that other theologians took notice of him and expressed their appreciation of him. The editor of the contemporary theological dictionary, the Swabian humanist Altenstaig dedicated his *Vocabularius Theologiae* (published in Hagenau, Alsace, in 1517) to Staupitz with these words: 'To the Reverend Father in Christ, Johann von Staupitz, most learned doctor of arts and theology, reformer of the cloisters and by apostolic authority Vicar General of the Observant Augustinians in Germany.'[182] Altenstaig was an Augustinian friar and possibly a student of the Tübingen humanist Heinrich Bebel. He and Staupitz knew each other from the times they both spent at Tübingen before the turn of the century. Altenstaig must have been very fond of Staupitz's preaching.[183]

At that same time, two other authors indicated that they held Staupitz in high esteem. Professor Karlstadt (*c*. 1480–1541), who taught Thomism for a while at Wittenberg, prefaced his commentary on Augustine's *De Spiritu et Litera* of 1517 with a dedication to Staupitz whom he called his 'teacher and patron' (*preceptor et patronus*). Karlstadt may have alluded to Staupitz being a professor at Wittenberg when he himself received his doctoral degree in 1510 there. He must also have had in mind his reading of Staupitz's Nuremberg sermons which had been published in the *Libellus* of February 1517. Karlstadt was especially impressed by Staupitz's sermonizing on the 'sweetness of Christ' with which Staupitz directed him to Augustine, as he attested in

---

[180] See Markwald, *A Mystic's Passion*, pp. 135–7 (Sermon 5).

[181] While it is not unlikely that Luther acquired this concept from Staupitz, it is more likely to have come through his own reading of Bernard's sermons, as Luther himself indicated: 'Blessed Bernard in a sermon on Advent: "O happy soul which always judges itself".' This line is found in Luther's first lecture on Psalm 109, in which he taught that nobody is 'justified by faith' except if he first confessed in humility that he is not yet just. 'Quia nemo per fidem iustificatur, nisi prius per humilitatem sese iniustum confiteatur' (*WA* 3. 345, 29f.); see also on Psalm 105, *WA* 4. 198, 19–21; and on Psalm 36 (gloss), *WA* 3. 208, 33–36. See also *WA* 4. 469, 16f.; *WA* 3. 185, 6; 288, 31–3; 370, 18; *WA* 1. 145, 28. See Posset, *Divus Bernhardus* (Kalamazoo, MI, 1999), p. 220 with n. 3.

[182] 'Reuerendo in Christo patri Ioanni de Staupitz / artium ac theologie doctori eruditissimo conuentuu reformator & observantie Augustiane per Germania apostolica auctoritate Vicario generali dignissimo patri obseruado Ioannes Altenstaig' (dedication preface).

[183] On Altenstaig from Mindelheim in Swabia, see Vonschott, *Geistiges Leben*, pp. 134–6; Oberman, 'Headwaters', pp. 37f.; Junghans, *Der junge Luther*, p. 26.

his preface. The other author was Friar Caspar Güttel who in the printed edition of his Lenten Sermons of 1518 (which were held at the friars' church at Eisleben) mentioned Staupitz's influence on him, when he indicated that he used ideas which Staupitz had expressed in his sermonizing.[184]

This influential Augustinian leader had become a guest preacher at Nuremberg, one of about 65 'Free and Imperial Cities' in the Holy Roman Empire of the German Nation that were directly subject to the Emperor. Nuremberg was the most important of them; not only the seat of the imperial government, in the absence of the Emperor, it was also at the forefront of modern technology at that time. The city was situated at the crossroads of 12 important trade routes which provided international connections: for example, to the Netherlands in the north-west for textiles; to Scandinavia and Russia in the north and north-east for fur and fish; to Silesia, Bohemia and Austria in the east for iron and metals; to Hungary in the south-east for cattle and grain; to Italy in the south for spices, gems, silk, paper and books; and to France and Spain in the south-east for wine and saffron.

In progressive cities such as Nuremberg, the humanist movement took root and the humanists formed informal literary societies ('sodalities'), dedicated to humanist scholarship. Likewise, at ecclesiastical courts such as at Salzburg, the humanist elements were particularly strong. Such societies were frequented not only by learned men but also by local politicians. 'One finds politicians and scholars together in the sodalities, those groups of humanists which developed at every place of any importance, in every significant imperial city, and at every fair-sized court.'[185]

Nuremberg's central significance in every regard – political, economic, cultural, technological, traffic-wise – was probably most attractive to Staupitz. As this city was the centre of attention, so was he with his unusual (that is reform-minded) sermons. Through Staupitz and other

---

[184] Karlstadt: 'Et tu, Reverende Pater [Staupitz] .... lectitavi epistolium, quo Christi dulcedinem ... pregustant ...' (Karlstadt's dedication preface in E. Kähler (ed.), *Karlstadt und Augustin. Der Kommentar des Andreas Bodenstein von Karlstadt zu Augustins Schrift De spiritu et litera* (Halle, 1952), pp. 5 and 9). See Lohse, 'Zum Wittenberger Augustinismus', pp. 90f.; Posset, 'The Sweetness of God', pp. 145f. Güttel: 'Jhesus // Ein fast fruchtbar buchlein von Adams wercken, und gottes genade mit unterricht wie recht beichte busszen, und das hochwirdigst Sacrament selig tzu entphahen im Augustiner Closter tzu sandt Anne vor Eislebe dise heiligste fasten gepredigt un gegeben 1518'; Kolde, *Die deutsche Augustiner-Congregation*, p. 310, n. 1.

[185] See B. Moeller, *Imperial Cities and the Reformation: three essays*, ed. and trans. H.C.E. Midelfort and M.U. Edwards, Jr. (Durham, NC, 1982), pp. 22 and 41; H. Böhme, 'Willibald Pirckheimer und Nürnberg' in Mehl and Schneider, *Reformatio et reformationes*, pp. 200f.

Augustinian friars, elements of a renewed theology infiltrated this leading city of the German Empire. About 1515/16 (possibly as early as 1512) the name of a 'Staupitz Society' emerged at Nuremberg, that is during the term of either Friar Besler's or Prior Volprecht's leadership as prior of the local friary. Reform ideas also entered with Friar Wenceslaus Linck. A close friend of Staupitz, he was the former prior of the friary of Wittenberg and dean of the theology faculty at the time when Luther earned his doctorate. Linck had been prior and preacher at Munich in 1515, and became now, in 1517, preacher and prior at the friary of Nuremberg, and thus a theological member of the Staupitz sodality. Staupitz had placed Luther at the budding friary and university of Wittenberg as a preacher and a professor, and now he placed as prior and preacher his other closer disciple, Linck, at Nuremberg, the quasi capital of the Empire.

Staupitz had numerous and influential friends in this most significant city. They became fans and called themselves 'Staupitzians' (*Staupiciani*), an expression first documented in a letter of 3 November 1517.[186] The group included important citizens: the city's two lord mayors or chief senators (*Losunger*), Jerome Ebner (d. 1532) and Anton Tucher (whose family funded famous art works in the city's churches), Kasper Nützel (Caspar Nuzel, d. 1529), Jerome Holzschuher (d. 1529), Andreas and Martin Tucher, Sigismund and Christoph Furer, the General Secretary of the City Council Lazarus Spengler (d. 1534), the artist Albrecht Dürer (*Albertus Durer* [sic], d. 1528), Germanus Appelles and Wolfgang Hoffman. Their names were listed by Scheurl in his letter to Staupitz of 7 January 1518, with a note that he himself belonged to it and that there were still more whose names escaped him momentarily; together they formed the 'Staupitz Sodality'.[187] These political, cultural and ecclesiastical leaders met at the Augustinian friary which may be considered the hotbed of the later (Lutheran) Reformation in Nuremberg. Here Friar Besler, who had come to know of similar humanist sodalities during his stay in Italy, was stationed. At Florence especially, from the fourteenth century, a sodality had existed in the Augustinian friary of Santo Spirito.[188] A 'Sodality of Basel' had been

---

[186] *Et alii plerique Staupiciani* (Scheurl's letter to Luther of 3 November 1517; *WABR* 1. 116, 12 (no. 49)).

[187] Scheurl's letter to Staupitz of 7 January 1518 had the designation *sodalitas Staupiciana*, used there for the first time for the group whose names he listed; see Soden and Knaake, *Christoph Scheurl's Briefbuch*, II, pp. 42f. (no. 159); Strauss, *Nuremberg in the Sixteenth Century*, pp. 160f.; H. Grimm, 'The Role of Nuremberg in the Spread of the Reformation', in Church and George, *Continuity and Discontinuity*, pp. 182–97. On the sodality member W. Pirckheimer, see Böhme, 'Willibald Pirckheimer und Nürnberg', in Mehl and Schneider, pp. 195–247. On Dürer, see for example J.C. Hutchison, *Albrecht Dürer. A Biography* (Princeton, NJ, 1990).

[188] See Machilek, 'Klosterhumanismus', p. 42.

formed in 1514 with Erasmus at its centre. At Heidelberg there was the literary sodality which Conrad Celtis had founded at the end of the fifteenth century, and to which Johann Reuchlin, Johann Trithemius and Jacob Wimpfeling belonged.[189] It seems that the Nurembergers wanted a sodality of their own, modelled after those in other cultural centres, as there was no university in Nuremberg.

At every one of the evening sessions of the Nuremberg sodality, Albrecht Dürer presented Staupitz with one of his pictures from his studio. It is not too far-fetched to assume a connection between the religious art of Albrecht Dürer and Staupitz's Christ-centred and cross-centred spirituality as he expressed it in his sermons and publications:

> His pictures have common elements with the preaching of his friend Staupitz. In his four series about the Lord's suffering and death, Dürer used the framework of traditional piety and filled it with new perspectives. In the garden of Gethsemane and on the Cross he gave to Christ an expression of triumph and majesty as the Lord suffered excruciating pains and in the scene before Pontius Pilate, the faces of Mary and John express hope and trust, as well as compassion and shared suffering. Thus it is fair to assume that the repeated preaching missions of Staupitz, the 'Primas' of the *Sodalitas Staupiciana*, in Nuremberg probably has had an effect on the work of Albrecht Dürer.[190]

The entire imperial city of Nuremberg was enthused about Staupitz who had now found his place among his humanist friends. His links with the 'establishment' of this imperial city were undoubtedly strongly forged. The reform movement was not carried out by the younger, more rebellious generation, but by those influential citizens who were in control of the city's political and cultural life. The humanism at Nuremberg was not only a 'Patrician Humanism', into which the nobleman Staupitz fitted quite well, but also a 'Monastic Humanism' into which Friar Staupitz squarely fitted as well.[191] Staupitz was so

---

[189] See Jeremias, *AELK*, p. 350. K. Garber et al. (eds), *Europäische Sozietätsbewegung und demokratische Tradition: Die europäischen Akademien der Frühen Neuzeit zwischen Frührenaissance und Spätaufklärung* (Tübingen, 1996).

[190] Markwald, *A Mystic's Passion*, Introduction, pp. 16f.

[191] See Vonschott, *Geistiges Leben*, pp. 151f. P.N. Bebb, 'Humanism and Reformation: The Nürnberg *Sodalitas* Revisited', in P.N. Bebb and S. Marshall (eds), *The Process of Change in Early Modern Europe: Essays in Honor of Miriam Usher Chrisman* (Athens, OH, 1988), pp. 59–79. On 'Patrician Humanism', see Hamm, 'Reichsstädtischer Humanismus in Nürnberg', pp. 168–72. However, Hamm's statement that Staupitz was 'no humanist' (p. 169) is too simplistic, as he disregards the fact that the Augustinian friary was the meeting place of humanists who formed the core of the 'Staupitz Sodality'. On *Klosterhumanismus*, see Machilek's essay with this notion in the title (in n. 110 above). In English, the term 'monastic humanism' is used, see N.L. Brann, *The Abbot Trithemius (1462–1516): The Renaissance of Monastic Humanism* (Leiden, 1981).

important to one of the leading men of Nuremberg, Lazarus Spengler, that he even recorded Staupitz's table talks; we know this from Scheurl's letter to Friar Caspar Güttel of 8 January 1518.[192] Staupitz came to the Nurembergers like a messiah to 'save the people of Israel', as Scheurl described to Staupitz the mood at Nuremberg after his sermons.[193] On 27 January 1517 Luther responded to Scheurl's letter of 2 January, thanking him for praising Staupitz's work at Nuremberg, and called Staupitz the instrument of Christ (whereby he used the Latin notion *organum*, which may designate a music instrument or a medical instrument for surgery!):

> What more pleasant news could you have sent me than your praising of Christ in his tool, the venerable father, our Vicarius [Staupitz] with such well deserved commendations. For nothing more precious can be told than that the Word of Christ is being preached, listened to and accepted. Yes, what is more, that it is being lived, felt and understood.[194]

It appears as if Scheurl had appointed himself to the position of a public relations manager for Staupitz, as he also sent Staupitz's *Libellus* to Bartholomäus Arnoldi von Usingen.[195] However, we do not know the latter's reaction and evaluation of it. On the other hand, we do know how the writer Hans Sachs of Nuremberg viewed the celebrated preacher. To him, Staupitz was an 'Evangelical', not a 'Lutheran', nor a 'Scholastic' (*Scholerischer*).[196] Later on, this poet compared Luther to a nightingale to whose songs all animals listen.

Incidentally, the contemporary designation 'Staupitzian' was in use before the notion 'Lutheran' was invented. The label 'Evangelical' stood for a reform movement early in the sixteenth century and cannot be identified with the term 'Lutheran', especially because the latter was not then in existence and when it was used later it was always in a derogatory way. The issue for Sachs in 1523/24 was not so much the contrast between 'Evangelical' and 'Lutheran', but between 'true Evangelical' and 'false Evangelical'.[197] However, the label 'Evangelicals'

---

[192] See Soden and Knaake, *Christoph Scheurl's Briefbuch*, II, p. 43 (no. 160). The table talks (known also as *sermones convivales*) were expected to be included in the as yet unpublished vol. 6 of the new critical Staupitz edition.

[193] 'Ac si tu is sis qui salvum faciet populum Israhel [*sic*]' (Scheurl's letter to Staupitz of 22 January 1517, Soden and Knaake, *Christoph Scheurl's Briefbuch*, II, p. 5 (no. 117)).

[194] 'Quid enim iucundius scribere potuisti, quam quod R. Patrem, imo Christum in organo suo, Vicario nostro, tam dignis extulisti praeconiis?' (*WABR* 1. 86, 6–9 (no. 33)).

[195] See R. Weijenborg, 'Neuentdeckte Dokumente im Zusammenhang mit Luthers Romreise', *Antonianum*, **32** (1957), pp. 147–202, (p. 148).

[196] See L. Keller, *Johann von Staupitz und die Anfänge der Reformation nach den Quellen dargestellt* (Nieuwkoop, 1967).

[197] It was after Easter 1519 that two followers of Luther (Thomas Müntzer and Franz Günther) were first called 'Lutherans' in a derogatory way, by the Franciscan Bernard

for reform-minded Catholics had also become suspect by 1523/24, when the 'Evangelicals' were disqualified as 'heralds of Luther's party' – as the conservative Augustinian Friar, Konrad Treger, informed his readership in the dedicatory preface to his book *Paradoxa centum*, published at Strasbourg.[198] 'Evangelical' was differentiated from 'Lutheran' also by the papal legate Aleander who complained in his report to Rome, at the end of the year 1523, that Germany was infested with 'Lutherans'. Because Luther's followers were supposedly so disgusted with his lifestyle, however, they allegedly preferred to call themselves *Evangelicos*.[199] In 1523 Staupitz would speak of 'evangelical people' as the true Christians.

Early in the spring of 1517, Staupitz stayed at Nuremberg, where he delivered Lenten sermons which were recorded by Lazarus Spengler, an eminent member of the Staupitz Sodality.[200] In these Staupitz talked about contrition, good works and other subjects related to Lent. He also took up the issue of 'free will' which he had already dealt with in his Tübingen sermons, relying on Egidio da Roma's commentary on the Sentences. At that time he had this to say about the cooperation of God and man: everything is God's doing and everything is also man's free will by consenting (*consentienter*). Everything is God's on principle and everything is man's free will as the instrument of God (*instrumentaliter*). Everything is God's because without his prevenient motion nothing is good; and it is also all man's because if we do not consent (*consentiamus*) to the divine motion, grace will not be poured into us. 'For it is God who justifies us, it is up to us

---

Dappe[n] in his report *Articuli contra Lutheranos* of May 1519 to the Bishop of Brandenburg; on this, see H. Junghans, 'Thomas Müntzer (1489–1989): A Short Biography on the Occasion of his 500th Birthday', in T. Dinovo and R. Kolb (eds), *Martin Luther in Two Centuries: The Sixteenth and the Twentieth*, trans. Katharina Gustavs (St Paul, MN, 1992), p. 50. In Sachs's view the 'false Evangelical' would be a 'Lutheran' – and Luther himself would probably have agreed with him! Luther himself was a 'Staupitzian' and thus a 'true Evangelical'. See G.G. Krodel, '"Evangelische Bewegung" – Luther – Anfänge der lutherischen Landeskirche: Die ersten Jahre der Reformation im Schnittpunkt von Kirchengeschichte und Sozialgeschichte', in W.-D. Hauschild, W.H. Neuser and C. Peters (eds), *Luthers Wirkung. Festschrift für Martin Brecht zum 60. Geburtstag* (Stuttgart, 1992) with n. 93 on pp. 40f. Luther appears to have used the term 'evangelical' for the first time during the Leipzig Disputation in 1519; see S.E. Buckwalter and B. Moeller (eds), *Die frühe Reformation in Deutschland als Umbruch. Wissenschaftliches Symposion des Vereins für Reformationsgeschichte 1996* (Gütersloh, 1998), p. 481.

[198] See A. Zumkeller, 'Konrad Treger OESA (ca. 1480–1542)', in E. Iserloh (ed.), *Katholische Theologen der Reformationszeit* (Münster, 1988), pp. 76–81.

[199] 'Nunc pertaesi hominis vitam non frugi se non Lutheranos, sed Evangelicos profitentur' ('Aleanders "libellus de personarum conditione",' in P. Kalkoff, *Aleander gegen Luther. Studien zu ungedruckten Aktenstücken aus Aleanders Nachlass* (Leipzig and New York, 1908), p. 137).

[200] Knaake, *Sämmtliche Werke*, pp. 15–42.

to consent.'[201] The solution with the concept of 'consent' had already been given by Bernard of Clairvaux: 'For to consent is to be saved.'[202] In his Advent sermons at Nuremberg in 1516, Staupitz had repeated this solution saying that the salvific election takes place by consent, as nobody is saved against their own will, and that the will and the reason are enslaved as a consequence of concupiscence, as Augustine had taught.[203] Now in his Lenten sermon of 1517, also delivered at Nuremberg, Staupitz insisted that we were created with 'free will', but he added that only if we rely on God's help as far as our works are concerned, will God give us the grace to do them willingly.[204] Staupitz here articulated awkwardly what Bernard said more eloquently: 'Free choice constitutes us *volentes* [willers]; grace, *benevolentes* [willers of the good].'[205]

Staupitz pointed out that there can be no Christian discipleship and no following Christ in suffering before one has experienced God's sweet mercy.[206] God's mercy is not denied to those who repent; it is always greater and more cordial. In this connection the preacher used the parable of the prodigal son (Luke 15) to illustrate his point. He also employed a unique metaphor in explaining what he meant: 'Just as a human being has to breathe in and to breathe out in order to live, so one needs to breathe out the stinking breath of one's sins, and turn to the cross and breathe in the fresh clean air of the merits of Christ's passion.'[207] One need not worry, not even about the punishment in purgatory, because God is not an executioner, but rather a shepherd who seeks the lost sheep. He is a loyal father who, nonetheless, disciplines his child. He is the most friendly, most merciful father whom we love, and whom we fear as a 'just, but mild judge'.[208]

---

[201] '... Iustificat enim deus nos, nobis consentientibus. Haec Aegidius de Roma in 2 Scripto distinctione 28 quaestione 1 quaestiuncula 3' (Staupitz, I. 270); Zumkeller, *Heilslehre*, p. 137.

[202] *SBOp*, III. 165–200; B. McGinn (ed.), *On Grace and Free Choice* (Kalamazoo, MI, 1977), p. 55.

[203] 'Aus dem erfolgt, das niemant wider seinen willen selig wirdet' (Staupitz, II. 237). 'Derhalb wirdet die sinreichkeit fengklich gefürt, der will ist gebunden ...' (Staupitz, II. 135). The Latin version has *ligata voluntas* for 'enslaved will' (Staupitz, II. 134); Zumkeller, *Heilslehre*, pp. 37–48.

[204] See Knaake, *Sämmtliche Werke*, p. 21; Zumkeller, *Heilslehre*, pp. 48 and 138.

[205] 'Itaque liberum arbitrium nos facit volentes, gratia benevolentes' (*SBOp*, III. 187); see McGinn, *On Grace and Free Choice*, p. 72. Staupitz, however, did not mention Bernard by name.

[206] See Knaake, *Sämmtliche Werke*, p. 28; Zumkeller, *Heilslehre*, p. 199.

[207] Knaake, *Sämmtliche Werke*, pp. 22–23; Zumkeller, *Heilslehre*, pp. 68 and 93. On Luke 15, see also his Sermon 11 of 1523, as quoted by Zumkeller, *Heilslehre*, p. 68, n. 428.

[208] 'Dorumb sollen wir Got lieben als den aller freuntlichsten parmherzigsten vater und forchten als ein gerechten milten richter' (Knaake, *Sämmtliche Werke*, p. 25; Zumkeller, *Heilslehre*, p. 71 and p. 144).

Staupitz took up again the theme of discipleship in suffering in his sermon that has the title 'That all our suffering and adversity becomes sweet and fruitful only through Christ's passion'.[209] Based on his Christo-centrism, he said that one's suffering is not fruitful without Christ's suffering. One's own suffering must be carried to the cross first and given to the crucified. The Christian who does this bites through the bitter shell of the nut (suffering) and finds the sweet kernel in it. The fruit consists of humility, obedience and patience. In Christ alone do we have hope for future blessedness, as we enter our suffering into the suffering of the saviour.[210]

As everything in Staupitz's spirituality is God-centred and Christ-centred, he attributes everything to God, including man's good works. In one of his previous sermons during Advent he had already said that nobody can do good works without Christ.[211] Now he reiterated that it is God who has given us the grace to do good works. They are not ours. They are divine works alone.[212] Therefore, one must not place any trust in one's own good works as some sort of investment for eternal salvation. Instead, one should despair over one's own works.[213]

Not even going to confession should be considered as earning merits, in Staupitz's view. He frowned on the custom of using confession booklets when going to private confession and objected if people used them just to busy themselves with listing their sins for the purpose of this promoting their own salvation. Going to confession should not be done with the attitude of earning more merits; rather, the confessing persons must place all their trust in God's mercy alone by which the sinners are justified. Staupitz did not want to belittle the sacrament of confession but to warn of false righteousness in preparing for it. Even after having received the sacrament of reconciliation, the Christian should pray to God that God may make him a true penitent (*pusser*) on the basis of the merits of Christ's passion.[214] Having dealt with issues of penance, good works, free will, discipleship and obedience, Staupitz brought his Lenten reflections at Nuremberg to a simple conclusion: the ultimate rule for human action is one's conscience. He quoted the scholastic axiom, 'whatever is done against one's conscience, leads to hell'.[215]

---

[209] 'Das alles unser leiden und widerwertigkait allein aus dem leiden Christi suß und fruchtbar wirdet' (Knaake, *Sämmtliche Werke*, p. 30; Zumkeller, *Heilslehre*, p. 93).

[210] See Knaake, *Sämmtliche Werke*, p. 30; Zumkeller, *Heilslehre*, p. 93.

[211] 'Neminem sine Christi gratia bene facere posse' (Staupitz, II. 94).

[212] 'Allain gotliche werk', Knaake, *Sämmtliche Werke*, p. 34; Zumkeller, *Heilslehre*, p. 185.

[213] See Knaake, *Sämmtliche Werke*, p. 39; Zumkeller, *Heilslehre*, p. 186.

[214] Staupitz's word for 'penitent' is *pusser* (in modern German, *Büsser*); see Knaake, *Sämmtliche Werke*, pp. 19f., 40; Zumkeller, *Heilslehre*, p. 176.

[215] 'Quidquid fit contra conscientiam, edificat ad gehennam' (Knaake, *Sämmtliche Werke*, p. 40; Zumkeller, *Heilslehre*, p. 43).

The general secretary of the imperial city Nuremberg, Lazarus Spengler, was a prominent member of the Staupitz Sodality, as already mentioned, and, as an eager listener to Staupitz's sermons, he even took notes on them.[216] Spengler used these notes when he composed his letter of consolation, 'A consoling, Christian prescription and medication for all adversities of life',[217] to his sister Margaretha who, knowing that her brother was a sympathizer of the reformers was concerned about his well-being. (The fate of the reformers appeared rather uncertain after the outcome of the Diet of Worms in the spring of 1521.) Spengler had his text published in two cities within the same year (1521), at Nuremberg by Friedrich Peypus, and at Augsburg by Jörg Nadler.[218] What Staupitz had said about the imitation of Christ[219] Spengler integrated into his letter of consolation.[220] What Staupitz reflected upon tribulations and temptations and how to deal with them in faith and patience,[221] Spengler repeated.[222] Staupitz's message that God becomes pleasing to man in faith, was also echoed in Spengler's words: 'Faith alone makes God nice and pleasing to us .... Faith alone turns all our tribulations into joy, makes all our burden easy, and all bitterness sweet.'[223] Spengler intertwined here Staupitz's thoughts with those of St Bernard, whom Spengler mentioned by name altogether eight times within this text. From these two spiritual authorities he learned that tribulations should lead to the knowledge of one's self as a sinner, that is to the acknowledgement of one's need for God's grace. 'Therefore, as St Bernard says, tribulation is quite useful and fruitful as it gives us reason to stand the test and [thus] leads us to the kingdom of heaven.'[224] Spengler referred to one of Bernard's sermons on Psalm 90, 'He who

---

[216] See Knaake, *Sämmtliche Werke*, pp. 15–50. On Spengler's life, see H. Grimm, *Lazarus Spengler: A Lay Leader of the Reformation* (Columbus, OH, 1978). On Spengler and city officials (*Stadtschreiber*) in other imperial cities such as Augsburg and Memmingen, see P. Frieß, 'Die Bedeutung der Stadtschreiber für die Reformation der süddeutschen Reichsstädte', *ARG*, **89** (1998), pp. 96–124.

[217] 'Ein trostliche Christenliche anweisung vnd artzney in allen widerwertikaiten', B. Hamm and W. Huber (eds), *Lazarus Spengler, Schriften, Band 1: Schriften der Jahre 1509 bis zum Juni 1525* (Gütersloh, 1995), p. 225; text edn pp. 226–43. The editors found about ten loci in this text where Spengler used Staupitzian thoughts, although he did not cite Staupitz's name.

[218] Hamm and Huber, *Lazarus Spengler*, p. 225.

[219] See Knaake, *Sämmtliche Werke*, pp. 31f.

[220] See Hamm and Huber (eds), *Lazarus Spengler*, pp. 228f.

[221] See Knaake, *Sämmtliche Werke*, pp. 21–6 and 31.

[222] See Hamm and Huber, *Lazarus Spengler*, pp. 231–3 and 241.

[223] 'Der glaub allein macht uns Got gefellig und angeneme.... Der [glaub] allein macht uns alle widerwerikait freudenreich, alle puerden leicht, und alle pitterkait sueß' (Hamm and Huber, *Lazarus Spengler*, p. 236).

[224] Ibid., pp. 237f.

dwells in the shelter of the Most High' (Vulgate, *Qui Habitat*), and to Rom. 5: 3–4, which Bernard had quoted in this connection, as did Spengler now.[225] He also invoked the same line from Job 1: 21 which Staupitz had loved to quote since his days at Tübingen: 'The Lord has given, and he has taken away. Blessed be the name of the Lord.'[226] Evidently, Staupitz the preacher and *Seelsorger* had a considerable spiritual impact on this leading layman of Nuremberg.

Preaching at Munich on the 'Love of God', 'Heavenly Sugar', and 'Heavenly Magnet' (Advent 1517)

Staupitz spent the Advent season of 1517 in Munich where he gave sermons about God's love. This topic appears to have been rather popular at that time, as a booklet in the vernacular by Thomas Peuntner (d. 1439), which bore a similar title, *Büchlein von der Liebhabung Gottes*, was reprinted in 1508 and 1518 after it had already been printed five times in the fifteenth century. Staupitz's vernacular sermons on this topic entered history as the famous treatise 'On the Love of God', published first by Johann Schobser in Munich in 1517/18, under the title *Ein seligs newes Jar von der lieb gottes.*[227] Staupitz dedicated it to the widowed Duchess Kunigunde of Bavaria, who was born the archduchess of Austria, the benefactress of the Augustinian friary at Munich. This book received a warm reception at Wittenberg from where Luther wrote

---

[225] 'Utilis tribulatio, quae probationem operatur, ducit ad gloriam' (Sermon 17, 3; *SBOp*, IV. 487, 20f).

[226] Slightly embellishing verse 21, Spengler wrote: 'Der Herr hat das "gluecklich" gegeben, der hat es auch wider genommen. Wie es ym gefallen, ist es geschehen. "Der name des Herrn sey gebenedeyet"' (Hamm and Huber, *Lazarus Spengler*, p. 242).

[227] Staupitz's vernacular version is known in the following prints: Leipzig: Melchior Lotter, 1517/18; Munich: Hans Schobser, 1517/18. The Latin version, *De amore Dei*, was published at Frankfurt in 1524. Later editions are by Caspar Schwenckfeld in 1547 (*Ain Seligs Newes Jar. Von der Liebe Gottes …*), by Daniel Sudermann in 1594, and by Johann Arndt in 1605. There are at least eight reprints between 1605 and 1630, according to Ludwig Keller, *Johann von Staupitz*, p. 393. Another Latin edition came out in Quedlinburg in 1706 as part of *Tetractys Tractatuum vere aureorum* (which also includes Staupitz's tract on the Christian faith, first published posthumously in 1525). A French translation came out in 1667, an English one in 1692, and a Danish version appeared in 1873. A German version was published in 1862, together with the tract on faith: *Von der Liebe Gottes und vom rechten christlichen Glauben. Aufs neue herausgegeben* (Stuttgart, 1862) (Knaake, *Sämmtliche Werke*, pp. 92–119). On Peuntner's printed editions, see B. Schnell, *Thomas Peuntner, Büchlein von der Liebhabung Gottes. Edition und Untersuchung* (Munich, 1984); R. Schwarz, 'Die Umformung des religiösen Prinzips der Gottesliebe in der frühen Reformation: Ein Beitrag zum Verständnis von Luthers Schrift "Von der Freiheit eines Christenmenschen"', in Buckwalter and Moeller, *Die frühe Reformation*, p. 135, n. 24.

to Scheurl in March 1518, that it should be reprinted soon, as he (Luther) hungers for it.[228] Before it was reprinted at Leipzig by Melchior Lotter, Luther gave his endorsement as the title-page of this edition shows: 'A wonderful instruction, written by D[octor] J[ohann] Staupitz, valued and approved by D[octor] Martin Luther, both of the Order of St Augustine.'[229] On Luther's recommendation the booklet was reprinted at Basel in 1520.[230] This book became Staupitz's best-known work. Luther sent a signed copy to his mother early in 1518 (see Plate 2).[231] The text is divided as follows into 21 chapters (sermons):

1 God is lovelier than anything.
2 God is to be loved above all things.
3 When God is not loved above all things he is not glorified as God.
4 To love God above all things cannot be learned from others.
5 To love God above all things cannot be learned from oneself.
6 To love God above all things cannot be learned from the letter of Scripture.
7 To love God above all things does not happen with a person unless the Holy Spirit previously dwells in that person.
8 From the indwelling of the Holy Spirit, the light of Christian faith first arises.
9 A person who has not been comforted by God's Spirit cannot hope to be consoled.
10 Our love for God is born from the revelation of God's love for us.
11 Love for God above all things is not given to every lover in the same measure.
12 How beginners love God above all things.
13 How the advanced ones love God above all things.
14 How the perfected ones love God above all things.
15 The stages of love for God above all things have an order among themselves, but are not always given by God in the same degree.
16 The stages of God's love undergo change according to the will of God's free love; how man is to know the same profitably.
17 The elect, who love God above all things, do what is best for all things.

---

[228] See *WABR* 1. 152, 30–32 (5 March 1518, no. 62).

[229] 'Ain wunder hüpsch Underrichtung beschriben durch [d]oktor J[ohann] Staupitz, bewert und approbirt durch Do[ctorem] Martinum Luther baide Augustinerordens'; quoted in Sallaberger, 'Johann von Staupitz, die Stiftsprediger', p. 262, n. 259; see also Schwarz, 'Die Umformung', p. 135, n. 25.

[230] *Von der liebe gottes, ... bewert vnnd approbiert durch D. Luther, beyde Augustiner ordens* (Basel: Adam Petri, 1520).

[231] See *WA* 48. 249; Kolde, *Die deutsche Augustiner-Congregation*, p. 298.

18 To those to whom it is not given to love God above all things, all other things are vain.
19 He who bears true love for God perfects all His commands.
20 Those who love God in the highest degree no longer find Christ's yoke and burden heavy to bear.
21 The surest sign, both of our whole love for God and of God's gracious love for us, is perfect emptiness of spirit.[232]

Staupitz presented the same message that he had proclaimed in his Advent sermons of the previous year, which had made such a great impression at Nuremberg. According to Staupitz, God's 'loveliness and friendliness' is seen only 'with the eyes of faith'. God is 'lovelier than anything', God is love beyond which nothing lovelier may be experienced. 'Yes, He is that love which adorns everything upon which it may fall. If it falls on a bitter enemy, he becomes a warm friend .... Whatever God loves cannot be ugly ...'. Thus, 'God is to be loved above all things', and if He is 'not loved above all things He is not glorified as God'. At this point Staupitz, the reformer of spirituality, inserted his criticism of improper praying. Today in Christendom, he said, we pray just as much to cattle, horses, silver, wood and to this world's goods as the pagans did a thousand years ago. Whoever does not love does not pray, even though speaking a thousand psalms. Whoever loves God, serves God. 'To love God above all things cannot be learned from others'.[233] He based his further reflections on Ps. 33: 9, arguing as follows:

> Things which can be known only from experience cannot be learned from others. No one can teach you how to see, hear, smell, taste, test, or experience, much less how to love, rejoice, bewail, and the like. We first try to experience before we love. First we must taste ourselves before God does it within us. This is why David said: 'Taste and see that the Lord is sweet ...' [Ps. 33: 9, Vulgate]. But we cannot learn to love God from someone else, much less to love him above all things. For love is a divine act, offered to one whose heart is within God's hand and whose will is in his power, to be turned where and when and how he wills.[234]

He continued that to love God cannot be learned from oneself nor 'from the letter of Scripture', since St Paul says that the letter kills (2 Cor.

---

[232] See translation by Stoudt, 'John Staupitz on God's Gracious Love'; see Posset, 'The Sweetness of God', pp. 161f.

[233] Chapters 1–4. Schwarz, 'Die Umformung', p. 145, points out the similarity of Staupitz's spirituality as expressed in these sermons to that of Gerhard Zerbolt of Zutphen (d. 1398).

[234] Stoudt, 'John Staupitz on God's Gracious Love', p. 229.

3: 6). From the Old Testament we learn God's written laws, and in trying to keep them we find out that we cannot keep them, that we are 'flecked' (*beflect*) with sin all over. 'No one can keep the law unless he loves God above all things'. We cannot in any way learn this from 'the letter' (*buechstab*). For if love for God above all things grew from the letter, then no one would have loved God as much as did 'the Jews who are stuffed full of the letter'. The letter of the old law produces nothing but the knowledge of the duty we have toward it, the knowledge of transgression, the knowledge of our inability to keep it, and the knowledge of eternal punishment which we have coming. Thus, the law helps to disclose our malady, but does not heal it. However, Staupitz is convinced that the 'spirit lies hidden under the letter', and 'that the old law is pregnant with and is bearing Christ'. Through Christ we are given grace so that we may love him above everything else, and thus to 'perfectly fulfil the law'. Those, who have found this spirit and recognized Christ hidden in the law, will have the Scriptures as a source of useful teaching and consolation. The letter of the Old Testament is meant to frighten us, which should lead us from nature to grace, from ourselves to the spirit in which we cry out to God: 'Abba, Father' (Rom. 8: 15). However, New Testament literalism is also a 'murderer of the soul' (*ein morder der selen*), and even more so than that of the Old Testament. Yet, the New Testament better points us to God as the one who redeemed us, and who for our sake became man and suffered on the cross; for this we should love him above all things.

Again, Staupitz emphasized self-accusation, that is the need to recognize and condemn ourselves as sinners. Although the New Testament brings Christ better before our eyes and his doctrine better to our ears, it cannot bring Christ's Spirit into our hearts; it serves only 'a heavier death' . 'The Jews' had Christ before their eyes, ears and hands, but they did not have Christ's Spirit in their hearts. Therefore they had been 'more condemnable than the heathens'. Staupitz had the Jews as Jesus' contemporaries in mind, as he used here the past tense (this can be observed also in his Lenten sermons of 1512). Here, in these 1517 sermons, he explained further that the Jews had more blessings from Christ than anyone else; yet they did not love him as much as he had blessed them. Staupitz then spoke of his own Christian contemporaries: 'So do we find it even to this day. Those who have Christ most on their tongues do not often find him in their hearts .... To love God above all things does not come to a person unless the Holy Spirit previously dwells in him.' Here Staupitz followed again St Paul who says in Rom. 5: 5 that our hearts are infused by the Spirit's love, given to us by the heavenly Father's Spirit, by Christ's Spirit; and the person who does not have it does not belong to Christ (*der ist nit Christi*), and this person thus cannot love God above all things. God must dwell in the believer as God did with Mary, the Mother of God, who received the Holy Spirit. In such a 'birth' the divine vitality overpowers the soul and all laws with love. Therefore, we are to ascribe all the good and holy acts to God alone, who fathers every good fruit within us.[235]

God is shown to us in the Bible as 'lovely' since he is the one who redeemed us, who for our sake became man, suffered, was crucified, died, and was buried. Therefore, we owe him our love. God's 'loveliness' can never be shown lovely enough, which happens when God reveals Himself to a person's heart. Staupitz contrasted the 'external doctrine' of the Scriptures which really cannot give us salvific understanding with the 'internal doctrine' through which the Holy Spirit grants the 'hidden understanding' (*heimlichen verstandt*). Christ must be moved from one's eyes to one's heart, from flesh to spirit, or else he cannot be known to us as our salvation. Again with the words of St Paul, Staupitz pointed out that 'neither [Paul's] nor the other apostles' teaching amounts to anything at all, if God himself does not teach into the heart' (*wo Got nit selbst ins herz lernt*). God brings himself into the soul as light enters into darkness where his 'loveliness and friendliness' are seen through the eyes of faith. Staupitz concluded the chapter with the statement: 'Knowledge of the Christian faith is pure divine grace.'[236]

God is revealed as the 'loveliest' through his inexpressible love for us, which is a great miracle that overwhelms us. Christ is 'most lovely and friendly', not because he suffered (in general), but because he suffered 'for us', because God who is merciful to humanity lets his Son be 'beaten' to death out of pure love 'for us'. Christ is the Rock who yields the fire to love, and he is the Rock who yields water. His life, suffering and death yield no enkindling spark (*zuntfeur*) to the soul unless the soul is stirred by the Holy Spirit. Only if God strikes the Rock in the chosen one's heart, fire rises and burns in love, 'the dead coals live, the black charcoal glows gold-yellow', enkindled by God's love. This happens without our own merits. 'To love God above all things is pure grace [*pur lautere gnad*], beyond all our arts and skills, beyond all our work and merit.' With these words Staupitz concluded Chapter 10.

The same strong emphasis on 'grace alone' is reiterated in the following sermons, especially in Chapter 15: as everything depends upon grace, it is not right for humans to ignore it. People who want to become righteous on their own are like worshippers who worship themselves as they want to make God inclined to them. They 'seek to draw God to

---

[235] See ibid., pp. 230f.; Zumkeller, *Heilslehre*, pp. 141f.
[236] Stoudt, 'John Staupitz on God's Gracious Love', p. 232.

themselves by their own piety as we bait the sparrow-hawk with a carcass'. They appropriate this image of God's mercy as their own due privilege, 'taking dirty linen to market and wanting to buy gold with muck' (*unflat*). Staupitz continued with his critical remarks as follows: 'Would to God that all the books in which people were taught to do virtuous deeds had been lost and only love survived!' A person is called perfect who 'conceives of God so lovely, sweetly, and amiably that it seems that there is nothing friendlier or lovelier than God'. Such a person is 'no longer a child of nature, but of grace'.[237] What Staupitz preached here is his earlier thesis rephrased, namely, that God's image is made sweet and pleasant to us by grace. It is not that we become pleasant to God, but that God becomes pleasant and sweet to us.

In these Advent sermons he also stressed with St Paul that all have been comprehended under unbelief and sin so that God might show his mercy to all. Sin was condoned in order that God's great mercy may appear in Christ the great Redeemer. Staupitz warned not to sin unabashedly. We must flee evil and sin. Ultimately, however, God is the one who 'covers up sin with mercy'. He alone can make evil good. 'We ourselves can fall, but we cannot lift ourselves up again. This rests on God's gracious mercy, which surpasses all his works.' With this phrase Staupitz concluded Chapter 17.

With words of his beloved Augustine, he pointed out that whoever bears true love for God perfects all his commands and keeps 'all that lies concealed in God's Word'. This is so, according to Augustine who said: 'Love God and do what you will.' Staupitz built on this Augustinian maxim in his conclusion to Chapter 19 which reads: 'Therefore one becomes educated only in the school of God's love. In it alone do we become doers of the divine Word [*wirker des gotlichen worts*]; all other arts make us nothing but hearers [*nichts denn horer*] ...' Whatever else we learn is nothing but labour and spiritual pain. No other art is necessary for salvation. God alone teaches us the 'art of love': 'Therefore, our Lord Jesus urged us not to seek any other master in the art of salvation but him.'[238]

In Chapter 20, the spiritual master reiterated that those who no longer love God inevitably find Christ's yoke a heavy burden. Sensuality can wear one down. Ingrained lust cannot be expunged by 'cassock and cowl, by cloister or church, by cell or dungeon, except if God's grace comes through our Lord Jesus Christ'.[239] After this cautious criticism of

---

[237] Ibid., pp. 234–36; Zumkeller, *Heilslehre*, pp. 46, 122f. and 187.

[238] Stoudt, 'John Staupitz on God's Gracious Love', pp. 237–41; Augustine's famous phrase is found in *Ep. Io. tract.* 7, 8; Zumkeller, *Heilslehre*, p. 143.

[239] Stoudt, 'John Staupitz on God's Gracious Love', p. 242.

misguided monasticism and church life, our reformer continued with the theme of the sweetness of God's grace. When God's grace comes, everything will be an easy task:

> For when [grace] sweetly forms God's inexpressible love in our hearts, then all other loves must cease .... It becomes so sweet that all creatures grow distasteful to us; then our iron-ribbed spirit grows soft, the heavy yoke sweet and the unbearable burden light because God's Spirit has stirred our spirit with loving-kindness.[240]

According to Staupitz, 'heavenly sugar' is at work in suffering. 'How can suffering not become sweet when it is strewn with the tasty heavenly sugar?' For God's nature is the spirit of unmediated love, and where it stirs it creates, where it points it leads, and where it is tasted it makes glad. He then added yet another image concerning God's love: 'Furthermore, its particular character is to deprive the flesh of its sweetness in the same way that the sun dims the candle's light. Moreover, its nature is also to sweeten pain.' His reflections culminate in exclamations and prayer:

> If temptations come from all sides to purge my virtues, they shall be like gold .... O Holy Spirit! O sweetest guest of the soul! O you life of man's life! ... In you we are moved to sanctity. And all this [is done] through Jesus Christ's merits, the one Saviour of the world, in whom God's inexpressible mercy and so great a love for us is revealed, and through you, Holy Spirit, [this love] is fashioned and firmly imprinted in our hearts .... Only from Christ does the fire of God's highest love show itself .... Only from him flow the waters of grace. And there is no other name by which one may be saved than in the most sweet name Jesus. To him do all of us who love God direct our desire, for in him do we find all that we need and must seek for our salvation.[241]

Toward the end of his booklet Staupitz wrote of the 'surest sign, both of our whole love for God and of God's gracious love for us'. It consists of 'perfect emptiness of spirit', that is empty of created matter, so that nothing but God may freely dwell in one's heart. When someone foresakes himself, seeks only God's honour, denies himself, exercises self-

---

[240] Ibid., p. 242.

[241] 'O Heiligister Geist, o sussister gast der selen, o einigs leben der menschen .... in dir werden wir seliglich bewegt [see Acts 17: 28]; und das alles von dem verdienen unsers herren Jesu Christi, des einigen erlosers der welt, in welchem uns die unaussprechliche barmherzigkeit Gottes und zu vil grosse lieb zu uns offenbar angezeigt und durch dich, Heiliger Geist, in unsere herz gebildet und so fest eingedruckt ist .... Auß Christo allein ... zeigt sich das feur der hochsten lieb Gottes, auß im einig fliessen die wasser der genaden; und ist kein ander namen, darinnen man mog selig werden [Acts 4:12], den der sueste namen Jesu' (Knaake, *Sämmtliche Werke*, pp. 116f.; Stoudt, 'John Staupitz on God's Gracious Love', pp. 242f.; Zumkeller, *Heilslehre*, pp. 90 and 120).

condemnation, then 'without doubt God dwells in that person who thus is full of God'.[242]

Staupitz worked here with yet another metaphor, that of the 'heavenly magnet', which he used as an illustration for God's attractiveness in Christ. In doing so the preacher most likely followed the medieval German spiritual writers Henry Suso, John Tauler and Rudolf of Biberach. Staupitz shared in particular with Suso and Rudolf the same vernacular term for 'magnet', that is *adamant/adamas* (while Tauler has *agestein*; an expression that Staupitz does not use):[243]

> Why is it that a magnet [*adamant*] follows heavy iron, and as soon as a basin containing iron is stirred by the loadstone and the iron is lifted up, it moves towards where the stone points? Show me how the stone can do this and it will not astonish you that the Creator of nature is the mighty mover of a free-willed creation and that the inexpressible loveliness of God [*liebligkeit gotes*] as sensed in the heart lifts up, enkindles, melts, and joyously raptures the spirit full of jubilation. Does not the stone draw the unmoved iron to itself? Then should the eternal heavenly Magnet [*adamant*] not draw the hardest and choked-up soul out of and above itself and guide it to Him?[244]

With this magnet metaphor Staupitz aimed at the relationship between God's loving suffering, on the one side, and the person who is drawn to it, on the other side. With this word picture of the 'magnet', Staupitz revealed his spiritual dependence upon earlier German preachers. Since this metaphor is otherwise very rare in religious texts, one may assume that he encountered it in, and copied it from, Henry Suso or Rudolf of Biberach. He probably learned it from Suso, as elsewhere he appears to have employed other expressions from Suso's *Horologium*.[245]

---

[242] Stoudt, 'John Staupitz on God's Gracious Love', pp. 243f.; see Posset, 'The Sweetness of God', pp. 161–4.

[243] See F. Posset, 'The Heavenly Magnet: On the Attractiveness of God in Western Christian Spirituality', *ABR*, **46** (1995), pp. 24–44. Other parallels between Staupitz and Suso are found in their use of the metaphor 'baking stove with warm bread'; or phrases like 'Christ as the most charming guest of the heart', or Christ is 'of my flesh and my Brother'. In contrast, Kolde, *Die deutsche Augustiner-Congregation*, p. 306 denied that there is any connection to the German mystics of the fourteenth century.

[244] Knaake, *Sämmtliche Werke*, pp. 115f.; Stoudt, 'John Staupitz on God's Gracious Love', p. 242, with a differing translation. This passage is quoted also by Keller, *Johann von Staupitz*, p. 49.

[245] See, for instance, the notion 'merry company' (*idcirce nec iucundae societati congruunt*) in Staupitz's Sermon 22 (no. 227), where he may have had in mind a passage from Suso's *Horologium*: *Iucundissima societas*, Book 1, ch. 11. The new critical edition of Staupitz's works makes an extra effort to integrate parallels to Suso's *Horologium* into the critical apparatus, as Suso may have been an additional source for Staupitz (see the Introduction in Staupitz, I. 38). However, the given parallels are insufficient proofs for dependence, especially because Staupitz does not refer to any source other than Augustine.

Since Staupitz also used the concept of Christ's cross being the real book from which we are to learn, which is also found in Suso (as mentioned above), one may give Suso some preference over Rudolf (and Tauler) as Staupitz's most probable source.

In continuation of Sermon 20, in which he dealt with the 'Heavenly Magnet', he stressed that the lover of God is taken over by God. Such a person is deified by grace; there is nothing left of 'God's wrath'.[246] Here he repeated in other words what he had said already, that we need to love God as 'the most friendly and most merciful father' and we should revere God as a 'just but mild judge'.[247] The same message was earlier conveyed in one of the sermons at Salzburg in 1512, when he had declared that God is the merciful judge, the 'judge of mercy'.[248]

Staupitz thus tamed the traditional concept of the wrath of God and also the image of Christ the Judge, and in so doing he fell in line with earlier German preachers like Suso, Tauler and Rudolf, none of whom presented Christ as the stern Judge. Suso, the earliest of them, in dealing with this image actually had converted the image of the judge into an image of sweetness. Although Suso was never quoted by Staupitz by name, Staupitz's spirituality appeared in close proximity to this German mystic of the fourteenth century, especially as far as the concept of the attractiveness of God and Christ is concerned. In the same way as these medieval mystics and preachers (Suso, Tauler and Rudolf), Staupitz featured the sweet Redeemer, not the Judge. In place of Christ the Judge, Staupitz showed his audience and readers Christ as the advocate and defender of the sinners. Since God is the Justifier, no accuser has a chance to accuse a sinner; therefore, it is impossible to conceive of God as a condemning Judge as long as Christ intercedes for us.[249]

The tremendous contribution which Staupitz made to the revision of the contemporary vulgar image of God and Christ is testified to by none other than the aged Luther. Twenty years after Staupitz's death, Luther wrote in his letter of 21 August 1544 to Spalatin that it was Staupitz who had consoled him when he (Luther) was in spiritual trouble; Staupitz had directed him to Christ the Saviour. That same advice Luther wished now to pass on to the depressed Father Spalatin, by quoting Staupitz from memory as follows:

---

[246] *Gottes zorn*, Knaake, *Sämmtliche Werke*, p. 118.

[247] Knaake, *Sämmtliche Werke*, p. 25; see above n. 208.

[248] *Richter der parmherzikait* (Sermon 12, Schneider-Lastin, *Salzburger Predigten 1512*, p. 123).

[249] 'Non habet accusatorem, quia deus ipse iustificat; non potest habere iudicem damnantem, quia habet Christum interpellantem' (Staupitz, II. 286); in his German version: *fursprecher* (ch. 23, Staupitz, II. 287).

This is how my Staupitz consoled me in my sadness at some time.
[Staupitz] said: '[If] You want to be a fake sinner, you [will have to]
make Christ even more so a fake Saviour. Get used to the fact that
Christ is the true Saviour, and that you are the true sinner. God does
not play games or play hide and seek, he did not joke when He sent
his Son and handed Him over [to die] for our sake.'[250]

Staupitz's booklet 'On the Love of God' may be his most mature and
popular work; after its publication, his popularity increased even further.
He was again invited to Nuremberg where he had already preached
during the previous Advent (1516), and Lent (1517), and where his
friends were waiting for him to give the next Lenten sermons. Scheurl
sent him the invitation in a letter of 7 January 1518, mentioning
explicitly the *sodalitas Staupiciana* that expected him to proclaim the
Word of God to them. Scheurl knew very well that he and his
Nuremberg friends had to compete with invitations from Munich and
Salzburg which Staupitz had also received.[251] Unfortunately, Scheurl's
invitation came too late – Staupitz was already scheduled to preach the
Lenten sermons in his beloved Salzburg.

Like other Augustinians, Staupitz's speciality had become the
preaching of the central themes of the Bible. This is true also of his
superior in Rome, General Egidio da Viterbo, who was one of the most
famous biblical preachers of the time. The first complete printing of the
Bible in Greek was dedicated to him when it was published in Venice in
1518.[252] The reputation of the Augustinians as great Bible scholars and
preachers spread even more when in the same year, in August 1518, an
encyclopaedia on Germany was published. This *Germaniae exegeseos
volumina dvodecim* was compiled by the young humanist, Franciscus
Irenicus (1495–1559), who would witness the famous disputation at
Heidelberg which Staupitz would order Luther to conduct at the
Augustinians' next chapter meeting in 1518. Irenicus's book was printed
with the printing privilege granted by none other than Pope Leo X, under
the date of 14 January 1518. The title-page shows two little angels each
carrying a banderole with the name 'Jesus', the one on the left in Greek
letters, while the one on the right in Hebrew. Ironically, in the second
volume of this work, on page 44v, the three friends of the reformed
Augustinian Order in Germany found honourable mention, although by

---

[250] 'Sic meus Stupitius me aliquando consolabatur ...' (*WABR* 10. 639, 37–41
(no. 4021)).

[251] '... vehementer obsecrem, quatinus hanc quadragesimam verbum dei apud nos
concionari digneris .... Scimus te quoque apud Monacenses [Munich] et Saltzburgenses
benigne foveri et excipi' (Soden and Knaake, *Christoph Scheurl's Briefbuch*, II. 42
(no. 159)). On Staupitz's booklet as his *reifste Schrift*, see Kolde, *Die deutsche Augustiner-
Congregation*, p. 297, and Kunzelmann, V, p. 475.

[252] See F.X. Martin, 'Giles of Viterbo', in *NCE*, VI, pp. 485–6.

that time they had made more than enough trouble for the pope and the Roman curia with their criticism of the indulgences. They were listed among the illustrious German scholars in the following grouping: Linck, M. Luder [sic], Staupitz.[253]

[253] Franciscus Irenicus, *Germaniae exegeseos volumina dvodecim* (Hagenau and Nuremberg: Anshelm; Koberger, 1518), XLIIIIv; see Junghans, *Der junge Luther*, p. 295. The title-page is reproduced in S. Rhein, A. Schlechter and U. Wennemuth (eds), *Philipp Melanchthon in Südwestdeutschland: Bildungsstationen eines Reformators* (Karlsruhe, 1997), p. 244 (exhibition catalogue of Badische Landesbibliothek).

CHAPTER FOUR

Coping with Challenges
(1514–20)

In the spring of 1515 Staupitz had once again been in the north of Germany visiting his mother in Dabrun, near Wittenberg, where his family owned land. From Dabrun he went to visit the friary at Wittenberg and from there accompanied the leading friars of the Order to Gotha for the chapter meeting of the reformed Augustinians from 29 April to 1 May 1515. Besler came from Nuremberg, Lang and Luther from Wittenberg. The friary at Gotha had been in existence since 1258, when the friars took over the building from the Cistercian nuns. Staupitz's humanist friend Mutianus who lived at Gotha was apparently present, at least occasionally, at their sessions. Staupitz, who was now in his fifth term as vicar general of the Reformed Congregation, presided, although he let Luther preach the solemn ceremonial sermon at the opening session before the assembled priors and select members of the Order. According to Chapter 32 of their Order's statutes which Staupitz had printed in Nuremberg in 1504, a sermon was to be preached on the first full day of the chapter meeting, after the morning Mass with the invocation of the Holy Spirit, and before any elections took place. Probably in consultation with Staupitz, Luther based his sermon on Chapter 44 of the constitutions of the reformed friars in which the sin of detraction was designated as diabolic; and thus dutifully scolded the vice of detraction. However, in his zeal Luther went overboard with his extreme acerbity and use of scatological language: 'A backbiter does nothing but chew with his teeth the excrements of other people and sniff at their filth like a swine. Thus, human faeces becomes the greatest pollutant, topped only by the devil's shit [*Teuffels Dreck*]'.[1] The chief backbiter is the devil himself whose name Luther referred to in humanist fashion in the three sacred languages: *satan* in Hebrew, *diabolos* in

---

[1] On Luther's 'election sermon', as Oberman calls it, and on the Order's constitutions, see H.A. Oberman, 'Teufelsdreck: Eschatology and Scatology in the "Old" Luther', *SCJ*, 19 (1988), p. 442; reprinted in H.A. Oberman, *The Impact of the Reformation* (Grand Rapids, MI, 1994), pp. 51–68. Oberman was able to use unpublished material in preparation for vol. 5 of the critical edition of Staupitz's works, 'in press' in 1988 (see his n. 21), but which did not appear until 2001. For Luther's elaborate use of (pseudo?)-Bernardine material in his sermon, see *WA* 1. 49, 38ff.; T. Bell, *Divus Bernhardus; Bernard von Clairvaux in Martin Luther's Schriften* (Mainz, 1993), pp. 76f. and 244.

Greek, and *detractor* in Latin. Luther had apparently spoken to Staupitz's satisfaction; the latter had suffered under recent attacks from the extremists among the reformed friars. While Luther's sermon was perceived as 'sharp', probably in the sense of 'aggressive', Staupitz himself was perceived as irenic according to Mutianus who spoke of him as the 'most welcome peacemaker'.[2] Luther's sermon evidently had made an impression as he was subsequently elected as the district vicar for almost a dozen reformed friaries in the territory of Meissen and Thuringia, for a three-year term. Among the friaries were those of Erfurt and Wittenberg, where the Order's study programmes were located, now also supervised by Luther. At the same meeting, a representative was to be chosen who would travel to the next general chapter meeting in Rome. It had been intended that Friar Nicholas Besler should be that man. He, however, adamantly refused because of the bad experience he had encountered several years before, when he was threatened with excommunication and imprisonment, while he had tried to do business there on behalf of his superior Staupitz in 1505/06 (see pp. 81–4). Instead, Besler was appointed district vicar of the reformed friaries in southern Germany. After the chapter meeting Staupitz had the honour of preaching to the general population on 3 May (Luther had preached only to the insiders, the friars). Unfortunately, Staupitz's sermon is not extant.[3]

Around the same time, perhaps as early as May or June 1515, Staupitz may have had his first discussions concerning the abuse of indulgences. This issue was not something that erupted all of a sudden at the end of October 1517. Adopting a critical attitude towards the indulgences was not uncommon at that time.[4] In France, the indulgence preachers were despised; 'indulgence sermons' were denounced as early as 1410.[5]

---

[2] 'Pacificator optatissimus' (Mutian to Lang about Staupitz, in C. Krause (ed.), *Der Briefwechsel des Mutianus Rufus* (Kassel, 1885), nos. 611 and 640, as quoted in *Staupitz*, II. VI, n. 4). On Staupitz and Mutian's friendship, see A. Jeremias, *Johann von Staupitz: Luthers Vater und Schüler* (Sannerz and Leipzig, 1926), p. 35.

[3] See T. Kolde, *Die deutsche Augustiner-Congregation und Johann von Staupitz* (Gotha, 1879), p. 263; Kunzelmann, V, pp. 470–71. On Luther in this context, see M. Schulze, *Fürsten und Reformation* (Tübingen, 1991), p. 168, n. 209.

[4] Gabriel Biel in his lesson 57 on the Mass (printed in 1488, perhaps without Biel's permission) had declared that indulgences are not effective in shortening the sufferings of the soul in purgatory; see H.A. Oberman and W.J. Courtenay (eds), *Canonis Misse Expositio*, 2 vols (Wiesbaden, 1963–67), II, pp. 399–410; M. Schulze, 'Tübinger Gegensätze. Gabriel Biel und Johannes von Staupitz', *Tübinger Blätter*, 72 (1985), 54–9 (p. 55). Luther's statement on Biel is found in WATR 3. 564, 4–7 (no. 3722, 2 February 1538); LW 54. 264; see Brecht, *Martin Luther, His Road to Reformation 1483–1521*, trans. J.L. Schaaf (Philadelphia, 1985) pp. 184f.

[5] See L. Taylor, *Soldiers of Christ: Preaching in Late Medieval and Reformation France* (New York and Oxford, 1992), p. 19.

Staupitz had his own view on the sacrament of penance and on the indulgences that are connected to the sacrament. He also had an uncomplicated attitude to the sacramental presence of Christ in the eucharistic bread (a concept which caused Luther considerable spiritual anguish).

In early summer 1515, at the Feast of Corpus Christi, Staupitz took Luther with him to Eisleben, the city of Luther's birth, for the opening of the new friary there on 18 June 1515. (The cloister building and St Anne's church are still in existence today.) The new religious community had been established three years earlier with Caspar Güttel from Munich as its prior. On that feast day Luther, although he was more than 30 years of age, was not spared a strange anxiety attack. As he and Staupitz, in their sacerdotal vestments, walked in the Corpus Christi procession with Staupitz carrying the monstrance that contained the Blessed Sacrament, Luther suddenly became frightened by the sacramental presence of Christ in the monstrance. As he recalled it many years later, he felt seized by terror, sweat and the fear of fainting, as he marched in the procession behind Staupitz. On mentioning this incident to Staupitz, he was corrected by him. Staupitz told Luther that Christ did not want him to be afraid: 'Your thought is not of Christ', since Christ is not present in the eucharistic bread as the Judge – as the rather confused 30-year-old man had apparently assumed. Staupitz did not let him get away with this mistaken assertion that it was Christ who frightened him. Here Staupitz's theology of the mercy of God was applied in a very pastoral and concrete way to Luther's problems as he corrected his twisted spiritual outlook. Staupitz, as an experienced spiritual director, knew exactly what spiritual advice he had to give to the younger friar at this point.[6]

---

6 See Kolde, *Die deutsche Augustiner-Congregation*, p. 264 (on Eisleben and Güttel). In Luther's account as told at table in December 1531: 'I was once terrified by the sacrament which Dr Staupitz carried in a procession in Eisleben on the feast of Corpus Christi. I went along in the procession and wore the garb of a priest. Afterwards I made confession to Dr Staupitz, and he said to me, "Your thought is not of Christ". With these words he comforted me well. This is the way we are. Christ offers himself to us together with the forgiveness of sins, and yet we flee from his face ... God gave us Christ with all his gifts, and yet we flee from him and regard him as our judge' (no. 137, recorded by Veit Dietrich, *WATR* 1. 59, 7–37; German version, lines 21f.) '*Ei, Euer Gedanken sind nicht Christus ...*'; see *LW* 54. 19f.; Similar accounts were recorded by Konrad Cordatus: 'Non est Christus, quod te terruit, quia Christus non terret, sed consolatur' (*WATR* 2. 417, 13–15 (no. 2318a)); 'Es ist nicht Christus, denn Christus schreckt nicht, sondern tröstet nur' (*WATR* 2. 417, 22f. (no. 2318b)); see E.H. Erikson, *Young Man Luther. A Study in Psychoanalysis and History* (New York, 1962), p. 37; Brecht, *Martin Luther, 1483–1521*, p. 75 simplistically speaks of Luther being 'overcome with horror about the sacrament'. Luther was not horrified about the sacrament, but mistakenly thought that Christ as the Judge was present in the consecrated bread in the monstrance.

Besides nurturing Luther's development, Staupitz had also kept an eye on Friar Wenceslaus Linck, who was the same age as Luther. After returning from visitations in the Netherlands and Belgium during the summer of 1516 (including one visit to Antwerp in June) Staupitz was at Mühlheim in August and perhaps also inspected the friaries at Magdeburg and Himmelpforten. At that time he appointed Linck as prior and preacher for the large Munich friary where, at the end of September 1516, Staupitz himself took up residency.[7] As his new home base, Munich had the advantage that it was relatively close to Chiemsee with its bishopric within the Salzburg realm of influence and a see which Staupitz may have wanted to fill should it become vacant. This position would have suited his pastoral experience and background, as he was of noble birth and easily able to play the role of an episcopal 'man of the world': 'Pious in church, courageous and cautious in council, pleasant and joyful at table and with the nobility',[8] as a saying of unknown origin about him went.

Aspiring to be Bishop at Salzburg-Chiemsee (1514–16)

Not much is known about Staupitz's activities for the period between May 1515 and summer 1516. We may assume that in regard to the well-known and contemporaneous Reuchlin controversy over the value of Judaism and Jewish books, Staupitz as an Augustinian sided with the famous Hebraist and humanist who had come under attack from the Dominicans at Cologne and especially from the inquisitor, Jacob von Hochstraten (c. 1454–1527). In this, Staupitz found himself in agreement with the prior general of his Order, Egidio da Viterbo, who himself was a famous humanist and Hebrew scholar, and thus a defender of their colleague, Reuchlin – who was also supported by the author(s) of the anonymous *Letters of Obscure Men*. The Augustinians with their leaders, including Egidio da Viterbo in Rome and Johann von Staupitz in Germany, were natural opponents of the Dominicans on this issue; humanists such as Mutian and Spalatin also supported Reuchlin.[9] There

---

[7] See J. Hemmerle, *Die Klöster der Augustinereremiten in Bayern* (Munich-Pasing, 1958), pp. 15–20. On the possible visit to the friary at Magdeburg, see Kunzelmann, V, p. 121; Kolde, *Die deutsche Augustiner-Congregation*, p. 270.

[8] See W. Graf, *Doktor Christoph Scheurl von Nürnberg* (Berlin and Leipzig, 1930), p. 65.

[9] On the letter from Spalatin to Staupitz about Staupitz's fondness for Reuchlin, see Kolde, *Die deutsche Augustiner-Congregation*, p. 272 (who follows Knaake on the issue of the addressee); Jeremias, *Johann von Staupitz*, p. 35 thought the letter was addressed to Mutian. On Egidio (Giles), see F.X. Martin, 'Giles of Viterbo,' *NCE*, VI, pp. 485–6 (with his portrait of 1523).

is reason to believe that Staupitz used Reuchlin's work *De verbo mirifico* in one of his Advent sermons which he delivered at Nuremberg in 1516 (see p. 163).

Before Staupitz had travelled to Nuremberg for the delivery of these Advent sermons, he had stayed at Salzburg and preached there during Lent 1516, as can be deduced from archive materials which show that he received payments, presumably for preaching. He earned 32 *pfund pfennig*, which was more than in January of 1515, when he was paid 21 *pfund pfennig*. The months in between Lent and Advent Staupitz filled with the inspection of the friaries in the lower Rhine Valley and in Belgium. During this trip he probably also incorporated the friary at Ghent into his own Reformed Congregation.[10] In addition, the elector of Saxony had commissioned him to obtain from the mother superior of St Ursula in Cologne the relics of the famed 'Eleven Thousand Virgins'. The well-informed Luther knew about this and reported to Spalatin at the elector's court:

> The Reverend Father Vicar has succeeded in getting permission from the Archbishop of Cologne to secure the relics for the sovereign .... Yet after the departure of the Reverend Father Vicar, the Mother Superior of St Ursula ... took shelter behind a papal prohibition; she argued that she could not with good conscience consent to release the relics without papal mandate or permission .... So if you [Spalatin] wish, you may inform the elector that he should either send there a well-authorized copy of the papal permission or else free the Reverend Father Vicar [from further obligations in this regard].[11]

While Staupitz appeared to be open to new developments such as the humanism of Reuchlin and others, he simultaneously had to deal with more conservatively minded people in high places such as Elector Frederick the Wise, who commissioned him to procure the relics from Cologne for his extensive collection. Previously, in 1509 the elector had printed a catalogue of this collection, produced by the court artist Lucas Cranach. He sought to add to it whenever possible. Among Frederick's prized possessions were small parts of the town where Jesus was born, of his swaddling clothes, of his crib, of his cradle, and of the hay and the straw on which Jesus slept. These relics were brought home from the Holy Land by Frederick himself, a journey which he had undertaken with his chamberlain, and Staupitz's friend, Degenhart Pfäffinger

---

[10] See Sallaberger, 'Johann von Staupitz, die Stiftsprediger und die Mendikanten-Termineien in Salzburg', *Studien und Mitteilungen zur Geschichte des Benediktinerordens und seiner Zweige*, **93** (1982), pp. 218–69 (pp. 254–55); Kunzelmann, p. 470; A. Zumkeller, 'Johann von Staupitz und die klösterliche Reformbewegung', *AAug*, 52 (1989), pp. 31–49 (p. 45).

[11] *WABR* 1. 78, 12–26 (no. 30); *LW* 48. 34. See *WABR* 1. 52, 30–39 (no. 20).

(d. 1519). Both Frederick and Degenhart, pious as they were, collected such relics as sacred souvenirs. However, while Frederick kept his collection at Wittenberg, Degenhart donated his to a village church in his home territory, that is at Salmanskirchen, near Mühldorf in Bavaria. Like Frederick, Degenhart also catalogued his relics, but never published his list as did his employer, who wanted to attract pilgrims to his church. Degenhart's home-made catalogue contains small paintings in water-colour, each page showing six relics. At the end of the catalogue are listed certain indulgences that could be obtained in connection with visiting these relics. One may assume that Staupitz was well aware of Degenhart's collection and that he himself saw it.

Degenhart's 'Catalogue of Relics and Indulgences', comprising 92 pages, is preserved at the museum in Mühldorf; however, the relics themselves are no longer extant. A typical page from the catalogue lists the following items:

A piece from the altar on which Christ was circumcised.
A piece from the spot where Christ fell when carrying the cross.
A piece from the spot at Caiphas' house where Christ was imprisoned.
A piece from the spot where Christ wept over Jerusalem.
A piece from the spot where Christ raised Lazarus from the dead.
A piece from the spot where Christ taught the eight beatitudes.

In those days, Staupitz was very busy with his visitation journeys, and his friends had a hard time tracking him down as he was constantly on the move. At the end of August 1516 Luther wrote to Prior Lang in Erfurt that he doubted whether he would find Staupitz in Munich at this time. The counts of Mansfeld, too, were eager to get in touch with Staupitz as they wanted him to be present in their midst for the dedication ceremony of the new Augustinian friary building at Eisleben. The prior of the Dordrecht friary also had written to Staupitz about the 'reformation' of the local friary which Staupitz was to carry out on the invitation of the local duke and the city council. On 5 October 1516 Luther informed Lang that Staupitz might now be found at Munich, and that although he (Luther) had hoped for a visit from him, Staupitz had run out of money to finance the trip and therefore had to stay where he was.[12]

During his visits to the friaries Staupitz was always on the lookout for potential students whom he would send to study at Wittenberg. However, there was so little room for them there that, in October 1516, Luther complained to Prior Lang at Erfurt that Staupitz was sending him all these friars and that he did not know how or where to

---

[12] '... se cogi manere, necessitate scilicet paupertatis' (*WABR* 1. 61, 21–3 (no. 24)).

accommodate them. At the very time when he was writing this letter, several student friars arrived from Cologne whom Staupitz had assigned to Wittenberg without asking Luther where they could stay. In fact, there were no cells available for them![13]

On his return from Belgium, Cologne and Ehrenbreitstein/Koblenz, Staupitz went south and stopped at Degenhart Pfäffinger's home in Salmanskirchen. Pfäffinger updated him with the latest news which he aquired from personal talks with Emperor Maximilian. Staupitz himself talked about these reports in his Nuremberg table talks of 1517.[14] It was from Salmanskirchen that Staupitz wrote to Luther on 8 October 1516, that he planned 'to enjoy a quiet winter in Munich',[15] presumably after the delivery of his Advent sermons of 1516 at Nuremberg which would make him so very famous.

During his conversations with Pfäffinger the topic of the nearby bishopric of Salzburg-Chiemsee must have been discussed. In June 1516, both the Elector Frederick and his advisor Pfäffinger may have pushed for Staupitz's appointment as bishop of Chiemsee. Staupitz's sister at the Cistercian nunnery at Nimbschen, also promoted his advancement to this position. Rumours about the resignation of the resident Bishop Berthold Pürstinger of Chiemsee (1465–1543; also 'Pirstinger', or simply 'Berthold von Chiemsee') must have been circulating at that time; he seems to have wanted to retire in order to do research and writing. Perhaps both Frederick and Staupitz were advised on this issue by Pfäffinger who was a native of that same region of Salmanskirchen/Wasserburg/Mühldorf in the Inn Valley; Chiemsee is located between Munich and Salzburg. In fact, by the time Pürstinger finally resigned from his episcopal office in 1525, towards the end of the Peasants' War in the Saltzburg lands, Staupitz was already dead.

---

[13] See *WABR* 1. 67, 75–80 (no. 26).

[14] See C.-J. Roepke, *Die Protestanten in Bayern* (Munich, 1972), p. 14; Sallaberger, 'Johann von Staupitz, die Stiftsprediger', p. 261. John Pfäffinger (1493–1573), a relative of Degenhart, was ordained to the priesthood in Salzburg, and became preacher at Passau in 1521, from where he had to flee to Wittenberg. Cranach's painting of the Last Supper (1565) shows John Pfäffinger at the Lord's table along with Luther and other Wittenberg reformers (but not Staupitz, who was long dead by the time the painting was commissioned); see P. Manns, *Martin Luther. An Illustrated Biography* (New York, 1983), plate 30 with the explanation on p. 81.

[15] 'Pater R. Vicarius [Staupitz] octava Octobris iterum ad me dedit literas ex Alberkirchen, id est ex domo Pfeffingeri [Degenhart Pfäffinger] .... Scribit se quiete per hiemem fruiturum in Monaco' (Luther's letter to Lang of 26 October 1516, *WABR* 1. 73, 54–58 (no. 28); *LW* 48. 32); Pfäffinger's home was at Salmanskirchen, not at Albertskirchen or Alberkirchen, as Luther's letter had it and also Kolde, *Die deutsche Augustiner-Congregation*, p. 270; on this, see Sallaberger's correction in 'Johann von Staupitz, die Stiftsprediger', p. 260.

It is notable that during each of the six years 1510 to 1516 Staupitz had managed to spend some time in Salzburg, for one reason or other. Perhaps he wanted to be close to the place where decisions were made, that is at the court of the archbishop of Salzburg, since Chiemsee was subordinated to the prince-bishop of Salzburg whose privilege it was to make the appointment to the Chiemsee bishopric.[16] Berthold Pürstinger had been bishop of Salzburg-Chiemsee since 1508. He was a reform-minded church leader whose outlook was probably similar to that of Staupitz. Although suffragan bishop of Chiemsee, Pürstinger did not reside at Chiemsee, but had to live at Salzburg in the so-called *Chiemseehof* (Chiemsee Court).[17] He may or may not have been the author of an anonymous book on the *Onus ecclesiae* ('Burden of the Church'), written in 1519 and published at Landshut in 1525. In it the burden which the Church loaded onto people was described: this included problems arising from the popes' and cardinals' avarice, the clergy's concubinage, the moral decay in the cloisters, and most of all the practice of indulgences which gave rise to superstition among the common people. The book explicitly referred to Luther's 1518 *Resolutions*, his explanations of his 1517 disputation theses on indulgences.[18] The author expected help only from a general church

---

[16] See M. Heim (ed.), *Quellen zur Geschichte des Bistums und Archidiakonats Chiemsee* (St. Ottilien, 1994), p. XI. On Staupitz's sister, Magdalena, and her role in promoting him, see Kolde, *Die deutsche Augustiner-Congregation*, p. 212.

[17] See M. Schulze, 'Onus Ecclesiae: Last der Kirche – Reformation der Kirche,' in P.A. Dykema and H.A. Oberman (eds), *Anticlericalism in Late Medieval and Early Modern Europe* (Leiden, New York and Cologne, 1993), pp. 317–42 (p. 319). Since the *Onus Ecclesiae* as edited by H. Werner in 1901 was not available to me, all the following references to it are quoted after Schulze's article, cited as *Onus* with chapter no. and pagination in Schulze. On the reform-minded Pürstinger's pastoral theology, see K. Amon, 'Der vortridentinische Salzburger Meßritus nach dem "Tewtsch Rational" des Bischofs Berthold Pürstinger von Chiemsee', *Heiliger Dienst*, **20** (1966), pp. 86–100 and 137–56. G. Marx, *Glaube, Werke und Sakramente im Dienste der Rechtfertigung in den Schriften von Berthold Pürstinger, Bischof von Chiemsee* (Leipzig, 1982); E.W. Zeeden, 'Berthold von Chiemsee (1465–1543)', in E. Iserloh (ed.), *Katholische Theologen der Reformationszeit 3*, (Münster, 1986), pp. 65–75; J. Sallaberger, 'Der Chiemseer Bischof Berthold Pürstinger (1464/65–1543). Biographische Daten zu seinem Leben und Werk', *Mitteilungen der Gesellschaft für Salzburger Landeskunde*, **130** (1990), pp. 427–84; V. Leppin, 'Pürstinger', in *Theologische Realenzyklopädie* 28, 1–3 (Berlin, 1997). The title-page of *Onus Ecclesiae* (Landshut 1524), University Library Salzburg, Sign. F II 56/1, is shown in J. Sallaberger, *Kardinal Matthäus Lang von Wellenburg (1468–1540)* (Salzburg, 1997), p. 164.

[18] Explicit mention of Luther is made in *Onus*, 15, 1, Schulze, pp. 334 and 340. See also Luther in *WA* 1. 534–6. The author no longer wanted to remain silent about the 'iniquity of Babylon' by which he meant the Roman curia's abuses. Luther used the name 'Babylon' for his own book on the criticism of the church: *The Babylonian Captivity of the Church* (1520). Following Bernard of Clairvaux and his criticism of papal misconduct, the author scolded the popes for acting more like successors of Constantine than of St Peter. Following

council without papal influence (as Luther also demanded) and from a clergy returning to apostolic poverty. He complained that the shepherds of the Church did not remain at their posts, but exacted heavy taxes in their absence. He prayed to Christ: 'Grant that the Church, which has been redeemed by Your blood, and is now, through our fault, near destruction, may be reformed!' The author critically evaluated also the contemporary academic studies which he saw being pursued for profit alone, while the truth was neglected: 'The worst stink of the world smells sweeter to us than the most sweet odour of God.' He lamented that, while the teachers of old were sent by God as lights to illuminate us about the mystical understanding of the *sacra scriptura*, today a fog blinds our spiritual eyes, and consequently the contemporary theologians want to understand the *sacra pagina* in a literal way only, that is the outer shell, and so they 'do not taste the inner marrow of the Scripture'.[19] The *Onus Ecclesiae* would later be condemned by the Council of Trent; Staupitz's works also ended up on the *Index of Forbidden Books* (see p. 362). Both Bishop Pürstinger and Vicar Staupitz were extraordinary representatives of the Catholic reform movement at that time; it was only during the later Tridentine Reformation that they were found to be unacceptable.

In 1528 Pürstinger wrote a summary of the Christian faith under the title *Tewtsche Theologey* ('German Theology') in his retirement at the Cistercian monastery Raitenhaslach, located north of Salzburg in the Salzach Valley. His publisher was the same Hans (Johann) Schobser at Munich who a decade earlier, in 1518, had printed the Advent sermons that Staupitz had delivered in Munich, known as the famous treatise *On the Love of God*. Cardinal Lang of Salzburg encouraged Pürstinger to publish a Latin version of his 'German Theology', which he did in 1531 at Augsburg under the title *Theologia Germanica*. In it Pürstinger presented the doctrine concerning the faith, the gospel, the virtues, and the sacraments, as all of those issues were debated controversially 'in these tempestuous times', as he put it in his Latin title-page.[20]

Brigitta of Sweden, he called for decisive reforms of the head of the church and of the religious Orders: 'Non est tacendum super iniquitatem Babylonis' (*Onus*, 19; Schulze, pp. 322f). On Bernardine style thoughts, see *Onus*, 19 (Schulze, however, does not recognize Bernard's matrix here); on Brigitta, see *Onus*, 19, 12 and 22, 3; Schulze, pp. 324–8.

[19] 'Dulcius sapit nobis foetor mundi pessimus quam odor Dei suavissimus' (*Onus*, 18, 4, Schulze, p. 337). 'Ideo isti intelligunt sacram paginam literaliter iuxta corticem exteriorem, non gustantes medullam scripturae' (*Onus*, 12, 7; Schulze, pp. 337f).

[20] *Theologia Germanica, in qua continentur articuli de fide, evangelio, virtutibus et sacramentis, quorum materia jam nostra tempestate controverti solet* (Augsburg: Alexander Weyssenhorn, 1531; reprinted at Basel, 1557; modern edn by W. Reithmeier, *Berthold Bischofs von Chiemsee Tewtsche Theologey*, with notes, vocabulary and biography (Munich, 1852). Pürstinger's book is not to be confused with the anonymous fourteenth-century work edited by Luther as his first publication. On Berthold's position concerning

As to Staupitz, he apparently saw a chance to become suffragan bishop of Salzburg-Chiemsee in 1516. In this, he was favoured by Degenhart Pfäffinger's sister, Ursula Pfäffinger, who had been the abbess at nearby Frauenchiemsee since 1494. She always held Staupitz in high esteem, and still later on provided him with fish from her ponds, knowing that Staupitz liked good food. (Incidentally, Scheurl, too, knew how to please Staupitz – he provided him with a shipment of oranges, as we know from their correspondence in 1515.[21]) Staupitz, as a bishop, would have loved the intellectual and spiritual climate which was created in that region between Munich and Salzburg under the influence of Catholic reformers like Pürstinger. It is not hard to imagine that Staupitz would have liked to succeed a bishop who analysed contemporary church life critically, as Pürstinger did, and who was more than ready for the general reform of the Church. There must have been a period of very active ecclesiastical renewal under way at that time as 35 new church buildings were dedicated between 1511 and 1524 in the Salzburg region alone, while, in the Chiemsee territory, Pürstinger himself consecrated about 200 new church buildings. In addition, the territory of Salzburg and Bavaria had felt the influence of the reform of the Benedictine monasteries under the leadership of the Melk monastery in Austria (west of Vienna), which had been developing since about 1418, in the wake of the recommendations of the Council of Constance.[22] All this must have looked quite attractive to Staupitz, and so it is not surprising that he preferred to stay in that region, awaiting possible assignment to the episcopal see.

The appointment, however, never came; partly perhaps because Luther did not wish it. Asked by the electoral court of Saxony to help persuade Staupitz to consider the Chiemsee bishopric, Luther expressed his strong opposition to such plans. In a letter of 8 June 1516 to his friend George Spalatin at the elector's court, Luther argued that this appointment was a bad idea because bishops were living in luxury and greed; he did not want his fatherly friend Staupitz to fall into such detrimental conditions. After asking Spalatin to do all that he could to dissuade Frederick the Wise, Luther continued in his letter: 'Even though

---

monasticism, see J. Schilling, *Klöster und Mönche in der hessischen Reformation* (Gütersloh, 1997), pp. 124–8. On Cardinal Lang urging Berthold to translate the book into Latin, see Sallaberger, *Kardinal*, p. 165, n. 55.

[21] On Staupitz receiving fish, see Sallaberger, 'Johann von Staupitz, die Stiftsprediger', p. 260; on Staupitz receiving oranges, see Scheurl's letter of 22 April 1514, in Soden and Knaake, *Christoph Scheurl's Briefbuch*, I, pp. 139f. (no. 91). On Ursula Pfäffinger, see *Allgemeine Deutsche Biographie*, Vol. XXV (Berlin, 1970), p. 596.

[22] See Zeeden, 'Berthold von Chiemsee (1465–1543)', p. 66; Roepke, *Die Protestanten in Bayern*, p. 13.

this man Staupitz is far from all these vices, do you want to see him dragged into the turmoil of the raging storms at the bishops' courts?'[23]

Staupitz was at Antwerp at that time and seemed to have been unaware of Luther's opinion and lack of support. The appointment never materialized, as Chiemsee did not become vacant until 1525. Since his plans for becoming a bishop there did not come to fruition in 1516, Staupitz had no further reason to remain in that region, neither at Salzburg nor at Munich. Staupitz departed for Nuremberg where he was invited to give his Advent sermons on 'predestination' in 1516 (see Chapter 3); he most likely made the friary there his temporary headquarters in 1516/17.

Travelling for the order: the indulgence issue (1516–17)

Soon after New Year 1517, Staupitz left Nuremberg in the company of Besler. They travelled first to Koburg to meet Elector Frederick for some reason and from there went on to inspect certain convents, including the Augustinian nunnery at Creuzburg (or Kreuzburg) on the Werra River between Eisenach and Eschwege, where they stayed on 23 March 1517. At the end of that month Staupitz was in Nuremberg again. Shortly after Easter 1517 he made a visit to the friary at Mindelheim, where he appointed Besler as the new prior, much against Besler's own wishes. Besler remained there as prior until the end of 1519. On his journeys Staupitz always eagerly promoted any potential scholars within his Order of learned men. He ordered Friar Gabriel Zwilling from the Wittenberg friary to study Greek under Friar John Lang at Erfurt; Luther therefore sent him there in March 1517.[24]

Although Staupitz was busy with his visitation journeys, his association with Nuremberg continued. Following success of his Advent sermons of 1516, he gave Lenten sermons in German on the Song of Songs there during March 1517; notes of which were preserved in Scheurl's library. Staupitz's table talks at Nuremberg were recorded by Lazarus Spengler later in 1517.[25] Apparently, the 'Augustinian family'

---

23 See *WABR* 1. 44f. (no. 16). In this letter, Chiemsee is mentioned explicitly, and also Pfäffinger; see Sallaberger, 'Johann von Staupitz, Luthers Vorgesetzter und Freund, und seine Beziehungen zu Salzburg', *Augustiniana*, 28 (1978), pp. 108–54 (pp. 131f.); and 'Johann von Staupitz, die Stiftsprediger', pp. 255–9.

24 See Kolde, *Die deutsche Augustiner-Congregation*, pp. 307–8. On Mindelheim and Besler, see also Hemmerle, *Die Klöster der Augustiner-Eremiten in Bayern*, p. 24; Kunzelmann, V, p. 475. On Luther, see *WABR* 1. 90, 5 (no. 35).

25 For the Lenten sermons of 1517, see Knaake's edition in *Sämmtliche Werke*, pp. 13–15, 49–50; *Sermones conviviales*, ibid., pp. 42–9.

at Nuremberg – that is, the 'Staupitzians'[26] – missed their spiritual leader who often had to be out of town. He was absent from Nuremberg later in spring 1517, as we know from Luther's announcement of 18 May 1517 to Friar Lang at Erfurt that Staupitz planned to come and see them soon. In that same letter Luther gave a brief status report as to the new theological trends at Wittenberg, which were quite in line with what Staupitz expected:

> Our theology and St Augustine are progressing well, and with God's help rule our university. Aristotle is gradually falling from his throne, and his final doom is only a matter of time. It is amazing how the lectures on the *Sentences* are disdained. Indeed no one can expect to have any students if he does not want to teach this theology, that is, lecture on the Bible or on St Augustine or another teacher of ecclesiastical eminence.[27]

On 11 June 1517, Staupitz met with Lang and Luther at Eisleben on the occasion of the Feast of Corpus Christi (the same place where, two years earlier, Staupitz had to deal with Luther's anxiety attack during the Corpus Christi procession). At their meeting Staupitz told Lang to continue his advanced theological studies. Staupitz also wanted several more young friars to prepare for their undergraduate studies under Prior Lang in Erfurt; Luther was expected to send them to Lang.

There is no doubt that Staupitz wanted well-trained friars to assist with the reform of piety and the church. When he met Luther next at the friary of Himmelpforten (near Wernigerode, north-west of Eisleben) in August 1517, he told Luther to remind Lang in writing to continue studying for the doctorate in theology (which he finally received in 1519). According to a plaque at the site of the former Augustinian friary of Himmelpforten, Staupitz and Luther met there on 6 August 1517 and discussed the indulgence issue.[28] Even earlier than that, two and a half years before Luther went public with his criticism of indulgences, Staupitz may have had congruous discussions with Luther and Linck (who had been dean of the theology faculty at the time of Luther's doctoral promotion) on this controversial subject – possibly as early as May or June 1515. Furthermore, the records of the city of Grimma and of Grimma parish indicate that in April 1516, about 18 months before the publication of Luther's famous *95 Theses*, such private discussions

---

[26] 'Augustiniana familia; et alii plerique Staupiciani' (Scheurl's letter of 3 November to Luther, *WABR* 1. 115, 1f. and 116, 12 (no. 49)).

[27] *WABR* 1. 99 (no. 41); *LW* 48. 41f.

[28] See *WABR* 1. 101f. (no. 43). On the meeting at Himmelpforten, see Kunzelmann, V, pp. 227 and 475; see also Institut für Denkmalpflege der DDR (ed.), *Martin Luther. Stätten seines Lebens und Wirkens*, p. 39.

had taken place between Staupitz, Linck and Luther. These three Augustinians formed a like-minded trio of reformers; all three were Bible scholars. By March 1517 Staupitz had appointed Linck to the prestigious position of preacher at the friary of Nuremberg. The conversations of these three friars were probably triggered by the activities of a member of the rival Dominican Order, John Tetzel, who had been involved in the indulgence business since 1502, and who, on 24 April 1516, had once again issued indulgence letters at Wurzen, which is to the north of Grimma and east of Leipzig.

In this situation, Staupitz decided to speak up against the false understanding of the papal indulgences (*der babstlichen indulgenz*). He had already voiced his criticism during one of his Advent sermons in 1516 in Nuremberg, and again in another sermon delivered there in early 1517. The latter is known under the title 'On the true and right contrition', and was recorded by Lazarus Spengler. In it Staupitz declared: 'The sound of the *gulden* which falls into the money chest will not free the sinner from sins.'[29] Only with true contrition will one obtain forgiveness of sins, that is 'without all those indulgences'. Staupitz wanted to set the record straight as far as the correct theological understanding of penance, contrition and indulgences was concerned. The person who wants to be truly contrite must know about the three kinds (not stages) of contrition. First, there needs to be some knowledge of the consequence of a misdeed, namely that one is hurting oneself; it is expressed in remorse, shame, and fear of punishment. Second, *Reue* (contrition) is a feeling that lets one feel sorry about having offended God, a feeling which he called an imperfect contrition. It is not an infinite contrition because any human contrition is finite and cannot blot out deadly sin. Third, and most important, is the contrition which is the 'suffering' (or *Reue*, 'contrition') which the innocent Christ felt (alluding to 1 Peter 2: 22). This is Christ's salvific 'contrition'; it alone is perfect, and based on it we can have our 'contrition'. It alone washes away the sins of thousands of worlds, Staupitz said. It is the work of the Redeemer

---

[29] 'Der klangk des guldens, so der in die geltkisten felt, wirdet den sunder seiner sunden nit entledigen' ('Von ainer waren rechten reu', in Knaake, *Sämmtliche Werke*, pp. 15–18; p. 18). See also A. Zumkeller, *Johann von Staupitz und seine christliche Heilslehre* (Würzburg, 1994), p. 174. (These sermons were expected to be included in the critical edition of Staupitz's works, as it was announced in 1979, but never appeared; one thus still depends on Knaake's text edition.) For the following elaborations on contrition, see L.G. zu Dohna and R. Wetzel, 'Die Reue Christi: Zum theologischen Ort der Busse bei Johann von Staupitz', *Studien und Mitteilungen zur Geschichte des Benediktinerordens und seiner Zweige*, **94** (1983), pp. 457–82; Zumkeller, *Heilslehre*, pp. 170–74.

(*seligmacher*). The fruit of Christ's suffering and contrition is a quieted conscience; it is the change of bitter tears into sweet ones (a wording based on Luke 22: 62); it is the joy and firm faith which is not tormented by doubts about Christ's (!) 'contrition' (*Reue*).

Staupitz developed here a strictly Christ-centred concept of 'contrition'. He declared further that some people live with the false hope that confession and the purchase of indulgences could achieve the absolution of sins. It is a false hope, because only the truly contrite heart is the real basis for the forgiveness of sins. Staupitz pointed this out against popular superstition, and in this he was able to rely on the official bulls on indulgences, which always stressed that indulgences work only for those who truly are contrite and confess. If indulgences were understood differently – and they probably were misunderstood by most of the people most of the time – they amounted to a 'Roman pestilence', Staupitz wrote to Spalatin in 1518.[30]

Staupitz's sermon pointed out what was expressed by an anonymous caricature of Tetzel as the commissioner of the German indulgences that showed him riding on a donkey, and two people offering their money for his coffers. The accompanying text runs as follows:

> O you Germans remember me well.
> I am the Holy Father's servant,
> And I alone bring you now
> Ten thousand and nine hundred years
> Of grace and indulgence from sin.
> You, your parents, wife and child,
> Shall benefit from it
> As much as you put into the collection box.
> As soon as the money in the chest rings
> The soul into heaven springs.[31]

There is a further report to the effect that, at another meeting in the Grimma friary, on 16 August 1517, Staupitz informed Luther about the dubious conduct of Tetzel who, as the official indulgence salesman, kept drumming up support for his business. Luther allegedly exclaimed: 'Now, God willing I shall punch a hole into Tetzel's drum'.[32] It certainly seems as though Luther was encouraged by Staupitz to do this, as Luther himself once observed that 'Doctor Staupitz incited me [Luther] against

---

[30] As mentioned by Jeremias, *Johann von Staupitz*, p. 44.

[31] Depiction with text appears in A.G. Dickens, *Reformation and Society in Sixteenth-Century Europe* (London, 1966), p. 61.

[32] For the conversations at Grimma in 1516, see O. Clemen, 'Paul Bachmann, Abt von Altzelle', In *Kleine Schriften*, II, pp. 279–80. Clemen also reported in this article that Abbot Bachmann preserved three of the utterances which Luther had made at Grimma; but he questions the early date of the conversation with Staupitz and Linck. I incline to let it stand.

the Pope', and that 'Junker Tetzel' forced him to leave the quiet friary in order to go public with his theological objections.[33]

Ridicule of, and objections to, the indulgences were not uncommon among the common people. A witness from the miners' town Annaberg observed:

> It is incredible what this ignorant and impudent friar gave out. He said that if a Christian had slept with his mother, and placed the sum of money in the pope's indulgence chest, the pope had power in heaven and earth to forgive the sin, and if he forgave it, God must do so also .... So soon as the coin rang in the chest, the soul for whom the money was paid would go straight-away to heaven.[34]

Staupitz's preaching against the vulgar concept of the indulgences sounded much like the anonyomous theological author(s) of what is known as the *Treatise on Indulgences*, which Luther 'edited', but never published. The Augustinian reform trio of Staupitz, Linck and Luther may have collaborated in articulating this text as early as April 1516, or as late as the summer of 1517. In the past, it was assumed to be Luther's sermon of 26 July 1516, in which he criticized the indulgence business; however, it does not fit very well into the sequence of sermons of that time, and it is now generally argued that this sermon is simply a *tractatus* by Luther. Yet, this general assumption of Luther's authorship is questinonable because the title of this text only indicates that it was 'edited' (*editus*) by Luther, which does not necessarily mean that it was also authored by him. The full title is as follows: *Tractatus de indulgentiis per Doctorem Martin ordinis s. Augustini Wittenbergae editus*.[35] The wording of this title, our knowledge about the earlier meetings at Grimma of the Augustinian trio, and also Luther's own statement (made to Scheurl) that he liked to talk controversial things over first with his closest friends before he proceeded with any action, all lead us to speculate that this text was not composed by Luther alone, but probably by that very trio, perhaps even by Staupitz himself. Luther indicated to Scheurl, after his *95 Theses* had become widely known, that he had first wanted to discuss them 'with a small group here and in

---

[33] '... et Doctor Staupitius me incitabat contra papam' (*WATR* 4. 440, 18f (no. 4707)). If it is true that Luther said this in his table talk of 1539, it is difficult to understand what Brecht wrote in regard to penance, indulgences, and the Reformation insights: 'But we cannot overlook the fact that, while the new insight released a powerful impulse in Luther's specific situation, there is no trace of anything like this with Staupitz' (Brecht, *Martin Luther, 1483–1521*, p. 230).

[34] Dickens, *Reformation and Society*, p. 61.

[35] See *WA* 1. 65ff. (allegedly, Luther's sermon of July 1516). See also *WABR* 12. 5–9 (no. 4212a, and no. 48).

the vicinity', and (based on the group's judgment) the theses then could have 'either been condemned and destroyed or approved and then published'.[36] One may assume that the 'small group' that he mentioned is identical (at least in its core) with the trio of Luther, Staupitz and Linck. It is furthermore notable that Luther, who published all kinds of things, never published this particular *Treatise*. The only known copy of it was found with the papers that make up the correspondence between Archbishop Albrecht and the theology faculty at the University of Mainz in December 1517.[37] It is not too far-fetched to assume that Luther sent this *Treatise* ('edited' by him) to the archbishop in support of his own *95 Theses* – which he qualified explicitly as his own.[38] The *Treatise* is 'quite different in tone'[39] from the *95 Theses*, which further supports the assumption that the text is not Luther's exclusively, but probably the result of teamwork, or Staupitz's own, or Linck's own. Luther enclosed the *Treatise* perhaps in order to suggest that it could become the basis for a new 'summary instruction' which should be given to all future indulgence preachers. As the Augustinians under Staupitz's leadership were instructed to improve pastoral care via preaching (in competition with the 'Order of Preachers', the Dominican friars who sold the new indulgences), Luther's shipment of these papers to the archbishop would fit squarely into the Augustinians' programme. The probability that the *Treatise* was not Luther's own, or at least not exclusively, is enhanced by another observation: if Luther were the sole author of that text, he would most likely have relied on it shortly afterwards when he had to explain his *95 Theses* in greater detail. At that point, however, he felt compelled to write his own, new *Resolutions* (in January 1518); he did not use the *Treatise*. In the introductory letter to his *Resolutions*, Luther gave credit to Staupitz for having led him to the correct understanding of penance,[40] which is the wider issue for any discussion of indulgences. He thus asserted that Staupitz's theology was the proper background for his own theologizing in this regard. This hint may also point perhaps to Staupitz as the author of the *Treatise*. Lastly, it is very difficult to consider Luther as the author of the *Treatise* when one reads in it the very positive

[36] '... sed cum paucis apud et circum nos habitantibus primum super ipsis conferri, ut sic multorum iudicio vel damnatae abolerentur vel probatae ederentur' (letter to Scheurl of 5 March 1518) (*WABR* 1. 152, 1–10 (no. 62)).

[37] See J. Wicks, 'Luther's Treatise', in *Luther's Reform: Studies on Conversion and the Church* (Mainz, 1992), pp. 87–116 (p. 89). Wicks assumes Luther is its author.

[38] 'Has meas disputationes' (see ibid., p. 92).

[39] Ibid., p. 93.

[40] 'Reverendo et vere patri svo Iohanni Stupitio [*sic*], S. T. professori, Augustiniae familiae Vicario' (*Resolutiones*, WA 1. 525, 1f).

statement that 'the granting of and gaining of indulgences is a most useful practice'.[41] Could Luther really have written such a sentence at that time? This statement is easier to accept if attributed to someone other than Luther, that is, to a more moderate and relaxed person – such as Staupitz is known to have been.

Here follow the main arguments of this all too neglected *Tractatus de indulgentiis*:

1 Although indulgences are the very merits of Christ and of his saints and so should be treated with all reverence, they have in fact become a shocking exercise of greed. The commissioners and preachers do nothing but extol indulgences and incite people to contribute. You hear no one instructing people about what indulgences are. The people come to think that by indulgences they are at once saved. Indulgences, however, do not confer the grace which makes a person righteous. They grant instead only the remission of penance and of imposed satisfaction.

2 We must therefore recall that grace is of two kinds, namely the grace of remission, and infused grace. It is irresponsible to proclaim that by these indulgences souls are released from purgatory. The pope would be cruel not to grant to suffering souls gratis what he is able to grant for money.

3 They themselves say that indulgences help only those who are contrite and have confessed.

4 The perfectly contrite person goes to heaven without indulgences. One cannot repent by natural power nor can the fire of purgatory free one from this sin without grace.

5 All works and merits of Christ and the Church are in the hands of the pope and he can apply whatever good works are done through Christ in the Church in three ways, as follows: first, as satisfaction; second, as a suffrage; and third, as a votive offering or sacrifice of praise. In this same way Christ by his deeds glorified God, took away our sins, and merited grace.

6 The pope cannot absolve or forgive the departed, but only make intercession that God will forgive and absolve them.

7 If the pope intercedes for souls as a mediator and not as one having jurisdiction, how can he be certain that a soul is freed? We must rely on 'Whatever you ask in prayer, believe that you receive it, and you will' (Mark 11: 24). Since this is the case, the granting of and gaining of indulgences is a most useful practice, in spite of the commerce and avarice which we fear is involved with them.

---

[41] Wicks, 'Luther's Treatise', p. 113.

8 Conclusion: Therefore, we must be quite earnest in preventing indulgences, that is, satisfactions, from becoming a cause of security, laziness, and neglect of interior grace. Instead, we must be diligent to cure fully the infection of our nature and thirst to come to God out of love for Him, hatred of this life, and disgust with ourselves. That is, we must incessantly seek God's healing grace. This is the end of this matter.[42]

Given that the group of close friends, under Staupitz's leadership, formulated this expert theological opinion on indulgences (called *Treatise*) some time between April 1516 and summer 1517, Luther must have felt assured in going public with his own criticism of the indulgences, as he did in a sermon at the beginning of the year 1517, in which he chided pastors for preferring fables and indulgences to the preaching of the gospel.[43] Given Luther's awareness of Staupitz's theology of grace as a back-up, it is more than likely that Staupitz, as the fatherly friend of both Luther and Linck, was the real instigator, behind the scenes, of criticism against abuses of the indulgence trade. Luther actually mentioned something to this effect in his *Resolutions,* when he wrote that he was not the only one who had doubts about the indulgences.[44] In fact, in a table talk of 1539 Luther openly blamed Staupitz for having encouraged him into acting as he did. He must have had in mind the talks with Staupitz on indulgences and penance at Grimma, and Tetzel's activities at that time; and perhaps he was also mindful of his editorial work on the *Treatise on Indulgences* (if the thesis is convincing that it was authored by Staupitz or by the Augustinian trio, and finally 'edited' by Luther, but not published).

By the sixteenth century, the indulgence business had undergone a long evolution since the Middle Ages when the theologians had accorded it a generally accepted dogmatic foundation. Theological aspects were quickly sidetracked, however, and public opinion began to focus on the economic and political implications. Staupitz's criticism and Luther's subsequent objections came at a time when Pope Leo X needed money for the construction of what is today St Peter's church in Rome, and when the German Cardinal Albrecht needed extra money as well. The

---

[42] English translation and commentary by Wicks ('Luther's Treatise', pp. 97–116).

[43] Luther's sermon on 4 January 1517 (*WA* 1. 509f).

[44] 'Non sum solus, sed veritas mecum et multi alii, scilicet qui dubitaverunt et adhuc dubitant, quid valeant indulgentiae' (*Resolutiones WA* 1. 608, 17–20). Concerning Linck as a member of the reform group, it is noteworthy that he received from Luther a letter dated 19 May 1518, which included Luther's reaction ('asterisks') to Eck's negative reactions ('obelisks') to their reform efforts concerning the indulgences. Linck was to send Luther's 'asterisks' on to Eck (see *WABR* 1. 178 (no. 77)).

leading banking house at that time was the Fugger Bank at Augsburg; it had lent large amounts of money to the church leaders, who planned to pay it back from the revenues raised through papal indulgences. The very fact that funds raised by the sale of indulgences had to be shared with Rome aggravated the existing anti-clerical and anti-Roman sentiment in Germany, especially in Saxony where Frederick the Wise steered a course with little regard for Rome. He avoided, for instance, sending any representatives to the Fifth Lateran Council.[45] Concerning the indulgence business, the contemporary Italian historian and papal official, Francesco Guicciardini (1483–1540), made this keen observation: 'In Germany many of the pope's ministers were seen selling, at a cheap price or gambling away in the taverns, the power of delivering the souls of the dead out of purgatory.'[46]

The Augustinian friars' criticism of the indulgence trade as it was conducted by the Dominicans fell on fertile ground. On 3 November 1517, days after the first publication of Luther's 95 Theses, the Staupitz Sodality at Nuremberg let it be known that they, too, were willing to 'restore Christ's theology and to walk in His law'. They even had the 95 Theses printed, in both Latin and the vernacular, a few months after their first publication. Also on 3 November 1517, Scheurl wrote to Luther that Staupitz was doing a great job at Nuremberg, and that Friar Linck was in town now, emulating their Vicar Staupitz. Remarkably, the indulgences were not discussed in their correspondence,[47] perhaps because they were not considered a matter of great theological importance.

However, the indulgence controversy began to strain Staupitz's relationship with his friend Frederick the Wise. Every year on the eve of All Saints' Day (31 October) Frederick put his collection of relics on public display (as already mentioned, he had even had Lucas Cranach produce an illustrated catalogue of them). Now his own theologians began to question the indulgences, some of which were connected to his own exhibition. Either Staupitz must have been summoned to give Frederick an explanation, or else he invited himself to see the elector

---

[45] See I. Ludolphy, *Friedrich der Weise Kurfürst von Sachsen 1463–1525* (Göttingen, 1984), pp. 373–5.

[46] See F. Guicciardini, *The History of Italy*, trans. S. Alexander (London, 1969), pp. 320–21. A fine description of the situation and the lacklustre income from the sales of indulgences is presented in R. Kiermayr, 'How Much Money was Actually in the Indulgence Chest?', *SCJ*, **17** (1986), pp. 303–18.

[47] *WABR* 1. 115, 1f. and 116, 12 (no. 49). On 11 December 1517, Luther thanked Scheurl for this letter with the information about Staupitz's popularity. The issue of Luther's *Theses* on indulgences was not mentioned, perhaps because it was not yet considered a hot topic (see *WABR* 1. 125f (no. 54)).

concerning this issue; in any case, rumours were spreading that Staupitz had fallen from grace; he therefore tried to see Frederick in person at Torgau, but the prince was elsewhere. It is not unreasonable to assume that Luther's public challenge of the indulgences, which had implications for the elector's exhibition of sacred souvenirs from the Holy Land, had something to do with Staupitz's summons to the electoral court. If there was no such connection, it is difficult to understand Luther's concern about Staupitz having annoyed the elector. Indeed, Luther was so worried that on 6 November 1517, less than a week after the opening of the exhibition of the relics at Wittenberg, and after the promulgation of his own *95 Theses*, he decided to write a letter to Frederick, pleading on behalf of Staupitz:

> Most Gracious Lord, ... I have been told by the prior at Erfurt [John Lang] ... that Your Grace is annoyed at Doctor Staupitz, our esteemed and dear father .... Therefore when [Doctor Staupitz] was here and sought Your Grace at Torgau, I talked to His honour and declared that I would not like to see Your Grace's displeasure come upon His honour. Truthfully, from the long conversation in which we discussed Your Grace all evening, I found out nothing else than that he has Your Grace in his inmost heart .... This was so much the case that he finally stated: I don't think that I have ever provoked my Most Gracious Lord .... Therefore, Most Gracious Lord, I plead on his behalf – as he has suggested to me several times – that Your Grace continue to favour and to be loyal to him, just as Your Grace had undoubtedly experienced his loyalty many times.[48]

This letter demonstrates that Staupitz and Luther formed a united front in reforming popular piety and correcting misinterpretations of indulgences. They even dared to draw their prince's anger on themselves.

Preaching at Salzburg on Christ's passion, on consolation, and also on Mary (1518)

At the time when Luther's *95 Theses* were disseminated through the German lands, Staupitz was in Salzburg where a change had occurred with regard to the preaching position at the city's main church. Father Paul Speratus (1484–1551), who had earned a doctoral degree in theology

---

[48] 'Wie das e[ur] f[ürstlich] g[naden] solt vngnade emfangen haben vber doctor Staupitz, vnnßen wirdigen lieben vatter, etlich schreybens halben' (*WABR* 1. 119f. (no. 51), *LW* 48. 50–52). Kolde, *Die deutsche Augustiner-Congregation*, p. 308, did not make the connection to the issue of indulgences. With Ludolphy, *Friedrich der Weise*, p. 390, one must assume that the friction between Frederick and Staupitz had something to do with the elector's collection of relics (and thus with the indulgences).

from Paris, had held the post for some time, but he then married, and left town. Therefore, on around 8 September 1517 an inventory had to be made, similar to the one written when Father Vitzthum had resigned; it showed that the proper payments to the departing preacher had been made.[49] In the following spring, 1518, Staupitz was apparently a substitute preacher at the city church of Salzburg. Here he delivered the well-paid Lenten sermons, which were recorded by the local Benedictine nuns.[50] While Staupitz remained in Salzburg, the Benedictine monks of St Peter's Abbey also took advantage of his expertise and invited him to preach for them, too. As the invoice of April 1518 shows, he was paid at first 10 *pfennig*, then another 32 *pfennig*.[51]

Earlier in his Tübingen Sermon 2, Staupitz had spoken of 'God's mercy alone' (*sola misericordia*);[52] 'mercy' had become a dominant theme in 1497/98. During Advent 1516, Staupitz had used similar terms both to his Nuremberg audience, and also in the written, published Latin version. He used phrases or notions that he qualified with an 'alone' (*allain* in Early New High German, *allein* in contemporary German) or 'unique' (*ainig*). He spoke of the first grace which proceeds from the will of God alone (*sola ... voluntate*) who wants our salvation.[53] By grace, God alone (*solum Deum*) is made pleasing to us, as Christ alone is the Lamb of God.[54] In 1517 he spoke of God as our 'only [*ainiger*] keeper, redeemer, and saviour'.[55] The salvation of humanity comes 'alone [*allain*] from God's love and grace, and from the merit of his holy passion'. Therefore, humans should not trust in their own works of, for instance, going to confession, but should trust 'in the perfect grace and mercy of God alone [*allain*] by which alone [*allain*] the sinner may be justified'.[56] No wonder that the Nurembergers praised him as the 'tongue of Paul' and 'the herald of the gospel'.[57]

---

[49] See Sallaberger, 'Johann von Staupitz, die Stiftsprediger', p. 249.

[50] See ibid., pp. 262–63.

[51] 'In Mense Aprili 1518 distributa: Item pro Stopiz [*sic*] dedi 10d; item pro Stopiz dedi 32 d.' (ibid., p. 263, n. 264).

[52] Staupitz, I. 56.

[53] 'prima gratia... sola benignissima liberrimaque Dei voluntate processit' (Staupitz, II. 96).

[54] 'Sed solum Deum ...' (Staupitz, II. 116); 'tu solus es agnus dei' (Staupitz, II. 158).

[55] 'Unser ainiger behalter, erloser und seligmacher' (Nuremberg sermon 1517, Knaake, *Sämmtliche Werke*, p. 20; Zumkeller, *Heilslehre*, p. 56).

[56] 'Allain aus Gots lieb und gnad und aus verdienstnus seines heiligen leidens .... allain in die volkomenhait der gnaden und parmherzigkait Gottes, dodurch der sunder allain gerechtfertigt werden mag' (Nuremberg sermon 1517, Knaake, *Sämmtliche Werke*, p. 40; Zumkeller, *Heilslehre*, p. 57).

[57] See Scheurl's letter to Luther of 2 January 1517 (Soden and Knaake), *Christoph Scheurl's Briefbuch*, II, p. 1 (no. 114), and *WABR* 1. 84, 3–16 (no. 32)).

During Lent 1518, Staupitz preached at Salzburg, as we know from the excerpts which were produced by nuns in the audience.[58] According to these notes, taken from several short Lenten sermons and also three Advent sermons, the Lenten sermons had the topic 'The Passion of Jesus Christ' and were delivered in the second half of the Lenten season.[59] Consistent with his biblical, God-centred and Christ-centred spirituality, Staupitz proclaimed Christ crucified as 'the bottomless ocean of mercy'.[60] Referring to Exodus 17, he interpreted Christ as the Rock who was severely beaten so that love may flow from him into our hearts.[61] The preacher let the crucified Christ speak to a dying person: 'O man, place your spirit into my Spirit, bring your dying into my death, die for my sake as I die for you. Thus you receive a blessed death which brings eternal life.'[62]

The Salzburg nuns' excerpts from the three Advent sermons reveal the same message of consolation for the sinners in the rhetorical question: 'How may the trustingly suffering Christian find any consolation?'[63] For an answer, the former professor of the Bible presented exemplary persons from the Scriptures who suffered hardship, such as the 'holy, royal prophet David' and the 'righteous and just Job'. However, consolation is to be sought from Christ alone, as there is no pain which he did not suffer. Christ is the model of *gelassenheit*, a disposition by which a person lets go of everything but remains under the power of the Holy Spirit and obedient to the will of God.[64] Christ will not desert anyone who puts hope in him, in his suffering, and in his merits. 'Our saviour on the cross' is truly the 'pure bronze serpent' (Num. 21: 8f.) by whom we are freed from all trials and suffering. In him 'alone' (*alain*) everybody will find the comfort of eternal salvation.[65]

In this context of Christ-centred preaching Staupitz incorporated a very high praise for Mary without finding any conflict in doing so. According to Staupitz, Christ gave to his mother under the cross the 'power' (*gewalt*) to be the 'mistress over all trials' (*anfechtung*) of all Christians, 'the mother of all graces and mercy'.[66] If anyone had to

---

[58] Staupitz's Salzburg sermons of 1518 were to have been included in vol. 4 of the new critical edition (scheduled for 1978–82), but did not appear. The manuscript is kept at St Peter's Abbey, Salzburg (Cod. b V 8. I); quoted here following Zumkeller, *Heilslehre*.

[59] 'Nach mitter fasten... auf das aller kürzist' (folio 66r; Zumkeller, *Heilslehre*, p. 12).

[60] 'Gruntloses mer der erparmung' (folio 69v; Zumkeller, *Heilslehre*, p. 84).

[61] Folio 72v; Zumkeller, *Heilslehre*, p. 123.

[62] Folio 72r; Zumkeller, *Heilslehre*, p. 199.

[63] Folio 61v; Zumkeller, *Heilslehre*, p. 93.

[64] Folio 62v; Zumkeller, *Heilslehre*, p. 200.

[65] Folio 62v–64r; Zumkeller, *Heilslehre*, p. 94.

[66] 'Maisterin über all anfechtung, das ist die mueter aller genaden und parmherzikait' (folio 69v–70r; Zumkeller, *Heilslehre*, p. 99).

endure trials, it was she; and she had mastered them all because Christ gave her the power to do so. Staupitz in 1518 also called her 'the clean, pure vase filled with all grace and virtue'.[67]

At this point a brief review of Staupitz's view of Mary is in order. Staupitz went along with the traditional use of high titles for Mary. In regard to the use of the rosary we may detect some mild criticism (see pp. 261f). Nonetheless, if one compares Staupitz's devotion to Mary with, for instance, that of Henry Suso in his *Little Book of Love*, one must conclude that Staupitz is far more subdued than Suso. Staupitz simply repeated the praises of Mary from the Church's *Lauretan Litany*. These showed up especially in his Sermon 11 of 1512 as the following comparison demonstrates:[68]

Lauretan Litany:	*Staupitz's original*:	*Translation*:
Dei genitrix	mueter gots	Mother of God
Mater Christi	muetter ... Jesu	Mother of Jesus
Regina Apostolorum	mit ... aposteln	Apostles
Regina prophetarum	propheten	Prophets
Mater divinae gratiae	mueter der gnaden	Mother of grace
	und all tugent,	and all virtues,
	muter der	Mother of
	barmherzickait	mercy
Regina sine labe originali	du rain	immaculately
concepta	entpfangen	conceived
Regina in coelum assumpta	künigin	Queen of
	der himmel	Heaven
Mater purissima	raine mueter	pure Mother
	rainist	most pure
	weib	woman
Refugium peccatorum	beschirm uns	be our refuge
Consolatrix afflictorum	trost	consolation
	zueversicht	confidence
Auxilium christianorum	Maria hilf	Mary help
	du bist ... zu hilf	you came to
	kommen	our help
Vas spirituale	rain lauter vas.	clean, pure
Vas honorabile.		vase.

---

[67] See Sermon 1518 (Zumkeller, *Heilslehre*, p. 97).

[68] See Schneider-Lastin, *Salzburger Predigten 1512*, pp. 122–3. On Suso, see his *The Little Book of Love* by *Heinrich Suso*, trans. P. Meister (Toronto, Ontario, 1989), pp. 24–8.

To Staupitz, Mary always remained the 'shrine of grace',[69] a title he derived from Luke 1: 28 ('full of grace'). We may assume that he grew up with an image of Mary identical, or at least close to, what is expressed in the litany of the Church and what was portrayed, for instance, in a painting of about 1486 that depicts his friend, the Elector Frederick, under the cloak of the 'Virgin of the Misericord' (*Schutzmantelmadonna*). Characteristic of the late fifteenth century, the painting represents Mary as a feudal protectress, indicated here by the contrast between her towering figure and the tiny persons under the protection of her cloak. The caption reads: *Fridericus dux Saxoniae Elector* (Frederick, Duke of Saxony, Elector). Frederick was a pious person who, as late as 1515, had Albrecht Dürer depict him in the pose of venerating the Virgin and Child.

This same elector one day asked his friend, the Bible scholar and spiritual leader Staupitz, about a disputed issue in Mariology. A friar (perhaps a Franciscan) had offered a 'Hail Mary' for the Elector Frederick, and then added a line unfamiliar to the elector at the end of his prayer, saying 'You, Mary, who are born without original sin'. Apparently, Frederick was surprised and so later asked Staupitz for spiritual and theological clarification. He wanted to know whether Staupitz agreed with this theological opinion that Mary was born without original sin. Supposedly Staupitz simply responded: 'This is fraudulence' (*betrigerey*),[70] a reaction that seems to indicate that, in his view, this doctrine was a mere theological speculation or fiction, probably because the scholar did not find it in the Bible – and in addition, perhaps, because it was developed by the rival Franciscans whom he did not like anyway, as Luther also reported in the table talk in which he told this story. If Luther's story about Staupitz's disqualifying statement is true, then it is difficult to maintain that Staupitz 'defended' the doctrine of the immaculate conception of the Virgin Mary, as Steinmetz contended. No statement strong enough to be construed as a forceful 'defence' of this doctrine is present in Staupitz's own works; nor was this doctrine spelled out by him in any aggressive way, as was done, for example, by Gabriel Biel.[71]

---

[69] 'Schrein der genaden' (Sermon 10, Schneider-Lastin, *Salzburger Predigten 1512*, p. 102).

[70] This story is preserved in an undated table talk of Luther, in macaronic language: 'Monachus quidam abtulit electori Friderico Ave Maria, et in fine papa addiderat: "Quae nata es sine peccato originali". Elector adhibuit in consilium Staupitium, interrogans, num probaret. Respondit Staupitius: Es ist betrigerey. Fuit bonum verbum, sive ex zelo quodam dixerit, sive ex odio. Denn er war den barfußern sehr feindt' (*WA* 48. 692, 29–32 (no. 7128)); this volume contains table talks not found in the volumes otherwise designated for Luther's talks. Staupitz's term *betrigerey* = modern German *Betrügerei/Betrug* ('fraud').

[71] 'Maria ab omni originalis peccati contagio fuit penitus preservata', as quoted by D.C. Steinmetz, *Misericordia Dei: The Theology of Johannes Staupitz in its Late Medieval Setting* (Leiden, 1968), p. 27, n. 2, see also p. 155.

Toward the end of the series of sermons of 1512 Staupitz had told his audience that Mary is the mother of all miserable sinners, of 'Heathens and Jews'.[72] She is the mother of graces. In this connection he had alluded to the medieval concept of the so-called 'double intercession' before the heavenly Father, which is also known in art history as the motif of the Tribunal of Mercy. People approach Mary who turns to her Son who turns to the Father, or as Staupitz has it: 'Christ came before the heavenly Father' in order to remind him that Mary is the 'mother of the entire Christian Church'.[73] In his 1515 book on discipleship, he had written of Mary as the 'spiritual heavenly mother', mother of the immortal Jesus and of all his members, apostles and prophets.[74] In it he also called upon Mary as 'mother of grace, mother of mercy' who was to 'protect us' from 'the enemy' (devil) in the ultimate necessity. 'You always were ready to help those who called upon you faithfully in truth. You make sure that we, miserable sinners, are forgiven.' If one does not want to be her child, one is not God's child either. 'She is the woman who bears the Christians, she is the mother who suckles them, who gives them food and drink; show love to her, ... or God does not love you.'[75] His reference to Mary's 'protection' was evoked most likely by images of Mary as the 'Virgin of the Misericord', such as the *Schutzmantelmadonna* showing Frederick the Wise under Mary's protective mantle.

In the concluding Sermon 12 of 1512, Staupitz had mentioned that Mary was free from any 'sin and inclination toward sin'.[76] This is not necessarily the full doctrine of the immaculate conception of Mary, but rather primarily the doctrine of her sinlessness. In his first sermon of 1512 Staupitz had let the Lord proclaim the following message about Mary: 'Everything that is pure with you [Mary] is so because of the purity of my body. That you are purely conceived and born is not something that stems from you, but from my mercy that has purified and adorned you.'[77] Characteristically, Staupitz also stressed the divine mercy

---

[72] 'Kain haiden noch jud wirt ausgeschlagen' (Sermon 11, Schneider-Lastin, *Salzburger Predigten 1512*, p. 113).

[73] 'Für [=Vor] den himlischen vater [ist Christus] kömen umb den sentenz: O himlischer vater, sprich aus, ob nit recht sei, das das weib, mein mueter, auch ain mueter sei der ganzen kristenlichen kirchen ...' (Sermon 11, ibid., p. 113).

[74] 'Geistlichen himlischen muetter ... ein muetter des ganzen unsterblichen Jesu mit allen seinen gliden, aposteln, propheten' (ch. 11, *Nachfolgung* in Knaake, *Sämmtliche Werke*, p. 77; Zumkeller, *Heilslehre*, p. 99).

[75] 'Wirstu ir kindt nicht sein, so saltu auch sein kindt nicht sein. Sie ist das weip, das cristen tregt, sie ist die mutter, die sie seugt, etzet unn trenket, hab sie liebe, ... ader Got hat dich nicht lieb' (Nachfolgung, in Knaake, *Sämmtliche Werke*, p. 77; Zumkeller, *Heilslehre*, p. 100).

[76] Schneider-Lastin, *Salzburger Predigten 1512*, pp. 122f.

[77] 'Alles das, was rain ist an dir, das ist alles aus rainikait meins leibs. Das du rain entpfangen und geporn pist, ist nit aus dir, sunder aus meiner parmherzikait, die dich also gerainigt hat und gezirt' (Sermon 1, ibid., p. 32).

in this regard. He explicitly used the notion 'purified' which refers to the purification after her conception, not preservation from original sin. Staupitz thus accepted the position which was developed within the Augustinian Order by none other than one of his favourite authors, Egidio da Roma (and, incidentally, by Henry of Friemar). Egidio da Roma taught that Mary was 'purified', not 'preserved' from original sin.[78] In contrast to this, the Franciscan theologian John Duns Scotus had developed the doctrine of Mary being without original sin – an opinion which was not shared, for instance, by St Bernard of Clairvaux nor St Thomas Aquinas. It appears that in 1512 Staupitz followed Friar Egidio of his own Order, and not the Franciscan, Scotus, although, from Staupitz's other inclinations toward Scotus one might have thought that he would also follow him in this mariological position. Indeed, this seems actually to be the case in Staupitz's *Libellus de executione*, as edited and translated by Scheurl in 1516–17. Here we read of Mary's sinlessness *per praeservationem* (*durch die fürenthaltung*, in the vernacular version) which is the Scotist articulation of this doctrine.[79] This means that Staupitz's sermonizing in 1516, as edited by the learned layman Scheurl, would demonstrate that he had departed from the 1512 position which mirrored Egidio da Roma's teaching, and would characterize him as a representative of the Scotist doctrine of the immaculate conception by preservation, not by purification. It is difficult to say whether Scheurl was aware of these scholastic distinctions and speculations when he worked on his edition of these sermons. Staupitz would appear to have accepted the change of viewpoint brought about within their own Augustinian Order by Friar Thomas of Strasbourg in the middle of the fourteenth century and by Friar John of Paltz in the fifteenth century, both of whom favoured the immaculate position.[80] However, Staupitz was not known for following any of them very closely.

Whose record of Staupitz's sermonizing is to be trusted more? The nuns' at Salzburg who in 1512 recorded him as having spoken of Mary as purified from original sin, or Scheurl's edition of the 1516 sermons at

---

[78] Zumkeller objects to Steinmetz's lumping together (*Misericordia Dei*, pp. 145–7) of Egidio da Roma and Henry of Friemar as alleged representatives of the doctrine on Mary being immaculately preserved; they teach purification after conception, not preservation (see Zumkeller, *Heilslehre*, p. 96).

[79] Advent sermon (ch. 12 in *Libellus De executione*, Staupitz II. 164).

[80] For Thomas of Strasbourg, see Schneider-Lastin, *Salzburger Predigten 1512*, p. 32, n. 57 (on Sermon 1). Paltz had presented his opinion in a sermon written on 28 August 1488, for the Augustinian Chapter meeting in Osnabrück on 8 September; see Paltz, 'De Conceptione Sive Praeservatione a Peccato Originali Sanctissimae Dei Genetricis Virginis Mariae' in C. Burger et al. (eds), *Opuscula* (Berlin and New York, 1989), pp. 142–54.

Nuremberg which contain the concept of 'preservation' from original sin? Was Staupitz more loyal to Egidio da Roma (and Henry of Friemar), or to Duns Scotus (and Thomas of Strasbourg and John of Paltz)? Did Staupitz really care much at all about this mariological issue? Apparently not, if one looks at it in the light of his priorities, the teaching about God's grace and mercy. Are there other Staupitzian texts that could help us? Evidently not, as no further cogent textual proofs for either one of these doctrines can be given from Staupitz's works.[81]

Perhaps one should let a theologian who was close to, and also very familiar with, Staupitz's teaching, make a final decision in this regard. This man would be Luther. If one gives credence to Luther's table talk (which, however, as has been mentioned, is undated, gives no date for the reported tale either, and is based on hearsay), one would have to conclude that Staupitz thought that all this quarrelling about the maculate or immaculate conception was 'fraudulence'. If that was indeed Staupitz's conviction, it would represent a reformed mariology with which he would have wanted to return to simpler concepts as found in the Scriptures. Regardless of all this speculation, and whether he thought it was fraudulent, he praised Mary as the model of modesty, virtue and humility, and as the one who 'daily drank from the fountain of the highest and eternal wisdom', as he said in 1517 to the Nurembergers.[82] The praise of her humility is found only on this one occasion in his sermons.

Otherwise she remained to him the *vorsprecherin* (in contemporary German: *Fürsprecherin*), the speaker for the sinners. All prayers to her are always answered, regardless for whom she intercedes. 'Nobody is saved without her help', Staupitz said in 1518.[83] He always found praise for Mary as the pure, sinless vessel (1518), the sinners' protectress against 'the enemy' (1515), the nurturer (1512, 1515), the Queen of Heaven (1512, 1518), and the Mother of God (1517), who under the cross remained filled with divine consolation and sweetness (1512) since the light of faith was never dimmed in her. She is the Virgin and Bride (1512), the Shrine (1512), and the heavenly Mother of the Church (1512, 1515). Yet, she is all this because of the mercy of God: 'That you are purely conceived and born is not something that stems from you, but from my mercy' (1512).

---

[81] Steinmetz (*Misericordia Dei*, p. 146, n. 5) quoted a locus in support of his interpretation which, however, is dubious from the point of view of textual criticism (see R.K. Markwald, *A Mystic's Passion: The Spirituality of Johannes von Staupitz in his 1520 Lenten Sermons* (New York, 1990), p. 106).

[82] See 'De compassione gloriose virginis Mariae' in Knaake, *Sämmtliche Werke*, pp. 34–5; Zumkeller, *Heilslehre*, p. 97.

[83] See 1518 sermon, as quoted by Zumkeller, *Heilslehre*, p. 99.

Involvement in the Luther affair (1518–19)

Reform-minded Augustinians wanted to correct the erroneous concepts of penance, confession and indulgences that were held by ordinary people. Staupitz was the key figure in these attempts, as Friar Caspar Güttel's publication of his 1518 sermons on 'Adam's Works and God's Grace' indicated. As mentioned above, Staupitz himself did not shy away from describing the Roman reactions to criticism as the 'Babylonian' or 'Roman pestilence'.[84] It may very well be that Luther had published his 95 Theses on the abuse of indulgences with Staupitz's approval.

In the spring of 1518, Staupitz invited Luther to come to Heidelberg for a disputation of his theology on the occasion of the Augustinians' chapter meeting. Staupitz had also received orders from the new general in Rome, Gabriel della Volta, to make sure that Luther appeared at the next chapter meeting in order to give account of himself. Volta had succeeded Egidio da Viterbo who resigned from the office of general of the Order on 25 January 1518, having become a cardinal on 1 July 1517. Volta had written to Staupitz on 3 February 1518, the same day that he himself had received orders from Pope Leo X to solve the problem of Luther. The papal letter to Volta was written in an elegant rhetorical style which reveals the influence of the learned Pietro Bembo, the Pope's humanist secretary. The letter insisted that the Augustinian Order must do something against Friar *Martinus Lutherius* who introduced 'novelties' in Germany and preached 'new dogmas to our peoples'. Volta should exercise his influence through a personal letter and 'through learned and probed mediators ... who can placate this man' [Luther].[85] Volta thought Staupitz would be the best person for this task and thus he asked him to intervene. Staupitz did this in his own way by letting Luther proclaim his theological convictions during the friars' disputation at Heidelberg which took place on 26 April 1518.

[84] On Güttel, see Kolde, *Die deutsche Augustiner-Congregation*, p. 310. On 'Roman pestilence', see Staupitz's letter to Spalatin of 7 September; see the edition by W. Grimm, 'De Joanne Staupitio ejusque in sacrorum Christianorum instaurationem meritis', in *Zeitschrift für die historische Theologie* (1839), issue 2, p. 119, as referred to by N. Paulus, 'Johann Staupitz. Seine vorgeblich protestantischen Gesinnungen' *Historisches Jahrbuch*, 12 (1891), p. 327, n. 3; see also Kolde, *Die deutsche Augustiner-Congregation*, pp. 316f.; Jeremias, *Johann von Staupitz*, p. 44; A. Zumkeller, 'Staupitz', *Dictionnaire*, XV, p. 1184.

[85] '... volo te eam curam suscipere, ut Martinum Luterium tuae societatis sacerdotem, quem scire te existimo in Germania novas res moliri, nova dogmata nostris populis tradere, quibus utantur, ab incepto, si potes, revoces auctoritate ea, quam tibi praefectura dat, cum scriptis ad eum literis, tum per doctos et probos internuntios, quos te illic habiturum multos puto, qui placare hominem conentur' (P. Fabisch and E. Iserloh (eds), *Dokumente zur Causa Lutheri (1517–1521), 2. Teil: Vom Augsburger Reichstag 1518 bis zum Wormser Edikt 1521* (Münster, 1991), p. 21).

Shortly before the meeting, Staupitz was made fully aware by Luther in a letter of 31 March (*pridie Kalen. Aprilis 1518*) that the latter had become a foe of the scholastics. Staupitz was assured that he, Luther, worked along the lines of Staupitz's own theology. Luther, who addressed Staupitz as 'my dear father in the Lord', pointed out that his own teaching was the same as found in the theology of Tauler and 'his book' (the *Theologia Germanica* of 'the Frankfurter', which he believed had been written by Tauler). Luther mentioned this text as being in print on Staupitz's order (printed by the Grunenberg Press, it came off the press on 4 June 1518). Simultaneously Luther admitted that his name was beginning to 'stink' in the world; he meant mainly in Rome. He also stated that people should trust in nothing but Christ, not in their own prayers, merits, or works. He was certain that Staupitz approved of his position as he added: 'But as I did not begin for the sake of fame, I shall not stop for infamy.' If the scholastics were allowed to question each other, why should he not also be entitled to do so? He was only following the Pauline advice, 'Prove all things, hold fast to that which is good'. Luther signed his letter in humanist style with *Fr. M. Eleutherius Aug[ustinianus]*.[86] One wonders why Luther used the humanist version of his name in this letter to Staupitz. Perhaps it was because Luther, who was inclined toward humanism, was writing to a man known as a friend of the humanists; and it may well have been fashionable for scholars to use humanist mannerisms.

Luther travelled from Wittenberg to Heidelberg via Würzburg, where he stayed overnight at the friary. In the company of its prior, Peter Wieglin, he continued his journey to the chapter meeting at Heidelberg. Here Staupitz either let Luther get away with circumventing any debate over the indulgences, or he himself was not interested in having the issue pursued. Luther was able to present his 'theology of the cross',[87] which he based on the Bible and the church fathers. It appears that the general

---

[86] 'Salutem. Occupatus plurimis cogor, mi pater in Domino, scribere paucissima. Primum valde credo nomen meum apud multos foetere .... Ego sane secutus theologiam Tauleri et eius libelli, quem tu nuper dedisti imprimendum Aurifabro nostro Christanno, doceo, ne homines in aliud quicquam confidant quam in solum Ihesum Christum .... Cur mihi non permittunt idem contra eos .... Fr. M. Eleutherius Aug.' (*WABR* 1. 160, 1–29 (no. 66)); see Fabisch and Iserloh, *Dokumente*, II, p. 19; E. Schwiebert, *Luther and his times: The Reformation from a new perspective* (St Louis, 1950), p. 326, still makes the questionable assumption (based on Knaake, *Sämmtliche Werke*, p. 90) that Staupitz had given *The Love of God* to the printer. The print was ready on 4 June 1518; see *WABR* 1. 161 with n. 5.

[87] See W. von Loewenich, *Luther's Theology of the Cross* (Minneapolis, 1976); A. McGrath, *Luther's Theology of the Cross* (Oxford, 1985); G.O. Forde, *On Being A Theologian of the Cross: Reflections on Luther's Heidelberg Disputation, 1518* (Grand Rapids, MI, and Cambridge, UK, 1997).

presider of this disputation was Friar Augustin Luft, the prior of the Heidelberg Augustinians, himself a theologian favourably inclined towards humanism. Luther's respondent was Friar Leonhard Beyer who had been a student at Wittenberg since 1514. The disputation took place in the lecture hall of the faculty of arts. Thus the disputation became an official event of the local university as well.[88]

At Heidelberg, Staupitz was re-elected to the position of head of the Order for a sixth term. Luther's three-year term as a district vicar had expired and, as district vicars could not stay in office for more than one term, he was replaced by Johann Lang. This change in office had the convenient side effect that Luther no longer held an exposed position within their Order. In addition, the political and ecclesiastical conditions were so uncertain that Frederick the Wise had felt compelled to write to Staupitz, on 9 April 1518, not to release Luther from his teaching duties at Wittenberg; apparently this was a possibility that had entered his and other peoples' minds. The elector reminded Staupitz that the latter had promised that Luther would be of service at Wittenberg for ever. Staupitz was told not to permit Luther to go anywhere else nor to delay his return: 'After you and other superiors of the Order of St Augustine summoned *doctor Martinum Luder* to the chapter meeting at Heidelberg, and if he is willing to obey ..., it is my wish, ... that he return immediately to this place, and that he not be dragged anywhere else nor held up anywhere else.'[89]

There is (occasional and unjustified, one might say) uncertainty over a letter that Luther sent to Staupitz on 31 March 1518. The concern seems to be that, if this letter was directed to Staupitz, it is surprising (to some people) that there is no mention made of the indulgence controversy.[90] But, perhaps this controversy was initially not as important then as it

---

[88] See Kolde, *Die deutsche Augustiner-Congregation,* p. 314; H. Vonschott, *Geistiges Leben im Augustinerorden am Ende des Mittelatters und zu Beginn der Neuzeit* (Vaduz, 1965), p. 136; R. Machilek, 'Klosterhumanismus in Nürnberg um 1500', *Mitteilungen des Vereins für Geschichte der Stadt Nürnberg,* **64** (1977), pp. 10–45 (p. 41). Heinz Scheible, '"Am gewohnten Ort": Luthers Heidelberger Disputation fand nicht im Augustinerkloster statt', *Rhein-Neckar-Zeitung: Heidelberger Nachrichten,* **39** (1982) no. 97, p. 2.

[89] 'Nachdem Ir und ander oberste des ordens Sancti Augustini doctor Martinum Luder zu eynem Capittel geyn haydelberg erforderth, so ist er willens ... gehorsam zu leisten .... so ist unnser Begern, ... das er ufs erst wider alher kom und mit vortzogen noch augehalten werde daran ...' (Frederick's letter to Staupitz of 9 April 1518, as edited by Kolde, *Die deutsche Augustiner-Congregation,* p. 314, n. 1; as quoted in Fabisch and Iserloh, *Dokumente,* I. p. 30). See Ludolphy, *Friedrich der Weise,* p. 399.

[90] See *WABR* 1. 160 (no. 66); see Brecht, *Martin Luther, 1483–1521,* pp. 213f. Luther mentioned in this letter that his name was beginning to stink since he was accused of rejecting popular prayers such as the rosary. He wrote that he preferred the Bible and the church fathers to the scholastics.

appears to us now. Alternatively, it may have been deliberately played down at that time. In any case, Staupitz helped to circumvent the entire issue of the indulgences and allowed Luther to enter the disputation at Heidelberg with much more fundamental theses that concerned the theology of the cross. As far as Staupitz was concerned, there was not much to be discussed regarding indulgences, especially since he and Luther concurred on this issue. Friar and Professor Arnoldi von Usingen, Luther's former teacher at Erfurt, submitted 12 counter-theses defending the scholastics against Luther.[91] Nonetheless, the indulgence controversy could not be totally ignored by Staupitz nor by the chapter members. A sharp communication from General Volta, addressed to Staupitz, had to be read to the assembly; however, no further official action was taken.[92] Apparently, the chapter meeting could not avoid the Luther affair altogether.[93]

All that fuss did not prevent the convivial Staupitz from enjoying himself at Heidelberg, where, as elsewhere, he was well connected to noble families. He and two Augustinian confrères, Luther and the district vicar John Lang, received an invitation from the local Count Wolfgang Wilhelm. They ate and drank, and there was good conversation. They also did some sightseeing as they 'viewed all the treasures of the castle chapel, and saw the armoury'.[94]

At the Heidelberg disputation, Luther had won Johann Brenz (d. 1570), Theobald Billican (d. 1554) and Martin Bucer (d. 1551) over to his anti-scholastic theology. Bucer was so impressed that almost two years after the event he wrote to Luther reminiscing about the spiritual banquet which both Staupitz and Luther had served them on that occasion. In this context Bucer called Staupitz 'a man of extraordinary piety'.[95] Bucer clearly perceived Staupitz and Luther as being united in battling for reform.

Concerning the aftermath of the indulgence controversy, nothing had happened at Heidelberg in 1518[96] as far as the reformed Augustinians were concerned. However, at the same time as the Heidelberg chapter meeting, the conventual Augustinians had held their provincial chapter meeting at Speyer. They elected as their new provincial the prior of the

---

[91] See Schwiebert, *Luther and his times*, p. 328.

[92] Ibid., p. 329.

[93] See Fabisch and Iserloh, *Dokumente*, I, p. 30.

[94] Luther's letter to Spalatin of 18 May 1518 (*WABR* 1. 173, 14–22 (no. 75); *LW* 48. 61); Schwiebert, *Luther and his times*, pp. 328f.

[95] 'Eximiae pietatis viro Io. Staubitz, vestro antistite' (*WABR* 1. 614, 8f. (no. 241)). *Antistes* means 'religious superior' in the contemporary humanist jargon, based on the classical Latin term for a 'high priest' of a pagan temple.

[96] See Brecht, *Martin Luther, 1483–1521*, p. 214.

Strasbourg friary, Konrad Treger, who would later become an opponent of the 'Evangelicals'.[97]

After the Heidelberg disputation, Staupitz received another letter from a grateful Luther, dated 30 May 1518. Because of Staupitz's explanations during previous conversations with him, the problem of 'penance' was solved for him now; penance appears 'sweet' to him, and Christ is his 'most sweet Saviour' and pardoner to whom Luther shall sing as long as he lives. This letter is a concise retrospective as Luther described Staupitz's impact on him:

> Reverend Father: I remember that during your most delightful and helpful talks, through which the Lord Jesus wonderfully consoled me, you sometimes mentioned the term *poenitentia*. I was then distressed by my conscience and by the tortures of those who through endless and insupportable precepts teach the so-called method of confession. Therefore I accepted you as a messenger from heaven when you said that *poenitentia* is genuine only if it begins with love for justice and for God .... Your word pierced me like the sharp arrow of the Mighty [Ps. 120: 4] ... Now no word sounds sweeter or more pleasant to me than *poenitentia*. The commandments of God become sweet when they are read not only in books but also in the wounds of the sweetest Saviour ....
>
> Continuing this line of reasoning, I became so bold as to believe that they were wrong who attributed so much to penitential works that they left us hardly anything of *poenitentia*, except some trivial satisfactions on the one hand and a most laborious confession on the other. It is evident that they were misled by the Latin term, because the expression *poenitentiam agere* [Mt. 4: 17, Vulgate] suggests more an action than a change in disposition; and in no way does this do justice to the Greek *metanoein*.
>
> While this thought was still agitating me, behold, suddenly around us the new war trumpets of indulgences and the bugles of pardon started to sound, even to blast, but they failed to evoke in us any prompt zeal for the battle .... Finally they taught impious, false, and heretical things with so much authority – temerity, I wanted to say – that if anyone muttered anything in protest he was immediately a heretic destined for the stake and guilty of eternal damnation.
>
> Since I was not able to counteract the furore of these men, I determined modestly to take issue with them and to pronounce their teachings as open to doubt [that is, the *95 Theses* of 1517].[98]

---

[97] See A. Zumkeller, 'Konrad Treger OESA (ca. 1480–1542), in E. Iserloh (ed.), *Katholische Theologen der Reformationszeit* (Münster, 1988), pp. 76–81.

[98] *WA* 1. 525–7; see his letter to the Pope (ibid., 527–9). *LW* 48. 64–70 has the English translation of Luther's entire letter. On the significance of Staupitz's theology for the young Luther, see M. Wriedt, 'Staupitz und Luther. Zur Bedeutung der seelsorgerlichen Theologie Johannes von Staupitz für den jungen Luther', in J. Heubach (ed), *Luther als Seelsorger* (Erlangen, 1991), pp. 67–95.

Staupitz was to Luther the discoverer of the true theology of penance. After Staupitz had given him the initial inspiration to rethink the concept of penance, as Luther claimed in this letter, he, in humanist fashion (and in following Erasmus), did some linguistic studies on his own on the Greek original of the concept (*metanoia*) and its Hebrew background. For Luther it was clear, as he stated in a talk at table, that it was Staupitz 'who started the doctrine'.[99] Staupitz received this letter as the cover letter to Luther's *Resolutions* concerning the indulgences which Staupitz was to pass on to Pope Leo X.

In June 1518, Staupitz declared that his Reformed Congregation had made the extra effort which the Order's general in Rome had expected of him – that is to clear up the Luther affair.[100] Staupitz sensed that Luther was in greater danger than ever. He expressed his feelings to Spalatin, the secretary of the elector, who in turn wrote to Luther on 5 September 1518 that Staupitz feared very much for Luther's 'head', while the other friends watch out for his 'health, reputation, and dignity'.[101] Two days later, on 7 September, Staupitz confirmed in his letter from Salzburg to Spalatin at the elector's court that he (Staupitz) and Luther are one heart and soul against the Roman 'pestilence': 'I know how much the Babylonian, or shall I say Roman, pestilence rages against those who contradict ...'.[102] We know that Staupitz spent the summer of 1518 partly on visitations of friaries and partly at Salzburg. However, it is not quite clear which location he meant when he sent his letter to Spalatin '*Ex Monasterio 7. Septembris* at Salzburg'.

For the Feast of the Assumption of Mary, on 15 August 1518, he was expected at Nuremberg, as Luther reported to Spalatin. On 1 September, Luther wrote to Staupitz, whom he expected to be in Nuremberg, that perhaps his *Resolutions* and the related text against the Dominican Friar Sylvester Prierias at the papal court were too liberal or daring in the eyes of Staupitz, and might not find his complete approval; certainly they would not be tolerable to the Romans.[103] As Staupitz sensed that Luther

---

[99] See *WATR* 1. 245: 9–12 (no. 526); *LW* 54. 97.

[100] See Fabisch and Iserloh, *Dokumente*, I, p. 31.

[101] 'Habes Patrem Reverendum Iohannem Staupitium pro tuo capite solicitissimum et reliquos omnes et ceteros pro tua salute, fama et dignitate vigilantissimos' (Spalatin's letter to Luther of 5 September 1518, *WABR* 1. 201, 46–8 (no. 92)); see I. Höss, *Georg Spalatin 1484–1545* (Weimar, 1989), p. 132.

[102] 'Ego novi, quantum saeviat Babylonica, ne dixerim Romana, pestis in eos, qui abusibus vendentium Christum contradicunt' (Staupitz's Latin letter of 7 September 1518 to Spalatin, in Keller, *Johann von Staupitz*, Appendix, pp. 399–400; p. 400). See Kolde, *Die deutsche Augustiner-Congregation*, pp. 316f.

[103] See Luther to Spalatin on 8 August 1518, *WABR* 1. 188, 16–19 (no. 85). 'In aliquot locis liberiores' (Luther to Staupitz on 1 September 1518, *WABR* 1. 194, 11–13 (no. 89)). On Staupitz's whereabouts, see Kolde, *Die deutsche Augustiner-Congregation*, pp. 315f.

was in imminent danger, he contacted the Elector Frederick via his secretary Spalatin by that letter of 7 September 1518. Staupitz asked Spalatin strongly to advise the elector not to tire of protecting the truth and not to be afraid of the lion's roaring (by 'lion' he meant Leo X). Staupitz thus may have been instrumental in preventing any authorities, ecclesiastical or secular, from taking Luther to Rome, who in a letter of 28 August 1518 was cited to appear before the general.[104]

Although Staupitz may have felt the dangers Luther was in and he himself by implication, the call for reform of the practice of indulgences was not all that dangerous in itself. That the Augustinians' reform ideas could still be considered 'good Catholic', we know from the fact that the Cistercian Abbot Valentine of Lehnin delivered to Luther a message to this effect from the bishop of Brandenburg. The letter referred to Luther's explanations of the indulgences in his *Resolutions* and stated that there were no errors contained in it, and that the bishop himself condemned the indiscreet and presumptuous manner in which recent preachers presented indulgences. Nevertheless, no more publications on this issue should be edited for the time being.[105]

During these months Staupitz must have spent considerable time on the road; he certainly travelled from Nuremberg to the Upper Alsace region, as a document of 28 August 1518 placed him there. The document was issued by Staupitz himself for the imperial governor for that region, Lord William of Rappoltstein, as part of the routine business of the Order that he had to take care of while the Luther affair was developing further. He drew up the document concerning the reception of William of Rappoltstein and his family into the *confraternitas* of the Augustinians. Such an acceptance was usually granted to any great benefactor of the Order. Apparently, in 1518, Staupitz had no problems with this practice; but, by 1523, when he was no longer an Augustinian superior, he had become very critical of it, as his Sermon 16 of that year shows. He then objected to the promise which an Order made in such cases, namely that the benefactors would benefit from 'all the good works, fasting, vigils, and prayers' which were performed by the friars. He now saw in this practice the selling of the friars' good works, based on the wrong theological opinion that good works, done by righteous

---

[104] See Keller, *Johann von Staupitz und die Anfänge der Reformation* (Nieuwkoop, 1967), p. 400. Ludolphy, *Friedrich der Weise*, p. 404, gives excerpts of Staupitz's letter of 7 September 1518. The letter of citation says: 'Citamus fratrem Martinum Lutherum et si non compareat, excommunicatum declaramus rebellumque nostrum et sedis apostolicae, quoniam dogmatizat de auctoritate papae, de indulgentiis etc.' (as quoted in Kunzelmann, V, p. 478, n. 2352).

[105] See H. Boehmer, *Martin Luther: Road to Reformation*, trans. J.W. Doberstein and T.G. Tappert (New York, 1960), p. 199.

persons, could be shared in terms of earning/meriting salvation. The comment in his sermon was: 'We cannot do anything that is good for ourselves and which would lead to our salvation, and [now] we want to save other people with our works!'[106]

If Staupitz actually resided anywhere at all for a longer period of time, it must have been at Salzburg. Not, however, primarily because he was called to this city by the archbishop, as has been assumed in the past, but mostly because he himself chose to live there. If this is so, it makes the invitation, which Staupitz extended to Luther at that time – namely to move in with him (and with the Friars Besler and Mayr?) at the Salzburg *terminus* – easier to understand. Staupitz anticipated persecution for Luther, as he wrote to him in his letter from Salzburg, dated 14 September 1518, the feast day of the Triumph of the Cross: 'As far as I can see, you have only the cross to expect, that is martyrdom. Leave Wittenberg, therefore, while there is still time, and come to me so that we may live together and die together. It is agreeable to the prince.' Staupitz signed this letter with 'Your Brother Johannes Staupitius D[octor].[107] Luther, however, remained in Wittenberg. He would have needed Frederick's permission to leave his post at the university to which he had been assigned for life. Previously the elector had insisted that Luther remain at his university. However, Staupitz may have persuaded him to release Luther under the given circumstances, and that he would have been able to provide a place for him at Salzburg.

---

[106] See Kolde, *Die deutsche Augustiner-Congregation*, pp. 441f. for the document of 28 August 1518. The critical Sermon 16 (1523) is quoted by Zumkeller, *Heilslehre*, p. 107 as follows: 'wir künen uns selbs nit ain werch tüen, damit wir uns sälig möchten machen, und wellen ander leut mit unsern werchen sälig machen' (folio 145r, in the sermons of 1523 in Salzburg's archive).

[107] 'Placet mihi, ut Wittembergam ad tempus deseras meque accedas, ut simul vivamus moriamurque. Id ipsum et Principi complacitum est .... Datum Saltzburgae, die Exaltationis sanctissimae crucis, anno M. D. XVIII. Frater tuus Iohannes Staupitius D.' (*WABR* 1. 267, 9–14 (no. 119)). See J. Sallaberger, 'Die Einladung Martin Luthers nach Salzburg im Herbst 1518', in H. Paarhammer and F.-M. Schmölz (eds), *Uni Trinoque Domino: Karl Berg. Bischof im Dienste der Einheit. Eine Festgabe Erzbischof Karl Berg zum 80. Geburtstag* (Thaur/Tyrolia, 1989), pp. 445–67. Boehmer (*Martin Luther*, p. 229), thought *princeps* refcrrcd to Cardinal Lang, but this is unlikely as Lang was not yet archbishop. More likely it was Staupitz's good friend Archbishop Keutschach of Salzburg who, at that time, was not on good terms with the Roman authorities, and might have been prepared to tolerate Luther in Salzburg. Luther, who knew of the friendship between Staupitz and Keutschach, was amenable to this archbishop acting as a mediator between him and the pope/emperor. However, Luther's move to Salzburg never happened because in May of 1519 Keutschach died (see Sallaberger, *Kardinal*, p. 243). Another possible *princeps* is the Elector Frederick the Wise, as posited by the editor of *WA* (footnote on p. 267). The redating of this letter as proposed in *WA* is not justified; see Brecht, *Martin Luther, 1483–1521*, p. 514, n. 28. To speak of Staupitz at Salzburg being 'in exile', as in Staupitz, II. 7 (Introduction), is questionable.

Concerning Luther's conflict with Rome, one must assume that the Roman administrators of the Order considered it hopeless to ask Staupitz for further assistance in solving the Luther affair by having Luther arrested.[108] On 25 August the proto-magister of the Augustinians wrote a letter concerning this matter to the provincial of the Saxon province, Gerhard Hecker (*c.* 1470–1538), who, of course, was not Luther's immediate superior; Hecker was not an official in the reformed branch of the Order. The letter from Rome demanded action against Luther, and Hecker was to seize him:

> Therefore, we command you under pain of losing all your promotions, dignities and offices, when you receive this letter, to proceed to capture the said Brother Martin Luther, have him bound in chains, fetters and handcuffs, and detained under strict guard in prison at the instance of our Supreme Lord Leo X. And as he belongs to that Congregation which thinks itself free from your government, that he may have no way of escape, we give you in this matter all our authority . . . .[109]

Apparently the Roman authorities felt that such forceful language was necessary. Strangely enough, Staupitz did not receive a similarly threatening communication from Rome. Hecker's role is unclear. He may have informed Staupitz and Luther concerning their imminent arrest.

Meanwhile, Frederick the Wise had insisted that Luther should not be brought to Rome, but be interrogated instead by the papal legate at the forthcoming imperial diet at Augsburg. Thus, in the autumn of 1518, Luther together with Friar Beyer appeared at Augsburg before Cardinal Cajetan (d. 1534) the papal legate present at the diet (primarily in order to gather support for a tax with which to finance defence, or a crusade, against the Turks). Since the papal representative was in German lands, Staupitz had thought it opportune that Elector Frederick the Wise himself, being present at Augsburg, should talk the Roman cardinal into listening to what Luther had to say. According to Luther's own reminiscence in 1541, it was Staupitz who convinced Frederick to talk personally to the Roman cardinal on Luther's behalf. Staupitz himself planned to be at Luther's side in Augsburg on 10 October 1518 (when

---

[108] See Schwiebert, *Luther and his times*, p. 343; Brecht, *Martin Luther, 1483–1521*, p. 248.

[109] '. . . iccirco mandamus, sub poena privationis omnium tuorum graduum, dignitatum et officioum, ut praefatum fratrem Martinum Luther, his acceptis, capi et incarcerari cures faciasque in vinculis, compedibus et manicis ferreis, ad instantiam Sanctissimi D. N. Leonis decimi, sub arta custodia detineri' (Volta's letter to Gerhard Hecker of 25 August 1518, Fabisch and Iserloh, *Dokumente*, II, p. 27; the facsimile of this letter is provided ibid., p. 78). R. Bäumer, *Lutherprozess und Lutherbann: Vorgeschichte, Ergebnis, Nachwirkung* (Münster, 1972), p. 26, n. 31, considers this writing a falsification, but without explaining his reasons; see Brecht, *Martin Luther, 1483–1521*, p. 514, n. 11.

he was anxiously expected by Luther),[110] but he probably arrived two days later, perhaps during the night of 12/13 October, having travelled from Alsace, where he is known to have accepted William of Rappoltstein into the Augustinian confraternity on August 28 (see p. 234). Immediately upon his arrival on 13 October, Staupitz accompanied confrère Martin to the interrogation before Cardinal Cajetan, who was himself a member of the Dominican Order. Staupitz was impressed by Luther's argumentation, and felt that Cajetan unjustly dominated the conversation. The third member of the leading Augustinian trio, Friar Linck, also stood at Luther's side, having accompanied him from Nuremberg to Augsburg. Luther's outer appearance was so poor that Linck had to give him his own cowl to wear in order that he should give the impression of a proper Augustinian friar.[111] The Augustinians had to stay at the cloister of the Carmelites, who were sympathetic to Luther's cause because their own Order did not have a friary in Augsburg. The Saxon chancery office made arrangements so that their professor would be safe in Augsburg with John Frosch, the prior of the Carmelites. A good friend of Luther, Frosch had received his doctorate in theology from the University of Wittenberg in 1516.[112] In Staupitz's absence, Luther, together with his confidants Linck and Frosch, had already appeared before the cardinal on 12 October. They later ate lunch with the cardinal. Apparently Staupitz, Linck and Luther were generally regarded as a trio, because when Luther had refused to recant, the cardinal summoned not only the superior Staupitz, but also Prior Linck (although not Luther) to talk things over after lunch – for several hours – at the Fugger residence. The Fugger family were the most influential bankers of the then known world, charged with processing and compiling all the moneys from the sale of indulgences. They were so rich that they could afford to build for themselves the chapel that bears

---

[110] See Luther to Spalatin on 10 October, *WABR* 1. 210, 51–4 (no. 97). For Luther on Staupitz being instrumental in the hearing before Cajetan see: 'Aber da der Cardinal Caietanus auff dem Reichstage zu Augspurg komen war, Erlanget Doctor Staupitz, das der selb gute Fuerste, Hertzog Fridreich [*sic*], selbs zum Cardinal gieng vnd erwarb, das mich der Cardinal horen wolt' (*WA* 51. 543, 29–544, 1 (*Wider Hans Worst*, 1541)). See J. Wicks, 'Roman Reactions to Luther: The First Year (1518),' *Catholic Historical Review*, **69** (1983), pp. 521–62. On Cajetan, see J. Wicks, 'Thomas de Vio Cajetan (1469–1534)', and on Karlstadt, A. Zorzin, 'Andreas Bodenstein von Karlstadt', both in C. Lindberg (ed.), *The Reformation Theologians. An Introduction to Theology in the Early Modern Period* (Oxford, 2002), pp. 269–83 and pp. 327–37, respectively.

[111] See Luther to Spalatin on 14 October (*WABR* 1. 214, 39–41 (no. 99); *LW* 48. 86). 'Eo tempore ne obolum quidem habebam, cucullum Doctoris Linckii mutuo sumebam, cum proficiserer Augustam' (*WATR* 5. 78, 8f. (no. 5349, summer 1540)); see Brecht, *Martin Luther, 1483–1521*, pp. 256f.

[112] On Frosch, see Stupperich, pp. 83f.

their name in St Anne's church, the church of the Carmelites at Augsburg where the Augustinians stayed. The Fugger Chapel was finished in 1518, and Staupitz and the others must have seen this brand new building.

The cardinal asked Staupitz to procure Luther's retraction.[113] But the canny Staupitz resisted and declared that he had tried to do so many times before. The cardinal himself, Staupitz countered, being a famous scholar and debater, would be much better qualified for this challenging task. Staupitz also supported Luther's request to respond to the cardinal in writing. Thereafter, according to Luther, Cajetan boasted of having orders to throw him and Staupitz into jail.[114]

In this situation Luther felt he should inform his colleague Professor Karlstadt at Wittenberg that the cardinal had told Staupitz that Luther had no better friend than him (Staupitz) and that the cardinal would have liked nothing more than to hear him say only one single phrase, 'I recant'. Luther continued: 'But I will not become a heretic by recanting that through which I became a Christian; I would rather die, burn at the stake, be exiled, and condemned.'[115] Cajetan wrote to the elector how kindly he had treated Luther, but that Luther and Staupitz had secretly escaped. Reliable rumours had spread in town that those Augustinians were to be arrested by their own Order. One of the most important leaders of the city, the city's clerk Conrad Peutinger, apparently knew that Staupitz, too, was to be arrested.[116] Having become aware of this danger, Staupitz actually procured a horse for Luther's escape to Paris and also attempted to get some money for him. How could Staupitz get a horse so quickly? He probably asked for the one of Friar Martin Glaser of the friary at Ramsau, who was then in town. Luther himself recalled that 'Staupitz in Augsburg obtained a horse for me from a prior'.[117] This was Staupitz's second

---

[113] '"Revoco," das ist: "Ich widerrufe"' (*WABR* 1. 217, 60 (no. 100)).

[114] 'Ut et me [Luther] et vicarium [Staupitz] incarceraret' (*Acta Augustana*, 1518, WA 2. 17, 34).

[115] 'Aber ich will nicht zu einem Ketzer werden mit dem Widerspruch der Meinung, durch welchen ich bin zu einem Christen worden; ehe will ich sterben, verbrannt, vertrieben, und vermaledeiet werden etc.' (Luther's letter to Karlstadt of 14 October 1518, *WABR* 1. 217, 60–63); Brecht, *Martin Luther, 1483–1521*, pp. 248f., wrote that this statement was made to Staupitz, but this is incorrect.

[116] On Peutinger's knowledge of the imminent arrest of Staupitz and the others, see F. Roth, *Augsburgs Reformationsgeschichte 1517–1530* (Munich, 1901), p. 52.

[117] 'Stupitius Augustae mihi confecit equum a priore quodam' (*WATR* 5. 78, 12 (no. 5349, summer 1540)). Friar Glaser wanted his horse back, but Luther no longer had it, as he informed Glaser in his letter of 30 May 1519 (*WABR* 1. 408, 7f. (no. 182); *LW* 48. 125). Sallaberger, 'Johann von Staupitz, Abt von St. Peter (1522–1524) und die J. Salzburger Mendikantentermineien', *Studien und Mitteilungen zur Geschichte des Benediktinerordens und seiner Zweige*, **93** (1982) pp. 216–69 (p. 154), assumes that Staupitz travelled from Salzburg to Augsburg via Ramsau using a horse from Ramsau which Luther then rode back to Wittenberg.

attempt to get Luther out of the country, first to Salzburg, now to Paris. The Augustinian friary of Paris had been reformed for the past decade under pressure from its general, Egidio da Viterbo.[118]

The clever Staupitz made a tactical move by releasing Luther from religious obedience to him, perhaps to free both from each other, at least for the time being, and perhaps to relieve the Order from any further responsibility for Luther's actions. If Staupitz were ever pressured to arrest Luther, he would no longer have had any right or obligation to move against his dear protégé. Luther later remembered that Staupitz had told him on that occasion: 'Remember that you began this cause in the name of our Lord Jesus Christ.' In a table talk in the early 1530s he remembered, in typical Lutheran exaggeration:

> Three times have I been excommunicated. The first time was by Dr Staupitz, who absolved me from the observance and rule of the Augustinian Order so that, if the pope pressed him to imprison me or command me to be silent, he could excuse himself on the ground that I was not under his obedience. The second time was by the pope, and the third time was by the emperor.[119]

There is, of course, a qualitative difference between the so-called 'excommunication' as a tactical move by his 'closest friend' Staupitz (*a Staupitio familiarissimo amico*), and the formal excommunication by a pope and the 'ban' by an emperor. Luther never felt that Staupitz's 'excommunicating' him was for real. As late as 1545 Luther confirmed their united stand, saying: '[Staupitz] was first of all my father in this

---

[118] On the friary in Paris, see F.X. Martin, 'The Augustinian Order on the Eve of the Reformation,' *Miscellanea Historiae Ecclesiasticae. Bibliothèque de la Revue d'histoire ecclésiastique*, 44 (1967), 2, pp. 71–104 (pp. 93–6).

[119] Luther: 'Ego ter sum excommunicatus, primo a Doctore Staupizio, is Augustae me absolvit ab observatia et regula ordinis, ut, si papa urgeret, ut me caperet aut mihi mandaret silentium, posset se excusare, quod non essem sub sua oboediantia' (*WATR* 1. 96, 5–8 (no. 225, recorded by Veit Dietrich in Spring 1532)). 'Anno 18. absolvit me Doctor Stupitius ab oboedientia ordinis et reliquit me solum Augustae', *WATR* 1. 442, 1–5 (no. 884). This did not mean 'excommunication' nor dispensation from obeying the monastic Rule or religious vows in general, but from Staupitz as superior and from obedience to the Order: 'Staupicii verba fuerant: Absolvo te ab oboediantia mea et commendo te Domino Deo' (*WATR* 1. 177, 31–7, here 36f (no. 409, recorded by Veit Dietrich, December 1532); 'a Staupitio familiarissimo amico' (*WATR* 1. 597, 31 (no. 1203, recorded by Veit Dietrich and Nikolaus Medler, early 1530s)). 'Anno 18. absolvit me Doctor Staupitz ab ordinis oboedientia' (*WATR* 2. 376, 9f. (no. 2250, Cordatus's collection, Fall/Winter 1531)); see *WATR* 5, no. 5375); letter to Staupitz of 14 January 1521 (*WABR* 2. 245, 2–6 (no. 366); *LW* 48. 191); see R. Schwarz, *Luther* (Göttingen, 1986), pp. 60f. Egidio da Viterbo in his *Informatio* of 1521 wrote that Luther procured for himself release from obedience to his superiors; possibly Egidio either did not know of or did not want to mention, Staupitz's role in this separation: 'a suorum obedientia superiorum se eximi procuravit' (as quoted in H. Tüchle, 'Des Papstes und seiner Jünger Bücher ...' in Bäumer, *Lutherprozess*, p. 52, n. 12).

doctrine and had borne me in Christ'.[120] Furthermore, it would be an exaggeration to maintain that, when Staupitz released Luther from his religious obedience, in effect he dismissed him from the Order,[121] and that he would no longer be 'Martin Luther, Augustinian'. For a long time afterwards Luther continued to sign his letters with 'Martin Luther, Augustinian'.[122]

Staupitz and Linck fled Augsburg leaving Luther and Beyer behind. Luther did not go to Paris, but went home to Wittenberg. Before Staupitz departed he may have made contact with Cardinal Lang of Salzburg who was also at Augsburg for the diet. Cardinal Lang, like Cardinal Cajetan, had been appointed as papal legate to this diet. The two cardinals appeared to be on excellent terms at Augsburg; perhaps they plotted to separate Staupitz from Luther by drawing him closer and more permanently to Salzburg, and thus far away from Luther and Wittenberg, and perhaps also from the Augustinians. It is not impossible that Staupitz and Cardinal Lang had met previously, as they were about the same age. Nor is it inconceivable that at that time, early in the autumn of 1518, the cardinal of Salzburg was looking for a suitable candidate to succeed the recently deceased abbot of St Peter at Salzburg (who died 18 June 1518). However, Cardinal Lang's efforts to bring this abbey under his control were not to be immediately successful and, on 11 July 1518, the newly elected Abbot Simon Garchanetz was ordained. (Garchanetz would be forced out of his abbacy by Cardinal Lang a few years later, in order to make room for Staupitz, as we shall see in Chapter 6). We do not know what Cardinal Lang thought of Luther at that time; he did not stay at Augsburg long enough to learn of the results of Cajetan's interrogation of Luther. We do know, however, that Luther, and perhaps also Staupitz, were not unhappy that Cardinal Lang had left Augsburg when the emperor departed for Innsbruck, prior to their meeting with Cardinal Cajetan.[123]

---

[120] WABR 11. 67, 5–8 (no. 4088), see WABR 2. 67, 7f. (no. 266).

[121] As opined in R.D. Balge, 'Martin Luther, Augustinian', in E.C. Fredrich et al. (eds), *Luther Lives: Essays in Commemoration of the 500th Anniversary of Martin Luther's Birth* (Milwaukee, WI, 1983), p. 15.

[122] For Luther's 'Augustinian' signatures, see his letters to Dungersheim, late January 1520: *Martinus Luther, Augustinianus* (WABR 2. 23, 8 (no. 245)); to the elector, 7 May 1520: *Capellan D. Martin Luther, Augustiner* (WABR 2. 102 (no. 286); WABR 2. 392, 36f. (no. 431)); to Gabriel Zwilling, 17 April 1522: *frater Martinus Lutherus* (WABR 2. 506, 21 (no. 478)). Shortly after his abduction to Wartburg Castle after the Diet of Worms in 1521, Luther supposedly stopped referring to himself as an Augustinian friar; see T.J. Wengert, 'Martin Luther's Movement toward an Apostolic Self-Awareness As Reflected in His Early Letters', *Lutherjahrbuch*, **61** (1994), pp. 71–92 (p. 87).

[123] See Sallaberger, 'Johann von Staupitz, Luthers Vorgesetzter', pp. 136f.; Sallaberger, *Kardinal*, pp. 148–50, esp. n. 121f.; Fabisch and Iserloh, *Dokumente*, p. 131, n. 86.

It is not impossible that Staupitz had been under consideration as a worthy candidate for the abbacy in Salzburg in the summer of 1518. Although this position eluded him for the time being, another opportunity to stay in Salzburg presented itself. An important preaching position needed to be filled there and Staupitz appeared to be an ideal candidate for it. With these openings for Staupitz should he remain in Salzburg, his resignation from the Augustinian Order (see pp. 287ff) could be seen in a new light altogether. Quite possibly, he resigned not so much because of frustration with Luther and his cause, but rather because of the appeal of becoming the leading preacher in a great city with a monastic humanist culture and the seat of a very important prince-bishop, or of eventually becoming the leader of a great abbey, and last but not least of having in Bishop Pürstinger a great colleague who was as reform-minded as himself.

While all this may have been going through Staupitz's mind, he, along with Friar Linck, had encouraged Luther to send a letter to Cardinal Cajetan with an apology for his lack of respect. Luther wrote the letter, dated 17 October, the day after he had left Augsburg secretly on horseback, without bidding farewell to the cardinal. Beyer had to deliver it to Cajetan. In his letter Luther also stated that Staupitz was his father in Christ.[124] Cardinal Cajetan must have realized that Staupitz would not stop protecting Luther; while Luther himself was certain of Staupitz's protection, as he had written to Karlstadt and to Spalatin on 14 October 1518 (see above). Staupitz had written from Augsburg to the elector on 15 October that the papal legate, Cajetan, only uttered empty words since his mind was preoccupied with shutting Luther up, and that he wanted him to recant. Staupitz continued that both he and Luther had given the legate a written response, but that the cardinal was looking for ways to shed innocent blood. He also mentioned that Gabriel della Volta's directive for Luther's arrest had arrived in town and that, according to the local patrician, Dr Conrad Peutinger (1465–1547), his own imprisonment was imminent.[125]

Meanwhile Staupitz had escaped and, together with Linck, arrived safely in Nuremberg, where Luther joined them on 22 October. Back at home in Wittenberg, Luther was confronted with a copy of the cardinal's letter to the elector of 25 October, in which Staupitz was mentioned several times, recounting the fact that Staupitz appeared before him with Luther on 13 October and that he had asked him whether Luther could respond to him in writing. Cajetan also reported that he had a lengthy

---

[124] *WABR* 1. 220f. (no. 103); Brecht, *Martin Luther, 1483–1521*, pp. 258f.

[125] The letter, signed with 'Cappelan D. Johannes von Staupitz', is edited in Kolde, *Die deutsche Augustiner-Congregation*, pp. 443f.

conference with Staupitz and the others, and that Staupitz had departed without bidding him farewell.[126]

In his response, Luther described the events at Augsburg from his own perspective and confirmed what was said about Staupitz, especially that the latter, as soon as he had arrived in town, appeared with Luther before the cardinal. Luther also mentioned that he had become aware of the rumours that, by the command of the general of their Order, he was supposed to be captured and imprisoned if he did not recant. Luther acknowledged Staupitz's abrupt departure and excused him for doing so, on the grounds that Staupitz had not been called to appear in front of Cajetan in the first place: 'The vicar had not been summoned, [thus] nothing pertained to him in this [Luther's own] case. He [Staupitz] was free to go, return, leave, or come at any time, as he wished.'[127]

After making his response to the elector, and although *pro forma* he had been released by Staupitz from religious obedience, Luther dutifully wrote to the latter on 25 November 1518, addressing him in Latin as his 'most sweet father in Christ' (*in Christo suavissimo Patri*). He informed him that he arrived back home 'happy and healthy', and that the *Acta Augustana* would be published with the permission of the territorial lord, Frederick. Luther apparently was ready to emigrate to France if the *censura* went into effect; however, Frederick prompted Spalatin to talk him out of this plan. In his letter Luther wrote that he had to inform Staupitz that Frederick did not want him to leave Wittenberg. Had Frederick not objected, Luther might have followed Staupitz's advice and thus have ended up in Paris. Luther also let Staupitz know that Cardinal Cajetan had noticed their united front, because the cardinal made terrible accusations against them as he spoke of Luther and Staupitz and others as his 'associates'. Luther signed himself as 'Your Martin Luther, the very miserable'.[128]

Luther returned to Wittenberg, while Linck remained in Nuremberg, and Staupitz went on to Salzburg. Not long after the three friends had held their ground at Augsburg vis-à-vis the papal powers, Luther confided to Linck in a private letter of 18 December 1518 that he

---

[126] *WABR* 1. 233, 29 and 41, and 234, 54–61 (no. 110).

[127] *WABR* 1. 240, 184–6; 241, 205f. and 225–8; 246, 405–8 (no. 110).

[128] 'Dixi: "Si venerint censura, non manebo", dissuasitque, ne tam cito in Galliam irem' (*WABR* 1. 258, 19f. (no. 114)); quoting the cardinal's letter to the elector: 'Scripsit interea prolixam epistolam Reverendus Dominus Legatus Principi, in qua dire criminatur me et te et socios [ut vocat] meos' (*WABR* 1. 258, 8–10); Luther's signature: 'T. Martinus Luder [*sic*] pauperculus' (line 30); see also *WABR* 1. 232–5 (no. 110). Staupitz remained Luther's prime protector (*premier protecteur de Luther*), see L. Cristiani, 'Staupitz', in *Dictionnaire de Théologie Catholique* (Paris, 1941), XIV, 2. 2580–83. See also Ludolphy, *Friedrich der Weise*, p. 409.

suspected that the pope was the antichrist, worse than the Turks; and in his letter to the *Apostolicus Commissarius* Miltitz he doubted that Cardinal Cajetan was still a 'Catholic Christian'.[129] These suspicions emerged at a time when all three Augustinians felt their lives endangered.

At around Christmas 1518 Staupitz received a letter from Nuremberg's city lawyer and sodality member, Scheurl, saying that the Staupitz Sodality was quite concerned about Luther's fate. Scheurl mentioned that they were now listening to Friar Linck's sermons. (During Advent 1518, Linck delivered 30 sermons on the seven beatitudes in Nuremberg's Augustinian church; they were printed in 1519 by Gutknecht in Nuremberg.[130]) Among Linck's audience were Ebner, Nützel, Holzschuher, Spengler, Dürer, and Scheurl and his wife, all of whom sent their greetings, while they hoped very much that Friar Martin be safe. Prior Volprecht also hoped that Staupitz was 'very happy'.[131]

There is no question that public opinion in Nuremberg always viewed Staupitz as being on Luther's side. There is also no question that the three learned friars excelled in preaching in their respective cities: Linck in Nuremberg, Luther in Wittenberg and Staupitz in Salzburg. After all, good preaching was the chief task of Augustinian friars for which they primarily did their graduate work in theology. In 1518, while Linck was active in Nuremberg, the political centre of the empire, Staupitz preached his Advent sermons in Salzburg, one of the most important ecclesiastical centres of the time.

Concerning his relationship with Luther, there was little more that Staupitz could have done after he had allowed Luther to present his theology at Heidelberg, and then stood by his side before the Roman cardinal in Augsburg, evasively excusing his failure to get Luther under control. Staupitz himself had to carry on with his own preaching assignment at Salzburg. In his Advent sermons he spoke on the sacraments. He esteemed these highly throughout his life, although he did not talk much about them in his other sermonizing. He explained what the worthy receiving of the Eucharist meant, namely receiving it in

---

[129] 'Antichristum illum verum' (Luther to Linck (or Sinistrus) on 18 December 1518, *WABR* 1. 270, 12 (no. 121)). 'Ego [Luther] eum [Cardinal] dubito esse catholicum christianum' (Luther to Miltitz on 17 May 1519, *WABR* 1. 402, 39f. (no. 178)).

[130] See W. Reindell (ed.), *Wenzel Lincks Werke* (Marburg, 1894). J. Lorz (ed.), *Bibliographia Linckiana. Bibliographie der gedruckten Schriften Dr. Wenzeslaus Lincks (1483–1547)* (Nieuwkoop, 1977), pp. 26–8; G. Strauss, *Nuremberg in the Sixteenth Century*, (Bloomington, IN, and London, 1976) p. 162.

[131] 'Nos hic vivimus quiete, valemus recte: nam et Wenceslaus praedicat populo gratus; eius auditores te salutant, Je. Ebner. ... A. Durrer [*sic*], ... omnes salutis Martiniane cupidissimi.... Sed et meus prior V. Volprecht te cupit felicissimum ...' (Soden and Knaake, *Christoph Scheurls Briefbuch*, II, 78 (no. 188)).

firm faith, that is a faith in God's forgiveness of one's sins.[132] If one firmly believes in the forgiveness of sins as God had promised, and when in this faith one receives the 'divine food' of the sacrament, then the Holy Spirit lives in one's heart and it is this Holy Spirit who then works our good works. 'As the Father is in the Son and the Son in the Father, so is the well-disposed human spirit united with the Holy Spirit and the Holy Spirit is in him. Such a person does not want anything else but what God wants, in life and in death, in time and in eternity. Therefore, God is the doer of all his works.'[133]

The theme of 'God's Spirit at work in the human spirit' was carried over into Staupitz's Lenten sermons of 1519 which were also delivered in Salzburg. The scriptural text on which these were based was Jesus' farewell discourse, 'which Christ delivered at the last supper [before his passion] for his disciples'. Four of these sermons are partly preserved in notes taken by a local nun: 'When God's spirit thus reigns, works, and vivifies, one's heart jumps for joy, sweet love, and gratitude.'[134] Staupitz expounded John 14: 6 by saying that one must place all trust in Christ alone who is the truth. Christ is the way in whom one is to put one's hope and who leads one to the right goal and place. Christ is the life who comes to you in your greatest need, and in your final hour he takes you by your hand, gives you the wedding gown, which is coloured by his blood, and takes you to the predestined place which Christ has earned for you.[135] On John 14: 26, Staupitz commented that faith, hope and love are the three jewels which the Holy Spirit as the consoler (John 14: 26) grants to us. If one does not have these three at all times, one needs to be patient, as this is a period of spiritual dryness and trial which ultimately will pass. One must obediently take one's cross and bear the burden until divine consolation comes. A Christian who is obedient in this way may be assured that he loves God and that the Holy Spirit is in him.[136] With John 15: 4–6, on the vine and the branches, Staupitz illustrated the cooperation between God and man: Christ is the vine, we are the branches who bear the most sweet fruit toward eternal life, 'not by our own works, but by the works and merits of the blood of Jesus Christ'. Therefore, work-righteousness is detrimental to our eternal

---

[132] See Zumkeller, *Heilslehre*, p. 115.

[133] Ibid., p. 199.

[134] 'O wen der Geist Gots also regirt, würcht und lebentig macht, des herz springt in freiden süesser lieb und dankperkait' (Sermon 1, Zumkeller, *Heilslehre*, p. 120. As these sermons are not available in any critical edition, I rely on the quotations which Zumkeller provided in 1994. They form part of the manuscript containing the 1518 sermons; folios 73r–81r, see ibid., p. 12; Sallaberger, 'Johann von Staupitz, Abt von St. Peter, p. 153.

[135] See Sermon 1, Zumkeller, *Heilslehre*, p. 85, n. 550.

[136] See Sermons 2–4, ibid., pp. 124f.

salvation, including a good work such as a pilgrimage to Compostella, even if it were performed all the way on 'bare knees'.[137] Christ is the sole operator (*werkmeister*); we are his tool (*werkzeug*).[138]

For his preaching he was paid by St Peter's Abbey in the form of a good quantity of high quality wine from South Tyrol. The wine had most likely been given to the Augustinians' branch office (*terminus*) at Salzburg where other donated goods were stored. Apparently Staupitz's prestige had increased dramatically, as this honorarium was worth 180 times the value of his previous engagements as a preacher. The Augustinian friar was employed by the Benedictine monks for services in their churches as they were in charge of the pastoral care of certain parishes connected to their abbey.[139]

Staupitz had been in demand as a preacher in Salzburg, and he must have liked it there, as he spent the winter months of 1518/19 in the city. When Luther found out about Staupitz's definite preference for Salzburg, he lamented his 'patron's and superior's' absence from Wittenberg and his silence, in a letter of 20 February 1519.[140] Outwardly it seemed that Staupitz's attitude toward Luther had become reserved and distant following Cajetan's interrogation at Augsburg; perhaps indeed Staupitz wanted to give this impression to the general public. In April 1519 Luther expressed the belief that Staupitz had forgotten him, as he did not write at all.[141] Staupitz had received further information from Luther about the negotiations with the papal emissary, Carl von Miltitz, which took place at Altenburg. During those talks, the name of the Salzburg archbishop, suggested by Spalatin, surfaced as the one who was thought to be a good mediator in the Luther affair.[142] Luther readily accepted this proposal and reported to Staupitz that he (Luther) nominated the archbishops of Salzburg, Trier and Freising for this task.[143] Luther's nomination of the archbishop of Salzburg in the first place had something to do with the fact that Staupitz was on friendly terms with this prelate, Leonhard von

---

[137] 'Auf plossen knien gein sandt Jacob [de Compostella]' (Sermon 4 (1519), ibid., pp. 183 and 188).

[138] Sermons 1 and 4, ibid., pp. 183f.

[139] 'Anno D[omi]ni 1519: Item dedi D[omi]ni Doctori N. Stawbitz [*sic*] propter eius Sermones populo in nostris ecclesiis factas pro salario eius x urnas vini australis loco lb d xv computando urnam xii d in die Purificationis' as quoted by Sallaberger, 'Johann von Staupitz, die Stiftsprediger', pp. 264–5, n. 272.

[140] 'Etsi tu multum nobis et distas et taces, Reverende Pater . . .' (Letter of 20 February 1519, WABR 1. 344, 4 (no. 152); LW 48. 108–11).

[141] 'Reverendus Pater Vicarius oblitus est nostri, adeo nihil scribit' (WABR 1. 370, 87 (no. 167)).

[142] See Luther to the elector of 5 or 6 January 1519 (WABR 1. 289 (no. 128)).

[143] See Luther's letter to Staupitz on 20 February 1519 (WABR 1. 343–5 (no. 152), LW 48. 108–11).

Keutschach. However, the planned mediation never took place as Leonhard died on 8 June 1519.[144] Two months earlier, on 29 March 1519, Pope Leo X had written to Luther personally that he was elated by the letter he had received via Miltitz, and that he was sure things would work out after all; Luther should come to Rome and recant in front of the pope.[145]

Later that year, in June 1519, Staupitz was expected to appear at the Augustinian Order's general chapter meeting in Venice, Italy. He was supposed to clear up the issues surrounding the Luther affair; however, he missed the meeting – whether intentionally or not we do not know. The southern German friaries were advised not to associate any longer with Staupitz's Reformed Congregation. In fact, Gerhard Hecker, the provincial of the Saxon-Thuringian province, was also absent from the general assembly at Venice. Both Staupitz and Hecker had been asked by the Order's general to become commissioners of the indulgence sales in order to raise funds for their general chapter meeting in Venice with its 1100 participants.[146] Hecker had declined as he apparently sympathized with Staupitz, Luther and the others. By 1521, this Augustinian provincial would openly preach in the reformers' vein.[147] Whether or not Staupitz complied with the Roman wish is not known.

It may have been this lack of cooperation from the German leaders of the Augustinian Order that angered General Volta to such an extent that he cancelled Staupitz's jurisdiction over the five south German reformed friaries, in the Swabian region, Tübingen, Esslingen, Weil-der-Stadt, Alzey and Heidelberg. Volta placed them instead under Friar Konrad Treger as the provincial of the Rhenish-Swabian province, who was present at the meeting in Venice. By staying away from the gathering at Venice, Staupitz thus sacrificed (or simply lost) his previous achievements concerning the reforms in his Order. He did all this apparently in order to protect his younger friend, Friar Martin, who shared most of his theological opinions, even though Staupitz himself expressed them in a less aggressive way.

In July 1519 the famous Leipzig Disputation took place. This was originally intended to engage Dr Eck against Dr Karlstadt, however, Luther was also drawn into it. Arbitrators, chosen from the universities

---

[144] See Sallaberger, 'Johann von Staupitz, die Stiftsprediger', p. 267.

[145] *WABR* 1. 363–5 (no. 164).

[146] Letter of 16 February 1519, Kolde, *Die deutsche Augustiner-Congregation*, p. 323, n. 3. '... Magistro Ioanni Stupiz Vicario Congregationis significamus, quem Commissarium etiam facimus indulgentiarum Capituli', as quoted in Kunzelmann, V, p. 479, n. 2355.

[147] On Hecker, see H. Bornkamm, *Luther in Mid-Career 1521–1530*, ed. K. Bornkamm, trans. E.T. Bachmann (Philadelphia, 1983), p. 103. No money from any indulgence business was sent to Rome as of 24 August 1519 when the general in Rome asked to pay the debt; see Kolde, *Die deutsche Augustiner-Congregation*, p. 324.

of Erfurt and Paris, could not be members of either the Dominican or the Augustinian Order. This event lasted for more than three weeks with ten days of disputation.[148] After it was over, Luther was rather downhearted because Eck appeared as the winner according to public opinion. Luther was now very anxious to meet with Staupitz.[149] Apparently Staupitz had planned all along to meet with him after this disputation, as part of his visitation journey through Saxony accompanied by Linck. Indeed, the Augustinian trio of close friends – Staupitz, Linck and Luther – met at the end of July at Grimma, about 25 kilometres south-east of Leipzig. Evidently, the two leading German Augustinians, Staupitz and Linck, maintained contact with their friend who was in deep trouble, while at the same time keeping their distance from their own Order's leadership in Rome. Consequently the Order was unable to make any decisive move against Luther. Staupitz had shown himself as a great tactician in this regard. The meeting at Grimma was perhaps the last confidential meeting of the three friars and friends, although Luther and Staupitz kept in touch by letter. In the autumn of 1519, Staupitz received from Luther the academic theses for Melanchthon's theological baccalaureate. Apparently Luther wanted better to acquaint Staupitz with the latter's thinking. Luther commented on Melanchthon: 'He represents many Martins, he is a very strong enemy of the devil and scholasticism and knows their folly and Christ's rock as well.' Luther also kept Staupitz up to date about his own scholarly work; he sent along two copies of his *Commentary on Galatians*. In the same letter Luther wrote that he very much wanted to see Staupitz again:

> You leave me very much on my own. I was so sad about you, like a weaned baby about his mother .... Last night I had a dream about you. It was as if you said farewell to me. Then I wept bitterly and lamented. You then raised your hand and said that I should be quiet, and that you would return to me soon.[150]

What more intimate dependency could there be than the one Luther depicted here in his dream about Staupitz? Luther must desperately have needed Staupitz. However, Staupitz was rather busy himself. Nonetheless, it should not be presumed because Staupitz did not dedicate his entire time to Luther in distant Wittenberg, that he had undergone a change of attitude towards Luther in the sense of now being 'remarkably reserved and distant'.[151] Staupitz still had his job of inspecting friaries

---

[148] See Brecht, *Martin Luther, 1483–1521*, p. 313; Schwarz, *Luther*, pp. 66–72.

[149] See Luther's letter to Lang of 26 July 1519 (*WABR* 1. 432, 5–7 (no. 188)); 'R. P. Vicarium Stupitz in Grymmis inveni' (*WABR* 1. 424, 155 (no. 187)); see Kunzelmann, V, p. 210.

[150] Letter of 3 October 1519 (*WABR* 1. 514f. (no. 202)).

[151] Brecht, *Martin Luther, 1483–1521*, p. 336 (on Staupitz's alleged change of attitude toward Luther).

and nunneries to do: in October 1519, he had to spend time at the Creuzburg nunnery and at the Sangerhausen friary; in September he had been at Nuremberg, and later he stayed at Munich.[152] By 18 December 1519 Staupitz was at Salzburg again, 'healthy and honoured',[153] from where he informed Luther that their adversary Eck was being rejected in Salzburg. Clearly, there was no change in his relationship with Luther; they still formed a united front against Eck and their other opponents.

Meantime, in Salzburg Staupitz was respected. The increase in the honorarium for his preaching was substantial. The general spiritual climate was also to Staupitz's liking as this city had long been a centre of monastic humanism, radiating its influence across all of upper Austria, especially through the Benedictine monasteries and Augustinian friaries where the new scholarly spirit of the Renaissance had emerged. Above all, the Benedictines' library at St Peter was remarkable as it included German versions of Augustine, Bernard, Petrarch and Cicero. At the end of the fifteenth century, this library must have possessed most of the early printed editions of most Renaissance works.[154] It is no wonder that the learned Staupitz remained attracted to Salzburg with its great intellectual climate coupled with the higher salary and benefits that he received on top of the recognition and the prestige that he earned as a great preacher.

Also in 1519, the year of the Leipzig Disputation, Karlstadt published his commentary on Augustine's *De spiritu et littera,* with a preface that was dedicated to Staupitz as the one who had directed Karlstadt away from the scholastics toward the immediate study of Augustine. He called Staupitz the 'outstanding preacher of the grace of Christ'; Luther would later call Staupitz the 'herald of grace and cross'.[155] There is no question that both Karlstadt and Luther recognized Staupitz's significance in general, and for themselves in particular. However, we do not know of any close contacts between Staupitz and Karlstadt as the theological and political fronts hardened in German lands, and as Luther and Karlstadt drifted apart.

---

[152] See Luther's letter to Spalatin of 13 October 1519 (*WABR* 1. 530, 62–5 (no. 205)).

[153] [Staupitz] 'Reverendus Pater Vicarius Saltzburgae agit sanus et honoratus, scribens Eccium [Eck] ambire primores passim, sed Cardinali Langio Episcopo discplicere Eccianam modestiam' (*WABR* 1. 597, 37ff. (no. 232); *LW* 48. 138). The allusion to Eck's 'modesty' was, of course, sarcasm.

[154] See R. Newald, 'Beiträge zur Geschichte des Humanismus in Oberösterreich', in *Probleme und Gestalten des deutschen Humanismus* (Berlin, 1963), pp. 67–112.

[155] 'Eximius Christi gratiae predicator' (Preface, in E. Kähler, *Karlstadt und Augustin* (Halle, 1952), p. 6). Luther: 'Gratiae et crucis praeconem' (*WABR* 2. 264, 48 (no. 376; letter of 2 February 1521)).

'Standing up for the Evangelical Truth' (1520)

Every year from 1511 onwards, Staupitz spent some time in Salzburg, with the probable exception of 1517. He most likely resided at the Order's *terminus* facilities on Kaigasse, which the Augustinians of Munich had bought in 1407. This branch office with two buildings and a courtyard was adjacent to the magnificent building complex which Staupitz's friend, the Archbishop Leonhard von Keutschach, had built between 1497 and 1501 for his relatives.[1]

During the last two weeks before Easter 1520, starting on Wednesday 23 March, Staupitz gave six sermons in German on the biblical passion narrative in the church of St Mary. This was also the place of worship of the Benedictine nuns of St Peter, whose nunnery was attached to the monks' abbey. Today it is the church of the Franciscans, where mostly lay people worship.[2] The significance of 'St Peter's Ladies' lies in the fact that they produced numerous manuscripts, including recordings of sermons such as Staupitz's of Lent 1520.[3] These sermons dealt with the following topics:

1 God's love and human rebirth.
2 The imitation of Christ.
3 Jesus' suffering and human perseverance.
4 A mystical vision of the cross.
5 God's masterpiece.
6 Christ's perfect death works perfect salvation.

Staupitz always addressed his audience with the expression 'Friends of Christ'.[4] He pointed out that we will not be born again of God except by God's love, and only then also by our love of our neighbour. God's love is

---

[1] See J. Sallaberger, 'Johann von Staupitz, Abt von St. Peter (1522–1524) und die Salzburger Mendikantentermineien', *Studien und Mitteilungen zur Geschichte des Benediktinerordens und seiner Zweige*, **93** (1982), pp. 218–69 (pp. 243–5).

[2] The English translation is now available in R.K. Markwald, *A Mystic's Passion. The Spirituality of Johannes von Staupitz in his 1520 Lenten Sermons. Translation and Commentary* (New York, 1990); (p. 124, with n. 63).

[3] See ibid., p. 27, with n. 48. The source text is a transcript of 1540, produced by the nun Eva Trost (see ibid.).

[4] See ibid., pp. 33, 53, 69, 95, 129 and 157.

shown in the suffering of Christ for us, as Isaiah 53 and 63 teach us. The suffering of Christ has been prefigured by Job, who said: 'The Lord has given it, He has also taken it again, blessed be the name of the Lord' (Job 1: 21). Staupitz revived here his interest in Job as a prefiguration of the suffering Christ. He had preached 34 sermons in 1497/98 on Job, using Job 1: 21 as the leitmotif throughout his first series of sermons.

He often spoke of Christ as 'God', always thinking of the second person of the Trinity. He did this not just occasionally, but almost 50 times in these six Lenten sermons. 'Your God [Christ] stood highest when He was totally forsaken of all creatures and no one stood by Him but Mary, the devout woman, the treasure of all graces'. He applied the image of the wine presser of Isa. 63: 2–6 dramatically to Christ and his suffering:

> [God the Father] punished the Innocent One so fiercely on account of the sins of others because He speaks: 'In my fierce anger I have trodden the wine-press alone and forsaken' [Is. 63: 3]. There I have conquered all sin. Then I have jumped about and kneaded it 'til their blood' [Isa. 63: 3b] – that is, their sins – were pressed out of them by me. They all have soaked 'my garment' [Isa. 63: 3b], for I did not do any sin of my own.[5]

Staupitz continued that when humans suffer they should bring to mind the suffering of Christ. Suffering gives one the genuine comfort 'that God is the very closest to you, yea that you are one of the dearest persons to God'.[6] He concluded his first sermon with these words: 'He has placed His human nature into my faith, so that I have come to believe that He is the true God and the Saviour of all the world and with His divine nature He has fully enfolded me. Amen.'[7]

In his second sermon Staupitz focused on Christ's suffering at the Mount of Olives, and on the imitation of Christ. He inculcated the following in his first three points: (1) 'That your devout and most beloved God was arrested and bound ...'; (2) 'That your faithful God was led into the house of Annas and interrogated about His disciples and His doctrine'; (3) 'That the slap in the face He received from the servant, which your God suffered boldly, has not kept Him quiet ...'.[8] Then Staupitz defined 'imitation of Christ' as doing God's will in patience, and not, 'as several say', that the best way would be to sacrifice one's 'free will' and offer it to God. It is difficult to determine whom he had in mind with his mention of the 'several' others whose names were not given. He elaborated, however, his own position which sounded straight out of the

---

[5] Ibid., pp. 33–36.

[6] Ibid., p. 40, with the annotation in n. 21 that Staupitz may have been remembering Henry Suso's *Little Book of Eternal Wisdom*.

[7] Ibid., p. 40.

[8] Ibid., pp. 54–6.

Augustinian and Bernardine tradition: 'The point of all this is: the free will is perhaps the cause of people's fall and frailty, but to rise up and to march on: that is strength that truly man does not possess, except it be given to him by grace.'[9] It is the gift of grace rather than the gift of free will that he wanted his audience to be aware of. Staupitz continued and further defined, or actually redefined, the 'imitation of Christ' (nachvolgung) as 'standing up for the evangelical truth' (ewangelische warhait), which in his contemporary language meant 'the truth of the Gospel'. We have nothing to fear, 'neither force, nor beatings, nor death. We shall boldly insist upon the truth'. Staupitz's expression 'standing up' anticipated Luther's similar one in the following year at Worms, when he famously declaimed 'Here I stand!'[10]

The preacher carried on with three more points: (4) 'That your most beloved God has been so shamefully denied by Peter'; (5) 'That your kind God is being led to the high priest Caiaphas'; (6) 'How the wise men have gone to council and have turned your God over to the rascals'. Staupitz then closed his second sermon with the thought that Christ is our 'pioneer' who exercised 'all of His arms of virtue and love, so that we may recognize Him as our most affable God and Saviour'.[11] Staupitz always wanted to make sure that his listeners understood the divine Saviour properly.

Staupitz's third sermon focused further on God's suffering, as he developed his points (the first three of which were not elaborated according to the nuns' records): (1) What my God is suffering; (2) Why He is suffering innocently; (3) Who is suffering. His fourth point was that Christ was suffering out of love, as Isaiah clearly prophesied in Chapter 53.

Here then the preacher made use of the words of Cant. 1: 2 and 4; Cant. 3: 6; and Cant. 7: 9 in describing Christ's love for us and the soul's reactive love:

> 'He kisses me with the kiss of His own mouth' [Cant 1: 2] and 'draws me after you' [Cant. 1: 4], 'so I would run in your sweet smoke' [Cant. 3: 6; 'laden with myrrh, with frankincense, and with perfume ...], for 'out of your breast flows the sweetest wine' [paraphrasing Cant. 7: 9]. Since from the cross the sweetest wine has flowed in abundance, [therefore,] the cross gives us occasion to remember that He is the Saviour of the world. It leads us and shows us that we should love the Father and the Holy Spirit and the entire Holy Trinity, in witness that we were born of God.[12]

---

[9] Ibid., pp. 55f.

[10] Ibid., p. 55; and R. Bainton, Here I Stand: A Life of Martin Luther (New York, 1950).

[11] See Markwald, A Mystic's Passion, pp. 57–9.

[12] Ibid., pp. 70f.

This spiritual birth takes place in the believer's heart. 'Only see to it that you go to the sufferings of Christ, that God lives in your heart.' Going to see Christ's suffering is going to 'behold, how your innocent God stands there naked'. Staupitz took up again what he had discussed in his first publication concerning the imitation of the naked Jesus. In this regard he probably followed in the spiritual tradition of Henry Suso who wrote of this in a similar way in his *Large Book of Letters*.[13] Staupitz may also have had in mind the iconographic motif of 'Christ resting' on a rock: 'They undressed him and placed Him naked upon a rock and gave Him a mixed potion of myrrh and gall to drink.' Staupitz then described how Christ was scourged twice. As a Bible scholar he tried to harmonize the diverse biblical accounts; the concept of two flagellations and the motif of 'Christ resting' had both been used in his tenth sermon in 1512. As to the latter, he may have seen and perhaps been inspired by pictures such as Lucas Cranach's woodcut with this motif of 1515.[14]

At the end of his third sermon of 1520, Staupitz unfolded his fourth major point in ten brief thoughts about imitating Christ:

> We must note ten short points on the imitation:
>
> 1. The Eternal Light, the lustre and gleam of the Holy Trinity, has been placed before the judges of darkness. Oh, do not be concerned that you should be judged by one who does not know anything about your case.
> 2. The Eternal Wisdom has been made a laughing stock. Do not let it bother you if you are being offended by someone who is not very reasonable ...
> 3. The Highest Goodness has been reproached.
> 4. The Omnipotence has been scoffed.
> 5. The Majesty has been suppressed. Oh, don't let it burden you, even if you are reproached, rejected, and suppressed. Oh behold, how your innocent God stands there ...
> 6. The Gift has been rejected and destroyed ...
> 7. The Justice is being tried ...
> 8. The Life is being killed.

---

[13] Ibid., pp. 73f.; see Henry Suso, 'Grosses Briefbuch', no. 18.

[14] See Markwald, *A Mystic's Passion*, pp. 74–7. For the parallel thoughts in his tenth sermon of 1512, see Schneider-Lastin, *Salzburger Predigten 1512*, pp. 104f. (on 'Christ resting'); and p. 99 (on two separate flagellations). For the iconographic motif, see the entry 'Rast Christi', in E. Kirschbaum, *Lexikon der christlichen Ikonographie* 4 vols (Rome and Freiburg, 1968), III, pp. 496–8. Cranach's woodcut carries the title 'Saint Bernard's Meditation'; on this and the depiction of it, see Posset, 'Saint Bernard of Clairvaux in the Devotion, Theology, and Art of the Sixteenth Century', *LQ*, **11** (1997), pp. 306–52 (fig. 5 on p. 316). Staupitz's awareness of contemporary art can be inferred from his reference in Sermon 4 (1520) to artists who paint the suffering Job and his devout wife; see Markwald, *A Mystic's Passion*, p. 96.

9.   The Salvation is thrown out.
10. The Sweetness turns bitter. Oh, behold, how your Lord and
God, who gives fruitfulness and sweetness to all things, sits there the
poor man and the poorest of all.[15]

With these words and another reference to 'Christ resting' he both
ended his third sermon and established a connection with the following
sermon.

As he introduced the fourth sermon, Staupitz reminded his audience
that so far (that is, during the previous sermon), they have gone together
to the foot of the cross and that 'we ... sat him down naked at that place
.... Now, today, let us go to him again, for God's sake, because we still
find him sitting in the same place.' The preacher dramatized his
description by letting Christ speak: 'I am sitting: the Son of the Heavenly
Father .... I sit there like the bridegroom who is waiting for his beloved
bride .... Job says: "He sits as a wretched man, forsaken by God and by
all creatures". What a wicked bridegroom were I, if I abandoned my
bride, the great Church, [to whom I] was betrothed when I became man,
with whom I must now have intercourse on the cross and make her spirit
pregnant.'[16]

Staupitz advised further (still in Sermon 4) that all those who take
refuge in Christ's 'torn skin' (not 'torn hand') will be saved. It makes more
sense to think here of meditating on the chastised and crucified Christ with
his torn body and skin, under which his loving heart is found, than to
imply that he meant meditating on the 'torn hand' of Christ. Therefore
one needs to opt for the following reading, with Christ speaking to his
Father on behalf of the sinners: 'I entreat you that for all those who take
refuge in my torn skin, and appropriate my suffering, you would not
punish any of their sins by eternal death.'[17] Staupitz concluded his sermon
with a practical twist, by questioning popular piety and pilgrimages from
a reforming point of view; he let Christ speak as follows:

> Therefore, he who looks upon my suffering with the eyes of his
> hoping heart, will have no sin harm him or cause his death. You need
> neither go to Rome, nor Aachen, nor to St Peter's or St John's Lateran
> Churches for the indulgence of sin: you have it indeed already with
> you in your chamber, or bed, and you can [indeed] obtain forgiveness
> of all sins. Although I do in no way disdain the power and grace of the
> Church, yet the true Pope lives in your heart.[18]

---

[15] See ibid., pp. 79f.
[16] Ibid., pp. 95–8.
[17] Ibid., p. 102; on the alternative reading in *Codex Salzburgensis b* V8, see ibid., p. 120.
Sermon 5 presents the same difficulty with German *Haut* and *Hand*; see ibid., pp. 133 and 147.
[18] 'Der recht pabst want in deinem herzen' (Sermon 4, A. Zumkeller, *Johann von
Staupitz und seine christliche Heilslehre* (Würzburg, 1994), p. 108; Markwald, *A Mystic's
Passion*, p. 104).

With this carefully articulated God-centred spirituality, at a time when the authority of the pope in the Church was challenged, Staupitz revealed himself to his audience as a first-class spiritual reformer who knew what was essential for a faithful Christian's spirituality. Staupitz was critical of the pope when preaching that Christ/God is the only 'pope' who needs to reign in one's heart.

Let us here digress briefly in order to recall Staupitz's anti-Roman sentiment which was well known to Luther, mostly from the conversations at Grimma concerning indulgences. Therefore Luther could be very frank with Staupitz; on 30 May 1518 he had written to him: 'Christ may witness whether the words I utter are His or mine; without His power and will even the pope cannot speak.'[19] Staupitz's downplaying of questions of authority may have been generally known to his audience, as can be deduced for instance from his table talks at Nuremberg. On one occasion he told a joke (or anecdote) about the Council of Constance of 1414–18: when the Cardinals proceeded to elect a new pope, the emperor's jester suddenly appeared saying that he was sent by the Holy Spirit to tell them that He (the Holy Spirit) was momentarily so busy that He could not visit them. Therefore, they should cast their votes without Him.[20] This Staupitzian table conversation reveals not only something of his convivial personality, but also of his attitude toward authority, in particular how questionably he felt it was exercised at the Council of Constance, especially with regard to the case of John Hus of Bohemia. Staupitz had continued with the attempt to 'revise' this case which had apparently been started by his predecessor Andreas Proles, that is, to rehabilitate Hus at least within their own Augustinian Order, because one of their own friars had been instrumental in condemning Hus at the Council of Constance. Luther probably knew of this trend, and thus it was easily possible for Luther, in a letter of 14 February 1520, sarcastically to label himself and Staupitz – and even Augustine and Paul – as 'Hussites' (that is, followers of the condemned John Hus): 'We are all ignorant Hussites.'[21] By identifying

---

[19] See Luther's letter to Staupitz of 30 May 1518, enclosing the letter to be forwarded to Leo X (WA 1. 525–7); Luther: 'Doctor Staupitius me incitabat contra papam' (WATR 4. 440 (no. 4707)).

[20] See Knaake, Sämmtliche Werke, p. 47, as quoted in B. Hamm, 'Geistbegabte gegen Geistlose: Typen des pneumatologischen Antiklerikalismus – Zur Vielfalt der Luther-Rezeption in der frühen Reformationsbewegung (vor 1525)', in P.A. Dykema and H.A. Oberman (eds), Anticlericalism in Late Medieval and Early Modern Europe (Leiden, 1993), p. 384, n. 7.

[21] 'Docuit eadem imprudentia et Iohannes Staupitz. Breviter: summus omnes Hussitae ignorantes' (WABR 2. 42, 22–9 (no. 254); LW 48: 153); see W. Delius, 'Luther und Huß',

himself and the others with Hus, who had been burned at the stake during the Council of Constance, Luther recalled that Hus's condemnation was unjustly brought about by a friar from their own Augustinian Order, Johann Zachariae of Erfurt. (The stone slab covering Zachariae's grave is still in front of the high altar of the Augustinian church at Erfurt, on the very spot where friars who were to be accepted into the Order had to prostrate themselves, as Luther had done in 1506.) Some time after Staupitz's death, Luther remembered what Staupitz had once said about Hus and how Hus was 'mistreated' with a quotation taken from Ezek. 34:10 by their own fellow friar, Zachariae, at the Council of Constance, as he (Staupitz) had heard it from his predecessor, Andreas Proles. In 1536/37, when Luther's friend Johann Agricola translated and edited three letters of John Hus, Luther became more specific in his postscript to that edition. In it he again mentioned the changing position of Staupitz and the Augustinian Order toward Hus, due to Proles's insights into the case. Staupitz had once told Luther that Proles had insisted that John Hus was innocent and that he did not deserve to be burned at the stake. This means that it was Staupitz who was instrumental in relativizing the problem of authority in the Church and in changing Luther's perspective on Hus and on the issue of ecclesiastical authority and its relationship to the Scripture principle, since Hus was convicted partly as a result of Johann Zachariae's twisted biblical interpretation (Ezek. 34). Together with Proles and Staupitz, Johann Greiffenstein, another friar, the master of novices at Erfurt, was also of the opinion that Hus was condemned without any real proof of heresy. The German Augustinians of the early sixteenth century (Proles, Staupitz, Greiffenstein and, in following them, Luther) were ready to correct the record and to stand up for the 'evangelical truth' and thus also to speak in favour of John Hus.[22]

Lutherjahrbuch, 38 (1971), 9–25; R. Schwarz, *Luther* (Göttingen, 1986), p. 74; M. Brecht, *Martin Luther, His Road to Reformation 1483–1521*, trans. J. Schaaf (Philadelphia, 1985), p. 331–2; Zumkeller, *Heilslehre*, p. 101.

[22] (Ezek. 34: 10) 'quo Iohannes hus [sic] a Zacharia fuisse vexatus, retulit sese audisse Staupitius ex Andrea Proles' (*WABR* 3. 289, 6–9 (no. 742)). Luther wrote extensively on Hus, Zachariae, Proles and Greiffenstein in his *Von den neuen Eckischen Bullen und Lügen* (1520) (*WA* 6. 590, 18 – 591, 20). Later, in the postscript to Agricola's 1536/37 edition of the three letters of John Hus, Luther wrote that he felt compelled to share what Staupitz had told him about this case, and that he shared Staupitz's conviction: 'Ich mus hie aber mal erzelen, das ich von Doctor Staupitz selbs gehoret habe, wie sein vorfarn Andres Proles geredet hat .... – Wie es denn J. Staupitz auch dafur hielt. Und ich zwar auch' (postscript, 1536/37, *WA* 50. 36, 19 – 37, 22). Zachariae's grave is depicted in P. Manns, *Martin Luther: An Illustrated Biography* (New York, 1983), p. 33.

After this explanation of what lay behind Staupitz's mild-mannered criticism, let us return to his 1520 sermons where there is still a mariological issue to be discussed in connection with Sermon 4.

In this sermon, with its critical remarks on traditional perceptions Staupitz spoke of Mary, according to one source, as the 'immaculate-born'. However, the other manuscript that preserves this sermon offers a different version, one describing Mary as 'birth-giver'.[23] In the context, the latter makes more sense, as Staupitz presented here a fictional conversation between Mother Mary and her Son, a situation in which the issue of Mary being 'immaculate-born' is irrelevant. The disparity is probably an error on the part of the nun who recorded the sermon.

After ending his fourth sermon with some critical remarks on popular piety, Staupitz now took up this same thought in the opening of his fifth sermon, saying 'you have heard ... how our faithful God is our Pope and forgives us our sins'. This idea was matched by another theological reform principle he used in this sermon: salvation is by faith alone, and by it alone we will become children of God: 'We must through faith and nothing but [faith] become children of God. He also wants to be the father of all our works in such a way that He produces them in us and we are solely the mother and tool.'[24] Here again Staupitz demonstrated his provocative emphasis on faith alone – by which he meant 'trust' or 'confidence' as a child trusts his parent; he also held that our good works are not ours, but those of our heavenly Father. Staupitz, furthermore, operated here with the salvific value of the sinner's self-accusation which is so typical of St Augustine, St Bernard (and also of Luther). Towards the end of the fifth sermon, Staupitz interpreted the thief's dialogue with Christ on the cross in terms of self-accusation and salvation. Christ said to him: 'Because you have justified me and condemned yourself you shall never more be condemned, for the sentence for you is the blotting out of all your sins. Therefore, he who does not want to be condemned, let him always justify God and condemn himself, thus it will be impossible for him to be sentenced to eternal death.' Staupitz let Christ continue by declaring that the redemption of the thief is his own divine masterpiece: '"That suits me just fine, now I will solemnize my masterpiece: that you would not be condemned". This is a comfort for us: if we condemn ourselves, then

---

[23] *Codex Salzburgensis b V8, p. 90v.* Mary's title is 'birth giver', as Markwald points out in his commentary on Sermon 4 (*A Mystic's Passion*, p. 106, n. 30). Markwald, however, prefers the other option in his translation on p. 96, in following Steinmetz's line of thinking on this issue, which I question.

[24] '[Daß Jesus Christus] unser frumer Got, unser pabst ist und uns unser sündt vergibt ...' (Sermon 5; Zumkeller, *Heilslehre*, p. 108; Markwald, *A Mystic's Passion*, pp. 129 and 134; F. Posset, 'The Sweetness of God', *ABR*, 44 (1993) pp. 164–5).

we shall never more be condemned, no matter how many sins we have committed.'[25]

In previous sermons Staupitz had already used the concept of the 'sweetness of God'. Now, in these 1520 sermons he took it up again and preached about the sweetness of the cross, because 'from the cross the sweetest wine has flowed in abundance'.[26] He also said that Christ's yoke is sweet, and human suffering will become bearable 'if I see that God sweetens it for me with His sufferings, He who is true man and real God'. The suffering on the cross turns human suffering into sweetness: 'If you sweeten all your torment with the Holy Cross, then all your burden will float to the surface, and you will leave death, hell and purgatory in the torn skin of Christ.'[27]

As the preacher connected human suffering to Christ's salvific suffering, so did he tie good works to Christ's salvific work. Man's meritorious good works are acceptable to God only if they are handed to God through the hands of Christ, and not through the hands of humans, as Staupitz had declared to his Salzburg listeners in the previous year (1519), when he had let Christ say the following:

> The Father wants to receive meritorious works from my hands, and not from yours .... I am the ... eternal Word of the heavenly Father; I am the one who wants to take your works away from you, and having coloured them in my blood [*in meinem pluet geferbt*], I then show them to the Father. Then, the Father will owe eternal blessedness to you.[28]

The same Christo-centric view is found in Staupitz's final sermon of the Lenten season of 1520. The soul as the bride of Christ must become pregnant by the Holy Spirit and must 'suck' all good works from the love and suffering of Christ and let God be the father of all our works. Here once more, Staupitz unequivocally based his view of good works on the 'contrition' (*reu*) and 'heartrending suffering' of Christ himself:

> This is a direct rebuttal of those people who think that they can do something good [for their redemption] by their own effort. We have to talk a little about that: if you yourself want to be a master of your works, then you disgrace the suffering of Christ. If you were capable of any good without that suffering from which all goodness flows, then my faithful God has endured death and suffering in vain, neither need He even save you. If you are self-sufficient for good

---

[25] Markwald, *A Mystic's Passion*, pp. 135–7. Both Augustine and Bernard had utilized the concept of self-accusation. In 1523 Staupitz would make his conception of faith still more explicit.

[26] Ibid., p. 71.

[27] Ibid., pp. 130–33. It is preferable to translate with 'the torn skin of Christ', rather than 'torn hand' as in ibid., p. 133.

[28] Salzburg Sermon 3 (1519) (folio 77r; Zumkeller, *Heilslehre*, p. 184).

works, then you require none but yourself to save you. Therefore, isn't it a great detriment and disgust to the suffering of Christ if one thinks that someone is capable of one good work, yea one good thought without God?

... Therefore, all our hope is built on the merits of the sufferings of Jesus Christ alone. Here we find our salvation and [the assurance] that the works of God become our works which God produces in us and to our benefit ...

[Jesus]: Yes, it was such a repentence [reu] and heart-rending suffering that I have indeed been forsaken of God and all creation, [and] even as I am waiting for the judgment of eternal condemnation. And the divinity has – as it were – hid itself from me as if I were not the Son of God [Matt. 27: 46; Psalm 22].[29]

Here, in the last of his six sermons of Lent 1520, Staupitz also reiterated his idiosyncratic concept of 'repentance' or 'contrition' [reu], that he had previously expressed in 1512. Here, too, in the conclusion of this last Lenten sermon, the Augustinian preacher made a rare mention of the ecclesiastical authority whom he liked most, Augustine, in the context of his meditation on Christ's death:

But the Lord gently bows His head and says: 'Soul, just farewell!' From that hour it was gone. He breathes no more, rather it appears that He wants to fall softly and sweetly asleep. Thus the Word was fulfilled which He [Himself] spoke: 'No one takes my soul from me; but if I lay it down readily, then it must depart and I may take it again when I wish' [John 10: 18]. For neither the cross, nor Jews, nor Gentiles took [His soul] from Him; but when He inclined His head, and gave it permission, then it had to leave. St Augustine also said [it]: 'Who has ever departed this life so sweetly [as] Christ, when He died? Who has slipped so easily and quickly out of a dress, as Christ's soul has hurried out of His body? Who has ever taken a step ahead so lightly like the soul of Christ when it ascended from this world into that one?' Therefore the true lovers and followers of the suffering Christ must learn from His death how to die.[30]

Here, Staupitz took up the old theme of the art of dying which he had written about in an earlier booklet. The Augustinian text quoted here is found in the treatise on the Gospel of John (119: 6).[31] Shortly after this passage, Staupitz mentioned Augustine again in the concluding sentences

---

[29] Markwald, A Mystic's Passion, pp. 157–60. Staupitz used the vernacular notion reu (repentance) for the first time in his third sermon of 1512 (see Schneider-Lastin, Salzburger Predigten 1512, p. 43; Zumkeller, Heilslehre, p. 171). Staupitz gave a sermon in 1517 titled Von ainer waren rechten reu (Knaake, Sämmtliche Werke, p. 17; Zumkeller, Heilslehre, p. 154, n. 981). See L.G. zu Dohna and R. Wetzel, 'Die Reue Christi: Zum theologischen Ort der Busse bei Johann von Staupitz', Studien und Mitteilungen zur Geschichte des Benediktinerordens und seiner Zweige, 94 (1983), pp. 457–82.

[30] Markwald, A Mystic's Passion, pp. 165f.

[31] See Zumkeller, Heilslehre, p. 25, n. 108; see also p. 94.

of his entire cycle of sermons, quoting from Ps. 4: 9 and Augustine's comment on it in *Enarrationes in Psalmos* 4: 9f., saying:

> 'In you, peace, I will sleep and rest' [Ps. 4: 9a]. But this rest is nothing else but the hope and the trust to which we come through the contemplation of the suffering of my God, wherein we die as we fall sweetly and bravely asleep. However, Saint Augustine, if one views his writings superficially, may appear as a contributor to dissension when he said: 'the eternal salvation is rest'. But I believe that he would not differ [from] me, I would bring him to my understanding, for the Psalmist says in the following verse: 'For you have placed me into the rest of hope' [Ps. 4: 9b]. Thus Augustine also asserts that hope's rest begins here and lasts eternally. May God the Father, the Son and the Holy Spirit help you and me to [obtain] it! Amen.[32]

At the end of the manuscript containing these six sermons is an appendix of sorts consisting of what looks like a communal penance service which Staupitz conducted for his audience. The beginning of this reads: 'This is the open confession which the Reverend Father has spoken' (for us). Then follow his words: 'Make the sign of the holy cross and repeat after me: "I am a poor sinner and I confess to God that I have committed many sins against my Lord with many improper thoughts, words, and works".' (See p. 282, on communal penance services.)

After the completion of this series of sermons Staupitz left Salzburg. He first appears to have had a meeting sometime in April 1520 with Duke William IV of Bavaria who, upon the recommendation of the Elector Frederick the Wise, sought Staupitz's help in reforming the monasteries of the Premonstratensians within his territory. From Munich, Staupitz travelled via Nuremberg to the friary at Kulmbach where he had an appointment with the district vicar, Johann Lang of Erfurt, on 21 April 1520. The concerned Staupitz wanted to discuss the Luther affair with Lang.[33]

At Nuremberg he had time to write a number of letters. One was addressed to Luther who mentioned its arrival in his own letter to Spalatin of 1 May 1520. However, Staupitz's letter to Luther is lost and Luther's letter to Spalatin is the only evidence that we have for its existence. Luther was happy to report that Staupitz 'finally praises my cause and has a firmer hope for it, which is certainly different from what I used to hear'.[34] Luther must have been greatly relieved to find that his old friend still supported him, as there may have been reasons for

---

[32] Markwald, *A Mystic's Passion*, p. 167; Zumkeller, *Heilslehre*, p. 25, n. 108.

[33] See Staupitz's letter of 11 March 1520 from Salzburg to Johann Lang, as mentioned in Sallaberger, 'Johann von Staupitz, Abt von St. Peter', p. 156.

[34] 'Ex Nurmberga Staupitianas literas accepi, laudantes tandem ac firmius sperantes in causa mea, quam antea solitus sum audire' (*WABR* 2. 96, 23f. (no. 283); *LW* 48. 162).

Staupitz to express his displeasure as to the direction in which matters were going. Apparently, up till then Luther was uncertain as to where exactly Staupitz stood. Had he known of the Salzburg sermons of Lent 1520, Luther would have been totally certain that Staupitz was in general agreement with him.

By the papal bull of 15 June 1520, the pope tried to silence Luther through the threat of excommunication. By this time Luther also knew of Staupitz's intention to resign from the leadership of the Order. That same summer Staupitz was at Erfurt from where he wrote to Luther asking him not to publish his pamphlet *To the Christian Nobility of the German Nation Concerning the Reform of the Christian Estate.* (Luther mentioned this request in a letter of 19 August 1520 to their common friend, Linck.) However, the booklet, written in June 1520, had apparently already come off the printing press;[35] Staupitz's request came too late. We do not know what his reaction was.

On 17 July 1520 the pope sent to Germany two emissaries, Aleander and Eck, whose task was to try to publish the bull that threatened Luther with excommunication. The Elector of Saxony and the University of Wittenberg declined to promulgate it. Amazingly, Eck was authorized by Rome to add names to the list of excommunicated persons, which he did by including two members of the University of Wittenberg, Karlstadt and Melanchthon, and two members of the 'Staupitz Sodality' of Nuremberg, the humanists Willibald Pirckheimer and Lazarus Spengler – but not Staupitz! We do not know whether Staupitz ever read the text of this bull. He must nonetheless have been aware that he, too, was in danger, since the text clearly indicated that the excommunication included Luther's 'accomplices, protectors, adherents, and anyone receiving him'; and Staupitz was certainly Luther's protector. However, his name did not appear on Eck's list, although two other names of men sympathetic to Luther did: Johann Wildenauer (Sylvius Egranus, d. 1535) a preacher at Zwickau who had been involved in a controversy with the Franciscans; and Hans von Dolzig (Doltzeg) who was one of Frederick's lawyers and his marshal.[36]

---

[35] 'Reverendus pater Vicarius heri ex Erfordia mihi scripsit, rogans, ne ederem libellum de statu Christianorum emendando ...' (*WABR* 2. 168, 12–14 (no. 328)); see *WABR* 1. 597, 37–39 (no. 232), *LW* 48. 138; *WABR* 2. 96, 23–26 (no. 283), *LW* 48. 162; and *WABR* 2. 167f (no. 327).

[36] The texts of the bull that threatened Luther with excommunication and the bull of excommunication are found in Fabisch and Iserloh, *Dokumente zur Causa Lutheri (1517–1521, 2. Teil: Vom Augsburger Reichstag 1518 bis zum Wormser Edikt 1521* (Münster, 1991), II, pp. 364–484. For the wording of the bull concerning the inclusion of Luther's sympathizers, see ibid., 402f. With regard to Wildenauer and Doltzeg, see ibid., 334f. On Wildenauer, see 'Sylvius Egranus' in Stupperich, p. 74.

The fact that the 'Staupitz Sodality' was sympathetic to Luther's cause does not necessarily mean that they were all 'Lutherans' in the later sense. These sodality members were citizens in established positions in their city and participated in the local Catholic church life. The translator of Luther's *95 Theses* on indulgences, the sodality member Kaspar Nützel, even let his daughter join the convent of St Clare at Nuremberg; so did Jerome Ebner whose daughter entered the same cloister. Furthermore, sodality members were seen in public processions on ecclesiastical feast days. Scheurl himself had Masses celebrated for his benefit up to the autumn of 1520 at the All Saints Foundation at Wittenberg.[37] Thus, one could be both a practising Catholic and a sympathizer of the reformers, especially when they based their teaching and preaching on the Bible, and directed their criticism against abuses within the Church.

The same can be said of Staupitz and his devotion to the Virgin Mary. In his sermons of 1520 he largely remained with his mariology of previous years, when he spoke of Mary as the devout woman and treasure of all graces.[38] She was the only one of all creatures who did not forsake Christ: 'Wherever He turns He is forsaken of God and all creatures, except for a woman.'[39] She is Christ's bride who is pregnant with the faithful of the Church. She is the 'pure procreatress', who shall bear God's children and nurture them in the faith, as he said with John 1: 12: 'Those become children of God who believe in his name.' Staupitz concluded this train of thought by alluding to Luke 1: 32–8 that 'we must through faith and nothing but faith become children of God'.[40]

Having matured as an Augustinian friar and venerator of the Virgin Mary, he nevertheless kept his critical distance from one particular trait of the Dominican friars' Marian devotion. They promoted the prayers of the rosary with the help of 'rings and beads' as Staupitz noted in a rather derogatory manner. The use of a rosary was a recent custom, not even 50 years old at the time when Staupitz expressed his dislike for it. A coloured woodcut from around 1500 testifies to the Dominicans' devotional preference as it shows the rosary with Mary at the centre with the Dominicans and members of rosary fraternities gathered under her protective mantle. The caption of this woodcut reads: 'My wide

---

[37] See W. Graf, *Doktor Christoph Scheurl von Nürnberg* (Berlin and Leipzig, 1930), pp. 76 and 84. 'In honorem Divorum omnium vel unam missam pro me celebrare digneris' (Scheurl's letter to Spalatin in 1518, Soden and Knaake, *Christoph Scheurl's Briefbuch*, no. 149).

[38] Markwald, *A Mystic's Passion*, p. 96.

[39] Ibid., p. 39.

[40] Ibid., pp. 133f.

mantle is my mercy.'[41] Staupitz articulated his dislike of the display of one's piety 'on the outside of one's coat', as he put it, where some people show off their rosary. To his mind, this was 'foolish work'. He contemptuously called it 'rings and buttons prayers', and commented: 'I do not know to whom it would do any good.'[42] Staupitz himself promoted an internalized piety without external signs or outward activities. At the end of his fourth sermon of 1520 he had polemicized against pilgrimages that were undertaken for the purpose of gaining indulgences; instead he proclaimed (as quoted above), that Christ as 'the true Pope lives in your heart'.[43]

In 1523, shortly before his death, Staupitz still called Mary 'the treasury of all graces' (Sermon 19), as she is the 'pure Virgin Mary in whom Christ was conceived by the Holy Spirit'; in her, the 'pure Queen Mary, lived the divinity, in her who is of David's race' (Sermon 3). She is the 'Mother of God' (Sermons 19 and 22). She alone, by God's grace, did not lose faith under the cross of Christ (Sermon 19). Yet, in his last sermon of 1523 (Sermon 24), Staupitz repeated his derogatory remarks on the rosary (*rosen krenczel*).[44]

Here again, Staupitz put most of his emphasis on the mighty power of God in saving Mary from falling into despair under the cross: 'It was the most holy Mother of God, Mary, whom God in his especially mighty power and grace preserved from falling. In her, the light of faith was never dimmed.'[45] Thus, Mary's faith was always strong, and because of

---

[41] 'Mein breytter mantel ist mein barmhertzigkeyt.' See *Martin Luther und die Reformation in Deutschland. Ausstellung zum 500. Geburtstag Martin Luthers veranstaltet vom Germanischen Nationalmuseum Nürnberg in Zusammenarbeit mit dem Verein für Reformationsgeschichte* (Frankfurt, 1983), p. 347, illustration 462. See also H. van Os, *The Art of Devotion in the Late Middle Ages in Europe 1300–1500* (Princeton, NJ, 1994), p. 171, illustration 78. Today the picture is in the Staatsbibliothek Bamberg, Germany. The rosary is believed to have originated in the Carthusian monastery of Trier, Germany, in about 1475; see exhibition catalogue, *500 Jahre Rosenkranz, 1475* (Cologne, 1975).

[42] 'Ringt und knöpfel pet.... Ich wais nit, für wen es guet ist' (Sermon 4 (1520), Zumkeller, *Heilslehre*, p. 108; Markwald, *A Mystic's Passion*, p. 101).

[43] See Markwald, *A Mystic's Passion*, p. 104.

[44] Sermon 3 (1523) in H. Aumüller, 'Predigten von Staupitz in Salzburg', *Jahrbuch der Gesellschaft für die Geschichte des Protestantismus in Österreich*, 2 (1881), p. 115; Sermon 19 (1523), Blatt 178v–181v; Sermon 22 (1523), Blatt 220r; Zumkeller, *Heilslehre*, pp. 95–7. On the rosary, see Sermon 24 as edited by T. Kolde, *Die deutsche Augustiner-Congregation und Johann von Staupitz* (Gotha, 1879), pp. 452–6 (p. 453, on praying with the rosary as an external work).

[45] 'Das ist dy aller heiligist mueter gots Maria gewesen, dy got auch aus seiner sunderleicher gewaltigen kraft und gnad enthalten hat vor dem vall, das das liecht jn jr nye geswecht ist warden' (Sermon 19 (1523), as quoted by D.C. Steinmetz, *Misericordia Dei: The Theology of Johannes Staupitz in its Late Medieval Setting* (Leiden, 1968) p. 27, n. 2 and again p. 147, n. 1). Zumkeller (*Heilslehre*, p. 97) has a different spelling from Steinmetz's and he takes the immediate context into consideration (while Steinmetz does

its strength, by the grace of God, she did not fall away from Christ when he died on the cross, while the other disciples did. Against dubious interpretations one must point out that Staupitz's phrase was not a statement about Mary's immaculate conception, but about Mary's immaculate and strong faith, even under the cross. Sermon 22 of 1523 has the same Good Friday context (when everybody on earth had fallen away from the faith) in which the statement is found that Mary, Mother of God, was saved from 'this' (*davon*), that is from the 'fall' into disbelief: 'The tender Queen, Mary, Mother of God, was the only one who by the mighty and powerful grace of God was saved from it.'[46]

While Staupitz remained a devotee of Mary and acknowledged her intercession, the invocation of other saints was less certain to him on account of his Christo-centrism. In his booklet on the right Christian faith, which was published posthumously in 1525, he wrote that, if one petitioned God in the name of Jesus, one would not need any other intermediary (*fürbitter*). Yet, he clarified this immediately, saying that he did not want to criticize those who call upon the saints to pray for us to God. Nonetheless, he would see it as a perversion (*verkerung*) to prefer what is uncertain over what is certain. To invoke the saints is an uncertain matter while we possess the certainty of being heard by Christ through our faith: our certainty of being heard 'rests' on the faith in Christ. This is so because the intercession by saints for someone who does not have faith in Christ would be in vain. Thus, Staupitz thought it more useful and necessary to turn to Christ and to the Father directly, without any intermediaries.[47] With his principal Christo-centrism, he

---

not): Staupitz's context speaks of the Good Friday situation when 'the holy faith and the gospel' were given up by everybody, except Mary, whom God by his grace 'saved from the fall' (*enthalten hat vor dem vall*), that is the falling away from 'the holy faith and the gospel'. Therefore, one may doubt that Staupitz wanted to speak here of the 'fall' as the original sin from which Mary would have been saved.

[46] Sermon 22 (1523, Blatt 220r): 'llain dy zart künigin, Maria, dy mueter gotz, dy auch nur aus der gewaltigen und mächtigen genad gots enthalten davon ist warden', as quoted by Steinmetz (*Misericordia Dei*, p. 146, n.6, where, however, the context is disregarded); Zumkeller (*Heilslehre*, pp. 95–6) takes the context into consideration, as he points out that the source references with which Steinmetz *Misericordia Dei*, pp. 145–7 presented Staupitz as the representative of the doctrine of Mary's immaculate conception are 'insufficient' (*unzureichend*, p. 96, n. 618). Steinmetz's view that Staupitz was 'an ally on this point with Biel and Gerson, who are also defenders of the doctrine of the immaculate conception' (*Misericordia Dei*, p. 146, n. 5), is not entirely convincing. The third locus for possible proof of the doctrine of the immaculate conception, according to Steinmetz, is in Salzburg Sermon 4 of 1520; however, this is dubious from a text-critical point of view (see Markwald, *A Mystic's Passion*, p. 106). It would appear Staupitz did not so much 'defend' as simply go along with a high mariology (see pp. 222–7).

[47] See Chapter 9 in Knaake, *Sämmtliche Werke*, pp. 128–9; P. Zeller, 'Staupitz. Seine religiös-dogmatischen Anschauungen und dogmengeschichtliche Stellung', *Theologische Studien und Kritiken*, **52** (1879), p. 48; Zumkeller, *Heilslehre*, p. 166.

preferred to trust in Christ, and therefore he took up a position somewhere between the extreme fronts. However, he never published any treatise on Mary or the saints, while the Franciscan Caspar Schatzgeyer (d. 1527) did with a booklet 'on the veneration and invocation of the dear saints' (*Von der lieben heiligen Eerung und Anrueffung*) which was published at Munich in 1523. Schatzgeyer maintained (as did Staupitz) that Christ is the only mediator of redemption, but in addition said that Christ left to the saints, including Mary, the care of answering calls for help in the ordinary difficulties of the temporal sphere. This was the typical popular Catholic position; later Protestant developments would tend toward the position that saints should not be invoked at all.[48]

Leaving the Order of St Augustine (1520)

Staupitz may have had plans as early as 1518 to accept a position at Salzburg.[49] It is possible that contacts and arrangements for such an appointment were made then because the former preacher, Paul Speratus (d. 1551),[50] married and moved away in the late summer of 1517, and no suitable successor had been named. Speratus had been *Stiftsprediger* (foundation preacher) at the main church; the contemporary designation for this position was *concionator* (speaker). The preacher in this *Stift* position was also at times invited to preach at St Peter's Abbey; and he was paid, at some occasions, in terms of a certain number of chickens which the abbey itself received on a regular basis. Staupitz had occasionally in the past filled this vacant preaching position at the main church in Salzburg as a substitute. However, Staupitz's permanent

---

[48] See G.H. Tavard, *The Thousand Faces of the Virgin Mary* (Collegeville, MN, 1996), p. 115 (on Schatzgayer); and pp. 103–33 (on 'Mary in Protestantism').

[49] See Sallaberger, 'Johann von Staupitz, Luthers Vorgesetzter und Freund, und seine Beziehungen zu Salzburg', *Augustiniana*, **28** (1978), pp. 108–54 (pp. 136–7).

[50] In 1520 Speratus was a preacher at Würzburg, and on 12 January 1522 he gave his famous reformation sermon at St Stephen's Cathedral in Vienna (printed at Königsberg, Prussia, on 16 September 1524). In 1524 he translated into the vernacular Luther's book *De instituendis ministris ecclesiae ad senatum Pragensem Bohemiae* (published in November 1523) (*WA* 12. 169–96; English trans.: *Concerning the Ministry*, *LW* 40. 7–44). Speratus dedicated his translation to the Christians at Würzburg and Salzburg; see J. Sallaberger, 'Johann von Staupitz, die Stiftsprediger und die Mendikanten-Termineien in Salzburg', *Studien und Mitteilungen zur Geschichte des Benediktinerordens und seiner Zweige*, **93** (1982), pp. 218–69 (p. 249); H. Bornkamm, *Luther in Mid-Career 1521–1530*, ed. K. Bornkamm, trans. E.T. Bachmann (Philadelphia, 1983), pp. 127–8. In 1529 Speratus was a Lutheran bishop in Marienwerder, Southern Prussia; see H.J. König, *Paul Speratus. Reformator, Organisator des Kirchenwesens in Ostpreussen, evangelischer Bischof von Pomeranien 1484–1551*. Lebensbilder aus Schwaben und Franken 9 (Stuttgart, 1963).

residency in order to fill the position at Salzburg could not have been at the invitation of the new Archbishop, Cardinal Matthew Lang von Wellenburg, because the appointment of preachers to this position was not in the archbishop's competency. Rather it was an appointment in the hands of the Salzburg city government represented by a small selection committee.[51] Some people may interpret Staupitz's appointment as *Stiftsprediger* as his desertion of the reformation cause, but it was not. It was an attractive position and must have facilitated or contributed to Staupitz's desire to settle permanently in Salzburg; this, of course, meant that he first had to resign from the duties as leader of the Augustinians' Reformed Congregation. Under the given circumstances Staupitz's decision to seek permanent residency in Salzburg was not difficult. The post seemed to fit Staupitz's capacities and interests and the situation in Salzburg must have remained attractive enough for him to stay there, even after the death of his friend Archbishop Leonhard in June 1519.

Staupitz most likely resided at the Augustinian Order's branch office, the *terminus*, which (as has been said) was an extension of the friary of Munich. He had assigned his close associate, Friar Besler, to the important position of *terminarius* at this location in December 1519.[52] In addition, Besler may occasionally have had to assume the responsibility of preaching. Perhaps they toyed with the idea of developing the branch office into a full friary. One may speculate also whether the improvements of the Augustinians' facility in Salzburg may have had something to do with Staupitz's plans to settle permanently in the city. Such strategies may have been underway for there could have been contacts with the Salzburg cardinal, Matthew Lang, as early as the Diet of Augsburg in 1518. By January 1521, however, Friar Besler wanted to be released from the job of building up the *terminus*. In contrast, we know that Staupitz was doing fine in Salzburg, as Luther reported before Christmas 1519 to Lang in Erfurt and to Spalatin at the elector's court that Staupitz was 'healthy and honoured' in Salzburg.[53]

Staupitz tried to settle in at Salzburg in 1519/20, but still had to cope with the Luther affair. The general of the Order, Gabriel della Volta, put official and direct pressure on Staupitz in a long letter dated 15 March 1520, in which presuming correctly Staupitz's love for Luther and vice versa, he also alluded to the correspondence between Luther and

---

[51] See Sallaberger, 'Johann von Staupitz, die Stiftsprediger', pp. 226f. and 244–51; F. Posset, 'Preaching the Passion of Christ on the Eve of the Reformation', *Concordia Theological Quarterly*, 59 (1995), 279–300 (pp. 282f.).

[52] See Kolde, *Die deutsche Augustiner-Congregation*, p. 361; Kunzelmann, *Geschichte*, V, p. 508.

[53] *Sanus et honoratus* (Luther's letter to Spalatin, mid-December, WABR 1. 572, 9f. (no. 228); Luther's letter to Lang of 18 December).

Staupitz. (Volta probably knew of Luther's letter of 30 May 1518 to Pope Leo X which had been sent via Staupitz.) The Roman superior expected Staupitz to mitigate or prevent Luther's polemics against the Church, the pope, and indulgences, since the good reputation of the Augustinian Order was at stake. The letter said that Luther had brought shame onto their Order; yet, in contrast to the demand for Luther's incarceration which Volta had expressed in a letter to the Saxon provincial Gerhard Hecker two years earlier, he now wrote nothing of this sort to Staupitz. Rather, the letter spoke of 'conciliation with Luther'![54] In no uncertain terms Volta let Staupitz know that he had been missed at the general chapter meeting of the Order in Venice in June 1519, where the troublesome matters surrounding the Luther affair could have been talked about had Staupitz been present. However, he had not been. It is possible that the death of Staupitz's friend Archbishop Keutschach on 8 June 1519 could partly account for Staupitz's absence from Venice. Alternatively, Staupitz may deliberately have avoided this particular meeting lest he be compelled by the Roman leadership to distance himself from Friar Martin Luther. Volta made Staupitz fully aware of the possibility that his Reformed Congregation could lose all its 'indults, favours, privileges, exemptions, and immunities'. Furthermore, Volta revealed that he had learnt that the bull of excommunication had already been prepared against Luther (it was issued on 15 June 1520). If only Staupitz would choose to intervene! If Staupitz really wanted to save his Order from 'infamy and calamity', he should bring back Magister Luther to the Augustinian fold.

Volta's letter must have been the immediate cause of Staupitz's decision to resign, as he was apparently unwilling to sacrifice Luther and his theological positions – which were also largely his own. In short, he was ready to give up his own career in the Order rather than to make an official move against Luther. Having served as vicar of the Reformed Congregation for 17 consecutive years, Staupitz now preferred to risk 'infamy and calamity' for the Order than to sacrifice his younger friend.

Evidently Staupitz shared his intention of resigning with others immediately after Volta's letter of 15 March had reached him, because by 1 May 1520 Luther knew of Staupitz's plans and wrote to Spalatin at the elector's court to report that rumour had it that Staupitz would resign on the forthcoming feast day of St Augustine, 28 August. In this letter to Spalatin Luther also expressed his happiness that Staupitz had finally praised his cause. Four days later, on 5 May 1520, Luther confirmed:

---

[54] 'Magistro Johanni Stupitio pro conciliando Lutherio' (Fabisch and Iserloh, *Dokumente*, II, pp. 33–5; facsimile, ibid., p. 36). See W. Delius, 'Der Augustiner-Eremitenorden im Prozeß Luthers', *ARG*, **63** (1972), pp. 27–28; Sallaberger, 'Johann von Staupitz, Luthers Vorgesetzter', p. 136.

'Our Vicar has summoned our chapter meeting at Eisleben on the Feast Day of Augustine; he will be present and lay down the burden of his office.'[55]

The perennial aggravations with the 'reformation' of the friaries, the obstacles that lay in its way from the central administration in Rome, together with the direct pressure from Rome in the Luther affair may all have been significant factors contributing to Staupitz's resignation. He may have sensed what was coming (mainly Luther's excommunication) and saw a way out from this predicament by seeking a more tranquil life, perhaps in semi-retirement, at Salzburg.

At Wittenberg, meanwhile, Luther was gaining momentum and could no longer be stopped. He continued to publish – 4000 copies of his pamphlet *To the Christian Nobility of the German Nation Concerning the Reform of the Christian Estate* had already come off the press by August 1520, the date of its publication virtually coinciding with the extraordinary chapter meeting which took place on 28 August at the friary of St Anne at Eisleben, where Staupitz's resignation was expected. In this booklet, Luther criticized the Church, celibacy, and the cloister. Shortly afterwards, in October 1520, his *Babylonian Captivity of the Church* appeared, in which he treated the sacraments, including private confession, in a new light. Luther stressed that true contrition (*Reue*) comes from faith in Christ – here he sounded like Staupitz on Christ's 'contrition' (*Reue*), a topic which Staupitz had pursued in his sermons at Salzburg in 1512 and 1520.[56] Faced with such similarity, one may question whether there is a direct link between Luther's Reformation treatises of 1520 and Staupitz's decision to abdicate and join the Benedictines.

For the last time Staupitz presided over a meeting of his Augustinian Order. He resigned and handed over the office of vicar general of the German Reformed Congregation to his and Luther's confidant, Wenceslaus Linck. During the first week of September, Staupitz and Linck travelled to Wittenberg to see Luther and to ask him to write a conciliatory letter to the pope in which he should state that he had never undertaken anything personally against the pope. They undertook this journey at the request of the papal nuncio Carl von Miltitz who had met with them on the occasion of the chapter meeting at Eisleben.[57] However, this compliance with the nuncio's wish did not mean that Staupitz and

---

[55] 'Vicarius noster anticipavit Capitulum nostrum ad festum Augustini ad Islebenn venturus depositurusque ibi officii onus, ut dicitur' (*WABR* 2. 101, 8f. (no. 285, 5 May 1520)).

[56] *WA* 6. 545 (on contrition, *Reue*). See Dohna and Wetzel, 'Die Reue Christi', pp. 457–82.

[57] See Kolde, *Die deutsche Augustiner-Congregation*, pp. 327f.

Linck distanced themselves from their close friend. Luther was not a lone fighter; on the contrary, he always felt supported by good friends from within the Augustinian Order. Luther's letter to the pope, dated 6 September 1520, indeed confirmed what the nuncio had expected.

The meeting at Wittenberg was Staupitz's last personal encounter with both Linck and Luther together; this Augustinian trio would not be able to meet again. Luther reported to Spalatin about his meeting with Staupitz, Linck and other friars, saying that they 'were not displeased with my cause, while the Romans are'.[58] Luther felt assured of Staupitz's support. Thus, Staupitz's resignation is not to be blamed on Luther, although some people mistakenly believe that he was fed up with Luther's criticisms of the Church as they became public, especially following the Leipzig Disputation of 1519.

At times it is assumed that Staupitz recognized that Luther not only fought the abuses in the Church, but went beyond this in 1520 when he designed his alleged anti-ecclesiastical reform programme in his address *To the Christian Nobility*. Staupitz was supposedly not able to 'control the situation' any more and therefore called the extraordinary meeting at Eisleben and resigned.[59] One has reason to question this line of argument not only because it blames everything on Luther, which is surely unbalanced, but also because it fails to see that Staupitz and Luther (and Linck) always formed a theologically united front, even if they may not always have agreed on ecclesiastical tactics or politics. They kept up their correspondence after 1520; in it Staupitz recognized Luther's achievements as a preacher of the Gospel. Staupitz may have planned his abdication long before Luther's publication of his Reformation treatises – working in Salzburg was very attractive to him.

Another view concerns the papal bull by which Luther had been declared a heretic. It is sometimes supposed that since Staupitz evidently had been unable to avert it, he therefore resigned. Again, it is opined that Staupitz was no longer able to 'control the situation' which Luther had created.[60] Such an interpretation portrays Staupitz as a Roman Catholic and it seeks to deny the thesis that he had a 'Protestant mind'. While one may agree that he did not have a 'Protestant mind' as this term later came to be understood, he certainly had an 'Evangelical' mind in the sense of Hans Sachs's contemporary classifications (see p. 185). There is no doubt

---

[58] Letters to Spalatin of 1 September and 11 September 1520 (*WABR* 2. 180 (no. 335) and 184f. (no. 337)). In the latter, the lines 30f. read. 'Vicarius Staupitz et Wenceslaus, cum aliquot fratribus. Quibus omnibus causa mea non displicet autem Romanibus.'

[59] See Kunzelmann, V, p. 480; A. Zumkeller, 'Johannes von Staupitz und die klösterliche Reformbewegung', *AAug*, 52 (1989), pp. 31–49 (p. 48).

[60] See Kunzelmann, V, p. 480; Sallaberger, 'Johann von Staupitz, Luthers Vorgesetzter', p. 136.

that Staupitz was a Catholic (although, not an enthusiastic Romanist). A similar argument is that Staupitz resigned 'because the Order had become so heavily infiltrated by Reformation followers'.[61] While this statement is correct insofar as many Augustinian friars were sympathizers of Luther's reforms, it is incorrect to see in this fact the cause for Staupitz's resignation. Staupitz himself remained favourably inclined towards Luther and his cause – which indeed he may still have perceived as a valid extension of his own devotional theology.

What appears to be a correct assessment of his resignation is as follows. First, by resigning from office, he officially gave up his efforts and hopes regarding reforming the entire Augustinian Order in Germany, a task that had been begun by Andreas Proles in the previous century. Staupitz had encountered so much resistance over the years, both from certain overly zealous friars and occasionally from the central office in Rome, that there was little success to show with regard to the reform of the Church through the renewal of the religious Orders in particular, which had been his original intention. Secondly, Staupitz probably anticipated the imminent dissolution of the Reformed Congregation as he knew it, and may not have wanted to preside over its disintegration as the last vicar general. Thirdly, in addition, and probably only secondary to those conditions within the reformed Order, the Luther issue may have become bothersome and dangerous to him, although not because he disagreed with Luther on fundamental theological points (he did not), but because he probably misjudged the force with which both Luther, on the one side, and Rome and the Dominicans, on the other side, acted and reacted. Subsequently he saw Luther (and himself) losing the battle with Rome as long as the new General Volta and Pope Leo X were in office. In addition, Egidio da Viterbo had also turned against Luther. The threat which Volta had articulated in his letter of 15 March 1520, of revoking every privilege that Staupitz's Reformed Congregation possessed, together with the hint concerning the bull of excommunication, may have been the final straw. In this situation, the alternative of living in relative tranquillity and stability in Salzburg, with the prospect of being an admired preacher there, must have looked rather attractive to the ageing friar.

Although Staupitz left his leadership position in the Order of St Augustine, he remained a reform-minded, Evangelical (gospel-oriented), Catholic theologian as far as the basic theological principles of faith alone and grace alone for salvation, and as far as the issue of 'faith and good works' were concerned. He saw these axioms rooted in Scripture and in the theological tradition. If these axioms are claimed to be

---

[61] *LW* 48. 64, n. 1.

'Protestant'/'Evangelical,' then Staupitz may be claimed for the 'Protestant'/'Evangelical' camp. However, if these principles can also be shown to be Catholic principles (as they can), along the lines of the theology of St Augustine and St Bernard of Clairvaux, then both Staupitz and Luther may be claimed for the 'Catholic' reform movement. Whatever definition one applies, and whatever results one may achieve as to in which camp they belong, one thing cannot be done: that is to consider Staupitz and Luther as being opposed to each other, especially when one considers their shared central theological concerns. Their temper and tactics may have differed, but, without doubt, they positioned themselves on the same *theological* side and fought the same battle for spiritual, theological, and pastoral reforms. The only major differences between them were their views on religious vows (see pp. 325–7) and the degree to which the papacy was to be criticized. Staupitz had spoken of 'Roman pestilence', but not of the pope as 'antichrist'.

While Staupitz was in Salzburg, Luther took action in Wittenberg. Early in the morning of 10 December 1520, six months after its issue on 15 June, Luther burned in public the bull *Exsurge Domine* which threatened him with excommunication unless he recanted within 60 days. In performing this frivolous act Luther was 'trembling and praying'[62] initially, as he reported to Staupitz January 1521, but eventually he felt good about it. Staupitz was also informed by Luther that Jerome Emser and Thomas Murner had written against him and that Luther's effigy had been burned three times, at Louvain, at Cologne and at Mainz. The emperor had summoned him in a letter addressed to Frederick the Wise. Ulrich von Hutten had written a commentary on the papal bull of excommunication 'with the sharpest remarks against the pope'. Staupitz received further information about issues within their Augustianian Order, namely that the vicar general, Wenceslaus Linck, went to Nuremberg probably for a formal visitation, and that Prior Wolfgang von Zeschau of the friary at Grimma had supposedly left their Order.

This correspondence shows once more how close Luther was to Staupitz, since he did not hesitate to share his feelings with his fatherly friend concerning, for example, his rebellious act of burning the bull. Would Luther have told Staupitz about it if he had thought that Staupitz was no longer trustworthy or that he had distanced himself from him? Luther must still have felt in line with his reform-minded superior, even though Staupitz would probably never have conceived of performing such an act himself. At that same time, before Christmas 1520, Luther

---

[62] 'Exussi libros papae et bullam, primum trepidus et orans, sed nunc laetior...' (*WABR* 2. 245, 17–19 (no. 366); *LW* 48. 192; Brecht, *Martin Luther, 1483–1521*, pp. 424–8).

wrote his explanation for burning the Roman bull in which 41 sentences from his works were pulled out and condemned. He defended those sentences and postulated that 'common opinion' was on his side.[63]

At the 'Anus of The World' (1520/21)

Staupitz, still a member of the Augustinian Order, waited in Salzburg to see in which way the Luther issue would be resolved. Luther's recent actions did not make life any easier for Staupitz. During that same month of December 1520, when Luther had burned the papal bull at Wittenberg, Staupitz was summoned by the new Archbishop of Salzburg, Cardinal Lang, who wanted him to repudiate Luther's positions. Originally the cardinal had dismissed the Luther affair simply as 'friars' quarrels',[64] and a matter of no importance. Indeed, rivalry among the mendicant orders had been a significant factor for quite some time. Now, all of a sudden, things changed and the Luther affair became urgent. The cardinal even expected Staupitz's statement against Luther to be notarized by a notary public – evidently Lang himself was under pressure from Pope Leo X. However, Cardinal Lang and Staupitz came to a mutually satisfying agreement by which Staupitz was no longer expected to recant what he himself had not advanced (or at least not advanced in public). This being the grounds on which he asked to be excused from recantation, the cardinal evidently accepted. Staupitz reported all this to Linck, his successor in the Order of St Augustine, whom he now addressed as his *paternitas* (the formal address for the superior), in a letter from Salzburg, dated 4 January 1521:

> To Wenceslaus Linck, from the faithful son Johann von Staupitz, servant of Christ. Salvation and Recommendation! Our land is replete with rumours about Martin, and our eyes are unsure and full of anticipation as to what will prevail, power or the truth. The roaring of the Lion [Pope Leo] has reached us now, and he seeks a victim which he would like to devour. Thus, the Most Reverend Cardinal [Matthew Lang] was summoned to force me to declare that Martin's *Theses* are heretical, erroneous, and offensive to pious ears, and to do so in front of a notary public and other witnesses. Since, however, I am unable to recant what I have not said, I asked the lord Cardinal to consider me excused. What will happen now is not yet clear to me. This much I wanted to write you as my father as far as I am concerned. Yet I want to add one thing. I had thought to have

---

[63] Latin: *sensus communis* (WA 6. 101, 22); German: *gemeiner synn* (WA 6. 321, 35); Schwarz, *Luther*, p. 100; see also *WABR* 3. 155f. (no. 659).

[64] *Mönchsgezänk*, see H. Widmann, *Geschichte Salzburgs*, 3 vols (Gotha, 1914), III, p. 44, as referred to by Sallaberger, 'Johann von Staupitz, Luthers Vorgesetzter', p. 137.

more peace now. But now this dark temptation approaches. I cannot fly, as I do not excel in learnedness nor in sanctity. Nevertheless, in my judgment I think it is the greatest injustice when one departs from the truth. Therefore, I will accept the cup of salvation and proclaim the name of the Lord. And you, Reverend Father, assist me with your advice and help. Martin has started something difficult, and he is very courageous, illuminated by God. I, however, feel like a stammering child needing milk. Farewell, Reverend Father, and do not depart from us [in the inn] of the 'Dark Star' at the anus of the world. Greetings from my fellow prisoners, Father Mayer [Gregor Mayr] and Father Bessler [Nicholas Besler], who desire to see the face of your *paternitas*. They would like to drink some wine with you which elsewhere is better than here in Salzburg; yet they promise to bear adversity along with you.[65]

Staupitz indicated that leaving the office of vicar general did not bring him the peace he had longed for. The letter revealed Staupitz's dilemma, but also his conviction that Luther was 'illuminated by God'. While the 'illuminated one' was at Wittenberg, Staupitz and the two other friars felt that they in contrast were sitting in darkness, at the inn of 'the Dark Star at the anus of the world' (*zum finstern Stern in culo mundi*), as the noble Staupitz expressed himself in an ignoble mixture of Latin and German. Clearly, Staupitz felt keenly the difference between the good times he had enjoyed until quite recently, in that same city and the situation he was now stuck at the anus of the world! However, he spoke of the entire group that was with him, and not just of his personal situation. Convivially he added that elsewhere the wine would be better which they wanted to drink when they were united again; their friendship was unbroken. By contrast, the people at Wittenberg had the impression that Staupitz had submitted to the pope.[66]

In the letter quoted above, a worried Staupitz was reminded by Luther of their previous conversations:

When we were at Augsburg and discussed my case, Most Reverend Father, you said to me among other things, 'Remember, Friar, you began this in the name of our Lord Jesus Christ'. I have accepted this

---

[65] 'Valeat Tua Reverenda Paternitas, et nos zum finstern Stern in culo mundi ne deseras. Salutant te concaptivi mei, Patres Mayer und Bessler, cupientes videre faciem Reverendae Vestrae Paternitatis und simul gustare vinum, quod et quale Salzpurgae melius inveniri poterit, sed et adversa tecum aequanimiter ferre promittunt. Ex Salzpurga 4. Jan. 1521' (Staupitz's letter of 4 January 1521 to Linck). This Latin excerpt is found in Sallaberger, 'Johann von Staupitz, Abt von St. Peter', p. 159, n. 421, and parts of it in *WABR* 2. 246 (no. 366), n. 2. For a German translation of this letter, see Sallaberger, 'Johann von Staupitz, Luthers Vorgesetzter', pp. 137–9. Brecht, *Martin Luther, 1483–1521*, p. 428, claims that Staupitz 'expressly acknowledged the pope to be the judge'; his interpretation of this letter appears erroneous.

[66] See Kolde, *Die deutsche Augustiner-Congregation*, p. 331; Brecht, *Martin Luther, 1483–1521*, p. 428.

word not as coming from you but as spoken to me through you, and I have kept it firmly in mind ever since. Therefore I now challenge you with your own statement.[67]

No mention was made of the fact that, at the same time, Staupitz had released him from religious obedience. Apparently, Luther had fully understood at the time in Augsburg that Staupitz's release of him was a clever tactic which benefited them both. A few weeks later Staupitz received another letter from Luther, dated 9 February 1521, in which Luther still addressed him as a member of the Augustinian Order. Luther wondered whether or not his shipment of letters and books had arrived; in the same letter, he averred that the bull condemned everything that Staupitz had taught about the mercy of God, thus implying that Staupitz, too, was condemned. Rumour had it, Luther went on, that Leo X had pressured him (Staupitz) and that he had given in 'to that wolf'. This is clearly a reference to the pope's attempt to get at Staupitz via Cardinal Lang of Salzburg and to the popular perception of the situation, as Luther continued 'you [Staupitz] seem to deny me and my concerns altogether, after you professed him [the pope] to be your judge'.[68] It would seem there are no hard facts about such a 'submission' or what was meant by this statement. Perhaps the attempt to force Staupitz to notarize a statement against Luther, or perhaps the papal dispensation that he requested in order to switch religious Orders, or both, were interpreted by some people as a 'submission'. 'You are too humble, as I am too haughty', Luther continued, and added that it seemed to him that Staupitz was stuck between Christ and the pope (the antichrist, in Luther's perspective by this time).[69] Staupitz's supposed 'submission' to the pope had saddened him and shown him quite another face of Staupitz, so different from the one he knew as the 'herald of grace and cross'. Nevertheless, he signed this letter with 'Your son Martinus

---

[67] 'Cum Augustae essemus, reverendissime Pater, inter caetera, quae de hac mea ausa tractabamus, dicebas ad me: "Memor esto, frater, te ista in nomine Domini nostri Ihesu Christi incepisse; quod verbum non a te, sed per te mihi dictum accepi et memori valde mente repositum teneo. ..."' (*WABR* 2. 245, 1–8 (no. 366); *LW* 48. 191f).

[68] 'Miror literas et libellos meos ... ad te nondum pervenisse, quantum et tuis literis capio [this letter from Staupitz to Luther is lost] .... Non invitus audio, et te peti a Leone, ut et tu crucem, quam sic praedicasti, in exemplum erigas mundo .... Non enim vellem tuo responso contentum esse lupum illum .... Sic enim ea interpretabitur, quasi in totum neges me et omnia mea, postquam eum iudicem te passurum professus es .... Fidentius haec ad te scribo, quod valde timeo, ne inter Christum et papam medius haereas .... Vere nonnihil me contristavit ista tua submissio, et alium quendam mihi exhibuit, quam Staupitium illum gratiae et crucis praeconem' (*WABR* 2. 262f (no. 376)). Luther had to speak up even if it meant people would call him the 'anti-pope' (*antipapa*); ibid., 263, 34.

[69] See ibid.

Lutherus'.[70] He also pointed out to Staupitz that Frederick the Wise remained steadfast and reliable. Luther enclosed his defence against the bull, which he had composed before Christmas 1520.[71]

To Luther it may at times have appeared that Staupitz had abandoned him. In fact, although the archbishop of Salzburg probably wished that Staupitz and Luther had separated, Staupitz did not comply at all. In reality his heart and soul were with Luther, while his body was stuck 'at the anus of the world', although he was not a prisoner in the legal sense. Perhaps the archbishop's expectation that Staupitz would come out publicly against Luther needs to be seen as the cardinal's planned prelude to the Diet of Worms in 1521; it never materialized because Staupitz cleverly and evasively refused.

An assumed difference between Staupitz and Luther appears to have been read into their correspondence of that time by some historians. The alleged difference concerned the problem of ecclesiastical authority, and was not one of doctrine, as both remained united in terms of their theology.[72] Differences between the two cannot be assumed simply on the basis of Luther's remarks about certain rumours circulating at Wittenberg. It has been demonstrated that Staupitz's Salzburg Lenten sermons of 1520 represent a subtle distancing from the pope, expressed in terms of a Christ-centred spirituality. Luther, of course, had no access to these sermons. Staupitz felt as close to Luther, and as distant from the papacy, as before. This should have been clear to Luther all along because on 3 February 1521 the well-informed Luther himself wrote to Spalatin that the pope in his communication to the cardinal of Salzburg had accused Staupitz of siding with Luther, and that Staupitz had apparently reacted with the phrase: 'I do not know whether he should be eradicated', which Luther quoted.[73] In this situation Staupitz's evasive response may actually be taken as an endorsement of Luther; that he should *not* be 'eradicated'.

By 5 March 1521 Staupitz must have received the letter of 9 February, in which Luther wrote that the bull condemned everything that Staupitz had taught about the mercy of God (*de misericordia Dei*), and in which he implied that Staupitz, too, was condemned. On that day (5 March) Staupitz wrote to Linck as the new superior in the Order that he had responded to Luther since both Linck and Luther appeared to have had

---

[70] Ibid.

[71] See ibid; see also *WA* 6. 308–455; I. Ludolphy, *Friedrich der Weise, Kurfürst von Sachsen 1463–1525* (Göttingen, 1984) (ca. 1468 bis 1524)' in E. Iserloh (ed.), *Katholische Theologen der Reformationszeit* (Münster, 1988), pp. 11–31 (p. 433).

[72] See W. Günter, 'Johann von Staupitz' (p. 28).

[73] 'Ro[manus] Pontifex Stupitium nostrum accusauit ad Card[inalem] Saltzpurgensem, vt mecum habentem. Ille respondit, nescio an euellatur' (*WABR* 2. 260, 6–8 (no. 375)).

the feeling that he (Staupitz) was faint-hearted.[74] In fact, he was not timid (although he was very cautious!). In his letter to Linck, Staupitz revealed the situation in the Salzburg region concerning the 'Evangelicals' which looked promising to him as the archbishop of Salzburg had not yet taken any measures against Luther in his diocese. The papal nuncio Aleander in his own way concurred with this assessment as he complained that the entire entourage (*familiares*) of the prince-bishop of Salzburg at the Diet of Worms (April 1521) was 'Lutheran'. If they were not Lutheran, he insisted, they were definitely haters of the Roman Church.[75]

Staupitz must have continued to show an interest in what was happening at Wittenberg, as he asked Linck in a letter of 15 March 1521 for further information on and from Wittenberg.[76] He would not have asked for this had he intended to disassociate himself from Luther, and if he no longer cared for him and his fate. However, the shrewd and cautious Staupitz avoided direct contact with Luther at that time. Instead he tried to obtain news through the official channel, namely Linck, the new vicar general and his confidant.

The final meeting between Staupitz and Linck soon took place. Linck did what his predecessor Staupitz had done before him over the years; straight after his appointment in the autumn of 1520 Linck had begun to inspect all the friaries in Thuringia and Saxony. He and Staupitz remained in contact with each other and, following Staupitz's request of January 1521, Linck travelled before Easter to Munich to meet with him there once more, quite possibly to discuss the upcoming Diet of Worms in April 1521. Staupitz had come from Salzburg in company with Friar Besler. Incidentally, this mobility which Staupitz displayed here surely proves wrong the thesis that he was a real 'prisoner' at Salzburg. The description, in his letter to Linck of 4 January 1521, of himself and the other friars there as 'fellow prisoners' was a figure of speech which expressed Staupitz's discomfort and uneasiness about the situation in Salzburg. One cannot conclude on the strength of it that Staupitz was actually the cardinal's prisoner; for at no point was he restricted in his movements.[77]

---

[74] 'Respondeo Martino nostro, qui tecum sentiens meam arguit pusillanimitatem'; as quoted in the introduction to letter no. 376 in *WABR* 2. 263, the continuation of this letter is quoted by Sallaberger, 'Johann von Staupitz, Abt von St. Peter', p. 167 with n. 463, as: 'Nova apud nos non sunt'.

[75] On Aleander's observations, see P. Kalkoff, *Aleander gegen Luther* (Leipzig and New York, 1908), p. 138.

[76] 'Ex Witenberga' (Sallaberger, 'Johann von Staupitz, Luthers Vorgesetzter', p. 139).

[77] See Kolde, *Die deutsche Augustiner-Congregation*, p. 332; Günter, 'Johann von Staupitz', p. 28; Sallaberger, 'Johann von Staupitz Abt von St. Peter', p. 162 (against Jeremias' thesis that Staupitz was held captive at Salzburg).

In Worms, Luther appeared before the international assembly and refused to recant. Staupitz had proclaimed the previous year, in his 1520 Lenten sermons in Salzburg, that one should not be afraid to 'stand up for the evangelical truth'. This was exactly what his protégé did in Worms in front of the imperial assembly. Here Luther showed himself a true disciple of Staupitz. In the course of the last attempt to reach an agreement, during the session in the afternoon of 25 April, Luther suddenly referred to Staupitz's opinion that John Hus was unjustly condemned at the Council of Constance and that he expected Hus to be rehabilitated. However, reacting swiftly, the lawyer from Augsburg, Conrad Peutinger, changed the subject according to the report of his fellow lawyer, the Badenian Chancellor Jerome Vehus. This incident demonstrates how much Staupitz had influenced Friar Martin. The next day, Luther departed from Worms.[78]

As a result of Luther's refusal to recant, the Edict of Worms was issued in May 1521. According to this, anyone was allowed to capture Luther and no one was to help him. However, by a clever stratagem of Frederick the Wise, Luther was 'kidnapped' on his return journey and taken into hiding at Wartburg Castle, in some sort of 'protective custody'. Obviously, some of the secular authorities such as Frederick were not unsympathetic to Luther's cause. We do not know whether Staupitz knew of these events or where Luther was hiding. It is possible that he may have received confidential information about the events at Worms through his relative, Nicholas von Amsdorf (1488–1565), who had accompanied Luther there. The Reverend Amsdorf himself had to keep under cover at Worms because even before his arrival in the city the papal nuncio Aleander had threatened him. His presence would not be tolerated since he had dared to come without a safe-conduct which was guaranteed only to Luther. We may assume that Staupitz took a great interest in his nephew Nicholas's presence at Worms. He could expect new information first hand, as Nicholas, who was a confidant of both Staupitz and Luther, had shadowed the latter at every one of the Reformer's decisive public events, including the famous Leipzig debate, and now at the international assembly with the emperor at Worms. Whether Amsdorf followed Luther at Staupitz's request can only be surmised. After the diet, when Luther on his return trip from Worms was escorted to the Wartburg Castle, it was again Amsdorf who was the only person who knew of this clever plot.[79] Thus, we may assume that sooner or later Staupitz was informed as to Luther's whereabouts.

---

[78] See Sallaberger, 'Johann von Staupitz, Abt von St. Peter', p. 168.

[79] On Amsdorf's presence at Luther's side, see H. Boehmer, *Martin Luther: Road to Reformation*, trans. J.W. Doberstein and T.G. Tappert (New York, 1960, 3rd printing), pp. 411 and 428–30; Stupperich, pp. 25–7.

At about the time of the Diet of Worms, the Friars Linck and Besler emulated Staupitz in his visitation journeys. They inspected the friaries at Mindelheim, from where they travelled via Ulm, to the friary at Esslingen in south-western Germany, where they stayed on 1 May. From there they went to the Alsace region and visited the friary at Rappoltsweiler, while at Pentecost they stayed at the friary at Heidelberg. From there they journeyed to Flanders, Holland and Cologne, then on to Thuringia and Saxony, from where they returned to Nuremberg on August 15 and stayed there for the winter of 1521/22.[80] Staupitz was invited to Nuremberg, but could not accept the invitation since he was very busy.

In the autumn of 1521, Staupitz met with the 21-year-old Duke Ernest of Wittelsbach (1500–60) at Herrenchiemsee. The young Duke, at the age of 13, had competed against, and lost out to, the influential Matthew Lang for the archepiscopal see of Salzburg, one of the highest ecclesiastical offices in the German-speaking lands.[81] All that he could achieve was to become the administrator of the diocese of Passau (from 1516 to 1540), a suffragan of Salzburg (as was Chiemsee). After the meeting Staupitz came to the conclusion that Duke Ernest was on the side of the reformers like himself. On 16 October 1521 he reported from Herrenchiemsee to Vicar Linck that Luther even had a great friend in the young Duke Ernest, who, however, was a lifelong Catholic.[82] It was not until March 1522 that the Bavarian government prohibited the discussion of Luther's teachings. Any violations of that decree, called the 'Religion Mandate', were to be punished with imprisonment.[83]

From the correspondence between Staupitz, Linck and Luther, it can easily be seen that these three friars remained close friends through these most difficult times. Their friendship should not be underestimated, as it provided the necessary support for their reform efforts. In this situation, Staupitz had to watch his steps very carefully. He had apparently waited for a chance to be out of town, when on the said 16 October 1521 he prepared a letter from Herrenchiemsee, the cloister of the Augustinian canons, located in Bavarian territory, about 60 kilometres north-west of Salzburg. (Staupitz had a considerable amount of money invested in a

---

[80] See Kolde, *Die deutsche Augustiner-Congregation*, pp. 364f.

[81] See Sallaberger, 'Johann von Staupitz, Luthers Vorgesetzter', p. 140.

[82] On Duke Ernest, see Sallaberger, *Kardinal Matthäus Lang von Wellenburg (1968–1540)* (Salzburg, 1997) with portrait on p. 217; see also A. von Drüffel, 'Über die Aufnahme der Bulle "Exsurge Domine" – Leo X. gegen Luther – von Seiten einiger Süddeutschen Bischöfe', *Sitzungsberichte der Bayrischen Akademie der Wissenschaften, Historische Klasse* (Munich, 1880), pp. 571–97.

[83] See W. Landgraf, *Martin Luther. Reformator und Rebell. Biographie*, 2nd edn (Berlin, 1982), p. 230.

construction project there; and since it was a large sum he apparently wanted to see what was going on, and perhaps tried to get his money back.) In his letter Staupitz explained that he would have liked to accept Linck's invitation to join him in Nuremberg, but that he could not come because the Advent season was approaching, and he did not have anybody else to do his work in Salzburg (perhaps an allusion to his obligation as the 'foundation preacher' of Salzburg). He added the personal note that, although he had not been particularly afraid at the time when he left Salzburg, it was now harder for him to return to that city, and more dangerous, as the people say. He had been persuaded to depart from there, he wrote, but now he would have to return, 'almost forced'.[84]

Staupitz was required to return to Salzburg because there were plans to make him abbot of St Peter's Abbey, after the cardinal of Salzburg had managed to depose Abbot Simon Garchanetz on grounds of mismanagement.[85] A petition to the pope was already under way requesting permission for Staupitz to transfer from the Augustinians to the Benedictines of Salzburg. In November 1521, news was circulating among the Augustinians that their 'dearest Father Staupitz', their 'great man', was now an *aulicus*, that is 'a man of the court', meaning the court of Cardinal Lang in Salzburg.[86] On 26 April 1522 the transfer was granted by the Roman authorities.[87]

The papal bull against Luther was largely ignored in Germany, especially in southern Germany and in Austria. The learned Augustinian prior and provincial, Caspar Amman of Lauingen, south-western Germany, refused to publish it and was arrested for his refusal.[88] The bull was also not published in other southern regions including the territory of Salzburg. Cardinal Lang did not want to take any measures, at least not yet, against the so-called 'Evangelicals'. Perhaps it was Staupitz who saw to it, or who at least helped to prevent it, by his careful

---

[84] '... Accedit Adventus Domini, et non est alius subintrans labores meos. Non timui valde, quando reliqueram Salisburgam. Reditus mihi gravior est, et ut aiunt, periculosior .... Exivi persuasus, introibo fere coactus ...'; as quoted by Sallaberger, 'Johann von Staupitz, Abt von St. Peter', p. 169. On Staupitz's financial involvement at Herrenchiemsee, see ibid.

[85] See Kolde, *Die deutsche Augustiner-Congregation*, pp. 362–5.

[86] 'Audio autem eum idoli Salzburgensis aulicum esse, quod homini optimo invideo. Tu eum salutabis' (*WABR* 2. 415, 35f. (no. 446)); the American edition has: 'which makes me sad about this excellent man. Please greet him' (*LW* 48. 359). Luther called both men 'idol', the Cardinal of Salzburg and Cardinal Albrecht of Mainz with his collection of relics; see Luther's letter from Wartburg on 1 December 1521 (*WABR* 2. 395, 11f. (no. 434); 'Wider den Abgott [idol] zu Halle').

[87] See Kolde, *Die deutsche Augustiner-Congregation*, p. 333.

[88] See F. Posset, 'Amman, Caspar', in *BBKL* (Herzberg, 2000), XVI, pp. 49–52.

refusal to comply with any condemnation of Luther. The situation in Salzburg did not appear hopeless. Moreover, the officials of the Augustinian Order in Rome wanted to salvage whatever they could. They made one last effort to come to terms with Luther, even though he had been threatened with excommunication since 15 June 1520. With Staupitz no longer in charge of the Order's business, the leadership of the Order in Rome had to find other ways to deal with Luther. Therefore, some time after the Diet of Worms in April 1521 (where the imperial ban was pronounced against him), the Augustinian general sent the supervisor of the Augustinians' study programme at Paris, Arnald de Bornosio, to Wittenberg in order to talk to Luther, not knowing that he was no longer there but in hiding at Wartburg. Arnald talked with Karlstadt and Melanchthon instead, as he reported in December 1522.[89]

While Luther was at Wartburg, Staupitz's fellow friar, Gabriel Zwilling, conducted a new form of worship in Wittenberg on New Year's Day 1522. He preached against celebrating private Masses, attacked the religious vows, and called upon everyone to leave the cloister, claiming that it was impossible to enter heaven in a cowl. Zwilling left the Order and departed from Wittenberg. Iconoclasts took over and religious riots broke out. On Epiphany 1522 the Reformed Congregation of the Augustinians, under pressure from the Elector Frederick, held their chapter meeting at Wittenberg. It was summoned by Linck as Staupitz's successor. A few friars came from Saxony, Thuringia and Meissen. They evaluated the situation and decided to give each member the choice either to leave the Order quietly or to remain, but only under the condition that the remaining friars would provide for their own livelihood without 'begging'. Only Luther and the former prior, Eberhard Brisger, stayed at their friary in Wittenberg. The chapter decision became known as the 'Opinion of the Augustinian Synod Concerning the Freedom of Friars'.[90]

The following year, on 21 June 1523, the remnants of the reformed Augustinians gathered at the friary of Grimma in order to elect a new vicar, but failed to reach an agreement. On the following day, six representatives met at the Franciscan friary in Leipzig and signed a

---

[89] On Arnald, see A. Zumkeller, 'Martin Luther and his Order', in J.E. Rotelle (ed.) *Theology and History of the Augustinian School in the Middle Ages* (n.p., 1996), p. 278, with reference to D. Gutierrez, *La Ciudad de Dios*, vol. 168 (1956), p. 618.

[90] The decision made by the Augustinians assembled at Wittenberg on Epiphany 1522 was printed on one page by the Grunenberg press at Wittenberg as *Synodi Augustinianorum de Libertate Monachorum Sententia* (CR, I. no. 136); see O. Clemen, 'Miscellen zur Reformationsgeschichte', in *Kleine Schriften*, I, p. 207; Bornkamm, *Luther in Mid-Career*, p. 59; J. Schilling, *Klöster und Mönche in der hessischen Reformation* (Gütersloh, 1997), p. 138, n. 128.

declaration saying that it had not been their fault that no new vicar had been elected, and that they would not follow nor had they ever followed the new and alien teaching that is called 'Martinian' or 'Lutheran'. Those six friars were Professor Johann Nathin of Erfurt; Prior Johann Bethel von Spangenberg and Conrad Aldorff, both of Eschwege; Georg Doliatoris of Heidelberg; Caspar Pistatoris of Sternberg; and Nicholas Besler. Finally, on 8 September 1523 Prior Spangenberg was elected as the new vicar of the reformed Augustinians, by a handful of voters who gathered at the chapter meeting in Mühlheim. Spangenberg held this office until his resignation in 1529. He managed to preserve the reformed friary of Cologne which was broken off from Staupitz's Reformed Congregation and given back to the Augustinian province of Cologne in 1533. The Wittenberg friary was in dissolution. At Erfurt 15 friars, together with Prior Johann Lang, left the Order in spring 1522. At about the same time, the friary of Herzberg lost all its members. In Nuremberg, Wolfgang Volprecht (d. 1528) who was the last prior there, celebrated Mass in German and distributed Holy Communion in both kinds; for which, he was excommunicated by the local bishop. Before Christmas 1524 he handed over the entire friary to the city government, thus bringing to an end the religious life in that friary. After 1526 the Augustinian church where Staupitz had preached so successfully stood empty; it was razed in 1816. Other Augustinian friaries in the German-speaking lands that either dissolved themselves or were usurped by local lords about that time included Sternberg (1524), Magdeburg (1524), Gotha (1525), Windsheim (1525), Eschwege (1526), Mindelheim (1526), Rappoltsweiler (1527), Helmstedt (1527), Kulmbach (1528), Grimma (1529), Memmingen (1531) and Tübingen (1532). The friaries of Königsberg (Franconia) and Himmelpforten were destroyed in the Peasants' War of 1524–25.[91]

Staupitz may well have seen the early signs of the disintegration of his Reformed Congregation. Under the circumstances, its hardly surprising that he himself thought it more advantageous to remain in Salzburg, at some distance from the troubled Order. Staupitz's taking permanent residence in Salzburg should not therefore necessarily be understood as a deliberate attempt to distance himself from the person of Luther. Denominational lines as they came to be drawn had not yet been established at this time. Staupitz remained an Evangelical Catholic who was deeply concerned with the care of souls, as we shall see in the following section that takes us back to the year 1520.

---

[91] The document about the meeting at Leipzig is in the Staatsarchiv Magdeburg; ed. Kolde, *Die deutsche Augustiner-Congregation*, p. 451. On the dissolution, see D. Gutierrez, *The Augustinians in the Middle Ages (1357–1517)*, 2 vols (Villanova, 1879–83), II, pp. 28–32; J. Hemmerle, *Die Klöster der Augustiner-Eremiten in Bayern* (Munich-Pasing, 1958), pp. 14, 68; Zumkeller, 'Martin Luther and his Order', pp. 227 and 229–33.

Staupitz's services of communal penance (1520)

Staupitz was a popular preacher in Salzburg, so popular that his Lenten sermons of 1512, 1518, 1519 and 1520 had been recorded by nuns.[92] In his 1520 sermons Staupitz had taken issue with a late medieval spirituality that fostered pilgrimages and the indulgence business. In contrast to all that, he declared that 'the true Pope lives in our hearts' and that 'God is our Pope'. The manuscript volume which contains these sermons includes a text which has previously been totally ignored by historians, one that demonstrates that Staupitz conducted communal penance services for the nuns – and perhaps also for a wider congregation, since these nuns worshippd in the choir loft of the church of St Mary, where a wider population could have participated in his communal penance services. The macaronic (vernacular/Latin) text which 'the reverend Father spoke' to them is preserved under the headline *Die offen beicht* (literally: 'The open confession'). The identity of the transcriber is unknown. Staupitz opened the service with the sign of the cross and the invitation to confess oneself as being a miserable sinner. The act of contrition followed; it included the phrase *das ist mir treuliche laid* ('I am truly sorry'). The two Latin words *misereator* and *indulgentiam* which are incorporated into the otherwise vernacular text point to the priest's formula of absolution. The full Latin text of the absolution formula starts with *misereatur* (which in the nun's manuscript is mistakenly given as *misereator*): 'Misereatur tui omnipotens Deus, et dimissis peccatis tuis, perducat te ad vitam aeternam. Amen.' Our text thus simply indicates the first word of the first part of the formula which, of course, is known to every penitent who went to confession on a regular basis such as may be presumed in the case of the nuns. When, immediately after the first half of the formula, the confessor raised his hand for the sign of the cross over the penitent, he simultaneously used the second half of the formula of absolution from sins which starts with *indulgentiam*, which the recording nun indicated with her second Latin term within the vernacular context. The complete sentence of the second half of the formula says: 'Indulgentiam, absolutionem, et remissionem peccatorum tuorum tribuat tibi omnipotens et misericors Dominus. Amen.' After the absolution, the confessor gave the penitent some form of 'penance' to do. In this case, the penitents were to pray one Our Father, one Hail Mary, and the Creed. In the following transcript and translation, the full Latin formula is incorporated into the text and marked with [ ]:

---

[92] See G. Hayer, 'Die deutschen Handschriften des Mittelalters der Erzabtei St. Peter zu Salzburg', *Denkschriften der Österreichischen Akademie der Wissenschaften, philosophisch-historische Klasse, Denkschriften 154. Band* (Vienna, 1982), pp. 265–66.

Die offen peicht die der
wirdig vater gesprochen hat:

Pezaichent euch mit dem zaichen
des h[eiligen] + und sprecht mir
nach:
Ich armer sündiger mensch
pekenn got das ich vil gesündet
hab wider mein herren, mit vil
unzimlichen gedäncken worten
und werchen
wie und wievil ich das verpracht
hab, das ist mir treuliche laid,
köm heut und pitt genad,
gnad mir ewiger got, frist mir
mein leben also lang, pis ich
mein sünd müg gepüessen und
dein götliche huld
und genad erberbe.

Naigt eur haubt und herz zuo got.
pittet got umb genad und
parmhertzikeit.
Misereator [tui omnipotens Deus,
et dimissis peccatis tuis,
perducat te ad vitam aeternam. Amen];
indulgentiam [absolutionem, et
remissionem peccatorum tuorum
tribuat tibi omnipotens et
misericors Dominus. Amen.]

Halt euch auf als Maria Magdalena,
da ir der her vergab die sünd.
Zu hilf und trost der heiling [one word
crossed out] aller kristglauben seilen und
zumb vergebnüß eur sündt,
sprecht ain p[ate]r n[oster]
ave maria und ain glauben
da mit wir all zu unsern lesten
zeiten erfunden werden jn ainem
waren kristlichen glauben,
eret die werde muter gotz
mit in ave maria
jr h[eilige] empfänkniß,
damit si uns umb got erberg,
das wir nit in unsere sünde ersterben.
Ewr leib, sel, er und guet
secz ich unter die peschirmung
des h[eiligen] + jn nomine patris
et filij et sp[iritu]s sancti
Amen.[93]

The open confession which
the reverend father has spoken:

Make the sign of the
holy cross and repeat
after me:
I am a miserable sinner,
I confess to God that I have
committed many sins against my
Lord with many improper
thoughts, words, and works;
however and how much I have
done, I am truly sorry,
I come today and beg for grace,
eternal God, have mercy on me,
let me live long enough to
repent for my sins and
obtain your divine favour
and grace.

Bow your head and heart to God.
Ask God for grace and
mercy.
[The almighty God] have mercy [on
you, forgive you your sins,
and lead you to eternal life. Amen];
Indulgence, [absolution, and
remission of your sins
be granted to you by the almighty
and merciful Lord. Amen.]

Do as did Mary Magdalene, when
the Lord forgave her the sins.
For the help and comfort of all
Christian faithful souls, and
for the forgiveness of your sins,
say one Our Father,
Hail Mary, and the Creed,
so that at the end of our lives
we all are found in the true
Christian faith, give
honour to the dear Mother of God
with a Hail Mary,
her holy conception,
that she obtain from God
that we do not die in our sins.
I place your body, soul, honour,
and goods under the protection
of the holy + [cross], in the name
of the Father and of the Son and
of the Holy Spirit. Amen.

Staupitz granted full absolution in this communal penance service, which may seem rather surprising to Catholics today as it is now generally frowned upon. He dismissed the participants with words of blessing that probably included the making of the sign of the cross, as the Latin wording at the end would indicate. Staupitz's communal confession service demonstrates that he was not only a well-known preacher, but also a spiritual director and *Seelsorger* in Salzburg. He was evidently known both for his preaching and his spiritual directing; both of these activities were considered worth preserving by the nuns.

Staupitz probably also used this text when, as an abbot, in 1523 he conducted another penance service in connection with his last extant Advent sermon of that year. (The Advent season is also a penitential season in the traditional liturgical year.) The nuns recorded this event at the beginning of a manuscript which contains Staupitz's last known sermon. The title-page of that sermon includes the expression *gemayn peicht* ('communal confession') and reads: '[Staupitz] preached to us yet another useful sermon during Advent ..., when he held for us the communal confession'.[94]

Obviously, Staupitz's penance services consisted of a combination of preaching and general confession which he formulated for the congregation to repeat after him. Staupitz addressed the audience very cordially in almost every one of his 1523 sermons – for example, as 'devout, spiritual, dear sisters', or a variation of this phrase, or as 'Friends of Christ'.[95]

Staupitz's text is a rare witness to Catholic communal penance services of the sixteenth century. It is known to us only because of the recording efforts of the nuns in Salzburg. The practice of such services was situated in the reform-minded, yet Catholic, monastic (and probably also non-monastic) milieu. In this regard it is a shining example of Catholic reform efforts.

This Salzburg text is not unique, however, as a similar communal penance service exists in printed form from the year 1524, written by a

---

[93] Manuscript, *codex b V 8 (99r)*, see Hayer, 'Die deutschen Handschriften', p. 267. Unfortunately, this text is omitted from both the critical edition of Staupitz's works and the microfilm at the Hill Monastic Library at St John's University in Collegeville, MN. I am grateful to Dr Adolf Hahnl of the Bibliothek und Archiv der Erzabtei St Peter in Salzburg for providing me with a copy of that text. An edition and translation of this source is found in F. Posset, 'Communal Penance Services in the Context of Sixteenth-Century Reform Efforts', *Worship*, 69 (1995), pp. 334–45.

[94] 'Noch gar ain nuczen sermon hat er uns gepredigt im advent da er uns dy gemain peicht hat zuegesagt' (236r–246v); Hayer, 'Die deutschen Handschriften', p. 165. The sermon is edited by Kolde, *Die deutsche Augustiner-Congregation*, pp. 452–6.

[95] See *Staupitij ausslegung der evangelij*, (1*r) [*sic*], Hayer, 'Die deutschen Handschriften', pp. 163–5; *Freun[d]t Christi*, ibid., pp. 264–7.

reform-minded priest at Augsburg by the name of Michael Keller, whom the humanists called Michael Cellarius (d. 1548).[96] The difference between Staupitz and Keller is that Staupitz, both as elder friar and new Benedictine monk, remained within the wider Catholic Reform context at Salzburg, and he included elements of marian devotion in his service, while the Augsburg priest, Keller, worked in a rather advanced reformation context in this imperial city.

It cannot be determined whether such communal penance services were unusual at that time. Did Staupitz invent this devotional practice or did he follow the models of others? Was it a practice that grew out of the pastoral care of the Augustinians? We do not know the answers to these questions. Perhaps it was, indeed, an extraordinary event since the nuns kept written records of it. However, it would be a misconception to assume that Staupitz wanted to replace individual confession with such communal penance services, for he never gave any reason to support such a conclusion. Previously, in his Tübingen Sermon 11 he had spoken of the three parts of confession: contrition, confession and satisfaction.[97] At that time he had explained 'our justification' is happening 'through the sacraments', as he interpreted Rom. 8:30 (*Quos vero vocavit, hos et iustificavit*).[98] In connection with the art of dying, Staupitz had recommended that to receive the sacrament of reconciliation one should 'confess, do penance'.[99] To the people of Nuremberg he had said in a Lenten sermon of 1517 that true contrition in the heart should precede the oral confession.[100] Now in 1523, he told the nuns that when one feels true contrition, one should 'run to the priest and go to confession so that one will be despised, and God alone be loved, praised, and honoured'.[101] Staupitz continued that the mere tabulation of one's sins without contrition in one's heart is insufficient for obtaining absolution from sins.[102] He therefore instructed the audience of his concluding Sermon 24 of 1523 as follows:

---

[96] See O. Clemen, 'Formular der "offenen Schuld" von Michael Keller in Augsburg 1524', in *Kleine Schriften*, II, 99–100. In this text the expression *offen beycht* ('open confession') is found; which Staupitz had also used at Salzburg. Like Staupitz, Keller read the text and let the congregation repeat it. The text must date from the period after Keller had come from Wittenberg to Augsburg, where he became a preacher at a cloister church (*Barfüsser-Kirche*) in 1524; see Stupperich, p. 58.

[97] Staupitz, I. 204 (Sermon 11).

[98] 'Iustificationem nostram per sacramenta, in quibus virtus passionis domini nostri Iesu agit, recipimus' (Sermon 11, Staupitz, I. 203).

[99] 'Nachfolge' (Chapter 8; Knaake, *Sämmtliche Schriften*, p. 69; Zumkeller, *Heilslehre*, p. 169).

[100] '...der muntlichen peicht vorgen soll' (Knaake, *Sämmtliche Schriften*, p. 16; Zumkeller, *Heilslehre*, p. 169).

[101] 'Er lauft zum priester und peicht, damit er nur veracht wert, und Got ainig geliebt, gelobt und geert' (Sermon 15, *Heilslehre*, p. 170).

[102] See Sermon 17, Zumkeller, *Heilslehre*, p. 170.

After due examination of conscience, come before the priest and accuse yourself. However, confession is to be primarily a praise of God rather than you accusing yourself . . . . And when the priest says: I absolve you of your sins, take it as if Christ himself were present and absolved you. However, if one does not like to go to confession or become desperate, one has a sure sign that one does not have faith nor hope in Christ.[103]

After this last sermon, the nuns were well prepared to go to confession. Those who were unable to do so because of illness or weakness participated in the communal penance service which Staupitz conducted for them.

We have seen Staupitz here in action as a pastor to the nuns. Pastoral care, after all, was the purpose of his life as a friar and he continued with this care as a Benedictine abbot. When he saw his pastoral work within the Augustinian Order jeopardized by the turmoil created by the reform movement, he may have felt greater attraction to the duties of pastoral care of the Benedictines in Salzburg. After all, they provided from their ranks the pastors for the numerous parishes in their region.[104] These pastoral prospects in Salzburg may have facilitated Staupitz's decision to depart from the troubled Augustinian friars and enter the Benedictine Order in that city, since he saw these Benedictine monks involved in fruitful parish ministry.

---

[103] '. . . nach zimleicher erfarung des gewissens kum für den priester und peklag dich; doch sol di peicht mer sein ain lob Gots, dann du dich solt schelten . . .' (Sermon 24, Zumkeller, *Heilslehre*, p. 170).

[104] See F. Hermann OSB, 'Die Klosterpfarren', in Salzburger Landesregierung (ed.) *Das älteste Kloster im deutschen Sprachraum: St. Peter in Salzburg* (Salzburg, 1982), pp. 98–102.

CHAPTER SIX

Imposed as Abbot upon the Benedictines at Salzburg (1522–24)

Let us briefly recapitulate the situation in 1520–22. After the Diet of Worms in 1521, Emperor Charles V withdrew from the complicated religious scene in order to deal with his great rival for supremacy in Europe, Francis I of France. The Edict of Worms which banned Luther was largely ignored, the region of influence of the prince-bishop of Salzburg being no exception. After the death of Archbishop Leonhard von Keutschach in June 1519, Matthew Lang had become his successor at Salzburg; Lang had been coadjutor to Keutschach since 1512, and a cardinal since 1511. On 25 September 1519, Bishop Philip of Freising ordained him as a bishop. Encouraged by the Bavarian authorities, the new archbishop of Salzburg summoned a synod at Mühldorf (the Salzburg enclave surrounded by Bavaria) for the spring of 1522, for the purpose of initiating reforms in order to counteract the 'Lutheran sect' (*secta lutherana*) in the entire ecclesiastical province of Salzburg. The synod began on 26 May 1522. In attendance were Cardinal Lang (being also the bishop of Gurk), the two Bavarian bishops of the Wittelsbach dynasty, Philip of Freising and Ernest of Passau, Bishop Berthold Pürstinger of Salzburg-Chiemsee, several delegates from Brixen and Regensburg, and other prelates such as the humanist abbot of Aldersach, Bolfgangus Marius, who belonged to the entourage of the bishop of Passau. Staupitz was not part of this gathering. The synod had no real effects; because of its failure, Archbishop Lang perhaps made plans to recruit Staupitz, so that in the future the ecclesiastical reforms would be carried out expediently. Furthermore, Lang appears to have been pressured by Pope Leo X for some time to draw Staupitz to Salzburg, where he could be urged to distance himself from Luther; if Staupitz were to refuse, he ought to be imprisoned or punished in some other way (as we know from a letter of Erasmus of Rotterdam). The pope's letter was given to Cardinal Lang in September or October 1520 in Cologne.[1]

---

[1] See Erasmus' letter no. 1166, as referred to in J. Sallaberger, *Kardinal Matthäus Lang von Wellenburg (1468–1540)* (Salzburg, 1997), p. 160, n. 49; on Lang in Salzburg after 1519, see ibid., pp. 156ff; on the Synod of Mühldorf, see ibid., pp. 255–9; on the Cistercian Abbot Marius, see W. Hauer, 'Wolfgang Marius, der Humanistenabt von Aldersbach (1514–1544)', in *850 Jahre Zisterzienserkloster Aldersbach 1996* (Aldersbach, 1996), pp. 43–7 (p. 45). On the general situation, see E. Wolgast, 'Die deutschen Territorialfürsten

At Rome, the Dutchman Hadrian VI had become the new pope. He had first been a tutor at the imperial court, then the adviser, and finally the viceroy in Spain for Charles V. His pontificate was very short, lasting only from January 1522 to September 1523. He demanded that the Edict of Worms be carried out, as he thought Luther was a 'new Mohammed' who needed to be fought like any great sectarian. The Roman authorities also demanded that under the terms of the Diet of Worms the four leading preachers of the imperial city of Nuremberg and the prior of the Augustinian friary be imprisoned (since they had become known as supporters of Luther).[2] The new pope simultaneously and surprisingly admitted that considerable guilt for the present situation also lay with the Roman Church.

During Pope Hadrian's reign Staupitz became Cardinal Lang's councilman (*Rat*), on 11 March 1522. Lang was probably not aware of the fact that, in 1513, Staupitz had tried to intervene against him in Rome on behalf of Archbishp Keutschach. Staupitz's written declaration to be a loyal councilman to Lang was found recently by Johann Sallaberger. In it, Staupitz wrote that Cardinal Lang 'on his own motivation' had decided to 'promote' (*fürdern*) him to the abbacy of St Peter. In gratitude, Staupitz promised to be of lifelong service to the Cardinal in his function as the Abbot of St Peter, and also to be available as a *Rat* and as his delegate on pastoral visitations for the purpose of the 'reformation of the clergy' (*reformacion der gaystlichkayth*). A few weeks later, on 22 April 1522, Staupitz left the Order of St Augustine and joined the Order of St Benedict, with papal approval. The required papal dispensation was obtained through the Archbishop of Salzburg, Cardinal Matthew Lang, who in his petition cleverly avoided giving away the name of the candidate for whom this switch was to be arranged. The papal document granted the archbishop the option of transferring a religious from one Order to another, and allowed that such an individual could also become an abbot.[3]

Staupitz informed the Augustinian prior of Nuremberg, Wolfgan Volprecht, about this plan, who immediately must have passed on the information to Luther at Wittenberg, as Luther reacted with a letter to Staupitz on 27 June 1522, addressing his former superior simply as *D. Ioanni Staupitio, Ecclesiasti Salzburgensi* ('Dr Johann Staupitz, Preacher at Salzburg'). The title *ecclesiastes* may be an indication that Staupitz at

---

und die frühe Reformation', in S. Buckwalter and B. Moeller, *Die frühe Reformation in Deutschland als Umbruch* (Gütersloh, 1998), p. 422.

[2] See H. Bornkamm, *Luther in Mid-Career 1521–1530*, ed. K. Bornkamm, trans. E.T. Bachmann (Philadelphia, 1983), p. 297.

[3] Staupitz's autograph is now document 'B 405' in the Konsistorialarchiv at Salzburg; see Sallaberger, *Kardinal*, p. 262–4 (n. 54).

that time held either the position of Salzburg's 'foundation preacher' (*Stiftsprediger*) or of the *terminarius*. The former is perhaps more likely. There had been no exchange of letters between the two for more than a year. Now, Luther, in his spiritual attachment to his former' superior, took the initiative again and wrote:

> Grace and peace in Christ. Amen. Reverend and excellent Father: I have learned of your abbacy not only through the letter of the prior of Nuremberg [Volprecht], but also through a common rumour which affirms this so persistently that I would have been forced to believe it, even if I had not seen your letter [to the prior]. I suppose lies about us are carried to you by the same channels and in the same way. Although I do not want to interfere with God's will, nevertheless in my ignorance I cannot see how it can be God's will that you should become an abbot, nor do I think this advisable.[4]

Perhaps Luther knew that Staupitz had been pressured into the new position, and suspected that it was more the archbishop's will than anybody else's. This may actually have been the case; which would explain why Luther wrote saying that he could not believe that Staupitz's becoming an abbot was God's will. Luther also responded to a letter from Staupitz (now lost) which contained the charge that Luther was being praised by those who patronize brothels and that he caused 'many scandals with his recent writings'. Luther wrote back that all he wanted to do was to proclaim the pure gospel message, but that it was not in his power to control what people did with it. Furthermore, he stated that he wanted to drive out, 'by means of the Word, that unclean celibacy, the ungodliness of masses, the tyranny of the religious orders', and other human devices which were erected against 'sound teaching'. It is hard to say how offensive such talk would have been to Staupitz, but, as he knew Luther well, he probably took it in his stride. Luther boasted: 'My Father, I must destroy that kingdom of abomination and perdition which belongs to the pope, together with all his hangers-on.' In the same letter he expressed his fear to Staupitz that one of their reform-minded friars by the name of Jacob Probst (or Praepositus), the prior of Antwerp, whom Staupitz must have known from previous contacts, faced death for his convictions. In fact, Probst survived the persecution and died of old age in 1562 in Bremen, Germany. From Luther's reactions as

---

[4] '... Et quamquam nec ego velim Dei voluntati subtrahi, tamen pro mea ruditate plane nondum capio, si voluntas Dei esse possit, ut abbas fieres .... Destruendum est mihi, mi pater, regnum illud abominationis et perditionis Papae, cum toto corpore suo' (*WABR* 2. 566–8 (no. 512), dated 27 June 1522; *LW* 49. 10–13). On the issue of whether Staupitz was indeed the *Stiftsprediger*, see J. Sallaberger, 'Johann von Staupitz, Abt von St. Peter (1522–1524) und die Salzburger Mendikantentermineien', *Studien und Mitteilungen zur Geschichte des Benediktinerordens und seiner Zweige*, 93 (1982), pp. 218–69 (pp. 166–71).

expressed in this letter, one must conclude that this was the first time that Staupitz had criticzed Luther for something he said 'in recent writings'.[5]

Which Lutheran writings could Staupitz have meant? It was certainly not Luther's exposition of the *Magnificat* of 1521; perhaps he had in mind Luther's *To the Christian Nobility of the German Nation Concerning the Reform of the Christian Estate* or *The Babylonian Captivity of the Church* of 1520, and/or *The Judgment of Martin Luther on Monastic Vows* of 1521 – if indeed, had he been able to read them at Salzburg. The last named is most likely because the issue of vows was the only topic on which the two demonstrably disagreed. We definitely know, however, that at least one of the Benedictine monks of Salzburg, Father Rupert Freyschlag, was in possession of the collection of Luther's works which was published by Adam Petri in Basel in July 1520; an edition that included works by Luther published up to the Leipzig debate in 1519. We also know that Abbot Simon Garchanetz complained to Cardinal Lang in July or August 1521 that many books by Luther were being read in his abbey.[6]

Luther's letter must have arrived only a few weeks before Staupitz made his profession as a Benedictine monk on 1 August 1522. The document of his profession is preserved in Staupitz's own handwriting and is adorned with his own drawing of the Staupitzian 'horn' from his coat of arms (see Plate 3):

> I, Brother Joannes de Staupitz, till now called to be of the Order of the Hermits of St Augustine and by apostolic authority dismissed to join the Order of St Benedict, to the honour of the almighty God and the most blessed Virgin Mary, ... [do] promise [to observe] stability, lifestyle, and obedience according to the Rule of St Benedict before God and his saints.[7]

On the following day, 2 August, Staupitz was imposed on the monks of St Peter as their new Abbot John IV, after the archbishop of Salzburg had stripped the reigning abbot, Simon Garchanetz, of all his powers.

---

[5] 'Ex recentioribus scriptis meis' (*WABR* 2. 566–8 (no. 512); *LW* 49. 11), Luther referring to a lost letter, p. 172. On Probst, see Stupperich.

[6] 'Püecher Lutheri, der sy vill haben', as quoted in Sallaberger, *Kardinal*, p. 244, n. 24.

[7] Quoted after N. Paulus, 'Johann von Staupitz. Seine vorgeblich protestantischen Gesinnungen', *Historisches Jahrbuch*, 12 (1891), pp. 309–46 (p. 332, n. 1). This transfer to the Benedictine Order may have surprised some people as the man who for so long had tried to reform the Augustinian friaries by urging them to adhere more strictly to their Rule now entered a religious Order which, in terms of canon law, might be considered to have a more lax rule (*regula laxior*), as W. Günter, 'Johann von Staupitz (ca. 1468 bis 1524)', in E. Iserloh (ed.) *Katholische Theologen der Reformationszeit* (Münster, 1988) p. 28 opined. However, the comparison is inappropriate: Benedictines are 'monks' who are bound to the *stabilitas loci*, while Augustinians are mendicant 'friars' who are expected to be mobile. In addition, the Benedictines of St Peter were 'reformed'.

The archbishop was a declared enemy of the monks of St Peter's Abbey and he very much disliked their ancient privileges of self-determination.[8] He intimidated the monks by imprisoning in his fortress some of those who opposed him or by sending them away for 'correction' to other monasteries. During this process of an enforced abbatial election, five renegade monks were imprisoned and later exiled. Whether Staupitz knew any of the details surrounding his promotion to the abbacy and whether he approved of Archbishop Lang's machinations in this regard is hard to tell. In any case, he went along with the results of it and composed the declaration of loyalty mentioned above. The remaining 25 monks (24 priests and one deacon) were forced to petition the archbishop of Salzburg to confirm Staupitz as their new abbot, so that nobody could contest this forced 'election' in the future. The official text of the election speaks of the 'voluntary' resignation of Abbot Simon III, and of Staupitz declaring himself unworthy of the abbacy, but ultimately willing to accept the monks' petition to become their abbot. The monks led him to the high altar where they sang the *Te Deum*. From there his election was proclaimed to the people. This procedure was witnessed by Bishop Berthold Pürstinger of Chiemsee, by Abbot Johann Hagen of Mondsee, by the dean of the cathedral (the archdiocesan official), Dr Andreas von Trauttmansdorff, and by Dr Aegidius Rem, who was the chief adviser of Cardinal Lang and who would later become the bishop of Chiemsee. The monks formally asked the cardinal archbishop 'by his ordained authority' (*auctoritate sua ordinaria*) to confirm their choice. This petition was signed by the humanist Prior Chilian Pütricher (or Pietricher, Pitricher), who was warmly disposed towards Staupitz, in place of the two senior monks, Fathers Christoph and Benedict who were unavailable, and all electors. The notary public Leonhard Kummer confirmed the act.[9]

After these 'legalities' were taken care of, Staupitz sent his old friend and former fellow friar, Gregor Mayr, who apparently was employed as a preacher in Salzburg, to the Benedictine Abbess Ursula Pfäffinger at Frauenchiemsee, with an invitation to the celebration of his ordination as an abbot. The Bishop of Chiemsee, Berthold Pürstinger, whom we have already encountered as a reform-minded church leader, installed Staupitz

---

[8] See F. Hermann, 'St. Peter und das Salzburger Domkapitel', in Salzburger Landesregierung (ed.), *St. Peter in Salzburg: Das älteste Kloster im deutschen Sprachraum* (Salzburg, 1982), p. 74.

[9] See *Stiftsarchiv St Peter*, document 1995, in *Das älteste Kloster im deutschen Sprachraum*, p. 326 (no. 320). Cardinal Lang's confirmation (6 August) of the election is found in the same document. On the humanist Prior Chilian, see C. Bonorand, *Joachim Vadian und der Humanismus im Bereich des Erzbistums Salzburg* (St Gallen, 1980), pp. 75–89.

as abbot on 17 August 1522, in the presence of Cardinal Lang, Abbot Johann Hagen of Mondsee, who had only recently become an abbot himself, and Abbess Ursula.[10] Ironically, Staupitz was consecrated by the very bishop for whose position he had vied a few years earlier. It appears that since Staupitz could not become bishop of Salzburg-Chimesee, he instead – and perhaps as some sort of a consolation – was selected for the leadership position at St Peter's Abbey at Salzburg by Prince-Bishop Lang.

Staupitz kept records in his own handwriting of the sequence of events. He also recorded the expenses for the celebrations at the occasion of his consecration as abbot of St Peter's. He was forced to use the income from the regular collection:

> I, Johann von Staupitz, member of the Order of the glorious Bishop Augustine, transferred to the Order of Saint Benedict by papal dispense, made my profession in this church of Saint Pter's on 1 August 1522; in a canonically valid election I was unanimously elected as abbot on 2 August, confirmed [in this position] on 6 August, and consecrated on 17 August. For the celebrations I have spent for food the following ....[11]

The banquet was attended by Staupitz's close friend Dr Christoph Scheurl, the chief lawyer of the imperial city of Nuremberg. Staupitz had been present at Scheurl's graduation in Bologna and under his influence Scheurl, at the age of 25, had become a professor of law at Wittenberg. This had coincided with the time when Staupitz himself had been a member of the faculty of theology there. In spring 1522 Scheurl was a member of a delegation of the imperial government (with its headquarters in Nuremberg) who had to travel to the court at Vienna in order to meet Ferdinand I. On his way home from Vienna, Scheurl stopped at Salzburg in order to attend the celebration of his old friend's election as abbot of St Peter's.[12]

---

[10] See J. Sallaberger, 'Johann von Staupitz, Luthers Vorgesetzter und Freund und seine Beziehungen zu Salzburg', *Augustiniana*, **28** (1978), p. 144. Sallaberger, 'Johann von Staupitz, die Stiftsprediger und die Mendikanten-Termineien in Salzburg', *Studien und Mitteilungen zur Geschichte des Benediktinerordens und seiner Zweige*, **93** (1982), p. 260. Sallaberger, 'Der Chiemseer Bischof Berthold Pürstinger (1464/65–1543). Biographische Daten zu seinem Leben und Werk', *Mitteilungen der Gesellschaft für Salzburger Landeskunde*, **130** (1990) pp. 427–84 (p. 444). On Gregor Mayr as 'preacher of Salzburg' and lector in theology for the monks of St Peter in 1522, see Bonorand, *Joachim Vadian*, pp. 82f.

[11] 'Registrum omnium perceptorum et distributorum Domini Johannis Abbatis de anno 1522–23' (autograph, in *Das älteste Kloster im deutschen Sprachraum*, p. 327 (no. 321)). Around that time, the abbey was so deeply in debt that Staupitz had to sell off property in Lower Austria, on 29 May 1523; see T. Kolde, *Die deutsche Augustiner-Congregation und Johann von Staupitz* (Gotha, 1879), p. 334.

[12] See Sallaberger, 'Johann von Staupitz, Abt von St. Peter', p. 172–5.

Staupitz proved himself to be a loyal fatherly friend not only to Scheurl but also to Luther. After he had been abbot for about a year, Staupitz received a letter from Luther, dated 17 September 1523, who now addressed him as 'Abbot of St Peter's in the Benedictine Order at Salzburg' and still as his 'superior, father, and teacher in the Lord',[13] thus plainly expressing his close attachment to, and dependence upon, Staupitz in every regard. However, before an examination of its textual content, the historical context of this letter should first be considered. By this point, the cardinal of Salzburg had demonstrated his clear opposition to Luther and his followers within the Salzburg territory. Under the cardinal's leadership, the archdiocesan/provincial synod meeting of 31 May 1522 had taken place at Mühldorf, where it had been declared that any 'Lutheran' trends could no longer be tolerated. Moreover, at the Diet of Nuremberg, delayed to the end of 1522 and the beginning of 1523, Cardinal Lang, in his role as a member of the imperial government, even advised that force should be used against Luther's followers.[14]

It is not known how, if at all, Staupitz reacted to these new developments. He must have had certain mental reservations against any persecutions, because Luther's central theological views were always very close to his own, if not identical. However, Staupitz had expressed them in more digestible form, and he refrained from excessive polemics of the kind for which Luther was so well known. Actually, Luther's writings were read in Staupitz's Abbey of St Peter as we have seen, and, furthermore, at the request of some of the learned monks, Staupitz purchased for the cloister library the following books: Erasmus' New Testament edition in Greek, his *Paraphrases* and certain *Epistolae*, Valla's *Elegantiae*, Oecolampadius' *Grammatica Graeca*, and Melanchthon's *Loci Communes*.[15]

Luther was probably unaware that Staupitz had arranged all these purchases. All he seems to have known about Salzburg was that the cardinal was taking steps against those people who sympathized with his cause. For this reason Luther called the cardinal 'a monster', in a letter to Staupitz dated 17 September 1523:

> Grace and peace in Christ Jesus our Lord! Reverend Father in Christ: Your silence is quite unjust, and you can judge for yourself what I am forced to think of it. Yet even if I have lost your favour and good

---

[13] Luther's letter, *WABR* 3. 156 (no. 659); *LW* 49. 48.

[14] See Sallaberger, 'Johann von Staupitz, Luthers Vorgesetzter', p. 147.

[15] H. Widmann, *Geschichte Salzburgs*, 3 vols (Gotha, 1914), III, p. 47; as cited by G. Marx, *Glaube, Werke und Sakramente im Dienste der Rechtfertigung in den Schriften von Berthold Pürstinger, Bischof von Chiemsee* (Leipzig, 1982), p. 13, n. 67. On Staupitz buying these books, see Kolde, *Die deutsche Augustiner-Congregation*, p. 335, n. 1.

will, it would not be right for me to forget you or to be ungrateful to you, for it was through you that the light of the gospel first began to shine out of the darkness in our hearts.

I also have to say that it is true that it would have been more agreeable to me had you not become an abbot. But since you have, let us be considerate of each other, and each grant the other his understanding [Luther speaking with Rom. 14: 5 here]. I, indeed, together with your best friends, have not so much taken it ill that you are estranged from us as that you have put yourself into the hands of that infamous monster, your Cardinal .... Now you have to bear it and be silent. It will be a miracle if you do not fall into the danger of denying Christ. Therefore we earnestly wish and pray that you may be released from this tyrant's jail and given back to us, and we hope that this is also your intention. Insofar as I have known you up to this time, I am unable to make any sense out of these two contradictions: that you should still be the same man you were, yet have decided to stay there; or if you are still the same man, that you are not constantly planning to get away from there.[16]

As this letter shows, Luther saw things in stark contrasts. Staupitz had a different approach – he preferred to differentiate more than his younger friend. Luther's strong negative convictions about monasticism, which he now considered a 'symbol' for an anti-evangelical concept of righteousness, made it difficult for him to see Staupitz as the same person that he had always been, especially after Staupitz had switched to the Benedictines. By contrast, Staupitz, who did not share Luther's strong sentiments about religious vows, had no major problems with becoming an abbot. In transferring to another order, he did not necessarily have to change any of the theological convictions which he shared with Luther regarding grace, faith and good works. Furthermore, Staupitz was not 'in jail' but moved about as much as he wanted; although mentally he might have felt restricted in what he would say in public. It is quite probable that Luther's choice of words was metaphorical, that 'cloister' equalled 'prison' and 'monk' equalled 'prisoner'. This wording was used also for Achatius, the ex-monk from Salzburg whom Luther mentioned in his letter. Achatius had asked Luther to intercede for him for financial help from the new abbot at Salzburg. Luther closed his letter as follows:

---

[16] 'Per quem [Staupitz] primum coepit evangelii lux de tenebris splendescere in cordibus nostris .... Ego plane non desinam optare et orare, quam ut alienus a Cardinale tuo et papatu fias, sicut ego sum, imo sicut et tu fuisti. Filius tuus Martinus Luther' (*WABR* 3. 155f. (no. 659); *LW* 49. 48). My translation differs slightly from *LW* which has 'the light of the gospel first began to shine out of the darkness into my heart'. The restriction to the first person singular ('my heart') is not justified. Luther intended to include others who thought likewise and were taught by Staupitz. Luther's Latin explicitly says *in cordibus nostris* (and not *in corde mea*); and then in the following sentence he deliberately switches to the first person singular: 'Ego plane ... sicut ego sum ...'.

> I am sure you do not really despise us, although we may displease you in everything. I shall certainly not cease wishing and praying that you will be turned away from your cardinal and the papacy as I am, and as certainly you yourself once were.[17]

Luther hinted here at the fact that Staupitz was never a papist or a Romanist, but that he had kept his distance from the papacy; for Staupitz was the one who had instigated him against the papal indulgence business in the first place.

Staupitz in Salzburg must have felt the mounting pressures against the adherents of Luther. In neighbouring Bavaria, the reform-minded now felt the countermeasures as well. At the Munich friary where the young Staupitz had most likely made his profession as an Augustinian, things developed in a different direction from that at Wittenberg and the confrères at Munich began to distance themselves from the Wittenberg friars. In 1522, the same Augustinian Friar Leonhard Beier (= Beyer/ 'Bayer'; Leonhardus de Monaco, thus labelled as a Bavarian, or 'Bayer', who had accompanied Luther to Heidelberg and to Augsburg in 1518) wanted to take some scholarly theses concerning the reform of the Order to the friary at Munich. The secular authorities arrested and imprisoned him for about two or three years, releasing him some time between 1524 and 1525. He then married and became a reform-minded pastor at Guben in Holland. The year of his death is not known. Friar Wolfgang Kappelmaier (d. 1531) of Munich, who had received his doctorate in theology from the University of Wittenberg in 1509, and who taught alongside Luther at Wittenberg for some time, preserved the Munich friary for the old faith. In 1523, Pope Hadrian VI granted the Munich friars freedom from obedience to the Reformed Congregation which Staupitz had led until his resignation in 1520.[18] In this case, Counter-Reformation politics and the politics of the Augustinian Order neatly meshed, in favour of the Munich friary's independence.

There might be a kernel of truth in the charge that Staupitz 'undermined' the ecclesiastical authority of Rome and the central administration of the Order in Rome.[19] His own critical stance towards

---

[17] See *WABR* 3. 156, 23, 36–40 (no. 659); *LW* 49. 49. Sallaberger 'Johann von Staupitz, Luthers Vorgesetzter', p. 146, identified him with the humanist monk, Achatius von Wolsperg; see also Sallaberger, *Kardinal*, pp. 244f. Achatius had purchased several books for the library at St Peter's Abbey, including bibles, Greek grammars, and works of Erasmus; see Bonorand, *Joachim Vadian*, p. 77. It is not known whether Achatius was expelled from the abbey in connection with the manipulated abbatial election of Staupitz, or whether he left of his own accord in order to go to Wittenberg.

[18] See J. Hemmerle, *Geschichte des Augustinerklosters in München* (Munich-Pasing, 1956), pp. 15–20. On L. Beier, see Stupperich, p. 33.

[19] As Weijenborg correctly pointed out in 'Neuentdeckte Dokumente im Zusammenhang mit Luthers Romreise', *Antonianum*, 32 (1957), pp. 147–202, although he did not

the papacy and its trade in indulgences may have cleared the way for Luther to develop his extreme anti-Roman sentiments, especially when one takes into consideration Luther's recollection that Staupitz had 'instigated' him against Rome's indulgence business. However, the critical attitude which he adopted towards Rome in terms of church politics must not be confused with the theology and spirituality which Staupitz had developed along the lines of biblical theology and monastic humanism and by returning to Augustine. Staupitz's anti-Roman stance is understandable when one further takes into consideration his dealings with the central administration (of the Church Universal and of his own Order) during his several trips to Rome years before, which had resulted in limited success at best. On the other hand, he must have been pleased with the quick decision from Rome that allowed him to become an abbot, albeit that this may be attributable primarily to the power, significance and influence of the prince-bishop of Salzburg, Cardinal Lang.

After Luther had written to Staupitz on 19 December 1522, he also wrote to Linck, who by then had become Staupitz's successor in the Order, commenting on a now lost letter from Staupitz to Linck which Luther said he did not 'understand'. In this letter, Luther deplored Staupitz's 'most discouraged letters', by which he meant that they reflected a writer who was 'very much without courage'. If he (Luther) viewed things correctly, he said, these letters, if not completely without courage (or 'spirit'), are definitely not written in the way Staupitz used to think. The Lord may 'call him back'.[20] This was Luther's wording; it reveals his distorted perception that Staupitz's entry into the Benedictine Order reflected Staupitz's desire to distance himself from him. In reality, Staupitz never abandoned the central theological positions which Luther also held, namely salvation by grace alone and by faith alone; and religious vows were never of any central concern to him.

Probably also on 19 December, Luther sent a letter to Reverend Spalatin mentioning the letter to Linck in which Staupitz had written

---

really try to comprehend Staupitz's contribution to the renewal of spirituality and theology, his observations have some validity concerning the juridical problems which were involved; see on this W.A. Schulze, 'Ein neues katholisches Staupitz-Bild?', *Theologische Zeitschrift*, **13** (1957), pp. 352–4; F. Lau, 'Pere Reinoud und Luther. Bemerkungen zu Reinhold Weijenborgs Lutherstudien', *Lutherjahrbuch*, **27** (1960), pp. 64–122.

[20] 'Literas Staupitii non intelligo, nisi quod spiritu inanissimas video, ac non, ut solebat, scribit; Dominus revocet eum' (*WABR* 2. 632, 4f. (no. 557)). Here *spiritus* may mean 'courage', and not 'mind', or '[Holy] Spirit' (the latter translation is found in *LW* 49. 21). It is hard to imagine that Luther called his protector Staupitz 'most mindless', or 'completely void of the [Holy] Spirit'. Unfortunately, the letter from Staupitz to Linck that Luther referred to here is lost.

that he would soon deplore his stupid move (to the Benedictine Order); and that after leaving St Augustine's Order, he now underwent new labours, being 'canonically elected and called'. Again, Luther added that he did not understand any of this.[21] Apparently, by Christmas 1522, Staupitz already regretted that he had loaded more labours than necessary on to himself by becoming the abbot of St Peter's. He may have meant the increasing frustrations of the changed situation in which he found himself at Salzburg following the death of his friend Archbishop Keutschach in 1519, while he simultaneously tried to maintain his integrity by remaining a reform-minded evangelical theologian. Now, in addition, he had to cope with the stigma of being the former teacher and protector of a 'banned' person, Luther. Alternatively, he may have meant the troubles arising from the machinations of Archbishop Lang that brought him to the office of abbot, and the new duties which he promised the cardinal to fulfil. A further possibility is that Staupitz had in mind the extra work he had to carry out in his role as mediator – which he was asked to accept (together with Bishop Pürstinger) – in the popular revolt, the so-called 'Latin War' which had been waged between Cardinal Prince-Bishop Lang and the city of Salzburg since 1519.[22]

Meanwhile, there were many more rumours circulating in the Wittenberg area concerning Staupitz's position in the reform movement. It was suggested that he had fallen away from it, thus insinuating that Luther should be viewed in isolation from his former friends. Using such rumours, Thomas Müntzer (1488?–1525) wrote in the autumn of 1524 in his *Vindication and Refutation* (a response to Luther's *Letter to the Princes of Saxony Concerning the Rebellious Spirit* of July 1524, which was a statement inimical to Müntzer), that, at Augsburg, Luther had been immune to dangers, for he 'could lean on Staupitz as an oracle [source of wisdom]' to help him, 'though he has now deserted you [Luther] and has become an abbot'. Clearly, it suited Müntzer as the ideologue of the Saxon rebels to interpret Staupitz's relationship with Luther as having undergone a change for the worse (for Luther) in a situation where the relationship between Müntzer and Luther had soured already. He used the reference to Staupitz to emphasize Luther's

---

[21] 'Stupitius scripsit Venceslao [Linck], se suam stultitiam deinceps ploraturum, Et se nudiorem egressum ordinem S. August[ini], quam intrauerit, sese subiisse labores, licet canonice electum & vocatum. Ego nihil horum intelligo, quid velint. Mart. Luth' (*WABR* 2. 635, 16–636, 20 (no. 558)).

[22] See W. Hauthaler, 'Cardinal Matthäus Lang und die religiös-sociale Bewegung seiner Zeit. Zumeist nach Salzburger Archivalien. II. Theil', *Mitteilungen der Gesellschaft für Salzburger Landeskunde*, 36 (1896), pp. 317–402 (p. 321); Sallaberger, 'Der Chiemseer Bischof', p. 449.

isolation because Luther had turned against him (Müntzer). The rumour that Staupitz had both given up the cause of reform and given in to counter-reforms must have reached Melanchthon who, however, never accepted it. Instead, this young humanist insisted that 'Staupitz was no apostate' (that is from their cause) because 'he loved Luther very much'.[23]

Preaching the Word of God into the hearts (1523)

Preaching had always been one of the main tasks of the Augustinian friars. Early on, Staupitz and Luther were preachers in their Order. Friar Gregor Mayr became *Stift* preacher at Salzburg in 1523;[24] this was the position for which Staupitz had substituted in previous years. After Staupitz had become the abbot of St Peter's, he continued with his preaching, as we know from the notes taken by a Benedictine nun during his Lenten sermonizing which took place between 24 February (the feast day of St Matthias) and 15 March 1523. These were not public sermons, however, as 'the reverend lord and father, our prelate, Abbot Dr Johann von Staubicz' [*sic*] delivered them to the sisters in the 'ward for the sick'.[25] Staupitz wanted to comfort the nuns in their suffering, and to proclaim that in the end their 'suffering would become pure joy in Christ Jesus our Lord', as he stated in his first sermon.[26] He told them that their

---

[23] Müntzer: 'Dann Stupicianum oraculum stundt hart bey dir', as quoted in P. Matheson (ed. and trans.), *The Collected Works of Thomas Müntzer* (Edinburgh, 1988), p. 347, n. 233. E.W. Gritsch, *Thomas Müntzer: A Tragedy of Errors* (Minneapolis, 1989), does not mention Staupitz. On the idea that Müntzer may have been an Augustinian friar, and its rejection, see A. Zumkeller, 'Thomas Müntzer – Augustiner?', *AAug*, 9 (1959), pp. 380–85. On Melanchthon, see Jeremias, *AELK*, p. 346. In the preface to Melanchthon's works, as edited by John Manlius in 1562 under the title *Locorum communium collectanea*, is the note that Staupitz, the famous and noble man, 'loved Luther very much': 'Vicarius quidam Augustanus, clarus et nobilis vir, qui valde dilexit Lutherum, Tubingae doctor Theologiae factus ...', as quoted in Staupitz, I. 3 (Introduction).

[24] See Sallaberger, 'Johann von Staupitz, die Stiftsprediger', p. 243.

[25] 'In der siechstuben' (G. Hayer, 'Die deutschen Handschriften des Mittelalters der Erzabtei St. Peter zu Salzburg', *Denkschriften der Österreichen Akadamie der Wissenschaften philosophisch-historische Klasse, Denkschriften 154. Band* (Vienna, 1982), p. 163); Kolde, *Die deutsche Augustiner-Congregation*, pp. 335–46; H. Aumüller, 'Die ungedruckten Staupitz-Predigten in Salzburg', in *Jahrbuch der Gesellschaft für die Geschichte des Protestantismus in Oesterreich*, 2 (1881), pp. 49–60, and 11 (1890), pp. 113–32. Aumüller was a Protestant pastor at Salzburg; his edition contains seven of the 23 Salzburg sermons of 1523. See Sallaberger, 'Johann von Staupitz, Luthers Vorgesetzter', p. 151. There is an undated series of eight, and two series each of seven Lenten sermons, comprising altogether 22 sermons; and one undated Advent sermon; see Knaake, *Sämmtliche Schriften*, pp. 452–56.

[26] Hayer, 'Die deutschen Handschriften', p. 163.

names are entered into the book of life, not because of their holiness or their good works, but exclusively because of Christ's meritorious suffering.[27] Those whose names are entered in this book are the elect, who have received the first, prevenient grace, as Staupitz wrote in his last treatise on faith.[28] In the book of life, or better in the living book that is the crucified Christ, one finds one's election. Those who look to the cross for salvation are those who are entered into the book of life. Christ has opened the sealed book that is described in Apoc. 5: 1–5. One needs to read it since its pages are the skin of Christ, all torn up through his crucifixion: 'Now [the Book] is completely open and torn up; look into it [and look] through the torn up skin of Jesus Christ; then you truly will discover that you are chosen and that [your name] was entered into the book of life.'[29] One needs to meditate on the cross of Christ in stillness and silence: 'With such a prayer one need not babble much. Be silent and sit by yourself. God will tell you what to talk to him about. All you have to do is to be silent inside and outside and let him do the talking .... Listen to God, that he may have his friendly talk with you.'[30] 'The real Christians are those who live the Gospel and who recognize that being on their own they are damned, but because of Christ's passion they are completely safe and great', because they made his most bitter suffering their 'prayerbook' (*petpuechl*) from which they receive 'sweet taste' (*suessen gesmach*) which is the 'great love'.[31] 'Practise the most sweet meditation of the bitter suffering of Christ. I promise you: the more you do this, the more you will find the sweet taste'. This is so because God is 'sweet'.[32] Since the nuns observed fasting during Lent and were probably craving something sweet, Staupitz contrasted their bodily fasting with the spiritual nourishment with which he wanted to provide them at

---

[27] 'Ir saidt darein [in das lebentig puech] geschriben, nit aus eur heiligkeit oder werchen, nur allain aus dem verdiene meins leidens' (Sermon 1, Aumüller, 'Die ungedruckten Staupitz-Predigten', p. 51; A. Zumkeller, *Johann von Staupitz und seine christliche Heilslehre* (Würzburg, 1994), p. 73.

[28] See Zumkeller, *Heilslehre*, pp. 73f.

[29] 'Aber nun ist es ganz offen und zerrissen, da kuck hinein durch di zerrissen haut Jesu Christi, da wirstu warlich finden, das du erwelt und in das lebentig puech pist geschriben' (Sermon 1, Aumüller, 'Die ungedruckten Staupitz-Predigten', p. 52).

[30] *Zu diesem gepet bedarfs nit vil plapern. Sweig und sitz pei dir selbs* ... (Sermon 1, ibid., pp. 52f., Zumkeller, *Heilslehre*, p. 125).

[31] Sermon 1, Aumüller, 'Die ungedruckten Staupitz-Predigten', p. 53; Zumkeller, *Heilslehre*, pp. 194 and 198.

[32] 'Uebt euch in der allersuessisten petrachtung des pitern leidens Christi. Ich sage euch zue ye lenger jr euch daryn übt, ye mer werd jr darin suessen gesmack vinden', quoted by Steinmetz, *Misericordia Dei: The Theology of Johannes Staupitz in its Late Medieval Setting* (Leiden, 1968), p. 144, n. 5. Also in Sermon 1, Staupitz used the expression *der süsse Gott* ('the sweet God'); see F. Posset, 'The Sweetness of God', *ABR*, **44** (1993), pp. 143–78 (pp. 165–8).

this point.[33] In this meditation, one must make oneself small and humble; and one needs to acknowledge being a sinner who cannot redeem himself.

> Thus, my dear children, you must understand the Gospel as the consolation of your souls, that is that we know that we by ourselves cannot do anything, but in Christ we can do everything; by ourselves we are damned, but in Christ we are eternally blessed. Accuse yourselves, then Christ will excuse you; judge yourselves, then Christ will not judge you.[34]

Staupitz concluded his second sermon with the invitation to the nuns to 'become humble; then you will become true Christians and evangelical people'[35] (*evangelische leudt* [*Leute*, in contemporary German]). The expression 'evangelical people' is remarkable because, later on, it became synonymous with the term 'Lutherans', as today in 'Evangelical Lutheran Church'.

In Sermon 3 Staupitz dealt with the story of the Gentile woman whose daughter was tormented by an evil spirit (Matt. 15; Mark 7). He interpreted it as follows:

> Learn from the little woman, as she keeps running after Jesus and shouting: *miserere, miserere* [have pity, have pity]. Jesus remains silent. But do not ever think that we will not be granted our request immediately, if we say a prayer faithfully, even though we do not immediately feel and sense that we are listened to .... If you have prayed with all your heart, then do not think that you did not receive a hearing. But if you do not get an answer, then you are only wanting in your faith; it is never God's fault and it often happens that our prayers are being answered but we ourselves do not know it. Yes, [they are] answered in such a way that if we saw how sweetly God played within us, we would become haughty about it. If we had twenty hearts within us, all twenty of them would burst with joy; yet, so many times we do not know it, in fact almost never.[36]

Staupitz turned the story into what is almost a mystical treatise resonating with medieval trinitarian mysticism, when he said that the

---

[33] See Sermon 2, Aumüller, 'Die ungedruckten Staupitz-Predigten', pp. 55–9; Hayer, 'Die deutschen Handschriften', p. 163.

[34] 'Also, meine liebn kindt, muest irs Evangeli auch zu aim trost eurer sel versten, also das wir wissn, das wir in uns selbs nichts vermüegen, aber in Christo alle ding, in uns selber verdambt, aber in Christo ewig sälig. Beschuldigt euch selb, so wirt euch Christus entschuldigen, richt euch, so wirt euch Christus nit richten' (Sermon 2, Aumüller, 'Die ungedruckten Staupitz-Predigten', p. 57; Zumkeller, *Heilslehre*, pp. 168 and 194).

[35] 'Diemüetigt euch, so wert ir recht cristn und evangelische leudt' (Sermon 2, Aumüller, 'Die ungedruckten Staupitz-Predigten', p. 57; Zumkeller, *Heilslehre*, p. 194).

[36] Sermon 3, Aumüller, 'Die ungedruckten Staupitz-Predigten', pp. 113–17. I am indebted to Rudolf Markwald for his help with the translation. See Zumkeller, *Heilslehre*, p. 58.

Holy Trinity plays in the human heart (*spilt di heilig Drifaltikait*). Earlier, in his Tübingen Sermon 17, Staupitz expressed a similar thought, namely that the 'image of the Holy Trinity' is impressed on the human soul. However, it is almost impossible to pin down any direct influence from mystics such as Tauler (d. 1361), Suso (d. 1366) or Ruusbroec (d. 1381) in this regard. One may detect perhaps a similarity between Staupitz's trinitarian thinking and a text in John Ruusbroec's *A Mirror of Eternal Blessedness* about God having created each person's soul as a living mirror, on which he has impressed the image of his nature.[37] Yet there is no certainty that Staupitz ever read this work.

Staupitz continued with proclaiming God's friendliness as he inspired his listeners toward meditation upon the sufferings of Christ:

> Have faith and trust . . . . My dear child, why are you afraid of him? He is so friendly . . . . We do not have to be afraid of him . . . . See the miserable, torn apart, bleeding man. He has shed all his rose-coloured blood . . . so that we miserable, sick, needy, sinful people would have a miserable, needy and dying God.[38]

The preacher compared Christ's love and care for humanity to a stove in which wonderful bread is baked. Speaking to the divinity, he said:

> Yes, you, yourself, are the bread which you have baked in the baking stove of your burning love; you are the most tasty bread which you give to us when it is still warm, since you were born in Bethlehem which is called 'bread house' for you are the true and best bread and the most delectable food for those who are good . . . . But I know very well that we are not worthy to hear of this most tasty bread from your most sweet mouth.[39]

At this point the new Benedictine abbot paraphrased the *Prologue* of the *Rule of St Benedict*, which in its Latin version contains the notion of 'sweetness' which he tied to the message of God's sweetness that he proclaimed to the nuns:

> Our holy Father Benedict says in the *Prologue* to his *Rule*: [Therefore we intend to establish a school for the Lord's service. In drawing up its regulations] ah, I do not set down anything harsh,

---

[37] (Sermon 3), Aumüller, 'Die ungedruckten Staupitz-Predigten', p. 114; Zumkeller, *Heilslehre*, p. 58). See Tübingen Sermon 17 (Staupitz, I. 286). For Ruusbroec's text, see J.A. Wiseman (ed. and trans.), *John Ruusbroec: The Spiritual Espousals and Other Works* (New York, Mahwah and Toronto, 1985), p. 237. One may question the view that Staupitz was 'deeply influenced' by Ruusbroec and others, as found in M. Grossmann, *Humanism in Wittenberg 1485–1517* (Nieuwkoop, 1975), p. 45.

[38] 'Ach gelaubt & Vertraut . . . . Ach mein liebs kindt, warumb fürchstu dich vor jm, nun ist er doch gantz freuntleich' (Sermon 4, 1523, Aumüller, 'Die ungedruckten Staupitz-Predigten', p. 121; Steinmetz, *Misericordia Dei*, pp. 125f., n. 6; Zumkeller, *Heilslehre*, pp. 94–5).

[39] Sermon 3, Aumüller, 'Die ungedruckten Staupitz-Predigten', p. 116.

[nothing burdensome]. And when at first you are daunted you should not run away [from the road that leads to salvation ...], as ultimately everything will become so sweet that one does not have any need for a rule, since one does everything out of love.[40]

The former Augustinian who was so greatly inspired by Augustine's concept of the 'sweetness of God' and the axiom 'love and do what you wish' had now also found this theme in the *Rule of St Benedict*, as he preached about it in his new function as a Benedictine abbot.

In Sermon 6 Staupitz again combined Augustinian thought patterns and Benedictine spirituality, as he developed the sermon along the lines of Augustine's *On the Spirit and the Letter*. He advised that the 'gospel must be lived, not only read'. The gospel is to be read according to the spirit, and not according to the flesh. If one does not search and find Christ in the Scriptures, then Bible reading is altogether detrimental.[41] In criticizing contemporary developments he said that those who have the gospel in their mouths most of the time and who want to make use of the freedom according to the Scriptures do not find Christ in it. Among these so-called 'Evangelicals' there are more heretics than Christians. There are some who criticize monks and nuns because they wear special clothing, while these same people let bishops get away with their colourful clothes.

> Why should not Saint Benedict or any other dear saint clothe his followers in a certain colour? This does not matter at all. If I want to follow Christ, the cowl will not be an impediment to me .... But there are some who leave the cloisters; they think they cannot live according to the Gospel while wearing the cowl.[42]

In this same sermon he took the opportunity to clarify what was essential in Christianity, namely the correct concept of personal 'faith'. In doing so he echoed St Bernard's teaching in the *First Sermon on the Annunciation* and in his famous *Fasciculus Myrrhae* (*Sermon 43 on the Canticle*):

> O my dear children, read and listen to the Gospel in terms of spirit and life, and pray to Christ that he reveal and show himself to you .... If you elevate Jesus with his cross in your heart with all your faith so that you truly believe that he hangs on it, he who is true God and man, then you are in the right school. However, it is not enough simply to believe, because the devil and bad Christians also have that kind of belief, namely that he is true God and man and the saviour of the world. But with this belief they are not saved because they do not believe *confidently*. One not only has to believe [that is, a general

---

[40] Ibid., p. 117. See Posset, 'The Sweetness of God', p. 166.

[41] See Sermon 6, Aumüller, 'Die ungedruckten Staupitz-Predigten', p. 129; Zumkeller, *Heilslehre*, pp. 23, 143.

[42] Sermon 6, Aumüller, 'Die ungedruckten Staupitz-Predigten', p. 129; Zumkeller, *Heilslehre*, p. 19.

belief] that he is the saviour of the world, but *you* have to believe that he is *your* redeemer, and *your* saviour who loves you totally and cordially and who effects your salvation at every moment.[43]

Staupitz emphasized the 'you' as did St Bernard, and he showed himself simultaneously to be a critical reformer and a Catholic monastic preacher. Here, towards the end of his life, he had no problem synthesizing his lifelong Augustinian spirituality with his more recent insights into the Benedictine 'school for the service of the Lord'. He emphasized the 'you' because he wanted to preach into the hearts of his listeners. Therefore in Sermon 8 he asked how we would know that Christ himself preached into our hearts. His answer was: you know it when his preaching bears fruit in you which can be recognized by placing all one's love, faith and hope in God alone. When Christ preaches into your heart, then you believe that he is born for you, suffered for you, died for you, rose from the dead for you; then you trust that he wants to save you. Then the force of love is so strong that it burns away all earthly love and all false doctrine. Such love is like an explosive powder placed into the rock and ignited by God.[44] With this metaphor of the powder and the rock Staupitz may have alluded to the techiques that were used in mining, for which the people of the Salzburg mountain region were well known.

When preaching into the heart, Staupitz insisted, no philosophers are needed. Learned preachers who lacked experience in pastoral care would run the risk of 'dragging the gospel into Aristotle'.[45] He perhaps expressed here an aversion to Aristotelianism that as a young friar he may have acquired from the Tübingen humanists at the turn of the century. Such preachers, he continued, deny either the divinity of Christ or the humanity of Christ because with their own reasoning they cannot grasp that he is truly God and truly man. Their preaching is 'poison'. Staupitz repeated his reservations against the use of the philosophy of Aristotle later on, in Sermon 10.[46]

Staupitz always tried to keep the attention of his audience fixed on Christ. There is this 'exchange' between Christ and the believer in the

---

[43] Emphasis added. Sermon 6, Aumüller, 'Die ungedruckten Staupitz-Predigten', pp. 130–31; Zumkeller, *Heilslehre*, p. 156; Staupitz's Early New High German for 'confidently' is spelled *vertrawleich*; contemporary German would be *vertrauend*. On the great significance of Bernard's 'First Sermon on the Annunciation' for Reformation theology, especially for Luther, see F. Posset, *Pater Bernhardus: Martin Luther and Bernard of Clairvaux* (Kalamazoo, MI, 1999), pp. 163–75.

[44] See folios 67r–68v (Sermon 8). Sermons 8 to 23 are not available in a critical edition; from here on I refer to the unedited manuscript pages as quoted by Zumkeller; here *Heilslehre*, pp. 16 and 123.

[45] 'Evangeli in Aristotilis ziechen', folio 66r–v (Sermon 8); ibid., p. 18.

[46] See folio 89r–v (Sermon 10), ibid., p. 19.

sense of the patristic concept of the *admirabile commercium* ('wonderful exchange'): 'You know, that he is yours and you are his. Say [to yourself]: mercy and justice are mine. With this I can exist . . . . And my sins are his.'[47] He had said something to this effect already in Sermon 4: 'I know that his suffering and death are mine, his righteousness and mercy are mine, and my sins are his.'[48] God's suffering occurred because of his love that turns a sinner into his friend. 'Be happy that I let you taste some of the hell, so that you may have heaven for eternity.'[49] Staupitz carried this concept to the extreme when he let Christ say in his Sermon 14: 'I want to drink their sin-slime and filth so that they may drink my righteousness and the most pure water of my grace and love.'[50]

Staupitz was not only critical of the sophisticated preachers, but also of the unskilled preachers who lead people to desperation when they interpret the Scriptures 'to the letter' (in a 'fundamentalist' way, we might say today); in that way they kill the sinners with their extreme strictness. Such preachers only bring the anger of God to their listeners without any crumbs of mercy. They do not proclaim a gospel that is spirit-filled and life-giving. They will face judgment because they do not shepherd God's sheep properly, but instead torture them with cruelty. God will say to them: 'You did not like the miserable sinner and you wanted to throw him into desperation. You have shepherded my sheep with rage and cruelty.'[51] The Ten Commandments are to be preached together with the Gospel, he said, which is to be preached as a consolation.[52] God's mercy must not be abused in a supposedly 'Christian freedom' that would want to do away with fasting and praying and other good works. The believer is expected to be grateful, faithful and loving; and true love and faith are exercised in fasting, praying and doing other good works. He warned, however, that one should not 'place faith and hope in them'.[53] One must preach the Old Law together with the New Law. As a result one will then have 'tasty bread':

---

[47] Folio 77v (Sermon 9), ibid., p. 89.

[48] Aumüller, 'Die ungedruckten Staupitz-Predigten', p. 120; Zumkeller, *Heilslehre*, p. 89, n. 574.

[49] Folios 77v–78r (Sermon 9), Zumkeller, *Heilslehre*, p. 95.

[50] Folio 118r and folio 124r–v (Sermon 14), ibid., p. 88.

[51] 'Du hast den armen sünder nit leiden künen und hast in nur in verzagnüs wellen werfen. Du hast meine schäfel in grimm und grausamkait gewaidnet' (folios 78v–79r, Sermon 9, ibid., p. 17).

[52] See folios 79v–80r (Sermon 9), ibid., p. 140.

[53] 'Aber setz kainen glauben noch hoffnung darein' (folio 80r, Sermon 9, ibid., pp. 189; 20 and 70).

> If you want the crust alone, that is works, fasting, praying, and so on, you will break your teeth chewing on it. [The crust] is not tasty as it is burned .... The bread will turn out tasty when one brings together the law and the prophets, that is the promise which is given to us in the gospel. Then it will become an enjoyable bread [lustig prot], which is nourishing to man and which brings joy to the Son of God, and is well accepted by the heavenly Father. Its softness is inside, but the crust and hardness is on the outside.[54]

Concerning the 'Law and Gospel', he said that 'the Gospel ... is much older than the Law of Moses', because already in paradise after the fall the promise was made to Adam and Eve that a saviour will come [Gen. 3: 15], who is the seed born of 'the most noble woman, Mary'.[55] The Old and New Law are a protection for the Church which is the union and congregation of the elect who are gathered in the unity of faith.[56] Thus whoever is a believer is also elect. The Church is God's vineyard (Matt. 21) which is protected by a fence, namely the Old and New Law, which are tied together so tightly that they form one fence. If one does not preach the Law and the Gospel together, the vineyard will be destroyed by heathens, Jews, or heretics.[57] The wine from this vineyard is pressed out by Christ (see Isa. 63). However, the believer must first be pressed empty before being filled with the juice of the most lovely wine, which is a wine worthy to be presented to the heavenly Father'.[58] The watchtower in this garden (the Church) is staffed by the shepherds and 'evangelical preachers' who receive their teaching from above, from God, while others receive their wisdom not from the top of the tower, but from the 'art of Aristotle'. When the art of Aristotle and high wisdom are utilized to defend the faith, then every kind of rubbish is dumped into Christianity.[59] 'One must preach the Word of God alone, purely, without any additions.'[60] Only then will the vineyard of Christianity be fruitful.

Staupitz never lost sight of Christ as the centre of his proclamation, and so he continued that no human being and no angel could do what needed to be done by Christ alone: only he could do satisfaction for our sins.[61]

---

[54] Folios 80r–81r (Sermon 9), ibid., pp. 140–41.

[55] 'Des edelsten weibs, Maria' (folio 81r–v, Sermon 9, ibid., p. 141).

[56] See folio 83r (Sermon 10), ibid., pp. 73 and 101.

[57] See folio 84r–v (Sermon 10), ibid., p. 102.

[58] Folios 85v–87r (Sermon 10), ibid., p. 198.

[59] 'Alspald di kunst Aristotiles und die hoch weishait dazue ist kumen, das man den glauben damit wil verfechten, da ist aller unrat in di kristenhait gefallen' (folio 89r–v, Sermon 10, ibid., p. 19); see Kolde, Die deutsche Augustiner-Congregation, pp. 339–40.

[60] Folios 89r–90r (Sermon 10), Zumkeller, Heilslehre, pp. 16, 102.

[61] See folio 94v (Sermon 11), ibid., p. 86.

The Church's preachers have to convey this message and in doing so they must be preachers of consolation, not of desperation. The Church needs to let shine the light of the gospel which brings consolation to all sinners, wakes up all the sleepy ones and finds those who are lost.[62] Staupitz let the heavenly Father speak to the sinner as follows:

> My unique dear Child [Christ] did penance for all sins. All your iniquity was punished with my Son .... He has done enough. His blood was shed. You are already freed. All people are given back to me in grace through the bitter death of my unique dear Child. The lost Son has returned to the Father.[63]

Christ is also the Good Samaritan with all his mercy. With his cross he made the sick well and the foolish wise.[64] Here Staupitz wanted to offer the nuns 'a little piece of heavenly bread' by bringing them this 'holy and comforting gospel'. He wished that he and they might find the 'joy of the cross of Christ'.[65]

Although the Church is the assembly of the elect (as he said in Sermon 10), the Church is not an assembly of saints, but of sinners.[66] Even if one had committed a thousand deadly sins, the predestined are still saved.[67] Staupitz declared that Christ owed it to us to save us: 'My heavenly Father has given you to me. I must save you. Place all your faith, hope, and love and all your trust and confidence in me.'[68] In other words, Christ wanted to be the cornerstone of his Church whose members are tied to each other by the mortar (*kalich* = modern German *Kalk*) of faith, hope, and love in such a way that they cannot be taken apart.[69] The Church drinks of the living water of the Holy Spirit which is prevenient grace, a grace that makes the individual a personal believer, as Staupitz repeated himself (see above for Sermon 6 with its Bernardine background) about the Christ who is here 'for you':

> [Christ] must give us the prevenient grace, that is the faith that we truly believe that he has come to console us miserable sinners, that he is born for us, suffered for us, died for us and rose for us. From this it follows that we place all our hope and trust in him. Then we cry out and pray: O my dear Lord, give me the living water which is your Holy Spirit who really is love.[70]

---

62 See folio 95r–v (Sermon 11), ibid., pp. 22, 104.

63 Folio 96v (Sermon 11), ibid., p. 87.

64 See folios 98v and 101v (Sermon 11), ibid., p. 142, n. 909, and p. 92.

65 End of sermon 11; Hayer, 'Die deutschen Handschriften', p. 164.

66 See folio 107v (Sermon 12), Zumkeller, *Heilslehre*, p. 103.

67 See folios 108r–110v (Sermon 12), ibid., p. 104.

68 Folio 111r–v (Sermon 12), ibid., pp. 75, 92.

69 See folios 118v–119r (Sermon 14), ibid., pp. 105, 121.

70 Folio 120r (Sermon 14), ibid., pp. 157–8. See also Sermon 8 (as in n. 44 above).

Christ expects only one thing, namely that the sinners confess that they are sinners and are not able to keep the law. 'So that they prove me true from now on,'[71] One cannot remain undecided and stand still as one serves 'either God or the devil'.[72] Remaining with his Christo-centric focus, Staupitz explained in Sermon 15 that Christ clothes the soul with his own righteousness, without however implying a concept of forensic imputation of righteousness. We are dressed with the dress of the righteousness of Christ when we appear before the heavenly Father. In this outfit we are pleasing to God.[73] However, we must be ready to repent and accuse ourselves as sinners, 'that we know ourselves and scold ourselves and are inimical to ourselves and lament about ourselves and trust in his mercy alone'.[74] This is so because Christ alone is the innocent Lamb of God who was sacrificed for the entire world.[75] Therefore, one's good works do not add anything to this sacrifice; they are done in response to the grace received.[76] In Sermon 17 Staupitz continued this line of thinking concerning good works, stressing that our good works are in reality the works of Christ who fathered them. All we have to do is to be passive mothers and the agents of his action. We must simply consent as Mary consented.[77] He concluded that faith is the beginning and end of all works 'if they are to be good'.[78]

As everything else in Staupitz's spirituality was Christ-centred and grace-centred, so also was his thinking about 'free will'. In 1520, he had said in Sermon 2 that free will is affected by original sin, since free will is the cause for people's fall and frailty; but the ability to rise up and to march on comes from a strength that man does not possess except if it is 'given to him by grace'.[79] In 1523, he articulated this Augustinian/Bernardine insight in the following manner: 'I know very well that by myself I can do nothing but fall. However, with you [Christ] I can get up very well.'[80]

Sooner or later, Staupitz had to explain what he believed concerning those who are not elected by God, that is those whose names are not listed

---

[71] Folio 123v (Sermon 14), Zumkeller, *Heilslehre*, p. 195.

[72] Folio 128v (Sermon 14), ibid., p. 126.

[73] See folio 138r (Sermon 15), ibid., p. 150 (against Steinmetz).

[74] Folio 142v (Sermon 15), ibid., pp. 174–5.

[75] See folio 144r (Sermon 16), ibid., p. 85.

[76] 'Frei umbsunst allain auf genad' (folio 150v–151r, Sermon 16, ibid., p. 186).

[77] See folios 154r–156r (Sermon 17), ibid., p. 185.

[78] 'Das aller werch, süllen si anders guet sein, der anfang und das endt mueß der gelauben sein' (folio 161r, Sermon 17, ibid., pp. 116 and 161).

[79] 'Der frei will ist wol ain ursach zum fal und ain prechlichait; aber aufsten und für sich gen, das ist ain kraft, di warlich der mensch nit vermag, Got geb ims dann aus genad' (Sermon 2, 1520); see R.K. Markwald, *A Mystic's Passion* (New York, 1990), p. 56.

[80] 'Ich wais wol das ich aus mir selbs nichts kan dan fallen. Aber in dir kan ich auch wol aufsten' (folio 169r, Sermon 18, Zumkeller, *Heilslehre*, p. 134).

in the Book of Life: they can do as many external good works as they like, but they are still not friends of the saviour.[81] His final answer to this question was expressed in his testimony of faith (published posthumously in 1525): it is not up to us to ask why some are chosen and others are not. We should be happy to know that those who believe in Christ are taken care of.[82] 'God wants nothing more from us for our salvation than faith alone'. He wants to do everything else himself.[83] The criminal who was crucified with Christ had faith and was justified because he accused himself. 'He let God be righteous and judged himself.'[84] In sermon 2 of 1523 Staupitz said to the nuns: 'Remain humble, remain sinners for God's sake .... Remain sinners, then He must be your Justifier.'[85]

Being aware of the spiritual unrest which was provoked by numerous contemporary preachers, Staupitz told his audience that in these days God does not cease with his preaching into the hearts of the people, as there will always be somebody to explain the gospel in the right way. The present unrest among the preachers occurred for the sole purpose that the gospel will shine all the more. Staupitz may have thought of the numerous evangelical preachers among the reformed Augustinians, and especially of the case of Stephan Agricola (see pp. 312–19). He compared the situation to a fire which, fanned by the wind, burns much brighter.[86] May Christ himself be our 'master and preacher' who speaks to our hearts on how to understand his gospel, and how one can move from the letter to the spirit.[87] He warned though, that whoever uses the gospel for their own purposes, will be left with a bad taste in their mouth. Whoever accepts the gospel because of their own soul's necessity, will have it as food for eternal life.[88]

In another sermon he talked about the adulteress of Luke 7: 37–50. At this point he took the opportunity to address spiritual haughtiness. First he let a fictitious nun enumerate all her merits and proud accomplishments, only to decry her as a 'devil's saint' (teufelshailige)[89] because her

---

[81] Folios 176v–177r (Sermon 19, ibid., p. 80).

[82] 'Das die all versehen sind, die in Christum glauben' (Chapter 5, Knaake, Sämmtliche Werke, p. 125).

[83] 'Das Got nit mer von uns wil haben zu unser saligkait dan allain den glauben ...' (folios 181v–182r, Sermon 19, Zumkeller, Heilslehre, p. 158; Kolde, Die deutsche Augustiner-Congregation, p. 337).

[84] 'Rechtfertigt Got und gab ain urtail über sich selbst' (folios 185v–186r, Sermon 19, Zumkeller, Heilslehre, p. 195).

[85] 'Darumb, meine kindt, pleibt in diemütikait, pleibt sunder um Gots willn ... Pleibt ir nur sünder, so muess er euer gerechtmacher sein' (Aumüller, 'Die ungedruckten Staupitz-Predigten', p. 59; Zumkeller, Heilslehre, p. 195).

[86] See folio 192r–v (Sermon 20), Zumkeller, Heilslehre, p. 24.

[87] See folios 193v–194r (Sermon 20), ibid., p. 24.

[88] Folio 195r (Sermon 20), ibid., p. 24.

[89] Folio 200r (Sermon 21), ibid., p. 188.

works stink of haughtiness. All she did was to prepare God some filthy food. If works are used in order to accumulate merits, Christ would have died for us in vain. The highest honour is given to God if one lets him be the sole saviour. 'He must eternally be my saviour and grace-earner because outside Jesus there is no grace.'[90] In the pride of such a fictitious nun one may see the attitude of the 'Jewish rogue' (*jüdisch schalk*) who thought he could please God with his own works and would not owe him anything. With such an attitude one cannot love Christ very much because such a man thinks he can save himself; he does not need Christ as his saviour. He wants to feed Christ with his own human works; he does not want to be fed by Christ.[91]

Looking at God's mercy from yet another perspective, Staupitz continued that the heavenly Father sublimely mixed his mercy with his strict justice since he 'poured out the sweetness of mercy on us', while he let his dear only Son have his strict justice. He counted us as freed, while he demanded full payment for all our guilt from his own dear Child. The payment was so severe that he even let his Son die in order that we might be completely free through the works of Jesus Christ.[92] Rather surprisingly, Staupitz, who on numerous other occasions included references to, and praise for, the Virgin Mary, at this moment did not make use of the popular medieval allotment of mercy to the Mother Mary on the one side and of strict justice to Christ as the divine Judge on the other. Looking at salvation in this way, Staupitz concluded:

> you may freely despair over your own virtues and powers. However, have strong hope in the virtue, merit, and power of Jesus Christ. Hate yourselves. Acknowledge that you are poor, miserable, sinful, ill, and damned, completely incapable of doing anything good. But acknowledge Jesus as your redeemer, benefactor, healer, and eternal saviour.[93]

Once one has recognized oneself as a sinner, God's plan of salvation becomes clear: 'With great desire', Staupitz said, 'God had sought ways by which he would redeem us.' Since 'according to his divinity he could not suffer, while his justice demanded suffering and satisfaction', he

---

[90] 'Ach möchtestu mit deinen werchen genad umb Got verdienen, so wär Christus umbsunst für uns gestorben .... Der [Jesus] sol und mueß ewig mein erlöser und genad verdiener peleiben .... Dan ausserhalb Jesu ist kain genad' (folio 201r–v, Sermon 21, ibid., pp. 180 and 189; Kolde, *Die deutsche Augustiner-Congregation*, p. 338; Steinmetz, *Misericordia Dei*, p. 144).

[91] See folio 207v (Sermon 21), Zumkeller, *Heilslehre*, p. 189.

[92] '... auf uns gossen die süeß der parmherzikait, aber auf seinen lieben ainigen Sun sein strenge gerechtikait ...' (folios 206v–207r, Sermon 2, ibid., p. 87).

[93] '... erkent Jesum für eurn erlöser, guettuer, gesuntmacher und ewing saligmacher' (folios 224v–225r, Sermon 22, ibid., p. 195).

decided to take on the 'clothing of a slave and he placed our iniquity on himself'.[94] The preacher concluded that when we follow Christ to the cross and accept everything, then our suffering will become sweet, because although for Christ the cross is death, 'for us it is life'.[95] With this thought he ended his Lenten sermons of 1523.

These sermons demonstrate Staupitz's theological consistency over the many years of his preaching and thereby confute the thesis that Staupitz as an abbot in Salzburg turned away from his earlier views. There is an admirable theological continuity in Staupitz's spiritual outlook and theology,[96] which he succinctly expressed in 1520: 'We must through faith and nothing but [faith] become children of God.'[97] Similarly in 1523 he stressed that God does everything out of 'pure mercy' and God wants for our salvation nothing but our 'faith alone', as 'outside Jesus there is no grace'.

Staupitz reiterated this conviction in the posthumously published booklet of 1525 mentioned above: 'No person can be redeemed from sin except through faith in Christ, who is the Lamb of God .... There is no Redeemer except him'.[98] Because of his theological consistency concerning Christ alone, grace alone and faith alone, Staupitz kept his place on the side of those who truly were 'evangelical' theologians at that time. Not only did he emphasize faith, grace, and Christ 'alone', but also the 'Word of God' alone (*sola scriptura*): 'One must interpret and preach the words of God alone with pure intention [and] without any addition.'[99] He always pursued the goal of teaching his audience to seek comfort in the Word of God alone: 'Devout, dear sisters, many times you have heard during this Lenten season that we should seek comfort for ourselves in the Word of God', because his preaching was meant to serve the sole purpose of being 'fed towards eternal salvation'.[100]

Because of this declared sole purpose Staupitz always wanted to reach the hearts of his listeners; indeed, he often said that he wanted to 'preach

---

[94] '... wie er uns erlösen möcht. Und da er nach seiner gothait nit leiden mocht und doch sein gerachtikait ain leiden und genuegtueng erfadert .... da hat er des knechts röckel angezogen und hat unser missetat auf sich gelegt' (folio 229v, Sermon 23, ibid., p. 81).

[95] Folio 230v (Sermon 23, ibid., p. 199, see also p. 109).

[96] See L.G. zu Dohna and R. Wetzel, 'Die Reue Christi. Zum theologischen Ort der Busse bei Johann von Staupitz', *Studien und Mitteilungen zur Geschichte des Benediktinerordens und seiner Zweige*, 94 (1983), pp. 457–82.

[97] Lenten Sermon 5, Salzburg 1520; Markwald, *A Mystic's Passion*, p. 134.

[98] 'Ausserhalb sein ist kain erlöser' (1525), Knaake, *Sämmtliche Werke*, pp. 125f.; Steinmetz, *Misericordia Dei*, p. 144, n. 1.

[99] 'Man sol allain di wart Gots mit lautern grunt an allen zuesatz auslegen und predigen' (folios 89r–90r, Sermon 10, Zumkeller, *Heilslehre*, pp. 16 and 102).

[100] Sermon 14, Hayer, 'Die deutschen Handschriften', p. 164. 'Damit wir zu der weigen säligkait gespeist werden' (Sermon 16, ibid., p. 164).

into the hearts'. In this noble effort he was a brilliant representative of the 'rhetoric of the heart'.[101]

Reforming popular piety

Staupitz's advice to seek comfort in the Word of God alone is connected with his aversion to other kinds of comfort that may be derived from other devotions or religious practices. Much as he wanted to preach into the people's hearts for their comfort and consolation, he simultaneously wanted to achieve some practical reform by advocating the abolition of religious customs which he judged to be contrary to sound theological convictions. Thus, he included in his sermonizing attacks against the medieval custom of paying money to the confessor when one had received the comforting absolution of one's sins through private confession. The practice was called the payment of 'confession money' (*peichtgelt*; modern German *Beichtgeld*), which originally served the purpose of contributing to the livelihood of the father confessor. A pastor had the right to collect such funds from about the twelfth century onwards; however, a father confessor could not make such payments a condition for the absolution of sins. Staupitz objected on principle to this practice, as it came close to selling the sacrament of reconciliation, which he understood to be a sign given by God in free grace. Therefore, in Staupitz's judgment, 'the devil invented the confession money'.[102]

Staupitz was not only critical of this contemporary official practice relating to the sacrament of penance, but also of an unrelated, very peculiar and very private devotion which, as far as is known, was practised mostly in Dominican nunneries in connection with the veneration of the Christ Child. Staupitz probably did not have anybody specific in his audience of Benedictine nuns in mind. It was common for each Dominican nun to have a doll of the Infant Jesus in her cell, as we know from the example of the Dominican Margaret Ebner (d. 1351) who lived in the Maria-Medingen convent, near Dillingen in southern Germany. In her *Revelations* she recorded that she had a personal experience with the Christ Child doll, which she had received from a friend (and which is still preserved in the museum of her convent). She 'took the statue of the Child' and pressed it against her naked breast. 'At that I felt the movement of His mouth on my naked heart [breast] and I

---

[101] Here I transfer to Staupitz an expression applied to Luther in B. Stolt, *Martin Luthers Rhetorik des Herzens* (Tübingen, 2000), esp. pp. 59–57.

[102] Der teufel has das peichtgelt aufbracht (folio 148r, Sermon 16; Kolde, *Die deutsche Augustiner-Congregation*, p. 343; Zumkeller, *Heilslehre*, p. 106).

felt such a great holy fear that I sat a while and did nothing.' On another occasion she 'took Him out of the crib' and set Him on her lap, when 'He fell upon me with His little arms and embraced me and kissed me. After that I desired to know something about His holy circumcision.'[103] Such a cradle with a doll-like Christ Child had the function of assisting a nun in her private devotion of preparing for the spiritual birth of Christ in her soul. There were even books on this subject; one is known of 1488 from Antwerp, *On the Spiritual Childhood of Jesus*, which described this spiritual exercise: 'One now gathers up this sweet little Child Jesus and lifts Him from his crib. As He Himself said, one must lift up the Son of Man so that all those who believe in Him do not perish, but may have eternal life.'[104] Staupitz may have had this type of devotion in mind when, in his Sermon 9 of 1523, he told the nuns at Salzburg that he objected to such commotions with the little Jesus (*Jesukindlein*), that is, when they 'lift him up and put him down and fondle him'.[105] Staupitz may have brought up his criticism of this devotion, not so much because he suspected this practice among the Benedictine nuns in his audience, but more likely because it was known that Dominican nuns did this. This was a religious Order which Staupitz did not like at all; as we observed elswhere, he was critical of the Dominicans' ostentatious practice of prayer with 'rings and beads' (the rosary). In addition, he was opposed to the Dominican John Tetzel and his conduct of the indulgence sales.

Staupitz also included in his sermons of 1523 an attack on the common practice of donating candles, church decorations, chalices, altars, and even entire churches, if they were made for the wrong reason. He agreed with those radicals who said that 'God does not ask for candles'. However, he added that God expects to be loved and honoured, and that one should offer one's heart and prayers, body and goods for God's sake and service. It was important to Staupitz that people realized that they should not seek their own advantage and prestige from these donations, but God's honour. He objected to the mentality which

---

[103] L.P. Hindsley (ed. and trans.), *Margaret Ebner: Major Works* (New York and Mahwah, NJ, 1993), p. 134.

[104] A picture of a precious cradle with a doll of the infant Jesus in it (in French, a *Jésueau*) is provided in H. van Os, *The Art of Devotion in the Late Middle Ages in Europe 1300–1500* (Princeton, NJ, 1994), p. 103, and also in U. Rublack, 'Female Spirituality and the Infant Jesus in Late Medieval Dominican Convents', in B. Scribner and T. Johnson (eds), *Popular Religion*, pp. 16–37 (illustration on p. 24). The block-book (today in Utrecht) has the title: *Van die gheestelijker kintheyt Jesu*; see van Os, *The Art of Devotion*, p. 102; E. Honée, 'Image and Imagination in the Medieval Culture of Prayer: A Historical Perspective', in van Os, *The Art of Devotion*, pp. 166–7.

[105] '[Sie] machen ain solichs wesen mit dem Jesukindlein und heben ihn auf und legen ihn nieder und tescheln also mit im' (Sermon 9, folio 73r–74r; Zumkeller, *Heilslehre*, p. 108).

believed that a person's donation would result in God owing them a place in heaven. It would be better in such cases not to do any good works at all. On the other hand, Staupitz refuted the radical opinion that even those good works which are done for the greater honour of God should be abolished. People who maintained this position were like Judas who saw the anointing of the Lord with precious oils as a waste of money (Mark 14: 4f.).[106]

The evangelical abbot saves an evangelical friar (1523)

After having preached to the nuns in the ward for the sick during Lent of 1523, and perhaps being sick himself, Abbot Staupitz, the 'evangelical' theologian and preacher, was drawn into a controversy concerning his former fellow-friar, the learned Stephan Agricola (1491–1547), in the following spring. This friar's surname is the Latinized version of his original family name, Kastenbauer (or Kostenpauer, Castenpawr). He was born in lower Bavaria and probably entered the Augustinian Order at Regensburg (which was not affiliated with Staupitz's Reformed Congregation). In 1513 he studied in Vienna, where he was listed as 'Brother Steffanus Kostenpauer of Regensburg, of the Order of the Hermits of St Augustine', with the financial support of Cardinal Lang of Salzburg. He was a humanistically trained preacher, in good standing both in Vienna and in Regensburg. On 30 May 1515 at the general chapter at Rimini, Italy, the Order's general, Egidio da Viterbo, gave him permission to study for a graduate degree. To Friar Stephan were attributed the five volumes on the Acts of the Saviour, which was published in Basel in 1517. Their author relied heavily on the work of the Blessed Simon Fidati of Cascia (d. 1348) which bore the same title, *De gestis Domini salvatoris*, a religious tract following the four gospels. (Simon's theology is so close to Luther's that he has been described as a forerunner of Luther.)

On 18 June 1519, Agricola received his doctoral degree in theology from the University of Bologna through the general of his Order, having recently represented the Bavarian province of the Augustinians at the general chapter meeting in Venice (the meeting that Staupitz did not attend). Agricola returned to Regensburg where he became a lector in 1520. In the same year he published a booklet on worship, printed by Wolfgang Stoeckel at Leipzig, in which he proposed the use of the vernacular in the liturgy and questioned the language of 'sacrifice' for the Mass. From Regensburg he was transferred to the friary at Rattenberg,

---

[106] See Sermon 23, folio 231r–234r, ibid., p. 107.

Tyrol, in the Upper Inn Valley (which had been founded by friars from Munich), still within the territory of the Archdiocese of Salzburg. There he became prior in the spring of 1522, at the age of 31. It is unlikely that he was transferred from Regensburg to Rattenberg because in his sermonizing at Regensburg he already sounded like a 'Lutheran'.[107] Would a recognized 'Lutheran' really have been given leadership of a friary?

The sermons which Agricola delivered at Rattenberg were provocative, indeed, as they reflected the spirit of reform. By this time, the diocesan synodal decisions which had been drafted at Mühldorf had also been enacted in order to curb any 'Lutheran' influence. On both Ascension Day (29 May) and All Souls' Day 1522 Agricola gave controversial sermons, that he later admitted were inappropriate. He was denounced in a report to Archduke Ferdinand who ordered the imprisonment of this learned Augustinian preacher on 4 December 1522. Agricola was therefore arrested and in the spring of 1523 'shipped' down the Inn River to Mühldorf. He was considered to be a doctor 'of the Lutheran opinion', and was charged with the 'Lutheran' heresy. Agricola's defence is extant. He declared that to his knowledge, the anti-Lutheran Edict of Worms and the papal bull of excommunication were never proclaimed at Rattenberg. He never wanted 'to preach Luther's cause' (*des Luthers sach zu predigen*); all he admitted was that he relied on the writings of the ancient fathers such as Augustine, Jerome and Ambrose. 'Whoever calls me a "Lutheran" violates me; I proclaim and preach the Word of God.' He would follow Luther only at those points where he is in agreement with the Scriptures. He never preached on 'Luther's writings or teachings' (*des Luthers geschrifft oder leer*).[108] Agricola pleaded not guilty and stated that he relied on the Bible, particularly on St Paul. He wanted Staupitz and Pürstinger to be his judges. St Paul and St Augustine happened to be Staupitz's favourite authorities, too, so it is not surprising that Staupitz understood Agricola's position quite well.

---

[107] See Sallaberger, *Kardinal*, pp. 269f.; Kunzelmann, VI, p. 367. On the Rattenberg–Munich link, see J. Hemmerle, *Die Klöster der Augustiner-Eremiten in Bayern* (Munich-Pasing, 1958), p. 51. On Blessed Simon of Cascia, see A. Zumkeller, *Theology and History of the Augustinian School in the Middle Ages* (Villanova, 1996), p. 39. Friar Stephan Agricola (1491–1547) is not to be confused with John Agricola of Eisleben (1494–1566), as in Steinmetz, *Misericordia Dei*, p. 116. On the two Agricolas, see Stupperich, pp. 18–20. On Friar Stephan Agricola, see Bonorand, *Joachim Vadian*, pp. 51, 71 and 79; H. Roser, 'Stephan Agricola: Theologe der ersten Garnitur', in *Altbayern und Luther: 40 Portraits* (Munich, 1996), pp. 149–54.

[108] 'Doctor der von der Lutherischen opinion wegen bey denen von Rademberg [Rattenberg] am Yn in gefenngknus ligt' (Sallaberger, *Kardinal*, p. 271; Hauthaler, 'Cardinal Matthäus Lang', p. 347, n. 1).

Staupitz did not attend the conference of the Salzburg archdeacons at Mühldorf on 23 April 1523, when Agricola's case was discussed. He was unable to do so because he had scheduled for himself the medical treatment of blood-letting. Rather conveniently, this treatment provided him with a sound excuse not to attend this particular meeting where he was supposed to interrogate Agricola. Staupitz was known as a man well-versed in the Bible, and was perhaps regarded as the only one able to 'overcome' Agricola; however, his ill health prevented him from travelling to Mühldorf.

The Agricola case was dealt with again at the Salzburg government meeting in August 1523, when Abbot Staupitz was present as an adviser; presumably he was very cautious in his evaluations, as usual. The prisoner Agricola was to be interrogated at Salzburg which meant that he would have had to be transported from the Mühldorf enclave through Bavarian territory. For the delivery of the prisoner through their territory the Bavarians wanted to charge the Salzburg government 32 Rhenish gold *gulden*. In order to avoid such a politically unpopular and costly move, Agricola was first asked to recant at Mühldorf. He refused and wrote 'responses' to several points that were raised. These responses were presented to Staupitz at Salzburg who wrote his expert opinion on them, known as the *Consultatio super confessione fratris Stephani Agricolae*.[109] Staupitz accepted Agricola's principle that in matters of religion the Word of God is the main yardstick. Agricola had stated that the rights of the pope and of the emperor are of divine origin as long as they do not contradict the gospel. In his evaluation Staupitz had this to say, referring to Agricola as 'brother':

> The responses of Brother Stephan Agricola to the articles presented to him from the office of the consistorium are to be accepted up to no. 17. But some of them contain quite a few temerities which he adds several times. Nevertheless they are not offensive to piety; they are not adverse to the Gospel. In them he makes himself the judge and he gives priority to his judgment over any determinations of the Catholic Church. Such presumption originates, according to my

---

[109] See Hauthaler, 'Cardinal Matthäus Lang', pp. 321–9. The accusations and refutations were printed in 1523 by two printers at Augsburg, Jörg Nadler and Heinrich Steiner (under Stephan Agricola's name in the vernacular): *Artickel wider Doctor Steffan Castenpawr Eingelegt auch was er darauf geantwort hat, auß seiner gefencknus. Newlich von jm außgange. M. D. XXiij.*, as listed by O. Clemen, 'Ein Abhandlung Kaspar Ammans', in *Kleine Schriften*, II, p. 513; see also H.J. Köhler, *Bibliographie der Flugschriften des 16. Jahrhunderts*, 3 vols (Tübingen, 1991), I, nos. 63 and 64. The title-page of Agricola's booklet (extant at the Bayerische Staatsbibliothek, Munich) is shown in Sallaberger, *Kardinal*, p. 275. The critical edition of Staupitz's expert opinion is now available in vol. 5 of Staupitz's collected works (*Consultatio super confessione fratris Stephani Agricolae*, ed. L.G. zu Dohna).

judgment, from [his] ignorance of [his own] limitations. He does not understand what true piety is and what the Catholic Church is.[110]

Staupitz confirmed that Agricola was not teaching anything opposed to the evangelical message, but realized that his teaching was daring when it came to issues of authority. Agricola was ignorant of how the present Church operates. If he had known better, he would have been more careful in his statements. By stating that Agricola placed his own statements over that of the Church, Staupitz objected to his conceited subjectivism. The evaluation which Staupitz offered here was perceived as 'Protestant subjectivism' (as some scholars presumed), and therefore they decided to classify Staupitz's expert opinion as the opposite, namely that of a traditional, conservative Roman Catholic. Such a conclusion seems to be an over-interpretation of the given text because it disregards the other principle which Staupitz applied here, namely whether or not something is opposed to the gospel – a reformation axiom, Scripture alone. All in all, Staupitz approached the matter not so much in terms of dogmatics, but in terms of pastoral care, or perhaps pastoral carelessness as far as Agricola was concerned. By approaching the issue in this way, Staupitz cleverly avoided an evaluation which could have led to the charge of doctrinal heresy. He plainly and simply pointed out that Agricola's responses were not adverse to the gospel and criticized Agricola only for his immodesty in pastoral care and style. Staupitz summarized his evaluation on the basis of 1 Cor. 14 (on speaking in tongues and on rules of order), that Agricola should have been mindful of St Paul's advice that the Sacred Scriptures are not to be taught without modesty. A preacher must edify, not tear down; he must admonish, not instigate; he must console, not condemn. None of that was observed by Agricola in his pastoral activities. Staupitz pointed out, however, that Agricola spoke much of what is true, but little of what is edifying, encouraging, and consoling. Thus, Staupitz's expert opinion amounted to a criticism mostly of rhetorical style and pastoral carelessness. Such a flaw was, of course, insufficient reason to proceed with any heresy charges.

The archbishop's advisory council then deliberated as to whether Agricola should be confined to a cloister of his own Order in something like monastic imprisonment. For such a purpose he still had to be brought to Salzburg which meant travelling through Bavarian territory. Since this was difficult to do, the Salzburg officials repeatedly tried to persuade Agricola to recant without him actually being personally present at Salzburg. Agricola responded that he had always hoped that

---

[110] See N. Paulus, 'Ein Gutachten von Staupitz aus dem Jahre 1523', *Historisches Jahrbuch*, **12** (1891), p. 775.

Dr Staupitz and Bishop Pürstinger of Chiemsee would be able to show him in the Scriptures where he had erred. Only if they could prove him wrong from the Scriptures would he give in. As no recantation could be obtained from Agricola, it was decided, in January 1524, to suggest to the archbishop that since he had been imprisoned for quite some time already, one should have mercy on him and order him out of the Salzburg territory. He could name a number of cloisters where he might like to live. However, he should never be allowed to preach again. If the archbishop did not agree to that, the friar should be subjected to Abbot Staupitz and Bishop Pürstinger as judges whom he himself had named. Without doubt the archbishop's councillors thought that these two judges would be able to show him his errors, and that he would concede his errors to them. Apparently, Staupitz was perceived in Salzburg as a great theological expert.

 This solution was proposed in the awareness that a petition from the Archduchess Anna of Austria, and other noble ladies, had arrived in Salzburg on Agricola's behalf. Anna was an influential person connected to the House of Hapsburg; she was a lady of the high nobility, the wife of Ferdinand I of Austria who became Emperor Ferdinand I from 1558 to 1564. As the daughter of the king of Hungary she had employed Friar Agricola as her father confessor. This royal interference complicated matters for the prosecutors considerably, because now some very politically important women were exerting their influence on religious decisions. And Agricola would still have to be taken through Bavarian territory as Staupitz and Pürstinger recommended that he be brought from Mühldorf to the city of Salzburg. This plan was vetoed by the dean of the Salzburg cathedral, the humanist Dr Andreas von Trauttmansdorff (c. 1470–1525), third in command after the archbishop of Salzburg and the bishop of Chiemsee. Perhaps Staupitz had proposed Agricola's transport in anticipation of this veto. First, he had provided no good reasons for maintaining the heresy charges, and now he demanded the option which the Salzburg officials and politicians wanted to avoid at all costs, namely to ask the disliked Bavarian authorities for help in transporting the prisoner to Salzburg. It had become obvious that Friar Agricola had protectors and friends (if not sympathizers) in several high places, including the council of the archbishop of Salzburg, and the archduchess of Austria and other reform-minded noble ladies. It is not clear who those other ladies were; one of them might have been Argula von Grumbach (c. 1490–c. 1564) at the Bavarian court in Munich. Cardinal-Archbishop Lang now decided not to bring Prior Agricola to Salzburg. Given the 'Lutheran' unrest in the land, the only remaining alternative was to leave the preacher where he was, at the enclave of Mühldorf, and to dismiss him from there. The Salzburgers wanted to avoid a situation in which the Archduchess Anna would have to intervene on his behalf for a second time.[111]

Cardinal Lang himself was closely connected to the House of Hapsburg in whose service he had come to power; he had been the emperor's representative in Italy.[112] He apparently did not want to risk trouble with other influential people in very high places. Meanwhile, Father Agricola conceded that Staupitz was correct with regard to his improper approach to his pastoral responsibilities, and therefore, finally, he was released in summer 1524, after two years of imprisonment. The circumstances of his release are not known. He remained banned from all Salzburg territories.

Agricola had prepared for death at the stake by writing a 'sermon' on the art of dying with some considerations on the sufferings of Christ: 'A precious, good, and necessary sermon on dying, on how a person should prepare, together with some concluding remarks on the suffering of Christ'. Its printed edition of August 1523 stated in its title that is was issued by *Doctor Steffan Castenbaur Augustiner ordens* from his prison in Mühldorf. Agricola had given his text to Chaplain Wolfgang Ruß (also a persecuted, though not imprisoned, priest from Salzburg) who had visited him in prison, and who wrote a preface for it, which he dedicated to his own physician, Wolfgang Stamler at Ulm, Germany.[113]

A second expert opinion on Dr Agricola's position is in existence, which has often been attributed to Staupitz (and still is at times today)

---

[111] See ibid p. 775; Hauthaler, 'Cardinal Matthäus Lang', pp. 329–45; Roser, 'Stephan Agricola', p. 149. As to the reform-minded noble ladies, no names besides Anna's are mentioned by Hauthaler. For Argula von Grumbach, see Stupperich, pp. 90–91. Peter Matheson conjectures that as a young woman she might have met Staupitz at the Munich court; see 'Argula von Grumbach (*c.* 1490–*c.* 1564)', in C. Lindberg (ed.), *The Reformation Theologians*, pp. 94–108 (p. 96). For Dr Trauttmansdorff, see Sallaberger, *Kardinal*, pp. 166–8.

[112] See I. Friedhuber, 'Kaiser Maximilian I. und die Bemühungen Matthäus Langs um das Erzbistum Salzburg', in A. Novotny and O. Pickl (eds), *Festschrift Hermann Wiesflecker zum sechzigsten Geburtstag* (Graz, 1973), p. 125; Sallaberger, 'Johann von Staupitz, Luthers Vorgesetzter', p. 130.

[113] Agricola, *Ain kostlicher gutter notwendiger Sermon vom Sterben wie sich der mensch darzu schicken soll mit etlichen Schlüßreden vom leyden Christi. Außgangen Von Doctor Steffan Castenbaur Augustiner ordens in seiner gefancknuß vms gottes worts willenn, zu Müldorff. 1523* (Augsburg, printed by Heinrich Steiner). I am grateful to the staff at the Luther Seminary in St Paul, Minneapolis, for providing a copy of this text. On W. Ruß, see Sallaberger, *Kardinal*, pp. 275f. On Agricola's (Kastenbauer's) booklet on the art of dying, the suffering of Christ and the historical context of this text, see B. Moeller, 'Sterbekunst in der Reformation. Der "Köstliche, gute, norwendige Sermon vom Sterben" des Augustiner-Eremiten Stefan Kostenbaur', in F.J. Felten and N. Jaspert (eds), *Vita Religiosa im Mittelalter. Festschrift Kaspar Elm* (Berlin, 1999), pp. 739–65.

although quite wrongly.[114] This *Interrogatoria* (possibly dating from November 1523) was much more critical and threatening to Agricola's life, as it included the claim that he was a proven heretic according to the criteria that had been established: (1) Heretics are to be punished since the sheep need to be protected from wolves. (2) Followers of Luther are to be considered heretics according to the papal bull and the imperial edict. (3) Even if an author is demonstrated to be heretical in only one point alone, he is a heretic. Fortunately for Agricola, this document did not win the official support of the Salzburg authorities.

Besides Staupitz's cautious, non-accusatory evaluation, Trauttmansdorff's veto and Lady Anna's intervention, another factor may have contributed to Agricola's release. The city council of Rattenberg had sent one of its members, Judge Pilgram Marpeck, to Cardinal Lang in Salzburg in order to intercede for their former preacher. Marpeck also travelled to Mühldorf and paid Agricola a visit in prison.[115] Evidently, several people spoke up for Agricola. However, Staupitz's original, moderate, subtle, but effective defence of his former fellow friar may have been the decisive factor in Agricola's release from prison.

Agricola moved in with the Carmelites at Augsburg, in the same friary where Luther (and perhaps Staupitz) had stayed when he was summoned to appear before Cardinal Cajetan a few years before. The Carmelites at Augsburg had John Frosch, a graduate of Wittenberg University, as their superior from 1516. Apparently the Carmelites were sympathizers of the reform-minded Augustinians, and thus Agricola found employment in their midst. Doing what Augustinian friars do best, that is preaching, he became the preacher at the Carmelites' church of St Anna in Augsburg. Agricola enjoyed the official protection of the local government of the imperial city of Augsburg. Here he also found support from Dr Urbanus Rhegius (1489–1541), who held the most important preaching position in the Augsburg cathedral, until he was dismissed in 1530, under imperial pressure.[116] Agricola participated in the famous Marburg

---

[114] See Hauthaler, 'Cardinal Matthäus Lang', pp. 329–48. The author of the *Interrogatoria* is debated. Sallaberger in his 'Johann von Staupitz, Luthers Vorgesetzter', pp. 148–9, still attributed it to Staupitz; Lothar Graf zu Dohna disagrees (see his 'Staupitz and Luther: Continuity and Breakthrough at the Beginning of the Reformation', in H.A. Oberman and F.A. James (eds), *Via Augustini* (Leiden, 1991), pp. 116–29). I follow Dohna on this issue. In 1997, Sallaberger (*Kardinal*, p. 277) speculates that the author may be either Dr Rem or Dr Englmar of Cardinal Lang's court in Salzburg. On the humanist Aegidius Rem (*c.* 1485–1535), bishop of Chiemsee in 1525, see the biographical sketch in Bonorand, *Joachim Vadian*, pp. 178f.

[115] See E. Widmoser, 'Pilgram Marpeck', in G.F. von Pölnitz (ed.), *Lebensbilder aus dem Bayerischen Schwaben* (Munich, 1956), pp. 155–64 (p. 156). Marpeck later became an Anabaptist.

[116] See Stupperich, p. 176.

Colloquy in 1529, siding with Luther against Zwingli. Agricola ended his days at Eisleben (Luther's birthplace) where he died in 1547.[117]

Staupitz was spared the possible embarrassment of being confronted with this learned former fellow friar, with whom he probably sympathized to a large degree. He must have disliked confrontations and tried to avoid them if at all possible. As a result of Staupitz's shrewdness, Agricola had narrowly escaped being condemned as a heretic. Although it is not clear whether Staupitz ever visited Agricola in secret at the Mühldorf prison, it is not impossible, since we know that Staupitz travelled in that area, visiting his friends the Pfäffingers at their castle in the Inn Valley, at Salmanskirchen/Wasserburg, which is located in that same region.[118]

Esteemed adviser in troubled times

Reform measures were enacted in the ecclesiastical province of Salzburg from 1523 on. Ecclesiastical territories, such as Salzburg, felt that the end of their traditional status and role was approaching. This general ecclesiastical-political situation with the 'Lutheran sect' gaining ground was further complicated by the Turkish threat which was advancing from the south-east. The pope tried to raise taxes for a crusade against the Turks. The 'Lutheran sect' supposedly instigated opposition to this plan among the parish clergy who were to come up with the tax money, called the *tertia*, which was a third of their income.[119] Therefore, towards the end of 1523 the Salzburg government held a provincial council to deal with these issues. Abbot Staupitz was a member of the preparation committee.[120] At that meeting, which included the local bishops, the reform-minded were blamed for the decrease in revenues.[121] All the proposals of the council were submitted to the cardinal of Salzburg who passed them on to scholars and clerics for examination. After long deliberations, the cardinal declared them much too severe and rigorous, and even dangerous to the entire clerical estate (*geistlicher Stand*); he insisted on mitigation. Perhaps Staupitz's mellowing influence had an impact on the cardinal's decision. According to the decrees of the council meeting that were made public, the bishops wanted to do everything they could to eliminate any religious errors and improve general morality. However, the times were so evil that

---

[117] See Hauthaler, 'Cardinal Matthäus Lang', p. 349; Stupperich, p. 20; Roser, 'Stephan Agricola', p. 149.

[118] See pp. 103f.

[119] See Hauthaler, 'Cardinal Matthäus Lang', p. 351.

[120] See ibid., p. 351.

[121] See ibid., p. 353.

there was not much hope of improvement. Visitations and the reform of the clergy were ordered as a means of improving their performance as preachers. The 'Lutheran sect' was spreading day by day, while episcopal authority was fading. Pope Hadrian VI's demand for a 'Turk tax' was dismissed as an exaggerated pretext which would lead to nothing but the undermining of local ecclesiastical powers, and rebellion among the lower clergy. It would have been an 'impossible burden'.[122] They wanted to establish a lobby on their behalf in Rome.

In order to achieve the 'reformation of the clergy' a national council was to be called that would deal with this issue.[123] In order to create a consensus among the assembled bishops, Staupitz suggested that the princes and bishops should get together in person and deal with the issues. The next opportunity would be the Diet of Nuremberg in early April 1524. The cardinal followed Staupitz's advice.[124]

At about that time in 1523, when Staupitz had worked on the expert opinion in the Agricola case, the pope received reports from his nuncio, Aleander, that Cardinal Lang of Salzburg was permitting Staupitz to stay in Salzburg. Once before, in 1521, Leo X had protested at Cardinal Lang granting Staupitz residency in Salzburg,[125] however Lang had ignored the pope since he apparently trusted Staupitz and needed him at his side. The papal nuncio evaluated Staupitz's situation quite correctly, although he still referred to him as an Augustinian religious when he was already a Benedictine (with 'papal' approval of which the pope and his nuncio were apparently unaware!):

> This is most certain that [Cardinal Lang] keeps Staupitz of the Order of the [Augustinian] Hermits warm at his place; he who is Luther's teacher and who was the first to begin to speak up against the common school of theologians, although not with as much courage as Luther.[126]

Aleander was quite right to state that Staupitz was one of the first to oppose the 'common school of theology', that is medieval scholasticism. From his Roman perspective, Aleander saw in Archbishop Lang's inner circle nothing but 'Lutherans'. It appears that the cardinal of Salzburg had surrounded himself with reasonable advisers, who were inclined to

---

[122] 'Ain unmugliche Beschewerd' (ibid., p. 361).

[123] See ibid., pp. 356–63.

[124] See ibid., pp. 368–9.

[125] See Kalkoff, *Aleander gegen Luther* (Leipzig and New York, 1908), p. 121.

[126] 'Illud certissimum est. eum [Lang] domi fovere Stapitium [*sic*] ord. erem., Lutheri praeceptorem, qui primus contra communem theologorum scholam exercere linguam cepit, quamvis non tanto, quanto Lutherus spiritu. Iam vero cum Wormariae essemus, cardinalis sic omnes suos familiares ita Lutheranos habebat vel certe Romanae ecclesiae osores ...' (ibid., p. 138).

humanism, but also shrewd ones such as Staupitz, who stayed at Salzburg with papal approval. However, despite the papal nuncio's suspicions, not all of the cardinal's advisers were 'Lutherans', nor were they fanatical anti-Lutherans. The leading men carefully distinguished between the problem of religious errors in terms of dogmatic orthodoxy (theology and faith) on the one hand, and what they called the 'reformation of the clergy' by means of pastoral 'visitations' on the other.[127] These two issues are mingled in our modern notion of 'Reformation' with a capital 'R'. By 'reformation of the clergy' Staupitz and his contemporaries meant primarily the priestly lifestyle in terms of proper celibate behaviour and the fulfilment of pastoral tasks, a concern which the young Staupitz had developed as early as his days at Tübingen at the end of the previous century.

The fact that priests in rural areas were rather uneducated was understood as contributing to the rise of the 'Lutheran sect'.[128] Therefore, following the Nuremberg Diet of spring 1524, the Papal Legate Lorenzo Campeggi (1474–1539) together with the Archduke Ferdinand I summoned a convention at Regensburg in June that same year where this issue was to be brought up again. The Salzburg cardinal was also invited, with the express wish that he should participate in person or at least send trustworthy, experienced men who were not suspected of heresy.[129] Staupitz and a few others may have been meant here.

At Regensburg, the papal delegate met with political representatives from Austria and Bavaria, and with a dozen southern German and Austrian bishops including the bishops (or their representatives) of the then German cities of Trent and Brixen (both now in northern Italy), of Strasbourg (now in France), of Basel (in Switzerland), and of Vienna (in Austria).[130] The theologians Cochlaeus and Eck were also present at Regensburg. The original agenda of the meeting was threefold: (1) to find ways of enforcing the Edict of Worms against the Lutheran sect, (2) to deal with the complaints of the higher clergy against the secular powers and vice versa; and (3) to determine how to proceed further with regard to the still lingering issue of the Turk tax (*tertia*).[131] This was the first meeting which brought political leaders together on 'confessional grounds' by representing the old-time Catholic religion from the southern regions. A year later the 'evangelical side' formed the opposition League of Dessau, named after the town in the north of central Europe.[132]

---

[127] See Hauthaler, 'Cardinal Matthäus Lang', pp. 356 and 387.

[128] Ibid., p. 364.

[129] See ibid., p. 383; Sallaberger, *Kardinal*, pp. 302–8.

[130] See Hauthaler, 'Cardinal Matthäus Lang', p. 386.

[131] See ibid., p. 387.

[132] See Bornkamm, *Luther in Mid-Career*, p. 315.

At the Regensburg convention the cardinal of Salzburg gave 'a long nice speech',[133] while Duke William of Bavaria delivered 'a sharp speech on the reformation of the clergy',[134] which meant that he had added to the established agenda the issue of the 'reformation of the clergy'[135] as his main concern. They agreed to form two committees, one concerning the matter of faith and religion, the other concerning the 'reformation of the clergy'. The papal legate promised to convey, via the Archduke of Austria, the complaints about the 'Turk tax' to the pope who had proposed it.[136] The cardinal of Salzburg was the speaker of the committee on matters of religion and his report was unanimously accepted. The report of the second committee (on the 'reformation of the clergy') was not accepted on the grounds that it was not on the original agenda.[137] The meeting ended on 8 July 1524. The first result was the agreement on matters of faith and religion, which was called *Concordata*[138] (*Einung* in German) and which had been produced under the leadership of the prince-bishop of Salzburg. The *Concordata* contained the decrees of the Diet of Worms of 1521 and of the Diets of Nuremberg of 1523 and 1524.

According to this text the leaders made the following decisions:

1 To accept the holy gospel and other divine Scriptures 'according to the common Christian sense' as the saintly teachers interpret them and as they were accepted by the Church. No blaspheming of Christ, Mary, or the Saints was to be tolerated. Violators were to be prosecuted according to the Edict of Worms.
2 In their territories, no suspect preachers were to be tolerated. Only those who were examined by the ordinary and could produce the relevant certificate were accepted.
3 A printed version of the constitution on the 'reformation' which the papal delegate had presented concerning the abuses and the discipline of the clergy was to be produced. (Again, the notion of 'reformation' was associated not with what we call 'Reformation' today, but with the practical issues of clergy reform.)
4 No changes were to be made concerning the Mass and Christian customs such as fasting, praying and auricular confession. Lay people who wanted to receive the 'sacrament of the altar' without prior confession and absolution, and only in both kinds, were to be severely punished.

---

[133] 'Ain lange zierliche Red' (Hauthaler, 'Cardinal Matthäus Lang', p. 387).
[134] 'Ein scharffe Red auff di Reformation der Geistlichen' (ibid., p. 387).
[135] Ibid., p. 387.
[136] See ibid., p. 387.
[137] See ibid., p. 388.
[138] See ibid., p. 390.

5 Lent was to be observed; this was to include abstinence from consumption of meat. Violators were to be punished.
6 In their territories no runaway religious (namely friars) were to be tolerated; they had to be prosecuted.
7 The printing press business, including the printing of pictures (*Gemälde*) was to be censored.
8 No Lutheran or other heretical texts and pictures were to be bought or sold, donated or distributed. Violators were to be prosecuted according to the emperor's edict.
9 Any persons who were currently living in Wittenberg for the purpose of study (mostly theology students were meant here) must either return home within three months or enrol at another university. Violators would lose their financial support including any inheritance which they were owed. No graduate from the University of Wittenberg would find employment in their lands as a university teacher or pastor.
10 For the supervision of the execution of these measures, commissioners were to be installed as *superintendentes*.
11 They were to promise to comply with the Edict of Worms and the decisions made at Nuremberg. Violators were to be exiled, not only from any territory of one of the lords, but from all the territories of those who were represented at the Regensburg convention.[139]

This was now the ecclesiastical-political climate in which Staupitz lived. In this situation he dared to remain friends with Luther. No wonder Staupitz felt himself to be living 'at the anus of the world'.

The number of students at Wittenberg University declined steadily after 1519 to the lowest point in 1526, most likely due to the restrictions contained in no. 9 above, since graduates from Wittenberg now had little prospect of finding jobs in their home territories.[140] The second result of the Regensburg convention concerned the 'reformation mandate' (*reformatio cleri*), published on 7 July 1524, which was drafted by the papal legate, and reworked by the committee. The lifestyle of the clergy was to be reformed according to St Paul's guidelines: any abuses about which the lay people were complaining had to stop and 'all classes' of the clergy[141] must obey the 'reformation mandate'. A detailed list of 38 points was published. It included the decree that members of the religious Orders were no longer admitted to the pulpit without approbation by the local episcopal ordinary or his vicar. Sermons were

---

[139] See ibid., pp. 390–92; the account of the decrees in Sallaberger, *Kardinal*, p. 304, differs slightly.
[140] See Hauthaler, 'Cardinal Matthäus Lang', p. 393.
[141] See ibid., p. 395.

to be delivered according to the manner of the saintly fathers and teachers of the Church, whereby specifically the following were meant: Cyprian, Chrysostom, Ambrose, Jerome, Augustine and Gregory. Here now, the 'reformation mandate' dealt with reformation theological issues, but only insofar as guidelines for the practice of preaching were concerned. The clergy had to wear long clothes, and not bear arms except when travelling. They were to avoid taverns, drunkenness, gambling, blaspheming, quarrels, dances, theatres and public parties. No fees were to be exacted for the administration of the sacraments. Ordinarily, members of religious Orders were no longer allowed to work in parishes; violators were forced to go back to their cloisters. Such regulations would have hit Staupitz as an itinerant preacher very hard, had he still been a member of the mobile Augustinians. The mendicant Orders and their system of preaching and collecting alms remained under the control of the bishops, whereby apostolic concessions remained in place. Holy days were to be reduced, and the priests were told to 'eagerly read the New and the Old Testament'.[142] Secular priests with concubines were no longer tolerated.

The Austrian Archduke Ferdinand and the pope were pleased by these decisions of the *Concordata* or, as it was also called, the 'Regensburg Reformation'. By contrast, of course, Luther saw in them the persecution of his followers. He wrote about the new situation, saying that in Bavaria the persecution of the Word was fully under way.[143] At Salzburg under Cardinal Lang, the 'Regensburg Reformation' took effect as late as 5 October 1524. It is not known why this date was chosen. Perhaps the princes who promoted the 'Regensburg Reformation' wanted the other lords of the German lands to join them.[144] At any rate, they won over the Elector Albrecht of Mainz and Brandenburg, who was also the archbishop of Magdeburg and bishop of Halberstadt. Albrecht did not persecute the reformers with force. Indeed, as late as 1527 Melanchthon praised him as the ecclesiastical leader of Germany who, unlike other princes, did not use acts of violence against them.[145] Albrecht's assent was a significant advantage for the anti-Lutheran camp. Emperor Charles V expressed his great joy over the 'Regensburg Concordata' in a communication from Tordesillas of 31 October 1524, as it supposedly helped to restore unity

---

[142] Ibid., pp. 397–8.

[143] 'In Bavaria multum regnat crux et persecutio verbi' (Letter to Gottschalk Crusius of 30 October 1524, *WABR* 3. 366, 12f. (no. 788)); see Hauthaler, 'Cardinal Matthäus Lang', p. 399, n. 1.

[144] Hauthaler, 'Cardinal Matthäus Lang', pp. 400f.

[145] See B. Lohse, 'Albrecht von Brandenburg und Luther', in F. Jürgensmeier (ed.), *Erzbischof Albrecht von Brandenburg (1490–1545). Ein Kirchen- und Reichsfürst der Frühen Neuzeit* (Frankfurt, 1990), p. 81.

and extinguish the 'Lutheran Hydra'.[146] The Cardinal Lang was asked by
Ferdinand I of Austria, on 3 February 1525, to provide him with a list of
princes who should also be invited to join the 'Regensburg Reformation'.
In his response of 16 February 1525, the cardinal asked for a longer 'time
of reflection'.[147] The peasant revolt disrupted for quite some time the
progress of the traditional Catholic 'Regensburg Reformation', but the
chief reason for the delay of the list that was requested may have been
the loss of the cardinal's esteemed adviser, Staupitz, who had died a few
weeks earlier, in the closing days of 1524.

Religious vows: central or marginal?

After the Diet of Worms, Luther was confined in Wartburg Castle from
May 1521 to March 1522, and thus had time for reflection. Among
other things this included a review of the religious vows in the course of
which he came to the conclusion that they had no biblical theological
foundation.[148] At the end of June 1522, his colleagues Karlstadt and
Melanchthon published their opinions on the vows; this was at the time
when Luther expressed to Staupitz his disquiet about him becoming an
abbot.[149] He was honestly concerned about Staupitz having departed
from the gospel truth as he and the other Wittenbergers perceived it.
Whether Staupitz was aware of the heated debate on vows in which the
professors at Wittenberg were involved and whether he had any
accurate information about it is hard to tell. Luther himself still wore
the cowl in August 1523, as is evident from a report made by the bishop
of Ermland, John Dantiscus, that was sent to the king of Poland.
Dantiscus was the ambassador of the Polish king at the imperial court.
On his way home he had stopped at Wittenberg where he saw Luther in
his monastic habit.[150]

   While lengthy discussions on the vows went on at Wittenberg,
Staupitz never attributed much weight to them as far as one can tell from
the sources. He himself needed no liberation from his vows; he had no
distorted attitude toward them, nor did he consider them a big problem.
Staupitz disagreed with Luther's (and the other Wittenberg professors')
position in a noble way. He let Luther know that, in general, vows were

---

[146] Hauthaler, 'Cardinal Matthäus Lang', p. 401.

[147] Ibid., pp. 401–2.

[148] See WA 8. 573–66; LW 44. 245–400.

[149] See B. Lohse, 'Die Kritik am Mönchtum bei Luther und Melanchthon', in
Evangelium in der Geschichte. Studien zu Luther und der Reformation (Göttingen,
1988), pp. 80–96.

[150] See Bornkamm, Luther in Mid-Career, p. 292.

not all that important. Staupitz touched upon this issue in his 1523 Lenten sermons (which would appear to be his indirect reaction to the challenge by the Wittenberg professors), saying that those people who have the gospel in their mouths most of the time, and who wanted to make use of the freedom according to the Scriptures, do not find Christ in it. He was convinced that among the 'Evangelicals' were more heretics than Christians.[151]

In a similar vein he wrote to Luther on 1 April 1524, warning him not to confuse essential and non-essential issues. Luther saw in the religious vows and in the lifestyle which he experienced in the cloisters the essence and the symbol of an unbiblical work-righteousness which he detested; Staupitz viewed vows as a viable Christian option on one's way to salvation, without identifying monasticism with 'work-righteousness' in the way Luther did. Nevertheless, such disagreement could not separate the two friends. In this last communication which he sent to Luther, Staupitz still considered him to be his 'best friend' whom he loved more than a woman can love, speaking with words from 2 Sam. 1: 26. Staupitz called himself Luther's 'brother and disciple':

> To D[octor] M[artin] L[uther], his best friend and Christ's servant, your brother and disciple Johann, a servant of Christ. Jesus.
>
> My faith in Christ and in the gospel remains unchanged. But I am in need of prayer that Christ would help my unbelief, that I would have a disdain for human things and might not love the Church in a lukewarm fashion. For you I have a very steadfast love, passing the love of women [2 Sam. 1: 26], always unbroken. Pardon me if at times the slowness of my mind cannot grasp your [reasoning] and that I, therefore, pass over it in silence ....
>
> The hearts of the simple-minded are burdened, and anyway, what is it that made the cowl so objectionable to you, which most religious wear in holy Christian faith?.... One must not throw out something only because it incidentally was misused. Do not condemn things that are not so important and that can be harmonized with an upright faith .... But against matters that are in conflict with the faith, scream and do not stop. We owe a great deal to you, Martin, who have guided us back from the sows' troughs to the pasture of life, to the words of salvation. May the Lord Jesus grant that we at long last may live by the gospel, now heard with our ears, and constantly talked about by a lot of persons. For I see that countless numbers of people abuse the gospel for the freedom of the flesh. But the Spirit blows where it chooses [John 3: 8]; to you we owe a debt of gratitude because you have planted and watered, giving glory to God, to whom we attribute the power of making us God's children .... I have written enough; may it be

---

[151] See Aumüller, 'Die ungedruckten Staupitz-Predigten', pp. 129f.

granted that I could confer with you just one single hour and open the secrets of [my] heart. I commend to you, my dear brother, the one whom you see before you, who delivers this letter to you. I would appreciate you making him your disciple by your effort and influence. Also please see to it that he will soon get his Master's cap and be sent back to me .... May my unworthy requests have some weight with you, [for] in previous times I have been an advance guard of the holy evangelical teaching and have hated the Babylonian captivity as I still do today.[152]

This letter may be taken as Staupitz's response to Luther's letter of the previous year, dated 17 September 1523, in which Luther had addressed Staupitz as 'Reverend Father in Christ, Doctor John, Abbot of St Peter's Benedictine monastery in Salzburg, my superior, father, and teacher in the Lord', and had acknowledged Staupitz as the one through whom 'the light of the gospel first began to shine out of the darkness in our hearts'. He had signed his letter with 'your son Martin Luther'. He was appreciative of Staupitz, saying that even if he no longer enjoyed Staupitz's favour, he remained grateful to him. Luther had also expressed his theological difficulties with the vows and with the fact that Staupitz had placed himself 'into the hands of that infamous monster', the cardinal of Salzburg. Luther wished that Staupitz would distance himself from the cardinal and from the pope at this time, as he (Luther) himself and as Staupitz had done in previous years.[153]

With his letter Staupitz sent greetings to three other Wittenberg professors, Amsdorf, Schurff and Melanchthon; thus indicating that he wanted to be on friendly terms with them. This also means that Staupitz probably did not want to separate himself from the Wittenberg version of the reform movement which was represented by these figures. They remained friends, even if they disagreed over the (in)significance of vows; the proclamation of the gospel was more important. From Luther's perspective, however, the rejection of the legitimacy of the vows appeared essential, since it was derived from the gospel message as he interpreted it. Staupitz's perspective was more liberal, as he let the vows be what they are – not essential, but rather 'neutral',[154] as he wrote in his last letter. In Staupitz's view, Luther condemned many things that are not only 'neutral', like vows, but also 'external' and do not burden one's conscience.[155]

---

[152] *WABR* 3. 264 (no. 726). See R. Wetzel, '"Meine Liebe zu Dir ist beständiger als Frauenliebe": Johann von Staupitz (+1524) und Martin Luther', in P. Freybe (ed.), *Luther und seine Freunde* (Wittenberg, 1998), pp. 105–24.

[153] *WABR* 3. 155, 7–156, 1 (no. 659); see *LW* 49. 48–50.

[154] 'Quae neutra sunt' (*WABR* 3. 264 (no. 726)).

[155] See ibid.

Staupitz, nevertheless, readily acknowledged that Luther had 'led them back to the pasture of life, to the words of salvation'.[156] Remarkably, at the end of his letter, Staupitz described himself as the one who 'in times past' (*olim*) had been the *praecursor* of the evangelical doctrine. His self-designation implied that he was the advance guard, front-runner, guide, or harbinger who goes before to secure lodging.[157] It seems that Staupitz wanted to maintain a continuity in his labours between then (*olim*) and now (*hodie*). In referring to the present 'Babylonian captivity' he probably meant to include his current personal situation at Salzburg where conservative pressures were increasing. On 17 September 1523, Luther had reminded Staupitz of his earlier anti-Roman sentiments, when Staupitz had been an 'alien' to the papacy. To be connected to the papacy or not was of little significance for Staupitz, who was anti-Roman insofar as the abusive indulgence business was concerned – as Luther well remembered when he declared in retrospect in 1539 that it was Staupitz who 'instigated' him against the pope.[158] It is quite possible that Staupitz in using the notion of *captivitas babylonica* wanted to allude to Luther's work of 1520 by the same title, or to a line in Luther's text for the Leipzig Disputation of 1519.[159] If that is so, Staupitz was expressing his sympathy with Luther's position, even though he was not happy about Luther's published Reformation writings.

The disagreement over vows could not destroy the long friendship between the two men. Luther was glad of this friendship, as he forwarded to Spalatin Staupitz's letter of 1 April 1524 in which he had addressed Luther as his 'best friend and Christ's servant'. Luther sent it to Spalatin under the date of 29 April, which is probably the same day as he himself had received it (apparently the travelling time from Salzburg to Wittenberg was less than a month): 'I send you Dr Staupitz's letter, who "finally" and for once "revived" to greet us and communicate with us

---

[156] 'Debemus tibi, Martine, multa, qui nos a siliquis porcorum reduxist ad pascua vitae, ad verba salutis' (*WABR* 3. 264, 22–4 (no. 726)).

[157] '... qui olim praecursor extiti sanctae evangelicae doctrinae et quemadmodum etiam hodie exosam habui captivitatem babylonicam' *WABR* 3. 264, 34–6 (no. 726). On this, see H.A. Oberman, 'Captivitas Babylonica. Die Kirchenkritik des Johann von Staupitz', in A. Mehl and W.C. Schneider (eds), *Reformatio et reformationes* (Darmstadt, 1989), pp. 97–106; English translation in H.A. Oberman, *The Impact of the Reformation* (Grand Rapids, MI, 1994), pp. 26–34. One may question Oberman's translation of *praecursor* as *Vorläufer*, if it was meant in the sense of 'pre-reformer' (*Vorreformator*), while agreeing with him that Staupitz is not simply a prelude (*Vorspiel*) to the Reformation or its 'pre-history' (*Vorgeschichte*). His English translation of it as 'precursor' or 'forerunner' (p. 27) is equally questionable; I prefer to understand *praecursor* as standard-bearer of the gospel.

[158] See *WATR* 4. 440, 17–19 (no. 4707).

[159] 'Absit, absit ista plus quam Babylonica captivitas' (*WA* 2. 215, 2. See in *Operationes, Archiv WA* 2. 600, 10–12; *Resolutiones, WA* 1. 573, 25.

after so much silence and after [we] having written so many letters to him'.[160] Luther must have been glad and proud of Staupitz's compliment, and he must have thought it helpful to pass it on to Spalatin at the elector's court, even if this letter showed their disagreement over the evaluation of the vows, which Luther had considered to be central but which Staupitz played down as marginal. Luther in his letter to Spalatin paraphrased Phil. 4: 10 (in the Latin version) as he described his joy at the letter which he received from Staupitz: 'It gave me great joy in the Lord that now at last you revived your concern for me' (Phil. 4: 10).[161]

For further corroboration of their strong bonds of friendship and mutual trust in personal and theological matters (in case these were ever to be questioned, then or later), Staupitz sent a letter of recommendation to Luther for the letter carrier, Georg Führer, a student from Salzburg who was to finish his theological studies at Wittenberg.[162] Had Staupitz entertained major reservations against Luther and the recent developments in his theology, or against the theology which was promoted at Wittenberg in general, he would certainly not have recommended to Führer to conclude his studies there with a master's degree. Entrusting a student to this university was all the more risky at that time, since plans were in the making to cut off any ties to Wittenberg. Perhaps Staupitz was aware of these plans and therefore made sure that Führer would be able to get through to Wittenberg, and start working towards finishing his degree before it was openly prohibited. Only three months after he had sent this student to Luther, the traditionalist bishops and princes who gathered at Regensburg in the summer of 1524, decided that every one of their subjects presently living at Wittenberg had to return home within three months or enrol at another school, and that graduates of the Wittenberg University no longer would find employment (see p. 323). Three days after Führer had delivered Staupitz's letter and Luther had written to Spalatin, Luther sent another note to Spalatin, on 2 May, saying that he had not yet responded to Staupitz (a response was apparently still on his mind).[163] Unfortunately, this response to Staupitz did not survive.

---

[160] 'Mitto literas D. Staupitii, qui tandem semel refloruit nos salutare & alloqui post tot silentia & tot literas ad eum datas' (*WABR* 3. 280, 10–13 (no. 735)).

[161] Latin Bible version of Phil. 4: 10: 'quoniam tandem aliquando refloruistis pro me sentire, sicut et sentiebatis: occupati autem eratis'; Luther's wording: [Staupitz] 'qui tandem semel refloruit nos salutare.'

[162] See n. 17 in *WABR* 3. 264; see H.A. Oberman, *The Impact of the Reformation*, p. 39. On Georg Führer and other students from Salzburg at Wittenberg up to 1524, see Sallaberger, *Kardinal*, pp. 245–8.

[163] 'Staupitii nondum respondi' (*WABR* 3. 283, 18 (no. 738)).

With highly emotive words, Staupitz had expressed the hope that he might be granted to meet with Brother Martin at least one more time, for one hour, and then 'to open the secrets of [his] heart'.[164] This remark prompted later Lutheran scholars to call Staupitz an *anima naturaliter evangelica*, a soul naturally inclined to the Evangelical truth,[165] and to consider Staupitz really a 'Lutheran' at heart. The Catholic scholar Nikolaus Paulus strongly rejected this view.[166] Both may be right, if at the start of the twenty-first century we reach beyond the positionings of Lutherans and Catholics in the way it was done at the end of the nineteenth century. Staupitz was an Evangelical at heart, from whom Luther learned most of his Reformation theology, but he was not a 'Lutheran' in the sense that this label was used both then and today. Rather, Luther was a 'Staupitzian', except for his understanding of religious vows. Both were 'Evangelical souls' who wanted to be 'Catholics', but not 'papists' or Romanists. Each wanted to be friends with the other, and they indeed remained friends to the end.

This lasting friendship between the two is all the more remarkable when one considers that at the time when Staupitz sent his last letter to Luther on 1 April 1524, the Reformed Congregation of the Augustinian Order in Saxony and Thuringia was about to dissolve under Linck. Staupitz had worked for the reform and reorganization of the Order for 20 years, and he could easily have blamed Luther for its fate. However, Staupitz did not do that at all, instead confirming his friendship with Luther, regardless of their minor ideological difference concerning the vows. Staupitz's last word on the issue of the monastic life was his vision of the ideal-typical religious community which he described in his eighteenth sermon of the year 1523:

> O my dear children, see and remember what a great and blessed thing it is when a community lives together in the name of Christ. God is totally obliged to do what they desire. The only reason why cloisters came into existence is that in them we serve God and live together having one will, one spirit, one community, in the name of Jesus Christ. Then [Christ] will have to be in our midst always.[167]

For Staupitz the vows were never a big problem. Now as an abbot he had no time to enter into sophisticated theological discussions on that issue, since he was very busy with his administrative duties. These

---

[164] 'Sat scripsi, utinam vel unica hora liceret tibi colloqui et aperire secreta cordis' (*WABR* 3. 264, 29f. (no. 726)).

[165] See Kolde, *Die deutsche Augustiner-Congregation*, pp. 351–4.

[166] Paulus, 'Johann Staupitz. Seine vorgeblich protestantischen Gesinnungen', pp. 328–46. Paulus, 'Ein Gutachten von Staupitz', pp. 773–7.

[167] Sermon 18, as quoted in A. Zumkeller, 'Johannes von Staupitz und die klösterliche Reformbewegung', *AAug*, 52 (1989), pp. 31–49 (p. 49, n. 40).

included the supervision of numerous parishes and possessions, even of salt mines in the Alps. In September 1524 Abbot Staupitz was actually approached by the Roman curia regarding matters of mining with a request to dispatch mining experts from Salzburg (known throughout the world for their experitise) to the Papal Estates.[168] However, Staupitz never got around to complying with the Roman wish; in 1525 his successor promised to send two specialists to Italy.[169]

Among the abbey's parishes was the rather wealthy one at Hallein, a centre of the salt trade, where as an abbot of St Peter's he had to celebrate Mass twice a year, in order to demonstrate the abbey's claim to this parish.[170] The monastic parishes and other possessions which were connected to St Peter's Abbey were located as far away as the Danube Valley near Vienna.[171] His abbey was a centre of the regional economy, but also of spirituality, culture and education. This can be seen from the fact that in the year of his death, 1524, Abbot Staupitz was approached by Dr Urban Braun, the principal of St Peter's school, to establish a school for secondary education, that is a *gymnasium,* a project which was not carried out until much later, when the University of Salzburg came into existence.[172]

Last Sermon to 'St Peter's Ladies', Advent 1523

Staupitz's last known sermon was delivered to the Benedictine nuns of St Peter's during Advent 1523.[173] This may have been while he was working on his booklet on the 'right Christian faith' which contains the same message, and which was edited posthumously by Linck in 1525. There was no change in his theological views concerning faith and salvation in his later years. In that last sermon he had this to say to the nuns: 'My dear children .... The devil deceived us and did not leave us with anything but the name' [*Geistliche,* that is, 'spiritual' people]. They should not trust in their dress code, or in their praying, fasting, and bodily castigation in the monastery. Such works do not make a person 'spiritual'. Here he played

---

[168] See letter to Abbot Staupitz of 19 September 1524; Sallaberger, *Kardinal,* p. 263, n. 63.

[169] See letter of 25 January 1525 from Abbot Kilian Pütricher to the Roman secretary, Dr Philippus de Sernis; Sallaberger, *Kardinal,* p. 263, n. 63.

[170] See F. Koller, 'St. Peter als Salzproduzent', in Salzburger Landesregierung (ed.) *Das älteste Kloster im deutschen Sprachraum* (Salzburg, 1982), pp. 104–8.

[171] See F. Hermann, 'Die Klosterpfarren', in *Das älteste Kloster,* pp. 98–102; Koller, 'Die Grundherrschaft der Abtei St. Peter', ibid., pp. 109–16 (with two maps).

[172] See F. Hermann, 'Von der Peterschule zur Universität', in *Das älteste Kloster,* p. 196.

[173] Edited by Kolde, *Die deutsche Augustiner-Congregation,* pp. 452–6.

with this word, since in German the traditional designation for members of religious Orders or the clergy in general is *Geistliche* (literally, 'spirituals'). A person is not 'spiritual' by being conceited, or by looking stern and 'letting the head hang down', and someone who would assume that one could earn salvation with one's works. Rather, the preacher insisted, the term 'spiritual' is derived from 'Spirit' and means that our 'spirit' is to be united with God's Spirit. A person is not 'spiritual' when he thinks he is able to earn salvation with good works. Instead, the abbot recommended that one should call upon God 'in the Spirit' and pray as follows that God alone be pleasing to the human person:

> Do with me what you wish, so that you alone will be pleasing to me and I will love you alone and praise you. Grant me, my God, that I dislike myself, and love no one but you ...; that I stand firm in faith and trust that [Christ] will save us and make us righteous because of his merit and of pure mercy, and not at all because of our own external works ....[174]

At this point the preacher added the rhetorical question: 'Dear God, should faith alone really be enough?' His response to this sounded very much like a sentence from the Council of Trent on justification by faith: 'Yes, of course, it is enough! Have faith freely. Faith cannot be without fruit and work of love if it is a living faith'.[175] 'See to it, that you always have faith and trust .... This [faith] is what is first and what is the foundation.'[176] From this faith follows the praise of God for sending us his Son: 'Jesus is born for us, Jesus suffered for us, Jesus died for us, Jesus is risen for us.'[177]

From faith it also follows that we examine our conscience and recognize that we really are sinners who are in need of confession:

> O my righteous God, I come to you with so many sins, and I confess to you that being on my own I am a miserable hell fire and damned

---

[174] '... und in aym festen vertrauen, und gelauben stenn, das er uns wel Sälig und frum machen aus seym verdyen, und lauterr parmherczikait, und gar nichtcz aus unsern außern werchen' (ibid., p. 452; see Zumkeller, *Heilslehre*, p. 109).

[175] 'Ei lieber Got, solt es den alles genueg sein mit dem gelauben? Ja freilich ist es genueg. Gelaubt nur frei. Er kan nit an [ohne] frucht und werch der lieb sein, ist er anders lebentig' (Kolde, *Die deutsche Augustiner-Congregation*, p. 453; see Zumkeller, *Heilslehre*, p. 159; Steinmetz, *Misericodia Dei*, p. 118). The Council of Trent declared that 'faith is the beginning of human salvation, the foundation and root of all justification' (*Quia fides est humanae salutis initium, fundamentum et radix omnis justificationis*), Chapter 8; H.J. Schroeder (ed.), *Canons and Decrees of the Council of Trent* (St Louis, MO, and London, 1978), p. 313 (Latin text); pp. 34f. (English text). For Staupitz's wording, see n. 176 below.

[176] '... das ist das erst und das fundament' (Sermon 24); Kolde, *Die deutsche Augustiner-Congregation*, p. 453; see Zumkeller, *Heilslehre*, p. 156.

[177] Kolde, *Die deutsche Augustiner-Congregation*, p. 454.

dog (*armer hellprant und verdambter hunt*). However, in you I am one of the redeemed elect. Therefore I come to you. Since I cannot do anything else but commit sins and go to hell, your work will be to cleanse, have mercy and make righteous those who recognize themselves to be sinners.[178]

Staupitz ended his last sermon with this prayer to God: '... You promised me that you want to save me. Our Lord Jesus Christ help us; [it is] he from whom all and everything has its origin, beginning and end. Amen.'[179]

Staupitz's final days – at a time of turmoil

While travelling in spring 1524, Staupitz was taken ill at Braunau, about 25 miles from Mühldorf down the Inn Valley and about 45 miles north of Salzburg. He was there to settle some disagreements between his abbey and Archduke Ferdinand concerning the income from salt production. From Braunau he sent two letters to the prior of St Peter's, Chilian Pütricher, telling him about his illness and the difficulties with the salt business. Staupitz wrote that he did not feel well and that it was impossible for him to return to Salzburg by the expected date. He explained that he was in the care of Dr Georg Obsinger (or Hobsinger), who had been the personal physician of Archbishop Keutschach at Salzburg (now apparently living at Braunau), and that he took medication daily. He signed both letters with 'your Brother Johannes, Abbot, Servant of Christ'.[180]

Hardly anything is known about Staupitz's personal life during the rest of that year, or about his final days around Christmas 1524. However, we do know that in July and August 1524 he was in Bad Reichenhall, Bavaria, about 15 miles south of the city of Salzburg and within the archdiocese. There he received a letter, dated 5 August, from Prior Chilian. From this letter we learn that Staupitz's biblical scholarship and Scripture interpretation was greatly appreciated by St Peter's monks. Father Chilian wished for his speedy return to Salzburg 'so that we are no longer deprived of the consolation of your paternity's interpretation of the Scriptures'. In this same letter, he informed Staupitz of violent acts by those that are called 'Lutherans' against a Carthusian

---

[178] Ibid., p. 454; see Zumkeller, *Heilslehre*, p. 168.

[179] Kolde, *Die deutsche Augustiner-Congregation*, p. 456.

[180] Letters to Chilian Pütricher of 14 and 15 April 1524; in ibid., p. 448f. These letters are dated shortly after his last letter to Luther of 1 April 1524. See also ibid., p. 351; Bonorand, *Joachim Vadian*, p. 88; Sallaberger, 'Johann von Staupitz, Luthers Vorgesetzter', p. 152. On Obsinger, see Bonorand, *Joachim Vadian*, pp. 59 and 84.

monastery (probably the one at Ittingen/Thurgau) which was burned.[181]
Prior Chilian must have become a close friend of Staupitz, as he was
familiar with Staupitz's writings which he sent in the year 1524 to the
young humanist at Vienna, Georg Sayler (or Sailer).[182]

During one of the many trips with which he still loved to indulge his
wanderlust, Staupitz died in Bad Reichenhall on 28 December 1524.
Within the city Bad Reichenhall was a *terminus* of the Augustinians
which was connected to the Munich friary, so it is possible that Abbot
Staupitz was in town to refresh his connections to the Augustinians.
Alternatively, he may have been there to visit the city's spa for health
reasons. Or, he might have been on business for the Archdiocese of
Salzburg or he could have been trying to meet the priest John Pfäffinger
(1493–1573), who had been assigned to Bad Reichenhall.[183] A further
possibility is that Staupitz was on his way to the residence of the
Pfäffinger family near Pfaffing in Bavaria, a region which appeared to be
untouched by the Peasants' War, and thus would have been preferable to
Salzburg which seems to have been a focus for attack. We do not know
the precise reasons for his sojourn at Bad Reichenhall, but evidently he
had to, or wanted to, get out of Salzburg. Ludwig Keller (1885) was of
the opinion that Staupitz left his abbey in spring 1524 without officially
resigning from the abbacy, and never returned, supposing him to have
stopped preaching and settled at one of the cloister's possessions in
the Inn Valley.[184] Keller's opinion cannot be proven or disproven from
the available sources. However, it would not be too far-fetched to assume
that Staupitz thought it desirable to seek safer surroundings in the
neighbourhood of friends such as the Pfäffingers in Bavaria, given the

---

[181] 'Fertur Helvetia iurgiis variis inter se extorqueri et hos quos vocant Lutheranos
exussisse monasterium quoddam Carthusiensium. ... ne amplius in exilii miseriam
detrudamur et P[aternitatis] V[estrae] scripturarum interpretationis solatio destituamur'
(Kolde, *Die deutsche Augustiner-Congregation*, pp. 350f., n. 4), see also Paulus, 'Johann
von Staupitz. Seine vorgeblich protestantischen Gesinnungen', p. 336. For the identification
of the Carthusian monastery, see Bonorand, *Joachim Vadian*, p. 88.

[182] See A. Horawitz, 'Zur Geschichte des Humanismus in den Alpenländern',
Sitzungsberichte der philosophisch-historischen Classe der Akademie der Wissenschaften,
Band 114 (1887), II, pp. 386 and 388–91, as referred to by Bonorand, *Joachim Vadian*,
pp. 86 and 88.

[183] See E.W. Zeeden, 'Johann Pfeffinger', in *Lexikon für Theologie und Kirche*
(Freiburg, 1962), VIII, p. 416; B. Steimer, 'Pfeffinger, Johannes', in K. Ganzer and
B. Steimer (eds), *Lexikon der Reformationszeit* (Freiburg, 2002), col. 581. John left for
Wittenberg in 1523 and became a 'Lutheran'.

[184] See L. Keller, 'Johannes von Staupitz und das Waldenserthum', *Historisches
Taschenbuch*, 6 (1885), pp. 115–67 (p. 121); R. Wetzel, 'Staupitz und Luther. Annäherung
an eine Vorläufer-Figur', *Blätter für Pfälzische Kirchengeschichte und Religiöse
Volkskunde*, 58 (1991), pp. 369–95 (p. 395). Berndt Hamm assumes that Staupitz died
at his monastery in Salzburg ('Johann von Staupitz', *ARG*, **92** (2001), p. 15, n. 27.

social unrest that was beginning to spread, and the change of attitude toward the reformers that he saw looming.

Tidings of Staupitz's death undoubtedly came to Wittenberg at once, because as early as 23 January 1525 Luther shared the news with Staupitz's nephew, Nicholas von Amsdorf: 'Staupitz is gone from the living, after having suffered briefly under a dictatorship.'[185] Luther meant the conditions at Salzburg under Cardinal Lang as he imagined them.

---

[185] 'Staupitius excessit e vivis brevi functus potentatu' (*WABR* 3. 428, 5 (no. 821)).

CHAPTER SEVEN

The 'Golden Treatise':
Testament and Remembrance

The immediate historical context

Cardinal Matthew Lang, Prince-Bishop of Salzburg, had placed a heavy tax on the citizens of his territory in order to recoup the high assessment that he had to pay to the empire for its defence against the Turks. The higher clergy and the upper class refused to pay their contributions and therefore the city of Salzburg also refused. This conflict became known as the 'Latin War' between Cardinal Lang and the city of Salzburg. Only Bishop Pürstinger and Abbot Staupitz were willing to pay their shares. In June 1523 an uprising began among the people of Salzburg when no less than 1500 men, including 'priests, students, and sacristans', gathered with the intent 'to storm and plunder' (*zu stürmen und plündern*). Lang, who was out of town, called upon Archduke Ferdinand for help; he provided about 1000 soldiers. With them Cardinal Lang approached the city of Salzburg from the south and a military confrontation seemed imminent. In this situation, the two prelates, Staupitz and Pürstinger, stepped in as negotiators on behalf of the city, which was willing to give in. On 11 July 1523 the prince-bishop entered Salzburg with some hundred foot-soldiers. A bloody confrontation had been avoided. On 16 July 1523 the city had to recognize Lang as its lord with all his demands. An agreement was drawn up and signed, by Staupitz and Pürstinger among others. It included a tax on beer; however, Lang was willing to limit this tax to ten years.[1]

Staupitz died in December 1524, shortly before any major upheavals of another war, the 'Peasants' War' of 1524/25, reached the Salzburg region. Peasants' revolts had been erupting locally and intermittently for some time since 1491. Now a wave of unrest had begun to sweep across upper Germany into Austria (Salzburg, Tyrol and Carinthia), Alsace and Franconia, even reaching distant Thuringia and Saxony. According to certain reports, during the last year of Staupitz's life, in the hay-making season of summer 1524, a new outbreak arose far to the west of Salzburg when, on the Feast Day of St John the Baptist (24 June), the countess of

---

[1] See J. Sallaberger, *Kardinal Matthäus Lang von Wellenburg (1468–1540)* (Salzburg, 1997), pp. 282–5.

Lupfen, Helena of Rappoltstein, had ordered the peasants of her region around Stühlingen (outer Austria, west of Schaffhausen near the Swiss–German border) to collect snail shells for use in textile production. The peasants refused; they roamed about Lake Constance and the southern Black Forest, banded together, and on 14 December 1524, entered their first military confrontation at Donaueschingen, near the headwaters of the Danube River. Here 200 peasants were defeated and forced to flee. In their flight they sacked many castles and cloisters, their anticlericalism leading them to treat any monasteries, property-owning cathedral chapters and parsonages as prime targets. The revolt spread from the southern Black Forest eastwards, into other Hapsburg territories and reached the Benedictine monastery of Ochsenhausen (north of Memmingen, south of Ulm) and the territory of the influential prince-abbot of Kempten. The abbots of Kempten were infamous for their exploitation of the people; those unfortunate subjects of the Ochsen-hausen monastery complained that they were 'sold like cows and calves, although we have only one Lord' (Christ). By the time of Staupitz's death, the rebel bands had come close to the imperial cities of Memmingen and Augsburg; they reached them by the beginning of 1525. By April 1525 Innsbruck was under threat and by June Salzburg had been seized. One wonders how much information Staupitz had gathered concerning the rebels' intentions and actions. We know that Salzburg's citizens opened the city gates to the rebels, and Archbishop Lang had to take refuge in his castle-fortress high above Salzburg. The rebels demanded control of the city; rulers such as the archbishop of Salzburg were to be deprived of all power. The clerical government of Salzburg (and of other cities such as Würzburg or Bamberg) was to be staffed by members of the secular estates of nobles, burghers and peasants; clergymen were to be excluded. Regional representatives were to be elected and all authority except that of the emperor was to be abolished. Such were the specific demands in the Alpine lands of Salzburg and Tyrol, and in the Upper Rhine and Upper Swabia regions. At one point the people in the *Landschaft* (region) around Salzburg wanted to replace Cardinal Matthew Lang with a secular prince from neighbouring Bavaria and thereby to secularize the archbishopric. Archduke Ferdinand of Austria sought assistance from the Swabian League on 28 October 1524, in order to be able to deal with the peasants and the miners who had joined them. By May or June 1525, the rebels drew up their *Twenty-four Articles of the Common Territory of Salzburg*, in which they expressed their anticlericalism and arguments for their resistence against injustice – making their case on the basis of the gospel. The two-week siege of Salzburg led to a settlement with the rebels in early September 1525. Archbishop Lang was rescued by the troops of the Swabian League, but his residence was pillaged and the rebels extorted large sums of money from Salzburg's rich monasteries, both St Peter's and Nonnberg. Staupitz was spared this experience, as he was no longer alive. Possibly anticipation of such troubles had prompted his departure from Salzburg in 1524, leading him to seek safer surroundings outside the immediate vicinity of Salzburg and closer to Bavarian lands which remained untouched by the war. The Peasants' War turned out to be one of the greatest uprisings in European history and has been compared to the French and Russian Revolutions.[2]

This social unrest threatened monasteries and friaries alike, nor did the rebels distinguish between reformed and conventual cloisters. Perhaps the known stability of the Benedictine monasteries had contributed to Staupitz's original desire to depart from the restless life of a mendicant friar and to seek personal safety and economic security at a rich abbey such as St Peter's in Salzburg. After all, at the time he had been more than 50 years old. This idea of an eventual retirement in a contemplative monastery is not too far-fetched. We know, for example, that the Carthusian monastery at Nuremberg was the preferred cloister for older gentlemen from the upper classes to conclude their lives in religious surroundings.[3] Usually such men did not choose a friary of the mendicant orders, but specifically, in this case, the local Carthusian

---

[2] See the translations of documents such as 'The Austrian Government's View of the Situation in Autumn 1524: The Address of the Austrian Commissioners to the Assembly of the Swabian League in Ulm, 28 October 1524', 'Preamble to the Twenty-four Articles of the Common Territory of Salzburg, May–June 1525', and the 'Grievances of the Subjects of the Abbey of Kempten and the Reply of the Prince-Abbot, Sebastian von Breitenstein, to the Same, Presented at the Diet at Obergünzburg, January 1525', in T. Scott and B. Scribner (eds), *The German Peasants' War. A History in Documents* (Atlantic Highlands, NJ, and London, 1991), pp. 73–8; 105f.; 149f. K.-H. Ludwig, 'Miners, Pastors and the Peasant War in Upper Austria 1524–26', in J.M. Bak and G. Benecke (eds), *Religion and Rural Revolt. Papers Presented to the Fourth Interdisciplinary Workshop on Peasant Studies, University of British Columbia, 1982* (Manchester/Dover, NH, 1984), pp. 154–60. E.W. Zeeden, 'Salzburg', in A. Schindling and W. Ziegler (eds), *Die Territorien des Reichs im Zeitalter der Reformation und Konfessionalisierung. Land und Konfession 1500–1650, vol. 1: Der Südosten* (Münster, 1989), p. 77. On the origins of the Peasants' War, see W. Stolze, 'Die Stühlinger Erhebung des Jahres 1524 und ihre Gründe', *Historische Zeitschrift*, **139** (1929), pp. 273–302; R. Kolb, 'The Theologians and the Peasants: Conservative Evangelical Reactions to the German Peasants' Revolt', *ARG*, **69** (1978), pp. 103–31; B. Scribner and G. Benecke (eds), *The German Peasant War of 1525: New Viewpoints* (London, 1979), esp. H. Buszello (pp. 109–22), and J. Bücking (pp. 160–73); on Kempten, see H. Grisar, *Martin Luther: His Life and Work* (adapted from the 2nd German edn by Frank J. Elbe, ed. Arthur Preuss (Westminster, MD, The Newman Press, 1953), p. 280; on Müntzer, see E.W. Gritsch, *A Tragedy of Errors: Thomas Müntzer* (Minneapolis, 1989); H. Junghans, 'Thomas Müntzer (1489–1989)', in *Martin Luther in Two Centuries* (St Paul, MN, 1992), pp. 45–68.

[3] See I. Höss, 'Das religiös-geistige Leben in Nürnberg am Ende des 15. und am Ausgang des 16. Jahrhunderts' *Miscellanea Historiae Ecclesiasticae*, **2** (1967), p. 23.

monastery. That Staupitz should conclude his career at a Benedictine abbey such as the one at Salzburg fits squarely into this pattern. However, the times were changing, as the abbeys, formerly sound and strong in economic terms, came under attack from the peasants who fought for independence and freedom from exploitation.

Meanwhile, the dissolution of the Augustinian Reform Congregation was well under way. As the successor of Andreas Proles, Staupitz had led the reformed Augustinians north of the Alps. He was encouraged by Egidio da Viterbo, the most famous and learned general of the Order. Under his leadership, the Order had comprised 20 000 friars in 1000 friaries, organized into 26 provinces (four provinces for the German lands).[4] Staupitz, as the vicar of the Reformed Congregation, had played a decisive role in this Order. The observant movement among the Augustinians had spread to the Low Countries where, from 1437, a reformed congregation, called 'Vicarians', had comprised important Augustinian friaries under their own vicar. In 1493 a reform-minded group of Saxon Augustinians had founded the Haarlem friary. In 1513/14 the new friary of Antwerp had joined the reformed friaries and had received special attention from Staupitz during its period of formation. In the Low Countries the ground was well prepared for reform, not least because of the impact of Staupitz and like-minded reformers within the Order. Their reform efforts became known to the humanist Erasmus of Rotterdam who, in 1519, observed that 'in Antwerp there is a prior [Jacob Probst, d. 1562], in the friary, a genuine Christian with nothing false about him, who glows with love for you [Luther], ... He is virtually the only one who preaches Christ.'[5]

When the artist Albrecht Dürer lived in Antwerp in 1520/21, he liked to visit the Augustinians, as he also did in Nuremberg, especially when Staupitz was in town. Dürer (like Erasmus) held Prior Probst in high esteem; he even painted a portrait of him. Probst had studied at Wittenberg; the close contacts between the Augustinians of the Low Countries and the University of Wittenberg, which Staupitz had initiated, accelerated the spread of the reforms in that region. In general, from among the more than 100 Augustinians whom Staupitz had drawn to the University of Wittenberg during his term as vicar of the Order, a rich crop soon came out on Luther's side.

As fast as the Reformation movement gained ground, the counter-action from the papal and imperial camp matched it, in those areas

---

[4] See F.X. Martin, 'The Augustinian Order on the Eve of the Reformation', *Miscellanea historiae ecclesiasticae. Bibliothèque de la Revue d'histoire ecclesiastique*, **44** (Louvain, 1967), II, pp. 73–7.

[5] See H. Bornkamm, *Luther in Mid-Career 1521–1530*, ed. K. Bornkamm, trans. E.T. Bachmann (Philadelphia, 1983), pp. 100–103.

wherever the Edict of Worms was enforced. In January 1523, the Augustinian friary at Antwerp, known for its reformers, was actually levelled; only the church remained. This happened while Staupitz was still alive. Some of the reform-minded Augustinians from Staupitz's fold in the Low Countries were persecuted, including Friar Jacob Probst; while others were executed as heretics, including Friar John van den Essen (1494–1523) and Friar Johan Voss (d. 1523) in Brussels, and Friar Henry van Zutphen (1488–1524) in Meldorf in northern Germany.[6]

Staupitz may have seen the writing on the wall for his mendicant friars. There were certainly omens aplenty which he must have read. For example, by 1521 the friary of Wittenberg had lost 15 of its 41 friars, and in 1523 Luther was the only one left there.[7] The Augustinian friary at Grimma was deserted when its prior and several of his subordinates left the Order in 1522, the same year that Staupitz joined the Benedictines. In the south-west, around the same time, Staupitz's friend, Friar John Mantel, got into trouble in Stuttgart for his reformation preaching and was imprisoned for a while. Also in 1522, Friar John Lang, whom Staupitz had once asked to portray the Order favourably to the humanists in Nuremberg, left the Order. Then in 1523 the new friary at Eisleben, which Staupitz had helped to build, dissolved. However, its former prior, Caspar Güttel, who had esteemed Staupitz so highly, remained as a preacher in the city.[8]

The friaries in France at Toulouse, Narbonne, Bourges and Paris (where Staupitz had planned to send Luther in 1519 after his interrogation by Cajetan at Augsburg) had the reputation of being centres of heresy.[9] In Paris, the Augustinian Jean Vallière was burned at the stake in August 1523.[10] Luther might well have suffered the same fate, had he heeded Staupitz's well-meant advice to take refuge there. At Metz, the Augustinian Jean Chatelain died at the stake in 1524, and in the same year the Augustinian Friar Caspar Tauber suffered the same

---

[6] See O. Clemen, 'Das Antwerper Augustiner-Kloster bei Beginn der Reformation (1513–1523)', in *Kleine* Schriften, I, pp. 434–41; M. Gielis, 'Augustijnergeloof en Predikherengeloof: Het conflict tussen de reformatorische verkondiging van de Antwerpse augustijnen en de scholastieke leer van de Leuvense theologen (ca. 1520)', *Luther-Bulletin. Tijdschrift voor interconfessioneel Lutheronderzoek*, 6 (1997), pp. 46–57.

[7] See W. Ziegler, 'Reformation und Klosterauflösung. Ein ordensgeschichtlicher Vergleich' in K. Elm (ed.), *Reformbemühungen und Observanzbestrebungen im spätmittelalterlichen Ordenswesen* (Berlin, 1989), pp. 585–614 (hereafter referred to as: Ziegler, 'Reformation und Klosterauflösung').

[8] See Stupperich, pp. 93, 127 and 138.

[9] See Martin, 'The Augustinian Order on the Eve', pp. 73–7.

[10] On Jean Vallière as a Lutheran martyr, see A. Greiner, 'Martin Luther in Frankreich' *Luther*, 56 (1985), p. 71.

fate in Vienna.[11] We do not know whether Staupitz, as an abbot in Salzburg, was kept informed about the fate of the friars who were persecuted and who died for their convictions. It is conspicuous that no Augustinians were executed for their reform efforts in regions where Staupitz was able to make his expertise and influence felt.

However, not only the Order of the Augustinians was in turmoil. Nunneries were in uproar, too, as the sisters began to read anti-monastic writings. Sixteen Augustinian nuns escaped from their convent at Widerstedt near Mansfeld in June 1523. One of them became the wife of the ex-priest and peasants' leader, Thomas Müntzer. Staupitz's own sister, Magdalene, together with several other Cistercian nuns, fled from their cloister at Nimbschen, near Grimma in Saxony, with Luther's help, during Holy Saturday Night, on 4 April 1523. They had turned to him after their families refused to take them back. Luther found a reliable man from Torgau, who was ready to risk this abduction which carried the death penalty. This man, a relation of Nicholas von Amsdorf and thus distantly related to the Staupitz family, regularly delivered fish and beer in barrels, and other goods to the nuns in Nimbschen. At nightfall he loaded the nuns into the barrels and smuggled them out of their convent. A witty Austrian student, Wolfgang Schiefer, described the situation in a letter to Beatus Rhenanus on 4 May: 'Several days ago a wagon arrived here with a load of vestal virgins, as they are now called. They would like to marry as much as to stay alive. May God provide them with husbands so that in the course of time they won't run into greater need!' Staupitz's sister, who was a teacher at the convent, was recommended as a potential bride for Father Spalatin at the Elector's court, a friend of Staupitz and Luther. Among these Cistercian nuns was also Katharina von Bora, who became Luther's wife in June 1525.[12] We do not know anything of Staupitz's reactions to his sister's flight from the cloister. He was spared from learning of Luther's marriage since he died at the end of 1524, six months before it took place. As a family man, Luther continued to live in the friary building at Wittenberg with his wife and children until his death in 1546.[13]

Staupitz was also spared the dissolution of the Erfurt friary during the anticlerical upheaval in 1525. On July 31 of that year, Erfurt's last Augustinian prior, Adam Horn, received permission from his superior in

---

[11] See Martin, 'The Augustinian Order on the Eve', p. 72; on Caspar Tauber, see Grisar, *Martin Luther*, p. 338.

[12] See Luther's letter to Linck of 8 April, and to Spalatin of 10 April 1523 (*WABR* 3. 53f. (nos. 599, 600)); Grisar, *Martin Luther*, p. 234; Bornkamm, *Luther in Mid-Career*, p. 258f. On Katharina von Bora, see R.K. Markwald and M.M. Markwald, *Katharina von Bora* (St Louis, MO, 2002).

[13] See Bornkamm, *Luther in Mid-Career*, pp. 401–8.

the Order, the Vicar General Johann Bethel von Spangenberg (who was elected in September 1523, succeeding Linck), to abandon the friary, since he himself was no longer safe in it.[14] The Nuremberg friary, too, ceased to exist when the friars dissolved their cloister in 1524 and joined the Reformation. In 1525, the Nuremberg city government formally introduced the Reformation. Most friars had left the Order already; however, Friar Besler, Staupitz's long-time travel companion on visitation journeys and prior of the Nuremberg friary, did not join the reformers and was forced to leave the cloister and the city. Charitas Pirckheimer, that celebrated daughter of Nuremberg and sister of the great humanist Willibald, commented in her memoirs that 'the Augustinians were the beginning of all our misfortunes',[15] in effect blaming Staupitz's reform-minded Order for the Reformation in Nuremberg.

The Swabian friary at Tübingen, where Staupitz had begun his promising career as a preacher, did not receive the necessary support from the local rulers to ensure its survival. In 1520 the friary struggled to pay the bills for the remodelling of its buildings. By 1528, four years after Staupitz's death, the first evangelical sermons were heard there, delivered by Matias Remherr, an otherwise unknown friar; he was, however, chased away from Tübingen and later married. Moral and liturgical decadence had crept into the friary by 1530; by that point Masses were no longer celebrated. Clearly, the people of Tübingen no longer had any interest in retaining the Augustinian friary in their midst. By 1534, ten years after Staupitz's death, the friary was completely dissolved.[16] Other Augustinian cloisters, such as the one at Memmingen, where the 'Memmingen Bull' was promulgated, existed until 1538,[17] but, by about 1540, Staupitz's entire Reformed Congregation in Germany seems to have disappeared.[18]

---

[14] On the Erfurt friary, see O. Clemen, 'Miscellen zur Reformationsgeschichte', in *Kleine Schriften*, I, pp. 210–13; Clemen corrected Kolde who had thought that the Erfurt friary was already deserted by the time Spangenberg took office in 1523; the friary had friars until 1525.

[15] See F. Machilek, 'Klosterhumanismus in Nürnberg um 1500', *Mitteilungen des Vereins für Geschichte der Stadt Nürnberg*, **64** (1977), pp. 10–45, p. 33; A. Schindling, 'Nürnberg', in A. Schindling and W. Ziegler, *Die Territorien des Reichs*, pp. 36–7; G. Pfeiffer and W. Schwemmer (eds), *Geschichte Nürnbergs in Bilddokumenten* (Munich, 1970), p. 39; for C. Pirckheimer's memoirs, see G. Strauss, *Nuremberg in the Sixteenth Century* (Bloomington, IN, and London, 1976), p. 177.

[16] On the end of the Tübingen friary, see M. Brecht, 'Das Augustiner-Eremiten-Kloster zu Tübingen', in *Mittelalterliches Erbe* (Tübingen, 1962), pp. 85–9.

[17] See Ziegler, 'Reformation und Klosterauflösung'.

[18] See Kunzelmann; his three final chapters of vol. V cover the history of the German Augustinian friars and the dissolution of the Reform Congregation in Germany (1520–40).

The more legal protection a city or a noble family provided for a friary within its walls or under its patronage, the longer such a friary could survive. However, because the Augustinian friaries were not very well secured in this regard as a result of their constant reorganization and reform, they did not survive. Staupitz's good connections with the ruling class could not prevent these developments, especially once he had resigned from the Order. In addition, his resignation left a void among the Augustinians. Thus, the major factor in the disintegration was not so much the lack of theological clarity, but the juridical instability of the institutions as such, combined with the lack of committed leadership. The friaries' juridical foundations were weakened by their operating principle which relied on secular government (*Obrigkeit*), whose protection for the mendicant Orders began to fade away.[19] This decline took place to the same degree and at the same speed as previous reforms in the friaries had blossomed following invitations from local governments to reform those same friaries. Furthermore, the basis of their economy was eliminated when the friars were no longer welcome to preach and collect donations at any of their *terminus* locations.

While Staupitz's position as friar (and later as monk and abbot) meant that he did not or could not bequeath any physical-material inheritance to following generations, he left behind a 'personnel legacy' in the form of a mobile troop of men, friars and ex-friars, ready to preach the gospel to the world. Moreover, he handed down a spiritual testament concerning the Christian faith, something more precious than any well-oiled organization or network of reformed friars. Most significantly, Staupitz fathered a spiritual son in Martin Luther, whom he tried to protect as much as he could from attacks by the pope and others, such as the rival Dominican friars; although ultimately even Staupitz could not prevent Luther's excommunication and banning.

At Salzburg, the situation was different, at first. Staupitz had been able to save the life of Friar Stephan Agricola in the summer of 1524 by arguing wisely in his defence (see pp. 312–19). Agricola ended up at Nuremberg where the former friar and Staupitz's successor as vicar, Wenceslaus Linck took him in. Linck had become preacher at St Sebaldus at Nuremberg in April 1525, where he stayed for more than two decades until his death in 1547.[20] Linck, Luther and Staupitz had been close friends in the Order and remained so afterwards. When Luther was reminiscing in 1540, he said: 'When I wrote for the first time against

---

[19] See Ziegler, 'Reformation und Klosterauflösung'.

[20] See J. Lorz, *Das reformatorische Wirken Dr. Wenceslaus Lincks in Altenburg und Nürnberg (1523–1547)* (Nuremberg, 1978); Stupperich, pp. 132f.

Mass and Canon, I could not believe that anyone would agree with me. I had written it for myself, Staupitz, and Wenceslaus [Linck].'[21]

At Salzburg in the early 1520s, the spread of Lutheran ideas and possible action against them were discussed at the court of Cardinal Lang, and counter-measures began to take shape from the summer of 1523 in the form of visitations to local communities, similar to the well-known Lutheran visitations made in Saxony but with the opposite goal. We do not know what exact position Staupitz took, or what part he played during these discussions at the court. However, his role in the execution of some of the ten decrees of the bishops' conference that took place at Regensburg in the summer of 1524 (see pp. 321–5) is known. The first two decrees of this 'Regensburg Reformation' declared that the traditional Catholic faith was to be kept and the Edict of Worms was to be observed. Preachers and their sermonizing were to be strictly supervised. Staupitz, Pürstinger and one Herr Stephan (perhaps another learned councillor) were to design a *forma praedicandi*[22] – presumably a 'model for preaching' that the clergy had to follow. However, it is not known what this document looked like or what exactly it contained, or even if it was ever drafted. Some of the other decisions at Regensburg included the prohibition of marriage for secular priests and religious order priests; the requirement that anything to be printed must first be submitted for approval; the prohibition of the printing, purchase and sale, or any other distribution, of Lutheran writings; and the termination of any pursuit of studies at Wittenberg. It was in these circumstances that Staupitz's theological testament, to which we now turn our attention, came into existence.

'On the Holy Right Christian Faith'

It was the ex-friar Linck who created a literary memorial to his fatherly friend Staupitz by posthumously editing Staupitz's manuscript 'On the Holy Right Christian Faith'. Written in the vernacular, it was first printed in 1525 in Nuremberg by Jobst Gutknecht's press, then in Augsburg by Heinrich Steiner (who in 1523 had printed the sermon on dying by the persecuted friar, Stephan Agricola; pp. 312–19 above); and then, 20 years

---

[21] 'Cum ego primum scriberem contra missam et canonem, non potui credere quemquem mihi oboedire posse; mihi scripsi et Staupitzio et Vinceslao [Wenceslaus Linck]' (*WATR* 4. 606, 28f. (no. 4998)). Here Luther referred to the 1520s when he began to criticize the Mass practices; he wanted to make the point that Staupitz and Linck were his confidants.

[22] See Sallaberger, *Kardinal*, p. 312 (and p. 304 for the list of decrees); see also pp. 286, 290–317.

later, again in Nuremberg by Christoph Gutknecht in 1545.[23] Strangely, this book was not very well received by Luther who, on 7 February 1525, wrote to Linck as the prospective editor, that he returned the manuscript, and that it might be printed, but he (Luther) did not really like it. It is 'dull, as [Staupitz] always was, and of little passion. Do what you want with it. It is a book not unworthy of the light and of the public.'[24] What exactly Luther disliked is difficult to grasp. His review seems to have had more to do with style than content. If Staupitz had written something contrary to any Reformation theological positions, Luther would surely and vehemently have objected to its publication; yet he explicitly said that it was worthy of seeing the light of day. Luther evidently did not perceive this book to be at odds with any of his own opinions. Therefore, it is highly debatable whether Staupitz's last work was meant as a correction of the Lutheran theological concept of 'faith alone'. Perhaps it was a criticism of a misunderstood concept of faith of Lutheran epigones.[25] Another reason for Luther's reservations may have been the fact that Staupitz had signed off as a monastic author: 'Doctor Johannes Staubitz Abte zu sant Peter zu Salzburg.'

With this booklet we have Staupitz's spiritual testament on the right Christian concept of 'faith' in which he teaches the essential unity of faith and good works.[26] In his preface, Staupitz deplored that among

---

[23] *Von dem heyligen rechten Christlichen glauben. Johannes Staubitz Nach seinem abschayden an tag kumen vnd außgangen* (Nuremberg: Jobst Gutknecht, 1525); see J. Lorz (ed.), *Bibliographia Linckiana* (Nieuwkoop, 1977), p. 67. The Augsburg edition of 1525 by Steiner has the book title as: *Von dem hailigen rechtn Christennlichenn Glawben: Johanes Staubitz Nach seinem abschaydan an tag kumen vnnd außgangenn*. The 1545 edition has the first words transposed, as 'Right Holy Christian Faith' (*Vom rechten heyligen Christlichem glaube. Johannes Staubitz*). His family name was consistently spelled with 'b', as in *Staubitz*. The booklet was re-edited by Johann Arndt together with Staupitz's *Von der lieb gottes* in 1605; the combined volume was reprinted 30 times in the seventeenth and eighteenth centuries, including two Latin editions (1624 and 1706).

[24] 'Remitto Staupitium; frigidulis est, sicut semper fuit, et parum vehemens. Fac, quod libet; indignus non est luce et publico libellus' (*WABR* 3. 437, 8f. (no. 827)). Another of Luther's rare criticisms of Staupitz lumped him together with other learned men whose preaching was not very popular: 'Osiander, Mathesius, et Doctor Staupitius, vir doctissimus, talis erat odiosus contionator, et populus libentius audivit simplicem fratrem' (*WATR* 5. 644, 27f. (no. 6404, n.d.)).

[25] See N. Paulus, 'Johann Staupitz. Seine vorgeblich protestantischen Gesinnungen', *Historisches Jahrbuch*, 12 (1891), pp. 309–46. One may question the assumption made by D.C. Steinmetz that Staupitz wrote his booklet as 'his reply to Luther' (Staupitz', in H.J. Hillerbrand (ed.) *The Oxford Encyclopedia of the Reformation*, 4 vols (New York and Oxford, 19–), IV, p. 111).

[26] The concluding line about Abbot Staupitz is found in Print A of 1525; see Zumkeller, *Heilslehre*, p. 159, n. 1024. On Luther's teaching on the unity of faith and good works see his 1520 treatise *Von der Freyheyt eyniss Christen menschen* (The Freedom of a Christian), *WA* 7. 29, 31–34, 22. On a recent interpretation of Luther's treatise in relation to the

Christians who lived after the death of all the apostles there was so much ignorance concerning the faith without which no one is saved. Faith in Christ is the foundation of all that is good, the root of all virtue and the sole consolation of the elect.[27] Staupitz covered the following themes in 13 chapters: the duty to believe; the duty to believe in Christ; the promise of the blessing; the promise of illuminating the Christians; the assurance/certainty of eternal predestination; the freeing from sins; the freeing from damnable sins; the amount of merits; the certain fulfilment of prayers; the indissoluble union with Christ; the error of nominal Christians; the orderly infusion of the divine gifts; and Christian works.

In the opening pages, Staupitz emphasized that faith in God's promise and mercy is the only thing that is expected of a human being; there is no other consolation. This faith is the justifying faith which makes us children of God, and which takes away the anger of God. It is a saving faith, without the works of the law. Only the subsequent works that come from this faith are not in vain.[28] The last three chapters (Chapters 11 to 13) were written because Staupitz was urged by his friends (*familiares*) to do so. We do not know who they were, nor what their motivation was. Perhaps they were from his Augustinian 'family' of former confrères, since a former Augustinian became its editor.[29]

Staupitz had this to say to them: the devil works hard to form a 'stupid faith' in people's minds, a faith which is separate from the 'evangelical life', as if it were possible to have true faith without the gospel. True faith cannot be separated from good works. Discipleship in following Christ demands that one emulates him in suffering and in doing good works. The fools say: whoever believes in Christ does not need any works.[30] Luther expressed the same Staupitzian view in *The Freedom of*

---

earlier spiritual tradition, see R. Schwarz, 'Die Umformung des religiösen Prinzips der Gottesliebe in der frühen Reformation. Ein Beitrag zum Verständnis von Luthers Schrift "Von der Freiheit eines Christenmenschen"', in S.E. Buckwalter and B. Moeller (eds), *Die frühe Reformation in Deutschland als Umbruch. Wissenschaftliches Symposion des Vereins für Reformationsgeschichte 1996* (Gütersloh, 1998), pp. 128–48.

[27] I rely on Alfred Jeremias's modern German quotations and paraphrases, *Johann von Staupitz: Luthers Vater und Schüler. Sein Leben, sein Verhältnis zu Luther und eine Auswahl aus seinen Schriften* (Sannerz and Leipzig, 1926), pp. 292–9 (p. 292 for the preface); and also on a German version of 1862 (hereafter quoted as 'Edition (1862)'; here p. 63. Staupitz's preface is summarized also in T. Kolde, *Die deutsche Augustiner-Congregation und Johann von Staupitz* (Gotha, 1879), p. 346.

[28] See Edition (1862), pp. 65–82; Jeremias, *Johann von Staupitz*, p. 293.

[29] See Edition (1862), p. 82; Jeremias, *Johann von Staupitz*, pp. 293–4; see the Introduction to the critical edition of the *Libellus*, p. 9 with n. 34.

[30] See Edition (1862), p. 83; Jeremias, *Johann von Staupitz*, p. 294. Also paraphrased by A. Zumkeller, 'Das Ungenügen der menschlichen Werke bei den deutschen Predigern des Spätmittelalters', *Zeitschrift für Katholische Theologie*, 81 (1959), pp. 265–302. Staupitz is included among the significant German preachers who emphasized the insufficiency of

a Christian (Von der Freyheyt eyniss Christen menschen), where he had the 'wicked men' (Staupitz's 'stupid' ones) speak in the very same way about works. Luther said to them: 'Not so, you wicked men, not so.'[31]

Staupitz supported his statement with references to Matthew 11 and 19, John 12 and 14, and Psalm 14, saying that he who loves God indeed does what God commands. The Ten Commandments must be fulfilled in an 'evangelical' way so that they are fruits of faith. However, the evil spirit insinuates into the ears of carnal Christians that one may be justified without works – referring to Paul who allegedly had preached exactly that. Staupitz clarified: Paul indeed disputed against the works of the law when done in fear and without love. If they are done out of love for God, Paul did not criticize them, since he thought of them as necessary for salvation. Christ wants the fulfilment of the law (Matt. 5), and Paul, too, praised the Law, while the fools call it evil, because they do not have the taste of the Spirit (Rom. 8).[32]

The first divine gift which we call 'faith' comprises three things: (1) not to doubt God's love for the sinner; (2) salvation is by the Son of God alone; (3) to firmly believe that the Holy Spirit reigns in us. This is the correct faith and the first among the gifts. This gift needs to be planted by God into our hearts. No craft, nor experience, nor reasoning, nor work can do the job. Such faith is followed by love which is the second gift of God. This love enflames us to love God. It is ignited through the divine Word and the Holy Spirit. God so loved us that he sent his Son to die for us. He is our saviour (*Seligmacher*). The Holy Spirit creates love in return, a love so hot that it melts the soul like wax. The third gift is hope which is the indefatigable trust that no devil nor hell can overcome. These three gifts (which are the theological 'virtues' in traditional language) are the best gifts, among which faith is first and feeds the others. Faith in the *Seligmacher* must be first in order that love can go to work. There are inner and outer good works, which do not always come together. The outer works are not without the inner (Rom. 6), while the inner may exist without the outer. In the inner 'good works' (faith, hope, love) one fulfils the first three of the Ten Commandments. From them follows that the person who believes in Christ certainly fulfils these first three commandments. When that person is ready to do everything that these three command, then the other commandments can also be obeyed, insofar as they are connected to the inner person. This occurs in love for one's neighbour. The willingness to do so is decisive, even if one

---

human works for salvation; he, his faith and his doctrine are recognized as being Catholic. Zumkeller follows N. Paulus's interpretation in this regard.

[31] Latin version: 'Non sic, impii, non sic' (*WA* 7. 59, 28); German version: 'Neyn, lieber mensch, nicht so' (*WA* 7. 30, 2f.).

[32] See Edition (1862), pp. 83f.; Jeremias, *Johann von Staupitz*, pp. 295f.

is unable to do the works externally. To perform the latter, one needs the special grace of God.[33]

Luther referred to Staupitz's spiritual testament/testimony in the context of his statement about Staupitz having inspired him to speak up against the papacy in connection with the indulgence controversy. According to that table talk of 1539, Luther praised Staupitz's genius and sincerity, since he, as a nobleman, was always of noble mind, and never slavish. Then Luther said: '... I hope everything good for him; his testimony gives witness to that'. Luther spoke here of Staupitz's *confessio* according to the Latin version of the table talk, and of *Bekenntnis* according to the vernacular version.[34] There is no doubt that Luther appreciated Staupitz's final spiritual testament because it revealed once more their spiritual and theological kinship.

Because of their theological agreement, the question has been raised whether Staupitz was Luther's disciple (as Staupitz called himself in one of his last letters to Luther). If Staupitz really meant to say that he had learnt something from Luther, it might be the concept which is found in Luther's tract *The Freedom of a Christian* of November 1520. In it, Luther made the distinction between the inner and outer man, saying that the liberty of the inner man stems from the righteousness of faith, while the outer man does good works. Staupitz cherished the same concept in his treatise, as shown above. Staupitz's dependence upon Luther in this regard rests on the assumption that he knew the content of Luther's tract (which is not unlikely), and further that Staupitz's text was written well after 1520 (which most likely it was). Luther had declared in his conclusion: 'Faith does good works .... We do not, therefore, reject good works.'[35]

What Staupitz may have learned from Luther is the use of the concept of the inner and outer man as applied to the teaching on justification by faith alone and its relationship to doing good works. However, this elaboration was not a totally new insight which Staupitz would have had to learn; rather, it was a concept that he may have developed by degrees from the premises of his own earlier theology. Regardless of how one answers the question as to who was dependent on whom on the issue of faith and good works, it is evident that both Staupitz and Luther taught the same doctrine: the inner man is justified by faith which is followed by good works, performed by the outer man. Staupitz's text 'On the Holy

---

[33] See Edition (1862), pp. 85–90; Jeremias, *Johann von Staupitz*, pp. 296–8.

[34] 'Deinde commendabat Staupitii ingenium et sinceritatem .... Quamvis bona de illo spero, sicut illius confessio testatur' (*WATR* 4. 440, 21–6 (no. 4708, 16 July 1539)); German version: 'Wiewohl ich Guts von ihm hoffe, wie sein Bekenntniß zeuget' (*WATR* 4. 441, 1–9 (no. 4708)).

[35] See *The Freedom of a Christian* (p. 346f. above).

Right Christian Faith' is the last theological statement we have from him. It is thus his definitive theological testament for all 'Evangelicals' – be they Lutheran Catholics or Roman Catholics.

The train of thought concerning faith and good works does not have any traits that appear forced, and does not suggest that Staupitz had unwillingly added certain clarifications. What is expressed here is thoroughly Staupitzian. When his friends asked him to write this clarification, Staupitz did just that: he explained his position without adding anything contrary to what he had taught previously. Therefore, it is not surprising that the second print of the book, from later in 1525, no longer needed the note that his *familiares* had urged him to write those passages. Here is the summary of his position:

> Christian works are those alone which flow from the Christian faith. They alone are good, for they alone and no other ones are born of God. Therefore, when Christ was asked which works were divine works, he said: 'This is the work of God: have faith in the One whom he sent' [John 6: 29] .... From faith flow love, hope, obedience, peace, chastity, mildness, truth, struggle against concupiscence. In them all good works are contained and commanded by God. In them all commandments are fulfilled. What is not contained in the mentioned works, God did not command, is not good, and does not flow from the right Christian faith. This is the reason why God declared faith to be the only good, divine work, since the other works become divine in faith and through the faith.[36]

Staupitz concluded his 'On the Holy Right Christian Faith' with these thoughts:

> Accept this instruction which is meant to lead you to the exercise and testing of yourself in the right Christian faith, with great eagerness. In this faith one finds salvation and grace, without it there is no salvation. I let the works be in their own worth, but I insist that outside the faith in Christ they bear no fruit and are often detrimental. Faith is advantageous for everyone, and to nobody's disadvantage. Faith lives and brings life, is never idle, but is always active until we reach eternal life and possess it. God help us. Amen. Jesus, I am yours, save me. Doctor Johannes Staupitz, Abbot of St Peter's at Salzburg.[37]

We do not know exactly when Staupitz wrote this booklet which Linck edited posthumously. By comparison, we realize that Staupitz's last known sermon, which was delivered during Advent 1523, had the same message as found in this booklet. In that last sermon he warned the nuns against devilish deceit in trusting in their external dress code. Instead they must

---

[36] See Edition (1862), pp. 90f.; Jeremias, *Johann von Staupitz*, p. 298.
[37] See Edition (1862), p. 91; Jeremias, *Johann von Staupitz*, p. 299.

have faith as the true foundation for salvation.[38] There is no opposition in Staupitz's spirituality and teaching between faith and works. 'Faith cannot be without fruit or work of love if it is a living faith.'[39]

In Memoriam Johann von Staupitz by Martin Luther

Staupitz's closest friends from the Order of St Augustine, Linck and Luther, kept his memory alive among their contemporaries. Linck did so by editing Staupitz's manuscript 'On the Holy Right Christian Faith'; while Luther preserved Staupitz's memory in his own ways by regularly reminding his friends at table, and his audience or readership, of the man who had been both his promoter and protector. He even recalled the early days when he had come to Wittenberg in 1508, and the year 1509 when he went to Rome 'because of Staupitz's contention', and the year 1512 when he received his doctoral degree.

More than five years after Staupitz's death, Luther had to spend the summer at the Coburg fortress, while his friends participated in the Diet of Augsburg in 1530 where they produced the famous *Augsburg Confession*. One summer day, on 27 July 1530, he must again have recalled the conversations with Staupitz, as he mentioned his name and one of his memorable sayings in two letters of that same date. Luther remembered him saying that 'whom God wants to blind, He closes his eyes first'. We do not know when Staupitz said this, or to whom besides Luther. It is remarkable, however, that Luther recalled it five years after Staupitz's death, and that he found it worthy of passing on to two of his best friends, Philipp Melanchthon and Johann Agricola.[40]

Luther recalled in 1531/32 Staupitz's confession that he had lied to God a thousand times by promising to keep the commandments, a promise he had finally given up. When in 1531 Luther preached on 'the law and the gospel' in connection with interpreting John 7, he was reminded of what he learned from Staupitz's own spirituality concerning the fulfilment of the law:

---

[38] See Sermon 24 (Kolde, *Die deutsche Augustiner-Congregation*, p. 452; Zumkeller, *Heilslehre*, pp. 109 and 156).

[39] See Sermon 24 (Kolde, *Die deutsche Augustiner-Congregation*, p. 453; Zumkeller, *Heilslehre*, p. 159; D.C. Steinmetz, *Misericodia Dei: The Theology of Johannes Staupitz in its Late Medieval Setting* (Leiden, 1968), p. 118.

[40] 'Anno octavo veni Wittenbergam, nono Romam profectus sum causa contentionis Staupitii, 12. promotus sum in doctoratum' (*WATR* 2. 613, 20f. (no. 2717, Cordatus' collection, autumn 1532)). 'Staupitius noster dicebat: Wen Gott blenden will, dem tut er zuvor die Augen zu"' (Luther to Melanchthon from Coburg on 27 July 1530, *WABR* 5. 498, 3f. (no. 1659)); the same saying to John Agricola (*WABR* 5. 506, 12 (no. 1662)).

Doctor Staupitz once said to me: 'I lied to God more than a thousand times by promising to become righteous, but I never achieved it. Therefore, I will not undertake it [any more] wanting to be righteous [on my own] since I realize that I cannot do it.' The same thing happened to me [Luther].[41]

Here Luther credited his Reformation insight of the 'law and gospel' dynamics and the justification of the sinner to none but Staupitz. In Konrad Cordatus's collection of Luther's table talks of 1532, Luther quoted the same Staupitzian insights into 'the law and the gospel' and 'free choice':

Staupitz said this about free choice: I once confessed every day and proposed to myself to start to become righteous and remain righteous, and every day I failed in this. I did not want to lie any longer. I cannot achieve it. I want to wait for the right hour that God will come with his grace. If not, everything is lost. This is so, because a person's will brings forth either presumption or desperation and a person cannot fulfill or excel the law. It [the law] is a huge mountain which I am to climb. And the presumptuous flesh says: I want to climb it. The insight into sin responds: You cannot climb it. Despair says then: I give up. And so it is with the law. It either leads people to presumption or to despair. However, so that the people truly despair with regard to their salvation, we preach the law and then the faith, in order that people do not become slugglish.[42]

Luther remembered Staupitz several times in his lectures on Galatians of 1531. His reminiscences appeared in the printed version of his commentary on Galatians in 1535:

---

[41] 'Wie den Doctor Staupitz ein mahl zu mir sagete: Ich hab gott mehr denn tausendt mahl gelogen, das ich wolte from werden, und habs nie gethan, drumb will ich mirs nicht fursetzen, das ich from wolle sein, den ich sehe wohl, ich kans nicht halten. Also gieng mirs auch' (sermon on 7 John, 1531, WA 33. 431, 27–34; LW 23. 271).

[42] 'Staupicius de libero arbitrio ita dixit: ... Es ist ein grosser berck .... Ita se res habet cum lege; ideo vel praesumere facit homines vel desperare. Sed ut vere et ad salutem desperent, praedicamus legem et deinde post fidem quoque, ne segnes fiant homines' (WATR 2. 665, 28–666, 11 (no. 2797a, Cordatus' collection, autumn 1532); similar wordings in nos. 2797b and 2797c). See M. Brecht, *Martin Luther, his Road to Reformation 1483–1521*, trans. J.L. Schaaf (Philadelphia, 1985), p. 74 (with n. 24), where this reminiscence is situated in Luther's early monastic years. This placement may be correct, but one must add that, as he related this anecdote many years later, Staupitz's influence on Luther must have continued well into his later years. This aspect tends to be forgotten by Luther's biographers, who generally create the impression that Staupitz's influence was confined to the early years of Luther's monastic life. In fact, Luther was so impressed by Staupitz's thoughts that they show up again in his table talks: 'Ideo Doctor Staupitz dixit: Ich wil nit mehr frumb sein, ich hab unsern Hern Got zwuil geteuscht' (WATR 4. 525, 44f. (no. 4806, June 1542)). Mathesius mentioned the same thought in May 1540 (WATR 4. 563, 14–17 (no. 4868)). In the manuscript known as Clm. 943, in which table talks are preserved, Staupitz's confession is given in its Latin version (WATR 5. 322, 16–19 (no. 5687)).

> [On Gal. 1: 12] I recall that when my movement first began [*initio cause meae*], Dr. Staupitz, a very worthy man and the vicar of the Augustinian Order, said to me: 'It pleases me very much that this doctrine of ours gives glory and everything else solely to God and nothing at all to men; for it is as clear as day that it is impossible to ascribe too much glory, goodness, etc., to God'. So it was that he consoled me ...

> [On Gal. 2: 13] It is dangerous, as Dr. Staupitz used to warn us, to trust in our own strength, no matter how holy, erudite, or confident of our knowledge we may be. For in that which we know best we can err and fall, bringing not only ourselves but others as well into danger, as Peter did here.

> [On Gal. 5: 17] I remember that Staupitz used to say: 'More than a thousand times I have vowed to God that I would improve, but I have never performed what I have vowed. Hereafter I shall not make such vows, because I know perfectly well that I shall not live up to them. Unless God is gracious and merciful to me for the sake of Christ and grants me a blessed final hour when the time comes for me to depart from this miserable life, I shall not be able to stand before Him with all my vows and good works'. This despair is not only truthful but is godly and holy.[43]

Luther's table talks contain numerous other reminiscences of Staupitz's sayings, which can only mean that long after Staupitz had died he continued to have a significant effect on Luther's thinking. In his conversations at table, the aging Luther recalled Staupitz's conviction that everything is to be attributed to God, and that it would be 'dangerous to rely on our own forces'. Luther remembered a similar thought from Staupitz's interpretation of the Cant. 8: 12, 'My vineyard, my very own, is for myself':

> Staupitz used to quote this sentence from the Song of Solomon 8 [:12], and he used to interpret it to mean that God has taken the dominion upon himself so that not everybody would strut about haughtily. God says, 'I'll take care of everything by myself. I'll be the pastor, the rector, the man in the house, the wife who brings up the children, in short, I'll do everything alone'.[44]

---

[43] [Print] 'Sic memini D. Staupitium, tunc summum virum et vicarium ordinis Augustiniani, inicio cause meae ad me dixisse: Hoc me, inquit, consolatur, quod haec doctrina nostra gratiae totam gloriam et omnia soli Deo tribuit, hominibus nihil. ... Sic tum me consolabatur (In epistolam S. Pauli ad Galatas Commentarius)' (*WA* 40, 1. 131, 21–25; *LW* 26. 66). 'Ideo recte admonebat D. Staupitius periculosum esse nostris viribus confidere, etiamsi sancti ac doctissimi simus ...' (*WA* 40, 1.205, 17–21; *LW* 26. 114); 'Memini Staupicium dicere solitum: Ego plus quam milies Deo vovi me fore probiorem, sed nunquam praestiti, quod vovi ....' (*WA* 40, 2. 92, 24f; *LW* 27. 73). Luther also mentioned Staupitz during his lectures on Gal. 6: 2 in 1531; however, this was not included in the printed version of 1535: 'Quando Stauppitius [*sic*] imposuit Prioratum: non facient fratres, quod voletis, sed contra' (*WA* 40, 2:144, 8f.).

Here Staupitz expressed what is generally regarded as Luther's basic theological principle: 'Let God be God' and 'everything is grace'. In a table talk of November 1531 Luther recalled that Staupitz had told him that he needed a better image of God:

> While I was in Erfurt I once said to Dr Staupitz, 'Dear Doctor, our Lord God treats people too horribly. Who can serve him as long as he strikes people down right and left, as we see he does in many cases involving our adversaries?' Then Dr Staupitz answered, 'Dear fellow, learn to think of God differently ...' .[45]

This advice was concerned with the central issue of theology: the image of God. Staupitz succeeded in straightening out Luther's distorted understanding of God, and all its consequences. In addition, Luther's understanding of Christ in the Eucharist and as Judge also needed to be corrected by Staupitz.[46] Luther remembered that Staupitz had influenced his image of Christ as one from whom no one needs to flee because he is not an angry judge. On one occasion, during his late lectures on Genesis (1535–45), Luther spoke again about this central issue of the proper understanding of God and Christ. He did not mention Staupitz by name, but stated that a certain friar made an 'extraordinary statement' which was of great help to those brethren like himself who were caught up in spiritual conflicts. Luther probably meant Staupitz, as the content of the reminiscence (on Gen. 43: 19–22) is similar to what Luther mentioned elsewhere about Staupitz:

> In the same manner the conscience is affected toward God; for when He smiles and is most favourable toward us, it [conscience] fears His wrath in spite of this and thinks that He is hostile and angry. Therefore it was an extraordinary statement on the part of a certain brother in our friary who used to say to those who were afflicted and disturbed: 'God is not angry with you. Do not be angry with Him. For you are more likely to be in rage against Him'.[47]

Staupitz mediated to Luther an image of God that was fundamentally different from the one with which Luther had grown up. As one of the young Luther's confessors, it was Staupitz who had called Luther 'stupid'

---

[44] 'Staupizius solebat hanc sententiam Cant 8 ...' (*WATR* 5. 223, 1–6 (no. 5538), *LW* 54. 449). On the danger of relying on one's own forces, see *WATR* 6. 25, 16–19 (no. 6537, undated): 'Doctor Staupitz, der Augustiner Vicarius in Germanien, pflegte recht und wol zu sagen: Es wäre mißlich und fährlich, da wir uns auf unsere eigene Kräfte verließen.'

[45] '... Tunc Doctor Staupizius respondit mihi: Lieber, lerned ihr yhn anderst [ansehen]' (*WATR* 1. 35, 14–20 (no. 94)), *LW* 54. 11.

[46] '... Vestra cogitatio ist nit Christus' (*WATR* 1. 59, 7–37 (no. 137), here l. 12; German version: 'Ei, Euer Gedanken sind nicht Christus', L. 31–32; *LW* 54. 19f.).

[47] 'Itaque insignis vox fuit fratris ciusdam in nostro monasterio, qui solebat dicere afflictis et perturbatis: Deus non irascitur tibi, modo tu illi ne irascere. Gott zurnet nit mit dir, zurne du nit mit jm' (*WA* 44. 546, 9–15; *LW* 7. 332 (on Gen 43: 19–22)).

for confessing stupid sins, and Staupitz who added that 'God is not angry with you, but you with Him'. Luther also spoke of Staupitz not understanding him and his 'temptation', and that at one point Staupitz asked him over dinner why he was so sad. When Luther brought up the topic of 'temptation' in his answer, Staupitz told him that such 'temptation' was good for him so that something good may become of him.[48]

In the autumn of 1532, Luther recalled at table how Staupitz influenced his image of Christ and his understanding of predestination: 'This is how Doctor Staupitz often counselled and what he told me: "If you want to discuss predestination, start with the wounds of Christ, and at once all arguing on predestination will stop".' There are several other versions of this talk; according to one of them Staupitz added that 'it would be better not even to think about predestination', and one should not only start with the consideration of the wounds of Christ, but also internalize well the image of Christ. Luther traced Staupitz's recommendation to meditate upon Christ's wounds back to Bernard of Clairvaux: 'It is Bernard's saying: one must build nests in the wounds of Christ.'[49]

Luther also remembered that Staupitz stressed salvation by faith in Christ the Saviour, and that Staupitz wondered how St Jerome was saved since he displayed so little faith (as Luther saw it). Thus, early in 1533 Luther reported at table a conversation with Staupitz about St Jerome:

> I think Jerome has somehow been saved by his faith in Christ ....
> I know no doctor whom I hate so much, although I once loved him

---

[48] 'Dixit aliquando ad me meus confessor, cum subinde stulta peccata ad eum afferrem: Stultus es. Deus non succenset tibi, sed tu succenses ei. Deus non irascitur tecum, sed tu cum Deo. Magnificum verbum, quod tamen ille ante lucem euangelii dicebat' (*WATR* 1. 47, 21–25 (no. 122)), recorded by Veit Dietrich in November 1531. See P. Manns and R. Vinke, 'Martin Luther als Theologe der Liebe', in O. Bayer, R.W. Jenson and S. Knuuttila (eds), *Caritas Dei: Beiträge zum Verständnis Luthers und der gegenwärtigen Ökumene. Festschrift für Tuomo Mannermaa* (Helsinki, 1997), pp. 265–86 (p. 279), where the vernacular version is quoted: 'Doctor Staupitzen habe ich oft gebeichtet ...' .

[49] 'Staupitius: Si, inquiens, vis disputare de praedestinatione, incipe a vulneribus Christi ...' (*WATR* 1. 512, 19f. (no. 1017)); 'Doctor Staupitius mihi dixit: Wenn man will de praedestinatione disputirn, so were es besser, man dechte nicht daran, sondern hebe an a vulneribus Christi, und bilde dir den Christum wol ein, so ist praedestinatio schon hinweckh, quia Deus praevidit Filium suum passurum propter peccatores. Qui credit hoc, der sols sein; qui non credit, der sols nicht sein' (*WATR* 2. 227, 21–25 and 228, 5–7 (no. 1820, recorded by Schlaginhaufen, 1532)); see *WATR* 2. 582, 15–583, 2 (nos. 2654 a and b, recorded by Konrad Cordatus); *WATR* 5. 293, 28–30 (no. 5658a). On Bernard, see *WATR* 5. 395, 1f. (no. 5898); see F. Posset, 'Divus Bernhardus: Saint Bernard as Spiritual and Theological Mentor of the Reformer Martin Luther', in J.R. Sommerfeldt (ed.), *Bernardus Magister. Papers Presented at the Nonacentenary Celebration of the Birth of Saint Bernard of Clairvaux, Kalamazoo, Michigan* (Kalamazoo, MI, 1992), pp. 517–32 (p. 529).

ardently and read him voraciously. Surely there's more learning in Aesop['s Fables] than in all of Jerome. If only Jerome had encouraged the works of faith and the fruits of the Gospel! But he spoke only of fasting, etc. My dear Staupitz once said, 'I'd like to know how that man was saved!' And his predecessor Dr Proles said, 'I should not like to have had St Jerome as my prior!'[50]

It appears that Luther inherited his aversion to Jerome from his spiritual father, Staupitz, who so strongly stressed the priority of faith. Staupitz was also the originator of Luther's grace-centred and God/Christ-centred teaching, as Luther testified in spring 1533: 'But my Staupitz said: One must look at the man who is called Christ. Staupitz is the one who started the teaching', that is, the evangelical doctrine on Christ as the Saviour. 'I have everything from Staupitz,' Luther insisted.[51]

These bits and pieces from table conversations and other sources give us an inkling of Staupitz's devotional theology as it was recalled by Luther. Of no less significance to Luther was Staupitz's counselling (his pastoral advice), as Luther remembered in 1530 in a letter to a friend who needed counselling for 'temptations'. Luther passed on the same advice which he had received from Staupitz, namely: 'Martin, don't you know how useful and necessary temptation is to you. Be not afraid of God testing you in this way. You will see for what great things he will use you as his servant.'[52] In a table talk of 14 December 1531, Luther reported that Staupitz had told him that he himself had never sensed such temptations, 'but that they are necessary like food and drink'.[53] In another table talk in the spring of 1533, the issue came up again. On yet another occasion, Luther boldly elaborated: 'And if one is never exposed to such trials, one knows nothing.' Staupitz's advice concerning 'temptation' left such a lasting impression on Luther that he remembered as late as in 1539 that *tentatio* is a necessary experience for becoming a 'good theologian' (besides the necessity of prayer and

---

[50] 'Staupicius meus aliquando dicebat: Ich wolt gern wissen, wie der man wer selig worden! ...' (*WATR* 1. 194, 11–23 (no. 445, recorded by Veit Dietrich), *LW* 54. 72); a similar wording is found in *WATR* 1. 399, 15–19 (no. 824).

[51] 'Sed Staupicius meus dicebat: Man mus den man ansehen, der da heyst Christus. Staupicius hat die doctrinam angefangen' (*WATR* 1. 245, 9–12 (no. 526, recorded by Veit Dietrich, spring 1533); *LW* 54. 97. 'Ex Erasmo nihl habeo. Ich hab all mein ding von doctor Staupiz; der hatt mir occasionem geben' (*WATR* 1. 80, 16f. (no. 173, recorded by Veit Dietrich, spring 1532)).

[52] 'Nescis, Martine' *WABR* 5. 519, 30–32 (no. 1670, letter to Jerome Weller from Coburg Castle in July 1530).

[53] 'Cum igitur quererer apud Stupicium, dicebat quidem se eas nunquam sensisse; sed quantum intelligo, inquit, sunt vobis magis necessarie quam cibus et potus' (*WATR* 1. 62, 1–3 (no. 141)); see Manns and Vinke, 'Martin Luther als Theologe der Liebe', p. 279. A similar wording is found in *WATR* 2. 13, 25–26 (no. 1263).

meditation).[54] Not only was Staupitz of decisive help to Luther as regards to coming to grips with spiritual 'temptation', but also concerning his anxieties about predestination, as Luther again remembered in a table talk and in a letter of 1542, almost two decades after Staupitz's death: 'And if Dr. Staupitz, or better God through Dr. Staupitz, had not helped me [to get out from these anxieties], I would have drowned in them and ended up in hell.'[55] Furthermore, as late as in his last lectures on Genesis, Luther at one point told his audience that it was Staupitz who liberated him from these troubles by referring him to the meditation of the wounds of Christ.[56] It was also in these lectures on Genesis that the aging professor of the Bible remembered that Staupitz had guided him away from late medieval spirituality which marginalized the Bible in favour of visions and auditions. Apparently, Staupitz had told him not to become preoccupied with matters such as St Birgitta's 'satanic illusions'. Whether such a characterization of St Birgitta's revelations was Staupitz's or Luther's wording cannot be determined. We only have Luther's reference to Staupitz about this, in the context of interpreting Genesis 30.[57] Staupitz wanted to concentrate on the essentials of the Christian faith, and therefore private revelations (such as the Swedish saint's) were of little significance to him.

Similarly, Staupitz had little interest in secondary theological issues, such as the question of whether Mary was affected by original sin. Luther was obviously impressed by Staupitz's concentration on the essentials, as he also remembered Staupitz calling the Franciscan opinion that Mary was free from original sin their 'fiction'. Staupitz taught Luther to focus on nothing but God, Christ and the gracious forgiveness of sins.

Staupitz himself had been bothered by the overly sophisticated scholastic theology, which he must have perceived as largely nonbiblical,

---

[54] *WATR* 1. 240, 12–20 (no. 518, recorded by Veit Dietrich, spring 1533); *LW* 54. 94; see *WATR* 1. 26, 4–6 (no. 1288, December 1531); *LW* 54. 132f.; *WATR* 1. 47–50 (no. 122). See Manns and Vinke, 'Martin Luther als Theologe der Liebe', p. 279. 'Qui non est tentatus, nihil scit' (*WATR* 5. 592, 25 (no. 6305)).

[55] 'Undt wo mihr D. Staupitz, oder viel mehr Gott durch Doctor Staupitz, nicht heraus geholffen hette, so were ich darinn ersoffen vndt langst in der helle' (*WABR* 9. 627, 23–25 (no. 3716, letter to Duke Albrecht of Mansfeld 23 February 1542)). The same wording is found in a table talk, recorded in Latin: 'Ego etiam semel liberatus sum, ab hac cogitatione a Staupitio, alioquin iam diu flagrarem in inferno' (*WATR* 5. 293, 28–30 (no. 5658a)). In other table talks of the 1530s Luther made similar remarks about Staupitz who had helped him to conquer the problems in his spiritual life; see *WATR* 2. 112, 9–11 (no. 1490).

[56] 'Nisi Staupitius eadem me laborantem liberasset.... Staupitius his verbis me consolabatur...' *WA* 43. 461, 1–16 (on Gen. 26: 9).

[57] See *WA* 43. 667, 29–34 (on Gen. 30).

since he had asked to be liberated from such a distorting type of theology when he repeated Summenhart's question: 'Who will free me from that quarrelling theology?' Luther remembered Staupitz's appeal so well that he brought it up in one of his table talks during the summer of 1540. Staupitz is remembered as following Andreas Proles in this regard. Proles was known to have said that certain disputations made him think of a man sharpening his file continuously, but never using it in order to achieve anything. In the same way such disputations are useless, and nothing but mere words.[58] Luther also remembered well Staupitz's call to patience when reforms went too slowly, as he said in the context of some antipapal conversation in October 1540:

> The pope wants to be a judge and has found fault with us .... Just hold still! They must all go down .... This is what Staupitz said to me when he was overcome by sadness: 'God grant patience! After all, nothing remains unpunished. And all history testifies that God is coming'. This is the reason some take Luther to be a prophet and apostle, for he has prophesied that there's nothing good in a papist.[59]

In a similar comment, according to Luther's recollection, Staupitz resignedly said that 'nothing in this world goes right', and that this is the greatest knowledge which everyone must learn.[60] He also remembered clearly that Staupitz had warned him about challenging the ecclesiastical authorities when, during a conversation at table in August 1532, the humanist and lawyer Dr Justus Jonas brought up the issue of the 'reformation of the church'. Luther commented:

> I knew it well! For it was Doctor Staupitz who told me this: If you try to do that [reforming the church], you will stir up the entire world against us; and he added these words: the Church is founded, irrigated, and growing on blood, is watered, fertilized, and pruned [by it].[61]

Staupitz's name came to Luther's mind also when conversations turned to the scandalous lives of popes and bishops, as Luther remembered

---

[58] See *WATR* 6. 309, 21–29 (no. 6991); on Summenhart's saying, see *WATR* 5. 99, 14–16 (no. 5374).

[59] '... Sicut dixit ad me Staupitius, cum esset in maerore: Got verleihe gedult! Bleibt doch nichts vngestrafft. Und alle historien bezeugens, das Gott kumpt ...' (*WATR* 5. 44, 12–19 (no. 5284), *LW* 54. 405f.).

[60] 'Stopitz dixit summam scientiam esse, quam oporteat omnes discere: Das in dießer welt nicht recht zugehet' (*WATR* 2. 374, 1f. (no. 2241, Cordatus' collection, autumn or winter 1531)).

[61] '... Nam Doctor Staupitius ad me haec verba dixit: Si hoc tentaveris, totum mundum contra nos irritabis, addens haec verba: Ecclesia sanguine fundata est, irrigata et propagata, wirdt mit diesem blut begossen, getunget und geschneittelt' (*WATR* 2. 551, 23–26 and 552, 10–13 (no. 2621b); see ibid., no. 2621a).

Staupitz working towards real reforms in the lives of the clerics and the religious in the entire Church. However, Staupitz had turned his mild-mannered anti-Roman attitude and his hatred of the Babylonian captivity of the Church[62] into the positive spiritual advice that Christ alone should be the 'pope' who rules over the hearts of Christians.[63] This was Staupitz's way of saying that the pope's authority in Rome was not as decisive, after all, as people thought, or as the pope himself thought. One's own proper spirituality of the heart, in which Christ must be the 'pope', is more important for salvation than the acknowlegement of ecclesiastical authority. Luther embodied this very Staupitzian conviction. Unfortunately, the issue of authority in the Church was overwhelming at that time. Luther took up this issue and did not yield on it until it came to the permanent breach. Staupitz indirectly and Luther directly and openly dealt with it throughout their lives. They both also remembered well the famous case of John Hus at the Council of Constance of 1414–18, and the unfortunate role which one of their own friars had played at that time. It was from his predecessor Andreas Proles that Staupitz had received the idea that Hus was unjustly condemned, and Luther accepted Staupitz's revisionist position concerning Hus.

Luther, furthermore, remembered Staupitz's view of authority within religious Orders. As to the force and authority of monastic rules, Staupitz appreciated the reasonableness of the Rule of Augustine. This had also been recognized by the contemporary Bishop of Worms, Johann von Dalberg (1482–1503), who had once made a remark to Staupitz to that effect, regarding how exceptions to the rules might be permitted in the case of a friar's ill health. Staupitz's views on this theme were so important to Luther that he quoted him on this in his *On the Councils and the Church* of 1539: 'Dr Staupitz told me once that he had heard the Bishop of Worms, Dalberg, say about St Augustine's Rule that if he had not written anything else besides the Rule, one nevertheless would have to agree that he [Augustine] was a great wise man.' An Augustinian cloister was not meant to be a prison, 'but a free association of priests'.[64]

---

[62] *WATR* 3. 400, 8f. (no. 3548); *LW* 54. 229f. See L.G. zu Dohna, 'Staupitz and Luther: Continuity and Breakthrough at the Beginning of the Reformation', in H.A. Oberman and F.A. James (eds), *Via Augustini* (Leiden, 1991), pp. 116–29; H.A. Oberman, 'Captivitas Babylonica: Die Kirchenkritik des Johann von Staupitz' in A. Mehl and W.C. Schneider (eds), *Reformatio et reformationes* (Darmstadt, 1989), pp. 99–103.

[63] See Staupitz's fifth Salzburg sermon of 1520 in R.K. Markwald, *A Mystic's Passion* (New York, 1990), p. 129.

[64] See *WA* 50. 612, 17–30. For a historical portrait of Bishop Dalberg, see E. Mittler (ed.), *Heidelberg: Geschichte und Gestalt* (Heidelberg, 1996), p. 245.

In July 1539, Luther recalled his 'move' into the friary at Erfurt, and then he told his dinner guests his life story. He thought he would never leave the cloister, as he had died to the world until God thought it was time for a change, when the Dominican Friar Tetzel with his indulgence business drove him to a reaction, 'and Doctor Staupitz instigated me against the pope'.[65]

Staupitz had impressed Luther in every regard, be it with his understanding of monastic rules and ecclesiastical authority, his occasional statements against Rome, his style of leadership within the Order, his spiritual-pastoral counselling, or with his theological priorities as a Bible scholar.

The most significant contribution to theology and spirituality lies in Staupitz's theological principles which make up his theological straightforwardness. Church leaders recognized it without necessarily approving it. This was the case with the Papal Nuncio Aleander when he described Staupitz as having been 'the first' who went against the 'common school of theologians',[66] the scholastics, and who thus bypassed them on his way 'to the sources'. He was encouraged and cheered on by the biblical humanists. Luther remained gratefully aware of Staupitz's significance in this regard.

Staupitz always envisioned that he and his Augustinian friars would become good biblical preachers.[67] He made the friars prepare for this task by a course of solid theological studies designed by himself at the University of Wittenberg, where he had Luther and other capable candidates pursue their theological education, not so they would ultimately become scholars, but rather that they would become good preachers of the gospel. In this devotional, pastoral theology Staupitz did succeed. Luther again remembered him in this connection, during a conversation at table on 9 November 1538, saying that it was Staupitz who 'drove' him to the study of the Bible and theology: 'Many [at Erfurt] took umbrage at my getting the doctorate at the age of twenty-eight, when Staupitz drove me to it.'[68]

Staupitz influenced Luther's life decisively and contributed significantly to his theological development. Luther saw himself as the fulfilment of a 'prophecy' which Staupitz had uttered, namely that God needs Luther dead or alive: 'Staupitz's prophecy had to become true ... This prophetic

---

[65] '16. Iulii, in die Alexii, dicebat: Heute ist die jerige zeit, do ich in das kloster zu Erffurt gezogen.... et Doctor Staupitius me incitabat contra papam' (*WATR* 4. 440, 5–19 (no. 4707)). In the 1530s, Luther recalled that he had started to write against the papacy in the year 1516: 'Anno 16. incepi scribere contra papatum' (*WATR* 1. 441, 38 (no. 884)).

[66] P. Kalkoff, *Aleander gegen Luther* (Leipzig and New York, 1908), p. 138.

[67] See Dohna, 'Staupitz and Luther: Continuity and Breakthrough', pp. 116–29.

[68] 'Compulsus a Staupitio' (*WATR* 4. 130, 1 (no. 4091), *LW* 54. 320).

voice was fulfilled in me.'[69] On other occasions, Luther reported that Staupitz had heard a prophecy during his sojourn in Rome in 1510 which was a matter of common knowledge there, though generally decried: 'An Eremite [Augustinian friar] will rise up under Leo X and will oppose the papacy.'[70]

Almost 20 years after Staupitz's death, Luther wanted to call Staupitz's theological achievement to the minds of the younger generation of theologians whom he taught. Luther would not have done this had Staupitz's impact on him been only pastoral or marginal. Thus, in 1543 Luther arranged a doctoral disputation in which he let Staupitz's primary concerns be discussed, formulated as part of Johann Marbach's disputation that one must let God be God and that God is the forgiver of sins; as the Thesis 46 reads:

> Staupitz: You do not want to be a true sinner, you want to be righteous [even] before the remission [of your sins]. But you must confess [first] that you are an unworthy sinner, only then can God be the true forgiver.[71]

After his graduation, Johann Marbach (1521–81) returned to south Germany and became for a while the preacher for the imperial city of Isny, then at Strasbourg in 1545. In 1552, as a 'Lutheran', he represented the city of Strasbourg at the Council of Trent.[72]

---

[69] 'Anno 1510. doctor Staupitius Romae fuit, qui hanc prophetiam vulgatissimam Romae audivit ex omnium ore: Surget eremita sub Leone Decimo, qui papatui se opponet. Sed hic sermo ad completionem usque contemptus est' (*WATR* 5. 660, 1–4 (no. 6435, undated, Lauterbach's collection)). Another table talk speaks of the year 1511 when Staupitz heard the prophecy in Rome: 'Addidit et mihi animum Doctor Staupitz, qui cum Romae fuisset anno 1511, ibi in multorum ore fuisset haec prophetia Romae publicae pronunciata: Surget eremita et devastabit papatum …' (*WATR* 3. 439, 15–20 (no. 3593)).

[70] Veit Dietrich recorded the prophecy in a table talk in winter 1531/32: 'Prophetia Romae fore, ut heremita quidam Leonem papam graviter affligeret. Ibi Stupicius ad me: Sihe, ich dacht nit, das es so solt ein heremita sein, sed imaginabar barbatum pallidum prodeuntem ex silva etc.' (*WATR* 1. 69 (no. 147)); in another recording, the prophecy was mentioned by others, and then Luther reported more specifically that Staupitz had heard of a Minorite's dream in which virtually the same words as in the mentioned prophecy were used ('that an Eremite will rise up …'): 'Similiter Staupitius audivit somnium Minoritae: Surget eremita sub Leone Decimo, qui papatum adorietur' (*WATR* 5. 467, 19f (no. 6059, undated)). In July 1538 Luther yet again spoke of 'Staupitz's prophecy' that was fulfilled in him: 'Vaticinium Staupitcii …. Aber Doctor Staupitzen prophecei hat mussen war werden…. Haec vatidica vox in me impleta est' (*WATR* 4. 13, 30–35 (no. 3924)).

[71] 'Staupitius: Tu vis esse peccator non verus, tu vis esse iustus ante remissionem. Nam oportet te confiteri, te indignum esse peccatorem, ut Deus possit esse verus remissor' (*WA* 39, 2. 227, 31–33 (Doctoral disputation of Johann Marbach, 1543)).

[72] See Stupperich, pp. 138f. On the presence of a few Lutheran representatives from Germany at the Council of Trent in 1552, see R.E. McNally, 'The Council of Trent and the German Protestants', *Theological Studies*, **25** (1964), pp. 1–22; E. Iserloh, 'Luther and the Council of Trent', *Catholic Historical Review*, **69** (1983), pp. 563–76.

As for the issue of sinfulness, Luther also remembered well being almost scolded by Staupitz, when Luther 'wrote' to him about his sins. The relevant correspondence is not extant. Luther reported in a table talk what Staupitz had to say in his response:

> When I was a friar, I often wrote to Doctor Staupitz, and one time I wrote to him: O my sin, sin, sin! He responded to me: 'You want to be without sin, and you do not have a real sin. Christ is the forgiveness of real sins, such as killing one's parents, public blasphemy, despising God, adultery etc. These are the real sins. You need to have a list with real sins listed, if Christ is to help you. Don't deal with such junk and puppet sins, and don't make a sin out of every fart'.[73]

Only a fatherly friend could give Luther such direct advice without holding back. Only on the basis of a strong sympathy for Luther was the aging Staupitz able to admit frankly to Luther in retrospect: 'For you I have a very steadfast love, passing the love of women [2 Sam. 1: 26].'[74]

That Staupitz was an immeasurable source of consolation and wisdom to Luther was confirmed by an unexpected source, namely Thomas Müntzer, who (see p. 296f.) had said to Luther that Staupitz functioned like an *oraculum* for Luther, by which he meant that whenever Luther had asked for Staupitz's advice he received a wise response which he accepted as if it were of divine inspiration; literally: 'For the Staupitzian oracle stood close by you' (*Dann Stupicianum oraculum stundt hart bey dir*).

In Memoriam by counter-reformers; and Staupitz included on the *Index of Forbidden Books*

The monk Wolfgang Seidel (= Sedelius, 1492–1562) of the Benedictine abbey of Tegernsee, Bavaria, is known as a counter-Reformation preacher and participant in the Council of Trent. Nevertheless when he came across Staupitz's sermons on Job he recognized their value. They were found among his possessions at Tegernsee. Sedelius lived in the Augustinian friary at Munich from 1532 to 1548 and from 1555 to 1562, and at Salzburg between 1552 and 1555, so could have brought the manuscript with him from either place. Whatever the case, this

---

[73] 'Da ich ein Mönch war, schreib ich Doctor Staupitzen oft ... [du] mußt nicht mit solchem Humpelwerk und Puppensünden umbgehen und aus einem jglichen Bombart eine Sünde machen' (*WATR* 6. 106, 32–107, 3 (no. 6669, undated)); see Manns and Vinke, 'Martin Luther als Theologe der Liebe', pp. 280f.

[74] See *WABr* 3.264 (no. 726); R. Wetzel '"Meine Liebe zu Dir ist beständiger als Frauenliebe": Johann von Staupitz (+1524) und Martin Luther', in P. Freybe, *Luther and seine Freunde* (Wittenberg, 1998), pp. 105–24.

unique manuscript of Staupitz's Tubingen sermons ended up in the Bavarian State Library during the secularization of church property in the nineteenth century.[75] It is therefore most likely thanks to Sedelius that these sermons escaped the burning that would have been their probable fate had they remained in Salzburg.

The destruction of Staupitz's papers – books, manuscripts and letters – was ordered in 1584, 60 years after his death, by a later abbot of St Peter's Abbey, one Martin Hattinger, a convert from Brünn. The book-burning took place in the abbey's court and allegedly included letters from Luther's pen.[76] While Abbot Hattinger tried to erase the memory of his predecessor, the monk Sedelius (knowingly or not) helped to preserve it. The destruction of Staupitz's spiritual and theological legacy was based upon the fact that his works appeared in the re-updated *Index of Forbidden Books* which had been published in Munich in 1582, by the papal nuncio Feliciano Ninguarda. The first Roman *Index* of 1559 had included Staupitz, probably because his name was mentioned next to Luther's in Cochlaeus' *De actis Lutheri*.[77] Staupitz's name appeared in the first category – writers who are forbidden regardless of what they have written. The *Index* of the Council of Trent, edited in 1564, included him again in the same class.[78] Apparently, the authors of the Roman Church's *Index* agreed with Luther (and with Melanchthon) that Staupitz took his theological position on the Reformation side, and they therefore put his works on their *Index*. However, it should be noted that the Roman Church's decision in this regard was not justified. Staupitz represents solid Catholic theology, as it was always understood by Catholic researchers on Staupitz including the nineteenth-century scholar Nikolaus Paulus and the twentieth-century researcher Adolar Zumkeller. Both insist that placing Staupitz's writings on the *Index* was not justified.[79] It is not insignificant to note in this connection that Staupitz never called Luther's adherents 'heretics', although this was alleged for a long time, on the basis of a document falsely attributed to

---

[75] H. Pöhlein, *Wolfgang Seidel. 1492–1562. Benediktiner aus Tegernsee, Prediger zu München. Sein Leben und sein Werk* (Munich, 1951). See Staupitz, I. 3 (Introduction); Staupitz, II.10, n. 39 (Introduction).

[76] See J. Sallaberger, 'Johann von Staupitz, Luthers Vorgesetzter und Freund, und seine Beziehungen zu Salzburg', *Augustiniana*, **28** (1978), pp. 108–54 (p. 153, n. 200).

[77] See Staupitz, II. 10, n. 39 (Introduction).

[78] Index: 'Quorum universae conscriptiones, cuiuscumque argumenti sunt, omnino prohibentur'. See Paulus, 'Johannes von Staupitz. Seine vorgeblich protestantischen Gesinnungen,' pp. 345f.; Steinmetz, 'Staupitz', in *The Oxford Encyclopedia of the Reformation*, IV, p. 111.

[79] See Paulus, 'Johannes von Staupitz. Seine vorgeblich protestantischen Gesinnungen', pp. 309–46; 773–7; Paulus's position is defended by A. Zumkeller, 'Staupitz', *Dictionnaire*, XV, pp. 1184–96.

him – the second expert opinion on the Agricola affair, which does not stem from Staupitz's pen.[80]

In memoriam Johann von Staupitz by the nuns of Salzburg

It is easily forgotten that it was not the monks whose abbot Staupitz later was, but the nuns at Salzburg who held Staupitz in at least as high esteem as Luther did. It must have been under the leadership of Abbess Regina Pfäffinger (d. 1516) of Salzburg's Nonnberg convent that the local nuns (both at Nonnberg and at St Peter's) were made aware of Staupitz's significance with the result that from 1512 on they kept records of his sermons. The family of the abbess was on friendly terms with Staupitz, and he had visited their home in Bavaria on more than one occasion. Even after Regina's death, the nuns continued faithfully excerpting and recording Staupitz's sermons, indicating that he must have been an exceptional pastor and preacher to them. The nun, who had in 1512 recorded from memory his twelve Lenten sermons, humbly asked at the end of her notes that those who read these sermons of 'the worthy lord and father Johann Staubitz' [*sic*] pray for her for God's grace and reward. Another nun, perhaps by the name of Dorothea Meixner, copied the original excerpt, and her manuscript is now the only extant source for these 1512 Lenten sermons.[81] Six years later, excerpts of Staupitz's three Advent sermons of 1518 were also preserved by the nuns who esteemed his sermons so much that they recorded 'a few beautiful pieces'[82] from them, namely the esteemed sermons of the 'honourable father Johanns Staubicz' [*sic*]. This was their way of keeping Staupitz in their highest regards as he was the one who preached the gospel and the 'Suffering of Our Lord'[83] to them during Lent, and 'comforting, beautiful sermons'[84] during Advent. With the nuns' records of Staupitz's sermonizing in Salzburg (together with the records of members of the Staupitz Sodality at Nuremberg) a more objective understanding of

---

[80] See L.G. zu Dohna, 'Von der Ordensreform zur Reformation: Johann von Staupitz', in K. Elm (ed.), *Reformbemühungen und Observanzbestrebungen im spätmittelalterlichen Ordenswesen* (Berlin, 1989), pp. 571–84; see Chapter 6.

[81] Schneider-Lastin, *Salzburger Predigten 1512*, pp. 125 and 9–17.

[82] 'Etliche schöne stückel' (description of the sermon excerpts including the beginning and end of an excerpt (G. Hayer, 'Die deutschen Handschriften des Mittelalters der Erzabtei St. Peter zu Salzburg', in *Denkschriften der Österreichischen Akademie der Wissenschaften, philosophisch-historische Klasse, Denkschriften 154. Band* (Vienna, 1982), p. 265).

[83] Most of the 1512 Lenten sermons have the headline 'Sermon on the Suffering of Our Lord' (or 'of Christ'), see Hayer, 'Die deutschen Handschriften', pp. 264–5.

[84] 'Tröstliche schöne predig[t]' (1518 Advent sermon excerpts; Hayer, 'Die deutschen Handschriften', p. 265).

Staupitz's theology and impact on the Reformation can be obtained. The nuns' industrious recordings made it possible to study his sermons several centuries later. This is all the more important as Staupitz and his role in the early reform efforts were completely neglected by many historians of the German Reformation and by biographers of Luther, probably because of Melanchthon's and Mathesius's ignorance of Staupitz's immense significance to the Reformer. These two are the earliest Luther biographers and their view still largely determines our image of Luther and Staupitz's underexposed role in Luther's life up to this day.[85]

Not much is known of the direct reception of Staupitz's devotional theology later in the sixteenth century, except that one of his booklets continued to attract attention even beyond that century, mainly because it had been endorsed by Luther himself. Staupitz's *On Loving God* appeared in a Latin version, *De amore Dei*, in Frankfurt in 1524. Later editions were produced by Caspar Schwenckfeld in 1547, by Daniel Sudermann in 1594, and by Johann Arndt in 1605. Another Latin edition came out in Quedlinburg in 1706 as part of *Tetractys Tractatuum vere aureorum* which, among certain 'golden treatises', included Staupitz's tract 'On the Holy Right Christian Faith' (which Linck had published in 1525) along with the works of John Tauler. A French translation of *On Loving God* came out in 1667, an English one in 1692, and a Danish one in 1873. A German version was published in 1862, together with the tract on faith: *Von der Liebe Gottes und vom Rechten christlichen Glauben. Aufs neue herausgegeben* (Stuttgart, 1862). All these later editions were apparently published by Protestant printing presses. For most Roman Catholics access to Staupitz was blocked because his works were included in the *Index of Forbidden Books*, as was the book *Onus Ecclesiae* which is ascribed to Staupitz's later colleague, Bishop Pürstinger.

In Memoriam Johann von Staupitz and his 'Golden Treatise', by an eighteenth-century Augustinian

Staupitz's testament 'On the Holy Right Christian Faith' was claimed by the Protestant reformers' camp as an expression of their doctrine of justification by faith; to them it was one of the 'golden treatises'. Apparently in spite of this Protestant evaluation, and of the fact that it was listed in the *Index of Forbidden Books*, the Catholic scholar Friar

---

[85] M. Foket, 'Luther et Staupitz (I)', in *La Foi et le Temps: Revue bimestrielle des diocèses francophones de Belgique*, **20** (Tournai, 1990), pp. 69–83.

Angelus Höggmayr of Munich read it and did not let either this Protestant claim or the ecclesiastical prohibition go unchallenged. In his description of the leaders of the Augustinian Order in Germany, *Catalogus Priorum Provincialium Ord. Erem. S. Aug. per Provinciam totius Germaniae deinde per Provinciam Bavaria* of 1729, he gave his Catholic appraisal of Staupitz's booklet: it is an *aureum tractatum*, a 'golden treatise'.[86]

---

[86] See Paulus, 'Johann von Staupitz. Seine vorgeblich protestantischen Gesinnungen', p. 337.

CHAPTER EIGHT

Conclusion

This study of Staupitz's life and work has sought to highlight 'a piece of theological micro-history with world-historical consequences'.[1] Staupitz was a reformer throughout his life: a reformer of the religious life in the friaries, of spirituality and pastoral care in general, and a *reformator* of the University of Wittenberg. As an organizer of the new university he relied for help on Christoph Scheurl and others. Scheurl was originally a sympathizer with the 'evangelical cause' of the reformed friars of the Order of St Augustine in Germany under Staupitz's leadership. However, by 1530, that is about five years after Staupitz's death, he had become an opponent of the Reformation.[2] Scheurl's turning away from the Reformation makes one wonder where Staupitz would have stood, had he still been alive at that point.

Concerning his reforms within the Augustinian Order, the observants' movement, there was no essential change in Staupitz's general outlook. When plans of unification with the reformed Lombard congregation failed, he moved on to an attempt to unify the conventuals (the non-reformed friaries), with his reformed branch (the observants). In all this he had limited success, although he was always ready to reorganize and to reform. In doing this he appears also to have accentuated, at various stages in his life, different aspects of religious life both within the friaries and outside them. Whether, however, there is a major difference between Staupitz's early and late view of the religious life is debatable.[3] It is

---

[1] B. Hamm, 'Von der Gottesliebe des Mittelalters zum Glauben Luthers: Ein Beitrag zur Bußgeschichte' in *Lutherjahrbuch*, **65** (1998), pp. 19–44 (p. 35): 'Dies ist ein Stück theologischer Mikrohistorie mit weltgeschichtlichen Konsequenzen.'

[2] See Wriedt, 'Scheurl', *BBKL*, IX, pp. 178–85.

[3] As Ralph Weinbrenner opines in *Klosterreform im 15. Jahrhundert zwischen Ideal und Praxis: Der Augustinereremit Andreas Proles (1429–1503) und die privilegierte Observanz* (Tübingen, 1996), p. 236. Weinbrenner thinks that there is a *Differenz* which is difficult to ignore, and criticizes the view put forward in 1989 by Zumkeller (see 'Johannes von Staupitz und die klösterliche Reformbewegung', *AAug*, **52**, pp. 31–49); however, his argument is unconvincing. Furthermore, Weinbrenner's greatest flaw is his failure to differentiate between 'monks' and 'friars', a mistake often made by German authors because the German language provides only a single expression, *Mönch*, which does not allow distinction between the two types of Orders. The English language has the advantage of two distinct notions for vowed religious personnel: 'monk' for members of the monastic

probable that there was no significant change in his basic attitude toward the professed religious life, be it as a friar or later as a monk and abbot.

Staupitz as a mendicant friar, reformer of pastoral care, and so-to-speak 'itinerant preacher' was attracted to the large cities of the empire, such as Nuremberg and Salzburg. They provided the audience that he, and the mendicant Orders in general, wanted to reach. Large cities had the means to invite capable preachers, especially for the Lenten and Advent seasons. Such Lenten sermons were called *quadragesimales* (for the 40 days of Lent).[4] Engaging guest preachers for Lent first caught on in the fourteenh century, and apparently remained popular up to Staupitz's time. So it happened that Staupitz became a prominent speaker during the seasons of Lent and Advent in Salzburg, Nuremberg and Munich.

Occasionally, scholars have analysed Staupitz's various writings in an attempt to trace the evolution of his teaching on his theological perspective. Most recently, his Nuremberg Advent sermons of 1516, published as *Libellus* in 1517, were declared his main theological work (*theologisches Hauptwerk*) and his Tübingen sermons on Job of 1497/98 an odd exception (*Ausnahme*) within the entire body of his output.[5] The criteria for such an evaluation are not clear. In contrast, one could argue that, on the basis of the popularity among contemporaries or among later generations of the sixteenth century, Staupitz's Advent sermons in Munich, *On the Love of God,* published in 1518, are the most important texts to come from his pen. One could also argue that the Salzburg Lenten sermons of 1512 are the most significant ones because they are his earliest sermons in the vernacular. However, instead of ranking one set of sermons above another, perhaps it would be more fruitful to determine which spiritual/theological insight was the most important one in all of Staupitz's work, from the early Tübingen sermons through to the last Salzburg sermons. Reviewing them all may bring us to the conclusion that his most important insight concerned the 'mercy of God' and the 'sweetness of God'; that God has been made 'sweet for us' and our salvation, as God is like 'heavenly sugar' that attracts us like a magnet.

---

tradition, that is the Benedictine tradition and its branches such as the Cistercians; 'friar' for all the others who are not bound by the *stabilitas loci*, such as the later medieval mendicant Orders of the Franciscans, Dominicans, Augustinians and so on. Weinbrenner at times lumps both together, and he may thus incorrectly speak of Staupitz's *Mönchtum* when he means Staupitz's life as an Augustinian friar.

[4] For the similar situation in France, see L. Taylor, *Soldiers of Christ: Preaching in Late Medieval and Reformation France* (New York and Oxford, 1992), p. 15.

[5] See M. Wriedt, 'Staupitz und Augustin: zur Kirchenväterrezeption am Vorabend der Reformation' in L. Grane et al. (eds) *Auctoritas Patrum* (Mainz, 1993), pp. 229, 242 and 250.

Staupitz's spirituality was definitely shaped by the study of the sacred scriptures and most likely by medieval sources which are coloured by Augustinian theology. With this spirituality he was able to reach the hearts of his listeners and to talk about the inner life of the 'heart'. He stressed the 'sweetness of God' in Christ and the need to experience it. He was indebted above all to Augustine, but also to Bernard, Tauler, Suso, Henry of Friemar and Gerson. In his sermons and publications from 1512 on he hardly mentioned any authorities by name, although there is the occasional exception, particularly Augustine, whose name is found, for example, in the margins of the Leipzig edition of his *Nachfolge* of 1515, twice in his *Libellus*, once in the Nuremberg sermons of 1517, and twice in the Salzburg sermons of 1520. Evidently Staupitz was so attached to this church father and the patron of his religious Order that he felt obliged to mention his name periodically.

In Staupitz's spiritual teaching, God and God's honour and glorification took centre stage. All human works are meant to glorify God. In connection with the glorification of God, man is to recognize his sinfulness in true humility. Those who humble themselves are the true 'evangelical people'. They are the ones who accuse themselves of their sins and thus receive their justification through God's grace in faith. They have the will to obtain conformity with Christ in all suffering, and they live with the attitude of *Gelassenheit*. In silence and quietness they will experience the sweet taste of God's love in their hearts. However, Staupitz was critical of extraordinary mystical experiences or visions like those that certain nuns claimed to have had of the Infant Jesus. Staupitz was also critical of external manifestations of popular religiosity, such as the reliance on indulgences or the showing off of one's rosaries.

Having emphasized the great significance of Augustine, one should quickly add that Staupitz always remained a scriptural scholar, even after he had resigned from his teaching position at Wittenberg to make room for Luther. In the print of his Nuremberg sermons, published as his *Libellus*, a total of 250 biblical source references are found, provided by Staupitz himself and not by later editors. He thus demonstrated his determination to present a concise concept of 'evangelical' theology for his sophisticated audience in Nuremberg. The turn towards Bible studies and the church fathers was promoted by the humanist movement, to the principles of which Staupitz was receptive from early on without, however, becoming much involved in the linguistic elements of that movement; he did not display any in-depth knowledge of the original biblical languages. Staupitz was an 'evangelical' theologian in the contemporary sense of the early sixteenth century, and the Nuremberg audience of his Advent sermons of 1516 recognized him correctly as the 'tongue of the Apostle Paul' and the 'herald of the gospel'. He may very well be called an Evangelical Catholic Reformer[6] who was open to ideas which were promoted by the Renaissance humanists inside and outside his reformed Augustinian Order.

From among the Scholastics, he appreciated much of Duns Scotus's theology although he hardly mentioned him by name. Yet as a young friar at Tübingen he had probably become familiar with the interpretation of Duns Scotus by Professor Paul Scriptoris. According to the rules of the Augustinian Order of 1290, Staupitz must have studied Egidio da Roma who was to be preferred over Gregory of Rimini. It would be of great interest to know whether, and to what degree, Staupitz studied Gregory's commentary on the Sentences. However, there is little that can be gleaned from the existing sources in this regard;[7] there is more evidence of his fondness for Egidio da Roma.

Certainly one may point out that Staupitz's theological thinking starts with predestination, and that he lets justification follow, as is the case with Gregory of Rimini; and that a person is justified before God and is able to do good works if he or she is first predestined by God. Furthermore, it is possible to observe in Staupitz the reception of the Scotist-Nominalist *pactum* theology for a predestination theology, and a new interpretation of the theology of grace. One may even agree that the Scotist *via antiqua* and the Nominalist *via moderna* share the same fundamental categories, namely the distinction of *potentia dei* and the emphasis on the *pactum dei* with the Church, for which his term *debitum* is revealing. Moreover, one may agree that Staupitz may have taken such notions from the covenant theology of Scotism as found at Tübingen, and that Staupitz and Gregory insist on Augustine's anti-Pelagian predestination doctrine. All this *may* be the case. More certain, however, is the observation that Staupitz does not go as far as Gregory of Rimini in teaching a predestination unto death.

Nevertheless, Staupitz reversed the interpretation of much of the medieval theology of grace as his interpretation does not appear to have any historical predecessors in scholastic theology. The framework of Thomism is no longer appropriate for categorizing Staupitz in terms of the history of theology.[8] With Steinmetz and others one may question the hypothesis that Staupitz was the mediator of the so-called *via Gregorii* at Wittenberg, that is the modern Augustinian school. He may have been in

---

[6] See H.A. Oberman in the preface of Staupitz II. p. IX.

[7] See A. Zumkeller, *Johann von Staupitz und seine christliche Heilslehre* (Würzburg, 1994), pp. 211 and 215–16.

[8] See M. Schulze, '"Via Gregorii" in Forschung und Quellen', in H.A. Oberman (ed.), *Gregor von Rimini. Werk und Wirkung bis zur Reformation* (Berlin and New York, 1981), pp. 1–126, esp. pp. 109–26.

agreement with Gregory of Rimini on several questions, but he did not quote him at all; the strongest Augustinian opinions which Staupitz cited are those of Augustine himself. The scholastic references which abound in Staupitz's early phase (in his sermons on the book of Job and in *Decisio*) disappear in the later writings where the Scriptures and Augustine take over as the decisive authorities.[9] Steinmetz rightly objects to the characterization of Staupitz as a Thomist. Staupitz's thinking was more akin to the Franciscan orientation of the theological faculty at Tübingen; whatever else he was, he was not the link to the world of Thomism. In fact, Staupitz was more a representative of the older Augustinian school than of the alleged school of Gregory of Rimini.[10] Moreover, Staupitz shared the humanists' distaste for the *rixosa theologia* of the Scholastics in general.

Although Gabriel Biel's theology appeared to be of great influence at the end of the fifteenth century, one must agree with Zumkeller that Staupitz was not influenced by him. As the prior at Tübingen, Staupitz made his friars take the lectures of Paulus Scriptoris who was known as 'the sharpest Scotist',[11] so perhaps Scotus may have been of greater influence on the young Staupitz's theological outlook. Staupitz's Augustinian grounding would have kept him at a distance from the relatively optimistic opinion concerning the consequences of original sin as found in Scotus, Ockham and the *via moderna*. Staupitz did not follow the teaching of Scotus and Biel that man is capable of loving God on natural grounds without grace. In this regard he sided, deliberately or not, with Gregory of Rimini and other theologians of the Augustinian Order.[12] According to Staupitz, good works are always done through grace and in faith, as nobody can do good works without Christ's grace.[13] Nobody can earn the justifying grace. Staupitz always taught with 1 John 1: 8 that all humans are sinners and in need of redemption; he referred to this Bible verse as early as his Tübingen Sermon 26.

Deeper investigation into the history of spirituality and theology, we arrive at Bernard of Clairvaux and the concept of a 'right to heaven'

---

[9] See Steinmetz, 'Luther and the Late Medieval Augustinians. Another Look', *Concordia Theological Monthly*, **44** (1973) pp. 245–60. M. Wriedt, 'Via Guilelmi – via Gregorii. Zur Frage einer Augustinerschule im Gefolge Gregors von Rimini unter besonderer Berücksichtigung Johannes von Staupitz' in R. Melville et al. (eds) *Deutschland und Europa in der Neuzeit* (Stuttgart, 1988), pp. 111–31; Wriedt questions the thesis of Oberman and Schulze.

[10] See D.C. Steinmetz, *Luther and Staupitz* (Durham, NC, 1980).

[11] 'Acutissimus Scotista', as quoted by A. Zumkeller, *Erbsünde, Gnade, Rechtfertigung und Verdienst nach der Lehre der Erfurter Augustinertheologen des Spätmittelalters* (Würzburg, 1984), p. 459; Zumkeller, *Heilslehre*, p. 213.

[12] See Zumkeller, *Heilslehre*, pp. 39, 122 and 210.

[13] See ibid., pp. 47f. and 179.

which was surely used by Staupitz in the formation of his spirituality.[14] He must be seen closer to the monastic theology of St Bernard than to any scholastic theology. This observation may be corroborated by the often overlooked fact that St Bernard was a widely published spiritual author before and during Staupitz's lifetime.[15] It is, therefore, not too far-fetched to assume that Staupitz was familiar with Bernardine writings, some of which he quoted.[16]

Staupitz's theology cannot be identified with one individual school of thought. He may best be grouped together with the slightly older religious thinkers at Tübingen around 1500, Konrad Summenhart (d. 1502) and Paulus Scriptoris (d. 1505). They were relatively independent in their theological reflections and made great efforts in reforming theology, spirituality and the Church at the turn of the fifteenth century, when Staupitz lived and worked in the friary at Tübingen.

It appears that Staupitz's theology had little in common with that of his confrère at Erfurt, Johannes von Paltz (d. 1511) who is characterized as the 'most extreme' representative of sacramentalism.[17] Departing from the theological thinking that was represented by Paltz, Staupitz gathered around himself like-minded younger friars from his own Reformed Congregation. His inner circle included above all Martin Luther, but also Wenceslaus Linck who had become his successor as leader of the observant Augustinians. Staupitz, Linck and Luther formed a theological trio.

On Staupitz and Luther: our study of the life and work of Staupitz has brought with it a new perspective that no longer allows us to see Staupitz simply as a mediocre theologian who may have had some pastoral influence on the young Luther; nor can one see Staupitz as incapable of realizing the ramifications of his, and Luther's, theology. Staupitz's devotional theology, in the service of piety, turned out to be of great significance for the early Reformation. The closeness of Staupitz's and Luther's theological positions is evident.

While friends of Staupitz at Salzburg and at Nuremberg (the 'Staupitz Sodality') kept records that enable us to gain a fairly accurate picture of Staupitz the theologian and preacher, it was most of all the older Luther who kept the memory of his revered fatherly friend alive among his

---

[14] See F. Posset, 'St Bernard's Influence on Two Reformers: John von Staupitz and Martin Luther', *Cistercian Studies*, 25 (1990), pp. 175–87.

[15] See Posset, 'Saint Bernard of Clairvaux in the Devotion, Theology and Art of the Sixteenth Century', *LQ*, 11 (1997) pp. 309–52.

[16] 'Bernardus ad Eugenium libro De consideratione: Tu, pastor ...' (Sermon 19, Staupitz, I. 311).

[17] 'Extremste Gestalt' (Hamm, 'Von der Gottesliebe des Mittelalters zum Glauben Luthers', p. 33, n. 43).

students and colleagues. In his sermons, publications and table talks, Luther displayed fond memories of Staupitz, and through him we are reminded that the Reformation in Germany was first of all a theological, spiritual, and pastoral renewal; as such it is unthinkable without Staupitz. The very early Reformation was largely a movement that aimed at the renewal of preaching by focusing on the central message of the gospel. Staupitz, as a religious superior, saw to it that his reformed Augustinian Order (the 'Observants') produced well-educated friars with doctoral degrees in theology whom he could, in good conscience, appoint as qualified preachers at churches in major centres of population, and thus contribute to the renewal of Christianity.

One must agree with Wetzel when he warns of playing down the great significance of Staupitz for Luther for the sake of safeguarding the Reformer's originality; a tendency which Wetzel sees at work in Steinmetz's monograph of 1980. Wetzel elaborates on two major areas of Staupitz's influence on Luther: predestination and penance. Luther readily admitted that Staupitz's concept of penance impressed him and remained with him like a 'sharp arrow' (Ps. 119: 4). Wetzel connects Luther's insights to Staupitz's Chapter 6 on the justification of the sinner in his book *De exsecutione*, a passage which so far has not been considered in the context of the connections between Staupitz and Luther. In it, Staupitz spoke of justification by grace as the recognition of the true God in faith so that God is pleasing to man (*ut deus sibi placeat*). As for the question of attrition and contrition for the absolution of sins, Staupitz taught the necessity of contrition, thereby deviating from Scotus and his school. In Staupitz's work, contrition is the centrepiece of penance; it is the love in return which flows from Christ and his action and passion. Luther was led by Staupitz to see penitence as 'sweeter' than anything else, and the commandments of God as 'sweet', if they are read not in books, but in the wounds of Christ 'our most sweet Saviour'. Luther spoke of this insight concerning penance in 1518 in the same manner in which he described in 1545 his insights concerning the proper meaning of the righteousness of God (Rom. 1: 17). Luther preached Staupitzian insights when he proclaimed that 'God will become so lovely, pleasing, and sweet'.[18]

The second major discovery which Luther received from Staupitz concerned the doctrine of predestination (Eccles. 9: 1), as the older Luther himself testified: certitude in matters of salvation cannot be gained by speculating about the hidden will of God, and thus disregarding the revealed word, as Staupitz explained in Chapter 23 of his Advent sermons of 1516. With regard to the issue of the certitude

---

[18] *WA* 8. 379, 12–21.

of salvation, we feel compelled, along with Wetzel, to see Luther and Staupitz as being much closer together than did either Steinmetz in his study of 1968, or Oberman in his *Werden and Wertung* of 1977. There are further parallels between Staupitz and Luther including the concept of *resignatio ad infernum* in Staupitz's *Nachfolgung* of 1515 (Chapter 12), and in Luther's scholium on Rom. 9: 3 in 1515/16; or in the concept of the 'joyous exchange' in Staupitz's *De exsecutione* (Chapters 9–11) and in Luther's *On Christian Liberty* of 1520. Thus the question remains: is Staupitz the Reformation?[19] The answer is 'yes' in terms of the central theological issues which Staupitz and Luther shared, although at the same time it must, of course, be stated that neither Luther nor Staupitz in himself represented the entire 'Reformation theology'. Staupitz was the older, leading reform spirit, from whom Luther learned 'everything' according to his own testimony. Luther was very much a Staupitzian: he insisted not only that Staupitz was his 'closest friend' and 'father' in the faith, but that he was also 'the preacher of grace and cross'. Thus, we may very well accept Luther's own view of Staupitz's significance for him. One would have to say (as a further result of this investigation) that Staupitz is not properly placed if he is situated between the medieval mystical theology and preaching of the cross on the one side and the early Reformation theology and preaching of the cross on the other (as Ernst Wolf argued in the 1920s). Instead, following Oberman's later view, Staupitz should be placed among the 'Masters of the Reformation' of both the Catholic and the Protestant Reformations, since he was one of the most eminent preachers of grace and the cross. Both Staupitz and Luther were essentially gospel-oriented theologians. They both eventually became anti-papal, albeit to differing degrees, when they recognized the distorted spirituality and theology which lay behind the papal indulgence business; and, most of all, when the papacy interfered with their preaching of the gospel and their pastoral care, instigated by representatives of the Dominican Order in Rome and at home.

This view does not mean that Staupitz invented what has become known as 'Reformation theology'. A case could be made for the view that central elements precisely of the 'Reformation theology' are to be found in medieval theologies, which would only prove that Luther's and Staupitz's theologies are not 'revolutionary' at all, but soundly 'Catholic'. There is a continuity in Staupitz's Catholic and evangelical thinking. The elder Staupitz wrote in April 1524 that up to the present day he despised the 'Babylonian captivity' of the Church. To Luther's question as to

---

[19] See R. Wetzel, 'Staupitz und Luther', in V. Press and D. Stievermann (eds), *Martin Luther: Probleme seiner Zeit* (Stuttgart, 1986), pp. 75–87.

whether Staupitz distanced himself from the gospel and from him, Staupitz responded that he did not. Staupitz was always Luther's father and teacher. It would not be correct to weaken this statement of a clear dependence by claiming that the influence of each on the other was mutual and equal. Such a view could hardly be supported by the sources. Staupitz's use of the notion 'Babylonian captivity' in his Nuremberg sermons of 1516/17 is medieval, and probably based on Augustine and Jerome; it is used also by the Erfurt Augustinian Johann von Paltz (1503), and only later, in 1519, by Luther in his *Operationes in Psalmos*. Staupitz's criticism of the Church remained consistent with his own thoughts. This does not necessarily mean that his standpoint was identical with Luther's; he may have alluded deliberately to Luther's famous programmatic work which bore the same title. However, unlike Luther, Staupitz did not draw the consequence of rejecting the papacy altogether, even though both shared the same basic analysis of their contemporary situation under the popes of the Renaissance. Staupitz's differing position should not be interpreted psychologically as his 'weakness'[20] in contrast to Luther's strength and greatness.

Even with such strong evidence of 'Reformation theology' in Staupitz's thinking as is revealed above, one may nevertheless state with Hamm and Zumkeller that he remained within the wider framework of the teachings of 'the old Church'.[21] This is also true for much of Luther's thinking, especially when he knew himself to be in agreement with Staupitz, as he often was. In terms of theology and spirituality Staupitz's reform efforts come very close to Luther's. If, however, 'Reformation' is understood primarily in terms of its objections to positions in Catholic ecclesiology – such as concerning monastic/religious vows, priestly celibacy, and the papacy – then Staupitz was not a major agent in the

---

[20] See H.A. Oberman, 'Captivitas Babylonica: Die Kirchenkritik des Johann von Staupitz', in A. Mehl and W.C. Schneider (eds), *Reformatio et reformationes*, pp. 97–106.

[21] See Hamm, 'Reichsstädtischer Humanismus in Nürnberg', in Mehl and Schneider, *Reformatio et reformationes*, pp. 131–93, esp. pp. 168–72 and n. 127; Zumkeller, *Heilslehre*, p. 230. However, Hamm is not convincing when he views Staupitz with a 'late medieval horizon' in order to build up a contrast with Luther (as in 'Von der Gottesliebe des Mittelalters zum Glauben Luthers', p. 38). He is more persuasive when he emphasizes a certain continuity between medieval and late medieval spirituality and Luther's Reformation theology, as in his 'Warum wurde für Luther der Glaube zum Zentralbegriff des christlichen Lebens?', in S. Buckwalter and B. Moeller (eds), *Die frühe Reformation in Deutschland als Umbruch* (Gütersloh, 1998), pp. 103–27. One must also agree with Hamm that Reformation research needs to be approached from a medieval perspective (see his opening paragraph of 'Von der Gottesliebe des Mittelalters zum Glauben Luthers', p. 19). Finally in 2001, and correctly so, Hamm sees Staupitz as the 'Father of the Reformation'; see his 'Johann von Staupitz (ca. 1468–1524) – spätmittelalterlicher Reformer und "Vater" der Reformation', *ARG*, **92** (2001), pp. 6–42.

history of the 'Reformation'. It was in the later course of the early Reformation controversies that the opponents of Staupitz and Luther turned central theological issues into debates on ecclesiastical authority, and to a degree which the two reformers never originally intended. In the course of events, Luther became aggressively anti-papal, while Staupitz stayed quiet and let his criticisms be known more subtly. Provocation and polemic were not Staupitz's strengths.

Much as he claimed and blamed Staupitz for his spiritual and theological coming of age, Luther always felt that he himself was God's chief instrument in all the reform efforts. When one day Luther at table had talked about himself and Staupitz, and about the prophecy which the latter had heard in Rome about a 'hermit' who should bring down the papacy, Luther added immediately: 'Thus God drives the cause [of the reform] miraculously and He drives me, innocent that I am, into this cause; and He alone brought it to the point where we and the Pope cannot get along.'[22]

Within the wide range of the controversial field of 'religious authority', one point of difference remained between the two friends, and that was the issue of how to weigh monastic vows; and these only in regard to the question as to whether vows are important, or whether they should be treated as 'neutral'. Luther took them as important enough to viciously attack their legitimacy. Staupitz took them less seriously, apparently considering them more or less marginal, or 'neutral' if compared to other more central theological concerns.

If 'Reformation' primarily means church politics and the rejection of papal authority and religious vows, Staupitz would remain relatively insignificant, and could not be considered a serious agent of the 'Reformation' since he did not concern himself much about these issues. It was not his view of ecclesiology, but his theology of salvation, the doctrine of justification, that made him the father of the Reformation in Germany. Anyone whose view of the Reformation is primarily focused on church politics is likely to underestimate the force of theology and spirituality which Staupitz promoted and which Luther accepted (as he stated that Staupitz had started this doctrine, and that he owed everything to him), and thus would correctly dismiss Staupitz as insignificant.

Our closer look at Staupitz's life and theology, however, resulted in the observation that, to their contemporaries, Staupitz and Luther

---

22 '... prophetia Romae publicae pronunciata: Surget eremita et devastabit papatum. Quae visio cuidam Romae minoritae visa est. Also treib Got die sach wunderlich und treib mich unschuldig in die sache, und er allain hats also weit bracht, das es zwischen dem bapst und uns nit kan vertragen werden' (*WATR* 3. 439, 15–20 (no. 3593)).

represented largely the same theological opinions. This united front found contemporary visual expression in the remarkable fact that, in its layout and decoration, the title-page of Luther's *German Catechism* of 1529 is almost identical with that of Staupitz's 1545 edition 'On the Right, Holy Christian Faith', which their friend Linck, as the ex-friar, published.

Staupitz's chief theological convictions may be summarized in the following points:

1 Theological orientation must be based on the Sacred Scriptures, supported by Augustine's theology. Such biblical orientation leads to a thinking and preaching which is God-/Christ-centred.
2 This centring on the Bible and on God and Christ leads to the revision of contemporary distorted images of God/Christ (distortions which the young Luther had displayed in an exemplary way). It appears that Staupitz and the maturing Luther share the same 'Reformational' conception of Christian theology, and in this regard Staupitz's impact 'hardly can be overestimated'.[23] Staupitz corrected the distorted type of piety by stressing that God is sweet and pleasing to man, and that therefore the need of man to be pleasing to God becomes a secondary issue. God does not demand achievements based on human efforts in order to merit salvation.
3 This is so because everything depends upon grace.
4 Everything depends on faith alone in terms of trust in God alone.
5 From this Christian trust (faith) all good works flow. The good works of a Christian are not his, but God's. Man cannot rely on his own works; human beings are sinners and in need of salvation.

If these five Staupitzian axioms – (1) scripture-based theology and spirituality; (2) Christocentrism in terms of Christ as the sweet Saviour alone (and not the stern Judge); (3) salvation being obtained through divine grace alone and (4) through faith alone, with (5) good works flowing from faith – are indeed the theological foundation of what we call the 'Reformation' in the sixteenth century, then Staupitz is essentially a Reformation theologian and the front-runner of that movement. He

---

[23] M. Brecht, *Martin Luther, His Road to Reformation 1483–1521*, trans. J.L. Schaaf (Philadelphia, 1985), I, p. 79. However, Brecht's thesis that 'in no way was Staupitz's conception of Christ the Reformation[al] one, but rather a different sort of the medieval one' is not convincing. Of course, much depends on how 'Reformation' is defined. On a new discussion of this issue, see B. Hamm, 'Was ist reformatorische Rechtfertigungslehre?' *Zeitschrift für Theologie und Kirche*, 83 (1986), 1–38; Hamm, 'Von der spätmittelalterlichen reformatio zur Reformation: der Prozess normativer Zentrierung von Religion und Gesellschaft in Deutschland,' *ARG*, 84 (1993), pp. 7–81.

consequently should be regarded as a major force in the early 'evangelical movement' at the beginning of that century. He was a central figure as an 'Evangelical' Catholic in the theological tradition of St Augustine within the contemporary context of biblical humanism, monastic humanism, and the devotional theology (*Frömmigkeitstheologie*), all of which went back to the ancient sources of the faith – that is to the Bible and the church fathers.

In terms of a theology in the service of spirituality and piety, Luther and Staupitz were of one accord and one team, and Staupitz initially was Luther's coach. Perhaps it would be more appropriate to call Luther (in terms of theology) a Staupitzian than to call Staupitz a Lutheran. Staupitz remained essentially consistent throughout his career in his theological statements, whenever he incorporated them into his proclamations from the pulpit. In a way, one could say that the young Luther accepted the chief concerns which Staupitz expressed, and that he applied this Staupitzian theology to everyday religious practices and evaluated them critically from a biblical point of view (*sola scriptura*). This meant a criticism of activities such as the selling of indulgences which was done on the basis of a distorted late medieval spirituality and ecclesiastical economics. Staupitz had instigated Luther against the indulgence business.

In terms of rhetoric, pastoral care, politics and tactics, Staupitz was much more careful and cautious than Luther. Indeed, Staupitz's evaluation of their fellow Friar Stephan Agricola as being imprudent and immodest in his pastoral style might have been repeated had Staupitz ever been compelled to make a similar judgment on Friar Martin Luther. Under Staupitz's supervision, the Augustinian friars, Luther and Linck, and many of their friends, preached the gospel to people inside and outside the cloisters and thus in the 'world'. In doing so they had to leave the academic language of Latin behind and translate their theological convictions into the vernacular, which they did successfully.

What has at times complicated our investigation is the fact that we are not used to the much wider sphere which the Catholic Church appears to have occupied around the year 1500, one in which various theologies and spiritualities had been accommodated. There is still the tendency today to project back on earlier times the Catholicism defined by the Council of Trent later in the sixteenth century and beyond. Within the Church of the early sixteenth century, Staupitz's biblical theology, which remained fairly consistent even later on when he was a Benedictine abbot, was one such Catholic theological possibility. Thus, if it is true that Staupitz's theology was simultaneously Catholic and Reformational, then at least the younger Luther, who to a large degree accepted and interiorized Staupitz's theological principles, must also be considered a real Catholic possibility at that time. In other words, Staupitz and Luther were both Catholic Reform theologians until Luther later went his own way with regard to church politics. Staupitz was originally trying to reform the Church through the reform of the religious Orders, a reform which had been under way since the fifteenth century with Andreas Proles and others. The Augustinian friars' 'tool of reform' was preaching, not so much addressed to their own friars, but to the ordinary people in the cities' churches. This was why the friars built their friaries in cities and not in remote areas. Staupitz himself initiated and helped build up the friaries in such developing cities as Wittenberg, Eisleben and Antwerp.

It should also be remembered that in 1512, when Staupitz started to preach in German at Salzburg, Luther had not yet received the doctoral degree necessary to qualify him as a good preacher in the eyes of his Order. At that time Staupitz's 'Reformation' theology was a real Catholic option, and Luther saw it this way, too, since it was based on the Bible and the church fathers, and was in close affinity to some of the medieval monastics and mystics of the Church.

Such a perspective on the interrelationship of Staupitz and Luther as developed here is understandable only if one is willing to give up the misconception that Thomistic theology was the only form (and norm) of medieval Catholic theology. Once we learn to see that there was a distinct monastic theology and a devotional theology, based on patristic/ Augustinian theology, in addition to the then dominant scholastic theology, then we realize that Staupitz's notion of theology and spirituality was at that time – and is still today – a genuine Catholic possibility in proximity to Augustine. This also applies to a large degree to Luther's theology, especially if the wider context and such central theological concerns as his Christology, the Trinitarian dogma, and the priority of grace and faith are taken into consideration. Occasionally Luther may have sharpened Staupitz's theological axioms. He definitely applied them to the daily life of ordinary Christians in his teaching and preaching, and this application made him, Luther, the pastoral, practical reformer, the *Seelsorger* (curate) of the Germans, as he too carried the gospel message outside the monastic walls, and more forcefully so than did Staupitz. In delivering his sermons, Luther fulfilled, in his own peculiar way, Staupitz's vision of reforming the Church through the reform of preaching.

Staupitz may not have included in his plans and visions the dissolution of his reformed friaries, which was the painful (and not entirely necessary) by-product of the type of Reformation theology which Luther developed in the 1520s to a point where the ageing Staupitz would have hesitated – that is, the rejection of monastic or religious vows. Staupitz did, however, adapt to the changing situation as regards mendicants in that he gave up the institutional and organizational reforms of his Augustinian Order of mendicant friars and joined the Benedictine monks at Salzburg. After his lack of success in going down the route of reforming institutions (friaries), Staupitz's reform efforts became more spiritualized through his concentration on the effective proclamation of the good news from the pulpit, whenever and wherever he was invited to preach. The observants' movement had run its course; but this was not the case with the renewal of the gospel message.

Staupitz was not very interested in customs and rituals; at times he made critical remarks about such practices as praying with the rosary. In his preaching and teaching of the sacraments, the Mass remained in the background, and his sermons indicate hardly any liturgical interests at all. As for the realm of sacramental celebrations and possible reforms of them, the younger reformers, such as Karlstadt, Müntzer and Luther became much more active.

When the Augustinian reformed Order deteriorated, Staupitz saw in the pastorally minded Benedictine monks of Austria a second chance to reform pastoral care and preaching, a chance which he had already grasped in 1518/19 when the Benedictines employed him as a preacher in the churches under their control, as we know from the invoices of St Peter's Abbey.[24] He continued as a *Seelsorger* after he had become their chief executive officer, the abbot of St Peter's, with its parishes that now were entrusted to him. He remained a preacher and 'pastor' of souls for friars, monks, nuns and for the educated citizens of the major cities at his time.

All in all, without Staupitz and his reform efforts there probably would not have been the Reformation in Germany as we know it. Without such monastics and friars there would be 'no Reformation'.[25] Staupitz does not belong with the pre-reformers,[26] as he is the theological front-runner and herald of the Reformation. Contrary to Steinmetz,[27] one may consider the 'forerunner' issue as having run its course.

---

[24] See *Abteirechnungen St. Peter 1518–1521*, in Salzburger Landesregiering (ed.) *Das älteste Kloster im deutschen Sprachraum: St. Peter in Salzburg*, exhibition catalogue, (Salzburg, 1982), no. 315.

[25] I apply here to Staupitz's life and work the slogan which appears in J. Schilling, *Klöster und Mönche in der hessischen Reformation* (Gütersloh, 1997), p. 11: 'Ohne Mönchtum keine Reformation.'

[26] With right, Benrath did not include Staupitz in his considerations on the so-called 'pre-reformers' (see G.A. Benrath, 'Die sogenannten Vorreformatoren in ihrer Bedeutung für die frühe Reformation', in Buckwalter and Moeller, *Die frühe Reformation*, pp. 157–66.

[27] D.C. Steinmetz, 'Luther and Staupitz: The Unresolved Problem of the Forerunner', in T. Maschke et al. (eds), *Ad fontes Lutheri: Toward the Recovery of the Real Luther. Essays in Honor of Kenneth Hagen's Sixty-Fifth Birthday* (Milwaukee, WI, 2001), pp. 270–80.

Staupitz's life and work are best summarized by the epitaph on his grave at St Peter's Abbey at Salzburg, which highlights the central role of the 'Sacred Page', the Bible, in his life and work (see Plate 4):

> Behold, mortal one, the graves of the dead,
> See what arrogance and riches are worth.
> You will recognize dry bones without marrow.
> You may see for yourself what you can trust in.
> He who distinguished himself by integrity,
> by venerable faith, by honesty, who held fast to
> whatever the sacred page teaches, is Abbot Staupitz
> who rests in this grave. I pray that he may rest in
> the heavenly realm.

> This Doctor Johann von Staupitz, Abbot of this monastery died on 28 December in the year of the Lord 1524.[28]

---

[28] The Latin text is found in *Das älteste Kloster im deutschen Sprachraum*, no. 326; also in J. Sallaberger, 'Johann von Staupitz, Luthers Vorgesetzter und Freund, und seine Beziehungen zu Salzburg', *Augustiniana*, **28** (1978), p. 152; Zumkeller, *Heilslehre*, p. 7; Markwald, *A Mystic's Passion*, p. 189 (in a slightly abbreviated and differing English translation). According to modern dating, the year of Staupitz's death was 1524.

Staupitz's Works
(in Chronological Order)

With the exception of the extant autograph of the Tübingen sermons, 'manuscripts' of Staupitz's works are in the form of sermon notes recorded by his listeners.

c. 1497–98   Tübingen Sermons.

c. 1500   *Decisio quaestionis de audientia miss[a]e in parochiali ecclesia dominicis et festivis diebus. Cum ceteris annexis* (Tübingen, Othmar, 1500); 2nd edn (Nuremberg: Weissenburger, *c.* 1511).

c. 1504–06   *Constitutiones fratrum Eremitarum sancti Augustini ad apostolicorum privilegiorum formam pro reformatione Alemanniae,* edited by Staupitz (Nuremberg, 1504–06).

1512   Salzburg Sermons.

1515   *Ein büchlein von der nachfolgung des willigen sterbens Christi* (Leipzig, 1515); 2nd edn, *Eyn buchleyn von der nachfolgung des willigen sterbens Christi. Beschriben durch den wol wirdigenn vatter Johannem vonn Staupitz. Der heyligen geschrifft Doctorem. Der Brüder einsidler Ordens sancti Augustini* (Nuremberg, 1523).

1517   *Libellus de executione aeternae praedestinationis* (Nuremberg, 1517); German translation by Christoph Scheurl, *Ein nutzbarliches büchlein von der entlichen volziehung ewiger fürsehung ... Joannes von Staupitz, Doctor, vnd der reformirten Augustiner Vicarius, Das heilig Adue[n]t das 1516 Jars, zu Nurmberg, got zu lob vnd gemeiner wolphart gepredigt hat* (Nuremberg, 1517). For second German printing, see 1518 below.
'Concionum epitomae. sententiae. sermones convivales: Nürnberger Predigt- und Lehrstücke, Nürnberger Tischreden'.

1518   *Ein seligs newes Jar von der lieb gottes: Gegeben von dem hochgelarten wirdigen hern Doctori Johanni von Staupitz Augustiner ordens* (Leipzig, 1518); 2nd edn, combined with second German edition of *Ein nutzbarliches büchlein von der entlichen volziehung ewiger*

fürsehung (Munich, 1518); 3rd edn, *Vo[n] der liebe gottes ein wu[n]der hübsch vnderrichtung beschriben durch D. Johan Staupitz; bewert vnnd approbiert durch D. Martinum Luther; Beyde Augustiner ordens* (Basel, 1520). For Latin edition see 1524 below.
Salzburg Sermons.

1519   Salzburg Sermons.

1520   Salzburg Sermons.
'Die offen beicht.'

1523   Salzburg Sermons.
'Consultatio super confessione fratris Stephani Agricolae.'

1524   *De amore Dei* (Frankfurt, 1524).

1525   *Von dem heyligen rechten Christlichen glauben. Johannes Staubitz [sic] Nach seinem abschayden an tag kumen vnd außgangen*, posthumously edited by Wenceslaus Linck (Nuremberg, 1525); *Von dem hailigen rechten Christennlichen Glauwben Johannes Staubitz [sic]* (Augsburg, 1525).

Select Bibliography

Primary Sources

Older Editions

Aumüller, Heinrich, 'Predigten von Staupitz in Salzburg', *Jahrbuch der Gesellschaft für die Geschichte des Protestantismus in Österreich*, 2 (1881), pp. 51–9; and 11 (1890), pp. 113–32.

Buchwald, Georg and Wolf, Ernst (eds), *Staupitz Tübinger Predigten* (Leipzig, 1927; reprinted New York and London, 1971).

Gärtner, C. (ed.), 'Consultatio super confessione fratris Stephani Agricolae', in *Salzburgische gelehrte Unterhaltungen* (1812), Heft 2, pp. 67–72.

Jeremias, Alfred, *Johannes Staupitz. Luthers Vater und Schüler. Sein Leben, sein Verhältnis zu Luther und eine Auswahl aus seinen Schriften* (Sannerz and Leipzig, 1926).

Knaake, Joachim Karl Friedrich (ed.), *Johann von Staupitzens sämmtliche Werke. Erster Band: Deutsche Schriften* (Potsdam, 1867). This edition was intended to contain all of the available writings of Staupitz. However, due to the lack of both funds and interest at that time, only the first volume, 'German Writings', appeared in print. It comprised the following with their titles given in Latin: (1) *Concionum epitomae. Sententiae. Sermones conviviales* (Nuremberg sermons, 1517); (2) *De imitanda morte Jesu Christi libellus* (1515); (3) *De amore dei libellus* (1518); (4) *De sancta fide Christiana libellus* (1524); (5) *Libellus de exsecutione eternae praedestinationis* (1517).

Kolde, Theodor, 'Bruderschaftsbrief des Joh. von Staupitz für Christoph Scheurl den Älteren und seine Familie, 1511, 6. Oct.', *ZKG*, 6 (1884), pp. 296–8.

———, *Die Deutsche Augustiner-Congregation und Johann von Staupitz. Ein Beitrag zur Ordens- und Reformationsgeschichte nach meistens ungedruckten Quellen* (Gotha, 1879), pp. 452–6 (includes one Advent Sermon of 1523).

Von Soden, Franz Freiherr and Knaake, Joachim Karl Friedrich (eds), *Christoph Scheurl's Briefbuch, ein Beitrag zur Geschichte der Reformation und ihrer Zeit. Erster Band.: Briefe von 1505–1516; Zweiter Band: Briefe von 1517–1540* (Potsdam, 1867–72; reprinted Aalen, 1962).

The unfinished critical edition of Staupitz's works

Dohna, Lothar Graf zu and Wetzel, Richard (eds), *Johann von Staupitz: Sämtliche Schriften. Abhandlungen, Predigten, Zeugnisse* (Berlin and New York, 1979–):

Volume 1, *Tübinger Predigten*, ed. Richard Wetzel (1987).
Volume 2, *Libellus de exsecutione aeternae praedestinationis*, mit der Übertragung von Christoph Scheurl: *Ein nutzbarliches Büchlein von der entlichen Volziehung ewiger Fürsehung*, ed. Lothar Graf zu Dohna and Richard Wetzel (1979).
Volume 5, *Gutachten und Satzungen*, Lothar Graf zu Dohna and Richard Wetzel (2001).

To date, only the above volumes have appeared. Staupitz's Salzburg Sermons of 1512 are also available in a separate critical edition:

Schneider-Lastin, Wolfram (ed.), *Johann von Staupitz: Salzburger Predigten 1512. Eine textkritische Edition* (Tübingen, 1990).

English translations

Markwald, Rudolf K., *A Mystic's Passion. The Spirituality of Johannes von Staupitz in his 1520 Lenten Sermons. Translation and Commentary* (New York, Bern, Frankfurt am Main and Paris, 1990).
Oberman, Heiko A., *Forerunners of the Reformation. The Shape of Late Medieval Thought, Illustrated by Key Documents*, trans. Paul L. Nyhus (New York, Chicago and San Francisco, 1966; London, 1967; Philadelphia, 1981), pp. 175–203 (selections of Staupitz's Advent Sermons of 1516 at Nuremberg).
Posset, Franz, 'Communal Penance Services in the Context of Sixteenth Century Reform Efforts', *Worship,* **69** (1995), pp. 334–45 (includes the source edition *Die offen peicht*).
Stoudt, John Joseph, 'John Staupitz on God's Gracious Love', *LQ*, 8 (1956), pp. 225–44 (*Von der lieb gottes*, 1518).

Secondary Literature

Staupitz bibliography

Markwald, Rudolf K. and Posset, Franz, *125 Years of Staupitz Research (Since 1867): An Annotated Bibliography of Studies on Johannes von Staupitz (C. 1468–1524). Sixteenth Century Bibliography 31* (Saint Louis, MO, 1995).

Select literature

Bebb, Phillip N., 'Humanism and Reformation: The Nürnberg *Sodalitas* Revisited', in Bebb, Phillip N. and Marshall, Sherrin (eds), *The Process of Change in Early Modern Europe: Essays in Honor of Miriam Usher Chrisman* (Athens, OH, 1988), pp. 59–79.

Bonorand, Conradin, *Joachim Vadian und der Humanismus im Bereich des Erzbistums Salzburg* (St Gallen, 1980).

Buckwalter, Stephen and Moeller, Bernd (eds), *Die frühe Reformation in Deutschland als Umbruch. Wissenschaftliches Symposium des Vereins für Reformationsgeschichte 1996* (Gütersloh, 1998).

Demme, Dietrich, *Martin Luthers Weg ins Kloster. Eine wissenschaftliche Untersuchung in Aufsätzen* (Regensburg, 1991).

Dieckhoff, August Wilhelm, 'Die Theologie des Johann von Staupitz', *Zeitschrift für Kirchliche Wissenschaft und Kirchliches Leben*, 8 (1887), pp. 169–180 and 232–44.

Dohna, Lothar Graf zu, 'Staupitz und Luther: Kontinuität und Umbruch in den Anfängen der Reformation', *Pastoraltheologie*, 74 (1985), 452–65. Reprinted in Dohna, Lothar Graf zu and Mokrosch, Reinhold (eds), *Werden und Wirkung der Reformation* (Darmstadt, 1986), pp. 95–116. English translation: 'Staupitz and Luther: Continuity and Breakthrough at the Beginning of the Reformation', in Oberman, Heiko A. and James, Frank A. (eds), *Via Augustini. Augustine in the Later Middle Ages, Renaissance and Reformation. Essays in Honor of Damasus Trapp, O.S.A.* (Leiden, New York, Copenhagen and Cologne, 1991), pp. 116–29.

———, 'Von der Ordensreform zur Reformation: Johann von Staupitz', in Elm, Kaspar (ed.), *Reformbemühungen und Observanzbestrebungen im spätmittelalterlichen Ordenswesen* (Berlin, 1989), pp. 571–84.

Dohna, Lothar Graf zu and Wetzel, Richard, 'Die Reue Christi: Zum theologischen Ort der Busse bei Johann von Staupitz', *Studien und Mitteilungen zur Geschichte des Benediktinerordens und seiner Zweige,* 94 (1983), pp. 457–82.

Eckermann, Willigis, 'Neue Dokumente zur Auseinandersetzung zwischen Johann Staupitz und der sächsischen Reformkongregation', *AAug*, 40 (1977), pp. 279–96.

Endriss, Albrecht, 'Nachfolgung des willigen Sterbens Christi. Interpretation des Staupitztraktates von 1515 und Versuch einer Einordnung in den frömmigkeitsgeschichtlichen Kontext', in Nolte, Josef, Tompert, Hella et al. (eds), *Kontinuität und Umbruch. Theologie und Frömmigkeit in Flugschriften und Kleinliteratur an der Wende vom 15. zum 16. Jahrhundert. Beiträge zum Tübinger*

Kolloquium des Sonderforschungsbereichs 8 'Spätmittelalter und Reformation' (31. Mai–2. Juni 1975) (Stuttgart, 1977), pp. 93–141.

Fasola, Carlo, *Die Sprache des Johann von Staupitz. I. Lautlehre*, Philosophical disseration, Marburg, 1892.

Favre, Ernest, 'Deux Phases de la Vie de Staupitz', *La Liberté Chrétienne*, **6** (1903), pp. 17–31.

Feld, Helmut, 'Konrad Summenhart: Theologe der kirchlichen Reform vor der Reformation', *Rottenburger Jahrbuch für Kirchengeschichte*, **11** (1992), 85–116.

Foket, Monique, 'Luther et Staupitz (I)', *La Foi et le Temps: Revue bimestrielle des diocèses francophones de Belgique* 20 (Tournai, 1990), pp. 69–83.

Geuder, Antonius Daniel, *Vita Ioannis Staupitii* (Dissertation, Göttingen, 1837).

Goetzius, G.H., *Commentatio de Joanne Staupitio* (Lübeck, 1715).

Grimm, Karl Ludwig Willibald, 'De Ioanne Staupitio eiusque in sacrorum christianorum instaurationem meritis,' *Zeitschrift für die historische Theologie*, Neue Folge, **1** (1837), pp. 58–126.

Guenter, Ilse, 'Staupitz', in Bietenholz, Peter G. and Deutscher, Thomas B. (eds), *Contemporaries of Erasmus*, 3 vols (Toronto, 1987), III, pp. 282ff.

Günter, Wolfgang, 'Johann von Staupitz (ca. 1468 bis 1524)', in Iserloh, Erwin (ed.), *Katholische Theologen der Reformationszeit*. Katholisches Leben und Kirchenreform im Zeitalter der Glaubensspaltung 48 (Münster, 1988), 11–31.

Gutierrez, David, *Los Agustinos en la edad media 1357–1517. Historia de la Orden de San Agustin*, 2 vols (Rome, 1977). English translation: Thomas Martin, *The Augustinians in the Middle Ages 1357–1517. History of the Order of St. Augustine*, I, 2 vols (Villanova, 1979–83).

Hamm, Berndt, 'Reichsstädtischer Humanismus in Nürnberg', in Mehl, Andreas and Schneider, Wolfgang Christian (eds), *Reformatio et reformationes. Festschrift für Lothar Graf zu Dohna zum 65. Geburtstag* (Darmstadt, 1989), pp. 131–93.

———, 'Von der Gottesliebe des Mittelalters zum Glauben Luthers', *Lutherjahrbuch* **65** (1998), pp. 19–44.

———, 'Johann von Staupitz (ca. 1468–1524) – spätmittelalterlicher Reformer und "Vater" der Reformation', *ARG*, **92** (2001), pp. 6–42.

Hansen Utne, Erling, 'Joannes von Staupitz' teologi', *Tidsskrift for teologi og Kirche*, **19** (1948), pp. 186–205.

Hemmerle, Josef, *Geschichte des Augustinerklosters in München* (Munich-Pasing, 1956).

———, *Die Klöster der Augustiner-Eremiten in Bayern* (Munich-Pasing, 1958).

Henry, Arthur L., 'Catholicity and Predestination in the Theologies of Johann Eck and Johannes von Staupitz, 1513–1517' (Th.D. dissertation, Berkeley, CA, 1971, on microfilm).

Hillerbrand, Hans J. (ed.), *The Oxford Encyclopaedia of the Reformation*, 4 vols (New York and Oxford, 1996).

Hümpfner, Winfried, 'Äussere Geschichte der Augustiner-Eremiten in Deutschland (Von den Anfängen bis zur Säkularisation)', in Deutsche Provinz der Augustiner-Eremiten, *St. Augustin 430–1930. Zur Jahrhundertfeier dargeboten von der deutschen Provinz der Augustiner-Eremiten* (Würzburg, 1930), pp. 147–96.

Junghans, Helmar, *Der junge Luther und die Humanisten* (Weimar, 1984; Göttingen, 1985).

Kalkoff, Paul, *Aleander gegen Luther. Studien zu ungedruckten Aktenstücken aus Aleanders Nachlass* (Leipzig and New York, 1908), pp. 137–40.

Keller, Ludwig, *Johann von Staupitz und die Anfänge der Reformation. Nach den Quellen dargestellt* (Leipzig, 1888; reprinted Nieuwkoop, 1967).

Köstlin, Julius, 'Luthers letzter Verkehr mit Staupitz', *Theologische Studien und Kritiken*, **52** (1879), pp. 703–5.

Kunzelmann, Adalbero, *Geschichte der deutschen Augustiner-Eremiten. Fünfter Teil: Die sächsisch-thüringische Provinz und die sächsische Reformkongregation bis zum Untergang der beiden* (Würzburg, 1974).

Lohse, Bernhard, 'Zum Wittenberger Augustinismus – Augustins Schrift De Spiritu et Littera in der Auslegung bei Staupitz, Luther und Karlstadt', in Hagen, Kenneth (ed.), *Augustine, the Harvest, and Theology (1300–1650). Essays Dedicated to Heiko Augustinus Oberman in Honor of his Sixtieth Birthday* (Leiden, 1990), pp. 89–109.

Martin, Francis Xavier, 'The Augustinian Order on the Eve of the Reformation', *Miscellanea historiae ecclesiasticae. Bibliothèque de la Revue d'histoire ecclesiastique*, **44** (Louvain, 1967), II, pp. 71–104.

———, 'The Augustinian Observant Movement', in Elm, Kaspar (ed.), *Reformbemühungen und Observanzbestrebungen im spätmittelalter-lichen Ordenswesen* (Berlin, 1989), pp. 325–45.

Moeller, Bernd and Buckwalter, Stephen (eds), *Die frühe Reformation in Deutschland als Umbruch. Wissenschaftliches Symposion des Vereins für Reformationsgeschichte 1996* (Gütersloh, 1998).

Oberman, Heiko A., '"Tuus sum, salvum me fac". Augustinreveil zwischen Renaissance und Reformation', in Mayer, Cornelius Petrus and Eckermann, Willigis (eds), *'Scientia Augustiniana.' Studien über Augustinus, den Augustinismus und den Augustinerorden. Festschrift P. Dr. theol. Dr. phil. Adolar Zumkeller OSA zum 60. Geburtstag* (Würzburg, 1975), pp. 349–94.

————, *Werden und Wertung der Reformation* (Tübingen, 1977; 2nd edn, 1979; 3rd edn, 1989). English translation: Dennis Martin, *Masters of the Reformation. The Emergence of a New Intellectual Climate in Europe* (Cambridge and London, 1981).

————, 'Captivitas Babylonica: Die Kirchenkritik des Johann von Staupitz', in Mehl, Andreas and Schneider, Wolfgang Christian, *Reformatio et reformationes. Festschrift für Lothar Graf zu Dohna zum 65. Geburtstag* (Darmstadt, 1989), pp. 97–106.

————, 'Duplex misericordia: Der Teufel und die Kirche in der Theologie des jungen Johann von Staupitz', *Theologische Zeitschrift*, **45** (1989), pp. 231–43. English translation: 'The Devil and the Church in the Early Theology of Johann von Staupitz', in *The Impact of the Reformation: Essays* (Grand Rapids, MI, 1994).

Paulus, Nikolaus, 'Ein Gutachten Staupitz' aus dem Jahre 1523', *Historisches Jahrbuch*, **12** (1891), pp. 773–7.

————, 'Johann Staupitz. Seine vorgeblich protestantischen Gesinnungen', *Historisches Jahrbuch*, **12** (1891), pp. 309–46.

————, 'Johann v. Staupitz', in *Wetzer und Welte's Kirchenlexikon* (1899), XI, pp. 746ff.

Posset, Franz, 'St. Bernard's Influence on Two Reformers: John von Staupitz and Luther', *CSQ*, **25** (1990), pp. 175–87.

————, 'The Sweetness of God', *ABR*, **44** (1993), pp. 143–78.

————, 'Pater et Doctor Meus Est, Immo Sanctae Ecclesiae Intellectu Profundissimus', in Van Fleteren, Frederick, Schnaubelt, Joseph C. et al. (eds), *Collectanea Augustiniana. Augustine Mystic and Mystagogue* (New York, 1994), pp. 513–43.

————, 'Preaching the Passion of Christ on the Eve of the Reformation', *Concordia Theological Quarterly*, **59** (1995), pp. 279–300.

————, 'Saint Bernard of Clairvaux in the Devotion, Theology, and Art of the Sixteenth Century', *LQ*, **11** (1997), pp. 306–52.

————, 'Sensing God with the 'Palate of the Heart' According to Augustine and Other Spiritual Authors', *ABR*, **49** (1998), pp. 356–86.

————, 'The "Palate of the Heart" in St. Augustine and Medieval Spirituality' in Frederick Van Fleteren and Joseph C. Schnaubelt (eds), *Augustine Biblical Exegete* (New York, 2001), pp. 253–78.

————, '"Rock" and "Recognition": Martin Luther's Catholic Interpretation of "You are Peter and on this rock I will build my Church" (Matthew 16: 18) and the Friendly Criticism from the Point of View of the "Hebrew Truth" by his Confrère, Caspar Amman, Doctor of the "Sacred Page"', in Maschke, Timothy, Posset, Franz and Skocir, Joan (eds), *Ad fontes Lutheri: Toward the Recovery of the Real Luther. Essays in Honor of Kenneth Hagen's Sixty-Fifth Birthday* (Milwaukee, WI, 2001), pp. 214–52.

————, 'The "Double Right to Heaven": Saint Bernard's Impact in the Sixteenth Century', *CSQ*, **38** (2003).

Rosenthal-Metzger, Julie, 'Das Augustinerkloster in Nürnberg', *Mitteilungen des Vereins für Geschichte der Stadt Nürnberg*, **30** (1931), pp. 1–103.

Rotelle, John E. (ed.), Theology and History of the Augustinian School in the Middle Ages (n.p., Augustinian Press, 1996).

Sallaberger, Johann, 'Johann von Staupitz, Luthers Vorgesetzter und Freund, und seine Beziehungen zu Salzburg', *Augustiniana*, **28** (1978), pp. 108–54.

————, 'Abt Johann von Staupitz (1522–1524), Luthers einstiger Vorgesetzter und Freund', in Salzburger Landesregierung, *Das älteste Kloster im deutschen Sprachraum: Sankt Peter in Salzburg* (3. Landesausstellung 15. Mai–26. Okt. 1982: Schätze europäischer Kunst und Kultur), pp. 91–98.

————, 'Johann von Staupitz, die Stiftsprediger und die Mendikanten-Termineien in Salzburg', *Studien und Mitteilungen zur Geschichte des Benediktinerordens und seiner Zweige*, **93** (1982), pp. 218–69.

————, 'Die Einladung Martin Luthers nach Salzburg im Herbst 1518', in Paarhammer, Hans, and Schmölz, Franz-Martin (eds), *Uni Trinoque Domino. Karl Berg. Bischof im Dienste der Einheit. Eine Festgabe Erzbischof Karl Berg zum 80. Geburtag* (Thaur, Tirol, 1989), pp. 445–67.

————, 'Johann von Staupitz, Abt von St. Peter (1522–1524) und die Salzburger Mendikantentermineien', *Studien und Mitteilungen zur Geschichte des Benediktinerordens und seiner Zweige*, **103** (1992), pp. 87–188.

————, *Kardinal Matthäus Lang von Wellenburg (1468–1540): Staatsmann und Kirchenfürst im Zeitalter von Renaissance, Reformation und Bauernkriegen* (Salzburg, 1997).

Schmidt, Martin Anton, 'Rechtfertigungslehre in Staupitz' "Nachfolgung": (Korrekturthesen zu Albrecht Endriss)', in Nolte, Josef, Tompert, Hella et al. (eds), *Kontinuität und Umbruch. Theologie und Frömmigkeit in Flugschriften und Kleinliteratur an der Wende vom 15. zum 16. Jahrhundert. Beiträge zum Tübinger Kolloquium des Sonderforschungsbereichs 8 'Spätmittelalter und Reformation' (31. Mai–2. Juni 1975)* (Stuttgart, 1977), pp. 142–44.

Schulze, Manfred, '"Via Gregorii" in Forschung und Quellen', in Oberman, Heiko A., (ed.), *Gregor von Rimini. Werk und Wirkung bis zur Reformation* (Berlin and New York, 1981), pp. 1–126.

————, 'Tübinger Gegenätze. Gabriel Biel und Johannes von Staupitz: von spätmittelalterlicher Reform zu Luthers Reformation', *Tübinger Blätter*, **72** (1985), pp. 54–9.

————, 'Der Hiob-Prediger Johannes von Staupitz auf der Kanzel der Tübinger Augustinerkirche', in Hagen, Kenneth (ed.), *Augustine, the Harvest, and Theology (1300–1650). Essays Dedicated to Heiko Augustinus Oberman in Honor of his Sixtieth Birthday* (Leiden, 1990), pp. 60–88.

————, *Fürsten und Reformation. Geistliche Reformpolitik weltlicher Fürsten vor der Reformation* (Tübingen, 1991).

Schulze, Wilhelm August, 'Ein neues katholisches Staupitz-Bild'? *Theologische Zeitschrift*, **13** (1957), pp. 352–4.

Steinmetz, David Curtis, *Misericordia Dei: The Theology of Johannes Staupitz in its Late Medieval Setting* (Leiden, 1968).

————, *Reformers in the Wings* (Philadelphia, 1971).

————, 'Luther and the Late Medieval Augustinians. Another Look', *Concordia Theological Monthly*, **44** (1973), pp. 245–60.

————, 'Hermeneutic and Old Testament Interpretation in Staupitz and the Young Luther', *ARG*, **70** (1979), pp. 24–58.

————, *Luther and Staupitz: An Essay in the Intellectual Origins of the Protestant Reformation* (Durham, NC, 1980).

————, 'Religious Exstasy in Staupitz and the Young Luther', *SCJ*, **11** (1980), pp. 23–37.

————, 'Staupitz, Johann von', in Hillerbrand, Hans J. (ed.), *The Oxford Encyclopaedia of the Reformation*, 4 vols (New York and Oxford, 1996), IV, pp. 109–11.

————, 'Luther and Staupitz: The Unresolved Problem of the Forerunner', in Maschke, Timothy, Posset, Franz and Skocir, Joan (eds), *Ad fontes Lutheri: Toward the Recovery of the Real Luther. Essays in Honor of Kenneth Hagen's Sixty-Fifth Birthday* (Milwaukee, WI, 2001), pp. 270–80.

Urban, Wolfgang, 'Vom Astrolabium, dem Vacuum und der Vielzahl der Welten. Paul Scriptoris und Konrad Summenhart: Zwei Gelehrte zwischen Scholastik und Humanismus', *Attempto*, **69** (1983), pp. 49–55.

Walsh, Katherine, 'The Observance: Sources for a History of the Observant Reform Movement in the Order of Augustinian Friars in the Fourteenth and Fifteenth Centuries', *Rivista di Storia della chiesa in Italia*, **31** (1977), pp. 40–67.

Wernicke, Michael, 'Die deutschen Augustiner von 1500 bis 1520', in *Egidio da Viterbo, O.S.A, e il suo tempo: atti del V Convegno dell'Instituto Storico Agostiniano, Roma-Viterbo, 20–23 ottobre 1982* (Rome, 1983), pp. 9–25.

Weijenborg, Reinhold, 'Neuentdeckte Dokumente im Zusammenhang mit Luthers Romreise', *Antonianum*, **32** (1957), pp. 147–202.

————, 'Staupitz', in Höfer, Josef and Rahner, Karl (eds) *Lexikon für Theologie und Kirche*, 2nd edn (Freiburg, 1957–67), IX, p. 1026.

————, 'Review of *Johann von Staupitz, Sämtliche Schriften*, vol. 2', *Revue d'Histoire Ecclesiastique*, **76** (1981), pp. 394–400.

Wetzel, Richard, 'Staupitz und Luther', in Press, Volker and Stievermann, Dieter (eds), *Martin Luther: Probleme seiner Zeit* (Stuttgart, 1986), pp. 75–87.

————, 'Staupitz antibarbarus. Beobachtungen zur Rezeption heidnischer Antike in seinen Tübinger Predigten', in Mehl, Andreas and Schneider, Wolfgang Christian (eds), *Reformatio et reformationes. Festschrift für Lothar Graf zu Dohna zum 65. Geburtstag* (Darmstadt, 1989), pp. 107–30.

————, 'Staupitz Augustinianus: An Account of the Reception of Augustine in his Tübingen Sermons', in Oberman, Heiko A. and James, Frank A., III (eds), *Via Augustini. Augustine in the Later Middle Ages, Renaissance and Reformation. Essays in Honor of Damasus Trapp, O.S.A.* (Leiden, 1991), pp. 72–115.

————, 'Staupitz und Luther. Annäherung an eine Vorläufer-Figur', *Blätter für Pfälzische Kirchengeschichte und Religiöse Volkskunde*, **58** (1991), pp. 369–95.

————, '"Meine Liebe zu Dir ist beständiger als Frauenliebe": Johann von Staupitz (+1524) und Martin Luther', in Freybe, Peter (ed.), *Luther und seine Freunde* (Wittenberg, 1998), pp. 105–24.

Wolf, Ernst, *Staupitz und Luther: Ein Beitrag zur Theologie des Johannes Staupitz und deren Bedeutung für Luthers theologischen Werdegang* (Leipzig, 1927; reprinted New York, London, 1971).

————, 'Johann Staupitz und die theologischen Anfänge Luthers', *Lutherjahrbuch*, **11** (1929), pp. 43–85.

Wriedt, Markus, 'Ist der "Libellus auro praestantior de animae praeparatione in extremo laborantis, deque praedestinatione et tentatione fidei" eine Lutherschrift?' *Lutherjahrbuch*, **54** (1987), pp. 48–83.

————, 'Via Guilelmi – via Gregorii. Zur Frage einer Augustinerschule im Gefolge Gregors von Rimini unter besonderer Berücksichtigung Johannes von Staupitz', in Melville, Ralph, Scharf, Klaus et al. (eds), *Deutschland und Europa in der Neuzeit. Festschrift für Karl Otmar Freiherr von Aretin zum 65. Geburtstag. 1. Halbband* (Stuttgart, 1988), pp. 111–31.

————, *Gnade und Erwählung: Eine Untersuchung zu Johann von Staupitz und Martin Luther* (Mainz, 1991).

————, 'Staupitz und Luther – Zur Bedeutung der seelsorgerlichen Theologie Johanns von Staupitz für den jungen Martin Luther', in Heubach, Joachim (ed.), *Luther als Seelsorger* (Erlangen, 1991), pp. 67–108.

————, 'Staupitz und Augustin: zur Kirchenväterrezeption am Vorabend der Reformation', in Grane, Leif, Schindler, Alfred et al. (eds),

Auctoritas Patrum. Contributions on the Reception of the Church Fathers in the 15th and 16th Century (Mainz, 1993), pp. 227–57.

——, 'Seelsorgerliche Theologie am Vorabend der Reformation: Johann Staupitz als Fastenprediger in Nürnberg', *Zeitschrift für Bayerische Kirchengeschichte*, **63** (1994), pp. 1–12.

——, 'Johannes von Staupitz als Gründungsmitglied der Wittenberger Universität', in Oehming, Stefan (ed.), *700 Jahre Wittenberg: Stadt, Universität, Reformation* (Weimar, 1995), pp. 174–86.

——, 'Johann von Staupitz (ca. 1465–1524)', in Möller, Christian (ed.), *Geschichte der Seelsorge in Einzelporträts*, 3 vols (Göttingen, 1994–96), II, pp. 46–64.

Zeller, Paul, 'Staupitz. Seine religiös-dogmatischen Anschauungen und dogmengeschichtliche Stellung', *Theologische Studien und Kritiken*, **52** (1879), pp. 7–65.

Ziegler, Walter, 'Reformation und Klosterauflösung. Ein ordensgeschichtlicher Vergleich', in Elm, Kaspar (ed.), *Reformbemühungen und Observanzbestrebungen im spätmittelalterlichen Ordenswesen* (Berlin, 1989), pp. 585–614.

Zumkeller, Adolar, 'Das Ungenügen der menschlichen Werke bei den deutschen Predigern des Spätmittelalters', *Zeitschrift für Katholische Theologie*, **81** (1959), pp. 265–302.

——, 'Martin Luther und sein Orden', *AAug*, **25** (1962), pp. 254–90.

——, *Erbsünde, Gnade, Rechtfertigung und Verdienst nach der Lehre der Erfurter Augustinertheologen des Spätmittelalters* (Würzburg, 1984).

——, 'Johannes von Staupitz und die klösterliche Reformbewegung', *AAug*, **52** (1989), pp. 31–49.

——, 'Staupitz (Jean de)', in Villar, Marcel, S.J. et al. (eds), *Dictionnaire de Spiritualité Ascétique et Mystique: Doctrine et Histoire*, 17 vols (Paris, 1937–95), XV, pp. 1184–96.

——, *Johann von Staupitz und seine christliche Heilslehre* (Würzburg, 1994).

Index of Names